AN INTRODUCTION
TO THEOLOGY IN
GLOBAL PERSPECTIVE

At the beginning of a new millennium, the *Theology in Global Perspective* Series responds to the challenge to reexamine the foundational and doctrinal themes of Christianity in light of the new global reality. While traditional Catholic theology has assumed an essentially European or Western point of view, *Theology in Global Perspective* takes account of insights and experience of churches in Africa, Asia, Latin America, Oceania, as well as in Europe and North America. Noting the pervasiveness of changes brought about by science and technologies, and growing concerns about the sustainability of Earth, it seeks to embody insights from studies in these areas as well.

Though rooted in the Catholic tradition, volumes in the series are written with an eye to the ecumenical implications of Protestant, Orthodox, and Pentecostal theologies for Catholicism, and vice versa. In addition, authors will explore insights from other religious traditions with the potential to enrich Christian theology and self-understanding.

Books in this series will provide reliable introductions to the major theological topics, tracing their roots in Scripture and their development in later tradition, exploring when possible the implications of new thinking on gender and sociocultural identities. And they will relate these themes to the challenges confronting the peoples of the world in the wake of globalization, particularly the implications of Christian faith for justice, peace, and the integrity of creation.

Other Books Published in the Series

Orders and Ministries: Leadership in a Global Church, Kenan Osborne, O.F.M.
Trinity: Nexus of the Mysteries of Christian Faith, Anne Hunt
Eschatology and Hope, Anthony Kelly, C.Ss.R.
Meeting Mystery: Liturgy Worship, Sacraments, Nathan D. Mitchell
Creation, Grace and Redemption, Neil Ormerod
Globalization, Spirituality and Justice, Daniel G. Groody, C.S.C.
Christianity and Science: Toward a Theology of Nature, John F. Haught
Ecclesiology for a Global Church: A People Called and Sent, Richard R. Gaillardetz

THEOLOGY IN GLOBAL PERSPECTIVE SERIES
Peter C. Phan, General Editor

AN INTRODUCTION TO THEOLOGY IN GLOBAL PERSPECTIVE

STEPHEN B. BEVANS

ORBIS BOOKS
Maryknoll, New York 10545

Library of Congress Cataloging in Publication Data

Bevans, Stephen B., 1944-
  An introduction to theology in global perspective / Stephen B. Bevans.
      p. cm. — (Theology in global perspective series)
  Includes bibliographical references and index.
  ISBN 978-1-57075-852-2 (pbk. : alk. paper)
  1. Theology, Doctrinal. 2. Catholic Church—Doctrines. I. Title.
  BX1751.3.B48 2009
  230'.201—dc22
                                                                2009009584

ISBN 1-57075-852-2

To my students in Introduction to Theology
at
Vigan
Tagaytay
Catholic Theological Union
Yarra Theological Union
Broken Bay Institute

Docendo discimus!

Contents

Part IV
Faith Seeking through the Ages
Theology, History, and Culture

Abbreviations

AAS	*Acta Apostolicae Sedis*
AG	*Ad Gentes* (Vatican Council II, decree on the Church's Missionary Activity)
DS	H. Denzinger, rev. A. Schönmetzer, *Enchiridion Symbolorum, Definitionum et Declarationum de Rebus Fidei et Morum,* 36th ed. (Freiburg: Herder, 1976)
DThC	*Dictionnaire de Théologie Catholique*
DV	*Dei Verbum* (Vatican Council II, Dogmatic Constitution of Divine Revelation)
EiA	John Paul II, Apostolic Exhortation *Ecclesia in Asia* (1999)
EiAf	John Paul II, Apostolic Exhortation *Ecclesia in Africa* (1995)
EiAm	John Paul II, Apostolic Exhortation *Ecclesia in America* (1999)
EiE	John Paul II, Apostolic Exhortation *Ecclesia in Europa* (2003)
EiO	John Paul II, Apostolic Exhortation *Ecclesia in Oceania* (2001)
EN	Paul VI, Apostolic Exhortation *Evangelii Nuntiandi* (1975)
FC	John Paul II, Apostolic Exhortation *Familiaris Consortio* (1981)
FR	John Paul II, Encyclical Letter *Fides et Ratio* (1998)
GS	*Gaudium et Spes* (Vatican Council II, Pastoral Constitution on Church in the Modern World)
LG	*Lumen Gentium* (Vatican Council II, Dogmatic Constitution on the Church)
ND	Jacob Neuner and Jacques Dupuis, eds., *The Christian Faith in the Doctrinal Documents of the Catholic Church,* 7th rev. and enlarged ed., ed. Jacques Dupuis (New York: Alba House; Bangalore: Theological Publications in India, 2001)
PG	*Patrologia cursus completus, series Graeca,* ed. J.-P. Migne, 162 vols. (Paris, 1857-86)
PL	*Patrologia cursus completus, series Latina,* ed. J.-P. Migne, 217 vols. (Paris 1844-64)
RM	John Paul II, Encylical Letter *Redemptoris Missio* (1990)
SC	*Sacrosanctum Concilium* (Vatican Council II, Constitution on the Sacred Liturgy)

Foreword

by Peter C. Phan

When an academic discipline is in crisis, often questions are raised not so much about what is said but rather about *how* what is said can be known at all. In other words, attention is shifted from content to method. That Christian theology has been in crisis for quite some time now is being widely recognized, signaled by the fact that the erstwhile consensus has vanished and drastically divergent answers are given to such fundamental issues as the nature of God, the role of Christ, and the mission of the church, even in churches known for their insistence on uniformity and orthodoxy such as the Catholic Church. This crisis is brought about not only by intra-ecclesial mutations but also by external circumstances over which the church has no control, such as cultural and sociopolitical changes, migration, and globalization.

Recognition of this ongoing crisis in Christian theology provided the impetus for the undertaking of this new Theology in Global Perspective series. Previously published works in this series have hinted at the need for a new methodological approach. However, their primary interest was to develop more appropriate and adequate answers to old problems for the new context rather than exploring the method by which these answers are formulated.

This latter task is now taken up by a theologian whose qualifications for it are unexcelled in all respects. As its author Stephen Bevans says, *An Introduction to Theology in Global Perspective* has been thirty-five years in the making, a long gestation by any measure. We are deeply grateful to the author for bringing the work to birth, for it is the culmination of decades of not only teaching all over the globe but also of missionary and pastoral work. It also brings together Bevans's groundbreaking and prolific scholarship on contextual theologies and missiology.

What makes this work especially helpful to theology students, beginning as well as advanced, is that it does not discuss theological method in the abstract but shows how theology is actually *done*. The goal is not simply to inform students' minds with theological contents, however important, but to form them into *theologians*. Doing theology in this way, Bevans consistently points out, is not a do-it-yourself job. Rather it is a communal—more precisely, ecclesial—enterprise, carried out with all kinds of people, professional and nonacademic, in a humble yet critical dialogue with Scripture and Tradition, and for Catholics, under the guidance of the magisterium.

Moreover, in an increasingly globalized world, the context and audience of theology are not only the church but also diverse cultures and different religious traditions. Here Bevans offers a masterful survey of various contextual theologies, to be taken not as mutually exclusive but as complementary ways of responding to the most urgent challenges to theology in our time.

Lastly, the theologian's eyes must look out not only horizontally as it were, to the contemporary world, but also vertically, to the past: How has theology been done? Who are the theological ancestors and what can be learned from their works? We all stand on the shoulders of other theologians—giants or not—so we can see farther and perhaps better. What is most interesting in Bevans's gaze on the history of theology is that it espies not only the familiar faces, mostly from the Greek, Latin, European, and North American worlds, but also strange and tongue-twisting names—from Latin America, Africa, Asia, Australia, Oceania, and New Zealand, of all races and ethnicities, young and old, women and men, of all theological tendencies and church denominations—truly a global theology for a globalized world, a foretaste of the Heavenly Jerusalem!

Bevans dedicates his work to his students, past and present, in all the places he has taught. Humbly he admits: *Docendo discimus* (we learn by teaching). My hope is that in perusing this book, global in perspective, theologically informative and balanced, pastorally sensitive, lucidly and engagingly written, we may be able to teach by learning—*discendo docemus*.

Acknowledgments

In a real sense, I have been writing this book since 1974, when I first began teaching the course "Introduction to Theology" at the Archdiocesan Major Seminary (now Immaculate Conception School of Theology) in Vigan, Ilocos Sur, Philippines. Since that time I have taught "Intro" many times—in Vigan; at Divine Word Seminary (now Divine Word School of Theology) Tagaytay City, Philippines; at Catholic Theological Union in Chicago; and, as the book was in the press, at Yarra Theological Union in Melbourne and the Broken Bay Institute in Sydney, Australia. First of all, therefore, I need to acknowledge the patience, the wisdom, the enthusiasm, and even the misgivings and disagreements with my students throughout the last thirty-five years. When the legendary Casey Stengel of the New York Yankees was congratulated for winning yet another World Series in the 1950s he is said to have remarked: "I couldn't have done it without the players." I have similar sentiments in regard to my students, and this is why this book is dedicated to them.

The large number of footnotes at the end of the book is also a testimony to the fact that what I have written in these pages could not have been written without the wisdom of many women and men down through the ages. I have always been convinced—as I have written in chapter 4—that theology is a communal, ecclesial endeavor. But this conviction has increased a hundredfold as I have completed this work. I am incredibly grateful for the conversations I have had with the likes of Isaiah and Paul, Ephrem and Augustine, Aquinas and Bonaventure, Hildegard and Mechtilde, Luther and Calvin, Teresa and Sor Juana, Newman and Oman, Johnson, Ruether, Gutiérrez, Cone, Phan, Magesa, Fabella, and many, many others.

Colleagues and friends have supported me in this project in ways that I'm sure they will never fully know. Let me mention first of all Peter Phan, the editor of this series, whose enthusiasm and patience were always an inspiration and a consolation for me as I worked on and completed my work. Not far behind Peter in receiving my gratitude is Bill Burrows of Orbis Books, now happily retired and working on his own research project. Bill has been my best friend and theological conversation partner for almost a half century now, and the home of Bill and his wife Linda in Cortlandt Manor, New York, has become a wonderful place of refuge and refreshment over the years. The staff of the library at Catholic Theological Union has been unfailing in their help with my research, especially Library Director Melody McMahon and former Library Director Ken O'Malley. Very helpful, as well, has been Miranda McDermott of the St. Paschal Library at Yarra Theological Union,

Melbourne. Among many colleagues let me mention Robert J. Schreiter, James Okoye, Dianne Bergant, Claude-Marie Barbour, Richard McCarron, Barbara Bowe, Barbara Reid, Eleanor Doidge, Carmen Nanko-Fernández, Orlando Espín, Edmund Chia, van Thanh Nguyen, Gary Riebe-Estrella and Richard R. Gaillardetz. Among many friends let me mention Mark Schramm, Stan Uroda, Judy Logue, Mark Weber, Jim Bergin, Judy Borchers, John Cockayne, Susan Smith, Neil Darragh, and John Dunn.

Dr. Christie Billups was kind—and brave—enough to use the manuscript as a textbook in her Introduction to Theology class at Lewis University in Joliet, Illinois. Adam Setmeyer was an incredible help as he chased down foot-notes during the summer of 2008. Gil Ostiek was a wealth of wisdom and knowledge as I asked him question after question about Latin phrases, liturgy, and history. My dear friend and sometime writing and teaching partner Roger Schroeder generously allowed me to include chapters 10 through 13 in the reading assignment for our course "Tradition: Sources through History" in the fall semester of 2008. Thanks, too, for the feedback from our students in that course. Thanks, finally, to my friends in the St. Giles Family Mass Community in Oak Park, Illinois, for whom and with whom it has been my privilege to minister and be ministered to in the last seven years. Without the spiritual nourishment that they have provided, writing this book—labor of love that it has been—would have been much more difficult indeed.

Introduction

THIS BOOK IS AN INTRODUCTION to doing Catholic systematic theology in global perspective, and each one of these terms needs a bit of an explanation.

DOING THEOLOGY

First of all, this is a book about *doing* theology. Some introductions to theology—for example, German theologian Dorothee Sölle's (1929-2003) wonderful book *Thinking about God*, the fine volumes edited by U.S. Anglos Peter Hodgson and Robert King or by British Evangelical theologian Alister McGrath—provide basic introductions to the *content* of theology by offering an overview of the history and meaning of the central doctrines of Christianity.[1] This is also what many courses of introduction to theology at the undergraduate level—Theo 101—do as well. Other introductions to theology focus on the *process* or *method* of theology—for example, the introduction published in India by Kuncheria Pathil and Dominic Veliath, British Dominican Aidan Nichols's *The Shape of Catholic Theology*, or Filipino José de Mesa and Belgian Lode Wostyn's *Doing Theology* published in the Philippines.[2]

This book will employ the second approach, focus on process or method. As I will emphasize again and again in these pages, it is important to understand theology not so much as a particular *content*, but as an *activity*, a process. And so, I believe, while it is important to get an overview of the basic content of Christian faith, it is much more important to learn how to *do* theology, to become a *theologian*.

DOING *CATHOLIC* THEOLOGY

Second, this is a book about doing *Catholic* theology. When I say this I do not mean that doing Catholic theology is the *only* way to do theology, or the only *valid* way. Not at all. As the reader will see, I will make use of many ideas of Christians from other traditions, and occasionally I will reflect on ideas from people of other faith traditions altogether (Buddhism, Hinduism, for example). What I mean is rather that I have a very particular perspective as I do theology. As a Catholic, for example, I will place strong emphasis on Tradition, and not just on Scripture. In the same way, a Catholic does theology always in dialogue with the church's teaching authority, the magisterium. And Catholics have some basic theological and philosophical convictions as

1

they do theology. As U.S. Anglo theologian Richard McBrien expresses it, Catholics are convinced of the *sacramentality* of the world, where anything and everything—an event, an object, a person—can become transparent to God's presence, a vehicle of God's grace. They are convinced as well of the value of *community*—Catholicism is not an understanding of Christianity that is exclusively based on "taking Jesus as your personal Savior," but one in which Christians are formed by age-old traditions, cherished practices, and constant elbow-rubbing with others. Finally, says McBrien, Catholicism is about *mediation*. This follows from the idea of both sacramentality and community, for while, on the one hand, Christians *do* have immediate access to God (and vice versa!), God can also be approached through others (holy women and men, saints), God's will and teaching are ordinarily channeled through those in authority (the magisterium), and others (again, holy women and men, saints) can be occasion for a special manifestation of God's presence. For Catholics, as we will see in the following pages, especially in chapter 4, theology is best done in the context of community, whether in face-to-face conversation, in scholarly dialogue, or in critical dialogue with the church's tradition and teaching office.[3] There is, indeed, a "Catholic imagination."[4]

DOING CATHOLIC *SYSTEMATIC* THEOLOGY

Third, this is an introduction to doing Catholic *systematic* theology. In the past, Catholics spoke of *dogmatic* theology; more recently we speak of *doctrinal* theology, but the term *systematic* theology expresses best what this book will try to introduce students to. The terms dogmatic or doctrinal theology point to the kind of theology I will talk about in these pages: a reflection on and in dialogue with the doctrinal tradition of Catholic thought. However, the term *systematic* points to the fact that this doctrinal tradition is not just an unconnected "laundry list" of "facts" or "beliefs." On the contrary, every doctrine is connected with every other doctrine, and every doctrine is a kind of lens or prism with which to view THE Christian doctrine: the reality that God, Holy Mystery, has revealed God's true self to women and men in the warp and woof of history, through the presence of the Spirit and in the life, death/resurrection, and especially the person of Jesus of Nazareth, and calls them into friendship and partnership.[5] In other words, the Christian doctrinal tradition is a *system*, with every doctrine explaining every other one, and each explaining and being explained by THE doctrine, THE Mystery, at the center (see figure on p. 3). This is the point that the First Vatican Council made in 1870, when it spoke about one of the chief ways in which we come to an understanding of a doctrine: by reflecting on the connection of the doctrines with each other.[6]

Furthermore, the doctrines can be *formed* into a system, depending on where one starts with one's theology, or how one gives emphasis to a particu-

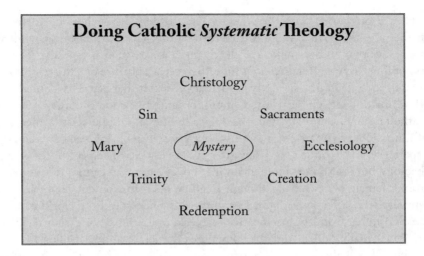

lar doctrine or doctrines. For example, if one would start one's theology from the perspective of the doctrine of the Trinity—how God is in God's deepest self an overflowing community-in-mission, one's theology would look quite different from one that began with an understanding of the human person as corrupted by sin, or if one started from the perspective of God's incarnation in Jesus Christ. Similarly, if one's ecclesiology were either open or exclusive, that would change the way one understood the person and work of Jesus, the nature of sin, or the entire doctrine of creation, not to mention one's understanding of The Mystery in the center. In her book on the Holy Spirit from a feminist perspective, Rebecca Button Prichard warns how a particular structuring of theology that starts from "God-the-Father-Almighty" establishes "a pattern that resists creative thinking, imagination, and novelty—the very gifts the Spirit offers."[7] Such a structure—the structure of the creeds for the most part—certainly has provided "an order and an agenda, but they also limit and exclude."[8] So we speak of *systematic* theology, not only reflecting on the doctrines of Christianity themselves, but on how they affect and are affected by all the others.

DOING CATHOLIC SYSTEMATIC THEOLOGY
IN GLOBAL PERSPECTIVE

Finally, this book is an introduction to doing Catholic systematic theology *in global perspective*. Such a perspective is key to this series of textbooks in Catholic theology and is, I believe, essential for doing Catholic systematic theology as such. Let me try to explain this global perspective briefly here.

On the one hand, theology must be rooted in a *particular* culture or context—something that I will insist on again and again as this book unfolds. I believe strongly that, in reality, there is no "theology" as such—no "universal theology"—there are only contextual theologies.[9] "Context," however, while it is a reality that allows one to see clearly from a particular perspective, is also something that can, if not *blindfold* one, then certainly cause one to wear blinders that severely limit vision. My particular context is that of a sixty-something white male living in the United States, ordained (for almost forty years) a Catholic priest, well-educated, theologically liberal, middle class, a member of a missionary congregation, and with a good number of years' missionary experience. This context, as I say, gives me a very rich perspective for doing theology, but it also puts blinders on me. Try as I might, I cannot do theology from a female perspective, although I can be open to women's concerns and feminist issues. Try as I might, I cannot really understand the world or read the Scriptures from the perspective of black, or Latino/a, or Asian realities, nor can I really understand the sometimes desperate and risk-filled lives of the poor. I will always be a U.S. American; I will always have the privilege of a white, ordained man, and I will inevitably fall into the trap of allowing that perspective to shape my understanding of Christian faith.

Therefore, in order to see past the blinders of my own context, I need to listen carefully to those other cultures, contexts, and social locations. I can never speak as one of them—as neither can a black male speak for an Asian woman—but I can listen, and expand my understanding, and I can approach my own thinking with what third world and feminist theologians have called a "hermeneutics of suspicion"—a recognition that, try as I might, my particular theological perspective is also a biased one.[10] Theology today should not be done by steeping oneself in only one tradition—whether it be Nigerian, Malaysian, Brazilian, or Roman. Theology today needs to be done in a dialogue with one's own contextual perspective and the broad and deep tradition of the Christian church, and in a dialogue as well with the results of this interaction and the perspectives of Christians from every part of our world.

Like me, readers of this book will each come out of their particular contexts—Latino college students, white middle-aged, middle-class women, African and Asian seminarians, Filipino or Asian lay men and women. Like my context, their context will give them a clear, penetrating lens with which to read the Scriptures and interpret the Christian tradition. However, like me as well, they also are limited by the same context that so enriches them, and they will also need to listen carefully to women and men from cultures and contexts that differ—often quite considerably—from theirs.

This is why I am writing—and the reader should be reading—in *global perspective*. We live in a church today, as Karl Rahner pointed out over a quarter century ago, that for the first time is really *catholic*, really a world church.[11] There is no longer a European and North Atlantic center and a third world periphery—indeed, as we will see in part 4, this has never been so. But especially today, the church is fully established and flourishing in every sense, with few exceptions, in every part of the world. Furthermore, since the end of the twentieth century, the "center of gravity" of Christianity has shifted from the white, affluent world of Europe, North America, and Australia/New Zealand to the world of black, brown, and Asian Christians, and theology is flourishing there. This is why, throughout my career as a teacher and a theologian and in writing this book, I have tried, as much as possible, to "listen to all the voices" as I do theology from my own particular yet limited perspective.

What I have tried to present in these pages is an introduction to doing systematic theology that is, on the one hand, fairly traditional in its shape and content. It deals with very traditional questions with which every theologian—formally trained or not—needs to grapple: revelation, faith, tradition, magisterium, method, history. On the other hand, I have tried to write this book by listening to theologians—both their insights and their challenges—from many cultures in my own country and throughout the entire world as well. And so, while the *questions* may be traditional, much of the organization of the book and the answers to the questions discussed have been profoundly influenced by this commitment to listen to the wider church.

What I ask of my readers is that they read this book from the perspective of their own context, but also try to expand that context and avoid the blinders that their context provides by "listening to all the voices" themselves. In this way they will be introduced to doing a truly *catholic* theology in quite another sense—although a complementary one—than what I described above: they will learn how to be faithful to their own particular culture, gender, generation, national identity while at the same time expanding their understanding beyond their own particularity to embrace, learn from, and even challenge other ways of thinking and expression. In order to highlight the contexts from which theologians come, the first time I refer to or quote a theologian in this book I will try to describe her or him in terms of her or his cultural context, social location, or national affiliation (the reader will notice that I have done this already). Such designations might seem a bit awkward, but in doing theology in global perspective it is important to know the basic contextual situation of every dialogue partner.

Theology today, I firmly believe, must be done in this global perspective. It *must* be contextual; but it must also be in dialogue, open to the other, ready to change, ready to challenge, ready to enrich and be enriched. This is what this series hopes to do for theology in general. This is what I hope to do as women and men are introduced to the art of doing Catholic systematic theology in the pages that follow.

Part I

Faith Seeking Understanding

The Nature of Theology

WHAT, REALLY, *IS* THEOLOGY? It is certainly "knowledge about God," as the roots of the word "theology" imply, but it is much more. God is ultimately unknowable in human concepts and images, and so the "knowledge" we have of God in theology is a knowledge that is the result of our own free response to God's offer of relationship and friendship with Godself. The purpose of part 1 of this book, then, is to come to a *definition* and *understanding* of theology in the light of the fact that any knowledge we have of God is really the result of God's gift. Theology, in other words, is the result of grace!

In chapter 1 we will approach a *definition* of theology by reflecting in a kind of first step on the incomprehensible and ineffable Mystery of God, always and everywhere present in the whole of creation and in human history, who offers women and men a personal relationship and, indeed, friendship through the offer and gift of revelation. Then, in a kind of second and third step, chapter 2 will reflect on the human response to revelation—the act of faith—and then on how that response inevitably moves toward a deeper understanding that involves the entire person. When this move happens, theology—or theologizing—has begun.

The best *definition* of theology, I will suggest, is an old one. It comes from the writings of the eleventh-century monk and bishop Anselm of Canterbury, who describes the act of theologizing as "faith seeking understanding." Chapter 2 will then move to a deeper *understanding* of our definition by showing how each one of the three words in this definition is important, and why "faith" and "understanding," in Catholic thought, need always to be kept together.

Chapter 3 will then draw out eight implications of our definition in a kind of variation on a musical theme in the light of the reality of today's world church. Theology, we will see, is much more than simply "knowledge about God." It is a special *kind* of knowledge—true, and yet always incomplete— that is discovered when *any* Christian seeks to understand her or his faith, but it is best discovered when this seeking is done in the context of the community of other Christian believers. It is always a seeking for understanding in a particular culture, always inspired by and directed to ministry and mission, always nourished by and nourishing in turn our spirituality. Theology, as we will see finally, cannot be confined to logical discursive thinking, or even to words. Christians do theology in poetry, in drama, in the visual and the musical arts. However and whenever faithful Christians seek to understand their faith, with whatever resources are available, they have begun to do theology.

1

Mystery and Revelation

"THEOLOGY," ALMOST ANY EDUCATED PERSON KNOWS, is derived from two Greek words: *theos*, which means "God," and *logos*, which means "word" or "thought." Etymologically, then, theology means a word or thought, or speaking or thinking *about God*. A number of years ago, the Scottish theologian John Macquarrie wrote a book about the nature of theology and entitled it according to this etymological thinking: *God-talk*; or, to refer to the title of a groundbreaking book by U.S. feminist scholar Rosemary Radford Ruether, *feminist* theology is developed by reflecting on *Sexism and God-Talk*.[1]

In his classic introduction to theology, the Quebecois Jesuit René Latourelle gives a more *scholastic* definition. Theology, he says, is knowledge that has God as its object, or knowledge of God.[2] So if *anthropology* is knowledge about the human person (*anthropos*), and *biology* is knowledge about *bios*, or life, and *sociology* is knowledge about society or social groups, theology is knowledge about God, knowledge that has God for its object.

Now, these two ways of defining theology—etymologically and in the context of scholastic theology—are quite traditional, true, and in many ways very helpful. They are very close to the way Thomas Aquinas (1225-1274) talks about theology in the *Summa Theologiae*.[3] A theological textbook that was widely used in the 1950s teaches that theology "according to its etymology, means 'teaching concerning God,'" and the text refers to no less an authority than St. Augustine's *City of God* (8.1) and concludes that "Thus theology is the science of God."[4]

As I say, these ways of defining theology are very traditional, certainly true, in many ways very helpful. They are certainly very neat and clear. There is, however, one big problem with this kind of approach: *God is not and can never be an object!* As Indian theologian Stanley J. Samartha expresses it, "God is never the object of human knowledge. God always remains the eternal subject."[5] Or, as Chilean Ronaldo Muñoz writes, "We cannot make God into an 'object' in the scientific sense of the word, something we can place in front of ourselves, to examine its contours and understand it intellectually."[6] God can only be subject; God is always ineffable Holy Mystery.

KNOWING THE UNKNOWABLE GOD

When we do theology we *do* really speak of God, and we *do* have real knowledge about God. This is indeed what theology is, for if we *can't* speak of or have knowledge of God theology would be impossible! But when we say this we also need to recognize that, ultimately, God can *never* be adequately grasped or understood with human concepts or logic. What this means is that, right from the beginning, we have to understand what theology is within the long tradition in Christianity—and in other religious ways as well—of *negative*, or *apophatic*, theology (*apophatic* from *apophainomai* in Greek, which means "to refuse").

In Christianity, this tradition of negative theology is deeply rooted in the Bible. In the Book of Exodus, for example, Moses at one point asks God to show him the divine glory (33:18)—in other words, God's deepest reality. In response, God says, "I will make all my goodness pass before you, and will proclaim before you the name, 'The Lord'. . . . But . . . you cannot see my face; for no one shall see me and live" (33:19-20). So God shelters Moses in the cleft of a rock, covers him with the divine hand, and then passes by him with all the divine glory. And, God says, after passing by: "I will take away my hand, and you shall see my back; but my face shall not be seen" (33:23). Moses, in other words, could have *indirect* knowledge of God—knowledge of God's "back"— but, as a human being, he cannot have direct, face-to-face knowledge.

Other examples from the Old Testament might be cited from Isaiah 6, the great scene of Isaiah's vocation as a prophet, where the prophet comes face to face with the ineffable majesty of God; or from Isaiah 45:15, where God is described as a hidden God; or from the magnificent scene toward the end of the Book of Job, when Job, after hearing of God's wonders, can only respond: "I lay my hand on my mouth" (Job 40:4; see also chapters 38-39). In the New Testament, as well, we read in John's Gospel that, despite the fact that God is revealed in Jesus Christ, "No one has ever seen God" (John 1:8). Indeed, even though we know God in Christ, we still know dimly, as if looking in a mirror (1 Cor. 13:12); God in Godself "dwells in unapproachable light" (1 Tim. 6:16). At the end of a long reflection on how, after Jesus, God will still be faithful to Israel, Paul ends by basically throwing up his hands: "O the depth of the riches and wisdom and knowledge of God! How unsearchable are God's judgments and how inscrutable God's ways!" (Rom. 11:33).

This biblical insight about God's radical ineffability is articulated throughout the Christian tradition as well, both in the East and in the West. Gregory of Nyssa (335?-394?), one of the great Cappadocian theologians of the fourth century (along with his brother and sister Basil of Caesarea and Macrina the Younger, together with their friend Gregory of Nazianzen), spoke of God as "that smooth, steep and sheer rock, on which the mind can find no secure resting place to get a grip or to lift ourselves up. . . . In spite of every effort our minds cannot approach him."[7] Augustine, bishop of Hippo in North Africa (354-430), perhaps the most influential theologian in the Western church, says in a famous passage in one of his sermons that "if you have understood, then this is not God. If you were able to understand, then you understood something else instead of God. If you were able to understand even partially, then you have deceived yourself with your own thoughts."[8] And another Western theologian, Isidore of Seville (d. 636), wrote in the seventh century that "God is known correctly only when we deny that he can be known perfectly."[9]

In the Middle Ages in the West, perhaps theology's greatest achievement was Thomas Aquinas's *Summa Theologiae*. Right in the beginning of this work, after he has demonstrated the existence of God with his famous "five ways" (part I, question 2, article 3), Aquinas begins question 3 with a short but important prologue. He says that ordinarily, once we have proved the *existence* of something, we would proceed to answer "the further question of the manner of its existence, in order that we may know its essence." But in the case of God, he says, that is impossible. "Because we cannot know what God is, but rather what He is not, we have no means of considering how God is, but rather how He is not."[10] Aquinas then spends questions 3 to 11 speaking in largely *negative* terms about God: God's simplicity, goodness, unity, infinity, eternity, omnipresence, immutability. Then, in questions 12 and 13, he goes on to reflect on how God can be known and named. God, says Aquinas, cannot be known "univocally," that is, what we say about God is never *exactly* the way God is. But, on the other hand, God is not known "equivocally," meaning that what we say about God does indeed bear some truth. Therefore, our knowledge of God is always by "analogy,"[11] meaning that language about God can express what God is really like, but never *completely* what God is like. In fact, it says more about what God is *not* like than what God is like—or, as one of my teachers once put it, analogy is like an arrow that always hits the target, but never hits the bull's-eye![12]

Aquinas goes on to examine virtually the whole Christian doctrinal and ethical tradition in the rest of the work, but always, it must be presumed, with the kind of respect for the apophatic tradition that he evidences in his treatment of God. Apparently, however, his caution was not enough. One day, the story goes, Thomas had a vision of Christ while he was celebrating Mass, and from that day forward never wrote again. "I cannot go on," he said. "All that I have written seems like so much straw compared to what I have seen and what has been revealed to me."[13] He died soon after.

The tradition of negative theology continued into the late Middle Ages and up until our own day. The German mystic Meister Eckhart (1260-1329) spoke of the importance, for true knowledge of God, of taking leave of God for the sake of God—in other words, recognizing that radical inability of our own efforts to express God's reality adequately.[14] Another late medieval German mystic, Nicholas of Cusa (1401-1464), spoke of the best knowledge of God as being a "learned ignorance" (*docta ignorantia*), "because he was sure that it was 'learned' to admit to ignorance about the One who thus transcends all human thinking, about the Trinity who transcends all human numbering, about the divine perfection 'beyond the best.'"[15]

The early modern French philosopher Blaise Pascal (1623-1662), who had his own experience of God's ineffability as "'God of Abraham, God of Isaac, God of Jacob,' not of philosophers and scholars,"[16] wrote that "a religion that does not affirm that God is hidden is not true."[17] And two centuries later, the great Danish philosopher and theologian Søren Kierkegaard (1813-1855), reacting to the rationalism of the philosopher Georg Wilhelm Friedrich Hegel (1770-1831), insisted that there exists between God and humanity an infinite qualitative difference—an idea that influenced Swiss theologian Karl Barth's (1886-1968) theology as well.[18] (Barth, it is said, used to joke that the angels would smile when they read his theology. Obviously the man who was arguably the greatest theologian of the twentieth century recognized that he also needed to do theology in the apophatic tradition!) Barth's German contemporary Paul Tillich (1886-1965) did theology in a very different way, but he certainly agreed with Barth in terms of being cautious regarding language about God. Tillich wrote that "one can only speak of the ultimate in a language which at the same time denies the possibility of speaking about it."[19]

Articulations of the apophatic tradition can sometimes come from surprising sources. Writing in *America* magazine in 2004, U.S. Anglo philosopher Michael McCauley relates an incident in his class when a "shadowy figure with one name [Dooley] who slides in and out of class and oblivious to all assignments" remarks "when we give God a name, when we call Him 'God,' we shrink him."[20]

Let me conclude this rather whirlwind tour of the Christian apophatic tradition with a passage from the contemporary U.S. Catholic feminist scholar Elizabeth Johnson. For Johnson, the tradition of divine ineffability is an important foundation for the construction of language about God that goes beyond the almost exclusively *male* language and imagery to include other imagery (e.g., rock), but *especially* female imagery. And so she summarizes the apophatic tradition as follows:

> In essence, God's unlikeness to the corporal and spiritual finite world is total. Hence, human beings simply cannot understand God. No human concept, word, or image, all of which originate in experience of created reality, can circumscribe divine reality, nor can any human construct express with any measure of adequacy the mystery of God who is ineffable.
>
> . . . This sense of an unfathomable depth of mystery, of a vastness of God's glory too great for the human mind to grasp, undergirds the religious significance of speech about God. Such speech never definitively possesses or masters its subject but leads the speakers ever more profoundly into attitudes of awe and adoration.[21]

As I mentioned earlier, this apophatic tradition is not confined to Christianity. It seems that in *every* religious tradition there is a strong, often subaltern, tradition of mysticism and caution about the language used about God or about what is most real in existence. A very famous phrase from Buddhism commands the religious person to *kill* the Buddha if you actually meet him.[22] In the Kena Upanishad, one of the scriptures of Hinduism, we read about the knowledge of Brahman in a way that recalls Nicholas of Cusa's idea of "learned ignorance": "I cannot imagine 'I know him well,' and yet I cannot say 'I know him not.' Who of us knows this, knows him; and not who says 'I know him not'. He comes to the thought of those who know him beyond thought, not to those who imagine he can be attained by thought. He is unknown to the learned and known to the simple."[23] The Chinese classic the *Tao Te Ching* begins with the famous lines: "The Tao that can be told is not the eternal Tao. / The name that can be named is not the eternal name."[24] Sura 18:109 of the Qur'an reads: "Say: if the ocean were to turn into ink (for writing) the (creative) Words of my Lord, the ocean would be expended before the Words of my Lord are—even if we were to bring another ocean like it."[25] In Judaism, finally, an example of the apophatic tradition is articulated by the great German Jewish philosopher and theologian Martin Buber (1878-1965): "God, the eternal Presence, does not permit Himself to be held. Woe to the man so possessed that he thinks he possesses God!"[26]

KNOWING THE MYSTERY

So the first step in understanding the nature of theology is to recognize, with the Christian tradition and with traditions of all the great religions of the world, that God is incomprehensible and ineffable: no thought, no image, no concept can adequately grasp God's reality, and, really, the deepest knowledge of God is *to know we cannot ever know*. As Gregory of Nyssa says so beautifully: "For the one who runs toward the Lord, there is no lack of space. The one who ascends never stops, going from beginning to beginning, by beginnings that never cease."[27]

Paradoxically, however, as even the apophatic tradition hints, this does not mean that God cannot be known by human beings. At least in our Christian tradition we say that God is fully known in the person and ministry of Jesus Christ. Yes, as John says, "No one has ever seen God"; but he goes on to say that "it is God the only Son, who is close to the Father's heart, who has made him known" (1:18). As U.S. Anglo theologian John Sanders writes, "Jesus manifests the real nature of God. . . . The God who comes to us in history is a God who relates, adapts, responds and loves. That is what God is actually like."[28] What the Christian tradition of negative theology means is *not* that we cannot know God at all, but rather that we always know God as Mystery, THE Mystery,

ABSOLUTE Mystery, or HOLY Mystery. Hilary of Poitiers (d. 368) put it profoundly: "I possess the Reality although I do not understand it" (*quod ignoro iam teneo*).[29]

Even in Jesus, God is Mystery, and so we need to ask just what a Mystery is, and how we can *know* such a mystery?

Problem and Mystery

A first step, I think, in approaching an understanding of Mystery is to distinguish, as does the twentieth-century French Catholic existentialist philosopher Gabriel Marcel (1888-1973), between a "problem" and a "mystery." For Marcel, a "problem" is something that is unknown, but that somehow, eventually, through human intelligence or just serendipity, I can figure out or solve: it is "something I meet, which I find complete before me, but which I can therefore lay siege or reduce."[30] For example, I have a problem with my computer, or with my car, or with a difficult theology book. With enough work, or study, or (most probably) knowing the right person to ask to help me, I can figure out why my computer keeps freezing, or how to change a flat tire, or how to understand Karl Rahner. I can *solve* problems, and basically move on.

A "mystery," says Marcel, is very different. A mystery isn't something *unknown* or *unknowable* but something that is already *known*, but absolutely impossible to be figured out, solved, or controlled. It is, we might say, *super-knowable*—something *so* knowable that, like the Energizer Bunny in U.S. television commercials, I keep "going and going and going" into my understanding of it. A mystery, says Marcel, "is something in which I myself am involved."[31] Solving a *problem*, in other words, is like going from the dark into the light. Knowing a mystery is like being blinded by the light—there is a line in an old hymn that says when we know God "'tis only the splendor of light hideth thee."[32] Or, as U.S. Anglo theologian John Haught expresses it:

> Instead of vanishing as we grow wiser, [mystery] actually appears to loom larger and deeper. The realm of mystery keeps on expanding before us as we solve our particular problems. It resembles a horizon that recedes into the distance as we advance. Unlike problems, it has no clear boundaries. While problems can eventually be removed, the encompassing domain of mystery remains a constantly receding frontier the deeper we advance into it.[33]

So the question is not that Mystery is unknowable, but how we come to know Mystery. One can know Mystery, but in a very different way than one comes to know the solution to a problem. This is what we need to reflect on a bit here.

The Knowledge of Revelation

I think the best way to explain how we come to know THE Mystery is to reflect on how we come to know Mystery in our everyday, ordinary experience—how, in other words, we come to know the mystery of a human person. Like God, human persons can never be reduced to objects. We can try to reduce them, of course. We see this every day in the news: think of atrocities like the Holocaust, the Vietnam War, or the genocide in Rwanda or Sudan. Nevertheless, when we treat a person as an object we are not really dealing with a human being as a *person*. As Martin Buber put it famously, when we do this we treat a human person not as they deserve—as a "Thou"—but as a thing, as an "It."[34] An indication of this is the common experience of trying to describe someone to another. I can describe the person until I'm blue in the face—what kind of eyes she has, the way she wears her hair, the way she walks, how kind she is, and so forth. But in the end I give up and say "You'll just have to meet her!" In other words, we have to encounter persons in their mystery to really know them; we have to meet them in person, we have to experience them for ourselves.

But even then we can't get at the full mystery of the person. That happens only if that person *allows* me to know him or her—or, to put it another way, it happens only through a self-gift of the person's self, in other words, a *revelation*. Naturally, we can get to know *some* aspects of a person by being given information, or by observation or deduction—for example, the color of a person's eyes, the set of the chin, a sense of the person's physical strength. But to know a person as a person that person has to *let* you know him or her; that person has to reveal himself or herself to the other. As Scottish philosopher John Macmurray puts it:

> I can know another person *as a person* only by entering into personal relation with him. Without this I can know him only by observation and inference; only objectively. The knowledge which I can obtain in this way is valid knowledge; my conclusions from observations can be true or false, they can be verified or falsified by further observation or by experiment. But it is abstract knowledge, since it constructs its object by limitation of attention to what can be known about other persons without entering into personal relations with them.[35]

And so it is, by analogy with knowledge of THE Mystery, God. Like our knowledge of human persons, God, says U.S. feminist theologian Catherine LaCugna, is mystery precisely because God is *personal*—and in fact the *origin* of all personhood.[36] We can know *some* things about God—objective data—by ourselves, by "natural reason," as the First Vatican Council teaches (DS 3004). God as God is in Godself, in the depth of who God is, in God's Mystery, can only be known through self-gift and self-revelation, and this is a free gift on God's part. Knowing God as God really is the result of grace. God always takes the first step toward human beings.

THE MYSTERY OF REVELATION

But how does this self-gift, this revelation take place? Let's look how it takes place between human persons; then it will be clear how it happens between human persons and God. Let me start with two very personal examples.

The first example is an incident that took place almost forty years ago when I was a student in Rome. I had left the United States with both excitement and regret several months before. I was excited about seeing Europe and especially the center of Catholicism, but I also left behind some wonderful friends whom I had gotten to know very deeply and intimately in the year or so before I departed. One day I sat down and wrote a long letter to one of these friends, really opening up my heart, and telling him a few things about myself that I had told almost nobody else before. A week or so after mailing the letter, about five in the morning, there was a knock at my door, and the brother who was in charge of answering the phone at our Collegio del Verbo Divino informed me that I had a telephone call from the United States. I didn't know what to think—were my parents OK? Had something happened in the family? Or to one of my friends? No—it was the friend to whom I had written several days before, with another close friend, calling to say that they were staying up late in Chicago and were talking about me, and that they just wanted to call and say they had read the letter and that I was still their friend!

A second example took place much later in my life, perhaps about fifteen years ago now. A friend of mine who had been mentor to me over the years was leaving the United States to live and work in Australia, and our community in Chicago was celebrating a last Christmas with him. When it came time for the exchange of gifts, this man had a special gift for me. I opened the envelope and inside was a year's membership to the Art Institute of Chicago—something I had wanted to get for myself for a very long time but just had never gotten around to it. It was a simple gesture, but I can't express how much it meant to me. It expressed in ways that words could never do my friend's care and concern for me.

In these moments I experienced something like magic and really came face to face with the mystery of these friends in a way that I recall all these years later. In moments like these, through very small and really ordinary things—a phone call, a gift, something *objective*—somehow the *subjective*, the mystery of a *person* was communicated. I knew these friends then—as I know them now—in a totally different way than I knew them before: I knew *them*; in a real sense, I had encountered their *mystery*. And I was able to do it because they had *allowed* me to know them; they had *revealed themselves* to me.

The same dynamic takes place when God reveals Godself to women and men. At certain times in our lives, God's gracious presence becomes manifest in our lives as God communicates God's *subjectivity* through *objectivity*. Through concrete events in our lives, or concrete persons, or particular words—very ordinary things—God becomes present and palpable to us in all God's incomprehensible, inexpressible, mysterious reality. The third-century Syrian-born theologian Irenaeus (ca. 130-200) expressed it well when he wrote about the Israelites that "God kept calling them to what was primary by means of what was secondary."[37] This is the pattern of divine revelation: the finite reveals the infinite, the objective reveals the subjective, what is ordinary reveals what is Mystery.

It's important to understand, however, that as gracious as God's revelation is, and as free as God is in revealing Godself, we shouldn't conceive of it as God, as it were, "zipping in" and "zipping out" of our lives. Rather, revelation simply points to the fact that at certain graced, really unexplainable moments, *we become aware of God's constant presence within our world, and within our lives*. It is at these times that we realize, with the French novelist Georges Bernanos, that "all is grace"; or as the poet Gerard Manley Hopkins wrote "the world is charged with the grandeur of God."[38]

A wonderful example of how this revelation takes place is found in the work of the U.S. American artist Bev Doolittle. In many of her paintings what one sees at first glance is only a very superficial view of what is actually there. For example, in one of her paintings, entitled *Hide and Seek*, we see at first the words "hide and seek," painted in a dappled pattern of brown and white. As we look closer, though, we begin to see hidden in the painting one brown and white pinto horse, and then another, and then another. The painting at first hides the images of the horses, but as one looks more and more carefully, they become clearer and clearer to the observer. The horses were there all the time, we just needed to pay more attention so that the painting could reveal them to us (see Bev Doolittle's art at http://www.galleryone.com/doolittle_prints .htm; see *Hide and Seek* at http://www.galleryone.com/images/doolittle/doo little%20-%20hideseek.jpg).

In a similar way, early-twentieth-century British theologian John Oman (1860-1939) gives a striking example from his own experience. One day, he writes, he had been driven around the county of Suffolk in eastern England. The weather had been perfect, the spring was in full bloom, and "the variety of greens and browns infinite, the light of unearthly perfection," and the farms and villages he had seen were "a panorama of varied beauty." At one point he arrived at Flatford Mill, the place where the nineteenth-century artist John Constable had lived and worked as a young man. Oman entered the millhouse and looked out of the window, seeing what he thought Constable might have seen "any time he lifted his head from his work" at the mill. What was framed in the window was, after all the glories of the day, a rather commonplace scene. And yet it was the scene of one of Constable's masterpieces: *The Hay Wain*. In one sense, as Constable saw the scene day after day, it was always "there." But it was not until he saw it with his artist's eyes that he actually *saw* it. It was not simply a matter of the beauty of the scene "breaking in" on the artist. It was because of his artist's sensitivity and openness to the reality of nature that he could see the ordinary as it really is: something of extraordinary beauty.[39] (See *The Hay Wain* at http://www.nationalgallery.org.uk/cgi-bin/WebObjects.dll/CollectionPublisher.woa/wa/work?workNumber=NG1207.)

It is something like this that happens in a moment of divine revelation. We become "aware" of the divine presence that is always already there; we *see* it again for the first time. Speaking of the Holy Spirit—who is always the agent of God's revelation—British bishop John V. Taylor says that although we speak about the Spirit "as a source of *power*," what is really going on is that the Spirit "enables us not by making us supernaturally strong, but by opening our eyes."[40]

WHERE REVELATION IS FOUND

This experience or manifestation of God's presence is found chiefly in three "places" in our lives: in our everyday experience, in the experience of reading or hearing the Word of God in Scripture, and in the experience of the meaning of the Christian Tradition.

Human Experience

First and foremost, God manifests Godself to us in our *everyday experience*. "The mystery of existence is always showing through the texture of ordinary lives," wrote U.S. Southern white novelist Flannery O'Connor.[41] Malaysian theologian Edmund Chia quotes U.S. Anglo theologian Robert J. Schreiter: "Revelation does not drop out of the sky as a series of truths; it comes to us in experience in concrete, existential encounter."[42] In moments of prayer or quiet, for example, a thought or a realization might "jump out" at us. I remember vividly one time at prayer when I was struggling with a particular bad habit in my life. As I thought and prayed over the matter, suddenly without warning I "heard" deep within my heart a kind of voice saying "don't worry—I understand—I am patient." All at once a great peace surrounded me and I realized that despite my struggles I was loved and accepted by God in a way that only grace could accomplish.

Often in the events of our lives we might experience a sense that God is present and near. Sometimes these experiences are "up" experiences—e.g., the birth of a child, passing an exam, a close call in a car when we narrowly avoid an accident. Such experiences we might name "limit *of*" experiences.[43] In these moments we realize that our experience, as it were, opens up a doorway to a whole other dimension of existence. These are experiences that "take our breath away" and give us a glimpse of the incredible depth of reality.

My Vietnamese students often tell stories of how they know God was near when they escaped Vietnam on the high seas, braving storms and attacks by pirates. I remember an experience I had floating one day off the beach at Anzio, Italy, in the Mediterranean Sea; as I was floating, kicking up drops of water that were catching the rays of the noonday sun I was all of a sudden overcome by a sense of certainty that all was well with my life—indeed, all was well with the world. God might be manifest in the beauty of nature—my brother once confessed that after he had seen Yosemite National Park in California he had to believe in God. Or perhaps we experience a sense of God's reality in the context of world events—many Filipinos claimed to experience this in the 1986 EDSA Revolution that ousted the dictator Marcos.[44]

We can also speak about "down" experiences, or what we might call "limit *to*" experiences—times when we experience a failure in life, such as not getting accepted for perpetual vows in our community or breaking up with a spouse or lover, or a tragedy or death in our family, or the news that we have a life-threatening disease like cancer. These are times when we recognize the extreme contingency or *limitedness* of our lives; it's like a door being slammed in our face in the opposite experience of the "limit of" experience.[45] But so often in these bleak moments we can experience the presence and strength of God who walks with us, suffers with us, even helps us bear our burden. These can also be moments of a profound sense of the presence of God in our lives.

Perhaps most of all, though, it is the people in our lives who are the occasions of God's revelation for us—those to whom and with whom we minister, those whom we love, even those we struggle to accept or get along with. These are our *abuelas*, our grandmothers, our uncles, our parents, *kababayan*, good friends, patients in the hospital who are dying with dignity, teachers who model to us what real integrity is. Years ago, when I was a missionary in the Philippines, I was giving a two-day retreat to Catholic school teachers in Binmaley, Pangasinan, in central Luzon. I was not pleased with the way my talks had gone the first day, but at the end of the day a woman approached me and poured out her heart concerning a daughter from whom she had been estranged. She asked me to pray for her so that she could forgive her daughter. Everyone went home for the night, and the next morning the woman came running up to me right before the retreat was to resume. I wouldn't believe it, she exclaimed. When she had returned home the previous evening her estranged daughter was there waiting for her, begging her forgiveness—and the woman said she had found it in her heart to forgive her. Here I was, worried about my performance, when God had allowed me to touch this woman deeply, despite myself! I certainly experienced the presence of God in this experience.

The point of this first "place" where God manifests Godself to us in revelation is that, at any moment, through *any* kind of object or experience or person, God reveals God's constant presence in our lives. This is precisely what we Catholics mean when we speak of the *sacramentality* of the world, of life, of the present moment. What Cuban-American theologian Roberto Goizueta says of human persons could also, I believe, be said about all of human experience: "To suggest that the particular mediates the universal is to suggest that there is no such thing as an isolated, individual entity that is not intrinsically related to others. . . . In other words, every 'individual' is a particular, unique mediation of the universal humanity, universal creation, and, in the last analysis, a unique mediation of the Absolute."[46] The world is indeed "charged with the grandeur of God."

Sacred Scripture

The second way that God manifests God's presence in our lives is through the Scriptures, when they are read or being proclaimed. It is important to note immediately, however, that the Scriptures do not mediate God's presence in any automatic or mechanical way.

In his wonderful sermon on Ezekiel's condemnation of the false shepherds in chapter 34, St. Augustine reflects on verses 13 and 14, about how Israel will be fed "on the mountains of Israel." The mountains of Israel, he says, are "the mountains of Holy Scripture." "There, are the things that will delight your hearts; there you will find nothing poisonous, nothing hostile; there the pastures are most plentiful. There you will be healthy sheep; you will feed safely on the mountain of Israel." But Augustine goes on to caution his listeners not to "place our hopes in the good mountains themselves. . . . For your help is *from the Lord who made heaven and earth*." What is important, in other words, is not Scripture itself, but the fact that Scripture reveals the person and presence of God. I like to think that at certain times in our reading or hearing of Scripture, Scripture *becomes* the word of God—it's as though God's Word is not so much in the *words* of Scripture, but *between the lines*.

It is the experience of God *through* the Scriptures—"on the mountains"—that God reveals Godself; not the Scriptures as such. The great medieval German mystic Hildegard of Bingen (1098-1179) attests to this in her work *Scivias:*

It happened that, in the eleven hundred and forty-first year of the Incarnation of the Son of God, Jesus Christ, . . . Heaven was opened and a fiery light of exceeding brilliance came and permeated my whole brain, and inflamed my whole heart and my whole breast, not like a burning but like a warming flame, as the sun warms anything its rays touch. And immediately I knew the meaning of the exposition of the Scriptures, namely the Psalter, the Gospel and the other catholic volumes of the Old and New Testaments. . . .[47]

At certain times, as I say, Scripture *becomes* God's word; the story of Scripture—*the* Story—becomes *my* story. Or the word touches us just where we need to be touched. Think of the famous moment of Augustine's conversion to Christianity: when he was in the midst of crisis he heard a child saying in the distance *tole, lege*—take up and read. And so he randomly opened the Scriptures to the passage in Paul's letter to the Romans (13:13-14): ". . . not in debauchery and licentiousness. . . . Instead, put on the Lord Jesus Christ, and make no provision for the flesh, to gratify its desires." Augustine writes, "I had no wish to read further, and no need. For in that instant, with the very ending of the sentence, it was as though a light of utter confidence shone in all my heart, and all the darkness and uncertainty vanished away."[48]

Scripture that becomes God's word can often satisfy our questions and needs in a particularly powerful way. Think of the two disciples on the way to Emmaus, and how Jesus answered their doubts and questions by opening their minds to the meaning of the Old Testament (Luke 24:13-35). "'Were not our hearts burning within us while he was talking with us on the road, while he was opening the scriptures to us?'" (24:32). Often as well, Scripture can challenge us in a particularly powerful way. A good example of this is the conversion experience of St. Antony of Egypt (251-356), one of the first Christian monks and an early African saint. Born into a wealthy family, he happened to hear read one day the line from Matthew 19:21 (from the Gospel story of the rich young man): ". . . go, sell your possessions, and give the money to the poor, and you will have treasure in heaven; then come, follow me." Robert Ellsberg, a U.S. Anglo spiritual writer, tells us that "it seemed to Antony that this text was addressed personally to him. He immediately sold all his possessions and donated the proceeds to the poor, keeping only what he required for himself and his sister. Later, hearing the gospel verse, 'Do not be anxious about tomorrow' [Matt. 6:34] he regretted even this minor concession to prudence. After settling his sister in a convent, he gave up all his holdings and dedicated himself entirely to God."[49]

Finally, Scripture can open up an experience of God's presence that was not in our lives before, as happened in the story of the Ethiopian eunuch (another early African saint) in the Acts of the Apostles. Puzzled by the passage about the Suffering Servant in Isaiah 53, the eunuch's mind and heart were enlightened by the preaching of Philip, whom the Spirit had inspired to go down the road to Gaza and run after the eunuch's chariot (see Acts 8:26-40).

"Faith looks *through* the Scriptures, not *at* them," writes Canadian theologian Douglas John Hall.[50] And as we look through the Scriptures, they reveal to us—in simple words, simple stories, and sometimes bumbling characters—the very mystery of God.

The Christian Tradition

The third way that God can manifest Godself in revelation is through the mediation of the Christian Tradition. In the same way that Scripture is not automatically or mechanically revelation itself, but becomes revelation at various graced times in our lives, so with the Christian doctrinal tradition. The origin of doctrines is a symbolic, "second order"[51] language about the Christian experience of mystery, and, at times in our lives, doctrines can also be the means by which that original experience is re-experienced by believers. Take, for example, the doctrine of the Council of Nicaea, articulated in 325, that Jesus is "of one substance with the Father" (*homoousios to Patri* in the original Greek; see DS 125). This is not an abstract statement, one that was formulated in the lonely studies of theologians. Rather, the doctrine is one that was formulated to protect Christian faith in the fact that, in Jesus, God really did walk among men and women on this earth, shared our experience and pain, our pleasures and our joys. Because of this, we can really know God as God is—not of course in a complete conceptual way, but in the deep knowledge of personal encounter. As Uruguayan liberation theologian Juan Luis Segundo (1925-1996) puts it: "God is like Jesus."[52] Or, as the champion of Nicaea, Athanasius (296-373), bishop of Alexandria in Egypt, put it, what has not been assumed has not been redeemed.[53]

And not only was the doctrine formulated at Nicaea to protect Christian faith. It actually articulated more clearly and deeply what Christians had come to understand and believe because of their *experience* of the God of Jesus Christ in their lives. The people objected to the theologian Arius, whose preaching that "there was a time when the Word was not"—i.e., Jesus was not fully God. This precipitated the crisis that led to Nicaea: how can this be *since we pray to Jesus as we pray to God?*[54]

I can well remember the first time that the meaning of the doctrine of the incarnation was revealed to me. I was a student in Rome, studying Christology, and the professor was expounding all the intricacies of the Arian heresy. At one point, as I remember it, my professor, the eminent Belgian Jesuit Jean Galot (1919-2008), explained that the whole *point* of the doctrine of *homoousios* was to express the fact that Jesus was *uno di noi*, one of us. That's when it hit me: Jesus was really just like us, and so his humanity was like a window to the very reality of God. It's hard to express my feelings and the new knowledge that this revelation gave me, but they were strong, deep feelings, and the reality of God opened up for me in a way that is still meaningful. At that moment I was touched by the always already presence of God, revealed in the doctrine of the divinity of Jesus Christ.

The tradition can also be revelatory of God's presence through the men and women who have both made and handed on the Christian tradition, both living and dead—in a real sense our "ancestors" (as Asians, Africans and Native Americans would appreciate) in the faith. Reading the writings or the lives of women and men like Perpetua and Felicity (the account of their martyrdom is the earliest known writing of a Christian woman), Monica and Augustine (African saints), Ephrem the Syrian, Hildegard of Bingen, Patrick, Vincent de Paul and Jeanne de Chantal (models of friendship), Martin de Porres and Rose of Lima, the Japanese, Ugandan and Vietnamese Martyrs, or more recent "saints" as Felix Varela (Cuban theologian and patriot), John Henry Newman, Mother Teresa, Oscar Romero, Thea Bowman, Dorothy Day or Janani Luwum (martyr in Uganda under Idi Amin)—these and many more can be real mediators of the mystery and infinite variety of God's presence and working in our world.

REVELATION AS PERSONAL ENCOUNTER

We often think of God's revelation as the communication of information, propositional knowledge about God. In fact this has been the popular, if not traditional, understanding of revelation in Catholic theology at least since the Middle Ages and the Protestant Reformation in the West. One of the most eminent Catholic theologians of the first half of the twentieth century, Reginald Garrigou-Lagrange, defined revelation concisely as *locutio Dei ad homines, per modum magisterii* ("speech of God to human beings, by means of teaching"). G. van Noort's *Tractatus de Vera Religione*, printed in an English translation in 1955, explains the meaning of revelation in the following way:

> Revelation, a word derived from Latin meaning "to remove a veil," has the general sense of making known some truth to another. In an active sense it is the operation whereby someone discloses a truth to another; in an objective sense it is the truth disclosed. When theologians use the term, they always mean a divine revelation: the disclosure of truth by God to an intelligent creature, particularly to man.[55]

To some extent, this more objective, propositional understanding of revelation is certainly true. But at its core, in its deepest sense, revelation is much more than this. In the way that we have been developing it so far, revelation is the very *self-communication* of God, the offer of God's very personhood *by means of objective data*: the events of our lives, the words of Sacred Scripture, and the content and persons of the Christian tradition. As British theologian Aidan Nichols puts it, "Revelation is not in the first place a matter of propositions but a new personal presence and relationship of God through Christ to humanity."[56]

Revelation, in other words, is a communication of knowledge that reveals the *person*, that is, the *mystery* of God. I would define revelation in this way: it is the communication of God's *subjectivity* by means of objectivity. Through what is finite and concrete—words, events, persons—God amazingly and graciously communicates and offers in relationship God's very self. In the Decree on Revelation of the Second Vatican Council we read what was a real breakthrough in Catholic theology: "By this revelation, then, the invisible God . . . from the abundance of divine love, speaks to men and women as friends . . . and lives among them . . . , in order to invite and receive them into God's own company" (DV 2).

God's ultimate goal in offering women and men revelation is not to expand their *knowledge* (as Catholic theologians and others thought prior to Vatican II); rather, God's goal is the offer of relationship and friendship. Certainly, God's revelation does expand our knowledge of God, but that is a knowledge not simply restricted to the mind or to human reason, but one that is grasped only as mind and heart work together. It is personal knowledge—the kind of knowing that knowledge of Mystery requires. Douglas John Hall sums all of this up eloquently:

> Against this propositional or positivistic conception of revelation, the idea of revelation in more recent theological thought claims that what is revealed in Christian revelation is not, in the first place, a *what* but a *who*. A presence! The hidden mystery unveiled in external and internal event is God's own person. The knowledge of God intended by the term "revelation," says Karl Barth, is knowledge of God "as a *Person*. . . . He is one who knows and wills, who acts and speaks, who as an 'I' calls me 'Thou,' and whom I can call 'Thou' in return."[57]

REVELATION IN CONTEXT

Before concluding these reflections on divine revelation as a first step toward understanding the nature of Christian theology, I need to acknowledge the fact that the ideas I have so far presented are—while I hope applicable to other cultural and social contexts—nevertheless ideas that have their origin in my own Western culture. In the introduction to his *Why Theology Is Never Far from Home*, Filipino José de Mesa narrates his own struggle to break out of Western thinking and to begin to think as a theologizing *Filipino*. While de Mesa did find the more personalistic turn of Western theology helpful, he found himself doing "more of a translation than a genuine rethinking."[58] What began to change his understanding, however, was that God's revelation and God's will were concepts that were closely interconnected in Filipino culture, woven together in the Filipino concept of *loob*. For Filipinos, *loob* is the "deepest within" of a human being, one's most authentic self. De Mesa began to conceive of revelation, therefore, as God revealing God's own *loob*. Furthermore he began to realize that God's *loob* is revealed—particularly in the life of Jesus—as *maganda*, literally, "beautiful": what is revealed is God's *kagandahang-loob*. For Filipinos, this expression has immense resonance, because "*kagandahang-loob*" denotes that which is not only ethically good, but also winsomely good. Perhaps, for Filipinos "*kagandahang-loob* is primarily pure goodness or positivity that captivates and wins people over. It refers to a goodness that is not cold, but warm; a kindness which is not enslaving, but liberating."[59]

Two things need to be noted here. First, this understanding of God's nature that is revealed in the context of Filipino culture is in real continuity with the ideas of Vatican II and its understanding of revelation, but it goes beyond them as well, or at least nuances them for this particular context. This kind of "thinking through" a particular theological concept, with the recognition that "theology is never far from home" is what needs to be done in every cultural context and social location, for theology is only *theology* when it begins to make sense to particular people at particular times and in particular places. Africans, people of Latin American descent, Asians—all need to "think through" the idea of revelation presented in the previous pages in their own contexts.

Second, however, this reflection on revelation out of Filipino culture is one that can enrich the admittedly Western understanding that I have presented in the last several pages. In fact, any genuine contextual understanding of Christian faith should be able to enrich *any* understanding of revelation from *any* context. In the end, therefore, what is particular to one's context needs to be put into dialogue with that of others.

This contextual, dialogical, and ultimately *ecclesial* understanding of the theological process is one that we will reflect on more deeply in other places throughout this book. My point here is only to suggest that in any theology that is done in global perspective, this contextual and dialogical aspect of theology must always be kept in mind.

CONCLUSION

Yes, theology is about knowledge of or speech about God, but it is a *special* kind of knowledge and language, one that is not dependent on human knowing alone, but on God's offer or gift of self in revelation. Right in the beginning of our study of the nature of theology we have to recognize that God, ultimately, is not a reality "out there" to be grasped and understood, but rather a person who freely offers and gives Godself to us—in our human experience with all its historical and cultural particularity, through the words of Sacred Scripture, and the doctrines and people of our tradition—as a person. As we try to bring this knowledge and language to expression, we have to recognize that, while true, it can only partially and always inadequately grasp the Reality who has been revealed to us. Recognizing and acknowledging this is a first, crucial step toward a definition and an understanding of theology.

QUESTIONS FOR REFLECTION

1. What are the advantages of beginning to understand theology's nature from the tradition of "negative theology"?
2. Have you ever had an experience of revealing yourself to another person, or have another person reveal himself/herself to you? If so, what was that experience like?
3. Have you ever encountered God in your ordinary experience? Try to describe that experience.
4. Have you ever encountered God while reading a passage of Scripture? Through insight into a Christian doctrine? Through another person? Try to describe those experiences.

SUGGESTIONS FOR FURTHER READING AND STUDY

José M. de Mesa, *Why Theology Is Never Far from Home* (Manila: De la Salle University Press, 2003), 5-12.

José M. de Mesa and Lode Wostyn, *Doing Theology: Basic Realities and Processes* (Quezon City, Philippines: Claretian Publications, 1990), chapter 3, "The Pole of the Judaeo-Christian Tradition," 47-70.

Avery Dulles, *Models of Revelation* (Garden City, N.Y.: Doubleday, 1983).

Roger Haight, *Dynamics of Theology* (Maryknoll, N.Y.: Orbis Books, 2001).

Jane Kopas, *Seeking the Hidden God* (Maryknoll, N.Y.: Orbis Books, 2005).

Michael McCauley, "The Deep Mystery of God," *America* 191, no. 11 (October 18, 2004): 16-18.

Gabriel Moran, *Theology of Revelation* (New York: Herder & Herder, 1966).

Gerald O'Collins, *Fundamental Theology* (New York: Paulist Press, 1981), chapters 2 and 3, "Human Experience" and "The Divine Self-Communication," 32-113.

Raimon Panikkar, *The Experience of God: Icons of the Mystery* (Minneapolis: Fortress Press, 2006).

Kuncheria Pathil and Dominic Veliath, *An Introduction to Theology*, Indian Theological Series (Bangalore: Theological Publications in India, 2003), chapter 2, "The Sources of Theology," 39-83.

2

Faith and Theology

THE GREAT TWENTIETH-CENTURY Dutch spiritual writer Henri Nouwen writes that "a gift only becomes a gift when it is received, and nothing we have to give—wealth, talents, competence, or just beauty—will ever be recognized as true gifts until someone opens his [or her] heart to accept them."[1] The same can be said about the notion of faith: to refer to Karl Barth's words at the end of the last chapter, only when we are able to call God "Thou" in return can revelation really happen, can God really give the gift of Godself. God's offer of revelation necessarily implies what St. Paul called "the obedience of faith" (Rom. 16:26; see DV 5).

Revelation and faith are *always* connected. As I just said, there can be no revelation without a person or a community *recognizing* it as such. God's saving presence is always *there* in history and in people's lives, but it only *reveals* when people become aware of it and acknowledge it as such. As José de Mesa and Lode Wostyn, writing from the Philippines, put it, "Revelation-faith are correlatives; that is, we cannot speak of one aspect without the other. Revelation as God's offer of life and love does not become revelation until that offer is experienced and accepted in faith. And Christian faith is not possible without God's offer of life and love to people."[2]

THE DYNAMICS OF FAITH

How do people come to faith? In the act of divine revelation, as we said in the previous section ("Step One"), God offers God's very self, God's "inside," as Filipinos would say, God's very *loob*. God does this *by means of* objective things: events in human life, events in history, through particular objects or persons. In the act of faith, human persons reciprocate. They reach out and *accept* God's offer *initially* and *continually* by accepting the objectivity by which God offers. Such acceptance is done in three ways. First, the objectivity by which God offers God's self is accepted as true (e.g., Jesus is risen from the dead) or meaningful (e.g., Jesus is the Good Shepherd, Eternal High Priest). Second, that objectivity is understood as a symbol of God's personal gift of self (e.g., I experience the incredible beauty of a starry night and am moved to praise and adoration of the Creator). Or, third, that objectivity is accepted as an invitation to growth and transformation (e.g., I recognize in Oscar Romero's own option for the poor of El Salvador God's call for *me* to offer my life in service to justice in the world).

Let's see if we can "unpack" this a bit more in detail. What I am trying to get at is that faith, like revelation, is also a gift of one's self. Furthermore, that gift of self can be given in three ways: by belief, by affectivity, and by personal conversion. The act of faith is not a one-time act, but something that we do constantly, daily, in our lives.

Offer of Gift

Relationship

Acceptance of Gift

Faith as Personal Relationship

First, the act of faith is the way that human persons are open to or offer their own personhood or subjectivity to God. Like the offer of revelation, by which God gives *God's* very self, God's very *Mystery* to women and men, the act of faith is the way that women and men give *themselves* by giving God something objective—assent to truth, personal commitment, a change of behavior (more about these when we reflect on the second point below). The *result* of this human offer of self, through objectivity, to God is what we mean by *grace*. Grace is not some *thing* outside of God, or some thing people possess when they relate to God. Grace, rather, is the relationship that is initiated when a person accepts God's revelation. We speak about being in the state of grace— grace is a *stance* of God toward human beings, and the *stance* of human beings toward the offering, inviting God.

An example might help here. In the illustration above we see a man offering flowers to a woman.[3] The point of the gift is not simply to give the woman *flowers*; the point is rather that in this concrete, symbolic way the man is offering his self, his *heart*, to the woman by means of the gift of flowers. The woman, then, is free to accept the flowers or not. Certainly, if she sends the flowers back to the man who sent them she is saying that she does not accept his offer of his self. On the other hand, if she accepts them she is not only accepting *him*; she is also giving *her self, her heart* to the man—thus initiating a relationship between them. This may be as simple as a friendship or as intimate as a love relationship, but this offer and acceptance of the flowers make this no mere transaction, but a rich personal event.

In the same way, God offers Godself to women and men by means of something objective—something in human experience, through the words of Scripture or in the Christian tradition. When the person says *yes* to this offer in some way, she or he has made an act of faith.

Three Aspects of Faith

The second aspect of our "unpacking" is that the act of faith has three aspects or dimensions: the intellectual, the affective, and the behavioral.

Faith, in the first place, has an *intellectual* dimension. In the act of faith, we accept something objective as true—either factual or meaningful. For example, when we assent to the fact that God is indeed the creator of the universe or recognize the meaning of the truth that God *really* is "my shepherd" (Ps. 23:1), we are involved in the intellectual aspect of faith. This is to accept that what God offers in revelation is objectively true. Classical theology speaks of this aspect of faith as accepting the truth of an event or a doctrine on the testimony of God as such—to "believe God" (the classic Latin phrase is *credere Deum*). Another classical expression referring to this aspect of faith is to speak of the "faith *that* is believed" or, in Latin, *fides quae creditur* (sometimes abbreviated as the *fides quae*).[4]

Faith has an affective, relational, or trusting dimension as well. We believe *that* something is true, but what we believe is "for us and for our salvation," as the Nicene Creed puts it. It is an act of trust in a God with whom women and men have relationship and friendship. The belief *that* God is creator of all calls us to trust in the kind, merciful, and (in John Haught's wonderful phrase) "humble" God.[5] We trust that God is at our side as we walk through "the valley of death" or the "dark valley" (Ps. 23:4). In classical theology, this aspect of faith as a deep trust in God is expressed as believing "in God" (*credere Deo*), as we would believe "in" a good friend or lover to stand by us in time of need or support us by her or his presence in our lives. The word "believe" has its roots in the English word "belove."[6] This is the aspect of faith that classical theologians speak of as the *fides qua creditur* (*fides qua*), or the "faith *by which* we believe."

Finally, faith has what I would call a behavioral aspect. When one "believes God" and puts full trust in God, a person commits herself or himself to a way of living and acting that is in accord with God's own acting in mercy, love, justice, and integrity. So, since God is affirmed as creator of the world, for example, and is our companion and strength through all of life's adventures and difficulties, we come to the realization that we need not live in reliance on wealth, prestige, or power and commit ourselves to live in that way. This aspect of faith is what is called "believing *into* God," or *credere in Deum*. As U.S. Anglo Cardinal Avery Dulles points out, this aspect of faith was not very prominent in theological thinking prior to the twentieth-century renewal in theology marked by the Second Vatican Council. Indeed, in Thomas Aquinas's understanding, faith was conceived much more as an intellectual act ("credere Deum") than as a move toward God in a personal relationship (*credere Deo*) or personal commitment (*credere in Deum*).[7] Today, this third aspect of faith has been particularly highlighted in liberation and feminist theologies or in what are sometimes called "practical theologies."[8] A person of faith is one who *does* justice, who embodies what he or she believes through a life of service and openness to others. As U.S. feminist theologian Joyce Ann Mercer expresses it, faith is "the praxis of God's love and justice in the context of particular communities of struggle and hope."[9]

In his treatment of the "nature and object" of faith, Avery Dulles provides a fine summary of these three important aspects of faith. "Insofar as it is assent," Dulles writes, "Faith means acceptance of a revealed message on the word of the divine revealer [what we have called the "intellectual aspect" of faith]. Insofar as it is trust, it involves self-surrender into the hands of God and confidence in God as the savior who is utterly faithful to his promises [our understanding of the "affective" aspect]. Insofar as it is commitment [what we have called the "behavioral" aspect], it involves an intention to conforms one's conduct to the values and norms established by revelation—to be a 'doer' and not simply a 'hearer' of the word (cf. Jas. 1:22)."[10]

The point of reflecting on these various aspects or dimensions of faith is to recognize that, finally, faith is a total response, one that involves a person's entire being, one's whole self. If in revelation one is touched by the presence of Mystery in one's daily life, or through the Scriptures or the Christian Tradition, in faith one *allows* this to happen. Earlier in this section I alluded to Vatican II's Decree on Revelation, paragraph 5. Here is the full quotation:

> "The obedience of faith" (Rom 16:26; cf. 1:5, 2 Cor 10:5-6) must be given to God who reveals, an obedience by which men and women entrust their whole selves freely to God, offering "the full submission of intellect and will to God who reveals," and freely assenting to the truth revealed.

In the edition of the council documents edited by U.S. Anglo theologian Walter M. Abbott, we read the following note of commentary:

> Note the general descriptions of faith, "by which men and women commit their whole selves": the Council desired to get away from a too intellectualist conception. Christian faith is not merely assent to a set of statements; it

is a personal engagement, a continuing act of loyalty and self-commitment, offered by men and women to God.[11]

Faith as an Ordinary Act and Constant Practice

I mentioned above that faith is accepting both *initially* and *continually* the offer of relationship and friendship that human beings experience in moments of revelation. In saying this, however, I did not want to create the impression that the invitation to faith comes exclusively in some kind of emotional or dramatic way. We certainly do read in the lives of some saints—St. Paul, for instance, or St. Augustine or John Wesley—experiences of conversion and faith that are quite emotional and dramatic. Oftentimes evangelical or charismatic Christians also speak of powerful moments when God's call and their response have been experienced in particularly memorable ways. But there are also examples of holy women and men, for example, Thérèse of Lisieux—who have been born in an atmosphere of faith and have not had any particularly strong experiences of being "born again" or "twice born" (this latter the phrase of the U.S. Anglo philosopher William James).[12] Or, to quote a famous passage in the diaries of former United Nations General Secretary Dag Hammerskjöld (from Sweden), many people may not be able to pinpoint a *moment* of conversion or coming to faith, but at some point they realize that they definitely have made that crucial decision in the warp and woof of their lives: "I don't know Who—or what—put the question, I don't know when it was put. I don't even remember answering. But at some moment I did answer *Yes* to Someone—or something—and from that hour I was certain that existence is meaningful and that, therefore, my life, in self-surrender, had a goal."[13]

What this quotation from Hammerskjöld points to is that often—if not most times—the act of faith is not simply something that we do once and then we never have to think about it again. Rather, faith is something that is continuous, something we are challenged to renew every day as we come in touch with revelatory events in our ordinary, daily lives. What the interplay between God's offer of self in revelation and our acceptance of God and subsequent gift of *our* selves in faith opens up is the possibility of a life lived in God's presence, a life that demands deeper reflection and prayer as we experience God's presence and challenge in our lives. It will be this kind of life that will be our starting point for understanding the nature of theology in the third and final section of this chapter.

FAITH AS GIFT/FAITH AND DOUBT

Before we move toward this final section of our chapter, however, I would like briefly to reflect on two additional aspects of faith: the notion of faith as the result of the gracious action of God, and the importance of struggle and doubt in our life of faith.

Faith as Gift

That faith is the result of a free, gracious gift of God is a doctrine of the church, laid down by a number of important councils in the church's history.[14] At the same time, this doctrine of the graciousness or "supernaturality" of faith must be understood over against another doctrine: that faith is a fully human act, and therefore a fully *free* act. God does not somehow "scramble our brains" or zap us with some kind of electric charge to force us to believe. Faith is not and can never be a gift in that sense—since anything that is imposed involuntarily would hardly be a gift anyway. As Dulles expresses it, reflecting on the teaching of the Council of Trent: "According to the Council . . . the will in coming to faith is indeed moved by God, but God does not move it coercively, as irrational creatures are moved, but freely, in such a way that it makes its own contribution."[15]

I would suggest that we understand the graciousness of God's gift of faith by reflecting on how human persons interact with one another. In a real sense, the only way that persons can enter into relationship with one another is by a free offer and a free gift one to another. There is no way, in other words, that one person can *make* or *force* the other to love or be friends with him or her. One can only invite, and wait for a free response. He or she can offer gifts, flattery or promises, and these can be seen—as in our example of the gift of flowers—as tokens of the gift of self, but none of these can "buy" a person's reciprocal gift of self.

On the other hand, however, if one is not invited, one cannot respond. A gift becomes a gift only if it is accepted—but a gift is a gift only if it is offered, not demanded or taken. What this means is that what is absolutely necessary for the act of faith is that it be a *response* to something that is offered. One does not *decide* to have faith; one can only have faith after one is touched—however dramatically or undramatically—by God's offer of revelation. I think what we can say is that *revelation* is the gift that makes the act of faith possible—and that is what makes faith a gift.

Faith and Doubt

Doubt, wrestling, questioning—these are always a part of genuine faith. As British theologian John Davies writes, "The enemy of faith is not doubt but the suppression of doubt."[16] While this might sound like a radical idea, if one thinks about it one will realize that in *all* the important decisions in life—getting married or ordained, taking up a profession or deciding to enter religious life, for example—there is never *absolute* certainty. We never know if we are really doing the right thing when we make these decisions. We can have virtual certainty or moral certainty, but we always take a risk that what we are doing is not the right thing for us, or for the person or persons we are committing ourselves to. The response of faith is on this same level. It always involves risk; it can only be an act that we do as a result of partial knowledge. As we will reflect on in our next chapter, this does *not* mean that faith is an *irrational* act, but it does point to the fact that it puts us at risk of being wrong or misled. Swiss theologian Hans Küng puts it eloquently when he says that

> unfortunately the "depth" (or "height") of a truth and . . . certainty in accepting it are in inverse ratio. The more banal the truth ("truism," "platitude"), the greater the certainty. The more significant the truth (for instance aesthetic, moral and religious truth by comparison with the arithmetical), the slighter the certainty. For the "deeper" the truth is for me, the more I must first lay myself open to it, inwardly prepare myself, attune myself to it intellectually, willingly, emotionally, in order to reach that genuine "certainty" which is somewhat different from assured "security." A *deep* truth, for me outwardly uncertain, threatened by doubts, which presupposes a generous commitment on my part, can possess much more cognitive value than a certain—or even an "absolutely certain"—*banal* truth.[17]

As the great twentieth-century German theologian Paul Tillich (1886-1965) writes in a classic book on faith, making an act of faith *necessarily* involves doubt because it involves our whole person in an existential choice. This is not "the permanent doubt of the scientist, and it is not the transitory doubt of the skeptic, but it is the doubt of him who is ultimately concerned about a concrete content. One could call it existential doubt. . . . It does not question whether a special proposition is true or false. . . . It is aware of the element of insecurity in every existential truth."[18] Because of this, says Tillich, the act of faith is an act of courage in the face of the possibility that what one is staking one's life on may not in fact be true. And so, in such "courageous standing of uncertainty, faith shows most visibly its dynamic character."[19]

THE NOTION OF THEOLOGY

So far we have reflected on the nature of revelation as God's absolutely free offer of relationship and friendship by which, through something objective, God's very Mystery is made manifest to women and men. We've reflected as well on the nature of faith as a person's full and free gift of self in response to God's offer. Having taken these first two important steps we are ready to understand the nature of theology.

Faith and the "Eros of the Mind"

In a very mysterious but real way, God offers God's self in revelation, and human beings respond with the gift of ourselves in the act of faith. But things don't stop there. A person who has made that all-encompassing, courageous, risk-filled act of faith necessarily wants to know more about the truth and person he or she has accepted, and that has claimed such complete obedience, such "full submission of intellect and will" (DV 5; see DS 3008). He or she wants to know more about the relationship that faith has initiated; he or she wants to know more about the tradition within which he or she accepts God. He or she wants to understand how this faith makes sense in his or her particular place or time or culture. Questions arise in the aftermath of faith; new doubts begin to be articulated; ways of expressing one's relationship with God need to be brought to speech.

This is simply the result of our human nature. Part of being human—and a major part—is the possession of a drive to understand and know more and more about who we are, what we do and why we do it. Karl Rahner speaks about this fact as *spirit*—the human person is always questing, always open, always asking more questions.[20] Canadian theologian Bernard Lonergan (1904-1984) speaks of a certain "eros of the mind," an "unrestricted desire to know" which "demands the intelligent and critical handling of every question."[21] In a famous line, Lonergan points to the difference between humans and animals by the fact that when an animal has nothing to do, it goes to sleep—whereas when a person has nothing to do he or she *may* ask questions.[22]

Such an "eros of the mind" might be illustrated by an advertisement that I came across in a magazine some time ago.[23] Inside a rough drawing of a piece of a jigsaw puzzle was written the following: "S'ti numah eaturn ot tanw ot eigurf shingt tuo." When I first saw this ad I immediately tried to figure out what the words said, only to realize that the line inside the piece of the puzzle says, when finally unraveled, "It's human nature to want to figure things out." Point well taken!

So our rational—Rahner would say *spiritual*—nature pushes us to further understanding of the act of faith that we have made. It pushes us to understand more deeply the objective truths that we have accepted as true and/or meaningful; it pushes us to understand more deeply the person who is revealed through this objectivity; and it pushes us to understand the commitment to growth and transformation that the acceptance of this person calls us to. In a passage that shows a strong influence of Thomas Aquinas, René Latourelle expresses this dynamic "push" of faith in this way:

> Faith is an initial possession, though an obscure and imperfect one, of the object we aspire to know. It reaches out towards a clear experience of the

living God whose witness it has received. It wishes to contemplate unveiled him whom it knows to be the cause of its happiness. For this reason there is within faith itself an appetite for vision, a desire to know and see. Adherence to what it has been told and a tending towards vision are the two essential aspects of the act of faith. Because it does not see, faith seeks to see, to understand.[24]

In fact, this need to understand is *so* important that if the effort to understand our faith is somehow thwarted, if one simply stops trying to understand why one believes, the whole relationship of faith will wither and eventually die: U.S. Americans have a proverb that applies here: "Use it or lose it!"

The Beginning of Theology

Now, when such an urge to further understand one's faith emerges—and it surfaces in every person who truly believes, in the form of questions, difficulties, doubts, curiosity, the hunger for more depth. And when a person begins to *deal* with this urge—however tentatively, however awkwardly—*that person has begun to theologize.*

What I am trying to say here is that doing theology, in its basic dynamic, *is not something that is exotic, or something highly intellectual or academic.* Rather—and on this we'll reflect more deeply in chapter 3—it is something that happens in any and every person who struggles to understand her or his faith; it is a process that goes on in the heart and mind of any sincere believer. Let me give some examples of this.

When I was working as a missionary in the Philippines, one of my colleagues in the seminary where I was teaching had over the years developed what he called a "Basic Bible Seminar" that he and several lay women would give to the simplest people in barrios or small villages all over the country. Inevitably, he told me, when they would finish the seminar and people had been able to get a fresh taste of the riches of the Bible and biblical faith, the people would ask the question "How can we know more?" The seminars had called them to deeper faith, and that deeper faith—through the dynamism of the human spirit—was calling them to go deeper into it. The people—as simply educated as they were—were doing theology. Similarly, I was always moved to see that women and men with whom I had worked on a marriage encounter, after the experience, inevitably wanted to know more about their faith. Their faith had been newly awakened by the marriage encounter experience, and they were ready for deeper knowledge—they began doing theology! And to give a third and final example, I recognize that many of the students— particularly older students—who enroll in my classes are men and women who have somewhat recently come to a new or fresh understanding of their faith through some kind of experience in their lives. This experience of faith is so strong that they are often impelled to enroll in a theology course just to figure out what has happened in their lives, or to get to know in a more intimate way this God who has lately become so real in their lives.

Again, my point is that theology is what is born in persons when they seek to further understand their faith—however simply, however awkwardly, oftentimes however implicitly. This, basically, is the same point made by Anselm of Canterbury (1033-1109) in the eleventh century. In the preface to his work *Proslogion,* Anselm spoke of theology as *fides quaerens intellectum*: "faith seeking understanding."[25] This is a definition of theology that, to my mind, is unsurpassed even after a thousand years, and it is the definition that I propose for theology to readers of this book. *Theology is faith seeking understanding.*

FAITH—SEEKING—UNDERSTANDING

Theology is faith seeking understanding—a simple definition, three simple words, but three words that need to be reflected on more deeply to grasp their full meaning. We need to acknowledge, therefore, that *each word* is an important element in the definition; we also need to acknowledge, second, that the first and last words ("faith" and "understanding") need always to be kept together in a dynamic relationship. Doing theology without *faith*, or without *seeking*, or without *understanding* is not doing *theology*; and overemphasizing either "faith" or "understanding" is to fall into one of the errors that have been persistent as theology has been done throughout the world and down through the ages.

Each Word Is Important

Faith Seeking Understanding

Theology is not mere curiosity about faith, nor is it an analysis of *someone else's* faith. It must be one's *own* faith one seeks to understand. In a Roman document that appeared some years ago regarding the theological formation of those to be ordained, there appears a Latin phrase that expresses this idea very well: to do theology is *cum assensu cogitare*,[26] which in translation means that doing theology is "to think within the context of personal assent to the offer of revelation."

This is something that U.S. theologian Richard McBrien has always insisted on in his writings. In his book *Catholicism*, McBrien writes that "*not all interpretations of faith are theological. Theology happens where there is an interpretation of one's own faith.* Apart from that faith, the exploration of faith is a philosophy of religion rather than a theology."[27] And in his 1998 encyclical on the relationship between faith and reason, Pope John Paul II (1920-2005) recalls the introduction of St. Bonaventure's (1221-1274) work *Itinararium Mentis ad Deum* (The Journey of the Mind to God), in which Bonaventure "invites the reader to recognize the inadequacy of 'reading without repentance, knowledge without devotion, research without the impulse of wonder, prudence without the ability to surrender to joy, action divorced from religion, learning sundered from love, intelligence without humility, study unsustained by divine grace, thought without the wisdom inspired by God.'"[28]

As McBrien put it above, one can do theology only in the context of one's personal faith. A philosophy of religion or a person schooled in "religious studies" can indeed reflect on the faith of someone else, or one can study a particular faith to which one does not personally subscribe—like a Christian studying Buddhism (or for that matter a Buddhist studying Christianity!). But if one is going to do *theology*, one must seek to understand one's faith—one's personal faith, or the faith of one's church or tradition.

Faith *Seeking* Understanding

"Seeking," on the one hand, points to the urgency in faith itself, a hunger to "go deeper" in one's understanding of one's faith. If there is not real seeking in this sense—if we are doing theology only to get a degree, or to pass an exam, or to fulfill the qualifications of ordination, or to get some kind of academic recognition—if there is no *passion* for understanding our faith, then what we are doing is not theology. Douglas John Hall expresses this urgency well:

> We ought to hear the verb "to seek" here in an almost aggressive sense. Like the defiant boldness of a lover, the doing of theology entails a search that will not be deterred by the many obstacles that are certainly in the way of it. The quest into which, by faith, we are initiated is no mild inquiry ("research"), but is a determined and unquenchable passion to comprehend. It *will know*. It will not be satisfied with simplistic answers to difficult questions. It will be like Jacob wrestling with the angel until dawn, until he is blessed and limps away from the encounter. There is a drive towards understanding built into faith itself, if it is really faith and not just sentimentality.[29]

In Latin American liberation theology, this urgency of faith is fueled by the fact that one's faith is always in a God who is absolutely on the side of the poor. One seeks passionately to see how God is speaking to women and men who are suffering under poverty and economic and political oppression, and yet who have glimpsed God's presence in their lives. Theology here is no "mild inquiry," but an almost desperate attempt to make sense out of a life surrounded by inhuman conditions and hopelessness.[30] African and Asian theologies are attempts to understand God's presence in the realities of their histories and cultures, and also in their sometimes overwhelming poverty. Sri Lankan theologian Aloysius Pieris has said famously that, for Asians, theology can be done only in a dialogue that has been baptized in the Jordan of Asian religions and crucified on the cross of Asian poverty.[31]

In sum, doing theology is serious business. It probes the meaning of life, and often does it in life-and-death situations.

But the notion that theology seeks to understand faith also implies that such seeking has a certain *tentativeness* to it. Dorothee Sölle connects such tentativeness to faith's "shadow," the ever-present element of doubt, emphasizing the fact that "faith without doubt is not stronger, but merely more ideological."[32] The knowledge we seek, from this perspective, is knowledge grasped in humility, one that is open for dialogue, and open as well for correction. Theological insights, insists Japanese theologian Kosuke Koyama, are always "*humble* theological insights."[33] So important is this attitude of tentativeness, humility, and openness that Robert Schreiter names such openness to correction as one of his five criteria for the genuineness of a particular theological expression.[34]

This tentativeness in our seeking after understanding also points to the fact that our work in theology is never finished. After all, as we have seen from chapter 1, theology is always seeking for the understanding of Mystery, which as such defies any kind of clear and clean formulation. The understanding we seek is always an understanding that can be open to deeper and deeper comprehension, and one that varies according to the particular historical situation or context in which understanding is sought. Theologians, writes David Tracy, should never claim "to provide pictures of the realities they describe." The only thing they can do is to try to "disclose such realities with varying degrees of adequacy."[35]

The truth of theology is not something "out there" that we can ultimately master; it is rather a constant project that can never be fully accomplished. As Aidan Nichols expresses it, one can never say that he or she has "finished" theology, and then is able to move on blithely to another area of academic interest:

There is a sense in which one might say something similar of Akkadian grammar or the family tree of the Hapsburg dynasty, but one cannot reasonably assert it of the exploration into God's revelation, which is, by definition infinite in its implications for human understanding. To be a theological student in the full sense of those words cannot be a temporary state or a preamble to something else, such as the ministerial priesthood or an all-around education. Rather, it is a solemn engagement to developing over a lifetime the gift of Christian wonder or curiosity, which is the specifically theological mode of faith. As theologians . . . we commit ourselves to the lifelong study and reflection which the satisfaction of such curiosity will need. Our faith is from now on, in St. Anslem's words, . . . "a faith that quests for understanding."

Faith Seeking *Understanding*

As with our previous point, to speak of the understanding that faith seeks also has two aspects to it. In the first place, we seek *understanding*, not proof; we seek a deepening of our faith, not certainty. I remember a professor of mine in Rome years ago, the Spaniard Juan Alfaro, who spoke of the task of theology to present *reasonable*, not *rational* arguments. The faith we seek to understand always remains faith, not rational certainty, and the knowledge and wisdom we achieve in theology are not a work of the mind alone, but mind and heart working together. The great seventeenth-century French philosopher Blaise Pascal (1588-1651) spoke of coming to know the "reasons of the heart." English Cardinal John Henry Newman (1801-1890) in the nineteenth century spoke of coming to truth through a method of "converging probabilities"; and twentieth-century Hungarian philosopher of science Michael Polanyi (1891-1976) spoke of the self-involving approach of "personal knowledge."[36] These are all ways of expressing what I am trying to get at here. Theological knowing, ultimately, says Douglas John Hall, "is the knowing of an encounter between two persons who indeed know that they will *never* know each other fully in the fact-knowledge sense, and will *never* acknowledge in one another fully everything that really *is* significant about the other, but who nevertheless determine to commit themselves to one another."[37]

From another perspective, however, we need also to insist that the understanding that faith seeks in theology is always the result of rigorous, serious thinking. Neither Pascal, Newman, nor Polanyi would suggest that their reasoning with mind and heart together is a "soft" kind of reasoning. On the contrary, their approach includes the use of all the tools available from philosophy, the social sciences, the physical sciences, history, and all the arts. We seek reasonability and understanding, not rationality and certainty, but this understanding needs as well to be *critical*. Theology always needs to reflect on whether, in *these* particular circumstances, the received wisdom of the past still makes sense. As liberation theologians and feminists have taught us over the last several decades, one needs to approach reflection on particular situations and doctrines with a "hermeneutics of suspicion," an attitude that a certain situation or theological formulation may actually support a position that is contrary to the deepest Christian values and practice. And even, as José de Mesa points out, some theologizing in some contexts should even call such hermeneutics of suspicion into question, giving way to what he calls a "hermeneutics of appreciation."[38]

And so *thinking* clearly and carefully is part of the way faith seeks under-standing as one does theology. Douglas John Hall quotes Swiss theologian Fritz Buri (1907-1995): "Christian faith cannot exist apart from thinking.... Thinking faith is Christian faith, and . . . today true Christian faith can only be thinking faith."[39] In *Fides et Ratio*, John Paul II quotes St. Augustine: "To believe is nothing other than to think with assent.... Believers are also think-ers: in believing they think and in thinking, they believe.... If faith does not think it is nothing."

Theology, therefore, can be done only in faith. It is an *urgent* search, not for certainty or rational clarity, but for an understanding that is firm yet humble and tentative. And while theologizing is not an activity of the mind alone, it espouses strict standards of scholarship and reason. Each word of our defini-tion of theology as faith–seeking–understanding is important.

Keeping "Faith" and "Understanding" Together

Throughout the history of Christianity there has always been a tendency to overemphasize either the *faith* aspect of theology or the *understanding* aspect—either one to the detriment of the entire theological task.

Fideism

If we overemphasize the *faith* aspect of theology, we fall into what is called *fide-ism*. Fideism, says Douglas John Hall, is a position based on "the assumption that the human intellect is incapable of attaining true knowledge of God."[40] It is a position that is suspicious of the powers of human reason to grasp in any adequate way the Mystery of God's offer of relationship and friendship, and one that, ultimately, is suspicious of human experience to come to any real knowledge of God.

One of the most classic fideists in Christian history is the North African-born theologian and (most probably) lawyer Tertullian (ca. 155-230). Writing about coming to faith in Jesus' resurrection, Tertullian wrote the famous words that "it is by all means to be believed, because it is absurd.... the fact is certain because it is impossible."[41] And in an equally famous passage Tertullian asks the question: "What does Jerusalem have to do with Athens, the Church with the academy, the Christian with the heretic?" He continued:

Our principles come from the Porch of Solomon, who had himself taught that the Lord is to be sought in simplicity of heart. . . . I have no use for a Stoic or a dialectic Christianity. After Jesus Christ we have no need of spec-ulation, after the Gospel no need of research. When we come to believe, we have no desire to believe anything else; for we begin by believing that there is nothing else which we have to believe.[42]

Other great theologians who fall within or close to the boundary of fideism are Bernard of Clairvaux (1090-1153), particularly in his debates with his contemporary Abelard (1079-1142); Martin Luther (1483-1546), who railed against the rationalistic Scholastic theology of his day; Søren Kierkegaard (1813-1855), who wrote so passionately about the risk and leap of faith; and Karl Barth (1886-1968), who was particularly suspicious of the powers of human reason—what is called "natural theology"—to come to the knowledge of God. In a particularly powerful passage, Barth wrote that "all the articles of our Christian belief are, when considered rationally, impossible and mendacious and preposterous. Faith, however, is completely abreast of the situation. It grips reason by the throat and strangles the beast."[43]

Today, fideists might include fundamentalist Christians or even some (not all!) Evangelicals and ultra-"traditionalist" Catholics. Fideism is also seen in the religiosity of the "ordinary" religious person, and often as well in persons just beginning the study of theology. One of my students told me that when she was explaining to her father that theology was about faith seeking *understanding*, he replied hotly: "Faith *needs* no understanding; that's why they call it faith!" And, from my experience, one of the great challenges of being a teacher of theology— and of being a minister as well—is to help people recognize the need to think *through* their faith, and not simply rely on "what the Bible says," or even "what the pope says." Reason, or the search for understanding, is crucial for our faith.

Rationalism

However, if the *understanding* aspect of theologizing is overemphasized, we fall into what is called *rationalism*. A rationalist is one who holds that "through the natural intellect" women and men "can indeed ascend even to a knowledge of theological and spiritual truths."[44] One of the first Christian theologians who tended toward rationalism was the lay theologian Clement of Alexandria (ca. 150-ca. 215), head of a theological school in Egypt in what was the Roman empire's unparalleled center of learning and philosophy. In his work of miscellaneous theological reflections entitled *Stromata* (literally translated, "miscellanies"), Clement wrote of academic learning in a much different spirit than did his fellow North African Tertullian:

> . . . philosophy does not ruin life by being the originator of false practices and base deeds, although some have calumniated it, though it be the clear image of the truth, a divine gift to the Greeks; nor does it drag us away from the faith, as if we were bewitched by some delusive art, but rather, so to speak, by the use of an ampler circuit, obtains a common exercise demonstrative of faith.[45]

Other famous rationalists in Christian history are Frenchmen Peter Abelard (1079-1142) and his espousal of "dialectics" or rational argument in theology; René Descartes (1596-1650), who searched for certainty about his own and God's existence through the "clear and distinct ideas" in his *Meditations*; John Toland (1670-1721) and his book *Christianity Not Mysterious*; and Georg Wilhelm Friedrich Hegel (1770-1831), the intellectual archenemy of Kierkegaard. Some forms of Scholastic theology, particularly Catholic theology as it developed after the Council of Trent and before the Second Vatican Council have a tendency toward rationalism; and, in a very different way, what is called "liberal Protestantism" and has a tendency to harmonize Christianity with nineteenth-century bourgeois culture. Today we might even say that some forms of theology that tend to dismiss the wisdom of the Christian tradition and, for Catholics, the teachings of the church's magisterium, might also fall within the rationalist camp. Harold O. J. Brown reports a remark made by eminent Greek Orthodox theologian Georges Florovsky about the atmosphere of faith at the Harvard Divinity School, where Florovsky was a professor: "Around here they call me a fundamentalist because I actually believe in God."[46] This points also to a type of rationalism that one finds in some university divinity schools and departments of religion.

Faith *and* Understanding

In the most common and orthodox strain of the Christian tradition, however—especially the Catholic tradition—*both* faith and reason are seen to be needed for theology to be genuine. Of course, there is always a tension between the two, but this tension is always a creative one. In the broad Christian tradition, theology is understood to be a *discipline* in the deepest sense of the word—it is a way of being a *disciple*, someone who is both student and loyal follower.

In the Catholic tradition in particular, solutions are almost *never* "either/or," but rather "both/and." As Richard McBrien points out, Catholic thinking prefers not to choose between Scripture *or* Tradition, but accepts Scripture *and* Tradition; not faith *or* works, but faith *and works*; not divine grace *or* human freedom, but grace *and* freedom; not Christ *or* Mary, but Christ *and* Mary.[47] And so with faith *and* reason, accepting what I have spoken of as the constant tension and avoiding the dangers of fideism on the one hand and rationalism on the other. The Catholic theologian develops what Aidan Nichols speaks of as the "theological habit of mind." It is "at the same time absolutely ordinary and natural, yet entirely extraordinary and supernatural. It is natural in that it draws on the human ability to study. It is supernatural in that its root and source is divinely given faith in the self-revealing God."[48]

All the great Christian theologians have always kept these two aspects together. Augustine emphasized the priority of faith for understanding: "Understanding is the reward of faith. Therefore seek not to understand that thou mayest believe, but believe that thou mayest understand."[49] Indeed, he argued that every attempt to gain knowledge without belief is futile. Nevertheless, he understood that faith is a stage on the way to full knowledge, and that faith by its nature seeks fuller understanding—"If faith does not think, it is nothing."[50] Thomas Aquinas (ca. 1225-1274), as Pope John Paul II points out, "had the great merit of giving pride of place to the harmony which exists between faith and reason. Both the light of reason and the light of faith come from God, he argued; hence there can be no contradiction between them" (FR 43). Aquinas is particularly outstanding in his use of the Greek philosopher Aristotle, and his dialogue with Jewish and Muslim thought, to more deeply understand the doctrines of Christianity—something that anticipates one of the important aspects of theology today (as we will see in the next chapter). In the seventeenth century, Blaise Pascal, whom we have already recognized as using both mind and heart in his own deeply religious thinking, wrote that "If we surrender everything to reason, our religion will lose all mystery and the supernatural. If we offend against the principles of reason, our religion will be absurd and ridiculous."[51] One could quote from the works of many other great theologians, including Hildegard of Bingen in the later Middle Ages, John Henry Newman in the nineteenth century, Karl Rahner and Bernard Lonergan in the twentieth century, and Elizabeth Johnson, Peter Phan, Shawn Copeland, or Gustavo Gutiérrez in our own day. All of them would agree substantially with what scientist Albert Einstein (1879-1955) said so powerfully in 1941: "Science without religion is lame; religion without science is blind."[52] Or, as Pope John Paul II summarizes the tradition in two chapters of his encyclical on faith and reason, on the one hand, a person must "believe in order to understand" (*credo ut intelligam* [FR, title of chapter II]); on the other, she or he must "understand in order to believe" (*intelligo ut credam* [FR, title of chapter III]).

CONCLUSION

As we have defined it, along with Anselm of Canterbury, theology is faith seeking understanding. Theology starts with God's revelation, illumining or challenging our lives with an invitation to relationship and friendship. If and when we respond in the act of faith, our stance of faith demands of us a further understanding, and that is the beginning of theology. Theology needs to be done in faith, with urgency and yet humility, and engages our whole mind and our whole heart. In our next chapter we will draw out a number of applications for our understanding of theology in today's global context and world church.

QUESTIONS FOR REFLECTION

1. Why is it important to understand faith as having three aspects: intellectual, affective, and behavioral?
2. Why is it important to recognize that faith is not something once-for-all, but a continual practice?
3. Why is having doubts about one's faith a good thing?
4. What are the advantages of speaking of theology as "faith seeking understanding"?

SUGGESTIONS FOR FURTHER READING AND STUDY

Avery Dulles, *The Assurance of Things Hoped For: A Theology of Christian Faith* (Oxford/ New York: Oxford University Press, 1994).

Roger Haight, *Dynamics of Theology* (Maryknoll, N.Y.: Orbis Books, 2001), chapter 1, "Faith as a Dimension of the Human," 15-31.

Joyce Ann Mercer, "Faith," in Letty M. Russell and J. Shannon Clarkson, eds., *Dictionary of Feminist Theologies* (Louisville, Ky.: Westminster John Knox Press, 1996), 96-97.

Ed L. Miller, ed., *Classical Statements on Faith and Reason* (New York: Random House, 1970).

Pablo Richard, "Theology in the Theology of Liberation," in Ignacio Ellacuría and Jon Sobrino, eds., *Mysterium Liberationis: Fundamental Concepts of Liberation Theology* (Maryknoll, N.Y.: Orbis Books, 1993), 154-60.

Howard W. Stone and James O. Duke, *How to Think Theologically* (Minneapolis: Fortress Press, 1996), chapter 1, "Faith, Understanding, and Reflection," 11-24.

Paul Tillich, *Dynamics of Faith* (New York: Harper Torchbooks, 1957).

3

Faith Seeking Understanding in a Global Church

"VARIATIONS" ON A THEOLOGICAL THEME

Aᴌᴛʜᴏᴜɢʜ ɪ ʜᴀᴠᴇ ᴍᴀᴅᴇ some references to the global nature of theology in this book, the way I have spoken of the nature of theology as faith seeking understanding and the way I have insisted on the balance between faith and reason have been relatively classical or traditional. In this chapter, however, I would like to draw out several implications of the understanding of theology that in a particular way pertain to the global perspective from which this series ("Theology in Global Perspective") has been conceived, and from which this book has been written. Since theology is faith seeking *understanding*, and since women and men seeking to understand their faith do it in *this* particular time of world Christianity and global consciousness, such a perspective needs not only to affect the *content* of theology but also the way theology is understood in general.

In many ways, the implications of Anselm's classic definition of theology for today can be compared to what in music—certainly in Western classical music, but also in jazz with its African and Latin American roots—can be called the "variation." In classical music in the West, a variation is written as a composer takes a simple theme, states it at the beginning, and then repeats it a number of times by elaborating on the melody, changing the key or even changing the tempo. The variation, I believe, is not just a minor musical exercise. Some of the greatest works in classical music are variations, and some have opened up new musical frontiers. Among my favorites are Brahms's "Variations on a Theme by Haydn," Tchaikovsky's "Variations on a Rococo Theme," Britten's "Variations on a Theme by William Purcell," and Vaughan Williams's "Fantasia on a Theme by Thomas Tallis." But there are many more. In jazz there is often a standard melody that is played first—Jacques Prévert's/Joseph Kosma's/Johnny Mercer's "Autumn Leaves," for example, or Duke Ellington's "Caravan"—followed by variations or "riffs" on that basic theme, often in turn by each instrument in the ensemble. Here the variation is pretty much of the essence of jazz. Even contemporary rock music might be said to use the form of the variation—think, for example, of Jimi Hendrix's controversial rendering of the "Star Spangled Banner." In other music around the world as well, it is quite common to take traditional melodies and forms from traditional cultures—for instance, the traditional folk songs of the Philippines or the drum rhythms of Cameroon, and mix them with contemporary rock or rap music to produce a totally new and yet deeply traditional sound. This is the music of reggae in the Carribean, or highlife in Ghana, the music of Sezen Aksu of Turkey,[1] Somalian hip hop artist K'nann,[2] or chicha music in Latin America (with its roots in Peru).[3]

The basic "theme" on which I would like to "compose" variations in this chapter is Anselm of Canterbury's classic definition. This phrase, as I have suggested in chapter 2, is unsurpassed as a definition of theology. As I've tried to show in chapter 2 as well, each word is supremely important: theology is rooted in *faith*; it is a *seeking* that is both urgent and tentative; and it a quest for *understanding*, not certainty, that is both intellectually rigorous and carried out within a tradition. Faith and understanding, moreover, need to be held together, avoiding, on the one hand, a blind fideism that in our day is expressed in a closed fundamentalism and avoiding, on the other, a bland rationalism that finds expression today in a rootless liberalism.

But Anselm's definition of theology as "faith seeking understanding" is also unsurpassed because of its ability to be interpreted—subjected to "variations"—within the context of today's world church. Just as, I believe, Haydn's, Purcell's, Ellington's, or a local culture's original themes have been greatly enriched—not superseded!—by the work of Brahms or Britten, a jazz sextet or a salsa band, so I believe Anselm's theme can be greatly enriched by the variations that I will offer here, many of which will come from the perspective of non-Western and third world Christians. These variations, however, will not only help us appreciate the depth of Anselm's definition; they will also help us understand more fully the nature of theology itself. This will be with the help of Christians from every part of the Christian world, who do theology with feet firmly planted in the wider faith of the church throughout the world and down through the ages and with a consciousness of theology's own ongoing dialogue with the cultural worlds and thought forms in which they live today.

On the theme, therefore, of "Faith Seeking Understanding" I offer eight implications or "variations."

Variation One:
Theology Is Not Exclusively an Academic Endeavor

"Theology," writes Indian theologian Michael Amaladoss, "is . . . not an abstract philosophical elaboration of eternal verities reserved to a few expert professionals. It is a discerning search for God in the here and now of history that is the concern of every one."[4] Defining theology as "faith seeking understanding" points to a dynamic in theologizing that belongs primarily to any and every Christian. Every Christian, whenever he or she prays, or when he or she tries to express personal faith and explain it to others or when he or she struggles with his or her own doubts is in fact already doing theology and is already a theologian. This is something we have seen already in the last chapter, but something I want particularly to emphasize here. As the great Renaissance Dutch humanist Erasmus (1466-1536) put it, "All can be Christian, all can be devout, and I shall boldly add—*all can be theologians.*"[5]

One does not have to look too far to discover that many untrained people of faith can and do bring startling insights into the life of faith. U.S. Anglo theologian Jack Shea brings this out in an article entitled "Theology at the Grassroots" when he writes about ordinary people he has encountered doing theology, in very ordinary ways—in a chance encounter at a hotel swimming pool, in a theological conversation among young volunteer workers, at a meeting of Chicago religious leaders in a church basement.[6] Nicaraguan Ernesto Cardenal's four volumes entitled *The Gospel in Solentiname* are a testimony to the fact that people with little education—peasants on the Nicaraguan island of Solentiname—but with much faith are able not only to achieve a penetrating understanding of scripture, but can even be inspirations to highly trained scholars. The late U.S. Anglo Scripture scholar Carroll Stuhlmueller (d. 1994), for instance, wrote that "upon reading this book, I want to . . . burn all my other books which at best seem like hay, soggy with mildew. . . . I know now *who* (not what) is the church and how to celebrate the eucharist."[7] Scots theologian Ian Fraser provides another testimony of the power of "grassroots theologizing" when he quotes a story told by a Belgian sister who had worked in Brazil:

> There are very poor people there, there was no water, there was no light, it was terrible. We had to go there because the bishop did not want to renew the contract with us. One of things which he said was: "You are not in the things which are holy." I told it to one of the women of Pueblo Joven and she was very angry. She said: "For the bishop what is holy is all that is happening inside the church. For me what is holy is the future of my people."[8]

But while it is indeed first and foremost an activity that is "the proper task of every Christian,"[9] if theological reflection is going to deepen and grow it needs to become more self-conscious, more systematic, more self-critical, more "disciplined"[10] and "deliberative."[11] On a kind of "second level" there emerges theology as a formal discipline, a topic of more formal reflection, study, and methodological procedure. René Latourelle explains this level of theological reflection as one that prolongs the spontaneous reflection that faith urges. It is a reflection that has become conscious of itself and seeks to understand faith in a more methodical and systematic fashion.[12] Theology at this level follows basic rules, submits to basic criteria, mines a long tradition, and is responsible to that tradition. To do theology at this level requires wide knowledge of the sources of theology, years of training, and a lot of practice.

That being said, however, it must always be kept in mind that, even if one is educated in this way, theology as such must never be seen as an esoteric, mainly academic science, but the work of every believing Christian. Academic, self-conscious theology—theology that is responsible to the wider tradition—*is* necessary, but it is only necessary as something that serves men and women in their fundamental efforts to understand their faith. Theology, writes Brazilian Clodovis Boff, has three levels: the popular, the ministerial, and the professional.[13] The only justification of the second two levels, however, is the service of the first. To paraphrase Peter Schineller, a U.S. Anglo Jesuit who has taught theology in Nigeria, theology is too important a task to be left only to the professionals![14]

The people, therefore—ordinary baptized Christian believers—are really the main theologians; the role of professionals—ministers, teachers, scholars, and authors—is subsidiary to the "real theologians," the people themselves. Filipino Leonardo Mercado speaks of the professional, trained theologian as the "midwife" who helps give birth to the theology of the common people; Samuel Amirtham (Indian) and John Pobee (Ghanaian) insist that "what the [trained] theologian does is *in the context of* and *with* the people, not *for* the people gathered as a community of faith."[15] But it is precisely *because* the people are the main theologians that the role of professionally trained pastors, teachers, and scholars is so important. They are necessary so that the community's understanding of faith can develop and flourish. As Patricia O'Connell Killen has astutely observed, assisting adults (and we might add *young* adults as well) is arguably "the single most significant work of the contemporary pastoral minister and religious educator."[16] Killen writes from her perspective as a white theologian in the United States, but I believe her insight is valid in all parts of the world today.[17]

Variation Two:
Theology Is Always Done in Community

As I have explained theology as "faith seeking understanding" so far in this book, I might have given the impression that theology is primarily the work of individuals seeking to understand their individual faith. U.S. Anglos Howard Stone and James Duke remind us, however, that while theology is something that is deeply *personal*—not casual reflection on religious experience in general but on *my* experience of God in my life—it is nevertheless never something that is merely *private*.[18] Christian faith, in other words, is ecclesial; we seek understanding of our faith only in the context of the community called church. Michael H. Taylor, writing in Britain but writing from the perspective of global Christianity, makes this point eloquently in a passage that has influenced my own thinking greatly over the past several years:

> If the theological task is a "do-it-yourself" job, it is not a "do-it-by-yourself" job. If it is local it must never be parochial. What we believe and decide to do must be exposed to what others believe and decide to do. Real heresy is not getting it wrong, but getting it wrong in isolation. The task must be done in critical conversation with the common wealth of the church.[19]

This basic communal or ecclesial dimension of theology, it seems to me, has three important implications: community is, first, the *source* of Christian theologizing; second, it both is the source of *and* sets the parameters for Christian theologizing; and third, it sets the *parameters* of Christian theologizing. Although these implications will be explained much more in detail in part 2 of this book, let me elaborate a bit on each of them here.

Theology, in the first place, is the *source* of theologizing. Christians never theologize as mere individuals because, according to Christian anthropology, individuals do not really exist. We are only who we are as human beings because of others. Others, our mothers and fathers, brought us into existence. Others, through culture and language, have given us a particular human identity. Only in relationship with others have we come to know ourselves as selves. Asian, African, Latin American cultures, as well as cultures in Oceania, know this instinctively. Rather than the Western Cartesian dictum "I think therefore I am," most cultures in the world establish identity according to the African proverb "I am because we are."[20]

In addition, we are Christians only because of others. No one can baptize him- or herself, and we are all together the people of God, the body of Christ, the temple of the Spirit in the world. Even the Christian understanding of the end of human existence is no vision of individuals enjoying God by themselves; rather, the Christian vision in both the Bible and the theological tradition is of a banquet, a liturgy, a community made up of women and men "from every race, nation, people and tongue" (Rev 7:9). Theology, whether explicitly in a reflection group or implicitly by the fact that, say, scholars read other theologians and communicate with them through their publications, is always a conversation, always done in some kind of communal or ecclesial milieu.

Second, however, while community can be the source of theologizing, it also sets limits to it. Theologians draw from the community's wealth of faith and its expression, but they also must be responsible to what the community believes. The Christian doctrine of tradition expresses this double function of community.[21] Tradition, on the one hand, is a rich source for theologizing. It is that milieu or atmosphere of faith in which Christians live and because of which Christians can interpret their present experience faithfully. It is through tradition understood in this "active" or "subjective" sense that the church "hands on to all generations all that she herself is, all that she believes" (DV 8). On the other hand, this Tradition (upper case) is made accessible by traditions (lower case)—objective texts, for example, in Scripture, liturgical books, or theological writings; works of art in the plastic arts, music, or architecture; women and men of outstanding learning, courage, or virtue like Francis of Assisi, Julian of Norwich, Black Elk, Josephine Bakhita, or Martin Luther King Jr. It is in conversation with and reflection on these sources—and sometimes even "talking back" to them, as U.S. feminist Letty M. Russell (1930-2007) notes[22]—that Christians are able to discover and rediscover ways of expressing their faith in a way that is both true to their experience and faithful to the past. As Dorothy Day (1897-1980) once said pointedly, "How anyone can persist in the search for God without the assistance of the church and the advice of her confessors, with the experience of generations behind them, I do not know."[23]

On the other hand, it is to tradition, in both its "subjective" and "objective" modes, that theologians need to remain responsible. There is a difference in being *traditional* and being a *traditionalist*. Tradition is the living faith of the dead; traditionalism is the dead faith of the living, as U.S. Greek Orthodox church historian Jaroslav Pelikan (1923-2006) once wrote famously.[24] Theologians nevertheless need to acknowledge and pay homage to the insights and accomplishments of their ancestors in the faith. While we may surely deepen and go beyond the past, we may never abandon it. This is certainly something that Christians from the "majority world" of Asia, Latin America and Africa can appreciate, and those of us from the "minority world" of North America, Europe and Australia/New Zealand can learn from such appreciation.

As U.S. Latino theologian Gary Riebe-Estrella writes, contemporary thinking on tradition has likened it more to a *conversation* than to a *content* or *deposit*. Using this analogy, theologians need always to keep within the bounds of that conversation. Rather than keeping us mired in the past, Latinos speak of Tradition as a way to break through to a *future* that is at the same time *faithful* to the past.[25]

In the third place, the specific Catholic understanding of the church's teaching office (magisterium) needs to be understood within our understanding of theology as a radically communal or ecclesial practice. Rightly understood, the church's teaching office—an office (i.e., a task) fulfilled in general by the *entire* church but concretely by the college of bishops in union with the pope—exists for the sake of protecting and defending the community's faith from an expression that would lead to wrong understandings of it. As such, the magisterium is a true service of the faith, setting the boundaries and parameters of orthodox expression. While theologians may certainly suggest new areas and expressions to explore, and while the magisterium needs to respect their important creative role in the church, they need to work *within* the parameters set by the magisterium, never against it.[26] Of course, this does not meant that Christians do not have the right and sometimes the obligation to disagree with certain exercises of the magisterium's teaching.[27] What it does mean, however, is that such teaching needs to be approached both with respect and a "hermeneutics of generosity." The magisterium is *supposed* to be a conservative force in the church. Its duty is to protect and preserve. It articulates, however, the community's wisdom, and such wisdom is not to be trivialized.

Variation Three:
Theology Is Not So Much a Body of Knowledge as It Is an Activity

Theology, Anselm says, is faith *seeking* understanding—in other words, it is an activity and not the *result* of an activity, a *process* rather than a *product*. It should perhaps be understood more as a *verb* rather than a *noun*. Theology is not the science of learning a lot of things—as though a correct theology existed somewhere "out there." Rather, if Anselm's definition is taken seriously, theology is more correctly conceived as the effort to come to a deeper understanding of God's self gift that was offered in revelation and accepted by means of an initial and continuing act of faith. It is not as if one can do theology by reading the right books or coming to know a particular body of knowledge—the contents of *Catechism of the Catholic Church*, for example, Denzinger's *Enchiridion Symbolorum*, or Jaroslav Pelikan's and Valerie Hotchkiss's marvelous collection of creeds and confessions.[28] What is much more important is that a person or community of persons become engaged in the process of trying to understand their faith by working to correlate it with what is going on in their lives.

What follows from this is that the task of any theological education is not so much to help students learn *theology* (i.e., a body of knowledge), but to help them learn to *do* theology. Of course, this does not mean that students of theology should not have to master a number of facts—the history of doctrines, the great figures in the tradition, the plurality of theological methods. What it does mean, however, is that mastering a content is not what is *primary* in theological education. The goal of such education is the acquisition of an attitude, what the scholastics called a *habitus*. The same thing was expressed by the U.S. Anglo author Eugene Kennedy when he spoke of one of the tasks of pastoral leadership as that of being the "theological person" in the community, the one who is able to interpret the day-to-day happenings in the world and in people's lives against the backdrop of the church's Scriptures and its rich, always pluriform tradition.[29]

I once saw a message scrawled on a wall: "E = MC squared," it read, under which was written "very good, Albert, but you didn't show your work!" Besides the lesson that one can find material for theological reflection absolutely anywhere, this scrawl is a little parable about the nature of theology as activity, not content. It is simply not enough to get the answers right in theology. Even less is it enough simply to parrot them from some authoritative source. "We have learned," says a group of U.S. feminist theologians who write collectively, "that to consume passively theologies produced by others is not to do theology."[30] Theological answers are only "correct" if they are the result of real engagement of men and women with the stuff of their lives and the wisdom of the tradition. Luther surely exaggerated, but he certainly says it powerfully: a theologian is not made by reading books, but by living, dying, even by being damned![31]

Variation Four:
Every Genuine Theology Is a Contextual Theology

Whether one speaks of "indigenization," "incarnation," "inculturation" or "contextualization," the basic tone of this variation is that every genuine theology is one that not only takes Scripture and Tradition seriously as the "experience of the past," but takes just as seriously "the experience of the present"—that is, context: theologians' social locations, their culture, their historical situation.[32] The point is that if theology is really faith seeking *understanding*, there can really be no such thing as a kind of generic theology, a theology of "one size fits all." There really is no such thing as "theology" as such; there can only be contextual theologies: feminist, African, North American, Roman, Asian, theology of first nations, and so on. A theology that might *claim* to be universal is really one that is *universalizing*—one that wants to impose a particular contextual theology on other ways of doing theology. As Robert Schreiter has pointed out, "All theologies have contexts, interests, relationships of power, special concerns—and to pretend that this is not the case is to be blind."[33]

Contextualization, I believe, is a theological imperative. It is not something exotic or marginal to the theological enterprise, but at its center. Any theologizing in the past that was worth its salt was a theology that took its context seriously, even though theologians' consciousness of their context was almost always more implicit than explicit. Nevertheless, we can see today how both the Old and New Testaments are products of various contexts in Israel's and the early church's history and circumstances; Origen's (ca. 185-ca. 254) greatness was precisely in the way he engaged the Neoplatonic thought forms of his time; Ephrem the Syrian (309-373) theologized within the Persian genre of the poem and song; Aquinas's theology in his day hinged on his dialogue with the newly rediscovered manuscripts of Aristotle; and Luther's (1483-1546) genius was to have articulated the growing understanding in the West of an individual's human dignity and responsible conscience. Missionaries such as Alopen in seventh-century China, Cyril and Methodius in the Slavic nations in the ninth century, and Matteo Ricci in the China of the sixteenth century certainly thought contextually. Doctrines such as Nicaea's *homoousios*, Scholasticism's transubstantiation, and the French school's understanding of ordained ministry are all results of theologians' deep encounters with culture and history. Today we are more conscious of the need for theology to engage context, and so papal and magisterial documents as well as contemporary theological thought have emphasized the importance of contextualizing and inculturating Christian faith in every situation. Pope John Paul II is often quoted as saying that "the synthesis between culture and faith is not just a demand of culture, but also of faith. A faith that does not become culture is a faith which has not been fully received, not thoroughly thought through, not fully lived out."[34]

One additional theme in this variation would be the fact that a contextual theology demands of theologizing that it be thoroughly interdisciplinary. While philosophy is still important in the theologizing process, it cannot be theology's sole dialogue partner. Dialogue with the "hard sciences" (e.g., biology, physics) and the social sciences (e.g., anthropology, sociology) is a *sine qua non* of theologizing today, as is a keen knowledge of literature, music, and the other arts. Contextual theology is about discerning the "signs of the times," and it will be these tools that help in the discernment.

Doing contextual theology, there is no doubt, puts theology at great risk of betraying the tradition by developing a false and unevangelical syncretism (i.e., focusing more on the context and culture than on the gospel message and/or the person of Jesus). But, as Scottish church historian Andrew Walls points out, there never has been any safe theology. The risks involved, for example, in developing an orthodox Christology in the fourth century by "thinking in Greek, using indigenous vocabulary, categories of thought, and methods of debate" were enormous. But such risks "led to discoveries (true discoveries, though not necessarily the final ones) about who Christ is, that could never have been achieved using traditional categories, such as Messiah, alone." Doing such radical rethinking of the meaning of Jesus nevertheless "did not mean abandoning the past; Messiah and the other traditional titles continue to mean what they always did. It did not mean abandoning Scripture; the process made clear things that were in Scripture all the time, but clearly seen only when they were brought out by translation."[35] Contextualizing theology is risky—yes. But definitely worth it.

Variation Five:
Theology Is about Personal and Communal Transformation

Classical theology, as we have seen, spoke of three dimensions of faith—an intellectual dimension (*credere Deum*), an affective dimension (*credere Deo*) and a transformative or behavioral dimension (*credere in Deum*).[36] What this fifth

variation of "faith seeking understanding" focuses on is the third dimension—
the fact that, in the phrase Karl Barth, "only the doer of the Word is its real
hearer,"[37] an idea particularly important in Latin American and other liberation theologies throughout the world. Theological knowledge cannot simply
consist of intellectual clarification or religious affection. The knowledge that
is the result of our theologizing is a knowledge that leads to the transformation both of ourselves and of our world. As theologians from the third
world declared at a meeting in Dar es Salaam, Tanzania, in 1976, "We reject
as irrelevant an academic type of theology that is divorced from action. We are
prepared for a radical break in epistemology which makes commitment the
first act of theology and engages in critical reflection on praxis of the reality
of the Third World."[38]

Theology, first, leads to the transformation of ourselves. A colleague of
mine once remarked that his aim in teaching was not just to impart knowledge of his subject of moral theology or ethics. His aim was nothing less than
to make his students more virtuous. This same sentiment, I think, is expressed
by Karl Rahner in an essay addressed to young theological students. A person
should not study theology, Rahner insisted, "unless one is prepared to open
all the areas of one's life to the realities which are the object of theological
reflection."[39]

But self-transformation is ultimately not for the enhancement of self but
for the transformation of the world. Perhaps the greatest contribution of liberation theology—Latin American, feminist, African, Asian— in the last several decades has been its insistence that genuine theology is always a "critical
reflection on Christian praxis in the light of the Word."[40] "Praxis," the liberation theologians insist, is not simply "practice," but a process by which action,
analysis, and reflection work together in a constant hermeneutical circle or—
better—spiral. For them, theology is only theology if it issues forth in liberating, transforming action that is subsequently analyzed and reflected upon
to produce even more intelligent and faithful action. In a way, this modifies
Anselm's definition into "faith seeking intelligent action." "To be the genuine
article," Ian Fraser writes, "Theology has to be put to work to change history."[41] "Political theology" is not just a *type* of theology, but a perspective, like
contextualization, that must be at theology's heart.

Variation Six:
Theology Affects Both Spirituality and Ministry

It should be fairly obvious at this point that the work of theology in not a mere
intellectual exercise, but an activity that affects the whole of people's lives. As
such, theology both nourishes and is nourished by our spirituality and our pastoral ministry. While one can rightly *distinguish* among them, how one does

theology, lives a spirituality, and performs ministry are all aspects of one reality. Spirituality and ministry are both theological acts, and theology has both a spiritual and a ministerial component if it is to be genuine faith, genuinely seeking genuine understanding.

Theology, then, has strong connections to Christian spirituality. On the one hand, theological reflection gives spirituality substance. One danger of spirituality is a danger of *fideism*, that is, as I explained it in chapter 2, a deep mistrust of human reason and disciplined reflection in a person's or a community's journey toward God. I remember once listening to an ardent adherent to the Catholic Charismatic movement say with confidence that, should he happen to trip on a flight of stairs, all he would have to do to be safe would be to recite verses 11 and 12 of Psalm 91: "For to his angels he has given command about you, that they guard you in all your ways. Upon their hands they shall bear you up, lest you dash your foot against a stone." In contrast to this, I remember one of my own spiritual directees thanking me several years ago for being a systematic theologian as well as a spiritual director. He felt that my ability to approach spiritual direction as a kind of theological reflection had really been helpful in his own discernment process. As one of my students once put it in regard to this interface between theology and spirituality: "The head moves the heart along."

On the other hand—and perhaps even more importantly—our spirituality gives life to our theology. Aidan Nichols paraphrases the well-known dictum of Evagrius Ponticus (345-399) of Asia Minor: "If you do not pray, then you are not a theologian,"[42] and Geoffrey Wainwright insists that theology is most properly done as "doxology," and so is deeply imbued with the experience of prayer and especially liturgy.[43] Theology, as it were, is to be learned and done on one's knees. Karl Barth writes that "the first and basic act of theological work is *prayer*. . . . In view of the danger to which theology is exposed and to the hope that is enclosed within its work, it is natural that without prayer there can be no theological work."[44] It is for this reason that Douglas John Hall speaks of theology as "thought-in-relationship" and as "persistent prayer." Referring to Anselm's definition, Hall writes that "the participle 'seeking' . . . comes very close to depicting the whole posture of theology as prayer. The attitude of theology is an inquiring one—and not in the sense of polite or detached curiosity, but as a quest upon whose outcome everything depends."[45]

Theology has equally strong connections to pastoral ministry. Theology, first, gives both depth and substance to ministry. French theologian and cardinal Charles Journet (1891-1975) relates how Ignatius Loyola (1491-1556), after his conversion and recognition of his vocation, realized that if he was to be of real spiritual assistance to people he would have to study. Consequently he went to the University of Paris and endured the humiliation of sitting with schoolboys to learn Latin in preparation for theological studies.[46] This story is echoed in a line from the great Anglican churchman Charles Gore (1853-1932), who insisted that "only those who know from the ground up what they believe, and why they believe, are able to help those who seek them out."[47] Ministry, as a friend of mine once put it, is not founded on the "theology of being nice," but on real theological expertise. Henri Nouwen insists that "the Christian leaders of the future have to be theologians. . . ."[48]

Conversely, however, pastoral ministry needs to be a major source of our theology. David Tracy's refinement of Paul Tillich's understanding that theology employs a "method of correlation" points in this direction. The correlation, says Tracy, must be "mutually critical" in that not only does the Christian tradition offer answers to questions that arise in Christian life and ministry, but such questions also refine and refocus Christians' understanding of the tradition as well.[49] Such is also the insight of U.S. Anglos James and Evelyn Whitehead in their proposal of a model and method of theological reflection for ministry. A minister's task in theological reflection is first to listen attentively to the data of personal and communal experience, that of the church's tradition, and the data of the context or culture in which one ministers as well. One proceeds by bringing these three elements of the model into mutually critical conversation with one another, with the desired result of discerning the concrete pastoral implications of that conversation.[50] In this way ministry becomes a theological act; theologizing becomes an indistinguishable part of ministry.

Variation Seven:
Theology Is Always Done with a "Missiological Imagination"

At its origins, theology emerged as a reflection on the church's missionary activity. Mission was the "mother of theology," German Scripture scholar Martin Kähler wrote; the first theology was a mission theology, and the first church history was a history of mission.[51] With the legitimization of Christianity under Constantine, however—at least in the West—church life and theology began to turn in upon themselves and mission began to be relegated to the fringes of the church's life while theology began to concern itself almost totally with "the knowledge of God and the things of God."[52] Only in the 1930s, with the theology of Karl Barth and Karl Hartenstein (1894-1952) and the Willingen Conference of the World Council of Churches in 1952, did an understanding of the church emerge that saw mission—as the participation of the church in the *missio Dei*—not so much as *having* a mission but as *being* mission in its very essence.[53] Consequently, as British theologian Andrew Kirk has expressed it, mission must inform the doing theology itself, since theology exists not for its own sake, but to be of service to a missionary church. Mission, writes Kirk, should not only be "the roof of the building that completes the whole structure, already constructed by blocks that stand on their own, but both the foundation and the mortar in the joints, which cements together everything else."[54]

Systematic theology, I believe, needs to be done with a thoroughly "missiological imagination."[55] In terms of *theological method*, the employment of such an imagination would mean that systematic theology would conceive of itself as "practical theology." It would be anchored, in other words, within the experience of a local community and would seek to serve that community's pastoral and evangelizing activity. Another methodological implication would be a sustained and serious effort to "listen to all the voices" in the doing of theology. Not just the great and prominent Western voices would be normative, but also voices of women theologians, theologians from the third world, and theologians from the grassroots. It is with this attitude that this book is being written. In addition, as I have already mentioned above, inculturation or contextualization would be at the heart of theologizing. The issue would not be *if* one is doing a contextual theology, but what particular model of contextual theology one would employ. A "missiological imagination" would change the *content* of systematic theology as well. To give a few examples: no reflection on God would be complete without taking into account the way the divine is understood and imaged in other religious traditions. Christology would tend to draw heavily on the traditions of "Spirit Christology," focusing much more on the "Jesus of history" and how he carried out his ministry "under the sway of the Spirit of God," as Asian theologians have put it.[56] In addition, issues about Christ's uniqueness—in the context of the validity of the world's religions—would be wrestled with. Ecclesiology would be constructed from the perspective of mission, and the major images and dimensions (marks) of the church would be developed in a missiological way.[57]

German theologian Wilhelm Andersen wrote that the doctrine of mission is always "the great agitation in the life of the church."[58] I want to suggest as well that mission will always be the great agitation in the doing of theology. Faith seeks understanding not for its own sake but for the service of the church; and faith seeks understanding so that the great mystery of God's love can be *understandable*. Doing theology with a "missiological imagination" is at the heart of a theology where faith seeks understanding today.

Variation Eight:
Theology Is Not Only Done Discursively

Christians tend to think of theology as something that is done discursively—in homilies, in articles or books, in a classroom discussion or lecture, in class presentations or assignments. It is important to point out, however, that there is a variety of other ways in which theology can be done, ways that may even be more profound than prose.

Some of the best theology, therefore, appears in literature. The novels and stories of Alice Walker, Graham Greene, Susan Howatch, Walker Percy, Soshaku Endo, Flannery O'Connor, and Chinua Achebe all make powerful theological statements. Dante's *Divine Comedy* must surely be rated as one of the most powerful and influential works in the history of theology. There is hardly a eucharistic theology in the Middle Ages more sublime than Thomas Aquinas's "Pange Lingua." And the poetry of Gerard Manley Hopkins, T. S. Eliot, Rainer Maria Rilke, George Herbert, and Denise Levertov contain truth and beauty that no prose can come close to expressing.

Robert Ellsberg writes that "Bach's spirituality, reflected in his music, is not for the cloister but for the world. Consequently, it is a remarkable fact that any place his music is performed seems instantly to be transformed into sacred space."[59] Works like Brahms's *A German Requiem*, Mendelssohn's *Reformation Symphony*, Mozart's *Requiem*—and the requiems of Verdi and Fauré—are only a few examples of almost overwhelming insights into God's mysterious presence in human life and history. Popular music also offers a rich expression of theology, as the works of Bruce Springsteen and U2 attest.

What Mariology can match Michelangelo's *Pietà*? Or what eschatology is more powerful than his painting of the last judgment? No written liberation theology can express the agony of the poor better than the crucifix by Peruvian Edilberto Merida that appeared on the cover of Gutiérrez's *A Theology of Liberation*. Asian landscape paintings present an entire theology of ecology, as nature in the paintings dwarfs the humans in them. And the marvelous carvings of *Ujamá* by anonymous Kenyan woodcarvers speak eloquently of human connectedness and the communion of saints. The pain and hope of South African women in the midst of the AIDS epidemic are expressed powerfully and exquisitely in the Keiskamma Altarpiece.[60] Film, drama, architecture, and dance all speak clearly and powerfully in ways that books (like this one!) can only stammer to say. Theology is embodied in rituals like those that take place in Native American sweat lodges; it is embodied as well in the wisdom of tribal elders and in community's myths and proverbs. Faith has many more ways of seeking understanding than that of cold prose and human words.

CONCLUSION

In his discussion of "The Classic" in *The Analogical Imagination*, David Tracy suggests a way by which we might know that a particular text is a "classic." Most of us, he says, can remember reading a particular novel, poem, or essay years before that had a deep impact on our lives at the time. If years later we should reread that text and it still has the same power, "It is a candidate for classic status." If not, "then we are better off with our memories. We will be thankful for its former contribution yet we will read it now, if at all, only as a helpful, nostalgic reminder of what life was like back then, not what life means now."[61]

My contention is that Anselm's definition of theology as "faith seeking understanding" is one that is indeed a classic. Like any classic, it needs to be interpreted for new times, but like any classic its basic truth is disclosive of an enduring surplus of meaning that is accessible in various ways in various changing contexts. The variations presented here, I hope, have given us a glimpse of that surplus of meaning for today and for today's world church. This is the meaning that can still guide us in the future.

QUESTIONS FOR REFLECTION

1. This chapter claims that every Christian is a theologian. Describe a time when you actually did theology, perhaps not even knowing it at the time.
2. Why do you think it is important to describe theology more as an *activity* than as a *body of knowledge*?
3. What are the advantages of saying that every theology is actually a *contextual* theology?
4. How do you think theology affects our spirituality and our work in ministry?
5. What are some songs, movies, television shows, or novels that can be examples of theology that is not discursive.
6. Why is it important to do theology with a "missiological imagination"?

SUGGESTIONS FOR FURTHER READING AND STUDY

Samuel Amirtham and John S. Pobee, eds., *Theology by the People: Reflections on Doing Theology in Community* (Geneva: World Council of Churches, 1986).

Stephen B. Bevans, *Models of Contextual Theology* (Maryknoll, N.Y.: Orbis Books, 2002), chapter 1, "Contextual Theology as a Theological Imperative," 3-15.

———, "Wisdom from the Margins: Systematic Theology and the Missiological Imagination," in Richard C. Sparks, ed., *Proceedings of the Fifty-sixth Annual Convention, The Catholic Theological Society of America* (Berkeley, Calif.: Catholic Theological Society of America, 2001), 21-42.

Ernesto Cardenal, *The Gospel of Solentiname*, 4 vols. (Maryknoll, N.Y.: Orbis Books, 1976, 1978, 1979, 1982).

José M. de Mesa, *Why Theology Is Never Far from Home* (Manila: De La Salle University Press, 2003).

Karl Rahner, "A Theology That We Can Live With," *Theological Investigations XXI* (New York: Crossroad, 1988), 99-112.

Clemens Sedmak, *Doing Local Theology: A Guide for Artisans of a New Humanity* (Maryknoll, N.Y.: Orbis Books, 2002).

John Shea, "Theology at the Grassroots," *Church* 3 (Spring 1989): 3-7.

Fredrica Harris Thompsett, *We Are Theologians: Strengthening the People of the Episcopal Church* (Cambridge, Mass.: Cowley, 1989).

On the Keiskamma Altarpiece, see http://www.saintjamescathedral.org/keiskamma .asp.

Part II

Faith Seeking Together

The Ecclesial Nature of Theology

I N THE SECOND PART of this book we are going to reflect more deeply on the fact that theology as faith seeking understanding is not just the work of *individual* believers seeking *individual* understanding of their faith, something dealt with briefly in the previous chapter.

On the one hand—certainly—theology *is* the work of individuals, people of personal faith. To be more accurate, however, it is not the work of individuals *as* individuals. Rather, theology is the work of *individuals* (that is, women and men who are *personally* trying to understand their faith) *in the context of a community*, a believing community, the church. In fact, in the *fullest* sense of the word, theology is the act of a community—the church. What we are going to focus on in this section, therefore, is the *ecclesial dimension of all theological reflection*. To understand our definition more fully, we must say that theology is faith seeking understanding *together*.

This is something that a number of theologians recognize today. Peruvian theologian Gustavo Gutiérrez, for example, writes that "theology is not an individual task, it is an ecclesial function. It is done from the Word of God received and experienced in the Church, and for the sake of its proclamation to every human being and especially the disinherited of this world."[1] Eminent German theologian Helmut Thielicke (1908-1986) insists that "insofar as we are determined to be true theologians, we think within the community of God's people, and for that community, and in the name of that community:—how shall I say it?—we think as part of the community itself."[2] British theologian Geoffrey Wainwright expresses the balance between individual and community in theology: "The doing of theology is inescapably individual: just as the act and attitude of faith require personal commitment, so we cannot avoid personal accountability in theological reflection upon faith. But the doing of theology, though individual, is not individualistic. The believer-theologian lives and works within the fellowship of the Church, draws sustenance from the Church, and seeks to serve the Church."[3] Finally, let me quote once again (as I did in chapter 3) from Michael H. Taylor's important essay in a book edited by Indian Samuel Amirtham and Ghanaian John Pobee: "If the theological task is a 'do-it- yourself' job, it is not a 'do-it-by-yourself' job. If it is local it must never be parochial. What we believe and decide to do must be exposed to what others believe and decide to do. Real heresy is not getting it wrong, but getting it wrong in isolation. The task must be done in critical conversation with the common wealth of the church."[4]

When we speak of this "common wealth of the church," it seems to me, we need to speak in reference to the church both *diachronically* (the church through history, both past and present) and *synchronically* (the church as both local and universal community, the church in its dimension as *catholic*). For theology to be true to its communal or ecclesial nature, in other words, it needs to be in a conversation with both present and past Christians, and with both the local community and the many local communities that make up the global church.

In addition, as we reflect on this ecclesial, communal dimension of theology, I think it is important to recognize two dimensions of this "*critical conversation with the common wealth of the church.*"

On the one hand, the community of believers is the *source* of theology. The community, in other words, is the source of theology as an *activity*. It is always done in some sort of dialogue or conversation with other believers, those living and those "gone before us marked with the sign of faith" as the Catholic Eucharistic Prayer I puts it, those in one's local, particular community (sharing the same culture, social location, or physical location) as well as those in other communities throughout the world. The ecclesial community—present and past, local and universal—is also the source of theology's *content*. The questions that theology wrestles with, the doctrines and symbols theology tries to interpret and understand more deeply, the emphases or perspectives that a particular local theology might develop—all of these sources of content come from a particular community (a fourth-century community in North Africa struggling with how to express Jesus' identity as both human and divine, or a twenty-first century Thai community trying to understand justification in the light of the Asian understanding of harmony). At the same time, the community's past also contributes to theology's content—for example, how the traditional image of the church as the body of Christ can shape a particular community's understanding of the mission of the church in its own specific context.

On the other hand, the community of faith also provides limits or parameters to theological inquiry and theological expression. Because a particular theological expression needs to "measure up" to the collective wisdom of the community, past and present, theologians—and their communities—are safeguarded against overly individualistic or idiosyncratic theologies or interpretations. And individual communities, because they need to measure their theology and practice over against the *entire* community in all parts of the world, will be safeguarded from theologies and practices that are overly self-focused or even "tribal." Theology, in other words, is always response to the community—local or universal, past and present.

In this second part of the book, then, we will be focusing on both of these aspects of the ecclesial dimension of the theologizing process.

In the first chapter of part 2, the focus will be on the *community as the source of theologizing*. Community is the source of theology because of the communal nature of human beings as such, and therefore theology must always, at some level at least, be done in the context of a conversation, a dialogue.

In the second chapter of part 2, the focus will be on the *community as **both** the source and the parameter of theologizing*. What this will involve is a reflection on the nature and importance of tradition in theologizing—particularly in the context of *Catholic* theology.

In a third chapter, our focus will be on the *community as parameter of theologizing*. This will point to the role of the church's teaching office or magisterium in the task of theologizing—again, an important aspect of particularly *Catholic* theological activity.

Let me end this introduction to part 2 with a quotation from U.S. American bishop James Malone of Youngstown, Ohio. In a reflection on the relationship between bishops and theologians, Malone wrote wisely of the need of the wider community both as a source and as a parameter-setter for theologians' work: "The theologian needs the community as a point of reference for his or her work, as a source of questions and commentary, and as a constituency which manifests the meaning of the word of God by the quality of witness in the world."[5] The understanding of the communal, ecclesial nature of theology is truly a *sine qua non* for a theology that is done today in authentic global perspective.

4

The Community as Source
of Theology

Doing Theology in Community

T HIS CHAPTER WILL BE DIVIDED into two main sections. In the first section
we will investigate the theological foundations for theology's communal
nature, focusing on contemporary reflections on theological anthropology,
or the understanding of the nature of women and men from the perspective of faith; contemporary understandings of the church that point to the
nature of theology as the work of communities of faith; and the important,
recently reemerged doctrine of the "sense of the faithful" or recognition of the
basic theological authority of the Christian community of believers. Then, in
a second section, we will explore a few concrete examples of how, indeed, the
Christian community, the church, is an authentic *source* of our theologizing.
This recognition of theology as the work of Christians *together* is an important
foundation for the refocusing of theology as an activity of the global church:
from seeing theology as something produced by a relatively elite group of
Christians (and mostly men) to seeing theology as a task engaged in by all
Christian women and men in every part of the world.

THEOLOGICAL FOUNDATIONS

The Social Nature of Human Persons

The Person as Individual
Especially since the dawn of Western modernity in the fifteenth century,
the understanding of theology (which has been fairly dominated by Western thought) has been based on the anthropology or the understanding of
the human person implied in the works of thinkers such as René Descartes
(whom we have already met in these pages), Thomas Hobbes (1588-1679),
John Locke (1632-1704), and Immanuel Kant (1724-1804). Descartes in particular, with his conviction that human identity lay with individual experience,

can be seen, in the words of German-American theologian Reinhold Niebuhr (1892-1971), as "the fountain source of modern culture."[1]

For Descartes, the final proof that he actually existed was based on his undeniable and undoubted experience that *I* think, therefore I am.[2] Everything in philosophy, everything in science, everything in society is based on what he considered this rock-solid fact. *Individual* existence is the foundation of everything. Such "ontological individualism"[3] was foreshadowed in terms of religion in the previous century by Martin Luther's famous declaration at the Diet of Worms (1521) that he could not go against his conscience ("Here I stand. I cannot do other").[4] The perspective was expressed as well in the eighteenth century in terms of epistemology and ethics by Immanuel Kant in his short but influential essay "What Is Enlightenment?" As Kant expressed it, it is the individual, using reason alone, not the influence of others, that makes one "enlightened," and therefore able really to *know* something and be capable of a truly *moral act*:

> Enlightenment is man's release from his self-incurred tutelage. Tutelage is man's inability to make use of his understanding without direction from another. Self-incurred is this tutelage when its cause lies not in lack of reason but in lack of resolution and courage to use it without direction from another. *Sapere aude!* "Have courage to use your own reason!"—that is the motto of enlightenment.[5]

This emphasis on the individual, however, did not mean that he or she did not need relationships or community. Human individuals certainly had relationships with others, and needed them. But the individual, in Western thinking and deep within the modern Western psyche, was the most important reality, the primary reality, the foundation of human existence. Relationships and community were seen as important, but definitely *secondary* to and supportive of the individual. Community is established *for the sake* of the individual and serves and protects individual rights. Whether community or society is formed, as Thomas Hobbes argued, to regulate what would be inevitable conflict among humans, or, according to Locke's thought, to promote human beings' best self-interest, what is basic is that human communal or societal life is the result of a kind of "contract" that is entered into—or departed from—by free and autonomous individuals.[6]

We might look to the text of the founding document of that great experiment in the new form of government that would guarantee individual rights—the United States' Declaration of Independence—to see how such a contractual understanding of community or society is expressed. Thomas Jefferson (1743-1826), the declaration's principal author, was particularly influenced by Locke's basic convictions of human equality and freedom, and we see this clearly in the Declaration in the famous words "We hold these truths to be self-evident, that all men are created equal, that they are endowed by their Creator with certain unalienable Rights, that among these are Life, Liberty and the pursuit of Happiness." The Declaration goes on to say that "to secure these rights, Governments are instituted among Men, deriving their just powers from the consent of the governed," and that whenever a government is not able or refuses to allow people to claim their rights, "It is the Right of the People to alter or to abolish it, and to institute new Government, laying its foundation on such principles and organizing its powers in such form, as to them shall seem most likely to effect their Safety and Happiness."[7] Such a foundation of "ontological individualism" was the basis for all the democratic movements that revolutionized Western politics in the nineteenth century and was the basis as well—somewhat ironically—for the great independence and anti-colonial movements that swept the world in the twentieth century.

This last statement points to the fact that the emergence of the individual, with individual rights, in the West in the last five hundred years was not *all* a negative movement. It has revolutionized human beings' understanding of themselves and has provided a vision of equality and freedom—economic, political, and religious—for peoples whose rights and dignity have been trampled on not only by the West but by their own governments and cultures. Ironically, once again it has been the rise of the Western understanding of the individual dignity of human beings that has been responsible for the emergence of a truly Catholic, global church and the kind of theology to which this book seeks to introduce its readers.

Nevertheless, in the last century or so another understanding of what it means to be human has been emerging in the West, one that—in yet another irony—reveals a new validity to more communal and communitarian understandings of human nature in Asian, African, Latin American, Middle Eastern cultures, the cultures of Oceania, and people of indigenous cultures in North America, Australia, and New Zealand. It is to this development that we turn in this chapter, because I believe that this more communal understanding of human beings can greatly and deeply affect the way Christians can live their lives and reflect on their Christian faith in the act of theologizing.

The Person as Communal

In the first decades of the twentieth century a number of significant voices were raised in Western thought that challenged the idea that human beings were, at base, inviolable and impenetrable individuals, and that one's "personhood" was best achieved as one achieved complete autonomy and independence. In many of his writings, Scots theologian John Wood Oman (1860-1939) emphasized the importance of the Enlightenment for a deeper understanding of the nature of the human person, writing that "the essential quality of a moral person is moral independence and an ideal person would be of absolute moral independence."[8] Nevertheless, he cautioned, this is only partly true. In a paradoxical way, a person can become an *independent* person only by becoming conscious of his or her deep connection with other people and, indeed, with the entire universe. As one becomes more and more "dependent," one realizes that reality actually calls one to true freedom and autonomy. The world, Oman argues, is radically personal, because it has as its deepest center the radically personal God. Authentic individual autonomy is ultimately something one achieves by asserting independence not over against reality but in relationship with it.[9]

In many ways, Oman anticipates the German Jewish philosopher Martin Buber's (1878-1965) more well-known development of the notion that it is our relationships that constitute us as true human beings, as persons; only when I acknowledge the presence and importance of another (treating another as a person, what he names a "Thou") can I truly be myself as a person. In a famous passage in his 1923 work *I and Thou*, Buber insists: "I become through my relation to the *Thou*; as I become *I*, I say *Thou*. All real living is meeting."[10]

In his 1913 work *The Problem of Christianity*, the U.S. philosopher Josiah Royce (1855-1916) argued the position that, counterintuitively for the Western mind, a human being achieved his or her individuality not so much by seeking one's independence, but by being a member of a community. As one rooted oneself in a particular past (in a "community of memory") and gave oneself over to a common vision of the future (in a "community of hope"), as one expanded oneself beyond oneself in this way, a person could reach his or her true potential.[11] As Royce scholar Frank Oppenheim (a U.S. Anglo) notes, writing in the context of a critique of U.S. individualism, Royce "identifies both community and individual as coequally ultimate realities. His 'special realism' sharply counters the current belief of most Americans that the world's primary realities are individuals only and that all communities simply derive from individuals' choices and so are not ultimate realities."[12]

In the 1950s the Scots philosopher John Macmurray (1891-1976) argued at length for the relational, communal nature of the self. For him, the basic proof of one's existence is not Descartes' "I think, therefore I am"; it is rather the recognition that "I *do*, therefore I am." In other words, the basic task in philosophy is "to transfer the centre of gravity . . . from thought to action,"[13] to shift one's thinking from the self as "thinker" to the self as "agent." Building on this fundamental shift, Macmurray points to the fact that if human beings are agents, then to speak of human beings as self-constituted is contradictory. This is because "any agent is necessarily in relation to the Other. Apart from this essential relation he does not exist. But, further, the Other in this constitutive relation must itself be personal. Persons, therefore, are constituted by their mutual relation to one another. 'I' exist only as one element in the complex 'You and I.'"[14] In very much the same way as Oman, Buber, and Royce, Macmurray makes the case that only to the extent that one moves out of oneself, ceases to fear the Other, and embraces real mutuality, can one achieve any kind of authenticity in her or his life. Human fulfillment hinges on authentic relationships, on commitment to community.[15]

What Western thought has begun to rediscover, of course, is part and parcel of the worldview of many—if not most!—of the world's cultures. In his pioneering work *Elements of Filipino Theology*, Filipino theologian Leonardo Mercado writes that although Filipinos/as have a keen sense of self, they find that sense of self in the context of some kind of "reference group" or (in Tagalog) a *sakop*.[16] The *sakop* is primarily a person's family, understood not so much as the Western nuclear family but the wider, extended family of aunts, uncles, and cousins as well as parents, grandparents, and brothers and sisters. Filipino languages express the connection between family members in organic terms. A relative is spoken of as a *kadugo* (Tagalog) or *kadara* (Ilocano—one of the three major languages), which literally means one who shares the same blood. Brothers and sisters are *kapatid* in Tagalog and *kabagis* in Ilocano, literally, one who shares the same intestines.

In my own experience of almost nine years working in the Philippines, I was always impressed that when two Filipinos/as met one another they would often question one another for several minutes to see if, by any chance, they are related. Filipinos/as also practice what is called "ritual kinship" or "fictive kinship,"[17] by which people become part of the family through being godparents or sponsors at weddings and baptisms. Unlike the prevailing custom in my own country of the United States where one has a number of one's friends to be groomsmen and maids of honor, a baptism or wedding in the Philippines may have five, six, or more sponsors. These sponsors are often significant people in the community (people of wealth, politicians) in order that the couple or child might increase their family connections with other families. But in all their relations Filipinos/as form other groups in which they belong—one's peer group or *barkada*, one's *compadres*, people from one's town or language group.

Filipinos/as, Mercado points out, are almost never alone. If they go somewhere, they look for a companion (in Tagalog, *kasama*); One always has a companion when one is sick, and in the hospital (rooms always come with a cot for the companion), and even in death there is always someone to watch the corpse. All of these examples point to the strongly communal nature of Filipinos/as, and such a communal sense, where the individual is first identified or even subordinate to the group, is a shared sense among Asians in general.[18]

In several of his writings, Mexican-American theologian Gary Riebe-Estrella has recourse to a seminal article by anthropologists Richard Shweder and Edmund Bourne in which the authors distinguish an "ego-centric" culture—such as that of the modern West, from a culture that is "socio-centric."[19]

Here "ego-centric" does not mean the same as selfish, but simply points to what we reflected on earlier about the primacy of the individual over a set of relationships like family or friends. "Socio-centric" cultures are found in Asia, Latin America, and Africa, and include also traditional (e.g., Native American, Inuit, Maori, Aboriginal) cultures as well as some Latinos/as or people of African or Asian descent in Western countries like the United States or Canada. In such cultures, "One's identity is rooted in the group (first, usually, in the primary group, which is the family). One individuates by accepting and perhaps redefining one's role *within* the group, but never by stepping outside the group."[20]

Riebe-Estrella gives several examples of socio-centric behavior from his own Mexican-American background. Among Latinos/as, relationships are of primary value. If a person is running late for a meeting, for example, and someone drops by the house on one's way out, the person going to the meeting would rather be late or even miss the meeting altogether rather than be inhospitable to her or his visitor. In the same way, when a Latino/a greets someone warmly and is given only a quick and perfunctory "fine" in response (as Westerners are prone to do, in the context of a totally different cultural world), the Latino/a is offended, for she or he would expect the person— especially someone that she or he has a relationship with—to stop and answer the question more fully.[21] Even the use of names to identify oneself differs in a culture where the group rather than the individual determines one's identity. As Riebe-Estrella points out, when you meet someone from the United States you are greeted with something like "Hi, I'm Fred." But "when you meet a Latino/a, you're given a whole string of last names as the person identifies for you who she or he is: 'Soy Josefina González Obregon.' The Latino use of two last names (*el doble apellido*) is a way by which persons identify the two primary groups of belonging which found their identity, that is, their father's family and their mother's family."[22] In many Asian cultures as well, family names may often come before the "given" name, as in Nguyen Duc Cao (Vietnamese), or Jung Young Lee (Korean).

Let me give one last example of an expression of the communal nature of human persons from the African context, namely, Botswana. In an essay that compares the notion of corporate personality in the Bible (which we will discuss below) and in the culture of Botswana, Bernice Letlhare quotes the proverb *motho ke motho ka batho*, which can be translated variously as "a person is a person through people," or "a human being is a human being through human beings." A variation of the proverb is *motho ke motho ka batho ba bangue*, which means "a human being is human because of other human beings," or "a person is a person because of other persons/people." "Through this proverb, then," Letlhare writes, "the indigenous Motswana recognised that the process of shaping and forming the 'one' is the product of 'others.'"[23] Among the people of Botswana, a newborn child is considered a gift from the ancestors, and a child only fully becomes a human being (a man or a woman) after the process of initiation, when the stories and customs of the group have been transmitted to them.[24]

In his apostolic exhortation *Ecclesia in Africa*, Pope John Paul II aptly sums up this African worldview in these words:

> African cultures have an acute sense of solidarity and community life. In Africa it is unthinkable to celebrate a feast without the participation of the whole village. Indeed, community life in African societies expresses the extended family. It is my ardent hope and prayer that Africa will always preserve this priceless cultural heritage and never succumb to the temptation to individualism, which is so alien to its best traditions.[25]

Reality as Communal

In his book *The Courage to Teach*, popular U.S. Anglo writer and speaker Parker Palmer tells of a personal experience that leads him to a reflection on the fact that not only are *humans* essentially communal, but that *reality itself* is communal. Everything in the universe is actually related to everything else. One day, Palmer says, he was lecturing at a large, prestigious university on his idea that the goal of education is nothing less than the creation "of a space in which the community of truth is practiced."[26] As he spoke, his attention was drawn to a distinguished-looking, elderly man near the front of the audience, and as soon as his lecture was finished and the floor was open for discussion, this man "rose quickly and introduced himself: 'I am Dr. Smith, Distinguished Such-and-Such Professor of Biology, Emeritus.'" Palmer's first reaction to this somewhat stuffy introduction was to steel himself to a vicious, academic attack on his ideas by this scientist. He thought, "He intends to have me for lunch—as an entrée, not a guest."

But what the professor said was stunning: "I am not sure I understand all this fuss about community in higher education. After all, it's only good biology." After that Palmer and the professor had a wonderful exchange about what the latter had said.[27] The account of this incident gave way to the following reflection, which I will quote in full:

> Two or three generations ago, no professor of biology would have claimed that community was good science. On the contrary, the biologist of an earlier era would have mocked my case for educational community as a romantic fallacy that violated the cardinal principle of the discipline: life is a ceaseless round of warfare between individuals, a win-lose arena of combat and death. For that earlier generation of biologists, nature was, in Tennyson's famous phrase, "red in tooth and claw." For the Social Darwinists

who built on that image of nature, human relations were no more than the survival of the fittest, thinly coated with a veneer of civilization.

But today, our images of biological reality have been transformed. Ecological studies offer a picture of nature less focused on the terrors of combat than on the dance of communal collaboration, a picture of the great web of being. Struggle and death have not disappeared from the natural world, but death is now understood as a factor in the ongoing life of the community rather than a failure in the life of the individual.[28]

A bit further on in the chapter from which this quotation is taken, Palmer refers to noted British philosopher Ian Barbour, who names three stages in how human beings have attempted to image reality. In premodern times, reality was imaged as "mental and material substance, or 'stuff.'" Think of Aristotle's conception of "prime matter." Then, with Isaac Newton (1643-1727) in the modern era (roughly contemporary with the philosophies of Descartes, Hobbes, and Locke) the image was atomistic, with reality consisting of basic, irreducible particles of matter. But, says Barbour, today reality is understood as "relational, ecological, and interdependent." The image, rather than "stuff" or "particles," is that of a "historical community of interdependent beings."[29]

What all of this points to is that there has been a kind of revolution in thinking not only about human beings but about the whole of reality itself. Human beings are constituted by their relationships to one another and find their fullest expression as they participate in a community that is rooted in the past and poised toward the future, as Royce would say. Thus, this deep communal nature of humanity simply mirrors everything else in the universe, and so women and men are also called to live in harmony not just with each other but with all of creation. As theologians such as Australian Denis Edwards have argued eloquently from their own study of contemporary science, human beings are *part of* not *over against* the universe, made of the universe's very elements.

> The living creatures of Earth are made up of molecules composed of atoms of carbon, hydrogen, oxygen, nitrogen, and phosphorus. Every atom of each of these elements, apart from hydrogen, has been made by nuclear fusion in stars. Every atom of every body found on Earth originates in a star. Life is intimately related to the stars. If there were no stars there could be no trees, flowers, kangaroos, or human beings. We are all made from stardust.[30]

Christianity as Communal

The revolution in Western thought, as well as the fresh recognition of the wisdom of Asian, Latin American, and African cultures, is at the same time a fresh insight into the rich communal nature of Christianity, which, under the influence of modern Western thought in the last five hundred years, was conceived very much as a religion for the sanctification of individuals. In the biblical worldview, however, we see that human beings are regarded not first as individuals, but primarily as members of particular groups—families, tribes, nations. Scholars speak of the notion of "corporate personality" to describe the concept of humanity in the Scriptures. Because of this notion of corporate personality, one person could stand for or symbolize an entire family or people, or an entire group could be summed up in the person of one individual. The word "adam," for example, is not a proper name in Genesis, but the Hebrew word for humankind in general. It refers only secondarily, says Swiss New Testament scholar Eduard Schweizer, to an individual.[31] God called Abram (Abraham) not just for himself, or even for his family, but to be the father of many nations (Gen. 17:6)—indeed, to be the one in whom *all* nations will find blessing (Gen. 12:3). The names "Israel" and "Ephraim" refer both to individuals (the name God gives to Jacob [Gen. 32:29] and the name of the second of Joseph's sons [Gen. 41:52]) and to the whole people of Israel and one of its tribes. The kings of Israel, by their obedience or disobedience to the covenant that God made with Israel at Sinai, embodied the obedience or disobedience of the entire people of Israel. As British Old Testament scholar H. Wheeler Robinson argued in a classic article on the corporate personality, the "I" of the psalms and the individual "suffering servant" in Second Isaiah both refer to the entire people of Israel and to concrete individuals as well.[32]

In the New Testament, we see Jesus preaching about and embodying in his action and personal behavior the presence of "the Reign of God," a community that is both forgiving and forgiven and one that excludes no one (see, e.g., Matt. 18:10-35; Luke 15).[33] After Jesus' death and resurrection, and the descent of the Holy Spirit upon the small group that made up the "Jesus movement," the group is described by Luke as a tight-knit community "of one heart and mind," sharing all things in common and praying together daily (Acts 4:32; 2:42-47). Paul reflected on believers' relationship with Christ and among one another in the image of the church as the body of Christ. The church in its deepest reality is a community endowed by the Spirit with a variety of gifts of mutual service that blossom into service of women and men beyond its boundaries (see 1 Corinthians 12). Through Baptism, Paul writes, we participate in Christ's death and resurrection in such a way that we are united in Christ's life (Rom. 6:3-11). And when Christians celebrate the Eucharist, they are united to the body and blood—the very person—of Christ: "Because the loaf of bread is one, we, though many, are one body, for we all partake of the one loaf" (1 Cor. 10:17).

That Christianity is essentially a communal religion is borne out by the fact that one can never become a Christian—at least in the fullest sense— by oneself. One must *be baptized* by another; one cannot baptize oneself; the celebration of the Eucharist, as we have discovered in the liturgical renewal of the last fifty years, is not an action done only by the priest, but an action of the entire assembled community. Vatican II's Constitution on the Sacred Liturgy (*Sacrosanctum Concilium*) speaks of every liturgical celebration as "an action of Christ the priest and of His Body the Church" (SC 7). Being a Christian, contrary to the slogan of popular religious culture like "taking Jesus as my personal savior," is about recognizing that one's full relationship to God as a human person is to be a person in community, a person in relationship with God through a relationship with others.

In several significant passages, the Second Vatican Council speaks of the essential communal nature of women and men, and points to this reality as the reason for the church's existence as "sign and instrument" of salvation (see LG 1). In its Dogmatic Constitution on the Church (*Lumen Gentium*), in the introduction to the key chapter on the church as "people of God," the council speaks of the fact that God has always been welcoming of individuals who live their lives in sincerity; however, God's will has been fully manifested in the fact that God makes women and men holy and saves them "not merely as individuals without any mutual bonds, but by making them into a single people, a people which acknowledges God in truth and serves God in holiness" (LG 9). In the final document promulgated by the council, the Pastoral Constitution on the Church in the Modern World (*Gaudium et Spes*), we read in paragraph 12 that "by their innermost natures human persons are social beings, and unless they relate themselves to others they can neither live nor develop their potential." And, a bit further on in the document we read a passage that points to the connection between the communal nature of humanity and the church's strong teaching on social justice and social transformation:

> The social nature of the human person shows that there is an interdependence between personal betterment and the improvement of society. Insofar as the human persons by their very nature stand completely in need of life in society, they are and they ought to be the beginning, the subject and the object of every social organization. Life in society is not something accessory to people themselves; through their dealings with others, through mutual service, and through brotherly and sisterly dialogue, men and women develop all their talents and become able to rise to their destiny. (GS 25)

Salvation as Communal

This "destiny," referred to in GS 25 quoted above, or what is called in Christian theological terms "salvation," needs also to be seen in terms of humanity's essentially communal nature. In the end, in "heaven" or in the full inauguration of the Reign of God, women and men will not participate in a kind of "private showing" of the "beatific vision" consisting of "me and Jesus." As U.S. theologian Mark Heim writes, salvation will not be "the self-contained condition of a subject, a pure experience (like bliss or 'pure consciousness'). A picture of a limitless line of individuals, each 'perfect' in her/his own independent happiness, is not an image of salvation."[34] Jesus compared the Reign of God to a great banquet (Luke 14:15-24; Matt. 22:1-14). His feeding of the five/four thousand in the wilderness was clearly drawn as an image of the fullness of the Reign of God to which his ministry witnessed (Matt. 14:13-21; Mark 6:34-44//Mark 8:1-9; Luke 9:10-17; John 6:1-15). This Gospel narrative—the only miracle story related in all four Gospels—was obviously inspired by Isaiah's vision of choice wines and juicy meats on God's "holy mountain," and God removes the veil that covers all peoples (Isa. 25:6-8; see 2:2-4). In the Apocalypse, the final, dramatic book of the New Testament, the image of final salvation is of a lively, peaceful meeting of peoples before God "from every nation, race, people and tongue" (Rev. 7:9). The scriptural witness, in sum, would suggest that Christians move from an idea of salvation as "personal immortality" to understanding it as the full reality of a "new creation" in which we will experience a universal communion with God, with other human beings—of all times and cultures—and with the whole of created reality in a way that is not possible in the present time.

In a conference on the creed, Thomas Aquinas spoke of this communal Christian hope when he said that "eternal life consists of the joyous community of all the blessed, a community of supreme delight, since everyone will share all that is good with all the blessed. Everyone will love everyone else as himself, and therefore will rejoice in another's good as in his own. So it follows that the happiness and joy of each grows in proportion to the good of all."[35] This powerful, beautiful image of the Christian understanding of salvation is mirrored in Dante Alighieri's (1265-1321) great theological portrait of heaven in his *Paradiso*. As Mark Heim summarizes:

> One of the dramatic things about paradise as Dante describes it is the overflowing variety there. The blessed plainly recognize these differences among themselves and yet the distinctions are no occasion for distress. They are causes for joy and delight.
>
> ... the relation with God that characterizes heaven is one that is unhesitatingly open to other's relation to God and to the various dimensions of God's relation with creation. What is not complete or ideal in one individual is not filled out to bring them into conformity with some single mold. The deficiency is supplied through participation in communion with others who each have their own unique grasp of aspects of God. It is each one's relation with God that makes possible and sustains this intercommunion among them....[36]

In contrast to this vitality of persons in communion is Dante's picture of Satan, "the emperor of the despondent kingdom," who lives at the very bottom of hell, half-encased in ice. As Heim comments, Satan is "the coolest, most solitary 'I' of all."[37] Toward the end of his famous play *No Exit*, French existentialist philosopher Jean-Paul Sartre has one of his characters, Garcin, exclaim, "Hell is other people!" But, if Christianity is right, Sartre is completely wrong: *Heaven*, the fullness of God's reign, is other people.

God as Communal

The deepest reason for the truth of the radical communal nature of men and women, and even the communal nature of reality itself goes to the very center of Christian faith: the doctrine of God as Trinity. Often we think of this doctrine as an impenetrable "mystery" (in this case, really what we have called a "problem" in chapter 1) of how one equals three or three equals one. However, the real key to the trinitarian Mystery (in the proper sense) is that God, who is revealed in history (since the beginning of time in the Spirit, and then in the concreteness of history in Jesus of Nazareth) is calling humanity and all creation to relationship and communion with Godself, with other human beings, and with all things in the universe—this God who calls to community is in God's deepest inner being relationship and communion itself. As Brazilian Leonardo Boff expresses it, "Christianity's most transcendent assertion may well be this: In the beginning is not the solitude of One, but the communion of Three eternal Persons: Father, Son and Holy Spirit. In the remotest beginning, communion prevails."[38] For Boff, the Trinity is the true icon of authentic existence. The openness of the three persons of the Trinity to each other, their total giving and total receiving in what is classically called *perichorēsis*—a Greek word that means circling around, but can be used in a wordplay with the Greek word "to dance"—is a model and challenge of how human beings should exist with one another. Feminist theologians as well point to the Trinity as the foundation for equality between women and men, calling for a relational, not an essentially hierarchical or patriarchal (rule by "fathers," i.e., by males), vision of reality.[39]

We read in the Book of Genesis (1:26) that God created humanity—male and female—in the divine image. What many commentators would point out today is that the way that human beings bear that image is in the fact of their relationality to each other and to God as such. For feminists who read the Scriptures, U.S. feminist Scripture scholar Susan Niditch observes, "No more interesting and telegraphic comment exists on the nature of being human and on the nature of God" than Genesis 1:26.[40] Human beings, then, exist as communal beings not on some divine whim, but to be God's representatives in the midst of creation in a particular, special way. All reality certainly mirrors God's inner, relational nature; human beings do this consciously, and grow more and more into what they have been created to be. It is immensely fitting, in sum— it is even imperative, I would argue—that human beings seek understanding of their faith in the God of relationship in a way that draws from their communal nature as a wellspring or source of that theologizing.

From Hierarchical to Community Consciousness

It was especially at the Second Vatican Council that the church, and theologians within it, became conscious of the social and communal nature of human persons as we have sketched out above. Theologians had certainly been conscious of this before, but it was present more implicitly than explicitly, and was eclipsed by the emergence of the individual with Western modernity and particularly with the Enlightenment in the eighteenth century. At Vatican II this fuller social understanding of human beings was claimed and appropriated in the light of twentieth-century personalist philosophies like that of Martin Buber, Emmanuel Mounier (1905-1950), and Gabriel Marcel (1889-1973).

One of the most far-reaching effects of this move to an understanding of the communal nature of human beings was a basic change in the understanding of the church. Particularly after the Protestant Reformation, when the visibility of the church and the authenticity of the papacy had come under attack, and as a result of the rise of governments that threatened the church's sovereignty—often in the name of the emerging understanding of individual dignity and rights—the church more and more imaged itself in terms of a visible institution and a sovereign state. The church saw itself, in the famous words of St. Robert Bellarmine (1542-1621) "as visible and palpable as . . . the Kingdom of France, or the Republic of Venice,"[41] or as a "perfect society."[42] But at Vatican II, while certainly not abandoning the truth that the church has a visible dimension (see LG 8), the church began to understand itself much more fundamentally as a community, a communion of persons who share the life of the communion that is God as such (see LG 4; AG 2). James Whitehead speaks of this change of understanding in terms of a *conversion*: a conversion from an essentially *hierarchical* understanding of the church to a consciousness that is rooted in the understanding of the church as a *community*.[43]

Where this conversion is most evident is in the centrality of the image of the church as "people of God" in the council documents. Sometimes this term is used to refer to laypeople in the church—in phrases such as "let us pray for the pope, the bishops, and the entire people of God." But this usage is incorrect. The term, as the council intended it, refers to the fact that, before they are anything else—before they are laymen or laywomen, religious, ordained, pope, and so on—and even before Christians are male or female, Indian, Fijian, Congolese, or Argentinian, they are all equally members of the church, equal members of the people of God.[44] This "fundamental equality" of the people of God is brought out very clearly in the council's Dogmatic Constitution on the Church (LG), paragraph 32:

> There is, therefore, one chosen People of God: "one Lord, one faith, one baptism" (Eph 4:5). As members, they share a common dignity from their

rebirth in Christ. They have the same filial grace and the same vocation to perfection. They possess in common one salvation, one hope, and one undivided charity. Hence, there is in Christ and in the Church no inequality on the basis of race or nationality, social condition or sex, because "there is neither Jew nor Greek; there is neither slave nor free; there is neither male nor female. For you are all "one" in Christ Jesus" (Gal 3:28, Greek text; see Col 3:11).

If therefore everyone in the Church does not proceed by the same path, nevertheless all are called to sanctity and have received an equal privilege of faith through the justice of God (see 2Pet 1:1). And if by the will of Christ some are made teachers, dispensers of mysteries, and shepherds on behalf of others, yet all share a true equality with regard to the dignity and to the activity common to all the faithful for the building up of the Body of Christ.

Leonardo Boff expresses this basic conversion from hierarchical to community consciousness in a diagram that he borrows from Yves Congar (and which I have adapted as well).[45] Instead of what we might call a "linear" understanding of the church (God sending the Son, who sends the Spirit first upon the hierarchy, who pass on grace to the laity), Vatican II presents us with a "circular" understanding (God lavishes the Spirit through Jesus upon the whole community directly in terms of particular ministries). These quite different ways of understanding the church have profound implications for doing theology, for who is able to engage in theological activity, for who is competent to judge the validity of theological expressions, and for the way theology is done. If one is possessed of the more hierarchical consciousness implicit in the "linear" model, it would follow quite naturally that only special people in the church (e.g., the ordained or the very specially trained) can do theology in specialized ways and judge its validity. If one is possessed of the more communitarian understanding of the church reflected in the basic direction that Vatican II takes, it is at least possible that all Christians have the potentiality to engage in theology as "faith seeking understanding," and that all Christians have some kind of say in terms of the validity of particular theological expressions. Theology in this perspective is the task of all Christians—not individuals but in the context of community—and not just "trickled down" from the top.

The Sensus Fidei *or* Sensus Fidelium

Because of this shift of consciousness expressed in the documents of Vatican II, an old doctrine—one that perhaps had been almost forgotten—emerged. This was the doctrine of the *sensus fidei* or *sensus fidelium* (the "sense of the faith" or the "sense of the faithful"). The idea, along with the term *sensus fidei*, is expressed in LG 12, where the document talks about the fact that the entire people of God share in Jesus' *prophetic* office (the document says elsewhere that Christians share in Jesus' *priestly* [LG 10-11] and—at least to some extent—his *kingly* office [LG 12-13] as well).[46] "The body of the faithful as a whole," the document says, "anointed as they are by the Holy One (see Jn 2:20, 27), cannot err in matters of belief. Thanks to a supernatural sense of the faith [*sensus fidei*] that characterizes the People as a whole, it manifests this unerring quality when, 'from the bishops down to the last member of the laity' [this is a quote from Augustine], it shows universal agreement in matters of faith and morals." The Abbott edition of the document speaks of this as the "sense of the faithful" in the footnote on this passage.[47]

As this doctrine has been developed, it points to the fact that, admittedly in some mysterious way, the church *as a whole*, as the entire community of believers, has a kind of "nose" or "sense" of what the true expression of the faith of the church actually is. We can speak about this "sense of the faithful" as a kind of "collective faith consciousness,"[48] or as "a peculiarly Christian tact, a deep sure-guiding feeling" that preserves the People of God in the truth.[49] Cardinal John Henry Newman described this "sense" as "a sort of instinct . . . deep within the bosom of the mystical body of Christ."[50] Cuban-American theologian Orlando Espín suggests that the "sense of the faithful" might be accessed in some way in the popular religiosity that people experience in devotions such as those to the crucified Christ or the Virgin of Guadalupe.[51]

What is involved here is not a matter of taking a poll or taking a vote; it is not finding out what the majority "Christian" or "Catholic opinion" is on a particular issue like Christ's real presence in the Eucharist or whether women should be admitted to ordination for diaconate or priesthood. Rather, in a much more subtle way, the "sense of the faithful" works as an understanding of how a particular issue or doctrine begins to take root in the church as a whole. It might take centuries, like the gradual realization—articulated by Pius XII in 1952—of the truth of Mary's bodily assumption into heaven. It might come relatively quickly, like the official recognition by the church, less than ten years after her death, of the sanctity of Mother Teresa of Calcutta.

The "sense of the faithful" is always operative in the church, but it emerges in a particular way when the church finds itself in times of crisis. A famous example of such an experience is reported by Cardinal Newman about the Arian crisis in the fourth century. This crisis could well be the most important theological controversy in the history of Christian theology, and it was, as we would say today, a crisis in inculturation.[52] The issue, ultimately, was how far Christianity could go in accepting Greek culture and Greek thought forms as the basis for explaining Christian doctrine. Arius, the brilliant theologian and preacher in Alexandria—the intellectual center of the Roman empire—

judged that to confess Jesus as truly divine would be a breach of the logic demanded by Neoplatonist philosophy. Neoplatonism insisted that God was so removed from the material world that it would be impossible for God to become human. It would be beneath the divine dignity to do so and would compromise God's nature. Jesus could perhaps be the first of all creatures, even *semi-divine*. But in no way could he be of the same substance as that of the divinity. The Council of Nicaea, called to mediate the dispute that was tearing Constantine's newly united empire apart, judged against Arius and said that, indeed, Jesus was God: *homoousios tō patri*, "one in being with the Father." But still the controversy raged, and many bishops sided with the Arian position until, on several occasions, the *laity* insisted on the orthodox formulation. If it were not for the laity and the sense of the faithful, argued Newman, the key doctrine of Jesus' divinity would not have been upheld.[53]

Today there are a number of issues that, despite official insistence that the cases are closed, people seem determined to keep alive in continued discussion and even disagreement. These issues range from the reception of Paul VI's 1968 encyclical *Humanae Vitae*, which forbade the use of artificial contraception, through the opposition to mandatory clerical celibacy in the Latin rite churches, to the thorny question of the ordination of women in Roman Catholicism. On the other hand, there seems to be widespread acceptance of several episcopal statements in the last several decades, notably the U.S. bishops' statements on peace (1983) and the economy (1986), even though there remains a strong and vocal opposition within the church as well.[54] Could the dynamic of the *sensus fidei/sensus fidelium* be at work in these continuing controversies?

One wonders as well if this doctrine of the church's "nose" for faithfulness might be tapped as we think of theology not just as the task or privilege of an elite few but as the task of every Christian. There is no doubt that the ordinary Christian by herself or himself does not possess the learning or the skill to mine the tradition or to engage in sophisticated correlation of experience with sociological or anthropological data or philosophical reflection. Nevertheless, when Christians come together *in* faith to seek deeper *understanding* of faith, might we not be convinced that God's Spirit is among them, that Jesus' presence can guide them (see Matt. 18:20), and that with such guidance these gathered Christians can penetrate deeply into the Mystery that invites them to faith? Such, I believe, is the case, and this is why the community can be a fertile source for theologizing—not just in the halls of Oxford, Maryhill School of Theology in Manila, or Tangaza College in Nairobi, but in the barrios of Mexico City and the villages of Ghana as well.

Our next section will explore ways in which theology, by its very nature, is always an activity in community, and how the community is always a source for authentic theologizing.

DOING THEOLOGY IN COMMUNITY

Because of the radical communal nature of human beings, a nature that is "perfected"[55] by Christian baptism and the practice of Christian ecclesial life, it is important to recognize that no matter who does theology, or when or where it is done, theology is *always* a communal, ecclesial enterprise. To my mind, theology is best done in the context of a community—when a group of Christians, conscious of their communal nature as human beings and as members of God's people share with one another, or work at writing together, or reflect on their faith or a Bible passage with one another. This might be in small groups in a base ecclesial community (or a small Christian community, as these are called in Africa), or by pastors and their entire pastoral team reflecting on their ministry together in weekly staff meetings, or by professional theologians writing or teaching together. Teaching as well, at any level, needs to be such that it is more than one or several experts simply communicating ideas or facts to passive students. As Parker Palmer argues eloquently, teaching should aim ultimately at creating a space for the emergence of a community of learners.[56] The communal nature of doing theology is the fundamental reason why professional theologians like myself or like many readers of this book need to be active in dialogue with others in their field through writing, attending conferences, and writing reviews of their colleagues' work. Finally, we have to see that the "lone" theologian at his or her desk is hardly alone as she or he reads or reflects on or argues through the thoughts of others. Deepening these ideas will be the purpose of this section as we conclude this chapter on the community as the *source* of our theologizing.

The Community as Theologian

Sharing Wisdom, by U.S. Anglo Benedictine Mary Benet McKinney, is a book that comes out of the author's many years of helping groups like parish councils, school boards, chapters of religious orders, and even academic faculties make important decisions by means of a method of discernment in the context of community discussion, reflection, and prayer. McKinney's focus is on how to make *decisions* as a community, but I have always thought that her method could just as well be employed in doing theological reflection. I believe her method is one that demonstrates how members of a community that really listen to one another, and listen to the word of God present through the community, can come to understand their common faith in new and fresh ways.

What doing theology in community is *not*, if one follows McKinney's method, is proceeding by some democratic or parliamentary model, where an idea or an issue is discussed, and then argued over until a vote is taken, with the majority winning the day. Discernment or "shared wisdom," as she calls it is quite another thing. It is a process done in the presence of God, who is present in the group and shapes the group. This God is the "God of the gathering."[57] A group or community goes about theologizing by first being open to God's presence and to God's Word, and then by being open to others in the group, open to mutual challenge, and always open to change—being open to the *sensus fidei* or *sensus fidelium* as it is made concrete within this particular group of people, at this time, in this particular culture. When this happens, the *community itself*, not just the individuals in it, becomes the theologian. As McKinney puts it:

> As we come together as a council, board, senate, team or whatever, the Spirit, in order to share with us the very wisdom of God, promises to each of us a piece of the wisdom. Repeat: a piece! No one can contain all the wisdom of God, for that would be to be God. However, the Spirit desires to share as much of the wisdom as the group can handle at any given time. To do this, different pieces of that wisdom will be given to different folks.[58]

To say that each person in the group has a "piece of the wisdom" is to say three things. First, it points to the fact that *no one has all the wisdom*. No one knows everything there is to know, even if that person is a trained theologian or an experienced pastor. Second, the wisdom is present in the variety of the group—*everyone has a different piece*. What this means is that at times there will be differences of opinion, conflicting experiences, or different theological perspectives, and these all have to be faced honestly and respectfully. A third point is then the fact that *everyone has some of the wisdom*. There is no person in the group who has nothing to say; any person in the group—according to McKinney's Benedictine tradition, even the youngest or simplest in the group—might hold the key insight that will lead the group to a deeper understanding.[59]

McKinney likens the process of discernment—for us, theologizing—to making a good pot of vegetable soup. For the soup to be really tasty, all kinds of ingredients need to be added: carrots, potatoes, celery, cabbage, spices like salt and pepper, and the like. Each one of these ingredients is important for the savor of the soup as a whole. Too much salt, too little turnip, not enough vegetable stock could spoil the soup. And when the ingredients have all been added, the soup has to simmer—for hours—until it is ready, until all the flavors have melded together and the taste of the soup is not just carrot, or tomato, or onion, but *vegetable*. In the same way, all the opinions, all the perspectives, all the questions and doubts of the group need to be expressed in the group. And then the issue has to "simmer" as the group expresses concerns, points to how a particular solution or expression is helpful, spends time in prayer and reflection, takes a sounding or two (or more), and gradually moves toward a consensus.

More than one time I have participated in a process like this, and I don't remember a time when I was not amazed at the result. When I have worked with a group writing a document for my religious congregation, or in a group that came up with a bold new design for the curriculum at the school where I teach, or just with one other companion to write an article or a book together, marvelous things happened. Ideas developed that no one of us could have come up with had we worked only by ourselves. Critiques of approaches and challenges were surfaced that no one of us could have discerned. All of us felt the presence of the "God of the gathering" as we sought understanding for our faith together.

What I have been talking about in this section is what U.S. Hispanic/Latino/a theologians have spoken of as *teología en conjunto* or *teología de conjunto* (translated very loosely as doing theology together, but really untranslatable). The term reflects another relatively untranslatable phrase, *pastoral de conjunto*, which is a way of doing pastoral ministry that is rooted in collaboration and in the importance of relationships about which we spoke earlier in this chapter.[60] For Latino/a theologians, any theologizing has to be done as much as possible with consultation at every level. In fact, the *process* as much as or even more than the *result* is what is important. One of the most important Latino theologians today, Orlando Espín, has served as co-editor of two volumes of Latino/a systematic theology (the first with fellow Latino Miguel Díaz, the second with his Anglo colleague Gary Macy) that are products of long and rich conversations and correspondence among all the contributors. These volumes are not mere collections of essays, but true fruits of collaboration.[61] In the same way, annual meetings of ACHTUS, or the Academy of Catholic Hispanic Theologians in the United States, are not gatherings where papers are merely read and responded to. The papers are distributed to the participants beforehand, and all the members participate in lively discussions of each one.

In his marvelous survey of systematic theology from a Hispanic perspective, Justo González names this collaborative, communal approach as "Fuenteovejuna theology." This is in reference to the play *Fuente Ovejuna* by the sixteenth/seventeenth-century Spanish playwright Lope de Vega (1562-1635). The play tells the story of a village, Fuente Ovejuna, that is ruled by a cruel and corrupt "commander" or military mayor. After the commander has raped several women, and while he is in the act of torturing the young husband of one of the raped women, the people of the village storm his residence and kill him, and then raise a banner over the town which proclaims, *todos a una* (all as one). When investigators arrive from King Ferdinand and Queen Isabella and ask who has killed the commander, one villager after another, even under torture, answer "Fuente Ovejuna, Señor." Everyone together in the village takes responsibility for the killing of the oppressive commander, and because his evil is recognized and all are responsible, Ferdinand and Isabella pardon all the villagers and promise them a new and better commander.

González reflects on the significance of the play's story for the doing of theology. "Fuenteovejuna theology," he says

> is a call for a different style of doing theology—a Fuenteovejuna style. If theology is the task of the church, and the church is by definition a community, there should be no such thing as an individual theology. The best theology is a communal enterprise.
>
> This is a contribution that Hispanics can bring to theology. Western theology—especially that which takes place in academic circles—has long suffered from an exaggerated individualism. Theologians, like medieval knights, joust with one another, while their peers cheer from the stands where they occupy places of honor and the plebes look at the contest from a distance—if they look at all. The methodology of a Hispanic "Fuenteovejuna" theology will contrast to this. Ours is not a tradition that values individualism, as does that of the North Atlantic. Indeed, ours is a language that does not even have a word for that "privacy" which the dominant North American culture so values. Coming out of that tradition, our theology will result from a constant dialogue among the entire community. In the end, to the degree that it is true to the faith and experience of that community, to that very degree will it be impossible for any of us to speak of "my" theology or "your" theology. It will not be a theology of theologians, but a theology of the believing and practicing community.[62]

Let me just refer briefly to two other examples of doing theology in the context of community. The first is a powerful image. In her book *Saving Work: Feminist Practices of Theological Education*, Rebecca Chopp offers the metaphor of theology as engaging in the practice of quilting (borrowing this image from a student paper by Megan Beverley, who uses it to describe the process of feminist preaching).[63] Quilting is a process of making a product from a number of different pieces of cloth—a bedspread, a pillow cover, or even a piece of decorative art. Although one can make a quilt by oneself, one of the traditions of quilting is that a number of workers—usually women—work together on a quilt, sharing news and stories while they work. Although quilts can have figures on them—for example, a tree or a house—some of the most beautiful ones are of wonderful geometric patterns. Megan Beverley says that her favorite kind of quilt, however, is the "crazy quilt," fashioned from all sorts of scraps of cloth sown together in no ordered pattern, but simply fitting odd-shaped scraps together with others. Such is a powerful image of theology done in community, and done by ordinary folk as well. People come together and bring whatever they have, and in sharing faith together and reflecting on it in the context of each others' lives, something new and beautiful is created, something unique, never to be repeated, something that comes from the group but which relates to a long tradition of the craft.

Several years ago, when our faculty at Catholic Theological Union moved into a new building and new offices, a friend of mine, Judy Borchers, gave me a "housewarming" present of a tapestry with four quilt patterns on it. Judy *thought* that the legend on the tapestry read "Blessed are the peacemakers" from Matthew 5:9, but she had misread it. What it actually said was "blessed are the PIECE makers," that is, those who make quilts. It was a fortunate mistake—it now hangs in my office as a reminder that the best way to do theology is to do it in community. Theologians, like quilters, are "piece makers."

My final example is from the epilogue of U.S. Anglo Vincent Donovan's (1926-2000) book *The Church in the Midst of Creation*.[64] In what Donovan told me personally is a true story, we read about the development of a Bible study group of African American Catholics, from its humble, hesitant beginnings through its growth and development and eventual division into three groups that would have constant communication with each other. The key to the group's success was that it was really a group of ordinary people sharing their life and faith with one another. It began under the leadership of the parish priest, but soon he was only part of the group, an equal among them. As Donovan describes it:

> The reality of community took on an importance that it never seemed to have had under parish auspices. The members grew very close to one another and shared many things that they had never shared before. They began to look on community as the essential element in the whole process. ... They began to look on the community not only as the heart of what they were doing, but as one of the sources of its correctness, of its inspiration, of its revelation. The other source was the Bible—the gospel.[65]

This might sound like an extraordinary group of people, but not as Donovan describes them. This was a group led by the Spirit, tapping into the "sense of the faithful," realizing their potential as church as they shared their faith, experiencing their community as theologian.

Professional Theologians in Community

As we come to the end of this chapter on the community as source of theology, let me speak briefly of the importance of community for those of us who are professional theologians. In the first place, we can speak of how a professional theologian—either a pastoral minister or an academic theologian—draws from and contributes to a group of ordinary Christians. My own experience of this was at a workshop I participated in a number of years ago with several other theologians and pastors and a large group of laypeople on the Caribbean island of St. Lucia. Our task was to develop a pastoral plan for the archdiocese of Caceres, the capital of the island, and we did it in two weeks. The first week we worked with laypeople, asking them to develop their understanding of the church as we theologians and pastors helped them to connect their ideas with the ideas of the Second Vatican Council. The second week was with the clergy of the archdiocese and a number of religious women, and we helped them engage with what the laity had spoken of and dreamed about the church and to put this into a concrete pastoral plan. The plan as it finally emerged was not a perfect one—it was not the plan that I would have drawn up as a trained theologian. Nevertheless, *it was their plan*, and it was one that they were committed to. What we theologians and pastors had done—besides learning a lot of ecclesiology and pastoral theology from our interaction with the people and leadership of the St. Lucia church—was to act as facilitators or midwives for the entire church. The theology was done by the women and men of St. Lucia themselves as they interacted with one another and discovered new ways—their ways—of being church.

Second, those of us who are teachers have to realize that we do theology not simply by transmitting ideas in a classroom. Every teacher worthy of the name will confess how much she or he has learned from his or her students, because good teaching is not just the transmission of knowledge; it is the discovery of knowledge by students and teachers alike as the class engages in reflection together, wrestling with questions, and moving in directions that were not part of a lesson plan or preparation time. I would suggest that this is even more true for theology, since theology, as we have said, is not a content "out there" that needs to be mastered but an activity that is engaged in as one searches for an understanding of the mystery that surrounds us all. What I have become more and more convinced of over the years is that discussion sessions, theological reflections, and spontaneous question-and-answer sessions are as much a part of the teaching process as are impeccably presented lectures. Teaching is doing theology in community, with students and teacher teaching and learning together.

I have also come to believe that the best way to engage in teaching is by team-teaching. This is a process that often takes much more time than solo teaching, but it is, in my experience, amazingly enriching for both teachers and students alike. To have to decide the content of a particular course together, to plan each class together and to interact with each other in the context of the class—and then with class discussion—is tapping deeply into community as a theological source.

Professional theologians who are academics often come under the "publish or perish" rule of academic institutions. This might seem like a harsh "survival of the fittest" regulation, but at its heart it is a recognition of the communitarian nature of the entire theological enterprise. By publishing articles, books, book reviews, CDs, DVDs, or podcasts, theologians enter into conversation with the wider community of theologians. Writing a book or an article is always engaging in conversation with other theologians, and conversing as well with former teachers and students. With the final products, ideas are tested with peers, one's best insights are shared with others, another's wisdom is brought to bear on another's work. The same is true with the regulation or strong encouragement for academics to join professional groups of theologians (e.g., the Catholic Theological Society of America, the College Theology Society, the Academy of Catholic Hispanic Theologians in the United States, the Sociedad Argentina de Teología, the Association des Théologiens Catholiques du Bénin, or the Ecclesia of Women in Asia) and to take an active part in them by presenting papers at annual meetings. Once again, this is an opportunity for theologians to enter into a wider conversation and to draw deeply from the source of one's peers. Through scholarly interaction wonderful friendships can emerge, which can issue in mutually enriching theological discussions. Some of my best friends—notably William Burrows, Darrell Whiteman (U.S. Anglos), and Gary Riebe-Estrella (whose thoughts I have borrowed above)—have led me into understandings of my faith that I could never otherwise have imagined.

Finally, as I have pointed out already in the introduction to this section of our chapter, just the act of reading is itself a conversation with others—great thinkers like Augustine or Hildegard (1098-1179); great religious figures like Catherine of Siena (1347-1380) or Martin Luther; or contemporaries like U.S. feminist Anne Carr (d. 2008), Vietnamese-American Peter Phan, Kenyan John Mbiti, womanist Shawn Copeland, Chilean and Peruvian missionary Diego Irarrázaval or Chinese feminist Kwok Pui-lan. Theological dialogue can be done from one's desk or easy chair as well as at the discussion table. As eminent U.S. Anglo theologian David Tracy observes: "We converse with one another. We can also converse with texts. If we read well, then we are conversing with the text. No human being is simply a passive recipient of texts. We inquire. We question. We converse. Just as there is no purely anonymous text, so too there is no purely passive reader. There is only that interaction named conversation."[66]

CONCLUSION

In this chapter we have reflected on the possibilities for doing theology that the Christian community affords. These possibilities are rooted in the radical, communal nature of human beings, and in the communal nature as well of Christianity. Human nature and Christian existence are not things we make by ourselves; they are given by others. Because of this, seeking understanding for faith is something that is best done in conversation with others—in fact in many ways it is *always* done with others. The next two chapters in this second part of the book will explore other ways that this conversation is participated in by Christians reflecting together. Our next chapter, on Tradition, will help us see the community as both source and governing framework for theological reflection, as theologians tap into the wisdom of their ancestors in the faith. Chapter 6, on the magisterium, will help us see how the church's fidelity to God's offer of God's self in revelation serves as a safeguard to the authenticity of our theologizing. Theology is faith seeking understanding *together*—in conversation with the living voices of the past, and in fidelity to the church's duty to preserve the present for the future.

QUESTIONS FOR REFLECTION

1. What are your thoughts about the communal nature of persons that this chapter proposes?
2. How does the communal nature of Christianity change the way you think about the church? About salvation? About God? About theology?
3. Describe an experience you have had of doing theology in community.
4. This chapter proposes that theology is best done in community rather than individually. Why might you agree or disagree?

SUGGESTIONS FOR FURTHER READING AND STUDY

Samuel Amirtham and John S. Pobee, eds., *Theology by the People: Reflections on Doing Theology in Community* (Geneva: World Council of Churches, 1986).

Patricia Fox, "The Trinity as Transforming Symbol: Exploring the Trinitarian Theology of Two Roman Catholic Feminist Theologians," *Pacifica* 7 (1994): 273-94.

Roberto S. Goizueta, *Caminemos con Jesús: Toward a Hispanic/Latino Theology of Accompaniment* (Maryknoll, N.Y.: Orbis Books, 1995), chapter 3, "*Nosotros*: Community as the Birthplace of the Self," 47-76.

Frank G. Kirkpatrick, *Community: A Trinity of Models* (Washington, D.C.: Georgetown University Press, 1986).

Mary Benet McKinney, *Sharing Wisdom: A Process for Group Decision Making* (Valencia, Calif.: Tabor, 1987).

Frank Oppenheim, "A Roycean Response to the Challenge of Individualism," in Donald L. Gelpi, ed., *Beyond Individualism: Toward a Retrieval of Moral Discourse in America* (Notre Dame, Ind.: University of Notre Dame Press, 1989), 87-119.

Gary Riebe-Estrella, "*Pueblo* and Church," in Orlando O. Espín and Miguel H. Díaz, eds., *From the Heart of Our People: Latino/a Explorations in Catholic Systematic Theology* (Maryknoll, N.Y.: Orbis Books, 1999), 172-88.

Richard A. Shweder and Edmund J. Bourne, "Does the Concept of Person Vary Cross-Culturally?" in Richard A. Shweder and Edmund J. Bourne, eds., *Culture Theory: Essays on Mind, Self and Emotion* (Cambridge: Cambridge University Press, 1984), 158-99.

5

Community as Source and Parameter of Theology

Theology and Tradition

W E SAID IN THE INTRODUCTION to this second part of the book that the communal nature of theology that we are exploring here provides both the *source* of our theologizing and the *parameters* or boundaries of it as well. Theology, in other words, is always done—at least in some sense—*within* a community of faith, but it is also *accountable* to that community. In the context of Christian theology, particularly in the context of *Catholic* theology that we are developing here, both of these aspects of theology's communal nature are expressed in the notion or doctrine of *tradition*. On the one hand, "tradition" refers to the milieu or faith-atmosphere in which a member or members of the church engage in the work of theology. It refers also to the collection of "classics" that can fuel and inspire theologians as they seek to understand their faith by being nourished by the wisdom of the past.[1] On the other hand, Tradition refers to these "classics"—as a set of expressions and doctrines—to which theologians need to be faithful, careful to preserve and be accountable.

The term "tradition" comes from the Latin word *tradere*, which means to "hand over," "hand down," or "hand on." The point that I want to make in our reflections here, in the context of theology done in the community of faith, is that *human existence as such*, and therefore Christian faith as an essential part of human existence, is something that is radically *traditional*. Our humanity itself, and our faith as part of our humanity, is always the result of being "handed on" or "traditioned," and always seeks to "hand on" what it has received. Theology is the result of the traditioning process and is fully involved in it.

In the pages that follow, we are going to approach our understanding of tradition in four steps. First, we will reflect on the fact that *human existence* itself is something that is traditional, and then recognize the fact that all traditioning has a twofold nature—"active" and "passive." Third, we will speak about the nature of our specifically *Christian* tradition, and then, finally, we will reflect on the possibility of the *development* of tradition, only to discover that tradition can be faithful to the past only if it changes and develops in the present and into the future.

HUMAN EXISTENCE AS TRADITIONAL

Australian theologian Gerald O'Collins puts it simply: "Human life is simply unthinkable without the element of tradition."[2] Without others to "tradition" (hand over) us, we would have no language; there would be no laws, no customs, and there would be no common signs or symbols (like flags, directional arrows, or traffic lights) for people to share, and so society would be in chaos. In short, without tradition and traditioning, there would be no culture. To refer to O'Collins once again, he points out that "even if members of a given society rarely stop to formulate and reflect on what they have taken over, they remain radically indebted to the past for the inherited values and expectations which give life its meaning and provide ideas to be striven for. Thus one generation passes on to another norms, attitudes and behavior patterns by which society has hitherto functioned and now seeks to perpetuate itself."[3] Stephen Still points out that even though tradition is something human and therefore relative, not absolute, even the way we experience depends on how we have been taught by the members of our families and culture. "There is no tradition," he says, "but an *experienced* tradition." And yet, "there is no experience, but a *traditional* experience."[4]

The Tswana theologian Gabriel M. Setiloane speaks of how, in initiation, girls are trained by elderly women and boys are trained by elderly men. Part of the initiation is the transmission by these leaders, through the initiation process, of the customs and laws of the society, particularly in relation to marriage and family life. With initiation, boys and girls pass from the stage of *bacha*, or youth, to that of full *botho*, or humanity. As the youth of Tswana society are entrusted with the traditions of their society, they achieve their full personhood.[5] Receiving and participating in tradition make one fully human, fully part of the group.

Without some kind of traditioning, on the other hand, there is something missing in our human lives. John Macmurray recalls Plato's answer to a dilemma posed to him by the sophists, a rival group of philosophers: Should people "live by nature or by custom?" Such a dilemma is absurd, said Plato, because "to live by nature is to live by custom. Human nature is social and custom is the bond of society."[6] Over the years a number of children have been found who have been raised—"traditioned"—by animals such as wolves, dogs, and monkeys. If the children had been brought into the animal group before they could speak, it would be almost impossible for them to learn to speak once they were found. Many of them walk and behave exactly like the animals by which they were raised and nurtured.[7]

Less dramatically, but in many ways much more tragic, are situations in which people are deprived of their traditions. A horrible example of this is the effects of one of the worst social sins ever committed: the practice of trading and owning slaves from Africa, which continued from the fifteenth through the end of the nineteenth century.[8] In the slave trade, women, men, and children were taken from their home villages in Africa and sent to North America, the Caribbean, and Europe with no thought to identifying their cultural roots or identity. As a result, millions and millions of human beings were deprived of any sense of their cultural, family, or religious heritage. U.S. Anglo historian Jon Butler speaks of this as the "African spiritual holocaust."[9] One can truly sympathize with African Americans who claim African clothing, African names, and have even invented an African holiday, Kwanzaa, in order to strengthen their identity and ties to ancestors in Africa. Such deprivation of any tradition explains the popularity of Alex Haley's book *Roots* and of the famous TV mini-series that was adapted from it.[10]

There might even be something physical about tradition. This would explain the deep need that many adopted children have to search for their birth-mothers, their natural fathers, or for other members of their biological families. Human beings need to be rooted in their past, connected to the people and places and cultures that gave them life.

My point here is simply that, even as a human phenomenon, the nature of tradition is to keep a culture, a society, a family, a group, or an individual alive to their identity. Without others to do the traditioning, people's identity will die. To allude to the title of a collection of essays by mostly U.S. Latino/a theologians, tradition "futures" us by linking us to a past.[11] We need others to tell us who we are—as British philosopher Alisdair McIntyre expresses it, the human being is the storytelling animal.[12] We need to know our story to know ourselves; and we need to tell that story to our families and to those who share our history as fellow citizens or members of our cultural group so that these groups can be rooted in their particular identities. German theologian Siegfried Widenhoffer sums this up admirably when he writes that "to live in and from traditions, to have traditions, to criticize traditions, to abandon traditions, to create traditions, to let traditions grow or decline, to be committed to traditions, to hate traditions, etc.—all that belongs to being a human being. Therefore, it could be said: 'Being human is being someone who has a tradition.'"[13]

THE TWOFOLD NATURE OF TRADITION

Every tradition has two aspects: what we can call an "active" or "subjective" aspect, and a "passive" or "objective" aspect. "Active" tradition is the very process of handing over, the act by persons ("subjects") "traditioning" others. Sometimes this is identifiable and explicit. It could be the act of passing on the history or customs or secret knowledge of a group of people in a ritual of initiation. It could take place as parents and grandparents tell family stories at the dinner table, or at an annual Christmas Eve celebration. I experienced this active traditioning very poignantly several times as my mother, in her last years, gave me articles that had been given her as wedding gifts, or that had been in the family for generations—some beautiful pieces of sterling sliver, for example, which I have recently handed on to my sister to hand on to her daughters. Graduation ceremonies are moments of traditioning, as women and men wear highly symbolic garb, receive degrees that have long histories in academic circles, and shake the hand of the institution's president or the chair of the board of trustees and "commence" their new life as educated persons.

At other times this "active" process is more subtle, and the traditioning takes place in an atmosphere or a milieu. As one lives one's daily life in a family, or in a religious community, or in a particular culture, one absorbs an identity and ways of acting in intangible but nevertheless real ways. There are some places, for example, the University of Notre Dame, where I studied for the Ph.D., where the tradition is almost palpable as one enters the campus, and it "rubs off" on a student in powerful ways as one lives and studies—and attends football games!—there.

"Passive" or "objective" tradition might best be recognized in the plural: it is the set of objective things, "traditions," that are handed over, "rubbed off," communicated, "traditioned" in the act of traditioning. These may be the secrets of a particular people revealed in an initiation rite, the stories of uncles or first jobs or courtship that are shared around the family dinner table, the beautiful serving fork that my mother gave me, the diplomas that signify the degrees passed on at a graduation ceremony.

Both of these aspects are essential to understand the concept of tradition in its full sense, and how Christian tradition—as Tradition and traditions, *traditio* and *tradita*, as act and content—expresses the communal, ecclesial nature of doing theology.

CHRISTIAN TRADITION

If tradition in general is the "handing on," the "traditioning" of an identity, keeping an identity alive, giving an identity a future by linking it to the past, then specifically *Christian* tradition is that reality that offers and ensures Christian identity down through the ages. Tradition, in other words, is the way that the faith we believe today is the same faith that Christians *have always* and *will always* believe—that our faith today is the faith of the "apostles," the apostolic community that knew and experienced Jesus. For this to be the case,

Christian tradition claims that it is a process and content guided by Jesus' Spirit, who despite the various changes in the faith's content and expression throughout history and through its encounters with various cultures, nevertheless preserves Christian faith in all its integrity and freshness. As German theologian Karl-Heinz Weger writes: "The mystery of Christ remains present in history because there is a fellowship of believers which in the vital process of life, doctrine and worship preserves the word of God, through the assistance of the Holy Spirit, through all the changes of history, and thus hands it on safely to all generations till the Lord comes in glory."[14]

Like tradition in general, there are both active or subjective aspects as well as passive or objective aspects to Christian tradition. Christians "tradition" one another in their life together, in their performance of ritual practices, in the mutual example they offer to each other. In this way doctrines, practices, and rituals are handed down from generation to generation—always influenced by a particular time and culture, and yet—by the guiding grace of the Spirit—always faithful and always fresh.

The Process of Traditioning

For centuries the active, traditioning aspect of tradition was almost forgotten, even though it clearly went on as mothers taught children to pray; as people were formed in faith through participation in novenas, processions, and practices throughout the liturgical year; and as women and men were inspired by the example of holy priests and nuns, relatives, and neighbors. But the emphasis was much more on knowing the content of doctrine, strictly observing customs (like bowing one's head at the name of Jesus, or crossing oneself when passing a church), or obeying moral commands to the letter. As Cuban-American theologian Miguel Díaz describes it, the focus was on the *what* of tradition.[15] The Council of Trent proposed what was interpreted as a "two source" theory of tradition, stating that revelation (which it conceived of in propositional terms) is contained "in the written books" of Scripture "and unwritten traditions which have come down to us, having been received by the apostles from the mouth of Christ himself or from the apostles by the dictation of the Holy Spirit, and have been transmitted as it were from hand to hand" (DS 1501; ND 210).

It was at Vatican II, however, where the notion of tradition as an active process was officially revived, even though theologians such as the German Johann Adam Möhler (1796-1838) and John Henry Newman in the nineteenth century and—building on their insights—Frenchmen Maurice Blondel (1861-1949) and Yves Congar in the twentieth century on the eve of the council had done the spadework. What Vatican II stresses is that tradition is *primarily* an active, subjective reality. Tradition is first of all, in other words, not what is handed on from one Christian to another, but the handing on itself. And this handing on takes place most especially in the day-to-day, *informal* life of the church—in what Latino theologian Orlando Espín calls "*lo cotidiano*."[16] It is the *atmosphere* of faith present in the church by which the living relationship of faith in Christ is passed on and given a future. As the council expresses it in its Constitution on Divine Revelation: "What was handed on to the apostles comprises everything that serves to make the People of God live their lives in holiness and increase their faith. In this way, the Church, in her doctrine, life and worship, perpetuates and transmits to every generation all that she herself is, all that she believes" (DV 8). Commenting on the passage, Karl-Heinz Weger explains it well:

> In the comprehensive sense, therefore, tradition is not primarily a "something," an objectified datum. It is not exclusively, when taken in its full sense, either the transmission of the word of God in Scripture or the handing on of truths and forms of piety not committed to writing. It is the faith of the Church in action, which is more than its expression in propositions both because Christ works in this faith and because not all that is done in faith is adequately accessible to reflection and expression.[17]

Avery Dulles makes two points about this active understanding of tradition articulated by Vatican II. In the first place, he connects the reality of active tradition to the "sense of the faith" or "sense of the faithful" that we discussed in the previous chapter. The Spirit is always active in the church, in other words, always creating it into a community of mutual love, and mutual inspiration, a space where the truth resides (not without, of course, distortion at times) and is communicated. Second, Dulles says, "Tradition is grasped through familiarity and participation as a result of dwelling within the Church, taking part in its worship, and behaving according to its standards."[18]

What Is Traditioned: Traditions

Nevertheless, as Espín wisely points out, "There is no traditioning . . . without tradition."[19] The way faith is handed on in the church, through the power of the Spirit, is by means of many objective things. These are the "*monuments* of tradition," the "theological sources," that help Christians get a grasp on the elusive "atmosphere" or "sense" of the faith that is present in the believing community. If we could say that traditioning is Tradition (spelled with a big "T"), then these "monuments" are tradition written with the "t" in lower case. Or, to refer to the title of Yves Congar's classic work, there is both "Tradition" and "traditions."[20]

In his book *The Analogical Imagination*, U.S. American theologian David Tracy speaks of the importance of *classics*—texts like novels or important philosophical or theological works, doctrinal expressions, or even the lives of certain people, all of which have proven through the centuries to have a certain power to reveal or manifest the truth of things or the depth of life.[21] These enduring classics—like Dante's *Divine Comedy*, Alice Walker's *The Color Purple*, Plato's dialogues, Gustavo Gutiérrez's *A Theology of Liberation*; or people like Jesus, or Mahatma Gandhi—not only open up new vistas of the present and the future by linking us with the wisdom of the past, but they set a standard of beauty, excellence, and morality to which we need to conform. The objects or "monuments of tradition," the sources of theology (technically called *loci theologici*) do the same thing. They provide expressions, symbols, and information from our ancestors in the faith that can help us come to a new depth and relevance as we seek to understand our faith more fully. But they also set parameters— standards of expression and truth to which we need to measure up and beyond which we cannot go too cavalierly.

These "classics" of Christian tradition can be grouped under several headings, and we will list them and reflect on them briefly in what follows.

First and fundamentally, there are the *Scriptures*, the Old and New Testaments. These are the primary way that we get to know the church's faith, and the primary measuring rod by which we can assess a theological expression's fidelity to revelation. The Scriptures are the records of Israel's experiences of faith over generations, and the relatively recent recollections of Christians who lived within a generation or two of Jesus, some of whom may even have known him personally. Christians believe that this collection of writings ("Bible" [*Biblia* in Greek means "books"]) "have God as their author and have been handed on as such to the Church itself" (DV 11). As such, they are the word of God— not in any mechanical sense, as we have seen in chapter 1. Because of this, again according to the teaching of the church, the Scriptures are inspired and "without error" in regard to what is about God's love and our salvation (DV 11). Aidan Nichols quotes the twelfth-century theologian Rupert of Deutz (1075-1129), who puts it well: "That woman, Ecclesia, drew the Scriptures from the well of truth, the well that is set in her midst and makes her the garden of the Lord."[22]

In the second place are the works and lives of the *Fathers (and Mothers) of the church*. These are the church's earliest theologians, many of whom were the disciples of the earliest Christians. These men and women are so close chronologically to the origins of Christianity that theology has always considered them privileged bearers of tradition. Nichols refers to the twelfth-century Franciscan theologian Hugh of St. Victor (1096-1141), who wrote that the early creeds of the church and texts of these theologians are nothing but "summaries of Scripture and commentaries upon Scripture, and so are necessary for the Scriptures' evaluation."[23] Theologians who merit inclusion here are those who lived during or just after the New Testament period (after 100 C.E.) into the seventh or eighth century. Pope Gregory the Great, who died in the early seventh century (604) is spoken of as the last father in the Western church, and John Damascene (or John of Damascus), who died in the mid or late eighth century, is considered the last of the fathers in the East.

Traditionally these theologians are called the "fathers" of the church, but current scholarship—particularly feminist scholarship—has insisted that women of this period, too, contributed very much to the development of theology in the ancient church. Women's contribution, however, was often ignored or erased from theological records, since history was most often written by men and for men. A closer examination of theological history, however, reveals that women indeed play a considerable part in theology of this period, and this reality needs to be reclaimed. And so while the works and lives of men like Ignatius of Antioch (50-d. 98-115), Polycarp (69-155), Gregory of Nyssa (d. 385/386), Augustine of Hippo, Ephrem the Syrian (309-373) and Athanasius of Alexandria (300-373)—to mention just a few—are classic sources of tradition and need to be consulted and studied carefully by theologians, there are a number of women whose lives and works need to be appreciated as well. The first writing by a Christian woman to be preserved is the *Passion of Perpetua and Felicitas*, written by Perpetua while imprisoned for her faith in the North African city of Carthage. Although we have no writings from Paula (347-404), Jerome's benefactor and companion in Bethlehem, he writes about her admiringly as someone steeped in the Scriptures and who, together with her daughter Eustochium (368-419), was highly learned in Hebrew. Some of the most important information we have about the fourth-century Holy Week liturgy comes from the pen of Egeria, a pilgrim to Jerusalem in the early 380s. Macrina (330-379), the elder sister of the great Cappadocian theologians Basil of Caesarea (329-379) and Gregory of Nyssa, did not put her great learning into writing, but "Gregory describes his older sister several times as being his teacher," in both spirituality and doctrine. These are just a few examples of important "mothers" of the church.[24]

A third set of important "monuments" of tradition are the so-called *doctors of the church*—men and women whose learning and holiness have given them a particular vantage point for understanding the Christian faith, and who are particularly rich traditioning sources for the theologizing process. The term "doctor of the church" is not an invention of the papacy, but since the time of the Protestant Reformation (sixteenth century), only the pope can officially add a name to the list, and at this moment in history there are thirty-three official doctors. Most of these are from Europe (e.g., Thomas Aquinas, Bonaventure [1217-1274], Anselm of Canterbury [1033-1109], and Anthony of Padua [1191-1231]), but three are from North Africa (Augustine, Athanasius of Alexandria [300-373], and Cyril of Alexandria [378-444]); four are from what we call today the Middle East—Asia—(Ephrem the Syrian [309-373], Cyril of Jerusalem [313-386], Basil of Caesarea, and Gregory Nazianzen [330-390]; and three are women (Catherine of Siena [1387-1380], Teresa of Avila [1515-1582], and Thérèse of Lisieux [1873-1897]). Only one (Hilary of Poitiers [d. 367]) was married.[25]

In addition to these "official" doctors, there are a number of learned holy women and men in history who have always been considered special fonts of wisdom for theologizing. Bartolomé de Las Casas (1474-1566) with his experience in Latin America, the English churchman and theologian John Henry Newman (1801-1890), and German theologian Karl Rahner (1904-1984) are good examples, as are the German preacher, mystic, and musician Hildegard of Bingen (1098-1179) and Sor Juana de la Cruz of Mexico (1648-1695). All of these except Sor Juana, Newman, and Rahner are canonized saints and Catholic, but we might mention others as well in today's ecumenical consciousness: Martin Luther (1483-1546), Karl Barth (1886-1968), the African American ex-slave Sojourner Truth (1797-1883), or the great Sri Lankan missiologist and theologian D. T. Niles (1908-1970).

One very important source of tradition, in the fourth place, is the *liturgy*. What I have in mind here is not so much *participation* in the liturgy—which is more an experience of the traditioning process or active tradition. Rather, here I mean the collections of liturgical texts and directions that exemplify the dictum of *lex orandi, lex credendi* (the law of prayer is the law of belief). This saying, which goes back to the fifth-century theologian Prosper of Aquitaine (390-455) points to the fact that we can perhaps best know what the Christian faith is all about if we look at the way Christians pray. For example (as we will see later in part 4), one of the arguments for Jesus' divinity during the Arian controversy in fourth-century North Africa (Arius denied that Jesus was God) was the fact that Christians *prayed* to Jesus as God and so therefore this is what Christians must believe. The Orthodox theologian Peter Mogila (seventeenth century) "quotes a hymn of the liturgy to prove the doctrine of Christ's descent into Hades 'although no mention is made thereof'" in the Nicene Creed. And even though the dogma of Mary's assumption was not made official until 1950, both the Eastern and Western church celebrated the feast for centuries.[26] The liturgy is a kind of *theologia prima* or "theology at a basic level." It is rich in what Aidan Nichols calls "implicit theology." As he says it so well:

> The texts of a wide variety of liturgies are all grist for the theologian's mill. However, the greater the agreement of these liturgies on a particular point, the stronger their evidential value for theology. If we think of the Christian liturgy as a sign system pointing to the truth of Tradition, it is where the signals flash most brightly that we can best follow them.[27]

Fifth, the texts of the *magisterium* are also important concrete expressions of the church's tradition. Whether these texts are instances of papal teaching, documents of the Roman curia, or the teaching of groups or individual bishops, they issue from the church's leadership and wisdom figures and so need to be taken seriously and treated with respect. They are the authoritative way that the church's tradition is articulated down through the ages. We will treat this source of tradition in much more detail in the chapter that follows.

Finally, the art and architecture of the various periods of the church are important monuments of tradition. A people's art captures its soul, and so artistic expressions—whether paintings on Roman catacombs, gothic cathedrals, Latin American altarpieces, southwestern U.S. *santeros*, or Ethiopian churches carved out of solid bedrock—are clues to discover how people have kept the faith through the ages. One of the most fascinating ways, for example, to discover the church's understanding of Christ or Mary is to study their images in various places and times in the church's history. The great U.S. Anglo church historian Jaroslav Pelikan (1923-2006) shows this wonderfully in his books on Jesus and Mary through the centuries.[28]

These monuments of tradition are the testimonies of hundreds of thousands—millions, even—of people from all over the globe who are our ancestors in the faith. They are witnesses in their own lives and works to what they themselves received from others in their past, and they have handed this on to us today—we who in turn must pass it on through our lives and works to generations in the future. As we ourselves do theology, we do not have to "reinvent the wheel," for women and men more intelligent and holier than we have left us a legacy that we can mine with great profit. And as we pass on this wisdom to generations after us, we ourselves need to be accountable to what has gone before us. The traditions we have received from our spiritual ancestors are standards we must live up to as we seek to understand our faith and pass it on to others. One of the great Christians of the twentieth century, Dorothy Day (1897-1980), expresses beautifully what we owe to those who have transmitted the tradition to us: "How any one can persist in the search for God without the assistance of the church and the advice of her confessors, with the experience of generations behind them, I do not know."[29]

THE DEVELOPMENT OF TRADITION

It is important, writes U.S. Latino theologian Gary Riebe-Estrella, *not* to imagine the traditioning process of handing on the faith to others as "something being passed by hand from one generation to the next, wherein the *thing* remains unchanged as it passes from one set of hands to another, rather like a box being handed from a postal clerk to the person whose name appears on the address label."[30] This way of thinking about tradition would greatly obscure its nature. Riebe-Estrella offers the image of tradition as a "conversation" in which ideas and attitudes are transmitted in an exchange among persons who express their understandings and commitments of faith out of their own cultural perspective and—at times—bias, who struggle to understand out of their own backgrounds and social locations, and who receive, reformulate, and retransmit these understandings and commitments in a way that the *same* faith is understood and transmitted, and yet understood and expressed differently. As Orlando Espín puts it, "Traditioning does something significant to tradition—historically and theologically."

What Riebe-Estrella and Espín point to is the complex, developing reality of tradition. Indeed, we are not maintaining the tradition if we simply parrot formulas or transmit ideas that have not been appropriated. Tradition as the legacy of the church's faith is something alive, something that, like ourselves, changes while remaining ever the same. Indeed, writes Brazilian theologian Ivone Gebara, "If we do repeat, it is because that is what today's situation demands, because it does touch the roots of our existence, because to some extent it responds to the problems that ongoing history sets before us." Ironically, Gebara points out, "What is normative is primarily the present . . . ; tradition is viewed in terms of the present."[31] In order to understand how to be both faithful and responsible to the tradition we have received and in turn pass on, we have to grasp tradition's vital, multidimensional nature. This is what we will try to do in this section. Tradition is (1) a radically pluriform reality that (2) develops by an appropriation of the past (3) in creative fidelity.

Tradition Is Radically Pluriform

In responding to a question at his 1997 Zenos Lectures at McCormick Theological Seminary in Chicago, Cuban-American church historian Justo González made use of the analogy of a landscape and the various perspectives of it to illustrate the fact of and the truth of a healthy pluralism in theology.[32] There is only *one* landscape, *one* topography of a particular place. And yet various people see various things in the landscape and judge their importance according to their interests at a particular time or in a particular circumstance. A river, for instance, can be seen by one person as water to boat on or to swim in by another person. Still another person, perhaps an engineer, would see it as a source of power. And yet a farmer might see it as a source of water for his crops, a poet might see it as a symbol of her journey toward God, and a tribal people might see it as a place to encounter the divine. A forest might be seen by a couple who are hikers as a cool place to walk in; a surveyor might see the same forest as a source for lumber or fuel. Mountains might be seen as difficult obstacles to get across, or a challenge that excites a group of vacationers.

Theology has the same diversity—Jesus, for example, can be understood as friend, savior, brother, ancestor, healer, or window into the reality of God.

A tradition can be pluriform as well. Building on the work of the U.S. American theologians James and Evelyn Whitehead, who speak of three senses in which a tradition is pluriform,[33] I suggest that it is pluriform in *five* respects.

In the first place, tradition is *pluriform in its origins.* The greatest and most basic record of tradition, the Bible, is amazingly diverse. The Old Testament is not simply one narrative or a witness to one theology. There are, to name only a few, a Yahwist perspective, a Deuteronomistic perspective, a priestly theology, and a wisdom theology—and these represent various interests in Israel, different time periods, and different circumstances. In the New Testament, says Justo González, referring to a passage of Irenaeus, it is no accident that there are four Gospels. There *must* be four Gospels, says Irenaeus, as an expression of the church's very catholicity, just like there must be four winds.[34] Each Gospel presents a different perspective on Jesus, weaving together and interpreting basic material in the context of the author's own understanding and the concerns of the community out of which the Gospel comes. And, as we see clearly in the entire New Testament, there is no monolithic understanding of ecclesiology or church order. Even the understanding of "apostle" is different in the Lucan understanding and the Pauline perspective.[35]

There is no such thing, in a real sense, as a (one) biblical tradition—there are only *many* biblical traditions, and they continued to be invented and to develop all through the biblical era, from the oldest oral traditions set to writing in the Old Testament to the various writings rooted in particular communities in the New Testament.

Second, the Christian tradition is *pluriform as it develops through history.* There is what we might call a *diachronic* plurality. This is because the expressions of the tradition, as the faith is handed on throughout history, are deeply dependent on the contexts in which that handing on is done. Augustine, for example, develops his theologies of grace and of original sin in the context of his own understanding of Neoplatonic philosophy, and within the context of his various disputes with the Donatists (who believed that sacramental grace could come only through the ministrations of a worthy minister) and the Pelagians (who believed that humanity takes the first step toward God, and then God helps women and men subsequently). His great work, *The City of God*—and one of the classics of Christian theology—was written in the context of the shocking news of sacking of Rome in 410 by the Visigoth chief Alaric. Thomas Aquinas, whom the Catholic tradition considers perhaps the greatest of Christian theologians, wrote his voluminous works inspired by the newly rediscovered works of Aristotle, and in a time when the church was experiencing what might have been the zenith of Christendom. Vatican II, to give just one more example, was held at a time when a strong optimism regarding economic development was pervasive throughout the world, and was influenced by the personalist philosophy of thinkers like Gabriel Marcel, Jacques Maritain (1882-1973), Emmanuel Mounier (1905-1950). It was an era when the Catholic Church had finally decided to come to grips with the "modern world." U.S. Anglo church historian Dale Irvin writes that seeing the diversity of the Western tradition leads us to posit the diversity and validity of other traditions in Christian history that may have been eclipsed until our own day.[36] What we have to recognize, in other words, is the rich plurality of traditions of Christian faith that have arisen through the ages in places like the Coptic church in Egypt, the Syrian church, the Latin American church, and among African Americans in the United States and Canada.

Third, Christian tradition is *pluriform in its contemporary expression*. It possesses a *synchronic* plurality. What this means is that in every age, even in the same place, there have been and continue to be quite different ways of expressing the reality of Christian faith. In the ancient church, for example, there existed simultaneously the Antioch school of Christology in western Asia and the Alexandrian school in North Africa. The former placed emphasis on Jesus' humanity; the latter on Jesus' divinity. There existed a good bit of tension between the two schools, but both were considered valid ways of approaching the same mystery of Christ. In twelfth-century Europe, the Dominican Thomas Aquinas, influenced by Aristotle, had a distinctly different approach to theology and spirituality than did his equally brilliant Franciscan colleague Bonaventure. Aquinas represented a more intellectual theological tradition, while Bonaventure represented an older, more contemplative, monastic tradition. In today's church, as a result of more positive understandings of culture and experience, we have a real flourishing of "contextual theologies" in every part of the world and within various socially located groups. Side by side today there are Filipino theologies, feminist theologies, Native American theologies, Japanese theologies, Fijian theologies—and of course many, many more. As these theologies interact with one another and with the traditions of the past, the entire tradition will grow in both depth and breadth. In today's church as well, there is tension between a theology more focused on the church as such, perhaps inspired by Vatican II's *Lumen Gentium*, and one, perhaps more influenced by Vatican II's *Gaudium et Spes*, that focuses on the role of the church in the world.[37]

Fourth, tradition is *pluriform in its value*. The process of traditioning, writes Orlando Espín—and I would add: the *content* of tradition—"*by itself* is not exclusive of doctrinal error."[38] Or, as James and Evelyn Whitehead put it, "Every religious heritage carries a history of both grace and malpractice."[39] There are powerful, life-giving doctrines that the Christian tradition has preserved—for instance, the constant insistence on Jesus' full divinity as true icon of the complete reality of God, or the Catholic vision of the sacramentality of the world, or Irenaeus's theology of the fullness of all things in Christ. In addition to this, there are some particular times when the church's stand was the right stand to take—like its difficult but necessary stand against "modern," anticlerical ideas in the nineteenth century. But there have existed stances and doctrines in the church's past that have been very harmful and, in today's light, even against the gospel: the Inquisition, insistence on the subordinate nature of women, tolerance for slavery, stubborn resistance to democracy in the nineteenth century, and the misunderstanding of Asian veneration of ancestors. As U.S. feminist theologian Anne Carr (1934-2008) writes,

> *Uses* of the Christ symbol in theological anthropology, ecclesiology, and ministerial theology to support political, social and ecclesiastical patriarchy are in fact a perversion of its positive religious content. These uses are a sobering reminder that no symbol, no tradition, is entirely pure but rather all are ambiguous, multivalent, open to both positive and negative human use. Hence there is a need for *both* new interpretations and critical theory, a hermeneutics of generosity *and* suspicion, or both analogical *and* metaphorical theology.[40]

Particularly because of the "malpractice" that has infected the church's tradition, therefore, it is important for the theologian to approach any tradition with a critical eye. Because of the pluriformity of tradition's value, we need to learn—in the words of U.S. feminist theologian Letty Russell—to "talk back" to it.[41] Critiquing, "talking back," shapes and develops tradition in the context of particular experiences and legitimate cultural and human interests.

Finally, tradition is *plural in its development*. Often the history of the Christian tradition is conceived as a gradual but cumulative growth in clarity, with the body of Christian doctrine growing more and more extensive as the "secrets" of tradition come to light. But this is hardly the case. Tradition develops in fits and starts; sometimes it betrays the very gospel it is supposed to protect (e.g., the Inquisition); sometimes developments that are legitimate and helpful in one age stay too long to be oppressive in another (e.g., a clerical mentality). Gary Riebe-Estrella, we have seen, has proposed that the process of traditioning be imaged as a "conversation." Dale Irvin speaks of tradition in terms of dialogue—"dialogues of faith in which we are engaged."[42] Perhaps in the light of the malpractice into which tradition often falls and the uneven and sometimes mistaken development that the process of traditioning takes, we might press these images to speak of tradition as an *argument*.[43] As one engages in this conversation/dialogue/argument, one is caught up in the process of traditioning, being open and yet critical, being (as Anne Carr suggests above) "generous" and at the same time "suspicious" in one's interpretation. Perhaps it is here—in the earnestness of conversation and the honesty of argument—that the Spirit that guides the traditioning process acts to lead us into "all truth" (see John 16:13).

Tradition Develops by Reappropriating the Past

Canadian Douglas John Hall points out that dramatic shifts in the evaluation and meaning of tradition occur especially in periods of radical transition in church and/or society. In these times of crisis, doubt, or surprising new insight, Christians are able to see the tradition with new eyes, and often what they see are aspects that have been forgotten or suppressed. During the crisis of the Protestant Reformation, for example, there was a "sudden resurgence" of interest in Augustine, whose thought had been contested with the rise of the influence of Aristotle and a decline in the interest of Platonic philosophy.[44] The Reformers, however, saw Augustine and his Platonism as a better way *in their age* to get at the experience that was in many ways the foundation of their theology. In the same way, as the Catholic Church struggled to come to terms with modernity and historical consciousness in the first half of the twentieth century, theologians such as Marie-Dominique Chenu (1895-1990), Yves Congar, and Henri de Lubac (1896-1991) employed the method of *ressourcement*—in particular, a study of the "patristic" tradition—to propose understandings of the church, the sacraments, and grace that possessed a real freshness and relevance in the twentieth century. Their careful scholarship of the past led to the renewal of Catholic theology that was marked by the Second Vatican Council.

In today's world as well, contemporary theology is profiting greatly from an appropriation of the past. Theologians engaged in developing theologies of liberation—in Latin America, in Asia, among gays and lesbians, or among feminists—can profit greatly by an appropriation of sources from the "left-wing" or radical reformation: the work of Anabaptists, or that of Thomas Müntzer (ca. 1489-1525). Feminists are reappraising movements such as Gnosticism and Montanism, in which the roles of women were more prominent than in the Christianity of the same time, and they have discovered the work of theologians and mystics like Julian of Norwich (1342-ca.1416) and Hildegard of Bingen.

What we see is that tradition develops not only by engagement with present concerns or issues (as it did, for example, in the Arian controversy, or as it is doing today as theology engages the contemporary science of evolution). It also develops as particular issues drive theologians to the past, to reexamine, rediscover, and reappropriate the great classics of tradition. In this sense the words of the great U.S. novelist William Faulkner ring truer than ever: "The past is not dead. In fact, it's not even past."[45]

Tradition Is Maintained through "Creative Fidelity"

In his essay "Creative Fidelity," philosopher Gabriel Marcel makes the crucial distinction between "constancy" and "fidelity." Constancy is a fidelity to a person or a cause that does not ever change, no matter what; fidelity, on the other hand, is always a creative commitment because, ultimately, it is not to a particular person or to a particular cause, but to God as such. Because of this, in the changing circumstances of life, fidelity may actually mean that we change and revise our commitment, precisely for the sake of that commitment.[46]

To be a Christian, and to be a Christian theologian, means to be faithful to the community of believers, faithful to our ancestors in the faith upon whose wisdom we constantly draw and to whom we need to be responsible. To be Christian, in other words, means to be faithful to the Christian tradition. But that fidelity—given the plurality of the tradition—has to be a *creative* one. Sometimes—and this is the particular task of theologians—for the sake of the tradition, we need to "abandon" the tradition and prove our fidelity to it by a creative reinterpretation. This is especially true today among theologians who work in cultures and contexts where "traditional" approaches (read: Western, male, white) do not make sense any more. Let me give a few examples of how creative fidelity might work.

A first example is an experience I had while attending an exhibition of the work of the French artist Edgar Degas (1834-1917) at the Art Institute of Chicago in 1996. As I listened to the guide to the exhibition on the headset, the narrator quoted Degas to the effect that an artist needs to study the "Old Masters" (e.g., Michelangelo, Rubens, David, Constable) *in order to surpass them*. In other words, real fidelity to the past (the "Old Masters") means not just being able to *reproduce* or copy them, but actually to improve on them—or to be as creative as they were in new circumstances. This is a wonderful description of theology, I believe, that is faithful to the tradition—studying the "Old Masters" like Luke, Athanasius, Hildegard—and yet engaging our contemporary world and our particular contexts with the same spirit with which they engaged their own. Dale Irvin quotes German-American thinker Eugen Rosenstock-Huessy (1888-1973), who writes very much in the same spirit: *"Each generation has to act differently in order to represent the same thing."*[47]

A second example is from a review of a 1997 book by Joan DeJean, *Ancients against Moderns: Culture Wars and the Making of a Fin de Siècle*. This book might seem a far cry from what we have been reflecting on in this chapter, but it is actually a book about tradition. It deals with a debate in late seventeenth- and early eighteenth-century France between the "ancients" and the "moderns"—that is, between those who upheld things the way they had "always been" and those who espoused the new authors, philosophers, and scientists of the early European Enlightenment. As the writer of the review summarizes the argument,

> The "ancients" pointed unwaveringly to classical antiquity, which had thought the best thoughts, perfected literary forms and produced mighty minds that posterity could only follow with humility. "Moderns" are but pygmies perched on the shoulders of giants. Pish! Said the moderns. Tradition is a gift; it should not be a burden. If Homer and company are indeed giants, which is doubtful, then anyone perching on their shoulders must be able to see further than they did.[48]

Once more, I think this passage is a fine illustration of a theology that is creatively faithful to the tradition. The way we see farther as theologians is to "stand on the shoulders" of the tradition; without the wisdom of the past we only see what is in front of us, but with its help we can see—perhaps—more keenly into the issues of our own times.

A third example comes from the work of the great Scottish theologian John Wood Oman (1860-1939). In the preface to the second edition of his book entitled *Vision and Authority*, Oman tells a parable about the meaning of the title. The context of the parable is that of the moors of northern England, where Oman lived at the time—vast, rolling plains filled with watery bogs— but my hope is that anyone can understand Oman's meaning:

> Suppose yourself on a wide moorland [Oman writes] without anything very distinctive, at any time, in any direction, and, in the dark, wholly without character or feature or visible landmarks, with the mist settling in the boggy hollows, and a sombre heaven above, with too few stars for any one to be identified with certainty. If, being accustomed to such a situation, you are still calmly assured that you will reach home safely, and even directly, to what guidance are you trusting?

Oman says that first of all, "there is the track trodden by those who have gone the same way before," and that "you are glad of its help so long as it serves." But you can't just follow it as such, because when it forks you have to decide yourself which way is the direction that is going to take you home. Eventually, the path that you have been following does not even help you at all, because it begins to go in another direction. When this happens, you have to "take the risk of leaving it and of faring forward as straight as you can," across the dangerous terrain. But it is the only way that you can get home, and you simply have to trust your instinct and experience of doing it on other occasions.[49]

What we can take from Oman's parable is that just as we find our way home in the dark with this double fidelity (to the authority of those who have gone before and to our own instincts as we move out on our own), so this is the way we need to live our faith, and, indeed, do our theology. The worn paths of tradition set us in the right direction, but they will do us no good in the final analysis if we just stick to them. Living our Christian life, and seeking deeper understanding for the living of that life in theology, demands that at some point we take the risk and leave the familiar paths.

Ironically, however, this freedom from tradition is really the tradition itself. This is what the great theologians were able to do—Paul in the New Testament, Justin Martyr in antiquity, Aquinas in the twelfth century, Luther in the sixteenth century, and James Cone, Gustavo Gutiérrez, and Rosemary Radford Ruether in our own day—and this is what we are called to do as theologians in U.S., Thai, Mexican, Ghanaian, or New Zealand culture. African American philosopher Cornel West quotes a passage from the writings of the U.S./British poet T. S. Eliot to this effect:

> . . . if the only form of tradition, of handing down, consisted in following the ways of the immediate generation before us in a blind or timid adherence to its successes, "tradition" should be positively discouraged. We have seen many such simple currents soon lost in the sand; and novelty is better than repetition. Tradition is a matter of much wider significance. It cannot be inherited, and if you want it you must attain it by great labour.[50]

CONCLUSION

Douglas John Hall believes that such "great labour" is well worth it. A healthy understanding of tradition, he writes, helps us avoid two pitfalls in theologizing—"modernism" on the one hand and "traditionalism" on the other.

For the modernist, the past is judged to be worthless, because either the present has overcome its significance or one's culture needs to be emphasized over anything else. The past is the work of "dead white men" and has nothing to do with where women or Africans or Latino/as are right now. Interestingly and ironically enough, this perspective dovetails almost exactly with individualism: only what makes sense to *me*, my experience now, my culture is what is worthwhile. There is no need to be burdened by the patriarchal, Western, clerical past. In contrast to this perspective is a remark made by Cornel West about his own creative work. He compares his work to that of a jazz artist, "at once deeply grounded and practiced in the tradition, but also radically open to spontaneity, improvisation and creativity."[51] West pointed out that he uses this image of a jazz musician when he speaks to youth. He warns them that what looks completely spontaneous and free is actually the result of immense discipline and knowledge of the standard tunes and music upon which the free-flowing jazz riffs are based.

The other pitfall of theology is traditionalism, where the past is preserved just for the sake of the past. As Jaroslav Pelikan has said famously, traditionalism could not be further from an authentic sense of tradition, for if "tradition is the living faith of the dead, traditionalism is the dead faith of the living."[52] Had the Council of Nicaea, for example, not taken the risk to go beyond biblical language and adopt the controversial philosophical language of *homoousios*, which expressed in clearer terms that Jesus was indeed divine, the church might be stuck in endless controversy over the matter. Biblical language—or the "tradition"—was simply not able to answer the question that Arius had posed for the first time. Had the Second Vatican Council refused to change its position on religious freedom, stating only its "traditional" position that "error has no rights," it would have actually betrayed the task set for it by Pope John XXIII to open up its doors and windows to the best developments of the contemporary world. To remain faithful to the "tradition" in these instances would not be to be faithful to it at all. It would simply to be stuck in traditionalism.

Hall says that theologians who take tradition seriously, therefore, need to develop an attitude of both *dependence* and *independence*, because tradition needs to be upheld and innovated upon at the same time. It is in the tension between these two attitudes that one grasps the tradition and is faithful to it. Hall writes beautifully of this tension and describes it as a third attitude "which knows how to be grateful for and responsible towards the authority of the tradition without using it as a refuge from intellectual and spiritual struggle":

> Anyone who has subjected herself or himself to the task of seeking to know, deeply, any of the great thinkers of the Christian past will realize how inconceivable it is for her or his generation to dispense with such testimony. But neither Augustine nor Aquinas, Calvin nor Luther, Barth nor Niebuhr can tell us what we have to understand as Christians today, as we face nuclear war and continental famine and racial strife and sexual tensions whose precise character none of these persons could have anticipated. From them, as from the Scriptures, we can receive inspiration and courage without which our own thought is impoverished, trivial, and literally impossible. But in the end it is we ourselves who must do theology.[53]

Yes, indeed. But we must do it ourselves *together*, listening to all the voices, which includes being in conversation—argument even—with the ancestors who have gone before us.

QUESTIONS FOR REFLECTION

1. Can you give some examples of tradition in your culture, your family?
2. Can you explain the difference between "Tradition" and "traditions"?
3. Why is Scripture *part* of Christian tradition?
4. Why is tradition best described as a "conversation"—or even an "argument"—carried on down through the ages?
5. What do you think G. K. Chesterton meant when he described tradition as the "democracy of the dead"?
6. Why do you think it is important that tradition changes and develops within history?

SUGGESTIONS FOR FURTHER READING AND STUDY

Yves Congar, *Tradition and Traditions: An Historical and a Theological Essay* (New York: Macmillan, 1967).

José M. de Mesa and Lode Wostyn, *Doing Theology: Basic Realities and Processes* (Quezon City, Philippines: Claretian Publications, 1990), chapter 3, "The Pole of the Judaeo-Christian Tradition," 47-70.

Orlando O. Espín and Gary Macy, eds., *Futuring Our Past: Explorations in the Theology of Tradition* (Maryknoll, N.Y.: Orbis Books, 2006).

Mary Catherine Hilkert, "Experience and Tradition: Can the Center Hold?" in Catherine Mowry LaCugna, ed., *Freeing Theology: The Essentials of Theology in Feminist Perspective* (San Francisco: HarperSanFrancisco, 1993), 59-82.

Dale T. Irvin, *Christian Histories, Christian Traditioning: Rendering Accounts* (Maryknoll, N.Y.: Orbis Books, 1998).

Gerald O'Collins, *Fundamental Theology* (Ramsey, N.J.: Paulist Press, 1981), chapter 7, "Tradition: The Ecumenical Convergence and Common Challenge," 192-207.

Jaroslav Pelikan, *The Vindication of Tradition* (New Haven, CT: Yale University Press, 1984).

6

Community as the Parameter of Theology

Theology and the Magisterium

A S WE HAVE SEEN in the last two chapters, the Christian community—the church—is a rich source for our theologizing. The best way to do theology is to do theology in community, to take advantage of the fact that those with whom one does theology all have "a piece of the wisdom." This communal nature of theology is also why professional theologians belong to "learned societies" and enter into conversation with other scholars through their publications. Even the lone scholar at her desk is participating in the communal nature of theology as she reads and reflects on the work of other scholars in books, journals, in podcasts, or on the Web.

But the communal nature of theology also extends the conversation partners in theologizing to the community of the past as theologians engage the Christian tradition. The importance of tradition in theology is based on the conviction that, in William Faulkner's words, the past "is not even past," and on T. S. Eliot's conviction as well that tradition is how "the dead poets (and) . . . ancestors assert their immortality most vigorously."[1] It is from this interaction with the community of the past that theologians draw the rich yet varied wisdom of the past, and at the same time it is a community to which they must make themselves accountable. Tradition points to the fact that community is the source of theology and it also sets its parameters.

In this present chapter we are going to reflect on how, in the Catholic tradition, theology's communal nature also functions in a way that simply sets the parameters for theologizing. To say this is to speak of the role of the magisterium in the church, the office or service within the church that has the task of setting the limits of adequate theological expression.

It is important to state at the beginning of these reflections that the magisterium is a reality that is thoroughly communal. It is never a voice that speaks *over against* the community, or *from above* the community. Even though it "is exercised in the name of Jesus Christ" (DV 10), it is a voice that, at least in its intention, speaks *within* the community as a divinely inspired *representative* of the community—which is the Lord's body on earth. This is why an understanding of theology that is essentially communal or ecclesial needs to take the authority of the magisterium into account.

We will proceed in our understanding of the magisterium in three steps. First, by a series of questions, we will investigate the *concept* of the magisterium. Second, we will reflect on the sometimes difficult but always necessary relationship between theology or theologians and the magisterium. Third, we will reflect on the sensitive question regarding whether and how much theologians can disagree with the church's teaching that is articulated by the magisterium.

THE CONCEPT OF THE MAGISTERIUM

What Is the Magisterium?

Magisterium is a Latin word that comes from the word *magister*, meaning someone who has authority—a master, like a "master of a ship" or a "master of a trade," or a "master of a knowledge"—a teacher.[2] In the context of theology, this meaning of "teacher" is what the term "magisterium" refers to, and so, etymologically speaking, "magisterium" has to do with *teaching*—in fact it is often called the "teaching office of the church." The word "office" comes from another Latin word, *officium*, which means "duty," "obligation," "service," "task," or even "charism" or "gift." So the idea of the magisterium refers to the task or duty of the church to teach (and preach) the fullness of the gospel, "in season and out of season" (see 2 Tim 4:2), and to do this with authority.

Who Is the Magisterium?

In the deepest and truest sense, the magisterium is the duty or charism *of the entire church*. In the first part of Part II we spoke of the doctrine of the *sensus fidelium*, or that "supernatural sense of the faith which characterizes the People as a whole" and gives them a share in the Christ's prophetic office (LG 12). The fact that the entire church is a prophetic people means that, in a fundamental sense, the entire church is endowed with the Holy Spirit and is responsible for teaching and preaching the gospel at all times and in all places. This is why Australian theologian Gerald O'Collins can say, "The divine self-communication comes to human beings who are essentially social, and hence it necessarily involves the community. In the language of the Second Vatican Council we have here 'the word of God which is entrusted to the Church'—that is to say 'the *entire* holy people' who are called to confess their faith and live by that word."[3]

This idea that the church's magisterium is fundamentally the task of all the people of God is the framework within which a proper approach to the church's teaching office needs to be understood. However, the church is a community of many particular gifts or charisms lavished upon it by the Holy Spirit (see 1 Cor. 12:4-11), and this means that particular tasks are done by those who are endowed with a particular charism. So while *all* Christians are called to teach in virtue of their sharing in Christ's prophetic office, some are called by the Spirit to do this in a particularly *authoritative* way.

In the twelfth and thirteenth centuries in the West, theologians spoke of two kinds of special magisterium in the church that were endowed with such a special charism. Thomas Aquinas, for example, spoke about the pastoral authority (or chair, since that was the symbol of authority) of the bishop (*magisterium cathedrae pastoralis*) and the academic authority or chair of the scholar (*magisterium cathedrae magistralis*).[4] Today, however, theologians most commonly speak of the magisterium as the college of bishops in union with the bishop of Rome, the pope. These are the Christians who have the special task of teaching and preaching the faith in a particularly authoritative way.

In our understanding today, in other words, magisterium is connected with those who participate in the leadership of the church as a result of having received the *sacrament of Order*. What this means is that certain Christians have been given the responsibility of leadership—have been *ordained*—in the church for caring for its "holy order."[5] They are responsible, in the first place, for the church's order of ministry. Since the whole church participates in Christ's office of kingship/servanthood, the church is a ministerial community, and so officeholders in the church must see to it that ministry—at all levels—thrives in the church. Second, those who are leaders in the church are responsible for the order of the church's worship, and so are the ones who (ordinarily) preside at the church's official moments of prayer—the liturgy—and are responsible for assuring that the liturgy is performed in a worthy manner. Third, the Christians who hold office in the church are responsible for the regulation and handing on of the church's faith—they are the guardians of the tradition—and so they are the ones who ordinarily preach at official gatherings of the church (e.g., give the homily at the Eucharist). It is in the context of this third responsibility for order that the bishops, in union with the "servant of the servants of God," the pope, exercise the teaching responsibility of the church in the sense that we understand it today: the magisterium.

More than three decades ago, Avery Dulles provided an apt image to express what we are trying to express here: that the magisterium belongs primarily to the entire church and yet it is the specific task of the church's leaders. The entire church, he says, is like a huge burst of diffused light, and its officeholders—the bishops of the church—function like a lens that concentrates and focuses that light:

In the total Church this light is widely diffused among individuals and groups which are differently gifted. The task of the hierarchy in any given region, and in the world at large, is to gather up all this radiance of light and bring it into focus. The official teaching of the Church emanates indeed from the episcopate, but not from the episcopate alone.... By gathering up and concentrating the diffused light, the hierarchy intensifies its splendor and enables it to be refracted, with greater power in the world.[6]

It is because of the light that has been given to the *whole* church that those who hold the office of teachers in the church need to be aware that theirs is a *service* to the church and for the church. As such, then, their task is much more along the line of tuning in, as Dulles puts it, "on the theological wisdom that is to be found in the community and bring[ing] it to expression."[7] German theologian Monika Hellwig (1929-2005) quotes a famous line of Pope John XXIII to make this same point: "I am not here to *tell* the church what the Spirit says, but to observe attentively and see *in* the Church what the Spirit is saying."[8]

The magisterium, as we understand it here, are the bishops of the church in union with the pope. But they do not act in their own name. They articulate the faith of the church, and so act with the authority of Christ (DV 10).

What Does the Magisterium Do?

The basic task of the magisterium—particularly as it is entrusted to the college of bishops in union with the pope—is to ensure that the faith of the church is faithfully taught, and that this faith remains *intact*. It is to ensure, in other words, that the ways in which Christians express their faith and communicate it to others—perhaps in different ways in the context of different cultures throughout the world—keep the faith's original apostolic freshness, to ensure that the gospel that the church preaches today *is the same gospel Jesus preached*, despite the way it has changed through the ages.

Much of this task, as we will see shortly, is positive—it is simply faithfully preaching the gospel. But some of it is inevitably corrective. The fact is, over time and in various contexts, expressions of faith—as sincere as they might be—can actually distort the gospel, the Christian story, and so part of the task of the magisterium is to make sure that those distortions are discovered and corrected. Let me give two very homey examples of how a faulty expression can distort a message.

A number of years ago, one of the seminarians in the formation community in which I was living was a Canadian from the French-speaking province of Quebec. He was living in the English-speaking United States for the first time and struggling with the language. One day he and I were in our dining room drinking coffee, and I remarked: "Boy, this coffee really curls the hair on your chest!" "What does that mean?" the seminarian asked. I explained how the expression means that the coffee was particularly strong, and particularly bitter. "Oh," he said.

A few days later, as I recall, I happened to walk into the dining room and my Quebecois friend was sitting at the table sipping coffee. "Boy!" he said, "this coffee really twists the fur on your breast!" Well, of course, I broke out laughing—he had *almost* gotten the English idiom right, but his use of the wrong expression totally miscommunicated his meaning.

Another example is from my years as a missionary in the Philippines. A friend of mine, a U.S. American, was a pastor in a parish in the northern part of Luzon, where the local language was Ilocano, and, like the French-speaking seminarian, he was struggling to master it. It was the feast of the Sacred Heart of Jesus in early June and he began the Mass of the day with these words: "Iti nagan ti ama, ken ti anak, ken ti Espiritu Santo. Amen. Ittatta nga aldaw rambakantayo ti piesta ti Nasantoan a *Pusa* . . ."—whereupon the entire congregation broke out laughing. My friend's mistake was the last word—*pusa*. In Ilocano *puso* is *heart*; *pusa* is *cat*. And so what my friend said was "In the name of the Father, and of the Son, and of the Holy Spirit. Amen. Today we celebrate the feast of the *Sacred Cat*." Again—close, but the meaning is totally wrong.

These examples have always reminded me of the difference between "*homoousios*" (of the same substance—the term of the Council of Nicaea) and "*homoiousios*" (of *similar* substance—the term of the heretical semi-Arians). The difference in the words is one *i* or *iota* in Greek, but the meaning is very different. The right words and the right expressions do matter and so it is the safeguarding of the "right words" that is the task of the magisterium.

Safeguarding the right words—by preaching them correctly and correcting ways that they are not—is another way of saying that what the magisterium does is safeguarding *doctrine*. So it is important that we try to understand the nature of doctrine if we are to understand the magisterium's task.

Understanding Doctrine

"Doctrine" is not an easy word to define, actually. Etymologically, the word comes from the Latin *docere*, which means "to teach," and so the sense of the English is that a doctrine is a teaching that carries authority. In secular usage we speak of things like the Monroe Doctrine (in 1823, U.S. president James Monroe said that the United States could intervene militarily if a European power interfered in the affairs of the nations of the Americas); in theology we speak of particular church teachings like the "doctrine of transubstantiation" (that the consecrated Eucharistic species *look* and *taste* like bread and wine, but their *substance* has been changed into the body and blood of Christ).

Perhaps the best way to understand the meaning of a doctrine is to lay out first two understandings that need to be avoided. On the one hand, doctrines are not simply *literal descriptions* of reality. They do not claim to be verifiable facts (although this *is* the position of some more conservative Christians). *Despite* the fact that Christians certainly do believe that Jesus rose from the dead and is not still buried in a tomb somewhere, the *point* of Jesus' resurrection is not something that could be recorded with a digital video recorder, or with someone's cell phone if she or he happened to be at the tomb on Easter morning. The point of Jesus' virginal conception is not the biological fact that Mary conceived Jesus without normal sexual intercourse, even though that may indeed have been the case. Doctrines are normative for Christians not because they are true facts (even though they might be!) but because they are *saving truths*, because they point beyond themselves to the Mystery of God who is involved with creation and acts to reconcile, heal, and enter into relationship with it. On the other hand, however, doctrines are not merely symbolic or poetic descriptions of some religious experience. They certainly *do* have symbolic significance, since they are human expressions that capture what is essentially an "un-capturable" reality, but they cannot be reduced to that significance. The resurrection, for example, is not just a poetic expression that "ultimately good triumphs over evil"—Jesus *really did* rise from the dead. Jesus' virginal conception is not just an expression of the "graciousness of God in human salvation"—Jesus truly was virginally conceived. We cannot just ignore these expressions or explain them away. They are not "just symbols."

A third way of explaining the nature of doctrine is proposed by the U.S. Lutheran Anglo theologian George Lindbeck. Lindbeck explains the nature of doctrine by using the analogy of normative rules of speech.[9] Doctrines, he might put it, are not a question of literal or symbolic speech, but provide the *parameters* of adequate and valid theological expression. They are "regulative, not informative."[10] Just as grammar is not a language itself, but provides the *rules* for the correct use of language—or just as a culture provides norms for particular kinds of behavior (greeting, for example, or relations between the sexes)—so doctrine provides a way or a space by which or in which our expressions in theology actually *express* and do not *distort* their understanding of God's Mystery. To refer to the example of my encounter with the Quebecois seminarian, there are many ways in English of talking about strong coffee (itself an idiom!): one could say, "This coffee is as thick as syrup," or "This coffee tastes like mud!" or "This coffee curls the hair on your chest;" but you *can't* say "This coffee is as thick *than* syrup," or "*These* coffee *taste* like mud!" or "*This coffee twists the fur on your breast.*" In the same way, *homoousios*, and not *homoiousios*, is a correct way to formulate the doctrine; and Pope Paul VI offered doubts as to whether the meaning of the doctrine of "transubstantiation" can be adequately expressed by the newer term "transignification."

To propose a more "homey" example than Lindbeck's comparison of doctrine with the rules of grammar we can refer to Justo González's comparison of doctrine to the foul lines on a baseball field. There is no rule, says González, that a player has to stand in a particular place on the field (e.g., that the second baseman would stand to the right of second base rather than left of it). There is no rule that says that a batter needs to hit the ball to left field—she or he can hit it anywhere that she or he can. But play has to take place within the foul lines (except, of course, unless a fielder catches a foul popup!). "As long as they stay within the foul lines, players have a great deal of freedom. The foul lines, however, do set limits to that freedom. . . . You may hit a ball as hard as you wish; but if it is foul it is not a home run. To try to legislate where each player must stand, and where the ball must be hit, would destroy the game; but to try to play without any sense of limits, without any foul lines, would also destroy the game."[11]

Lindbeck's and González's explanations of the nature of doctrine are basically correct, as most theologians today would agree. However, as Francis Sullivan points out, there is no intrinsic reason why doctrine cannot also express the truth of what we believe as well[12]—or, I would add, there is no reason why our doctrines cannot also, in their truth, be a kind of stammering expression of the way God encounters us in our lives. It seems to me that *all three* ways of understanding doctrine are valid, as long as our understanding is not *reduced* to the merely literal or the merely symbolic. It is perhaps in this more synthetic way that theologians could understand the definition of doctrine proposed by British Evangelical Alister McGrath: doctrines are "communally authoritative teachings regarded as essential to the identity of the Christian community."[13]

It is important to note here that *doctrine* needs to be distinguished from *dogma*. "Dogma" is from the Greek *dokein*, which means "to seem"—what "seems right"— and in theology, at least in the last two hundred years, a *dogma* is a *doctrine* that has been very explicitly and formally taught as infallibly true by the church's magisterium (we will speak about "infallibility" shortly).

Three Ways of Safeguarding Doctrine

There are three ways by which the magisterium works to safeguard the Christian community's doctrines. The first two are exercised quite frequently; the third way is quite rare.

First—and really most importantly—the magisterium witnesses to the truth of the Christian story by constantly teaching and preaching sound doctrine. This is done by the ordinary, day-to-day teaching and preaching of the bishops and their representatives (especially priests, deacons, and catechists) who in their homilies at the Eucharist and at the celebration of the other sacraments, in their teaching or supervision of religious education classes, in classes of sacramental preparation like the RCIA, or in pastoral letters or parish bulletins, are constantly articulating the church's faith in an accurate and faithful way. *This is the magisterium's primary task*, constantly to proclaim with conviction and accuracy the good news of God's love in Jesus, and how that is expressed in Scripture and the various doctrines of the church.

Second, the magisterium occasionally *clarifies* the meaning of a doctrine or a theological idea, so that Christians will know more clearly what a particular doctrine signifies. This can be the action of the Roman magisterium, of bishops' conferences, or of individual bishops as well. It was done, for example, in 1963 when Pope Paul VI published the encyclical *Mysterium Fidei* in which he cautioned that any eucharistic theology of real presence must start with and be faithful to the doctrine of transubstantiation. In the same way—although very controversially—Paul VI attempted to clarify the church's position on the regulation of birth in his 1968 encyclical *Humanae Vitae*. The Vatican Congregation for the Doctrine of the Faith regularly offers clarifications of doctrine, or warns of what it considers the dangerous positions of some theologians, for example, in its 2007 statement on "Regarding Some Questions of the Doctrine on the Church" and its warnings about the work of Belgian Jesuit Jacques Dupuis, whose approach to the theology of non-Christian religions was formed by many years of ministry in India. To give one more example of this kind of action by the magisterium at a more local level, we can point to the various statements of Conferences of Bishops in Latin America, Africa, and Asia.

A third—very rare—way that the magisterium acts is when it *defines* as exactly as possible (given the constraints of history and culture that are involved in any verbal expression) *what the faith of the church regarding a certain doctrine actually is*. In other words, the magisterium at times acts to make a doctrine a dogma. This can be done by means of a general council, when, with the approval of the pope, a particular doctrine is taught solemnly as calling for the assent of faith of all Christians. Or it can be done when the pope, acting as head of the episcopal college and head of the church solemnly declares a particular doctrine as infallibly true. An example of the former act of a council would be when the Council of Nicaea in 325 c.e. declared in no uncertain terms that Jesus was one substance (*homoousios*) with God the Father, or when the First Vatican Council in 1870 defined the universal primacy and infallibility of the pope.

Although the number of times a pope has exercised of papal infallibility is somewhat debated, it is certain that it has been done at least twice: in 1854, when Pius IX defined the doctrine of Mary's Immaculate Conception, and in 1950 when Pius XII defined the doctrine of Mary's Assumption.[14]

Infallibility

When this third, very rare, exercise of the magisterium takes place, what is taught in this very formal and solemn way is said to be taught *infallibly*. Because of this, the proper response of Christians is the assent of faith, because the doctrine—now dogma—is proposed to the church as an expression that can mediate God's saving presence *without error*. Infallibility, however, is a rather technical theological term that needs to be understood correctly.

A first point in a correct understanding of infallibility is that it is a *negative expression*. Infallibility—literally—means "immunity from error," or "not wrong." It does *not* mean that an infallible doctrine is an exhaustive expression of the truth, or irreformable in its *expression*.

Second, what is infallible and what needs to be believed is *what is asserted*, not necessarily how the assertion is expressed. That Mary was assumed into heaven, for example (see DS 3900-3904/ND 713-715), does not define that heaven is a place in the sky. That she sits at her son's right hand does not mean that Jesus literally sits on a throne. Or that she is "refulgent in glory" does not mean she actually emanates light (in the image of the old U.S. TV commercial, with a sort of "Alpo Glow"). My friend and colleague Barbara Bowe often refers to the practice of a former theology teacher in her college days who would make an assertion of theology like "Mary was assumed into heaven" and whisper up the ample sleeve of her habit: "whatever that means." I think this is a good way to express what we mean when we say that we need to believe only that which is asserted by a doctrine that is taught infallibly. This is not at all a cynical statement, but an admission that what we believe is what the doctrine really means to say—and that is often beyond our understanding.

A third and final point for a correct understanding of infallibility is that an infallible statement is always an articulation of *the infallibility of the faith of the church*. It is not a council or a pope that is infallible; it is the church that is infallible, and at a particular time a council or a pope discerns what the church does indeed infallibly believe. In an article in *America* magazine in 2000, the late bishop of Saginaw, Michigan (USA), Kenneth Untener points out that in the discussion on papal infallibility at Vatican I, "the title of the section on infallibility was changed from 'The Infallibility of the Roman Pontiff' to 'The Infallible *Magisterium* [i.e., teaching authority] of the Roman Pontiff.'"[15] If one reads the definition of infallibility carefully, one will notice that it teaches that when the pope speaks solemnly, as shepherd and teacher of all Christians, he "possesses through the divine assistance promised to him in the person of St. Peter, the infallibility with which the divine Redeemer willed his Church to be endowed . . ." (DS 3074/ND 839). As Untener summarizes papal infallibility, which I think is valid as well for infallibility exercised by a council: "Infallibility is a gift given to the church as a whole. It is exercised by the pope [or a council] when he [it] defines a doctrine to be believed by all the faithful, but it is not a gift given to the pope [or a council] as a personal quality."[16]

How Does the Magisterium Do What It Is Supposed To Do?

What is important to understand in answering this question is that *preservation* is not at all a matter of *mechanical repetition* of formulas, but, in the same way that the tradition as a whole develops (as we saw in chapter 5), of the adaptation and interpretation of doctrines to new and changing historical and cultural situations. Once more, a clear example of this is the adoption of Greek, nonbiblical, language at the Council of Nicaea. Another example is the way that Vatican II treated the traditional dictum "outside the church there is no salvation." The council did not quote it directly and spoke in more positive terms to the effect that while "the Church . . . is necessary for salvation" (LG 14), nevertheless salvation is possible for those "who through no fault of their own do not know the gospel of Christ or His Church, yet sincerely seek God and, moved by grace, strive by their deeds to do His will as it is known to them" (LG 16). As U.S. Anglo moral theologian Charles Curran expresses it: "Fidelity to the tradition does not mean merely repeating the very words of the Scripture or of older church teaching. The Christian tradition is a living tradition, and fidelity involves a creative fidelity which seeks to preserve in its own time and place the incarnational principle. Creative fidelity is the task of the church in bearing witness to the word and work of Jesus."[17]

Does This Mean That the Magisterium Teaches New Truths?

Contrary to what some people may naively think, the magisterium's function is *not* to produce new information or data of revelation. The function of the magisterium is *only* to preserve the integrity of revelation and to teach it faithfully by interpreting it creatively. Vatican II expresses this well in its Dogmatic Constitution on Divine Revelation (DV):

> . . . the task of giving an authentic interpretation to the Word of God . . . has been entrusted to the living teaching office of the Church alone. Its authority in this matter is exercised in the name of Jesus Christ. Yet this Magisterium is not superior to the word of God, but is its servant. It teaches only what has been handed on to it. At the divine command and with the help of the Holy Spirit, it listens to this devotedly, guards it with dedication, and expounds it faithfully. All that it proposes for belief as being divinely revealed is drawn from this single deposit of faith. (DV 10)

Spanish Jesuit Juan Alfaro also expresses it well. When it intends to assert that a doctrine is "*revealed*, the magisterium acknowledges the primacy of the 'authority' of God's Word as well as the primacy of the content of revelation. The content is not revealed because it is defined, but vice versa. The definition is not the word of God, but an authentic interpretation of that word."[18]

What we have said in answering this question as well as the previous one raises the question of whether revelation as such is closed. Traditionally we say that public revelation ceased "with the death of the last apostle." Or, as DV 4 puts it, "We now await no further new public revelation before the glorious manifestation of our Lord Jesus Christ (cf. 1 Tim 6:14 and Titus 2:13)." While this is absolutely true, we must also insist that revelation continues to be active and manifest in our lives, and so is constantly being revealed afresh in our historical and cultural contexts. This was the point of the first two chapters of this book, and it is what makes theology a reflection not just on the past but on our present lives. It is also what makes the church's magisterium a *living* magisterium, as we have just seen. How then do we solve this seeming contradiction?

I think a passage by Karl Rahner, echoing a line from the Spanish mystic John of the Cross (1542-1591), helps us very much here. Both appeal not so much to the *content* of revelation as to revelation as embodied in the person of Jesus of Nazareth. In him—this concrete person, born and living at a concrete time in history—we have the fullness of God's gift of Godself, but it will take the *rest* of history, and indeed all of eternity, to fathom the Mystery of this. Rahner says that

> it is because the definitive Reality which resolves history proper is already here that Revelation is "closed." Closed, because open to the concealed presence of divine plenitude in Christ. Nothing new remains to be said, not as though there were not still much to say, but because everything has been said, everything given in the Son of Love, in whom God and the world have become one, for ever without confusion, but for ever undivided.[19]

The line that Rahner echoes from John of the Cross is this: "In giving us his Son, his only Word (for he possesses no other) he spoke everything to us in this sole Word—and he has no more to say."[20]

Again, this is why we speak of the magisterium as working with creative fidelity. It must be faithful to what has already been said, but it must be able to communicate that "message" and interpret it in the context of the world's various cultures and the always-changing patterns of history.

How Authoritatively Does the Magisterium Teach?

If the magisterium teaches a doctrine that it says—through the pope or a council that is duly approved by the pope—expresses a reality that is at the core of the gospel, the Catholics are called to give to this the full assent of faith. As Vatican II expresses it: "When either the Roman Pontiff or the body of bishops together with him defines a judgement, they pronounce it in accord with revelation itself. All are obliged to maintain and be ruled by this revelation" (LG 25).

More often than not, however, the magisterium's teaching is not binding in this strict and solemn sense, even though it is always authoritative and should be taken very seriously and treated with utmost respect. LG speaks about how all of these non-infallible papal and episcopal statements need to be given what it calls *obsequium animi religiosum*, the first word of which, as Francis Sullivan judges, is to be translated as a bit less than "submission," a little more than "respect." Sullivan speaks of this "loyal submission . . . respect of the mind" as "an *attitude* toward teaching authority, which the Congregation for the Doctrine of the Faith has described as 'the willingness to submit loyally to the teaching of the magisterium on matters per se not irreformable'"[21] (that is, not infallible).

What this points to is that there are different levels on which the magisterium teaches, different kinds of authority that it exercises, and different kinds of response that it requires.[22] Since the nineteenth century it has been common in theology to make a distinction between the *ordinary* or non-solemn exercise of the magisterium and its *extraordinary* or solemn exercise. As a rule of thumb, we can say that *everything* articulated by the extraordinary magisterium is proposed to the church as infallible, and so requires a formal *assent* of faith; when the ordinary magisterium is exercised, in contrast, *most things* articulated are *not* infallible and so do not require the assent of faith, but in some cases the assent of faith is indeed called for.

An exercise of the extraordinary magisterium would be solemn statements of ecumenical councils, duly approved by the pope, such as those proposed by Nicaea on Jesus' divinity, by Chalcedon on the two natures and one person in Christ, or by Trent on the sacrificial nature of the eucharistic celebration. The only other exercise of the extraordinary magisterium is a definition of the pope pertaining to faith or morals and given *ex cathedra* or "from the 'chair' or papal throne"—that is given as shepherd and teacher of the church. As was said above, these have been very few in the entire history of the church—by the most "liberal" estimate twelve, but most likely fewer than that, perhaps as few as two.[23]

The various exercises of the ordinary magisterium, however, point to something more complex. It is, first of all, exercised in the daily preaching of the college of bishops in union with the pope, and from the perspective of a number of dogmas that have not been solemnly defined—for instance, Jesus' resurrection or the doctrine of the communion of saints—this preaching is infallible and calls for the assent of faith. Sometimes this is called an exercise of the "universal ordinary magisterium."[24] But the ordinary magisterium is exercised in all the non-infallible teachings of ecumenical councils, many of which laid down various disciplinary requirements or, in the case of Vatican II, expressly did not teach anything formally or solemnly. Papal encyclicals, such as Benedict XVI's *Deus Caritas Est*, or less formal documents such as apostolic exhortations or John Paul II's series of documents after the various regional synods before the close of the millennium (e.g., *Ecclesia in Africa*, *Ecclesia in Asia*, *Ecclesia in Oceania*), and papal discourses such as Benedict XVI's now-famous discourse to theologians in Regensburg, Germany, in 2006 are all exercises of the ordinary magisterium. Likewise, at a bit lower level, are statements made by Vatican Congregations and approved by the pope, like the Congregation for the Doctrine of the Faith's 2000 statement *Dominus Iesus*. At the episcopal level we have the marvelous statements of the Federation of Asian Bishops' Conferences (FABC) since its founding in 1974, the landmark documents from the Conference of Latin American Bishops (CELAM), especially those at Medellín, Colombia, in 1968, and pastoral letters on ecology by the bishops of the Philippines and Australia. Finally—although we are not being exhaustive in our listing—we can point to the statements of individual bishops, such as the groundbreaking pastoral letter on racism issued by Chicago, Illinois (USA), archbishop Cardinal Francis George.

When certain statements call for it—for example, in paragraph 7 of *Dominus Iesus*—certain positions must be "firmly held." Otherwise, non-infallible statements must be accepted with the "submission . . . respect" of *obsequium*, or, if they are disciplinary matters, they are to be given "conscientious obedience." The chart on page 122, adapted from the work of Richard R. Gaillardetz, lays this out clearly.[25] Here we see that there are four levels of authority of the magisterium. Each one demands a particular response—assent, firm acceptance, *obsequium*, or conscientious obedience—and, as we will see in the final section of this chapter, the last two responses leave room for a particular kind of disagreement.

In summary, to conclude the first section of this chapter, we can say that the magisterium is (1) the duty or charism of the *whole church* to preach the gospel constantly and faithfully, (2) which is exercised in a special way by the office-holders—the pastors—of the church, who are the college of bishops throughout the entire world, in union with the pope. (3) Their task is to safeguard the doctrinal expression of the Christian faith (4) not just by the repetition of traditional formulas but (5) by adapting the gospel message and witness to changing historical and cultural situations. As they do this (6) they exercise authority of different levels, both in an ordinary and an extraordinary way. The response to the magisterium's authority (7) is *always* one of respect and reverence, but at the highest level what is called for is the assent of faith. At times, the magisterium calls Christians to "firmly hold" a doctrine or statement; all other responses consist of that hard-to-translate action of *obsequium animi religiosum*, or conscientious oedience.

MAGISTERIUM: AUTHORITY, RESPONSE, DISSENT
(Adapted from Richard R. Gaillardetz, *Teaching with Authority: A Theology of the Magisterium of the Church* [Collegeville, Minn.: Liturgical Press, 1997], 271)

LEVELS OF CHURCH TEACHING	RESPONSE OF THE FAITHFUL	POSSIBILITY OF DISSENT OR DISAGREEMENT
Definitive Dogma e.g., Mary's Assumption	Assent of Faith (*the believer makes an act of faith, trusting that this teaching is revealed by God*)	None—although one can doubt the suitability of the concepts employed, felicity of expression, or persuasiveness of arguments
Definitive Doctrine e.g., only response to Christian revelation can be called faith (DI 7)	Firm Acceptance (*the believer "accepts and holds" these teachings to be true— "ecclesiastical faith"*)	None—with the same conditions as above
Nondefinitive, Authoritative Doctrine e.g., teaching of *Humanae Vitae*	*Obsequium* of Intellect and Will (*the believer strives to assimilate a teaching of the church into his or her religious stance, while recognizing the remote possibility of church error*)	Not dissent, but disagreement, after having engaged in a "docile attempt to assimilate the teaching" that ends in the inability to do so
Prudential Admonitions and Provisional Applications of Church Doctrine e.g., anti-modernistic decisions of the Pontifical Biblical Commission; pre-Vatican II stance on ecumenism	Conscientious Obedience (*the believer obeys [the spirit of] any church law or disciplinary action that does not lead to sin, even when questioning the ultimate value of the law or action*)	Disagreement, when one sees the fallacy or inopportuneness of the teaching

THEOLOGIANS AND THE MAGISTERIUM

History, and especially recent history, has shown that there exists a healthy tension (although it has sometimes been decidedly unhealthy!) between the church's scholars and the church's officeholders or pastors. I say "healthy tension" because the roles of both scholarship and cautious preservation of the expressions of faith are necessary in the entire theological enterprise, and so some reflection needs to be done on the complex relationship between the two. This is what I propose to do in this section.

We might say at the outset that there are two extremes to be avoided when we speak of the relationship between theologians and the magisterium—or, to use the categories of the Middle Ages in the Western church, between the magisterium of the church's scholars and the magisterium of the church's pastors.

One extreme would be somewhat akin to the *rationalist* position that we discussed in chapter 2. It would say that the *theologians*, the experts, should decide about matters of doctrine in the church. After all, they might say, bishops are usually pastors and are not trained in the history of theology or in the thought patterns of the contemporary world. Theologians worth their salt will be women and men who are constantly updated on the latest theological ideas and have their finger on the pulse of the women and men of their time and culture, and so they are the ones who should decide how the faith should be expressed. I'm not sure I know any theologians who would go this far, but it is certainly the fear of members of the magisterium, who will speak of their fear of a parallel magisterium of theologians like Rahner, Gutiérrez, or the Brazilian Ivone Gebarra.[26]

The other extreme is somewhat like the position of *fideism* or *traditionalism*. It would hold that the magisterium has all the say, and that theology should simply communicate or reflect on what the magisterium teaches. This position is basically the one of Pius XII in his 1950 encyclical *Humani Generis*, where the task of theologians is described as showing "how what is taught by the living magisterium is found, whether explicitly or implicitly, in sacred scripture and in divine tradition" (DS 3886).

Such an extreme position might be illustrated by a story told by the late U.S. Anglo Scripture scholar, Raymond Brown (1928-1998) in his book *Priest and Bishop*. A bishop (who is now deceased) was welcoming a group of Scripture scholars to speak to the clergy of his diocese. In his welcoming remarks the bishop said how much he envied the seminarians today for the good education they were getting in the study of the Scriptures. When he was going through the seminary, he said, his own training in exegesis was very poor, and he had never felt confident about his skills in interpreting the Scriptures as a preacher. "At the end of these kind words," Brown writes, "he cautioned the scholars that they should advise the audience that their conclusions about Scripture were only opinions, for the bishops were the only official theologians of the Church and only they could speak authoritatively about Scripture. Here was a man innocently claiming that he could speak authoritatively about a subject in which, as he had just admitted, he had not even elementary competence!"[27]

The true Catholic position, of course, is not that *either* theologians *or* the magisterium possesses the final competence in things theological. It is much more a question of *both/and*. Both theologians *and* the magisterium need each other and serve the church and its mission by respecting and cooperating with one another. In order to understand this more deeply, I would like to offer four theses.

Thesis One:
Theologians and the Magisterium Have Different
Yet Complementary Functions in the Church

I remember an occasion during my years in the Philippines when the then-archbishop of Manila, Cardinal Jaime Sin (1928-2005), spoke about the relationship between theologians and bishops, or the magisterium. In his usual humorous way, the Cardinal drew an analogy of a person driving a car: she or he needed to use both the gas pedal and brake, for if she only used the gas pedal she would certainly crash, but if he just kept his foot on the brake he would go nowhere! It is the same, he said, of theologians and the magisterium. Theologians provide the *motion* in understanding revelation more deeply—they have a tendency to keep their foot on the pedal, and some seem to have a lead foot! The bishops, however, like to be *safe*. Their tendency is to hit the brakes all the time, to slow things down, to be sure that they can make a sharp turn safely, to be sure that they don't go so fast that they run off the road. But this is why we need both theologians and bishops. Their task is different, but the church could not really move without both.[28]

Very much this same idea is expressed by Gerald O'Collins when he uses German sociologist Max Weber's (1864-1920) distinction between *institutional* and *charismatic* authority. While bishops are certainly endowed with charismatic authority, their authority as "authentic interpreters" (see DV 10) of God's word comes from their ordination into the worldwide body of bishops. And while theologians with their degrees and academic positions certainly possess an institutional authority, this really "rests on the quality of their theological gifts." Again, however, *both* types of authority are necessary, and anyone who knows church history or the history of doctrine knows how "the reciprocal relationship that has existed between the magisterium and theologians" has activated or reactivated "the saving revelation of God in people's lives."[29] Avery Dulles also says it well:

> . . . it must be recognized that there is a qualitative difference between the authentic magisterium of the hierarchy and the doctrinal magisterium of the scholar. The bishop and the theologian, while they are both teachers, have different roles. The bishop's task is to give public expression to the doctrine of the Church and thus to lay down norms for preaching, worship, and Christian life. . . . The theologian, on the other hand, is concerned with reflectively analyzing the present situation of the Church and of the faith, with a view to deepening the Church's understanding of revelation and in this way opening up new and fruitful channels of pastoral initiative. . . . [The theologian's] goal is not to spread doubt and confusion . . . but rather to face the real questions and to pioneer as best as he [or she] can the future paths of Christian thought and witness.[30]

There will always be tension between these two functions, but this tension should never be collapsed. In the language of the great Canadian theologian Bernard Lonergan (1904-1984), if a judgment is made without understanding, it is a poor judgment; but if we never judge, we can never come to the point where we can bring closure to our process of understanding and so be able to act.[31] Theologians' specialty is to provide "understanding"; the magisterium's is to offer "judgment." As U.S. bishop James Malone wisely said in a talk he gave some years ago at Marquette University in Milwaukee, Wisconsin, USA:

> Theologians without an appetite for creativity and development will not serve us well in an age where knowledge grows by quantum leaps; bishops without a courageous sense of responsibility to protect the deposit of faith will leave a gift we all need vulnerable to erosion and attack. The content of our responsibilities is complementary; the dynamic orientation of our responsibilities is different. Bishops and theologians need a sensitivity to each other's ministry in order that together we can share the treasure of the Catholic tradition and shape it for the future.[32]

Thesis Two:
Theologians Should Work within the Magisterium

There are two aspects of this thesis to reflect upon. First, the thesis refers to the fact that the magisterium provides the *parameters*, the framework, within which theologians theologize. What this means is that if a theologian realizes that she is moving beyond the basic doctrinal understanding of the faith in her work—or if he is warned explicitly by the magisterium—he has the obligation to pull back and rethink his position. He needs to take the parameters of the tradition seriously, in other words. After all, writes René Latourelle, the theologian "is, before everything else, a responsible servant of the Word of God, bound by a two-fold fidelity to Christ and to his bride, the Church. To seek the truth far away from the Magisterium by arbitrary and unauthorized ways would be to expose himself [or herself] to the danger of working in vain, without producing any fruit for the life of the community, or to run the risk of taking for truth the mirage of his [or her] questing imagination."[33]

In the second place, one of the task of theologians is to interpret the magisterium in ways that are understandable to the women and men of their time and their particular cultures. This is by all means not their exclusive task, as the International Theological Commission points out, but it does indeed "lend its aid to make the magisterium in its turn the enduring light and norm of the Church."[34] In his famous letter to the Duke of Norfolk, Cardinal Newman called this task of interpreting the magisterium the "charitable duty" of theologians, their "special work."[35]

Theologians in both their writing and their teaching certainly need to press forward in their theological research, looking for newer and more adequate ways to understand the faith in their particular contexts. But they also need to mediate the tradition that the magisterium guards. How does one interpret the doctrine of eucharistic "real presence," traditionally expressed in the Aristotelian categories of "substance" and "accident" in a world where science speaks in the language of quantum physics? How can Christians understand God's continuing creative activity in a world where Darwin's theory of evolution is now generally accepted, even by the church? How can the rich content of the documents of the Second Vatican Council be understood by women and men studying theology who were born a quarter century or more after those documents were published in 1965? Bishop Malone offers his own personal testimony to the important assistance that theologians have offered in his own teaching ministry:

> As a bishop in an episcopal conference which devoted substantial time and energy to the place of the church in the world, I can testify to the irreplaceable role of the theological enterprise. The pastoral letters on peace and the economy [issued by the U.S. bishops in the 1980s] drew extensively on the work of theologians. The public dialogue interpreting the letters to a multiplicity of audiences would have been impossible without the resources and personal engagement of the theological community.[36]

Thesis Three:
The Magisterium Should Listen to Theologians' Voices

Theologians *can* and *should* critique the magisterium, because criticism is not necessarily disloyalty but in many cases just the opposite.[37] While very often the magisterium does not appreciate critique, in the context of loyalty criticism can ultimately enhance the magisterium's authority and the cause of truth. When one looks at history, the critique of traditional ways of expressing some theological concepts in the opening decades of the twentieth century ultimately produced the rich renewal in the church that was marked by the Second Vatican Council in the early 1960s. Some theologians suffered very much in these decades and were even silenced by the Vatican after Pius XII's *Humani Generis* in 1950, but theologians like Yves Congar, Marie-Dominique Chenu, Henri de Lubac, Karl Rahner, Henri Bouillard (1908-1981) worked quietly throughout these decades. They were loyal to the magisterium, even though they critiqued its lack of historical sense, its rigidity, and its lack of sensitivity to the biblical and patristic texts. The U.S. Anglo theologian John Courtney Murray (1904-1967), in his important studies about the relationship between church and state, challenged the "traditional" teaching of the church that, where possible, Catholicism should be the established religion (based on the dictum "error has no rights"). His work at first met with suspicion and strong opposition in Rome but was eventually accepted and formed the basis for perhaps the most radical document of the council, the document on religious freedom. Let me once more quote the important talk of Bishop James Malone:

> The council was the work first of the Holy Spirit, second of the bishops who participated in it and third of the theologians who prepared the way for the teaching of Vatican II and who helped shape the specific content of that teaching. The role played by theologians was strikingly symbolized by the Mass Pope Paul VI concelebrated with the leading theologians at the close of Vatican II. Around the altar were Yves Congar, OP, Henri de Lubac, SJ, John Courtney Murray, SJ, and many others—most of whom had been silenced for part of their theological careers and had lived to see their work vindicated by the council. In human terms, it is difficult to think of Vatican II's achievement without the patient, meticulous scholarship of these theologians throughout the first half of the century.[38]

Paul VI himself acknowledged the help of theologians as they press beyond traditional and accepted ways of expressing the faith at an international conference of theologians the year after the council ended. Without theologians, he said, the magisterium could certainly do its job of teaching and safeguarding the faith, but it could not do it as thoroughly and faithfully as possible. "Deprived of the labor of theology, the Magisterium would lack the tools it needs to weld the Christian community into a unified concert of thought and action, as it must do for the Church to be a community which lives and thinks according to the principles and norms of Christ."[39]

Thesis Four:
Theologians Should Be Given Sufficient Freedom to Carry on Research

No less a figure than Cardinal Joseph Ratzinger, now Pope Benedict XVI, recognized the importance of the academic freedom of theologians in a talk he gave in Toronto, Canada, in 1986: "This vital link between theology and the church [i.e., the magisterium] must never be allowed to deteriorate to the point where theology goes to the other extreme and idolizes church teaching. The danger of a mean and cowardly vigilance is by no means a ghost in the closet. The history of the Modernist struggle is proof of this, even though simplistic judgements are made today which ignore the complexity of the period."[40] Especially in difficult matters, says Latourelle, theologians should be given the freedom to question and research.[41] Questions on the relationship between grace and freedom and the nature of original sin are classic problems that still need probing. Today the question of the role of Christ in the work of salvation is one of the most controverted and, despite statements like *Dominus Iesus*, theological thinking in this area has to continue. Other flashpoints of controversy in today's church are questions regarding the role of women in the church, or moral questions around the issues of cloning and stem cell research.

Certainly theologians can make mistakes, but if they do their theologizing with respect for the magisterium and its articulation of the church's tradition, and if they pursue their work with rigor and honesty and are in continued conversation with their own theological colleagues, they cannot go far wrong. We see here again the importance of theologians recognizing the communal, ecclesial nature of every theological effort.

In the chapter on the relationship between theologians and the magisterium in his small but important book on the role of authority in the church, Richard Gaillardetz writes of how contemporary documents of the magisterium have shifted away from a "dualism" of magisterium and theologians to an understanding of the issue based on Vatican II's ecclesiology of communion. Gaillardetz quotes Joseph Ratzinger's remarks on the 1990 Instruction of the Congregation for the Doctrine of the Faith on the ecclesial vocation of the theologian. Here the cardinal pointed out how the document begins with the fact that the truth of faith "is not given to isolated individuals, rather through it God wanted to give life to a history and to a people." Fundamentally, in other words, the faith of the church is neither the "property" of the magisterium, as much as its task is to preserve it; nor is the faith simply in the care of the church's theologians, as much as their task is to explain and interpret it. Rather, the faith of the church resides in the church, and so only constant conversation among the church's pastors, its theologians, and the people at large can truly advance the cause of "faith seeking understanding."[42] Every member of the church has "a piece of the wisdom," and, perhaps ironically, it is the role of the magisterium to safeguard that fact.

THE MAGISTERIUM AND DISSENT

An issue that has become an important one in theologizing today has been the question of whether a theologian, while basically being loyal to the magisterium, can nevertheless dissent or at least disagree with a particular pronouncement or set of pronouncements of the magisterium. In 1968, for example, many theologians in the United States and Europe especially publicly disagreed with the teaching on artificial contraception in Paul VI's encyclical *Humanae Vitae*. More recently, a good number of theologians—particularly feminist theologians—have strongly disagreed with the magisterium's statement that women's exclusion from ordained ministry is something to be "definitively held."[43] And in Asia, theologians have taken umbrage at the magisterium's statements in the area of Jesus' unique redemptive role.

Given the dialogical relationship among the magisterium, theologians, and the body of the faithful, how does this stance of dissent or disagreement function for theologians? This will be the question we will deal with in this final section of chapter 6.

The Notion of Reception

The notion of "reception" of doctrinal and moral teaching is an idea that has come under renewed investigation after Vatican II.[44] It is based on one of the key ideas found in the council's documents—that the church is not primarily a hierarchical society but a communion of persons. As such, as we have seen at the end of the previous section of this chapter, it is the *entire church* that is the primary recipient of God's word, not the pope and the bishops (and certainly not the church's theologians!). All Christians, at a fundamental level, are equal because of their baptism, and so the entire church is possessed of a *sensus fidei*, a "sense of the faith," as we discussed in chapter 4. The Holy Spirit, in other words, vivifies and inspires *every* member of the church. Although the gifts differ, everyone is endowed with "a piece of the wisdom."

Given this context, "reception" is the living process whereby some teaching, ritual, or discipline is assimilated into the life of the church, under the guidance of the Holy Spirit. I mentioned above that this process of reception has come under *renewed* investigation after Vatican II. This is because reception is not a *new* process but one that has always gone on in the church, even though it has sometimes been eclipsed. In the first millennium or so of the church's history, the process was very conscious and very much alive as the various local churches discerned and accepted teachings that came from other churches— we see this in the various christological controversies, and controversies over ritual issues such as the date for Easter. Another example might be the gradual development of the "monarchical episcopate": this form of church order seems to have been present in the Eastern part of the church around the turn of the second century C.E., replacing the rather fluid order in the various local churches reflected in the New Testament. By the third century, however, every local church was basically governed by one *episkopos* or bishop, assisted by deacons (*diakonoi*) and advised by a council of elders (*presbyteroi*).

In the Middle Ages (from about the ninth to the fifteenth century in the West), the church developed—for a number of reasons—a less communal and a more hierarchical structure, and so this notion of reception was greatly diminished and almost lost. It was in this context that theologians and the magisterium alike began speaking of the "teaching church" (*ecclesia docens*—the hierarchy, and possibly the theologians) and the "learning church" (*ecclesia discens*). The reality of reception was certainly still alive—we can see this, for example, after the Council of Trent as the church gradually renewed itself in the century that followed. But the predominance of the hierarchy and the gradual centralization of power in the church in the nineteenth century gave the impression—and it was taught by the magisterium—that the church was by nature "an unequal society" composed of "the pastors and the flock," and the flock had "no other duty but to allow itself to be led and to follow its pastors as a docile flock."[45]

But with the recovery of Vatican II of the understanding of the church as a community, it began to be recognized that the church was therefore a "'community of reception,' in which reception is not so much a juridical act of acceptance as it is an ongoing process in the life of the Church."[46] At least on the theological level, therefore, the church had moved from a kind of "trickle down theory" of authority to a more dialogical one, where individual Christians and Christian communities have a say in what the *entire* church teaches.

It is in this context that we need to understand the possibility of dissent or disagreement with the magisterium. In the understanding of the church as a "community of reception," every Christian has a right and even a duty to express her or his opinion—always of course in the context of faith and communion with the church and its leadership. And within this context as well we can see how theologians—as Christians first, but also trained and steeped in the church's tradition—might have a special responsibility to make their doubts about a particular teaching or discipline known.

The Possibility of Dissent

I have used the term "dissent" so far in this section because it is the usual word that is used when we talk about disagreeing with statements or teachings of the magisterium. As eminent Hungarian-American canonist Ladislaus Örsy observes, however, the term is so ambiguous and negative that it is really unsuitable for the best theological discourse. He would prefer that theologians use terms like "a different opinion" or "disagreement."[47] Indeed, the term "dissent" as the opposite of "assent" is certainly inappropriate, since it is not possible to dissent from church teachings that call for the assent of faith and still remain in the church.[48] So when we speak of dissent in this section we mean it in the "softer" sense that Örsy would prefer. We are not talking about disagreeing with or dissenting from teachings of the "extraordinary" magisterium, nor from teachings of the "ordinary universal" magisterium, but about disagreeing or not accepting teachings taught *authoritatively* but not *solemnly* or *infallibly*.

If we look at the four levels of the teaching of the magisterium that we sketched in the first section of this chapter, and which are outlined on the

chart on page 122, we can see that with the first two levels of teaching—
that of "definitive dogma" or "definitive doctrine"—no disagreement is possible. This is not because of any ideological reason, but because these teachings
which the magisterium proposes as infallibly true or definitively to be held
touch on the very heart of Christian faith—they are doctrines through which
God's Mystery are partially and yet *really* refracted. Theologians can, of course,
have doubts about how well or adequately a teaching is expressed, or about
the opportuneness of the definition, or even about whether the conditions
of infallibility (whether the pope *really did* speak *ex cathedra*, for example, or
whether the bishops of the world *really are* in agreement on this issue—have
been adequately met, but this is not dissent as such.[49]

It is on the third and fourth levels of teaching that the problem—and the
possibility—of disagreement arises. Gaillardetz (referring to the work of the
late U.S. Anglo moral theologian Richard McCormick [1922-2000]) lists four
conditions under which such disagreement can be legitimate.[50] In the first
place, a person must make an honest attempt to understand what the magisterium is teaching. Disagreement cannot be legitimate, for example, if a person
has only gleaned his information from a television program or a newspaper
account of the teaching, or disagrees with something that he knows little
about (e.g., a systematic theologian's ordinary knowledge about the intricacies
of stem cell research). Second, a person has to give careful consideration to
the magisterium's—and theologians'—arguments for and against the position.
One needs to weigh these arguments carefully, take them seriously, and not
just make a judgment on one's own experience or prejudices. Third, a person
who is deciding whether to agree or disagree with a particular teaching of the
magisterium that is not being proposed as infallibly taught needs to examine
her conscience to make sure that her hesitation is not due to bias. Just because
the acceptance of the teaching is *difficult* is ultimately no reason to disagree.
Finally, throughout this whole process, a person has to maintain respect for the
magisterium. We are dealing with a person who is basically *loyal* to the church
and is weighing whether to disagree in the context of a higher loyalty to the
truth as she honestly understands it. Disagreement, Örsy points out, could
really "be consenting wholeheartedly to the search for a better understanding
of the Christian mysteries."[51]

Deciding to disagree with the magisterium is serious business and should
never be done lightly. It is always important to recognize that, while one's
individual conscience and intellectual judgment are always to be respected,
one's faith is ultimately not really one's own, but something that each of us
holds in the context of the community. Important as well is the church's faith
that the magisterium—though its exercise certainly has been abused—is ultimately a service in the church for the sake of the gospel.

On the other hand, honest, respectful, and loyal "dissent" must sometimes be taken, especially by Christians who are perhaps more knowledgeable in theology, science, or even life experience than the authorities who have proposed a certain teaching. Had not Galileo continued to hold his views about the movement of the earth around the sun, and had not Cardinal Newman continued to argue for the sense of the faithful in the light of strong opposition from the English hierarchy, we would certainly be worse off today. If a Rahner, a Congar, or a Murray had not respectfully and persistently disagreed with certain church teachings prior to Vatican II, the great renewal that the council brought would not have happened. Who knows if the disagreement of a Charles Curran, a Leonardo Boff, or a Joan Chittister today to certain church teachings will not pave the way for a more faithful understanding of the gospel in the future. We must always "acknowledge the real possibility that legitimate dissent itself may be a manifestation of the Spirit in bringing the whole Church to truth."[52]

CONCLUSION

Theology is "faith seeking understanding," but that seeking is done together, in the context of a believing community. This means, on the one hand, says Gerald O'Collins, that "theologians would not genuinely serve the Church community if in a mechanical way they merely repeated the classic creeds, declarations of councils, the teachings of popes, and traditional pieces of doctrine. . . ." On the other hand, however, theologians should not become "lonely armadillos, encased in the narrow shell of their own ponderings." They need to seek and learn from the wisdom of the community, both past and present, and to respect those who are gifted by the Spirit with authority in the church. "Those who fail to listen to councils, popes and other official teachers and proclaimers of the Christian message will miss privileged and divinely endorsed instances of that message being interpreted and applied to the changing situations of both past and present."[53] The magisterium is not over against the church, we have insisted, but a service within the church for the sake of the gospel, and so any theologian who wants truly to serve the Christian people needs to work in dialogue with it. That dialogue needs to be honest and frank, serious and respectful, filled with creativity and trust, as theologians and the church's leaders seek understanding together.

QUESTIONS FOR REFLECTION

1. What do you think is the role of authority in the church?
2. Why do you think theological doctrines are important in the church?

3. What is the difference between the infallibility of the pope and the infallibility of the church?
4. Why are both the authority of the magisterium and the authority of theologians important in the church?
5. What are some of the areas in which you might disagree with the magisterium? Have your opinions changed after reading this chapter? Why?

SUGGESTIONS FOR FURTHER READING AND STUDY

José M. de Mesa and Lode Wostyn, *Doing Theology: Basic Realities and Processes* (Quezon City, Philippines: Claretian Publications, 1990), chapter 5, "Theology and Truth," 89-124.

Avery Dulles, *The Survival of Dogma: Faith, Authority and Dogma in a Changing World* (Garden City, N.Y.: Doubleday Image Books, 1973).

Congregation for the Doctrine of the Faith, *Instruction on the Ecclesial Vocation of the Theologian*, See http://www.vatican.va/roman_curia/congregations/cfaith/documents/rc_con_cfaith_doc_19900524_theologian-vocation_en.html.

Richard R. Gaillardetz, *By What Authority? A Primer on Scripture, the Magisterium, and the Sense of the Faithful* (Collegeville, Minn.: Liturgical Press, 2003).

———, *Teaching with Authority: A Theology of the Magisterium of the Church* (Collegeville, Minn.: The Liturgical Press, 1997).

George Lindbeck, *The Nature of Doctrine: Religion and Theology in a Post-Liberal Age* (Philadelphia: Fortress Press, 1984).

Robert McClory, *Faithful Dissenters: Stories of Men and Women Who Loved and Changed the Church* (Maryknoll, N.Y.: Orbis Books, 2000).

Gerald O'Collins, *Fundamental Theology* (New York/Ramsey, N.J.: Paulist Press, 1981), "Excursus: The Magisterium," 181-91.

Kuncheria Pathil and Dominic Veliath, *An Introduction to Theology* (Bangalore: Theological Publications in India, 2003), chapter 2, "The Sources of Theology," 39-83.

Francis A. Sullivan, *Creative Fidelity: Weighing and Interpreting Documents of the Magisterium* (New York/Mahwah, N.J.: Paulist Press, 1996).

———, *Magisterium: Teaching Authority in the Catholic Church* (New York/Ramsey, N.J.: Paulist Press, 1983).

Part III

The Way Faith Seeks

Theological Methods

"Theological method" or, as it is sometimes called, "theological methodology," is one of those terms that is thrown around quite a lot in contemporary theological circles. Frankly, if one theologian would like to impress another, he or she needs only to say something like "I think the real problem here is a lack of a coherent method." But like a lot of popular terms, "method" means different things to different people. René Latourelle and Richard McBrien speak of theological method as a *procedure*, as a *way of doing theology*, and, in a quite different but nevertheless related way, liberation theologians like Gustavo Gutiérrez, Leonardo Boff, and Juan Luis Segundo (a Spaniard who has worked many years in El Salvador) also speak of method in terms of procedure. More important, they say, than the content of theology is the way theology proceeds. If the process is correct—starting from the experience of the poor and moving toward action was consonant with the gospel to overcome the poor's oppression—the content will always end up being correct. As Gutiérrez puts it, "The theology of liberation offers us not so much a new theme for reflection as a *new way* to do theology."[1] Bernard Lonergan also speaks in this way of method in theology. For him, method is "a normative pattern of recurrent and related operations yielding cumulative and progressive results."[2]

On the other hand, U.S. Anglo theologian J. J. Mueller speaks of method in quite a different sense. For Mueller, method is determined by a theologian's basic, fundamental point of view or insight into the nature of the world and/or the nature of human persons. As he puts it, "Every theologian must be clear about his or her starting point, presuppositions and consequences of theology. This is what method tries to do."[3] This same perspective is expressed in an article on method by U.S. Anglo theologian Francis Schüssler Fiorenza in a multi-authored, two-volume work of Catholic systematic theology. For Schüssler Fiorenza, method is the theological starting point that "colors" the way one does theology.[4]

In our reflections here we will focus on *both* of these meanings of theological method. In the first chapter of this part (chapter 7) we will discuss method as procedure, outlining the more classical method of gathering data (positive method) and drawing out the implications of that method in theological reflection (speculative method). We will also indicate how this method is extended in the basic method used by the theologians of liberation (Latin Americans, feminists, black theologians, etc.). In the second and third chapters in this third part of the book (chapters 8 and 9) we will focus on method in terms of particular starting points that "color" the way theologians proceed in seeking understanding of their and the church's faith. Chapter 8 will examine various methods of contextual theology, and chapter 9 will reflect on what I call "Catholic method": the basic perspectives that ground the way Catholics approach the task of theology.

7

Historical Investigation and Theological Reflection

Classical and Contemporary Methods

IN THIS FIRST CHAPTER on the methods of theology we are going to look at two basic *procedures* in doing theology. The first method is a classical one. It consists of a twofold movement, the first of "positive" historical investigation and the second of theological reflection or "speculation." In this way, theologians come to a deeper understanding of an experience, a doctrine, or a theological theme. Building on this twofold movement toward the end of the chapter we will outline the method used in contemporary liberation theologies: the method of "critical reflection on praxis." The key to understanding this method is to recognize that it is built on a "new way of knowing" that seeks not so much intellectual understanding as an understanding that is built on reflective activity. This second way of doing theology pushes our understanding of theology from "faith seeking understanding" to "faith seeking action." It points to the fact that theology is ultimately not only about "right thinking" or "orthodoxy," but "right acting" or "orthopraxy."

This chapter will focus more closely on theological activity as *scholarly* activity. Nevertheless, we can never forget the communal, ecclesial nature of doing theology. Even a lone theologian working in her study or in a library is still dialoguing with the "cloud of witnesses" (see Heb. 12:1) that make up the monuments of tradition, and even scholarly investigation and reflection are best done as a team, since there is always so much ground to cover. Also, however, while a group of women and men in a pastoral setting may not always be doing the close scholarship that we will be talking about here, the *dynamic* of the way they proceed will be the same: experience needs to be analyzed, the tradition needs to be investigated, and reflection on the tradition needs to be done in an ordered way.

A TWOFOLD MOVEMENT:
HISTORICAL INVESTIGATION AND THEOLOGICAL REFLECTION

The most basic—and very traditional—way of proceeding in the doing of theology is to follow a twofold method, according, actually, to the basic twofold movement in the human process of understanding. The idea is that, since theology is *faith . . . seeking . . . understanding*, one proceeds in doing theology in the same way one proceeds in understanding anything.

In the first move, *data* must first be appropriated. We must find out what is believed—in other words, "get our facts straight." Second, however, we need to discern the *meaning* of what we believe—in other words, "so what?" Why is this particular datum of faith important for human life? How does it or might it enhance people's lives? What difference does believing this particular doctrine make in the way Christians should live?

If, for example, a theologian is investigating the Catholic doctrine of purgatory, he or she would ask, in a first move, what the church actually *believes* about purgatory—Is it a place? Is there *fire* there? Does it exist in time? But once these questions are clarified, the theologian needs to ask questions of meaning: How does purgatory make a difference in people's faith? What perspective does this doctrine give on the mystery of God? Thomas Aquinas put it succinctly: "Study . . . does not aim merely at finding out what others have thought but how the truth of things presents itself."[1]

In methodological terms, then, the first movement of fact gathering or historical investigation is called the moment of "positive theology." This is sometimes called the moment of *auditus fidei* or "hearing/listening to the faith." The second movement, trying to find meaning, is called the moment of "speculative theology" or theological reflection, referred to as the *intellectus fidei* or "understanding the faith," appropriating its meaning.[2] This is how Vatican II describes the way theological investigation is to proceed, and how a theological theme should be presented in a class of systematic (dogmatic[3]) theology:

> Dogmatic theology should be so arranged that the biblical themes are presented first. Students should be shown what the Fathers of the Eastern and Western Church contributed to the fruitful transmission and illumination of the individual truths of revelation, and also the later history of dogma and its relationship to the general history of the Church. Then, by way of making the mysteries of salvation known as thoroughly as they can be, students should learn to penetrate them with the help of speculative reason exercised under the tutelage of St. Thomas. Students should learn too how these mysteries are interconnected, and be taught to recognize their presence and activity in liturgical actions and in the whole life of the Church. Let them learn to search for solutions to human problems with the light of revelation, to apply eternal truths to the changing conditions of human

affairs, and to communicate such truths in a manner suited to contemporary women and men. (OT 16)

When this statement from the council's Decree on Priestly Formation was published, it was hailed as a real breakthrough in doing and teaching theology. The method it outlined—though it may seem fairly staid now—was a distinct departure from the way theology had been done throughout the nineteenth century and the first part of the twentieth. What is outlined in Vatican II's statement is an *inductive* approach to theologizing—starting from Scripture and proceeding to see how a particular doctrine or idea developed through a chronological and historical study of the "monuments of tradition."

How theology had proceeded previous to this was very *deductive*. The idea was basically to prove what the magisterium taught by amassing "proof texts" from Scripture and other theological texts from the magisterium, and then trying to see how these made sense from reason. The more inductive approach recommended by Vatican II allows the witness of Scripture, the wisdom of the tradition, and the reality of human experience to take the lead in theological reflection. In this way theologians are able to investigate how a particular doctrine or idea in theology actually developed, and what the factors were that led to that development.

Even though this was considered a breakthrough at the time, the method proposed by Vatican II—like many things proposed by the council—was hardly an *innovation* in theological method. It is actually a method that is found deep in the church's tradition. Augustine of Hippo, for instance, describes at the beginning of his great work on the Trinity how he is going to proceed: "With the help of God our Lord and to the best of our ability, we shall attempt to show . . . the reason why the Trinity is the one true God. . . . But we will first have to show by the authority of Holy Scripture that this is a matter of our faith."[4] The same double rhythm of theological method is reflected in a statement by Thomas Aquinas: "If a teacher settles a question by recourse to authority alone, his students will doubtless be convinced that the thing is true, but they will acquire no science or understanding and will go away without satisfying their intellects."[5] This is the same method that Aquinas used in his *Summa Theologiae*, beginning with sorting out the data (in the objections and answers to the objections), stating his position, and then explaining his position with the use of both data and philosophical and theological reasoning.

Historical Investigation:
The Auditus Fidei

The first movement, as we have said, in theological investigation is that of gathering the data, engaging in historical investigation. Theologians do this by investigating the various "theological sources" or *loci theologici*. Traditionally, as we saw in the first section of our course when we reflected on the nature of theology, these sources were understood to be Scripture and the various monuments of tradition. Today, however, we must also include *human experience* (i.e., historical events, a particular culture, one's "social location" as a man or woman, poor or middle class, Dalit or Brahmin, black, brown, or white) in our investigation of the sources of theology. James and Evelyn Whitehead list three "conversation partners" to be "listened to" when one does theology: experience, culture, and tradition (which, of course, includes Scripture).

A positive theological investigation can begin in several places. One could begin with the investigation of a particular doctrine—that of purgatory, for example, or of transubstantiation. The theologian would proceed by investigating the scriptural, traditional (patristic, historical, magisterial sources), and experiential foundations. One could also begin with a theme that appears in Scripture—e.g., reconciliation, Jesus, the church—and investigate how the theme develops throughout the tradition and what human experience might say about it today. Or one could also begin with a contemporary problem or incident—e.g., violence, immigration, the 1986 "People Power" revolt in the Philippines—and investigate how this might have a foundation in scriptural themes or themes in the tradition.

However theologians begin, the point of this moment in doing theology is to gather data, to see what Christians have said and thought down through the ages, to see how the church has acted to respond to a particular theme or to similar events.

What I would like to do in this section is to present each of these theological sources briefly and then mention some of the most important works in which these sources can be best investigated. I am presenting these sources in a way that might suggest the order of investigation, although not every historical study would necessarily focus on every area. As a theologian gains experience in research, he or she will discover the best way to proceed in individual studies. What is always true is that doing theology is more of a *craft* or an *art* than a strict method to be followed.

As I proceed, I want to acknowledge that there are many, many more references for investigation than the ones that I will list here, but I hope to offer the best ones that are available in English, although here and there I'll mention a few sources in other languages. Again, one learns by experience. As a theologian gets more and more practiced in theological investigation of the sources, he or she will discover new sources and establish certain ones as particularly reliable.

Scriptural Resources

As Vatican II advises, Scripture "ought to be the soul of theology" (OT 16) and so a first move in positive/historical theological research should be an investigation of the Scriptures. There is an abundance of material available in this area, and more works are being published all the time.

A major resource is the twelve-volume *New Interpreter's Bible* (Nashville, Tenn.: Abingdon Press), the first volume of which was published in 1994, followed by the other volumes throughout the 1990s, edited by the eminent New Testament scholar Leander Keck. The commentary is based on two English translations of the Bible, the New International Version (NIV) and the New Revised Standard Version (NRSV) which are printed in parallel columns in individual chapters or parts of chapters. Following the more technical commentary are short "Reflections," which are more pastoral and helpful for preaching. While most of the contributors are U.S. American white males, a good number of contributors are U.S. white women. An important feature of the first volume, however, are articles on various perspectival readings by Latino, Native American, Asian American, African American, and feminist authors. In 2005, two supplementary "Surveys" of both the Old and New Testaments were published. The *New Interpreter's Bible* is certainly one of the most important resources for biblical commentary that a theologian can consult. The commentaries are by the top U.S. biblical scholars of the late twentieth and early twenty-first centuries, and there are references throughout to articles and other commentaries on the biblical books. The twelve volumes of text and commentary are available from Abingdon Press also on CD ROM. Also worth consulting are the following commentary series: the extensive Anchor Bible (New York: Doubleday), volumes of which are still appearing periodically; the *Hermeneia* series (Minneapolis: Augsburg Fortress—a number of volumes of available on CD ROM); the *Ancient Christian Commentary on Scripture* (Downers Grove, Ill.: InterVarsity); *Sacra Pagina* (Collegeville, Minn.: Liturgical Press); and the *Catholic Commentary on Sacred Scripture* (Grand Rapids: Baker Academic).

There are a number of important one-volume commentaries that theologians might want to consult when investigating biblical themes and passages. A standard Catholic commentary is *The New Jerome Biblical Commentary* (Englewood Cliffs, N.J.: Prentice Hall, 1990), edited by the eminent Catholic biblical scholars Raymond E. Brown, Joseph A. Fitzmyer, and Roland E. Murphy. This is also a commentary written by mostly Anglo males, but it offers Catholic biblical scholarship at its finest and most balanced. A commentary with a more global outlook is *The International Bible Commentary* (Collegeville, Minn.: Liturgical Press, 1998), which includes both Catholic and Protestant contributors from all over the world. In 2004 Abingdon Press published *A Global Bible Commentary*, edited by French-born biblical scholar Daniel Patte, with co-editors from Africa, Latin America, and Asia and with two-thirds of the contributors from the third world. This is a shorter, less-detailed commentary than the *New Jerome* commentary, but essential for theologians who want to do theology from a more inclusive and global perspective. This volume will also point biblical researchers to more detailed work done by these scholars from around the world. One more single-volume commentary worth mentioning here is the expanded edition of *The Women's Bible Commentary* (Louisville, Ky.: Westminster John Knox Press, 1998), edited by Sharon H. Ringe and Carol A. Newsom. This commentary gathers many of the best feminist biblical scholars to comment on biblical texts that have bearing on women's issues.

In addition to commentaries, there are a good number of biblical dictionaries that trace biblical themes and identify persons in the Bible. It is often good to consult a dictionary at the beginning of one's biblical research to get the "lay of the land" and some important additional bibliographical information. Chief among these dictionaries is *The New Interpreter's Dictionary of the Bible* (Nashville, Tenn.: Abingdon Press), published in 2007 in five volumes, with contributors from some forty countries around the world, women and men, Catholic, Protestant, and Jewish scholars. The set is accompanied by a CD ROM. Still very important as well is *The Anchor Bible Dictionary* (New York: Doubleday, 1992) in six volumes, also available on CD ROM. Still unsurpassed for detail are the multivolume *Theological Dictionary of the Old Testament* and *Theological Dictionary of the New Testament*, both published by Eerdmans. A caution is in order in regard to the latter work, however: the original German was begun in the 1930s and does contain passages that speak of Jews in ways that are no longer acceptable in New Testament scholarship.

Resources from the Mothers and Fathers of the Church

After a study of biblical themes and sources, the positive/historical theologian would move on to study the works of the earliest theologians in the church. For a practitioner of theology from a global perspective, these sources are important since the earliest theologians lived in western Asia and North Africa. Although the object of this survey of resources is to present sources in English, it is important to mention at least several major collections of "patristic" texts in their original languages. The most eminent of these are the two collections edited by the nineteenth-century French priest and scholar Jacques-Paul Migne (1800-1875). The first of these collections is of the Greek Fathers (*Patrologia Cursus Completus, Series Graeca*); the second is of the Latin Fathers (*Patrologia Cursus Completus, Series Latina*). Both sets run to well over one hundred volumes each. This is a most amazing scholarly accomplishment, considering that Migne edited a good number of other multivolume works as well. The collections are referred to as "Migne," and are abbreviated PG and PL respectively.

Another important series of "patristic" texts in their original languages is that of the *Corpus Christianorum*. This set, begun in 1951, is the initiative of the Belgian publishing company Brepols and is often considered the contemporary equivalent to Migne. Its collection of early Greek theologians (*Series Graeca*) consists of 65 volumes and its collection of Latin theologians (*Series*

Latina) runs to 186 volumes. A third collection of patristic texts that needs mentioning here is the collection *Sources Chrétiennes*, founded in 1943 by Jean Daniélou, Claude Mondésert, and Henri de Lubac as part of their project of *ressourcement*. The collection is ongoing, but has already reached over five hundred volumes. Each volume is a critical edition of the original language with a French translation printed on the facing page, although some authors (e.g., those writing in Armenian) have been published only in translation.

There are three collections of "patristic" literature in English. The first is the nineteenth-century "Ante-Nicene Fathers" and the "Nicene and Post-Nicene Fathers." These volumes are available online on the Web page of The Ethereal Library: http://www.ccel.org/fathers.html. The second collection is entitled "The Fathers of the Church," and is published by The Catholic University of America. This ongoing series has produced thus far well over one hundred volumes. Third, Paulist Press publishes the series "Ancient Christian Writers," which now consists of some sixty volumes.

For excellent surveys of "patristic" times, the first volume of Jaroslav Pelikan's five-volume *The Christian Tradition: A History of the Development of Doctrine* (Chicago/London: University of Chicago Press, 1971) is a true classic. A wonderful feature of this work is that the text appears in a two-thirds width column on the right side of the page, and the left side of each page gives citations from primary sources so that the researcher can refer to the original text. The first volume as well of Justo González's *A History of Christian Thought* in the revised edition (Nashville, Tenn.: Abingdon Press, 1987) is also excellent. Three other classic "patristic" surveys that should be mentioned are J. N. D. Kelly's *Early Christian Doctrines* (San Francisco: Harper & Row, 1978) and *Early Christian Creeds* (New York: Continuum, 2006), and G. L. Prestige's *God in Patristic Thought* (London: SPCK, 1969 [1st ed., 1936]). The first part of the first volume of the monumental *Creeds and Confessions of Faith in the Christian Tradition*, edited by Jaroslav Pelikan and Valerie Hotchkiss (New Haven/London: Yale University Press, 2003) contains creeds from the earliest days of the church and is truly an invaluable collection.

I pointed out in chapter 5 that there is growing scholarship around the presence and contribution of women in the earliest centuries of the church. Much of the evidence of this can be accessed in the first volume of Mary Malone's *Women and Christianity* (Maryknoll, N.Y.: Orbis Books, 2000). The first pages of Barbara J. MacHaffie's *Her Story: Women in Christian Tradition* (Philadelphia: Fortress Press, 1986) also tell this story, and the companion volume that she edited, *Readings in Her Story: Women in Christian Tradition* (Minneapolis: Fortress Press, 1992), provides excerpts from texts by and about women in the early church. Kevin Madigan and Carolyn Osiek's groundbreaking study, *Ordained Women in the Early Church: A Documentary History* (Baltimore: Johns Hopkins University Press, 2005) is another important source of texts by and about women and their crucial role in the first centuries of Christianity.

The History of Theology

After an investigation of the scriptural and "patristic" traditions, a historical study of a particular theological theme should investigate how other important theologians in the Christian tradition—for example, Anselm of Canterbury, Thomas Aquinas, Bonaventure, Orthodox theologian Gregory Palamas (1296-1359), Martin Luther, John Calvin (1509-1564)—have dealt with the topic. In order to discover the relevant texts one might want to consult some of the histories of doctrine that have been published. We have already mentioned Jaroslav Pelikan's massive five-volume study *The Christian Tradition* and Justo González's *A History of Christian Thought*. Besides these, Justo González has published two shorter histories of doctrine. The first, *Christian Thought Revisited: Three Types of Theology*, rev. ed. (Maryknoll, N.Y.: Orbis Books, 1999), is written with a view toward understanding Latin American liberation theology. The second, *A Concise History of Christian Doctrine* (Nashville, Tenn.: Abingdon Press, 2005), surveys the history of doctrine in chapters that deal with themes such as "creation," "culture," "God," "salvation," and "tradition." This is an approach used as well in two very helpful older surveys of Christian doctrine: U.S. Anglo William Placher's *A History of Christian Theology: An Introduction* (Philadelphia: Westminster Press, 1983) and German theologian Bernhard Lohse's *A Short History of Christian Doctrine: From the First Century to the Present* (Philadelphia: Fortress Press, 1966). British Evangelical theologian Alister McGrath has a long section on the history of theology in his *Christian Theology: An Introduction*, 4th ed. (Malden, Mass./Oxford/Carlton, Australia: Blackwell, 2007), as does Aidan Nichols in his introduction to theology that we have quoted frequently in this book, *The Shape of Catholic Theology: An Introduction to Its Sources, Principles, and History* (Collegeville, Minn.: Liturgical Press, 1991). Finally, I might mention a more popular yet still substantial history of doctrine, Christopher M. Bellitto's *Ten Ways the Church Has Changed* (Boston: Pauline Books and Media, 2006). Bellitto surveys the development of themes like the church's organization, the sacraments, and the papacy through six periods of church history.

The Liturgy

As we have said in the section of chapter 5 on the "monuments of tradition," an important source of theological investigation is the *theologia prima*, or first-level theology, that is found in liturgical texts. Some histories of liturgy that can point the scholar toward the relevant themes and texts are Herman Wegman (German), *Christian Worship in East and West: A Study Guide to Liturgical History* (New York: Pueblo; Collegeville, Minn.: Liturgical Press, 1985); Marcel Metzger (German), *History of the Liturgy: The Major Stages* (Collegeville, Minn.: Liturgical Press, 1997); Italian liturgist Éric Palazzo, *A History of Liturgical Books: From the Beginning to the Thirteenth Century* (Collegeville, Minn./

New York: Liturgical Press, 1998); and Geoffrey Wainwright and Karen B. Westerfield Tucker, *The Oxford History of Christian Worship* (New York: Oxford University Press, 2006). There are many histories of the Eucharist, but one of the best and most accessible is Edward Foley's *From Age to Age: How Christians Celebrated the Eucharist* (Chicago: Liturgy Training Publications, 1991), which combines text and illustrations. An important source as well for liturgical history is *The New Dictionary of Sacramental Worship* (Collegeville, Minn.: Liturgical Press, 1990), edited by Peter E. Fink. This dictionary is available also on a CD ROM, which includes several other dictionaries as well that should also be helpful to the historical theologian: *The New Dictionary of Theology* (ed. Joseph A. Komonchak, Mary Collins, and Dermot A. Lane; Collegeville, Minn.: Liturgical Press, 1987), *The New Dictionary of Catholic Spirituality* (ed. Michael Downey; Collegeville, Minn.: Liturgical Press, 1993), *The New Dictionary of Catholic Social Thought* (ed. Judith A. Dwyer; Collegeville, Minn.: Liturgical Press, 1994), and James T. Bretzke, *Consecrated Phrases: A Latin Theological Dictionary* (Collegeville, Minn.: Liturgical Press, 2000).

The Magisterium

Catholic scholars who study the development of a doctrine or theological theme need also to investigate that doctrine/theme's treatment by the church's magisterium. Francis Sullivan points out that because a complete collection of the church's teachings would fill a library, "the student of theology will need to have at hand a manageable collection of the most significant of these documents."[6] In 1854 the German theologian Heinrich Denzinger published the first edition of such a "manageable" collection entitled *Enchiridion Symbolorum Definitionum et Declarationum de Rebus Fidei et Morum* (handbook of creeds, definitions, and declarations concerning faith and morals). The book has gone through thirty-seven editions in the century and a half of its existence, the latest done by German theologian Peter Hünermann, who for the first time provided a vernacular (German) translation of the Greek and Latin texts of the original. Although there have been English translations of "Denzinger" (as it is commonly called), the best one—done according to themes and not chronologically as in the original—is a volume edited by German Josef Neuner and Belgian Jacques Dupuis, both of whom taught in India and originally edited Denzinger for their Indian students. The book is entitled *The Christian Faith in the Doctrinal Documents of the Catholic Church*, 7th rev. and enl. ed. (Bangalore: Theological Publications in India, 2001; New York: Alba House, 2001). "Denzinger" is referred to as DS in most theological publications, even after Hünermann's edition, according to the major revision by Adolf Schönmetzer in the 1960s. Neuner and Dupuis' edition is referred to as ND.

In 1990 a two-volume English translation (together with the original languages, and where necessary, a Latin translation) of the decrees of all the ecumenical councils from Nicaea (325) to Vatican II (1962-1965) was published under the editorship of British church historian Norman Tanner (the original edition was edited by the Italian Giuseppe Alberigo): *The Decrees of the Ecumenical Councils* (London: Sheed & Ward; Washington, D.C.: Georgetown University Press). In 2006 the Belgian publisher Brepols began publishing a new edition, in Latin, of the decrees of the ecumenical councils, and this will most likely be considered the standard version in years to come. It is entitled *Conciliorum oecumenicorum generaliumque decreta.* A collection of the papal encyclicals (*The Papal Encyclicals*, 5 vols. [Wilmington, N.C.: McGrath Publishing, 1981]), edited by Claudia Carlen (1906-2004), is a collection of all the encyclicals, from the first by Pope Benedict XIV in 1740 until John Paul II's 1981 encyclical *Laborem Exercens.* To complete the papal encyclicals until the present day, the Vatican Web site (vatican.va) is a treasury of documents of the magisterium, including all the documents of Vatican II, the *Catechism of the Catholic Church*, and papal documents going back to Leo XIII (who reigned from 1878 to 1903). Two short and accessible histories of the ecumenical councils have been written by Norman Tanner (*The Councils of the Church: A Short History* [New York: Crossroad, 2001]) and Christopher M. Bellitto (*The General Councils: A History of the Twenty-One Church Councils from Nicaea to Vatican II* [New York/Mahwah, N.J.: Paulist Press, 2002]).

For scholars who are investigating the documents of the Second Vatican Council there are three major texts in English that I would recommend here, although the literature in all languages is extensive. First, there is the five-volume *Commentary on the Documents of Vatican II* (New York: Herder & Herder, 1967) edited by German theologian Herbert Vorgrimler. What is particularly valuable about this collection is that many if not all the commentaries were written by theologians (all male) who were *periti*, or theological experts, at the council. Beginning in 1995, Orbis Books published the English translation of editor Giuseppe Alberigo's massive five-volume *History of Vatican II* under the editorship of U.S. Anglo Joseph Komonchak. The final, fifth volume was published in 2005. Under the editorship of Christopher M. Bellitto, Paulist Press published a set of new commentaries on the documents of Vatican II by a number of noted scholars from the United States, England, Ireland, and Australia. The series is entitled "Rediscovering Vatican II," and the eight volumes in the series were published between 2005 and 2009. What is helpful in this work is that each volume follows the same pattern of (1) the history of the document under study, (2) a summary of its contents, (3) a survey of how it was implemented in the forty intervening years, and (4) the state of the questions that the document raised.

Scholarship on the magisterium, as readers will recognize, has been largely Eurocentric. However, especially in the past several decades, there has been a good bit of teaching by the local magisterium of bishops. A collection of the teachings of the Asian bishops is found in three volumes published by Claretian Publications in Manila, Philippines, under the title *For All the Peoples of Asia*. The first volume is edited by Filipinos Catalino G. Arévalo and Bishop Gaudencio Rosales; the second and third volumes are edited by German Franz-Joseph Eilers, a long-time missionary to the Philippines. The papers of the 1968 Latin American Bishops' Conference at Medellín, Colombia, were published by the United States Catholic Conference in 1970 under the title *The Church in the Present-Day Transformation of Latin America*. Orbis Books published the papers of the meetings of the Conference of Latin American Bishops at Puebla, Mexico (*Puebla and Beyond*, 1979), and Santo Domingo, Dominican Republic (held in 1992, published as *Santo Domingo and Beyond* in 1993).

Church History

The study of Scriptures, the "patristic" literature and history of theology, the documents and artifacts of the liturgy, and the documents of the magisterium should all take place in the context of understanding the historical context. This only a study of church history—in the context of broader secular history—can provide. Today many scholars prefer to speak of the "history of the world Christian movement" in recognition of the facts both that the history of Christianity at times goes beyond a history of the official church and that Christianity is truly a global reality. Two of the best histories that take this new perspective into account are the two-volume *History of the World Christian Movement* by Dale T. Irvin and Scott W. Sunquist (a U.S. Anglo with long experience as a missionary in Malaysia), published by Orbis Books in 2001 and 2009, and *Christianity: A Short Global History* (Oxford: OneWorld, 2002) by the highly respected U.S. Anglo "patristic" scholar and historian Frederick W. Norris. For histories written from a female/feminist point of view, theologians should consult the three volumes of Irish-Canadian historian Mary Malone, *Women and Christianity* (Maryknoll, N.Y.: Orbis Books, 2001, 2002, and 2003), and New Zealand theologian Susan Smith, *Women in Mission: From the New Testament to Today* (Maryknoll, N.Y.: Orbis Books, 2007).

The study of the World Christian Movement recognizes that much of that history is composed of the history of the church's mission, and so "church history" has begun to merge today with "mission history." An attempt to connect the history of doctrine and the history of the World Christian Movement is Anglo scholars Stephen Bevans and Roger Schroeder's *Constants in Context: A Theology of Mission for Today* (Maryknoll, N.Y.: Orbis Books, 2004). Much of the history of doctrine as well was forged in dialogue with churches outside Europe after the era of European discovery and exploration in the late fifteenth and early sixteenth centuries. Scholars in Latin America have formed a Commission for the Study of Church History in Latin America (CEHILA), and in 1992, under the leadership of Argentinian Enrique Dussel, a volume was published in English translation entitled *The Church in Latin America 1492-1992* (London: Burns & Oates; Maryknoll, N.Y.: Orbis Books). This volume is the work of over twenty Latin American and Caribbean historians and has a massive "Sources and Bibliography" section. The work of German historian Georg Evers entitled *The Churches in Asia* has been translated into English and published by ISPCK in Delhi, India. While the focus of this book is on Asian Christian communities after 1945, the study of each country begins with a historical overview and is prefaced by an ample bibliography. In 2000 Cambridge University Press published *A History of the Church in Africa* by the late Swedish scholar and long-time African missionary Bengt Sundkler (1909-1995) and British historian Christopher Steed. Nigerian Ogbu Kalu (d. 2009) has edited *African Christianity: An African Story* (Trenton, N.J./Asmara, Eritrea: Africa World Press, 2007), written mainly by Africans. Although it focuses chiefly on the history of the Protestant churches in the Pacific, Ian Breward's five-hundred-page *History of the Churches in Australasia* (Oxford: Oxford University Press, 2004) is certainly an authoritative work of the history of the church in this area.

Investigating Auxiliary Fields
During their investigations in a particular theological theme, theologians often need to investigate information found in fields auxiliary to systematic theology, such as philosophy, the history of art and architecture, or the social sciences. Listing sources in this area would certainly take us away from the main focus of this book and this chapter, but mention can be made of some of the leading works in these fields. If theologians are looking for information in the area of the history of religions or comparative theology, a good start for survey articles and bibliography would be the fifteen-volume second edition of *The Encyclopedia of Religion* (Detroit: Thomson Gale, 2005). The first edition of this extensive work was edited by the legendary historian of religion Mircea Eliade and was published in 1986; this second, updated edition is edited by Lindsay Jones. Edward Craig has edited the *Routledge Encyclopedia of Philosophy* (London/New York: Routledge), in ten volumes. This would also be a source for non-Western philosophies. A place to start for an inquiry into the history of art is the "Timeline of Art History" offered by New York's Metropolitan Museum of Art at http://www.metmuseum.org/toah/splash.htm. This site provides samples of art from around the world at all time periods and leads the inquirer to other source material as well. Dan Cruickshank has edited and updated the twentieth edition of *Sir Banister Fletcher's A History of Architecture* (Oxford: Architectural Press, 1996). This was originally published in 1896. Finally, let me mention the eighteen-volume *International Encyclopedia of the Social Sciences* (New York: Macmillan Company/Free Press, 2008), edited by David L. Sills. In 1991, Sills and Robert K. Merton issued volume 19, which is a collection of quotations. There is also an online version available.

Contemporary Systematic Theologies

As a theologian comes near to the end of "listening" to the theological tradition (*auditus fidei*), she or he might consult some contemporary systematic theologies to discover what contemporary thinkers are saying about the theme under investigation. Catholic theologians should always inquire what the thinking of German theologian Karl Rahner might be. He is debatably the most important Catholic thinker of our times, even though he died over a quarter century ago (some would argue that the "greatest" is the Canadian Bernard Lonergan), and has written on almost every topic in systematic theology. See the twenty-three volumes of his *Theological Investigations* (published by various publishers from 1961 until 1992) and his full systematic theology entitled *Foundations of Christian Faith* (New York: Seabury, 1978). One relatively recent Catholic systematic theology is the two-volume work by multiple authors (men and women but all from a more classical perspective), edited by Francis Schüssler Fiorenza and John Galvin (*Systematic Theology: Roman Catholic Perspectives* [Minneapolis: Fortress Press, 1991]). Perhaps the most important systematic theology produced in the last several decades is the three-volume work by Douglas John Hall, a member of the United Church of Canada. Hall has attempted to articulate a systematic theology from a North American perspective and he has named his volumes *Thinking the Faith* (Minneapolis: Fortress Press, 1989), *Professing the Faith* (1993), and *Confessing the Faith* (1996). A one-volume systematic theology from a more global and interreligious perspective is Ninian Smart and Steven Konstantine's *Christian Systematic Theology in a World Context* (Minneapolis: Fortress Press, 1991). A systematic theology from a Latin American, liberation theology perspective is the volume edited by Jon Sobrino and Ignacio Ellacuría entitled *Mysterium Liberationis: Fundamental Concepts of Liberation Theology* (Maryknoll, N.Y.: Orbis Books, 1993); the late Catherine Mowry LaCugna (1952-1997) edited a fine systematic theology from a feminist perspective entitled *Freeing Theology: The Essentials of Theology in Feminist Perspective* (San Francisco: HarperSanFrancisco, 1993).

Dictionaries and Encyclopedias

More generally, there are a number of important dictionaries and encyclopedias that theologians can consult. I will list a few of the most important here to close this section on positive/historical theological investigation. A standard theological encyclopedia for the last four decades has been *Sacramentum Mundi: An Encyclopedia of Theology* (New York: Herder & Herder; London: Burns & Oates, 1968). This work, which runs to six volumes, is edited by Karl Rahner and has contributions by all the leading German theologians of the time of Vatican II. Always important is *The Catholic Encyclopedia*. The original edition, in seventeen volumes, was published at the turn of the twentieth century, but some research experts believe that it is still unsurpassed in some areas.

It can be found on line at http://www.newadvent.org/cathen/index.html. A new edition, published in 1967 brings the researcher up to date with the theology of Vatican II (New York: McGraw Hill), and an even newer edition was published in 2003, in fourteen volumes (Detroit: Thomson Gale; Washington, D.C.: Catholic University of America Press). This newer version is also available on line by subscription.

Theological Reflection: The Intellectus Fidei

Having investigated *what* the church believes about a particular theological theme in terms of its history, its development, its current status among believers, and the seriousness with which the church teaches it, the theologian now turns to trying to *understand* the doctrine more deeply, to appropriate it for herself or himself, and to find ways to communicate the doctrine to others. This is the moment of theological reflection, or to use the more classical term, speculative theology.

When we hear the word "speculation" we often think of a process that's somewhat risky, somewhat abstract, or perhaps a matter of guesswork. We speak, for example of speculating on the stock market or we say things like "well, it might be true, but I think it's only speculation." When one thinks of speculating in theology she or he might associate this idea with the process of constructing abstract arguments, doing theology in an "ivory tower," or talking about things that have nothing to do with common, ordinary life or pastoral practice. The classic theme of speculative theology, people often think, is the supposed Western medieval question: How many angels can dance on the head of a pin?

"Speculative theology," as we understand it here, however, has a rather *technical* meaning in theology. It is, as we have said, that moment in theological investigation when theologians seek to understand a particular doctrine or theological theme in a way that makes sense of it in terms of their own time or their own culture. The Latin root of "speculation" is "specula" or "watch tower"—which *could* be an "ivory tower," but it could also be a vantage point from which to see the "big picture."[7] I personally like to play with the etymological root of "speculation" and link it to the Latin "speculum," which means "mirror"—and so "speculation" is looking at a theological theme as it is reflected in the "mirror of life."

The point is that "speculation" does not have to be obtuse or abstract, but very practical or pastoral in its ultimate intent. As Walter Kasper once put it, "To state it in methodological terms: dogmatic theology has exegesis as its starting point and missionary proclamation as its goal."[8] As we move through positive to speculative theology, in other words, the goal of doing theology is ultimately to be at the service of the church and its mission. In the same way,

Bernard Lonergan insists that the final goal of theologizing, although it goes through a rigorous journey of positive research and disciplined reflection, is the *communication* of the results of this process. In Lonergan's own words:

> After *research*, which assembles the data thought relevant, and *interpretation*, which ascertains their meaning, and *history*, which finds meanings incarnate in deeds and movements, and *dialectic*, which investigates the conflicting conclusions of historians, interpreters, researchers, and *foundations*, which objectifies the horizon effected by intellectual, moral, and religious conversion, and *doctrines*, which uses foundations as a guide in selecting from the alternatives presented by dialectic, and *systematics*, which seeks an ultimate clarification of the meaning of doctrine, there finally comes . . . the eighth functional speciality, *communications*.
>
> It is a major concern, for it is in this final stage that theological reflection bears fruit. Without the first seven stages, of course, there is no fruit to be borne. But without the last fruit the seven are in vain, for they fail to mature.[9]

In many ways, we can say that the "speculative" aspect of theology is actually more accessible to the ordinary believer than is the first aspect of historical investigation or positive theology. Lonergan refers to the abstract meaning of speculation when he speaks of systematic theology, but he denies that this moment of theology is abstract and impractical: "The systematic theology we advocate is really quite a homely affair."[10] One needs a lot of training to do accurate historical investigation, but any Christian can reflect in some way on the *meaning* of a particular doctrine in the light of his or her faith—and this might best be done, as we pointed out in chapter 4, in the context of community. The more one can "befriend the tradition," as James and Evelyn Whitehead put it, the more solid one's theology is. But this does not exclude the fact that our minds and hearts naturally want to understand what we believe more and more deeply, and connect it to our daily lives. It is this dynamic that we speak of when we speak of this second movement in theology as "theological reflection" or "speculation."[11]

Latourelle suggests that there are three general approaches to this second "speculative" moment of theological reflection: understanding, systematization, and judgment. We'll look briefly at each one of these.

Understanding

In its Dogmatic Constitution on the relationship between faith and reason (*Dei Filius*), Vatican Council I laid out what have become three classic ways that our theological reflection can come to an understanding of the mysteries to which doctrinal expressions attempt truly yet always inadequately to capture. These are (1) "from the analogy with the objects of [reason's] natural knowledge," (2) "from the connection of these mysteries with one another," and (3) from the connection of the particular doctrine under reflection "with our ultimate end" (DS 3016; ND 132).

The first of these ways, says Australian Anne Hunt, is by far the most used of the three.[12] Vatican I, I believe, uses the term "analogy" in a loose sense in that what it says could apply as well to the terms "simile" and "metaphor." All of these "figures of speech," as they are known technically, proceed toward an understanding of one thing by comparing with another, either explicitly (as with a simile—"I slept like a log," "he looks like Michael Jordan"), or implicitly (as with metaphors and analogies—"you're a prince to do this," "I had a deep sleep last night"). What is common in all three figures of speech is that understanding comes in a flash of recognition of similarities-in-difference, that something unlike another can lead one to understand that other thing. I am not a log, for example, but the solidness of the log expresses the depth of sleep I experience; sleep has no depth, but that expresses how well I slept. The difference between a simile or metaphor and an analogy is that in a simile or metaphor there is a consciousness of an unspoken "but not." My friend is a "prince" to help me, but of course he is not, literally, a prince, but a good friend.

As we move toward understanding a doctrine in theology, we could use all of these "analogical" ways. Legend has it that when St. Patrick evangelized Ireland, he used the simile of the shamrock to explain God's trinitarian nature: "God is like a shamrock. Just like the shamrock has three parts to the one leaf, this is the way God is—one nature, three persons." In her wonderful book *Models of God*, U.S. feminist Sallie McFague speaks of God in the metaphors of "Mother," "Lover," and "Friend." She reflects on what these words mean as we experience them in our lives, and her reflections take us deep into the reality of God and God's creative, passionate, and abiding love for us. But at the same time, God is *not* a mother—to use other metaphors that help us understand God's Mystery, God is a father, a rock. And God is not a lover and/or friend, but a coach, a dance, a stranger, a compassionate adversary, or fertile emptiness.[13] Thomas Aquinas tried to come to a deeper understanding of God through speaking of God as wise, or God as good—even though these words (as one of my teachers once explained it) are like arrows that hit a target but *never* hit the bull's-eye. Our own discussion about the nature of revelation was based on the analogy between the mystery of revelation and the mysterious nature of human relationships.

Much of the theology that is done in particular contexts is a search for good metaphorical or analogical language to express a local experience of faith adequately. African Christology has tried to make use of African images and experiences. Jesus is imaged, for example, as a master of initiation, or as an ancestor, healer or liberator,[14] and as theologians reflect on what these things mean in their own contexts, people can come to an understanding of who Jesus is for them. Filipino theologian José M. de Mesa tries to probe the mystery of Christ's resurrection by using the Pilipino (the Philippines' national language) term *pagbabangong-dangal*, roughly translated as "the raising up of one's honor."[15] And the word "liberation" is the "root metaphor" or analogy for Latin American theology that has been done over the last thirty-five years. "Liberation" is the way many Latin Americans—even today, despite significant changes in the Latin American context—understand salvation, image the church (community of liberation), and speak of the ministry of Jesus.[16]

In the introduction to this book, I made the point that the Christian doctrinal tradition is not a mere list of facts or a "laundry list" of what Christians believe. Rather, I said, all these doctrines are interconnected one with another, and one explains all of them and all explain each of them. In fact, the way that they are arranged—in terms of starting point and sequence—serves to explain the entire Christian mystery. This is why we speak of *systematic* theology: because theology is not about a list of doctrines but about a *system*.

It is this reality that is the basis for what Vatican I names as the second way we can approach an understanding of a particular doctrine. Since each doctrine is a way to explain the other, attempting to see how this is true is to engage in a deeper understanding. We understand the doctrine of the church through an understanding of the communion and mission of God as such, as Trinity. We further understand it by understanding how Jesus' two natures of human and divine are reflected in the church's all-too-human aspects but also its mystery as the foretaste, sign and instrument of God's reign. Anne Hunt's book on the Trinity in this series of "theology in global perspective" is a good example of how this form of theological reflection can work. Hunt proposes to understand the trinitarian nature of God by showing the connection between this foundational doctrine and other Christian doctrines—"Christology, creation, grace and the moral life, ecclesiology, the paschal mystery and soteriology, the world religions, spirituality and worship, and eschatology." She speaks of this method in the context of "faith seeking understanding" as "faith seeking connections."[17]

In many ways the third way of understanding in theological reflection—the connection with our ultimate end—is part of the second way we have just discussed. This way of understanding is a reflection on the *eschatological* implications of a doctrine, and the cluster of doctrines around the theme of "eschatology" ("the last things"—the Reign of God; the theology of history; the theology of death; and the theology of purgatory, heaven, and hell) are indeed doctrines. However, there is a particular dimension to these doctrines that sets them apart, since they refer not just to realities outside of us (the creation of the world, the nature of Christ, the mission of the church) but to realities that concern us very personally.

In this way of approaching theological understanding, we might come to a deeper appreciation of grace if we understand it, as did Thomas Aquinas, as "the seed of future glory."[18] Our relationship with God *now*, when we are in the "state of grace" will not be qualitatively different from the "beatitude" we will have in heaven or in the fully inaugurated Reign of God, since grace is really about relationship. As mentioned above as well, it is from the church being the already-not-yet reality of the coming Reign of God that it can be said to be a mysterious, divine reality. Or we may come to understand our own future in the light of Mary's Assumption, body and soul into heaven. We will be like she is now—fully ourselves, in our bodily natures (whatever, of course, they will look like!).

So a first way to engage in theological reflection is to find ways to "understand" a doctrine more fully, using our reason, using our experience, using our culture and our social location, and using the other doctrines in the Christian symbol system. But Latourelle suggests that there are other ways to approach an understanding of the doctrines we have established through our historical research.

Systematization

This approach is similar to the second and third ways of "speculating" as explained above. Again, it is important to recognize that the doctrines Christians believe are a system and so are all interconnected with one another. In this approach of coming to an understanding, the theologian attempts to understand one doctrine by placing it in the context of an overarching system, or, in other words, interpreting it through a "root metaphor." The great German-American theologian Paul Tillich, for instance, uses the basic experience of human alienation and God's coming into human life with New Being to construct his systematic theology. Every doctrine is explained in the light of these two dialectical concepts. Karl Rahner's very systematic thought is based on his analysis of the human person's radical openness to the transcendent as "Spirit in the World," and the fact that such openness is already God's gift of grace. He understands every Christian doctrine as a facet of that larger and foundational insight. What we said about the theology of liberation above might also be seen here as a way to understand a doctrine. Some Filipino theologians propose that basic to any coherent Filipino theology is the concept of *loob*—basically untranslatable, but standing for the true self, the "inside" of a person.[19] To give a another example from Asia, in 1995 the Theological Advisory Commission of the Federation of Asian Bishops' Conferences published a lengthy document on the theology of harmony. The commission wrote the document with the conviction that "the Asian search for harmony . . . will bring about a distinctive Asian theology."[20] The document shows how the Asian understanding of harmony—which Christians share with Asian peoples of other faiths—can help in a truly Asian understanding of doctrines such as the Reign of God, the redemptive activity of Jesus, and the church and its mission. Systematizing theology around this theme seems to be a very promising way to look into the "mirror of life" in Asia.

Judgment

The third way that we can propose for our theological reflection is to bring a particular explanation of a doctrine under scrutiny and judgment. What we do here is to compare a particular explanation or doctrinal expression with something that we already are sure is true. For example, in the beginning of her systematic theology from a feminist perspective, U.S. scholar Rosemary Radford Ruether articulates what she calls the "critical feminist principle." This principle can be stated both positively and negatively and proposes that (negatively) "whatever diminishes or denies the full humanity of women must be presumed not to reflect the divine or an authentic relation to the divine, or to reflect the authentic nature of things, or to be the message or work of an authentic redeemer or a community of redemption." Positively the principle states that "what does promote the full humanity of women is of the Holy, it does reflect true relation to the divine, it is the true nature of things, the authentic message of redemption and the mission of redemptive community."[21] When theologians attempt to match this principle to particular doctrines, the truth or adequacy of these doctrines comes to light.

To give a few examples of this, a comparison of the "critical feminist principle" with the doctrine of God's incomprehensibility and ineffability with which we began this book seems to compare favorably. This is because the statement that no image of God can adequately capture the reality of God lends itself to the idea that God can be just as "adequately" named in female images as in male or neutral images, and so Christians' minds can be nurtured more deeply into the divine mysteries by female images of God such as "mother" or "sister," or images from the Gospels like "baker woman" (Luke 13:20-21), the woman searching for a lost coin (Luke 15:8-10), or a "persistent widow" (Luke 18:1-7).[22] Similarly, feminists level a strong critique against an interpretation of Jesus' suffering and death on the cross that serves to legitimate women's suffering. Often, they say, women would be urged by religious leaders to bear spousal abuse with the motive to "suffer like Jesus on the cross." Some feminists, because of this, reject the cross altogether, whereas others have moved to interpretations of the cross as either God's solidarity with the poor and marginalized of the world, or as a symbol of the creative power of suffering as a conscious choice.[23] Perhaps an even more controversial example of this method of theological reflection at work would be to match current practices of exclusion of women from leadership in the church with the "critical feminist principle."

The idea of using judgment as a way of "speculating" in theology is one that is used, positively or negatively, in many third world contextual theologies. An African theologian, for example, might discern that a particular way of thinking just doesn't work with the African worldview—for example, the seeming isolation that Western theology might impose with some teachings on conscience. In a marvelous story the late missionary/theologian Vincent Donovan tells how at one point in evangelizing a group of Massai tribespeople in Tanzania, he announced that he thought that certain individuals in the group were ready for baptism. The elder in the group, however, disagreed. He said that the whole village had heard the gospel that Donovan had preached, and although some were more open than others, the elder said that all should be baptized because "we believe." He told Donovan that he should baptize everybody in the village or none at all. The judgment about the communal nature of faith and the communal nature of sacramental celebration could be a rich insight into how Africans might more deeply understand these realities.

The twofold movement that we have developed so far in this chapter is, as I have said, a very basic one, and a very traditional one. The movement is simple, based on the human process of understanding—gathering data and then appropriating it. It can be employed simply and even implicitly, as a group tries to grapple with an issue in a session of theological reflection. It can be used by a scholar in a fairly simple way, as in a book review where the reviewer first sketches out what the book says, and then how that book is helpful or not in understanding the faith. But it can also be used in a more complex way, as a theologian or group of theologians works out a full systematic understanding of a theological doctrine or contemporary issue. It can be used in a communal doing of theology, for example, in a theological reflection group; or it can be used by an individual theologian who is in conversation with the community of contemporary theologians or the voices of tradition. In the second, briefer section of this chapter, we will build on this basic method as we reflect on it from the more contemporary view of theology as a reflection on action or "praxis."

DOING THEOLOGY AS CRITICAL REFLECTION ON PRAXIS

Since the late 1960s, what can be called in general the "theology of liberation" has emerged in many parts of the world and has become one of the most vital forces in contemporary theology. It has many varieties—Latin American theology, black theology from the United States or Africa, feminist theology developed by U.S. white women, womanist theology articulated by African American women, *mujerista* theology proposed by some Latina women, Asian theology of liberation, Native American theology . . . and so on. While what is common in all these liberation theologies is their commitment to liberating their oppressed peoples from oppression and their solidarity with them as victims, what they also have in common, and what makes them especially distinctive, is a new *method* of doing theology.

This approach uses the more traditional method of positive and speculative moments we have outlined so far in this chapter, but it goes beyond that method by moving from mere intellectual understanding to an understanding that involves action. As pioneer liberation theologian Gustavo Gutiérrez insists, "The theology of liberation offers us not so much a new theme for reflection as a *new way* to do theology."[24] U.S. Anglo theologians Roger Haight and Robert McAfee Brown (1920-2001) echo this idea when they speak of liberation theology as an "alternative vision" or as doing theology in a "new key." And Uruguayan liberation theologian Juan Luis Segundo speaks of the theology of liberation as the "liberation of theology"—from out of the classrooms and world of the scholars into the world of ordinary people.[25]

Background: A New Way of Knowing

Key to understanding the difference between the more traditional method we have explained in this chapter and the more contemporary method of the various liberation theologies is the insight that *the highest level of knowing (or understanding) is intelligent and responsible doing.* The more traditional theological method we have reflected on up until now understands the theological process more in terms of *intellectual awareness*—that is, theology, ultimately, is a quest for meaning. In this perspective, action comes afterward, when you *apply* theology to concrete pastoral situations. Anselm's classic definition of "faith seeking understanding" in this context is interpreted as "faith seeking *meaning*," with meaning then seeking application.

Liberation theology would basically disagree with this approach, because it insists that theology cannot stop at the discovery of meaning. In fact, intellectual awareness doesn't discover the fullness of meaning at all—that is something that comes in the context of intelligent action, or what the New Testament calls "living" or "doing" the truth (John 3:21; Eph. 4:15). Let me explain this further.

In the mid-1970s, when liberation theology in Latin America was just emerging, one of the principal architects of the movement, Jon Sobrino (a Spaniard who worked in El Salvador) gave a talk in Mexico City in which he argued that any theology that could claim adequacy today needs to come to terms with two moments of thinking that developed in the nineteenth century.[26] The first of these moments is that of the European Enlightenment, when after the philosophies of René Descartes in the seventeenth century and Immanuel Kant in the late eighteenth, it was clear that human knowledge was a *profoundly personal or "subjective" activity*. What this means is that an individual knower actually has a real part in constructing the reality that is known. Knowledge is not of something that is objectively "out there already," in other words, but human knowers in their own historical or cultural conditionedness actually participate in seeing, understanding, and/or knowing what they see, understand, and/or know. I once ran across an example of this from the journals of the great historian of religion Mircea Eliade. Some development workers in African were showing a film in a village on how to dig more sanitary latrines. After the movie the workers asked the people what they saw, and after some hesitation one of them said "We saw a chicken flying." The development workers were shocked—is that all the people saw?—but when they played the film again there was a point in the film when, yes, a chicken did fly across the screen. The people in the village saw not what the Westerners wanted them to see, but what they were conditioned to see—and so saw the chicken and not much else.[27]

Because of the subjectivity of our knowledge, what the Enlightenment insisted on was that we only really *know* something if we have personally come to know it through a personal judgment. In other words, I don't really *know* something unless I can verify it for myself. I know something not simply because my teacher told me, or my parents or anyone else. I know something only when I take personal responsibility for it. And, in the same way, my actions are truly *moral* actions only when I myself have taken responsibility for them—I cannot morally do something simply because my parents told me to do it, or because the pope says to do it, or tradition mandates it. It is a right, moral action only if it is right in my own conscience. As early-twentieth-century Scottish theologian John Oman put it, what was really revolutionary about this first moment of modern consciousness "was the positive assertion that nothing is either true faith or right morality that is not our own; and that, in consequence, external authority is, in principle, an unsound basis, and individual judgement, not merely a right but a duty."[28]

Especially after Kant, theology's positive method of historical research, but especially its speculative method of theological reflection, had to show the meaningfulness of faith and the symbols of faith for human life. It was not enough, in other words, to say "this is what the church teaches"; one must say that it is truly meaningful to believe this teaching, for it enhances *my* life, it makes sense in *our* culture, it makes sense in *today's* world.

In his talk in Mexico City, Sobrino noted that this "turn to the subjective" was extremely revolutionary and certainly changed the nature of theology. However, he said, to stop here in our understanding of how to do theology would be a mistake, because there was in the nineteenth century a *second* revolutionary moment in philosophy. In addition to the moment of the Enlightenment and the turn to subjectivity, we need also to acknowledge a second moment embodied in the ideas of thinkers like Germans Max Scheler (1874-1928) and Karl Mannheim (1893-1947) and the French philosopher

Maurice Blondel (1861-1949)—but especially the German philosopher Karl Marx (1818-1883). The point of these thinkers, in one way or another, was that mere *intellectual knowledge* was not enough for a full understanding of something. The goal of knowledge is not simply the *intellectual understanding* of the world, but ultimately the world's *transformation*. This is perhaps best summed up in the famous sentence in one of Marx's earliest writings: "The philosophers have only interpreted the world in various ways; the point is to change it."[29]

Following from this even more revolutionary insight, says Sobrino, is that what the liberation theologians have discovered is that Christianity or Christian faith is *not primarily a system of personal and world meaning, but a system of personal and world construction, and, where needed, transformation.* Christianity is better described, therefore, not so much as a religion, but as a *way*, and the task of theology is to help Christians *live* that way, and so be a tool to give life to women and men and the structures in which they live. Furthermore, since these structures in many parts of the world and among many peoples are actually *oppressive* structures, the theme of any true Christian theology in these places needs to be the *transformation* or *liberation* of those structures. Theology, then, is not simply about providing *meaning* but about providing *transformation*, and this is why the goal of theology cannot just be right thinking or "orthodoxy," but right acting, or "orthopraxis."

As Sobrino puts it: "Fundamentally, Latin American theology has tried to recover the meaning of the profound biblical experiences concerning what it means to know theologically: to know the truth is to do the truth, to know Jesus is to follow Jesus, to know sin is to take away sin, to know suffering is to free the world from suffering, to know God is to go to God in justice." Commenting on this passage, U.S. Anglo Alfred T. Hennelly says that "the method [of liberation theology] is not to think about but actually to follow the way of Jesus, that is, Christ is 'truth' insofar as he is 'way.'"[30] As the great Argentinian Methodist theologian, José Miguez Bonino put it, for liberation theology "truth is at the level of history, not in the realm of ideas."[31]

With this important background, we can now lay out the method of liberation theology itself.

Foreground: Liberation Method

The method employed in liberation theology can be expressed perhaps most succinctly by describing it as "reflection on action and action on reflection." This constant movement between activity and reflection, each complementing the other, is what Gutiérrez means when he speaks about liberation theology as "critical reflection on praxis."[32] As Robert McAfee Brown puts it, "*Action forces me to look at theory again. . . . And theory forces me to look at action again.* This is a never-ending process."[33] We might imagine the basic movement of the method as a kind of spiral, as in the diagram below:

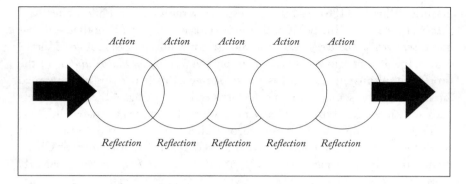

We might say a few words about the term "praxis." Often one hears the term as a kind of trendy way to say "practice" or "action"—that's all well and good, but how does it work in praxis? This is a mistaken use. Praxis, rather, is "action with reflection," both complementing each other and leading the one who acts with reflection to a higher level of knowledge. Praxis is reflected-upon action and acted-upon reflection, both rolled into one. In the diagram above, it is the entire process that is "praxis," not just the "action" part. Praxis is as much interested in reflection and theory as it is in action—the two are absolutely inseparable.

Nevertheless, there is a sense according to Gutiérrez in which reflection and theory are a kind of "second step" or "second act" in liberation theology. The first step—where one begins to do liberation theology—is action: a basic commitment, or a concrete action. As Gutiérrez expresses it, "Theology [i.e., reflection, theory] follows; it is the second step. What Hegel used to say about philosophy can likewise be applied to theology; it rises only at sundown."[34]

In liberation theology, one begins to do theology with a clear faith commitment, because, like all theology, liberation theology is faith seeking understanding. But the faith that is important here is not just in its intellectual sense of accepting something as true and/or meaningful. Rather it is the faith that is a commitment to acting on the vision that God's offer in revelation sets forth—a world of just and right relationships, where all peoples live in the friendship of God and of one another. This is much more a realization of the *credere in Deum* aspect of faith—faith in its behavioral aspect—than in its intellectual and fiduciary aspects of *credere Deum* or *credere Deo*. Liberation theology begins with a *commitment*: a commitment-in-faith to those who are marginalized and oppressed—God's *anawim*—be they the Latin American poor, women in various cultures, Native American peoples, Latinos/as, and so on. As Brazilian Clodovis Boff expresses it, "Theology [i.e., theory, reflection] (not the theologian) comes afterwards. First comes liberative practice."[35]

The second step in liberation theology method is *critical reflection* on some aspect of that life of committed action—a particular incident, an experience, a problem that the community has encountered with local government. This reflection has many forms, and they can intertwine, but it is here that the traditional twofold movement comes into play in the process. The "positive moment" of this reflection usually has two dimensions. First, there is a moment of *social analysis*, where one brings to bear on a particular situation the ideas of psychology, sociology, or perhaps anthropology or economics. Clodovis Boff calls this the moment of "socioanalytic mediation."[36] The point here is to try to discern what is really going on in a particular situation: why people are suffering, why they are not having success at achieving justice, who is really benefitting from this situation. The second dimension of this "positive moment" of reflection is the more narrowly theological one: a rereading of the Scriptures in the light of one's basic commitment, and a rereading of the theological tradition in the light of the same. What, in other words, does revelation have to say to this situation? What might the faith of the church contribute to understanding what is going on? This Boff calls the moment of "hermeneutical mediation."[37]

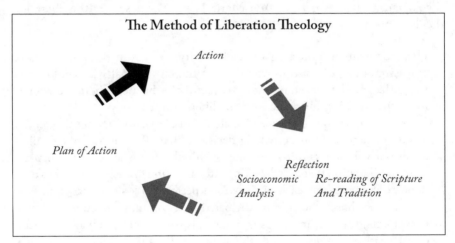

The Method of Liberation Theology

Action

Plan of Action

Reflection
Socioeconomic   Re-reading of Scripture
Analysis   And Tradition

Having analyzed the situation to which one is committed, the method moves to a third step, which is similar to that of theological reflection or speculation. But the ultimate question here is not, What does all this mean? but What can be done? In the light of our commitment, the sociological or economic reality of the situation, and the light that revelation sheds on things, how might we act in the most Christian way? What strategies must we take? How do we need to discipline ourselves, or express ourselves? This is the moment, in Boff's explanation, of "practical mediation."[38] In Boff's words:

> Liberation theology is anything but an inconclusive theology. It emerges from action and leads to action, and the round trip is steeped and wrapped

in the atmosphere of faith from start to finish. From an analysis of the reality of the oppressed, it moves through the word of God, finally to arrive at concrete practice. Back to Action is the motto of this theology.[39]

A fourth and final step is to act according to the plan that had been proposed, to put into motion the strategy that one's committed action and reflection on that action (praxis) have yielded. But this step is "final" only in the sense that it is one circle in the ongoing spiral. Liberation theology may not be "inconclusive," but it is certainly unending. The method that has been described might be illustrated by the diagram on page 161, keeping in mind that this is indeed one circle or cycle in an ongoing spiral.

I think it is important to point out, as we end this section, that in the method of liberation theology, whether it is Latin American, feminist, Latino/a or another variety, the *theology* is in the entire process, not just in the "reflection" step of the process. Gutiérrez and Boff both seem to distinguish between "action" and "theology," but I think they would really agree with how *mujerista* theologian, Cuban-American Ada María Isasi-Díaz describes the liberation theology process:

Hispanic women protesting the lack of city services in the South Bronx, emptying a bag of trash on the desk of the city official who could order the garbage to be picked up more frequently in the area where the women live—that is doing Hispanic women's liberation theology.

But the reflection that leads to such actions, reflection about self-identity, about our participation in making decisions that affect us and our families, about our willingness to risk—doing such reflection is also doing Hispanic women's liberation theology. Meeting after an action to analyze what has been done, to evaluate how each one involved performed assigned tasks, to hold accountable those who have participated in a community action/project—participating in such meetings is doing Hispanic women's liberation theology. To gather, to reflect on how the nature of Hispanic women's involvement either reflects or goes against important values and religious understandings—such reflection is doing Hispanic women's liberation theology.[40]

CONCLUSION

This chapter has focused on two related procedures in the doing of theology. The first procedure, which consists of the movements of positive historical research and "speculative" theological reflection, is a traditional, classical one, but its basic dynamic is not completely different from the more contemporary procedure of the theologies of liberation that we have sketched here as well. What both point toward is that, as procedure, theological method moves according to the processes of human understanding. As we understand, we need first to "get our facts straight" and focus on the data; only then can we proceed to the fuller understanding that deeper reflection and—ultimately—informed decision call for. Theology in its method always remains faith seeking understanding, both in terms of intellectual depth and integrity of action.

QUESTIONS FOR REFLECTION

1. Why do you think that the classical method of "Historical Investigation/ Theological Reflection" is a helpful one in studying and doing theology?
2. This chapter mentions many resources for theological investigation. Go to the library at your school and browse through the theology reference section. Note which resources that have been cited are there, and what other resources there are that might be helpful in learning more about a theological theme or issue.
3. As an exercise in theological reflection, list twenty-five or more metaphors or analogies for God (e.g., Father, Shepherd, Whirlwind). How do these images help you to understand the Mystery that you are reflecting upon?
4. Do you think that the method of "critical reflection on praxis" is an improvement on the classical method explained earlier in the chapter? In what ways?

SUGGESTIONS FOR FURTHER READING AND STUDY

Clodovis Boff, "Epistemology and Method of the Theology of Liberation," in Ignacio Ellacuría and Jon Sobrino, eds., *Mysterium Liberationis: Fundamental Concepts of Liberation Theology* (Maryknoll, N.Y.: Orbis Books, 1993), 57-85.

Neil Darragh, *Doing Theology Ourselves: A Guide to Research and Action* (Auckland, New Zealand: Accent, 1995).

Gustavo Gutiérrez, *A Theology of Liberation* (Maryknoll, N.Y.: Orbis Books, 1973).

Alfred T. Hennelly, "Theological Method: The Southern Exposure," *Theological Studies* 38, no. 4 (December 1977): 718-25.

Rosemary Radford Ruether, *Sexism and God-Talk: Toward a Feminist Theology*, Tenth Anniversary Edition (Boston: Beacon Press, 1993), chapter 1, "Feminist Theology: Methodology, Sources and Norms," 12-46.

Clemens Sedmak, *Doing Local Theology: A Guide for Artisans of a New Humanity* (Maryknoll, N.Y.: Orbis Books, 2002).

Howard W. Stone and James O. Duke, *How to Think Theologically* (Minneapolis: Fortress Press, 1996).

James D. Whitehead and Evelyn Eaton Whitehead, *Method in Ministry: Theological Reflection and Christian Ministry*, rev. ed. (Kansas City, Mo.: Sheed & Ward, 1995).

Lucretia B. Yaghjian, *Writing Theology Well: A Rhetoric for Theological and Biblical Writers* (New York: Continuum, 2006).

8

Contextual Methods

IN OUR LAST CHAPTER we sketched two ways by which theologians can *proceed* when they do theology—each distinct, yet closely related one to the other. In reflecting on procedure we focused on a first way of approaching an understanding of theological method. A very traditional yet basic way of doing theology is to begin with a movement of positive, historical research. One then moves to a process of theological reflection that can proceed (1) by trying more deeply to *understand* the doctrine or issue under consideration by proposing analogies, seeing the connection between various doctrines, or reflecting on the doctrine's or issue's eschatological implications; (2) by trying to see how the matter under consideration fits into or lends itself toward a *system*; or (3) by rendering a judgment about the doctrine's or issues' adequacy by *judging* it in the light of a conviction accepted as true. A more contemporary procedure that builds on this more basic one begins with the commitment to act justly in a particular situation, and then to reflect on this action in the light of sociocultural analysis and a rereading of Scripture and tradition. This having been done, a way of acting is developed and accomplished, and the entire process begins again. This is the method of "critical reflection on praxis" employed especially by the various theologies of liberation that have emerged in the last five decades throughout the world. This method is used as well by the emerging discipline of "practical theology."

In this chapter and the next we will approach the understanding of theological method from the perspective of some of the presuppositions that theologians might have as they begin to do theology. All theologians have certain presuppositions, and these determine many things methodologically. There is no purely "objective" theology. How a person regards the created world and human life—sinful but redeemed, good yet flawed, human nature as wounded or corrupt—makes a significant methodological difference in terms of what sources she or he takes seriously (human experience? the biblical text? the authority of the magisterium?) or where he or she might begin (translating a doctrine in terms of the context? approaching a culture with basic trust?). How a theologian understands revelation—a number of propositions? personal presence? an invitation to be a partner in working for justice?—can shape the way she or he connects one doctrine with another, or sees a doctrine in terms of creation's final end.

Although we might look at a number of these methodologically determining presuppositions (for example, the philosophical presuppositions dealt with by Francis Schüssler Fiorenza and J. J. Mueller in their fine works on method[1]), we are going to limit ourselves to two, both of which are relevant for doing theology from a global perspective. In this chapter we will sketch a number of approaches that theologians might take toward the context in which they theologize. In the next chapter we will focus on the basic worldview of theologians who do theology from the perspective of Catholic Christianity.

THEOLOGY AND CONTEXT

What theologians have come to realize in the decades since the opening of the Second Vatican Council especially is the large extent to which theology has been shaped by the times and by the cultures in which it has been articulated. In fact, many theologians would say that there really is no such thing as "theology"—a kind of "one-size-fits-all," universally valid and universally applicable expression of "faith seeking understanding." Instead, they would say that the only kind of theology that exists is "contextual theology"—theology, in other words, that is specific to a particular place, a particular time, a particular culture. There is only "Ghanaian theology," *mujerista* theology, Asian or European theology, theology done and written by white men, or poor Brazilian women. As I have tried to express more fully in another book, that theology is and must be "contextual"—that is, the attempt to understand Christian faith in terms of a context—is truly a "theological imperative."[2]

This understanding of theology is a relatively new one. Formerly, theology was understood as the reflection in faith of two theological "sources" or *loci theologici*: Scripture and Tradition. However, today, as we have expressed it a number of times in this book, theology also considers *present human experience* as a theological source or *locus theologicus*.

This third source, though, is not just "one more ingredient in the recipe." Not only is experience understood as equal to Scripture and Tradition; in a certain sense it has *priority* over them. Scripture and Tradition, of course, are absolutely normative for Christian faith and theology, as we have emphasized in chapter 4, but what theologians today have become aware of is that, on the one hand, these sources are the records of the faith *experiences* of the Hebrew people, of the early Christian church, and of the Christian people, and, on the other, the "space" in which the witness of Scripture and Tradition continues to live in every age and among every people. U.S. Anglo Evangelical theologian Charles Kraft has said that if a theology is perceived as irrelevant, it *is in fact* irrelevant.[3] What we realize today is that *our* experience in the present—interpreting and interpreted by our biblical and doctrinal tradition—is what ultimately validates *that* experience of the past.

This is why we can define "contextual theology" as a way of doing theology that takes into account two things. First, it takes into account the *experience of the past*, that is, the experience of our ancestors in the faith recorded in Scripture and the doctrinal Tradition both as a source and as a parameter of our Christian life and Christian theologizing. Second, it takes into account the *experience of the present* or, in other words, the *context* in which Christians of a concrete time and place find themselves. This context might be (1) a particular experience that a person or group of persons is having at the present time (e.g., a community of unemployed people in Lima, Peru; a Canadian woman going through a divorce; a village in Indonesia struggling to recover from a natural disaster). It could be (2) the culture—that network of meanings, values, and behaviors which gives shape to a people's world—in which an individual or a community lives, or (3) the social location (e.g., a poor black community in Jamaica, a Filipino member of the Society of the Divine Word) out of which an individual or a community theologizes. Or context could be recognized as the changing world (changed by the forces of globalization, migration, or secularization) that pushes Christians to reevaluate their faith.

What is new, therefore, about contextual theology is that theology is conceived as a dialogue—or as David Tracy would put it, a *mutually critical* dialogue—between the experiences of the past and the experience of the present. Both kinds of experiences are normative, and theology is done by allowing our experience today to be measured, judged, interpreted, and critiqued by the wisdom found in the classical sources, the "classics" of the Christian tradition, and by allowing those "classics" to be measured, judged, interpreted, and critiqued by the happenstances in our lives, by our cultural values, by our struggles and by the epochal changes that are shaping our world.

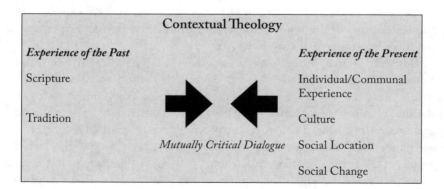

As we shall see in part 4 of this book, however, doing theology in a dialogue with the context is not something that is entirely new. In fact, it is deeply traditional—and part of the tradition. Context certainly played a part in the composition of the Bible. The colorful and anthropomorphic theology of the Yahwist in Israel's monarchical period, for example, differs quite dramatically from the rather liturgically centered and legalistic Priestly theology of the postexilic years; or the Christology implicit in Matthew's Gospel narrative expresses faith in Jesus' lordship from the perspective of the Christian community in Antioch in Syria, in contrast to the high Christology of the Johannine community in Ephesus. The liberal use of Greek philosophy in the work of Origen in the context of academic Alexandria in Egypt contrasts starkly with the Roman lawyer Tertullian's passionate rhetorical question "What does Jerusalem have to do with Athens?" Ephrem the Syrian's theology in hymnody comes out of the culture of the Persian empire in the fourth century C.E., the "Jesus Sutras" are attempts to interpret Christianity in terms of the culture of China in the eighth, and the *Heliand* speaks out of the culture of the Saxon peoples of ninth. The Protestant Reformation is largely unthinkable outside the context of the emerging individual of modernity, as is contemporary ecclesiology without the developments of the European Enlightenment values of human equality, on the one hand, and the appreciation of community so woven into the fabric of African, Asian, Latin American, and Oceanian cultures, on the other.

If we can say today that there really is no such thing as "theology," but only contextual theologies, we need to acknowledge that such has always been the case. We are perhaps more aware of the fact today that contextual theology is a "theological imperative," and that this is really the only way we can do theology. But any theology that was ever a valid theology was so because it was valid for its place and time, and for the people by whom and for whom it was articulated.

While some theologians prefer other terms to name the process we are referring to here—inculturation, local theology, or intercultural theology—the idea in all of these terms is very nearly the same. "Inculturation" is preferred in documents of the magisterium on the universal and local levels, but I prefer the term "contextual theology" because the word "context" points beyond culture or place to include social location (e.g., doing theology out of the experience of women) and social change (e.g., doing theology in the context of migration). What is important, however, is the recognition that theology has always and today must consciously be done in dialogue with women's and men's experience, and that such experience is seen as a privileged, Spirit-filled source ("*locus*") of theology.

MODELS OF CONTEXTUAL THEOLOGY

That theology has to be done contextually today is hardly disputed by contemporary theologians or even by the magisterium.[4] *How* contextual theology is done, however, is a question of considerable debate. One of the biggest issues is how the context functions as a theological source. Is it indeed equal to the other two sources of Scripture and Tradition, or will too much attention to the context work to *betray* the very faith that it seeks to express? Other questions cluster around the *agents* of contextualization. Can theologians outside the context (e.g., Irish missionaries in Kenya, or white feminists speaking for Latinas) do genuine contextual theology? Can professional theologians adequately represent grassroots folk? Or how does a person's basic theological perspective—more optimistic toward the world, or more cautious or suspicious toward it—affect the way theologians dialogue with the church's past and their situation in the present.

Models

Over the years various theologians have tried to answer these questions, both theoretically and concretely, and a number of "models" of contextual theology have been discerned. By models I mean a kind of pattern or template that offers a way of performing a task. To quote Avery Dulles, a model is "a relatively simple, artificially constructed case which is found to be useful and illuminating for dealing with realities that are more complex and differentiated."[5] Models, first of all, are streamlined, *artificially constructed* ways of thinking. Models do not exist as such in "real life," or in actual articulations of theology. However, when we discern a pattern in the way a number of theologians proceed in doing theology, we might find it *useful* to identify that pattern so we can use it in similar situations. Like symbols, to refer to a famous line of U.S. Anglo theologian Reinhold Niebuhr, they should be taken "seriously, but not literally."[6] On the other hand, models are not simply "useful fictions."[7] They do indeed disclose actual features in the matter under investigation, and they are truly disclosive of reality. Models provide a knowledge that is always partial and inadequate, but never false or merely subjective. While, for example, although the atom is not *actually* the kind of "solar system" depicted by Niels Bohr's famous model of the atom with its various "parts" like electrons and protons revolving around a nucleus, it really does—even though not fully—explain atomic structure. Avery Dulles's model of the church as an institution does not in any way capture the full reality of the church as both visible and invisible, human and yet in some way divine (see LG 8). And yet the institutional model points to a truth that cannot be denied as a valid aspect of the church and one that is indeed held by some Christians.

Models may be either *exclusive* or *complementary*. An example of exclusive models would be the U.S. Anglo theologian H. Richard Niebuhr's "ideal types" of the relation of Christ to culture in his classic book *Christ and Culture*.[8] One basically has to decide whether one will operate out of a conviction of Christ's identification with culture, or his opposition to it, or with the model of Christ above culture, Christ and culture in paradox, or Christ as transformer of culture. An example of a complementary model would be Avery Dulles's five models in his book *Models of the Church*.[9] For Dulles, a Christian could work out of a model of the church that is basically institutional, while still recognizing that the church is a mystical communion, or the servant of the Reign of God, a sacrament, a herald of God's Word.

Models *of* something might also be models *for* something. A model might be used, in other words, to demonstrate how several theologians approach, say, an understanding of revelation in distinct yet similar ways. For example, both Karl Rahner and José de Mesa understand revelation in terms of God's personal offer of Godself and *not* as propositional. Each employs the same model *of* revelation. However, Rahner's and de Mesa's model can serve not only to explain how they proceed in doing theology; it can also serve as a model *for* how Filipinos or Tanzanians can do theology. Theirs is a model *of* revelation that others can use in their own theologizing.

Six Models of Contextual Theology

The six models of *contextual theology* we will outline in the rest of this chapter tend to be understood as complementary or inclusive models. One might, for example, work basically with what we will call a "translation model," but be influenced by a "countercultural" perspective as well. In addition, the models *of* contextual theology can also be understood as "models *of*" that other theologians can use—and so are "models *for*" as well. A theologian might recognize that Gustavo Gutiérrez employs the "praxis model," and at the same time use it herself. The six models of contextual theology we will outline have been discerned from the work of contextual theologians and can be useful—especially if used in a complementary or inclusive way—for theologians as they themselves engage the process of constructing a theology that comes from and speaks to their context.

We have spoken of contextual theology as the dialogue in faith between the experience of the *past* that is recorded and preserved in Scripture and the church's tradition and the experience of the *present* that is found in one's *context*—what is happening in one's personal or communal life, one's cultural reality, one's social location—or in the process of change in one's culture or in our world. The *models* of how this process works have been discerned out of the *way* this dialogue takes place according to the basic attitudes one has toward both the past and present. The most "conservative" of the six models, the *countercultural model*, recognizes the importance of context but radically distrusts its sanctity and revelational power. The *translation model* is one that, while certainly taking account of experience, culture, social location, and social change, puts much more emphasis on fidelity to what it considers the essential content of Scripture and Tradition. The most "radical" of the models, the *anthropological model*, will emphasize cultural identity and its relevance for theology more than Scripture or Tradition, which it considers important, but a product of contextually relative theologies that have been hammered out in very particular contexts. The practitioner of the *praxis model* will zero in on the importance or need of social change as she or he articulates her or his faith. The one who prefers the *synthetic model* will attempt the extremely difficult task of keeping all of the elements (past, present, need for transforming action) in perfect balance, while profiting as well from a conversation with Christians from other cultures. Finally, the view of the *transcendental model* focuses not on a content to be articulated but on the person who is articulating. The hope here is that if one is personally authentic in one's faith and in one's being-in-the-world, one will be able to express one's faith in an authentically contextual manner. The chart below offers a kind of "map" of the models. The anthropological model, since it is the model that departs most from traditional theological content, is found on the far left. The countercultural model, since its concern is to challenge the context with the content of Scripture and Tradition, is located on the extreme right, with the other models falling in between—even though the transcendental model floats above all, since it is more concerned with the theologizing subject than with theological content.

It is important to say at the outset that each of these models represents a valid way of doing contextual theology. The question might be raised, however, of the *adequacy* of any of them in a particular context. The *translation model*, for example, might be best used in contexts where the theologian is a guest or where the gospel has been newly preached. The *anthropological model* might find the most resonance in contexts where a people's cultural identity has been repressed or disparaged. The *praxis model* might be most effectively employed in situations of oppression, and the *synthetic model* might be employed where Christianity has taken firm root but still needs to be thought out in terms of a people's contextual reality. I have found that the *transcendental model* is particularly effective in multicultural or intercultural situations, and I would suggest that the *countercultural model* might be the most relevant in the more secularized contexts of Europe, North America, Australia, and New Zealand.

For the sake of clarity, and so that the models can be compared with one another, we will proceed in the same way as we sketch out each model. After offering some alternative names of the model as a possible way of understanding it better, we will briefly discuss the basis that the model has in both Scripture and the church's Tradition. Then we will reflect on the presuppositions the model has in regard to revelation, to Scripture and Tradition, and to context. We will next discuss the actual way that the model under discussion proceeds, and then we will offer a horticultural analogy and a "bumper sticker" catch phrase that summarizes the model. Finally, we will offer a positive and negative critique of the model and mention a few theologians who might exemplify it.

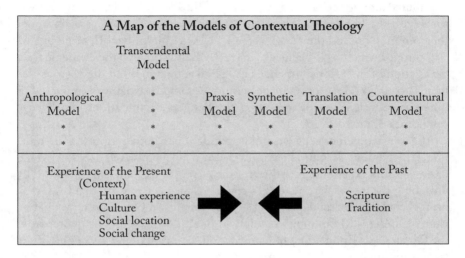

| A Map of the Models of Contextual Theology |

| Transcendental Model |
| * |
Anthropological Model	*	Praxis Model	Synthetic Model	Translation Model	Countercultural Model
*	*	*	*	*	*
*	*	*	*	*	*

Experience of the Present (Context)
  Human experience
  Culture
  Social location
  Social change

Experience of the Past
    Scripture
    Tradition

The Translation Model

When we speak of the *translation model*, we don't have in mind a kind of word-for-word translation, which is almost always awkward and wooden in any language. This is the kind of translation about which Charles Kraft speaks as "formal correspondence." What is needed, rather, is a translation that is creative and idiomatic—what Kraft calls translation by "functional" or "dynamic equivalence."[10] An example of such "dynamic equivalence translation" might be found in the United Bible Society's translation of the Bible into Ilokano, the language spoken by many people in northern Luzon in the Philippines. The original Hebrew in Genesis 1:1-2 speaks of the *ruach elohim* that moves over the surface of the watery chaos. The literal translation of this in English would be the Spirit of God moving over the waters, and indeed the original Ilokano version reads *ti Espiritu to Dios* moved over the waters. The newer, dynamic equivalence version, however, is less literal but much more faithful to the original Priestly author's intention when it translates *ruach elohim* as *ti pannakabalin ti Dios*, or "the *power* of God."

Nevertheless, a main presupposition of the translation model is that there is in Christianity a content that needs to be translated into other languages and other cultural terms. However creative this translation is, this content needs by all means to be preserved. This is why terms like "adaptation" and "accommodation" might also be used to describe the method that the translation model intends to employ. We can "adapt" the gospel to another culture; we can "accommodate" the Christian message in a particular context, but in the process the message we adapt, translate, or accommodate is not affected. In many ways this is the method of contextualization that Vatican II worked with when it spoke of being open to the "treasures [that] a bountiful God has distributed among the nations of the earth." The idea is "to illumine these treasures with the light of the gospel, to set them free, and to bring them under the dominion of God their Savior" (AG 11). Or, as John Paul II wrote in RM 53: "Groups which have been evangelized will thus provide the elements for a 'translation' of the Gospel message (EN 63), keeping in mind the positive elements acquired down through the centuries from Christianity's contact with different cultures and not forgetting the dangers of alterations which have sometimes occurred."

The translation model has an ample foundation in both Scripture and Tradition. Chief among scriptural passages that can be cited is Acts 17:2-31, which narrates Paul's experience in Athens at the Aereopagus. Paul ends up faithfully preaching the gospel, but he tries to couch his message in ways that his Greek hearers could understand. He speaks of the "unknown God" and how what he is proclaiming is whom they worship without knowing it, and he quotes from the Greek poets Epimenides of Knossos and Aratus of Soli.[11] Examples of the translation model in the church's tradition would be Saints Cyril (826-869) and Methodius (827-885), blood brothers who preached the gospel among the Slavs, translated the Bible into Slavonic, and were able to "transpose correctly biblical notions and Greek theological concepts into a very different context of thought and historical experience."[12] Two other famous examples of what we know today of the translation model are the great Jesuit missionaries Matteo Ricci (1552-1610) and Robert de Nobili (1577-1656). Ricci was a missionary to China in the late sixteenth and early seventeenth centuries and adapted Christianity to Chinese culture after mastering the language and the texts of the Taoist and Confucian scholars; de Nobili worked in India in the seventeenth century and attempted to translate the message of Christianity into the terms and values of Hindu culture. One more example from the church's tradition is Pope John XXIII, in his speech at the opening of the Second Vatican Council on October 11, 1962. The pope insisted on both fidelity to the past and openness to the present, because while "it is necessary first of all that the Church should never depart from the sacred patrimony of truth received from the Fathers . . . it must ever look to the present, to the new conditions and new forms of life introduced into the modern world. . . ." And this double fidelity is possible because "the substance of the ancient doctrine of the deposit of faith is one thing, and the way in which it is presented is another."[13]

For those who practice the translation model, revelation tends to be understood as propositional, containing a concrete message. That message is considered supracultural, even though it is expressed in cultural terms. There are, however, many expressions of the message that are not of the essence of the gospel, and so these may be adapted and translated. But the essential revelation cannot be compromised. Because of this, the translation model considers the Scriptures and the doctrinal Tradition both supracontextual and complete. *Supracontextual*, even though, as John XXIII would say, the substance and the way that substance is presented are two different things; *complete*, in that present human experience can add nothing to what has already been said and done in Christ. As the text from Vatican II quoted above indicated, context is regarded as basically good and trustworthy, although there may be aspects in it that need purifying and correcting in the light of the gospel. But the experiences and values of all peoples are worthy vehicles for the gospel.

Practitioners of the translation model speak of proceeding by first finding the essence of the gospel and then "clothing" it with the trappings of the culture or context into which one is translating it. The image often used is that of a grain of wheat or a grain of rice: one must first strip off the husk in order to find the kernel; then one can put on a new "husk" that will carry its meaning in its new context. In order to do this, one must study the context, know it well, master the local language, so that the gospel can be "inserted." In our horticultural image, the translation model would conceive of contextual theology as the theologian bringing seeds to a particular context and planting them there. These seeds are from "outside" the context, transcendent of it, but they will sprout and take root in the context's soil, and in this way become a part of it. As U.S. Anglo Evangelical theologian Bruce Fleming succinctly puts it, the process of contextualization is "putting the gospel into."[14]

Along with the countercultural model on which we will reflect below, this model of contextual theology takes the traditional content of the Christian message most seriously. Its task, while recognizing the importance of communicating the Christian message effectively, is to be at the same time *faithful* to it. It has a positive attitude to the context, even though it recognizes that in some ways it needs to be perfected and healed by the saving grace of the gospel message. Any Christian who has immersed himself or herself in the context into which the gospel is to be inserted can in fact translate that gospel in at least some adequate fashion, and so this is an ideal method for "outsiders" to use in a culture, or for missionaries to use in a situation of first evangelization.

A negative critique of this model of doing contextual theology is its somewhat naive understanding of both gospel message and context in terms of "kernel" and "husk." Is it really possible to get to an "essence of Christianity" in terms of its message? It seems that a notion of revelation that is overly propositional—as we have seen in chapter 1 of this book—is not very helpful, since the *words* of revelation are only the *way* by which God communicates Godself to us. And can a context—an experience, a culture, a social location—be stripped of its qualities to reveal something more basic? Critics of the translation model suggest that one should image an experience not as a grain of wheat or rice, but as an onion. The onion *is* its various layers; the layers do not cover an essential content. Contexts have components that are interchangeable and interconnected, and so we have to be careful in removing one or the other in an arbitrary way.

As we have already seen, Pope John Paul II clearly advocates for a contextual theology that attempts to translate the essence of the gospel without compromising it. As he puts it forcefully in RM 54: "Properly applied, inculturation must be guided by two principles: 'compatibility with the Gospel and communion with the universal Church' (FC 10). Bishops, as guardians of the 'deposit of faith,' will take care to ensure fidelity and, in particular, to provide discernment (EN 63-65), for which a deeply balanced approach is required. In fact, there is a risk of passing uncritically from a form of alienation from culture to an overestimation of culture." Protestant Evangelical theologians, in particular, are attracted to the translation model, both because of its insistence on safeguarding the content of revelation and for its positive and yet somewhat critical attitude toward human experience and context. Examples of such theologians are U.S. Anglos Charles Kraft and David Hesselgrave, African theologian Tite Tiénou, and Malaysian bishop and theologian Hwa Yung.

The Anthropological Model

If the primary concern of the translation model is the preservation of Christian identity while attempting to take the context seriously, the primary concern of the anthropological model is the establishment or preservation of the cultural identity by a person of Christian faith. What is important in this model is the understanding that Christianity is not so much about a particular message or set of doctrines, but is about human persons and their fulfillment. The practitioner of the anthropological model would wholeheartedly agree with Irenaeus's famous assertion that the glory of God is that of human persons fully alive. This model is "anthropological" in two senses: first, in the sense that the center of theology is *anthrōpos*, or the human person; second, in that this model more than any other uses the resources of the social science of anthropology or ethnography. This is why the alternative terms "indigenization" or the "ethnographic model" are apt descriptions of what this model is about.

This model, too, has a firm basis in both Scripture and Tradition. The stories of the Canaanite woman (Matt. 15:21-28) and the Syrophoenician woman (Mark 7:24-30)—which are basically the same story—make the point that this non-Jewish woman's faith actually changes Jesus' attitude toward her. What this might very well indicate is how even Jesus in his full humanity needs to have his horizon expanded beyond Jewish prejudices to the realization of the full implication of his gospel message.[15] If this is the case, those who espouse the anthropological model argue, perhaps our own understandings of the gospel also can be refined as we encounter new situations, other cultures, and others different from ourselves. Another important passage is the famous John 3:16 ("God so loved the world that God sent the only Son").

The world, says the evangelist, is one that is so loved by God that it is *worthy* of incarnation—a sign, say the practitioners of the anthropological model, of the world's goodness and capacity as so loved and graced as to be a place of God's revealing presence. In the tradition we find the important phrase of Justin Martyr, that throughout the world we can find the "seeds of the word" that point to God's presence in human history and human life even before the Word's incarnation.[16] Even though the terms "adaptation" and "accommodation" are used in GS 44, they appear in an important section of the document that is entitled "The Help Which the Church Receives from the Modern World." The entire paragraph is an important foundation for the anthropological model, but the following words are particularly important for its basis in the church's teaching: "With the help of the Holy Spirit, it is the task of the entire People of God, especially pastors and theologians, to hear, distinguish, and interpret the many voices of our age, and to judge them in the light of the divine Word. In this way, revealed truth can always be more deeply penetrated, better understood, and set forth to greater advantage." While AG 11 does seem to gravitate toward the more conservative translation model, it speaks of the need for a "sincere and patient dialogue" with the "treasures a bountiful God has distributed among the nations of the earth"; and in AG 22 we read how the local churches "borrow" "from the customs and traditions of their people, from their wisdom and their learning, from their arts and sciences," and thus make a contribution "to the glory of their Creator, the revelation of the Savior's grace, or the proper arrangement of Christian life."

The anthropological model tends to approach revelation not as a set of propositions to be preserved and guarded but as God's personal presence in history and human lives, offering women and men a life of relationship and friendship (see DV 2). Because of this, it is not so much a matter of *translating* something that is already expressed one way into another way as of listening carefully in faith to the context to see how this presence and relationship might be adequately expressed. Scripture and Tradition are certainly regarded as normative, but they are—like any theological expression of God's presence among us—thoroughly culturally conditioned, and as such are incomplete. We await no further revelation, for all has been given to us in Jesus of Nazareth, but we still have to mine the meaning of what that revelation means, and to do that will take all the riches that the cultures of the world and human experience can offer. Scottish church historian Andrew Walls, who speaks about the "infinite translatability"[17] of the gospel, but whose writings reflect more a sensitivity to the anthropological model, speaks about how, as Christianity extends to include all peoples, the vision of Ephesians 4:13 is fulfilled as our "faith and knowledge" grow into the "full stature of Christ." Context, therefore, is regarded as basically good and trustworthy, holy even, and so, when interpreted in dialogue with Scripture and Tradition, fully their equal as a theological source.

If a theologian employing the translation model would start with the message of Scripture and Tradition and find ways of "putting the gospel into" it, a practitioner of the anthropological model would start from the context and analyze it, listen to it, and discern the ways that God is speaking through it. One studies the context—with all the tools of social sciences like anthropology—in order to "pull the gospel out of it," as an anthropologist friend of mine once put it. It would be like a gardener who realizes that, despite a barren-looking plot, the seeds of beautiful flowers and succulent vegetables have already been planted in the ground and only need watering and cultivation for the garden to produce a surprising and beautiful yield. A powerful and often-quoted passage written by the British missiologist Max Warren sums up the attitude of the approach of this model:

> When we approach a man of another faith than our own it will be in a spirit of expectancy to find how God has been speaking to him and what new understandings of the grace and love of God we may ourselves discover in this encounter.
>
> Our first task in approaching another people, another culture, another religion, is to take off our shoes, for the place we are approaching is holy. Else we may find ourselves treading on men's dreams. More serious still, we may forget that God was here before our arrival.[18]

As the translation model guards the importance of the message of revelation contained in Scripture and Tradition, the anthropological model safeguards the presence of God in the warp and woof of people's lives in their experiences, cultures, and identities. It is able to provide fresh perspectives on Christianity, because it starts where people are. African theologians who study the various African cultures stretch Christology, for example, in new directions when they speak of Christ as master of initiation, or primal ancestor; Filipino theologian Leonardo Mercado raises new questions for theology when he suggests that Filipino faith healers are bearers of new ways of thinking about God's healing power and about the nature of Christian ministry. But this strength of the anthropological model is also its weakness. Its perspective on the goodness of human context is perhaps too naive, and doesn't recognize enough the sinfulness and error into which human beings can fall. There is a tendency as well to romanticize cultural practices and to forget that culture is something that is always changing as it encounters factors that challenge it and even subvert it.

I have already mentioned the name of Leonardo Mercado as an example of a theologian who employs the anthropological model. Through a series of books from the 1970s until today, Mercado has insisted that it is in a study of local culture, especially popular culture, and of local languages, where one finds God's Spirit inspiring the true theology that nourishes people's faith. The task of the theologian is to discover this theology and articulate it.[19] Other examples of theologians who tend to work out the anthropological model are Tanzanian Laurenti Magesa and Chilean and long-time Peruvian missionary Diego Irarrázaval.[20]

The Praxis Model

In many ways we have already reflected in some detail on the praxis model when in chapter 7 we spoke of the method of the theology of liberation as a distinct yet related method to the more traditional twofold movement of historical investigation and theological reflection. All theologies of liberation—Latin American, feminist, black, for example—work out of this third contextual model of doing theology. We speak of the *praxis* model here, however, for two reasons. First, the key insight of this model is the centrality of praxis, which, as we have pointed out, is a combination of *practice*, or action, and reflection on that action in a continuing spiral (it is *not* merely a fancy name for practice!). Second, this method can conceivably be done also in situations where oppression and marginalization do not make up the context in which persons theologize. Many methods of theological reflection on ministry employ the praxis model, but they are done in the context of pastoral care in a parish setting, or in a hospital. James and Evelyn Whitehead, for example, offer a three-step method of theological reflection that begins from practice, moves into a careful reflection on and analysis of this experience, of the culture in which it takes place and the Christian tradition that gives it theological depth, and then moves to a reflection on the possible pastoral implications of that experience and on how one might act more effectively and faithfully in the future.[21] And so, besides the alternate title of "liberation model," the names "situational model" or "theology of the signs of the times" might also help us see how the model functions.

One can point to the entire prophetic tradition in the Scriptures as a foundation for this kind of theologizing. The prophets called the women and men of Israel not just to right thinking or "orthodoxy" but to right acting or "orthopraxy." Isaiah cries out in God's name:

> When you spread out your hands,
>   I close my eyes to you;
> Though you pray the more,
>   I will not listen.
> Your hands are full of blood!
>   Wash yourselves clean!
> Put away your misdeeds from before my eyes;
>   Cease to do evil; learn to do good.
> Make justice your aim: redress the wronged,
>   Hear the orphan's plea, defend the widow.
>   (Isa. 1:15-16)

Or in the powerful words of Micah:

> Will the Lord be pleased with thousands of rams,
>   with myriad streams of oil?
> . . . . .
> You have been told . . . what is good,
>   and what the Lord requires of you:
> Only to do the right and to love goodness,
>   and to walk humbly with your God. (Mic. 6:7a-8)

It is in this prophetic tradition that we read the words of James (1:22): "Be doers of the word and not hearers only, deluding yourselves."

Justo González argues that some of what liberation theologians propose today is already anticipated by the more pastoral theologizing of Irenaeus, in contrast to the more legally oriented theology of a Tertullian, or a more intellectually oriented theology of an Origen.[22] Karl Barth insists that "only the doer of the word is the true hearer."[23]

Revelation in the view of the praxis model may certainly include a concrete message and an invitation to relationship. However, in keeping with the priority of action that the model holds central, revelation is more adequately conceived as a presence of God in the world that beckons to those who believe (*credere in Deum!*) to join God in God's liberating and saving activity within the weave of human and cosmic history. Not only are women and men called to be *friends* of God; they are called to be *partners* as well. Scripture and Tradition, therefore, rather than being simply *vehicles* of revelation are seen to be models of action, calling believers to that partnership, inviting all to the ministry of prophecy. While context can be good and trustworthy, and so offers us the experiences and cultural resources for theologizing adequately, it often needs to be critiqued and called to transformation. The point of theology, to paraphrase that famous phrase of Marx, is not simply to interpret the world, but to change it.

As we explained in chapter 7, the way this method proceeds—in terms of the various kinds of praxis concerns, sometimes distinct but always roughly similar—is to begin from a concrete committed action, then to analyze that action from a socioscientific perspective and a rereading of the tradition in light of that action, and then to formulate a new plan of action as a consequence of that analysis and reflection. This "critical reflection on praxis" is done over and over again in an unending spiral, and the *entire process* is the doing of theology—not, as is sometimes intimated, simply the intellectual moment of reflection. In terms of our ongoing analogy, we can say that engaging in the praxis model is like working in a garden that is always needing hoeing and weeding, because the work never ends. However, this constant practice of tending and watering serves to make one a better gardener as crop after crop is harvested and bunch after bunch of flowers is gathered. The phrase of Jon Sobrino can serve as a short phrase that discloses the whole point of this model: "To know Christ is to follow him."[24]

One of the most positive aspects of this model of doing contextual theology is its strong epistemological basis. What is important for the fullest knowledge is not simply intellectual knowledge of the truth, but a knowledge based on action and reflection on that action (praxis). Another positive factor, and one that recommends this as a model, is the response of theologians and simple people alike to this way of doing theology. If, as Robert Schreiter proposes, one of the criteria for a genuine theology is its impact on other theologies around the world, the impact of the variety of liberation theologies and the emergence of practical theology would point to the model's validity.[25] If there is a negative critique of this model, it might be, as a document from Rome suggested in 1984, that the model in its liberation theology version is perhaps sometimes too influenced by the ideology of Marxist thought.[26] It must be pointed out, however, that this is not at all the case in most theologies influenced by this model.

There are, of course, many practitioners of the praxis model. Among Latin American theologians we can name the "father" of liberation theology, Gustavo Gutiérrez. A leading African practitioner of this model is Cameroonian Jean-Marc Éla, and in Asia we should make mention of the Sri Lankan Aloysius Pieris. Among the leading feminists is German scripture scholar Elisabeth Schüssler Fiorenza, who has taught in the United States for many years. The Latina theologian who coined the term *mujerista* theology is Cuban-American Ada María Isasi-Díaz.[27] Special mention might also be made of the use of the praxis model by members of the Federation of Asian Bishops' Conferences (FABC). In a 1991 theological consultation held by the FABC's Office of Evangelization in Thailand, for example, the participants concluded that "since doing the truth comes before the formulation of doctrine, the Churches in Asia should not await a satisfactory theological answer before going further in the *praxis* of dialogue and proclamation. It is in the systematic reflection on sustained *praxis* that we shall discover what God is saying to the Churches."[28]

The Synthetic Model

While none of the three models that we have sketched so far is ever used exclusively by its practitioners—as we have insisted, these are *models*—the synthetic model that we will outline here is one that consciously tries to combine a translation approach, a stance of listening seriously to the context in which one theologizes, and which takes seriously as well the dynamic epistemology of the praxis model. In addition, it is a model that very deliberately is nourished by reading and exposing itself to other contextual theologies around the globe. This is why we can speak of this model as a "dialogical model." Or, as it compares one theology with another and profits from the similarity-in-difference that it discovers, we can speak of an "analogical model."

The synthetic model might rely for scriptural justification not so much on particular texts, but on the entire process of the formation of the various biblical books into what we now know as the Bible. The Bible came about gradually, through a collection of individual books, each of which was formed in the context of present concerns interacting with contemporary culture, neighboring cultures, concerns for fidelity to the tradition, and neighboring cultures. The synthetic model might rely as well on theories of doctrinal development that understand doctrine as emerging from the complex interaction of Christian faith and changes in culture and society. It could also invoke some passages of the Roman magisterium that try to walk the narrow path between mere adaptation, on the one hand, and an openness to new approaches and forms of expression on the other. Paul VI articulates some important aspects of what we are calling the synthetic model in EN 64:

> The more an individual Church is attached to the universal Church by solid bonds of communion, in charity and loyalty, in receptiveness to the Magisterium of Peter, in the unity of the *lex orandi* which is also the *lex credendi*, in the desire for unity with all the other Churches which make up the whole—the more such a Church will be capable of translating the treasure of faith into the legitimate variety of expressions of the profession of faith, of prayer and worship, of Christian life and conduct and of the spiritual influence on the people among which it dwells. The more will it also be truly evangelizing, that is to say capable of drawing upon the universal patrimony in order to enable its own people to profit from it, and capable too of communicating to the universal Church the experience and the life of this people, for the benefit of all.

It is true that the passage speaks in terms of *translating* the faith into other cultural contexts, but it seems to go beyond the translation model in that it acknowledges the fact that the contextual process involves the mutual enrichment of cultures, on the one hand—inculturation is not conceived as only a one-way process, and so we see a trace of the anthropological model here. On the other hand, there is a sense in the passage that the process concerns action as well, and so hints at the praxis model. In any case, the synthetic model is "both/and." It takes pains to keep the integrity of the traditional message while acknowledging the importance of taking all the aspects of the context seriously.

In trying to juggle all the values of the three previous models, the synthetic model would approach revelation with an acknowledgment of the validity of all three aspects of revelation. Revelation has a concrete message that can be expressed in propositions, but it also has elements that reflect God's personal presence and call to relationship. In addition, as is clear from a practitioner of the synthetic model like José M. de Mesa, revelation is an invitation as well to partner with God in working for justice. Scripture and Tradition, under the influence of the anthropological and praxis models, would be understood as open and incomplete, needing the wealth of experience from all peoples and situations fully to grasp the infinite riches of God. But for this model the context is incomplete as well, and needs to be redeemed, healed, and purified by the word of the gospel and by commitment to justice and continuing "right action" resulting from continuous evaluation and reflection. In addition, the synthetic model needs the "other" for a fuller understanding of one's faith in its particular context. Pope Paul VI's concern for the local church to keep contact with and fidelity to the universal church points to this openness as well.

The basic method of the synthetic model is that of dialogue or conversation—with the tradition, with the context, with the imperatives of praxis. Such dialogue or conversation is an art, demanding strong discipline, on the one hand, and immense creativity, on the other. In an often-quoted passage, David Tracy expresses the demands of conversation vividly:

> Conversation is a game with some hard rules: say only what you mean; say it as accurately as you can; listen to and respect what the other says, however different or other; be willing to correct or defend your opinions if challenged by the conversation partner; be willing to argue if necessary, to confront if demanded, to endure necessary conflict, to change your mind if the evidence suggests it.[29]

It is kind of conversation with all one's theological partners that might be expressed in the image of cross-pollination of the plants in one's garden. It is not enough to grow the plants; one wants to get the best from them all, and so one works to produce hybrids. In this way, each plant is recognized for its best qualities, but the result is something that comes from the best qualities of several. This is why the synthetic model might work most effectively in hybrid cultures—for instance, that of the Philippines. The great Filipino church historian Horacio de la Costa, once pointed out the significance of a diary written by the Filipino statesman José P. Laurel when he was being held at Sugamo Prison in Manila during World War II. Since there was no paper available, Laurel made his diary entries in the blank spaces between the lines of a Western book. De la Costa calls this fact "oddly symbolic" because it reveals something very meaningful about the Filipino condition and presents a kind of model for the construction of Filipino thought. As de la Costa comments: "We, as a nation, have received a rich intellectual legacy from the West: our religious faith from Spain, our democratic institutions from America. But this legacy, rich as it is, has blank spaces which, in the providence of God, we are meant to fill."[30] So, using the synthetic model, theologians try to write, as it were, "between the lines"—of the received tradition, of their experiences in their own contexts, of the demands of faith for intelligent action.

The strength of the synthetic model certainly lies in its approach to theology as an honest dialogue or conversation among all the partners. The synthetic model listens to all the voices, is open to all the elements that go into the theological process. Because of this, perhaps as much as the translation model, it would have the confidence of the institutional church and the guardians of the tradition. But it would also have the trust of members of the local culture, and those as well who are committed to the struggle for justice. Negatively, however, like the anthropological model, its strongest point can also be interpreted as a weakness. Every side might see practitioners of the synthetic model as "selling out" the other, of being "wishy-washy" in its commitment to traditional doctrine, or to God's presence in the local church, or to the demands of more effective action. The synthetic model is a "middle-of-the-road model," and so pays the price of those who live by attempting to recognize the value of all sides.

I have mentioned above the work of José M. de Mesa. He is a prime example of this model in his many books and articles, and he has come under fire from church authorities for his strong stance of trusting the culture and working with what he calls a "hermeneutics of appreciation."[31] Another fine example of a practitioner of the synthentic model is Japanese-American theologian Kosuke Koyama (1929-2009), whose many books and essays express Christian faith in creative, profound, and sometimes humorous ways.[32]

The Transcendental Model

The term "transcendental" in the title of this model does not mean that this model "points beyond," or deals with "transcendence." Rather, the term refers to the basic insight of the philosopher Immanuel Kant and his "transcendental method," which was developed in the twentieth century by thinkers such as French philosophers Pierre Rousselot (1878-1915), Joseph Maréchal (1878-1944), and theologians Karl Rahner and Bernard Lonergan in connection with the thought of Thomas Aquinas. Transcendental method insists on the centrality of the "subject" or human person in the act of knowledge: one only "knows" when one has weighed all the evidence and come to a personal judgment of the truth. Objectivity is not something that is simply "out there," but is something that is revealed to a person as he or she is open to experience, to various arguments, and especially to the deep drive to understand with which the human mind is gifted. "Genuine objectivity is the fruit of authentic subjectivity," Lonergan writes. Objective knowledge, knowledge of the real, can be achieved only by attaining to authentic subjectivity.[33]

This is why a possible alternative title to this model might be the "subjective model." The important thing in this model is not so much what one *produces*, what is objective. What is important is authentic subjectivity—authenticity as a believer, and authenticity as a person in a very specific cultural and historical context. Theology is conceived not as producing a content, but as being faithful to a process of honest and authentic inquiry. Bernard Lonergan would name this as being faithful to the "transcendental imperatives": "Be attentive, Be intelligent, Be reasonable, Be responsible," to which David Tracy adds "be loving, and, if necessary, change."[34]

"Subjectivity" is a thoroughly "modern" concept, and so it would be difficult to find a basis for this theological approach in the thoroughly premodern Scriptures. There is, however, one passage that has strong implications for subjectivity and opens up a constant theme in the scriptural witness that is relevant here: that of authentic conversion. The passage to which I refer is Mark 2:21-22, where Jesus tells the two parables of the unshrunken cloth that cannot be used to patch a cloak and the old wineskins that cannot hold new wine. No, Jesus says, one pours new wine into new wineskins. What Jesus is bringing, the parables imply, is something new, something that can be understood only with a complete change of mind—what the Gospels call *metanoia*, or "conversion." What is important is not simply being able to repeat something or accept something only on another's evidence; that would be sewing a new cloth on a garment and would only tear it, or putting wine in new skins, which would only burst them. What is need is a new cloak or new wineskins. What is important is being able to understand it and see it for oneself—and this is the key to both authentic religion and, for us here, authentic contextual theology.

It will come as no surprise that Revelation for this model is much more conceived as a personal presence that is encountered in a personal, subjective experience. And because experience is so central to this method, it is the way that Revelation is encountered as a person interprets Scripture and Tradition. One reads the Bible or studies the tradition and one discovers other subjects who, like oneself, experience and struggle with the presence of God. Their story is "my" story, and "my" story is their story, even though both stories are of a different time and a different context. Through *their* experience of God's personal presence and invitation to relationship, one discovers God's presence and invitation in one's own life. The tradition is not simply something complete that Christians accept passively. It constantly illumines and challenges their lives, as their lives open up new ways of understanding the great Christian heritage.

One's own context, then—one's personal experiences, one's culture, one's social location—is where one encounters God, and therefore that context is basically good and trustworthy. Context, though, is the clue to wider truth. The deeper one goes into oneself and finds one's own identity as a believer and a unique subject with *these* experiences, *this* culture and *this* social location, the more my expression of faith helps others to discover their own authenticity as a believer and cultural subject. On the personal level, the transcendental model proceeds along the analogy of a scissors: contextual theology—or better, *theologizing*—takes place as an authentic subject brings the "upper blade" of the experience of the past (Scripture and Tradition) together with the "lower blade" of context. Again, it is the *process* that is important; if this is followed, the authentic subjectivity of the person will naturally yield the objectivity of good theology.

As a person shares his or her theology with others, the model proceeds by the method of "sympathy" and "antipathy." As I share my own experience of faith, let's say, as an Australian woman, others to whom I speak or write and try to be true to their own subjectivity—whether they share my Australian identity or female gender—may resonate with what I say. They themselves will begin to take what I say and use it to develop an understanding of their faith according to their own identity. This is the way of "sympathy." But I may also speak or write to other persons who, try as they may, cannot resonate with my experience at all. Nevertheless, this "antipathy" can touch off a number of questions in their own minds, and help them discover—by discovering in what ways and how they disagree with me—what their own understanding of their faith is. In either case my own personal answers have helped the others begin their own personal search for a contextual understanding of their faith. I have not so much helped them articulate a theology, as I have helped them to begin the process of theologizing.

In our analogy of gardening, what practitioners of the transcendental model do is give an example. The cultivation of their garden inspires others to cultivate *their* gardens. Each one might care for it in a different way, grow different flowers or vegetables, and arrange it differently, but the creativity and industry of one has inspired the same in others. In distinct difference is found a genuine unity, and so, in a phrase of the U.S. Anglo psychologist Carl Rogers that somehow captures the truth of this model, "the most personal is the most general."[35]

The great advantage of the transcendental model is the way that it focuses on *process* rather than *product*. As we have argued in chapter 3, the authenticity with which one does theology is the most important thing. It is necessary to "show your work." This focus on process allows theologians to be creative and take risks, knowing that their faith and their rootedness in context, if they are faithful to the "transcendental imperatives," will keep them faithful as well to the faith of the church as a whole. One disadvantage of the model, however, is that it might *seem* too individualistic and too Western. This is not necessarily the case, since there is a real sense in which the model functions only when authentic individuals are brought into conversation. But the impression remains.

Although he is also a strong advocate of the praxis model, Justo González might be classified as a practitioner as well of the transcendental model. Especially in his 1990 work *Mañana: Christian Theology from a Hispanic Perspective*,[36] González attempts to do theology from an unabashedly contextual perspective. But to do this he brings to bear all his skill as an accomplished historian of doctrine and focuses not so much on Hispanic/Latino/a culture or practices as on how the tradition has resources for a theology rooted within the Latino context. He articulates this out of both his strong Christian faith and his clear identity as a Cuban-American. Another theologian we can identify as a practitioner of the transcendental model is U.S. feminist theologian Sallie McFague. In her powerful books on metaphor, naming God, and ecological responsibility,[37] McFague articulates a very North American and feminist theology, but she does it indirectly. The success of her work as contextual theology comes from a relatively unarticulated but very firm Christian faith interacting with her identity as a woman in the present U.S. context.

The Countercultural Model

The sixth and final contextual model that we will sketch out in this chapter is one that is somewhat different from the other five. In the first five models we have outlined, context is regarded as basically something positive. It might need to be perfected and healed; it may be somewhat ambiguous, but it is the "stuff" into which the gospel can be translated, or the stuff within which God makes Godself known. In the *countercultural* model, however, while the significance of context is certainly admitted, that context is regarded more as a hindrance to the gospel and the gospel message. Contextual theology, then, according to this model, is done as the gospel is proclaimed *over against* the context, and as the context is exposed as inimical to it. This is why alternative titles such as the "encounter" or "engagement" model might be proposed as well: contextual theology is done not as a translating of the gospel *into* the context, nor as allowing the context to provide new perspectives or the agenda for theological reflection, but as an "encounter" or "engagement" with the culture. The fact that the model is committed to a prophetic "telling forth" of the truth in the context of a "culture of death" might point to a term such as the "prophetic model" as an adequate name. Or the fact that the church in which Christians theologize is conceived by practitioners of this model as a "contrast community" might argue for naming it the "contrast model."[38]

This is certainly a model that has a strong basis in both Scripture and the church's tradition. Like the praxis model, the Bible's prophetic tradition is one of Israel's confrontation as it wants to settle in among the nations, borrowing their cultural traditions. Even though the Gospel of John speaks of the world in positive terms in 3:16, there are several other places where the world is something to be opposed or avoided (see John 17), and in the First Letter of

John we are cautioned: "Do not love the world or the things of the world. If anyone loves the world, the love of the Father is not in him" (2:15). Similarly, Paul writes in Romans 12:2 that Christians should not conform themselves to the age (the context) but should be renewed in their minds and do what is good, pleasing, and perfect. Tertullian is famous for his opposition to any cultural trappings that could obscure the gospel ("What does Jerusalem have to do with Athens?"), and the *Letter to Diognetus*, which describes Christians as living in "every foreign land" as "their homeland, and every homeland a foreign land."[39] We might also mention the very countercultural monastic tradition, the Anabaptist tradition within Protestantism, and powerful witnesses within the Christian peace tradition like Peter Maurin (1877-1949) and Dorothy Day.

In a way, revelation is conceived within this model as propositional, but it is perhaps more accurate to conceive of it more in terms of a narrative or a "story" in which one finds oneself confronted with the "fact" of Jesus Christ. This story is true; it claims our loyalty and calls us to live and act differently than the "world." Scripture and tradition provide women and men with the "clues" to the meaning of history, and it is in *that* sense that it is complete. It provides us with all we need to know, although we can plumb more of its depths as other cultures offer their own understandings of the gospel message and interpretations of the gospel story.[40] However, context needs to be regarded in this model with the utmost suspicion. It is radically ambiguous and usually resistant to the gospel. As U.S. Anglo practitioners of the countercultural model Stanley Hauerwas and William Willimon express it powerfully, "as Jesus demonstrated, the world, for all its beauty, is hostile to the truth."[41]

The method of the countercultural model proceeds by first recognizing the validity of the Christian story, embodied in the experience of the past within Scripture and Tradition as the clue to the meaning of human and cosmic history. This story is then used as a lens through which to interpret, engage, unmask, and challenge the experience of the present, the context of individual and social experience, human culture, social location, and the dynamics of social change. This is not a simple, one-time operation, but something that is ongoing and something that is both individual and communal. It is a process, too, that goes on not only within each individual believer but also within the church community—lest believers or the community be co-opted by the surrounding context. It is as though one's garden needs constantly to be weeded, constantly to be cared for, so that the plants can grow there in a healthy way. But weeds are persistent, and drought is ever-threatening.

Two phrases in particular capture what the countercultural model is about. The first is from the eminent U.S. Anglo missionary to India A. G. Hogg, who speaks of the gospel message as providing a "challenging relevance" in particular contexts, since in its challenge it actually calls the context to its full potential. The second is from the great Dutch missionary to Indonesia and theologian Hendrik Kraemer. Kraemer speaks of the gospel as providing a "subversive fulfillment," not accepting the context as it is but subverting it for its own good.[42]

To its credit, the countercultural model is able to combine a strong engagement of the context with fidelity to the gospel message, and this is particularly relevant in situations like Europe, North America, Australia, and New Zealand where the surrounding context and culture are indifferent to religion, and where the church itself has often been co-opted by the culture so as to find itself irrelevant within it. But the danger of being *countercultural* is to be anti-cultural, to despise the human and the created as corrupt and useless religiously. Such an attitude is diametrically opposed to what we will reflect on in the next chapter, the sacramental worldview of Catholicism.

There are several interesting groups of contemporary theologians—mostly North Americans, Europeans, Australians, and New Zealanders—who practice the countercultural model. These include The Gospel and Our Culture Network, whose Web page may be found at http://www.gocn.org/main.cfm, the Ecclesia Project (http://www.ekklesiaproject.org./), and Allelon (http://www.allelon.org/main.cfm). Some of the leaders in these groups are (all Anglos) George Hunsberger, Craig van Gelder, Lois Barrett, Alan Roxborough, Inagrace Dieterich, and Michael Budde.

CONCLUSION

To do theology from a global perspective, ironically, is to look to the local. Theology today does not need a *Summa Theologiae* or a *Church Dogmatics* that might claim to be valid in all human situations of today's world. What we need instead is the blossoming of theologies in every part of the world, in every historical situation, among every social group. "You may, and you must, have an African theology," Pope Paul VI cried out in a visit to Uganda in 1969,[43] and today we recognize that we may—and must—have feminist theologies, Mexican theologies, Maori theologies, theologies arising from deaf communities, and so on. How we understand our world, how we approach revelation, how we regard our Scriptures and doctrinal tradition play a crucial role in shaping the ways in which these contextual theologies will be developed. Whether we commit ourselves to translating the gospel into our contexts, or to finding fresh ways of expressing it by a deep listening to them, or to discovering the gospel message as we do the work of ministry or work for justice, or to entering into mutually enriching conversations or confronting our contexts with the power of the gospel, to do theology outside of our concrete situation today is no longer an option.

QUESTIONS FOR REFLECTION

1. Contextual theology, this chapter claims, is a "theological imperative." What does this mean? Why do you agree or disagree?
2. This chapter presents six "models" of contextual theology. Which one do you find the most adequate? Which one do you find the least adequate?
3. What are some important theological issues that arise out of your own context? What model(s) of contextual theology might best deal with each of them?

SUGGESTIONS FOR FURTHER READING AND STUDY

Stephen B. Bevans, *Models of Contextual Theology*, rev. and expanded ed. (Maryknoll, NY: Orbis Books, 2002).

José M. de Mesa, *Why Theology Is Never Far from Home* (Manila: De La Salle University Press, 2003)

Diego Irarrázaval, *Inculturation: New Dawn of the Church in Latin America* (Maryknoll, N.Y.: Orbis Books, 2000)

Laurenti Magesa, *Anatomy of Inculturation: Transforming the Church in Africa* (Maryknoll, N.Y.: Orbis Books, 2004).

James A. Scherer and Stephen B. Bevans, eds., *New Directions in Mission and Evangelization 3: Faith and Culture* (Maryknoll, N.Y.: Orbis Books, 1999).

Robert J. Schreiter, *Constructing Local Theologies* (Maryknoll, N.Y.: Orbis Books, 1985).

Andrew F. Walls, "Culture and Coherence in Christian History," in *The Missionary Movement in Christian History: Studies in the Transmission of Faith* (Maryknoll, N.Y.: Orbis Books, 1997), 16-25.

9

Catholic Method

IN THIS CHAPTER WE ARE GOING to reflect on what I call "Catholic Method": the basic presuppositions that shape the way Catholics seek to understand their faith. Catholics do theology in a very distinct way because they have a very distinct way of understanding or imagining the world in which they live. This understanding and imagination are something deep in the Catholic psyche, and, as U.S. Anglo sociologist Andrew Greeley argues, it is not something that Catholics can easily shake off, even if they *try* to leave the Catholic Church.[1] It is, however, something that Catholic theologians can and should embrace explicitly, and the more they do the more faithful they are to their Catholic tradition. When we speak about "Catholic method," of course, we intend to understand the word as beginning with a lower-case "c." Other Christians—for example, Orthodox, Coptics, Anglicans—also share the distinct "catholic" viewpoint, and so can both consciously and unconsciously do theology out of "catholic method" as well. In fact, as theologians in a "catholic" church, we would contend that doing theology from that perspective is, in the final analysis, the best way of seeking deeper understanding for our faith. Nevertheless, as Richard McBrien points out, Roman Catholics have this "catholic" viewpoint in a way that "one does not discover elsewhere and which commends Catholicism on its own merits, without regard for competing configurations."[2]

Our reflections in the following pages will be in three parts. First we will sketch out the "vision" of Catholicism, or that distinct worldview out of which Catholics do theology. Second, we will reflect on the tensions that such a vision necessarily entails, and that Catholics must always "reach for fidelity" to the fullness of the Catholic vision. In the third part we will reflect on the theological stance that is the direct opposite of Catholicism—fundamentalism—and how it can be countered by the Catholic spirit.[3]

THE VISION OF CATHOLICISM

"I regard the *analogia entis* [the "analogy of being"] as the intention of Antichrist, and I think that because of it one cannot become Catholic. Whereupon I at the same time allow myself to regard all other possible reasons for not becoming Catholic, as shortsighted and lacking in seriousness."[4] These are the famous words of Karl Barth, written in 1932 in the foreword to the first volume of his masterpiece *Church Dogmatics*, perhaps the greatest work of theology of the twentieth century. Barth mitigated this harsh judgment somewhat toward the end of his life in the essay "The Humanity of God" and in a message of reconciliation to his fellow theologian, the German Emil Brunner.[5] Catholic theologians would certainly deny that they work on a principle devised by the Antichrist, but in his basic intuition Barth was correct. The essence of Catholicism—and the main principle of catholic method—is the analogy of being, the principle that there exists a *continuity* between *our* being and *God's* being, and that knowledge of the things of this world can lead to a real, though imperfect, knowledge of God.

As important as is the Petrine ministry of the pope for Catholics, as important as are tradition and reason and the magisterium, as important as is the role of Mary in Catholic devotional life, none of these really holds the key to what being a Catholic means. They are all derivative. The principle on which Catholicism stands or falls is rather the conviction that the world, the human person, and human experience in the world are pluses and not minuses, that ordinary experience and finite reality of any kind have a capacity to be diaphanous of infinite meaning and bearers of God's revelation.[6] This is why, to do Catholic theology one must first of all be possessed with an "analogical imagination." One's basic worldview, in other words, must be one that can perceive "the profound similarities-in-difference in all reality," and can see in the individual and the particular the "disclosure of radical all pervasive grace."[7] The "analogical imagination" is, in the most profound sense, the "Catholic imagination."[8]

Sacramentality

The "analogy of being" is the philosophical concept that is, I believe, the lynchpin of the Catholic worldview. This is because it asserts the fact that *our* experience, *our* history, and the visible things of *this* creation—despite their real inadequacy, as we emphasized in chapter 1, to capture the Mystery of God—are nevertheless *clues* to what God and God's action in this world are like. It is the perception of *similarities* in the *difference* between ourselves and God.

Perhaps a less abstract and more accessible way of describing this genius of Catholicism, however, is to speak in terms of its basic *sacramental* principle. The Catholic vision, writes Richard McBrien in the conclusion of his book *Catholicism*, is one that discovers God in and through the things of this world. "The visible, the tangible, the finite, the historical—all these are actual or potential carriers of the divine presence. Indeed, it is only in and through these material realities that we can even encounter the invisible God."[9] A sacramental perspective is one in which the secular can reveal the sacred, the immanent can reveal the transcendent, the particular and partial can reveal the unity of the whole. A person, an event, or an object is clearly not to be identified with the divine—identification is a danger of the sacramental perspective and, as Protestants who work from a more "dialectical imagination" point out (e.g., Barth)—it can end in an un-Christian and unbiblical idolatry. But at certain graced times and in certain graced circumstances these created realities can manifest the power and glory of their creator. Julian of Norwich's conviction of God's universal love in her vision of "something smaller, no bigger than a hazelnut," Irish poet Joseph Mary Plunkett's ability to see Christ's blood on the rose, and British Jesuit Gerard Manley Hopkins's sense that "the world is charged with the grandeur of God"[10] are all eloquent expressions of a perspective that regards creation as a mystery "imbued with the hidden presence of God."[11]

If one understands this fundamental sacramental principle, one has come a long way in understanding Catholicism both as a social phenomenon and as a point of departure for doing theology. It is because of sacramentality that Catholicism values worship that appeals to every sense; and it is because of the same sacramental worldview that Catholics can profit from devotion to Mary as well as from activism for world peace or the right to life. Naturally, ceremony can become an end in itself, and "Mariology" can become "Mariolatry," and social activism can be reduced to mere humanism. But Catholics accept such a risk because they are convinced of the truth of the underlying principle that "transcendence can be, and most appropriately is, symbolized in and mediated through sensible realities,"[12] and they are convinced as well of "the more in the midst of the ordinary."[13] U.S. Latino/a theologians speak of a Catholicism rooted in *lo cotidiano*, the ebb and flow of everyday life.[14]

Because of Catholicism's belief that God's saving presence is mediated through the ordinary, the material, the human, Catholics can place great emphasis not only on the book of the church, the Bible (the Word of God in the words of women and men—see DV 12), but also on the church itself as a sacramental reality, visible and invisible, both human and divine (see LG 8). In a real sense, the insight of the nineteenth-century German theologian Friedrich Schleiermacher is correct. Catholics *do* believe that one's relationship to Christ does indeed depend on one's relation to the church.[15] But this is not to turn the church into a *substitute* for Christ, an idol. Rather, it is because the church *itself* is a sacrament, "a sign and instrument of communion with God and of unity among all" (LG 1). From the understanding of the sacramental nature of the church it is a small but logical step for Catholics to understand that the church's tradition, particularly—as we have seen in chapter 6—as it is articulated in the papal and episcopal exercise of the magisterium, must be taken with utmost seriousness both as a source and as a judge of all theologizing. And with the same sacramental point of view one can see why Catholic theology places such a premium on the role of reason in theological expression. As we have seen in chapter 2, Catholic theologizing avoids the extreme of *rationalism*, but it also avoids as well the other extreme of *fideism*— or as we will see in the third section of this chapter—*fundamentalism*. As Pope John Paul wrote eloquently, faith and reason are "like two wings on which the human spirit rises to the contemplation of truth" (FR, opening benediction). *Both* are needed to do theology. Especially today, the sacramental principle allows one to see why Catholic theology takes seriously, as a theological source on a par with both Scripture and Tradition, present human experience or context: the experiences of peoples from all cultures and social locations, and movements such as secularization, globalization, and migration that are constantly shaping these.

Catholicity

The perception of the sacramental nature of created reality is also the key to understanding the *word* "Catholic." To be a Catholic (from the Greek *kata holos*, "according to the whole") means to be radically open to "all truth and value."[16] Nothing that is truly good and really valuable can be excluded, for everything that is genuine can be a manifestation of the divine, and the divine reaches out to embrace all that is genuine. What this means is that every person, every nation, every culture, every race is included in the church because each has not only something to gain, but something to give as well.

It is because of this catholicity in all its richness of meaning that there exists a tolerance in the church, both in terms of quality of membership and plurality of theological expression. Catholicism is all-embracing, as inclusive as Jesus himself. The opposite of "catholic" is not really "Protestant"; it is rather a sectarianism or fundamentalism that insists on only one way to think of being Christian or doing theology. As British lay theologian Rosemary Haughton writes, catholicity means being open "not only to the highest but to the lowest, the repulsive, the self-hating; it can never be the cult of the beautiful, which is why it is not for the religious connoisseurs or the seekers after fulfillment."[17]

As we will see in part 4 of this book, there have always been a number of "schools" of theology within the Catholic tradition, and sometimes they have been in rather bitter opposition to each other: witness the different Christologies proposed by the North African Alexandrian school and the western Asian school of Antioch in Syria in the fourth century, or the sixteenth-century Molinist-Thomist controversy over the question of grace and freedom in Europe. Of equal significance is the existence in the Roman communion of a number of "rites" (Roman, Milanese, Ukrainian, Melchite [Middle East/western Asia], Maronite [Middle East/western Asia], Syro-Malabar [India],

Congolese—to name a few). Within these groups not only the style of worship differs, but the style of theologizing differs as well. Today, as the church begins critically to appropriate modernity's discovery of subjectivity and history, the plurality of theological expression has become even more evident. As we have seen in the previous chapter, there have emerged African and Asian theologies, Latin American, feminist, African American, and U.S. Latino/a theologies. Theologies based on philosophies that represent a genuine departure from the Aristotelianism that had become (but only from the twelfth century—or perhaps to be more accurate, only from the nineteenth!) the traditional basis for Catholic theologizing have also emerged. Asian philosophies or Western philosophies such as transcendental philosophy, U.S. pragmatism, or "process" philosophies could become the basis for very different theologies in the future.[18] Finally, a whole new kind of theology is being developed in the newly emerging discipline of "comparative theology."[19]

As both British theologian and spiritual writer Timothy Radcliffe and theologian and missiologist Robert Schreiter point out, there are two tendencies in Catholicism today that are in rather high tension.[20] The first is characterized by more openness to the world and shows interest in the movements of inculturation, liberation, dialogue, and reconciliation. Radcliffe calls this a kingdom-oriented perspective; both he and Schreiter would say that the basic document for "kingdom Catholics" would be Vatican II's Pastoral Constitution on the Church in the Modern World, *Gaudium et Spes*. The second approach to Catholicism Radcliffe calls a more "communio"-oriented perspective, but Schreiter speaks of it more in terms of a vision that has a more suspicious view of the world and would stress Catholic identity over against the world. The document that Schreiter sees as embodying this view would be Augustine's *City of God*, written in the context of the sack of Rome in 410 c.e. and emphasizing the importance of the church in a crumbling world order. Radcliffe argues that true catholicity would see the validity in *both* perspectives (the "both/and" that we will speak of below); each points to the richness of the Catholic vision. Schreiter, too, in proposing that catholicity today needs to be imaged in the form of communication, calls for these two competing visions to communicate with *each other*. Again we see how the genuine Catholic vision is one that has room for opinions and viewpoints that strongly differ with one another.

Of course, the tolerance demanded by catholicity has not always been put into practice, and Catholicism cannot deny a history of Inquisitions, cultural insensitivity, and active cooperation with European colonial designs. But these moments of intolerance must be looked upon as moments of *betrayal* of catholicity rather than expressions of it. As Rosemary Haughton writes, Catholicism is "the attempt to integrate the whole of human life in the search for the kingdom of God."[21] And, as Stephen Happel and David Tracy point out, when this attempt has failed, "Catholicism has cheated itself of its own universality."[22]

Catholicity has been characterized as having a "both-and" character, in contrast to classic Protestantism's "either-or."[23] While a key word in Protestantism is the intensive *solus* ("alone"), Catholicism's word is the comprehensive *et* ("and"). Catholicism emphasizes therefore faith *and* works, Scripture *and* Tradition, Christ *and* Mary, the human *and* the divine, God *and* humanity, the sacred *and* the secular, spiritual *and* material, nature *and* grace. It is not a question of authority *or* freedom, but authority nurturing freedom. It is not a question of past *tradita* (traditions) opposed to and preventing contemporary expression, but (as we have seen in chapter 5) the present against the background of the past, giving the present more depth, opening up the way to a future that is rooted in the riches of the past. Unity is not opposed to diversity, and it is not achieved by uniformity. Rather, true unity flourishes when diversity can be expressed. It is the tensive character of this "both-and," as we will see below, that provides the ideal and the challenge to Catholics as they do theology today.

Critical Realism

Over three decades ago, in an address to the annual convention of the Catholic Theological Society of America, U.S. Anglo theologian John J. Connelley tried to answer the question "Is there a Catholic theology?" by laying down several principles that shape theological reflection in a Catholic context.[24] Besides a sacramental principle that emphasizes the way the invisible is represented by the visible, and a dogmatic principle that emphasizes the role of authority in Catholic theology, Connelley proposes a third, *philosophical* principle. This philosophical principle is not the mere observation that one needs a philosophy in order to do theology; rather, Connelley insisted that the Catholic vision, rooted as it is in a sacramental worldview that takes the whole of reality with utmost seriousness, needs a philosophy to underpin and undergird what it articulates theologically. Connelley speaks of this philosophical principle in terms of a Catholic realism, but it is perhaps better known in philosophical terms as *critical* realism.

As Connelley expresses it, Catholic theology is based on the underlying philosophical conviction that our theological expressions, as much as they are products of various cultural and historical influences, express nevertheless what is objectively true; they are not just objectifications of mere subjective affections (as we have seen in our discussion of the nature of doctrine in chapter 7). Richard McBrien has explained this principle under the rubric of *Christian* realism and says that this critical realism is a position that avoids both the extremes of naïve realism or raw empiricism, on the one hand (i.e., what is "already out there now is real") and idealism ("what is real is what is in my mind"), on the other. Precisely because of its foundational principle of sacramentality, Catholicism holds that all knowledge, including the knowledge of God in revelational encounter, is an experience mediated by one's individual and cultural/historical context, but one that is also objective, and empirically and rationally verifiable.[25]

While the position of critical realism—along with the principle of the analogy of being—is the *foundation* of the sacramental principle, the comprehensiveness of catholicity, and the "both-and" character of the Catholic worldview, it also functions to bring to light several important aspects of Catholic theological method. Since critical realism avoids any naïve notion that reality is wholly "already out there now," any idea of a ready-made revelation or system of doctrines can find no real home within the Catholic vision. A fundamentalism, therefore (as we will see in the third part of this chapter), that believes only because "it's written in the Bible" or "taught by the church" is radically unacceptable to Catholic thinking or theological reflection. Similarly, a dogmatism that reads the tradition uncritically or obeys authority unthinkingly is—contrary to wide popular conception—profoundly un-Catholic. On the other hand, however, since the Catholic vision does not accept idealism, even in its critical form, any thinking and theology that do not grapple with the concrete biblical word, with particular teaching and traditions of the past, and with the legitimate claims of church authority, are thinking and theological reflection that cannot be called Catholic either. Critical realism is a philosophical position that takes seriously all of reality, the human *and* divine, the material *and* the spiritual. And it is convinced that our partial and always inadequate knowledge is still real knowledge. Critical realism knows that our knowledge does not provide a photograph of reality, but it does provide real insight into reality. Rather than a photograph, our knowledge provides a map. And although maps are not the reality itself, they do get us where we want to go.[26]

Incarnation

The philosphical principles of critical realism and the analogy of being are the foundations for the principles of sacramentality and catholicity, and they shape the way that Catholics approach life in general and the doing of theology in particular. Undergirding these philosophical principles, however, is a further, properly *theological* principle of incarnation. Jesus Christ, Word made flesh (John 1:14), truly God and truly human (DS 301; ND 614), is ultimately the reason for the sacramental and catholic worldview, why there is both continuity between the human and divine and why we can know truly with our historically and culturally conditioned minds. It is through Jesus' particularity—*this* person, of a specific height and weight, of a specific hair color and blood type, an Aramaic-speaking Jewish male in Roman-occupied Palestine during the reign of the Roman emperor Tiberius—that believers have, from the very beginning, experienced the full revelation of God. "God is like Jesus," says Juan Luis Segundo.[27] His very humanity is the key to knowing God rather than his fitting the description of what we think God is. "There is no other sacrament (*mysterium*) of God . . . but Christ," wrote Augustine. Jesus is the primordial "mystery" or sacrament, the "sacrament of the encounter with God," as Edward Schillebeeckx entitled one of his most important books.[28]

As we will see in part 4 of this book, the whole history of the development of classical Christology, from Nicaea through the Councils of Constantinople and Ephesus to the Council of Chalcedon, is not simply a game of "getting the facts straight" or getting the doctrine right. Rather, Christology developed as a struggle to maintain the balance that incarnation demands: Jesus is truly God, not merely a creature, and so in Jesus we have truly met God (Nicaea). Jesus is not two separate identities, and so humanity (wondrously) has a real role to play in its own salvation, symbolized by the doctrine that Mary is truly *theotokos*, the mother of *God* (Ephesus). Jesus has a fully human soul, and so God really has emptied Godself and has entered fully into human history (Constantinople I). Jesus is both human and divine (Chalcedon): the human is the vehicle for the expression of divinity, and the divinity has shown in the body and humanity of Jesus both the depth of God's love and the holiness and goodness of all that is created.

Catholicism claims nothing more than to take the incarnation with utmost seriousness. It is, as Thomas F. O'Meara puts it, an intense form of faith in the incarnation:

> Carthusian abbesses in mitre and stole, mischievous Peruvian acolytes in red cassocks and carrying silver reliquaries with saints' bones and hair (none of which is older than the ninth century), . . . the novels of Graham Greene or the short stories of Flannery O'Connor—these are figures in a procession whose source and goal are the one incarnation in many incarnations.[29]

Like the philosophical principles of the analogy of being and critical realism, this theological principle of incarnation has profound implications for Catholic theological method. Because God is manifested fully in the flesh of Jesus, nothing material and, a fortiori, truly human, can be incapable of leading men and women into relationship with God. Objects, events, or persons can become metaphors, analogies, or symbols of God's saving activity, and so can become partial but real tools for theological discourse. Persons and institutions can be invested with—if not total, then nevertheless real—holiness, and so must be respected and listened to. Human activity and human cultures can have real, if not ultimate, meaning, and so are able not only to be used as raw material for theological reflection but also in themselves to reflect a ray of God's luminous truth. The incarnation is more than a way of explaining who Jesus is—or a crude expression to be explained away. It is a symbol of the meaningfulness of human life in God's world and a cardinal principle of Catholic theologizing.

TENSIONS IN THE VISION

What has been presented so far in this chapter is what I have called the "vision" of Catholicism—Catholicism's ideal, the "idea" of what it means to be Catholic and to do Catholic theology. It is to this vision, I believe, that the best of Catholicism and Catholic theology attempts to be faithful, and it is because of these continued attempts at fidelity that Catholic theology has developed such a rich tradition. We will see this more in part 4, but it is the Catholic vision that inspired theologians like Justin in the second century and Origen in the third to draw on the wealth of Hellenistic philosophy. It inspired Ephrem to do theology in hymnody, Hildegard to speak of Jesus as mother and write her mystical music, Michelangelo to theologize in stone and frescoes. Today it still inspires people like Gustavo Gutiérrez to see God's presence in the Peruvian poor, Filipina Mary John Mananzan to theologize from the experience of Filipina women, or Andrew Greeley to theologize from the music of U.S. rock star Bruce Springsteen or the films of Martin Scorsese.

Real fidelity is a difficult enterprise, however, because the Catholic vision is one that contains an inbuilt tension. The Catholic "both-and" and the analogical imagination of being able to see similarity in difference are not easily maintained, and history is witness to constant compromises and betrayals for the sake of clarity and simplicity—or for the maintenance of power. The Catholic vision is one that demands the constant work of integration, and it does not promise a success that is easily achieved. This is particularly true in a church that is globally conscious, and for the construction of theologies that are rooted in the contexts of all peoples. As Pope John Paul II has said on several occasions, such a task of inculturation is a "lengthy" (RM 52), "difficult and delicate task" (EiA 62).

In her study of the idea ("thing") of Catholicism, Rosemary Haughton often has recourse to the interplay between two allegorical figures, whom she sketches at the beginning of her book.[30] The tension in this interplay, Haughton maintains, is the tension that is built into the Catholic vision itself.

The first figure in the allegory Haughton names "Mother Church," and she is a figure who stands for all that is institutional, traditional, and visible in the church. Mother Church is deeply dedicated to her children and is concerned about every detail of their welfare. She is a woman of long and deep experience, shocked no more by human wickedness, wise and full of many time-tested stories and proverbs. She is a wonderful housekeeper and has made her home beautiful and her life rich with the art and music of the centuries. However, says Haughton, Mother Church has a shadow side. She sometimes—and actually rather often—is inclined to confuse her wisdom with God's will, and she cares so much for her children and knows them so well that she tends to make decisions "for their own good." She knows the past so well and has been nourished so much by it that she is suspicious of anything new, and often simply suppresses it.

But Mother Church has a twin sister. Her name is "Sophia," the word for "wisdom" in Greek, but she is called many other names besides: Romantic Love, Mysticism, Superstition, Inspiration, Adventure, Imprudence, Sanctity, Folly. As these names imply, Sophia, like her sister, has both good and bad sides. She is a free spirit and wants everyone to be free. She prefers the new to the old, the risky to the tried and true, and the individual to the institution. She is completely unpredictable and often irresponsible. She writes and illustrates books that students read instead of doing their homework, and when she visits Mother Church and her family, she plays the piano for the children when they are supposed to be doing the dishes.

In many ways Mother Church and Sophia are opposites, and often Mother Church in her pushy way would like to get Sophia out of the picture. Then she could get on with providing what she knows is best. The truth is, though—and every once in a while even Mother Church acknowledges it—the two cannot get along without each other. Mother Church needs Sophia's freedom so she does not end up smothering her children; and Sophia needs Mother Church's discipline and experience so she will not make people totally confused and disorientated.

Strange as it may seem, the two sisters are really quite devoted to each other. The sad thing, says Haughton, is that their respective admirers do not always know this, and so they are always claiming one against the other instead of seeing the richness of the relationship that is beneath the surface.

The Catholic vision is one that emerges out of this "strange, yet essential" relationship between Mother Church and her twin sister Sophia: between institution and charism, authority and freedom, nature and grace. It is a vision that bears within it an inherent tension, and the tension has often failed to be maintained. The Catholic Church's respect for authority, based on its deep conviction that the visible and institutional can "re-present" the authority of Jesus, can and has become an authoritarianism that takes no account of the shared dignity and responsibilities of the people of God. The need to be faithful to the past, based on the conviction of the need to provide an understanding of its unity has often been perverted into a positivism that cannot provide a "cogent understanding of the contemporary."[31] The sacramental worldview of the sensible and the tactile can degenerate into an attitude of magic and superstition, the significance of culture for Christianity can become a "culture Christianity," and the value that Catholicism places on human partnership with God can fall into an almost Pelagian "good works" mentality.

Despite all its tension, however, and despite all the failures, Catholics still believe that the vision is worth reaching for. After all, God did manifest God-self fully in and through a particular person, and so present, material, and human reality must have a meaning. The vision might be difficult to maintain, but in trying to be faithful to it Catholics can—and in some uncanny way do—manifest the true face of God. It is this tension, this failure, and this continual reaching for fidelity that can explain the main characteristics of Roman Catholic theology and that can provide as well the key to understanding the diversity of theological opinion among Roman Catholic theologians throughout the world today.

Rooted in the philosophical principles of the analogy of being and critical realism, and in the foundational theological principle of incarnation, the sacramental, comprehensive, and "both-and" quality of the Catholic vision provides distinctive elements in Catholic theological method. As Catholics do theology, therefore, they are attentive to the scriptural witness but are also in contact with its interpretation by the wisdom of tradition. Their guide to such wisdom will be the teaching of the church, in particular the teaching of the papal and episcopal magisterium. But as they listen to the leadership of the church, theologians need also to listen with a critical ear, aware of the cultural, historical, and even ideological conditionedness of doctrinal expression and the contribution that can be made from their own historical and cultural situation and the way that God is speaking in their contemporary experience. Only in this way, Catholic theologians are convinced, can Christians do theology that is appropriate to the Christian tradition and adequate to Christians' experience in today's world church and globalized world.[32]

CATHOLICISM AND FUNDAMENTALISM

"Catholicism," writes Thomas F. O'Meara, "in its approach to Christian life, worship, church and culture is the polar opposite of every fundamentalism, Christian or other."[33] Fundamentalism may well be, as Richard McBrien argues, the most dangerous threat to Catholicism in his own country of the United States today[34]—and I would add that it poses a similar threat to any genuine Christianity in any part of the world. It has been estimated that in the U.S. state of Florida five Catholics enter fundamentalist churches every day, and a good portion of funding for fundamentalist television programs are said to come from Catholic pockets. Many, if not all of us, know a friend or a member of our family who has joined a fundamentalist church or cult.[35] Pope Benedict XVI recognized the inroads that fundamentalists are making among

Catholics in Latin America, as did the Latin American bishops at their 2007 conference in Aparecida, Brazil.[36] Pope John Paul II, in his various apostolic exhortations after the regional synods at the close of the second millennium also warned about the growing influence of fundamentalist groups. In *Ecclesia in Oceania*, for example, he acknowledged that "in some missionary areas, the Bishops are concerned about the effect that these religious groups or sects are having on the Catholic community" (EiO 24; see also EiAf 66, EiE 16, EiAm 73). The fastest growing churches in Africa are African Independent/Initiated/Indigenous Churches (AICs), and many of these have fundamentalist perspectives.

The Asian bishops also speak of the danger of fundamentalism, but speak of it in a way that includes fundamentalisms from other religious traditions as well.[37] In the first volume of their series on fundamentalism throughout the world (*Fundamentalisms Observed*), Martin Marty and R. Scott Appleby have collected articles about fundamentalists in Judaism, Islam, Hinduism, Sikhism, Buddhism, and Confucianism—and even in "traditionalist" Roman Catholicism![38] (Remember Pelikan's distinction between tradition and traditionalism!)

What Is Fundamentalism?

What *is* fundamentalism? In the first place, as the titles of the Marty and Appleby volumes indicate, there is no *one* form of fundamentalism. In fact, as these editors acknowledge, a number of the contributing authors to their volumes did not want their contributions to be named "fundamentalist." Nevertheless, Marty and Appleby recognized in all the varieties what the Austrian philosopher Ludwig Wittgenstein (1889-1951) called "family resemblances."[39]

Perhaps more helpful than a definition would be to list several distinguishing features that characterize all fundamentalisms—features that would also point to how such fundamentalisms are so opposed to the Catholic spirit. In the introduction to the first volume in their series, Marty and Appleby point to a kind of *militancy* that marks every kind of fundamentalism. Fundamentalists, they say, *fight back*, particularly against what they perceive as the relativism of modernity. Bruce Lawrence points out that while fundamentalists are *modern* in that they will not hesitate to use modern means (media, weapons) to achieve their purposes, they are not *modernists*.[40] They see the modern world as evil, destructive, ungodly. They *fight for* a particular vision of life, or religion, or liturgy, or government, often believed to be ancient, traditional, or original. They *fight with* "a particularly chosen repository of resources which one may think of as weapons."[41] These resources might be the Christian Bible, the Qur'an of Islam, or the Tridentine Mass of ultra-conservative Catholics. Fundamentalists *fight against* those who do not share their beliefs, be it the infidel, the promoter of liberal ideas, or those who seek compromise or dialogue—whether within the group or outside it. Fundamentalists are *sectarian* in the true sense of the word: *cut off* from others, identifying themselves *over against* others. Finally, suggest Marty and Appleby, fundamentalists *fight under God*, or in the name of some transcendent value (in the case of some Buddhist and Confucian fundamentalisms). Their fight, in other words, is divinely sanctioned and divinely commissioned, and so there is no question of their truth.

Fundamentalism and Catholicism

The Catholic spirit, however, whether of the more "conservative" "communio" variety or the more "liberal" "kingdom" perspective, sees the world in a very different way from any fundamentalism. In contrast to a stance that distrusts the world—especially the modern world—a truly Catholic perspective, while it does not embrace the world uncritically, recognizes that human experience, culture, the beauty of nature and its present dangerous situation, the movements of history, the miracles of technology are the raw materials of theological reflection. Theology is not just a mining of the past, but a constant discovery of history's richness and relevance for *this world, today*. In contrast to a belief that certain practices need to be restored that are "traditional" or "ancient" when often they are only a few centuries old, Catholicism has recourse to history.

As Thomas O'Meara affirms, "The Catholic Church is old" and "Catholicism takes the long view."[42] What this "long view" reveals is that there is very little that is really new, and that what might seem old is actually something developed in a relatively recent past. "History," says O'Meara again, "is the great enemy of every fundamentalism."[43] Catholicism's sense of history also counters any simplistic use or reading of a text or tradition. The Bible is not an answer book or scientific textbook, but a document that is the product of various authors in various periods of history, and each book reflects the culture and beliefs of the time in which it was written or finally edited. The Bible is inerrant, Vatican II teaches, insofar as it teaches "firmly, faithfully, and without error that truth which God wanted put in the sacred writings for the sake of our salvation" (DV 11). The Catholic theologian *interprets* the Bible according to various methods which reveal its meaning.[44]

As we have seen already in this chapter, Catholicism at its best is not at all sectarian, but inclusive, open, tolerant of various perspectives and theologies. There is room for *Gaudium et Spes* ("kingdom") Catholics as well as *City of God* ("communio") Catholics. There is room for Nigerian theology as well as Fijian theology, a more meditative "patristic" theology as well as a more analytical scholastic method. After Vatican II, it is clear that a theology that is Catholic needs to be in dialogue with theologies of other religious ways, while of course not capitulating to the temptation of thinking that "all religions are the same." Catholicism believes in a "wideness in God's mercy,"[45] because God's presence and grace are found not only *inside* the church but *outside* as well. In O'Meara's elegant words:

> Catholic tradition holds that grace as the inviting, intimate presence of God on earth is not tied to the three "Bs": baptism, belief, belonging to a church. While faith in the gospel and membership in the church are the central ways of God's grace working in history overall, grace exists outside Christianity. Christ died for all men and women, not just for a small, select group predestined by an unpredictable and unpleasant deity millions of years ago. Although Jesus Christ is unique, intense center and cause of grace, the presence celebrated by Christmas, Good Friday and Easter contacts all men and women in the silence of their lives and in their own religions. Here too Catholicism is the opposite of a fundamentalism which proclaims the landslide of most people—God's images—into hell.[46]

Ultimately, says O'Meara, there are three basic differences between Catholicism and fundamentalism, and these profoundly affect the way Catholics do theology.[47] First, while fundamentalists believe in a demanding, rigid God, Catholics insist on believing in a God who, while utterly mysterious, has revealed the divine fullness in the ordinary life and brutal death of the carpenter of Nazareth. The closeness and ordinariness of God's grace, then, are a basic theme of Catholic theologizing. Second, though human existence is shot through with sinfulness, we are at our core basically good, basically holy—as is our world, and as is all of creation. Human experience, therefore, is a worthy source of theological truth, when put into dialogue with the church's rich and long tradition. Third, the church, while not the exclusive place where God's grace is revealed, is nevertheless a privileged place, and so theology needs to be deeply ecclesial. Tradition matters, magisterium matters, theological debate matters.

CONCLUSION

Catholics do theology in a unique way, and so we can indeed speak of a "catholic method." What has been clear from this chapter, however, is that this method, rather than producing a *universal* theology, or one way of understanding Christian faith, actually gives way to what is often a bewildering but always a stimulating variety of expressions. Since Catholics treasure the concrete—in experience, in culture, in history—Catholic theology provides various ways in which peoples from various cultures can interact with Christianity's past as they seek its relevance for their present. The understanding of faith that Catholics seek is truly one grounded in the reality of the incarnation—God's becoming and revealed in human flesh, human history.

QUESTIONS FOR REFLECTION

1. How would you characterize the "vision of Catholicism"?
2. Where do you see "Mother Church" and "Sophia" in tension in today's church?
3. Why do you think people are attracted to fundamentalism?
4. Why are fundamentalism and Catholicism opposite theological perspectives?

SUGGESTIONS FOR FURTHER READING AND STUDY

Lawrence Cunningham, *The Catholic Experience* (New York: Crossroad, 1985).

Roberto S. Goizueta, *Caminemos con Jesús: Toward a Hispanic/Latino Theology of Accompaniment* (Maryknoll, N.Y.: Orbis Books, 1995), chapter 3, "*Nosotros*: Community as the Birthplace of the Self," 47-76.

Andrew M. Greeley, *The Catholic Imagination* (Berkeley/Los Angeles/London: University of California Press, 2000).

———, "The Catholic Imagination of Bruce Springsteen," *America* 158, no. 5 (February 6, 1988): 110-14.

———, "The Last Catholic Novelist: The Grace-filled Fiction of Jon Hassler," *America* 199, no. 14 (November 3, 2008): 21-25.

Thomas H. Groome, *What Makes Us Catholic: Eight Gifts for Life* (San Francisco: HarperSanFrancisco, 2002).

Stephen Happel and David Tracy, *A Catholic Vision* (Philadelphia: Fortress Press, 1984).

Rosemary Haughton, *The Catholic Thing* (Springfield, Ill.: Templegate, 1979).

Thomas F. O'Meara, *Fundamentalism: A Catholic Perspective* (New York: Paulist Press, 1990).

David Tracy, *The Analogical Imagination: Christian Theology and the Culture of Pluralism* (New York: Crossroad, 1981).

Part IV

Faith Seeking through the Ages

Theology, History, and Culture

A T THE BEGINNING of his masterful introduction to theology, British Evangelical theologian Alister McGrath quotes the great twentieth-century Swiss theologian Karl Barth concerning the livingness of Christian tradition:

> We cannot be in the church without taking as much responsibility for the theology of the past as for the theology of the present. Augustine, Thomas Aquinas, Luther, Schleiermacher and all the rest are not dead but living. They still speak and demand a hearing as living voices, as surely as we know that they and we belong together in the church.[1]

Because of this, McGrath says, "It is . . . of importance that the reader [or we could say, the Christian as such] becomes familiar with the Christian past, which provides vital reference points for the modern debate."[2]

In order to *do* theology, in other words, theologians—at least on the level of the professional theologian or minister—have to have at least a *general grasp* of the history of theology, or "befriend the tradition," as James and Evelyn Whitehead put it so well.[3] What this general grasp or "befriending" means is that theologians need to know at least the main historical and cultural forces that have given shape to the church's particular theological doctrines; know the main theological questions and issues that have emerged through the ages, and the historical and cultural contexts that have produced them; know the main theological personages and their particular contributions to theology; know the general movement of the history of theology, its major periods and developments; realize that Christian theologizing is not now and never has been a monolithic, purely *Western* reality, but from the beginning has been pluriform and multicultural in shape. If we can become aware not only of the *facts* of the past but of some of the major *factors* of its development, we will be in good shape to do theology ourselves in a way that speaks to and emerges out of the burning historical and cultural issues of our own day, in today's global church.

This is what I propose to do in these four concluding chapters. Chapter 10 will outline the development of theology from the beginnings of the world Christian movement till about the year 1000. Chapter 11 will focus on theology from the eleventh to the eighteenth century, sketching in particular the amazing theological activity of Scholasticism in the West, the creative theologizing of missionaries and new Christians in the sixteenth and seventeenth centuries in Latin America and Asia, and briefly on the movements of the Reformation in the sixteenth and seventeenth centuries in Europe. The final chapters will summarize the immense amount of theological activity in all parts of the world from 1700 to 1900 (chapter 12) and from 1900 to the present (chapter 13). Theology has always been the work of a world church; it is, however, only in the last century that we can speak of theology beginning to be done "in global perspective."

10

Christian Theology from
the Beginnings to 1000

THE FIRST ONE THOUSAND YEARS of the world Christian movement were years of truly remarkable growth and theological reflection. Within the first three hundred years, the number of Christians grew from a minuscule minority on the geographical margins of the Roman empire to members of a church that had grown 40 percent per decade. In this way, by the year 300 C.E., Christians comprised fully 10 percent of the empire.[1] Christians were found everywhere, but they were concentrated particularly in what is today Turkey and Greece, in Egypt, and along the coast of North Africa, largely due to the efforts of ordinary Christians and their excitement to "gossip the gospel."[2]

In 301, Gregory the Illuminator (257-330) had baptized King Tiridates I, and the king declared Armenia a Christian country.[3] Christianity had spread eastward into western Asia and the Persian empire and then south into India.[4] It had also spread westward into Spain and Britain. By the fourth century the gospel had been preached in Ethiopia, and in the fifth century Patrick (387-493 [460/61]) had evangelized Ireland, with the subsequent growth of monasticism and evangelical activity of Celtic monks throughout Europe. The sixth century saw the beginning of the European monastic movement as monasteries for both men and women under the Benedictine rule grew to thousands throughout the continent. In the seventh century Christianity's very existence was threatened by the phenomenal growth of Islam, but it also had spread along the Silk Road throughout Asia through East Syrian monks as well as merchants and soldiers, and reached China by 635.[5] In the ninth century the brothers Cyril (d. 869) and Methodius (d. 885) evangelized the Slavs, and by 988 Russia had been converted as well.[6]

The first centuries of Christianity were times of significant theological activity, and Christian theologizing is present in the Christian Scriptures themselves. The amount of theologizing, however, multiplied especially after Christianity was legalized and recognized as the Roman empire's official religion toward the end of the fourth century.

Theology was not done only in the West (i.e., Alexandria, Antioch, Rome), however. Wherever there were Christians—in Syria, in China, in India, in Ethiopia—Christians sought to express, justify, explain, and defend their faith both to non-Christians and fellow Christians alike, using the experience of their time in history and the culture in which they lived and ministered. Theology was not done only discursively or in writing. It was done as Christians preached, sang hymns, decorated Roman catacombs and churches, prayed with one another, or "gossiped the gospel" to friends, spouses, or neighbors.[7]

In the first ten centuries of Christianity we meet some of the most influential theologians in the Christian tradition—women, men, Africans, Asians, Celts, Europeans, monks, bishops, layfolk: Perpetua and Felicity, Augustine, Macrina, Ephrem the Syrian, Egeria, Evagrios of Pontos, Jerome, and Paula. In addition, we encounter the formation of perhaps the most crucial doctrinal expressions in our tradition: doctrines in Christology, grace, ecclesiology, Mariology, sacraments, ministry. The following summary of the development of theology in Christianity's first millennium will only scratch the surface of how Christians in all parts of the Christian world sought to understand their faith in terms of their history and culture. What I hope, however, is that it will help readers to begin to get enough knowledge to "befriend" the bewildering richness of how the earliest Christians did theology, and to begin to treasure that tradition as much as it deserves.

THEOLOGY IN THE NEW TESTAMENT

We often don't think of the writings of the New Testament as *theology*, but that is what they are—as are the rich variety of the Jewish Scriptures from which the New Testament took so much imagery and content.[8] Of course, the Bible constitutes a *normative source* of theology (along with as we have seen in previous chapters, human experience and Christian tradition). The Bible is absolutely guaranteed by the church to present the person and message of Jesus faithfully, and that is why we speak of the Bible as both *inspired* and *inerrant* (see DV 11). It does not represent just *another* theological opinion, like a work of Augustine, or Catherine of Siena (1347-1380), or Cuban American theologian Orlando Espín.

Nevertheless, the fact remains that the writings of the New Testament were written by people who were trying to understand their faith in Jesus of Nazareth and his impact on their lives, on the world, and on history. Because of this, there is really no other way to describe what the writings of the New Testament are except as theology—or perhaps we should say *theologies*.

The New Testament—like the Old Testament before it—is really a collection of theological writings. As such, it represents a number of ways of expressing the meaning of Jesus and faith in the God of Jesus Christ, each of which comes out of a particular cultural or geographical context, and each of which is directed to a different audience. The New Testament, in other words, is a collection of *contextual* theologies, and one of the normative aspects of this New Testament theology is that it points to the fact that *all* Christian theology needs to be contextual. As we have insisted throughout this book, theology to be authentic must come out of particular situations and address particular kinds of people.

Paul's writings are prime examples of this. His distinct theology of grace, of the church, of the Spirit, and of Jesus the Christ almost always is rooted in his effort to deal with problems in the churches to which he writes. What is also distinctive is that he almost never begins his reflections with the *historical* Jesus, and almost never refers to him. One time that he *does* quote Jesus—"it is more blessed to give than to receive" (according to Acts 20:35, not his own writings)—the saying was not even quoted in the Gospels. And so it is from his own experience of the risen Lord that Paul develops his ideas of faith and justification, the church as the body of Christ (for the usage in 1 Corinthians 12 and Romans 12 he borrows a well-known parable from Hellenistic culture), and the nature of the church as inclusive of Jew and Gentile (describing this in—for Jews—the scandalous way of speaking of the church as the "new" and "true" Israel).

Each of the four Gospels offers a distinct portrait of Christ and comes from a very concrete situation. As Aidan Nichols handily summarizes these distinctions, **Mark** presents Jesus as the "Son of Man, or the designated divine mediator," who "could only fulfill his destiny through suffering in which his disciples must expect to follow him." **Matthew** is perhaps the most "Jewish" of the Gospels and paints a portrait of Jesus the Messiah who "fulfills the Law by reexpressing it in the new code of his kingdom, which his disciples are to take to the ends of the earth." **Luke's** theology is perhaps the most influenced by a Gentile worldview. For him, says Nichols, Jesus is the king who reigns over human history, and "the saving efficacy of this reign is found in the foundation and miraculous spread of the Church in the (Lucan) Acts of the Apostles." Finally, the most overtly theological of the Gospels is **John**, which presents Jesus "as preexistent Word who enters history and returns to his Father with the promise that there his disciples will join him."[9] What Raymond Brown writes might serve as an apt summary: "The evangelists emerge as authors, shaping, developing, pruning the transmitted Jesus material, and as theologians, orienting that material to a particular goal."[10]

Other books of the New Testament present yet other theological perspectives and arise out of other particular circumstances. A famous example of a difference in theologies within the New Testament is the **Letter of James**, especially 2:24, which seems to be a direct contradiction to Paul's statements in, for example, Romans 4:5-6. The **First Letter of Peter** and the **Book of Revelation** are strongly countercultural and seem to contradict Paul's more accommodationist stance in Romans 13:1-7. **Hebrews** develops a Christology very different from anything in the New Testament and is the only book that speaks specifically of Christ as High Priest.

The Christian Scriptures are not systematic in their presentation of Christology, ecclesiology, or eschatology. They are more narrative and occasional in character. Nevertheless, they are theologies, and contextual theologies at that. Not only are they normative in terms of content; they are normative in terms of their composition and method. They are not like the Qur'an, which can never be officially translated or investigated with rigorous historical-critical methods. They are sure guides to the apostolic faith, but that faith has also to be nurtured by continuing to be in dialogue with the living Christian community, the living presence of Jesus in the church, and the living presence of the Spirit in history and culture.

THEOLOGY IN THE SECOND AND THIRD CENTURIES

The second and third centuries are often referred to as the "early patristic period," for this is the time of the early "fathers" of the church. While it is certainly true that these theologians—presbyter-bishops, monks, laymen, martyrs—are important Christian ancestors, the term "patristic" and "fathers" is entirely too exclusive, because there were women theologians who served as "mothers" of the church as well.[11] Feminist scholarship is recovering more and more evidence of the strong presence of women and women's leadership in the first centuries of the church, but we are still at a point where the overwhelming amount of writing that we know from this period is by men. More evidence of women's writing may indeed surface in the future. Most likely, however, given the constraints on women's education and freedom in the Hellenistic and west Asian cultures to which Christianity spread, most Christian authors were indeed men.

In any case, these two centuries, and the "golden age" that followed in the next period represent, as Alister McGrath says, "one of the most exciting and creative periods in the history of Christian thought."[12] And, as eminent twentieth-century French theologian (and cardinal) Henri de Lubac (1896-1991) has said, there has never been a movement of renewal or reform in the church without a fresh discovery of the witness of the men (and we would also say women) who are its earliest theologians.[13] All the more reason to highlight the few samples of writing by women.

It is also important to point out that in the second and third centuries most of the theological "action" took place outside of western Europe. The major centers of Christian theology were in western Asia—in Antioch in Syria, Edessa in Oshroene—and in North Africa, especially in Alexandria, the intellectual capital of the Roman empire. This would basically be the case through the fourth and fifth centuries as well.

The **Didache**, *the Letters of Ignatius of Antioch, and Other Accounts of Martyrdom*

In 1873, Greek Orthodox archbishop Philotheos Bryennios was browsing in the library of the Holy Sepulchre monastery in Istanbul, Turkey, when he came across a manuscript, signed and dated June 11, 1056, by "Leon the notary and sinner." The manuscript, published ten years later to the general astonishment of scholars, was a copy of a document that incorporated written and oral sources that go back to the first half of the first century, and was written in Greek, probably in Syria at the beginning of the second century. It is most likely the oldest Christian document in existence outside of the New Testament, and may even predate some of the New Testament books.

This document is known as the ***Didache***, after its opening line: "The Lord's teaching (*didache*) to the heathen by the Twelve Apostles."[14] It has a strong Jewish flavor, especially in the opening lines of chapter 1, which speaks of "two Ways, one of Life and one of Death" (1.1—see Deut. 30:15-20 and Psalm 1), although it was written, it seems, at a time when Christians in Syria were in the process of separating themselves from Judaism: the Jews are called "hypocrites" in 8.1 and 2. There is a version of the Lord's Prayer in 8.2 that follows the version of the prayer in Matthew's gospel (see Matt. 6:9-13), gives instructions for baptism (including a trinitarian formula—chapter 7), and has a beautiful version of a Eucharistic Prayer (without words of institution—chapters 9 and 10).

Another important aspect of the document is the glimpse it gives into the church order of a Jewish Christian, Syrian community at the beginning of the second century. The document speaks in chapters 11-13 of wandering teachers, apostles, and prophets who seem to have very much prestige in the community—although if the prophet asks for money the community should not give it to him (or presumably "her" in the light of Acts 21:9). Prophets are called "high priests" (13.3) and they may improvise at Eucharist (10.7). Scholars say, however, that the *Didache* community is one in transition in terms of ministerial structure. The era of wandering charismatics may be nearing an end, for the community is urged to appoint bishops (*episkopoi*) and deacons, and not to despise them, for "they also minister to you in the ministry of the prophets and teachers," 15.1). Perhaps a new church order is in the making— one attested to by the letters of Ignatius of Antioch, to which we now turn.

Sometime in the first decade of the second century (between 107 and 110, some scholars say), **Ignatius**, the bishop (*episkopos*) of Antioch in Syria, the third largest city in the Roman empire, was arrested and sentenced to death in Rome. He was taken overland through Asia Minor—what is today Turkey—to Smyrna, where he received visitors from Ephesus, Magnesia, and Tralles, wrote to those communities, and wrote a letter as well to the Christian community in Rome. Then he reached Troas, where he wrote to the Philadelphians, to the Smyrnaeans, and to the bishop of Smyrna, Polycarp. From Troas his guards put him on board a ship and they traveled to Philippi in Greece, and from Philippi to Rome where, presumably, he was martyred in a Roman amphitheater, possibly the famed Colosseum.[15]

Three important theological themes run throughout the letters, the first of which is the church order that Ignatius reflects rather matter-of-factly. What seems to have developed in Syria and Asia Minor—and this is the first evidence that we have of it—is that the rather fluid structure of ministry and church order that we find reflected in the Pauline letters[16] is beginning "to coalesce around a single leader of each eucharistic community, known as *episkopos*, or 'overseer,' rendered in modern English as 'bishop.'"[17] The same structure—one bishop, surrounded by a group of advisors (elders, *presbyteroi*) and deacons—seems to be present in each of the churches to which Ignatius writes. The only exception—very interestingly—is the church of Rome. Ignatius writes to the *church* of Rome (*Romans*, introduction). While the development of church leadership into one of "monarchical episcopate"—that is, one bishop—seems to have been complete in West Asia and Asia Minor (Syria and Turkey), it had not yet developed in Rome.

A second theme that runs through the letters is both an insistence on the true humanity of Jesus, against one of the earliest heresies in the church, "Docetism" (from the Greek word *dokein*, "to seem"—Jesus only *seemed* human), and an insistence on the discreteness of Christianity over against Judaism. To give just one example from the text for each of these, let me first cite a text that some scholars think is from an early Christian hymn:

> Very flesh, yet Spirit too;
> Uncreated, and yet born;
> God-and-Human in One agreed
> Very-Life-in-Death indeed
> Fruit of God and Mary's seed;
> At once impassible and torn
> By pain and suffering here below:
> Jesus Christ, whom as our Lord we know.
> (*Ephesians* 7)[18]

Against Judaizing, Ignatius writes in a way that Christians would find insensitive today, but which unfortunately is more common than not in early Christian theologizing: "It is monstrous to talk of Jesus Christ and to practice Judaism. For Christianity does not base its faith on Judaism, but Judaism on Christianity, and every tongue believing on God was brought together in it" (*Magnesians* 10).

A third theme—and one that had a tremendous impact on the church over the centuries—is Ignatius's embrace of martyrdom. Contrary to popular opinion, the Roman empire did not persecute Christians all that systematically, and Rodney Stark quotes eminent church historian W. H. C. Frend's conclusion that the number of martyrs in the three hundred years before Constantine legalized Christianity was really in the "hundreds, not thousands."[19] Frend's estimate is perhaps a bit of an exaggeration, but the point is that the number of martyrs was probably *far* fewer than we have been led to believe in the past from books and movies like *Quo Vadis* or *The Robe*. What happened, however, was that Roman authorities found Christians dangerous and subversive, since they would not offer sacrifice to the emperor and the state gods. Their tactic was to try to intimidate Christians by executing their leaders, like Ignatius, or Polycarp, or Cyprian. Of course this did not work. As Tertullian said famously, "The blood of Christians is seed."[20] Ignatius's writings no doubt fueled the hearts and the imagination of Christians who would give their lives in testimony to Christ, and eventually a rich cult of martyrs developed in all parts of the church. From the many places in Ignatius's letters where he writes eloquently of martyrdom, let me quote here only the most famous: In *Romans* 4, Ignatius wrote:

> For my part, I am writing to all the churches and assuring them that I am truly in earnest about dying for God — if only you yourselves put no obstacles in the way, I must implore you to do me no such untimely kindness; pray leave me to be a meal for the beasts, for it is they who can provide my way to God. I am His wheat, ground fine by the lions' teeth to be made purest bread for Christ. Better still, incite the creatures to become a sepulchre for me; let them not leave the smallest scrap of my flesh, so that I need not be a burden to anyone after I fall asleep.

Three other accounts of martyrdom from this period are also quite significant. The first is that of the **Martyrdom of Polycarp**, bishop of Smyrna. It too had a great influence on the theological imagination of the early church.[21] Perhaps lesser known, but extremely important in the history of theology are the accounts of **Perpetua and Felicity** and of the **Marytrs of Lyons**, especially **Blandina**. The account of Perpetua and Felicity, written at Carthage in North Africa in 203 by the noblewoman Vibia Perpetua, represents the earliest Christian writing by a woman.[22] The martyrdom of Blandina and her companions took place in Lyons in Gaul in 177 and was preserved by Eusebius of Caesarea (263-339) in his *Ecclesiastical History*, written in the fourth century after Christianity had been legalized by Constantine in the Roman empire.[23] Of particular importance in the account is a wonderful theological reflection by Blandina's companions as they saw her executed before them:

> But Blandina was suspended on a stake, and exposed to be devoured by the wild beasts who should attack her. And because she appeared as if hanging

on a cross, and because of her earnest prayers, she inspired the combatants with great zeal. For they looked on her in her conflict, and beheld with their outward eyes, in the form of their sister, him who was crucified for them . . . . (41)

The Apologists

In the first several centuries we find a number of theologians who attempt to defend Christianity (*apologia* in Greek means "defense") from misunderstandings by Roman authorities and Hellenistic philosophers. They are important for the history of theology because in trying to make their defense they have recourse to ideas in Hellenistic culture and philosophy—and so are early examples of what we call today "inculturation." One of the earliest apologists is the lay theologian **Justin Martyr** (100-165). He was born in Palestine of Greek parents, but traveled as a philosopher to Greece and then Rome. It was in Rome that he became a Christian, claiming that in Christianity he had found the true philosophy. Many of his works have been lost, but because of what survives—his *First Apology*, *Second Apology*, and the *Dialogue with Trypho the Jew*—he is considered the most important Greek apologist of the second century.[24] Justin's first and second apologies were addressed to Emperor Marcus Aurelius and to the Roman Senate, respectively, and they argued that Rome had nothing to fear from Christianity, for Christians believed what was fully true, which former philosophers only glimpsed previously. They could glimpse the truth—and they could even be called Christians.[25] This was because of the presence of God's Word (*logos*), which was spread throughout the world and in human hearts and minds in a partial way. Christians, however, know that Word—incarnate in Jesus—in its entirety.[26] In the *Dialogue with Trypho*, Justin argues how the Old Testament is fulfilled in the New. This is seen particularly by the fact that the Old Testament presents us with "types" or "figures," which will later be fully realized. Thus, the paschal lamb of Exodus is a type of Christ crucified, and the lamb's blood is the blood of Christ by which we are saved. Justin's "typological" interpretation of the Old Testament will take on great importance in the next several centuries and in patristic theology.

Another prominent lay apologist is **Clement of Alexandria** (ca. 150-ca. 215). Clement was converted by Pantaenus, who was the founder of the famous school of theology known as the Catechetical School in Alexandria (and who possibly ended his life as a missionary to India).[27] Clement succeeded Pantaenus as head of the school and was even more open to non-Christian religions and philosophies as ways to understand the riches of Christian faith—so much so that some even see him as an early rationalist (see our treatment of rationalism in chapter 2). For Clement, who was acquainted with Hinduism, Buddhism, and Persian, Egyptian, and Greek religions, all of these could serve as preparations for the gospel. This was because "any wisdom or philosophy that teaches righteousness can be understood as having come from God."[28] As he wrote in one of his major works, the *Miscellanies*: "Philosophy, therefore, was a preparation, paving the way for him who is perfected in Christ. . . . The way of truth is therefore one. But into it, as into a perennial river, streams flow from all sides."[29]

Clement's greatest pupil at the Catechetical School was to become Christianity's first true systematic theologian, **Origen of Alexandria** (ca. 185-ca. 254). British church historian David Edwards calls Origen "the early church's greatest theologian,"[30] and Hans Küng calls him "the only real genius among the church fathers, a man with an insatiable thirst for knowledge, a wide-ranging education and tremendous creative power."[31] Küng adds that Eusebius, writing in the fourth century, numbers Origen's books at two thousand; Justo González says that Epiphanius of Salamis (after 310-403) lists them at *six* thousand![32] Unfortunately, however, because of his being accused of heresy, most of these are now lost (how rich would our Christian tradition be if Christians had had more tolerance!).

A first work that should be mentioned here is Origen's attempt to establish the original text of Scripture, the *Hexapla*. The work, of which only fragments remain, gives six translations (*hex* in Greek = six) side by side, beginning with the Hebrew in the Old Testament, so that the scholar could decide which was most original and the best translation.[33] Origen's great defense of Christianity was the *Contra Celsum* (Against Celsus). Celsus was a Greek philosopher who mounted one of the most serious attacks yet made against Christianity, and Origen refuted Celsus's opinions one by one.[34] Origen's brilliant systematic work was entitled *Peri Archon* or *On the First Principles*, most of which has survived in a Latin translation. For Origen, as for all Platonic philosophy with which he was imbued, God was absolutely transcendent, above all change and beyond all time. Human beings had been created to enjoy God's transcendence, but when they "strayed from the contemplation of the One,"[35] they fell into sin. The divine mercy, however, provided fallen creatures with the material universe, where they might find their way back to wholeness, and Jesus was given to humankind as a way that finite minds might somehow grasp God's reality. Through Jesus, God would eventually bring all creation back into harmony with Godself. Origen posited a doctrine of universal salvation by which, at the end of time, even those in hell would be released—a doctrine that got him condemned after his death.

Nevertheless, Origen stands as one of the great giants in Christian theology. He was committed to the importance of reason and philosophy in theological work and was the first great system builder, against whom "later Christian theology would be judged in both its range and its level of philosophical argument."[36] But his faith was not just on the intellectual level. In 250 he was arrested and brutally tortured by the Roman authorities at Caesarea in Palestine (where he had fled after having been ordained a presbyter illegally). He did not die in captivity, but died soon after from his wounds, and the church has given him the title of martyr.

No history of the theology of the second and third centuries would be complete without recalling **Tertullian** (160-235), a native of North Africa and, from the strong legal cast of much of his theology, most likely trained in Roman law. Tertullian is one of the earliest, if not *the* earliest Christian theologian to write in Latin, and González calls him "the founder of Western Christian theology."[37] He was a layman and a prolific writer, and among his major contributions to future theology in the West was his use of a number of Latin terms that would become standard in later theology: *meritum* (merit), *persona* (person), *sacramentum* (sacrament), *trinitas* (trinity),[38] *substantia* (substance). He is also famous for many quotable phrases that have come down to Christians today: "We are little fishes called after our great fish Jesus Christ" (*ichthus*, the Greek word for "fish" is a kind of acronym signifying "Jesus Christ Son of God, Savior"); "We are born in water and can survive only by staying in water"; "The soul is naturally Christian"; "The blood of martyrs is seed"; "I believe because it is impossible"; "What does Athens have to do with Jerusalem."[39]

Because of these last two sayings, in some ways Tertullian might be best spoken of as a *confessor*, not an *apologist*. Nevertheless, he did defend the faith before the Roman authorities, and even though he did join the heretical Montanist sect toward the end of his life, he did die a martyr's death.

For Tertullian, God is described as a lawgiver and a judge. This is similar to how another early Western writer, Clement (in the latter part of the first century, in a letter to the church at Corinth), described God as the "despot" (or ruler) of the universe.[40] Creation is conceived as wholly complete after a certain order, and sin is described as going against this order and breaking the divine law. Human beings are born into this world as sinners, having inherited sinfulness from the first parents, who originally broke God's law and disrupted the world's order.[41] Jesus is depicted as the new Moses and the gospel a new law, which is a new law of repentance. If men and women submit to that law in baptism, they will be saved and so avoid God's punishment, provided they obey the laws of God's church and the prescriptions of Scripture. At the end, God will resurrect and judge the entire human race, and those to be saved will be with God forever in a state where order will be fully restored.[42]

Justo González speaks of Origen and Tertullian as exemplifying two basic types of theology that have persisted down through the ages to our own day. Tertullian represents a recurring concern for order in Christian life and theology, and González dubs this "Type A" theology, which focuses on order and/or law. Origen's commitment to philosophy and systematic thinking points to a more abstract and academic cast to theology, and González speaks of this type of theology as "Type B," a theology that searches to discover Truth wherever it is found. González identifies a third type of theology—"Type C"—which has its earliest exemplar in another major figure in early Christian theology: the Syrian-born bishop of the church in Lyons in Gaul, **Irenaeus** (ca. 130-200).

Even though Irenaeus was a bishop in the West, he wrote in Greek, and was more Eastern in spirit than his contemporary Tertullian. In his major works, a first entitled *Adversus Haereses* (Against Heresies) and a second entitled *Demonstration of the Apostolic Preaching*, Irenaeus is not systematic but pastoral. He is more rooted in Scripture for his image of God, whom he saw as a Shepherd rather than as a cosmic Lawgiver or transcendent Being.[43] Irenaeus clearly understood God as trinitarian, and he spoke famously of the Son and the Spirit as the Father's two hands, reaching out to creation.[44] One of Irenaeus's chief contributions to theology was his idea, no doubt inspired by Paul, of a final "recapitulation" of all in Christ at the end of time. For Irenaeus, creation was something "in process," and human beings and all creation were moving toward greater and greater perfection. Humanity was created in God's image and likeness and because of the first couple's immaturity, lost that likeness through their disobedience. God in God's mercy, however, offered Jesus as an exemplar of human perfection, and under his lead humanity would once again reflect God's image and likeness perfectly.

Irenaeus's more historical, more pastoral view, says González, has always been a minority view in the history of Christian theology, but most recently it has found new life both in the visionary theology of the twentieth-century French scientist Pierre Teilhard de Chardin (1881-1955), and in the variety of theologies of liberation that have their roots in late-twentieth-century Latin American theology.

Early Theology in East Syria and the Persian Empire

The Christian center of Edessa, modern Urfa in Turkey, came into contact with Christianity as early as 150 c.e., while it was still part of the Persian empire.[45] It was the capital of a small state between the Roman and Persian empires named Oshroene and throughout the second, third, and fourth centuries was conquered by Rome or Persia several times. The church in Edessa was connected to the Greek-speaking church of Antioch, but the language that was used in its literature and liturgy was Syriac, and there developed a substantial Christian literature in that language.

It was at Edessa that there lived the remarkable theologian, philosopher, and poet **Bardaisan** (154-222). His name means "Son of the Daisan," the river on which Edessa is located.[46] Born of Persian parents in Edessa, he was converted to Christianity as a young man and wrote voluminously. Almost all his works have been destroyed, however, since he was denounced as a heretic after his death by another influential Syrian theologian, Ephrem (306-373), whom we will treat in the next section. Like Ephrem, Bardaisan wrote some of his theology in hymnody, particularly his *Book of Psalms*, but he also wrote works against Marcion and the Gnostic Valentinus, and a work entitled *Book* *of the Laws of the Countries*, in which he showed a positive attitude toward local cultures and histories as fulfilled and reconciled in Christ. It was perhaps this more positive perspective that brought him under the charge of heresy, but Dale Irvin and Scott Sunquist see him as "one of the most Catholic thinkers of the early third century. . . . Bardaisan wrote of the ways of the Chinese, Indians, Persians, Arabs, Greeks, Germans, and Britons. He saw the means by which Jesus Christ, the First Thought of God, could bring about redemption of all without the displacement of their various laws and cultures. . . ."[47]

Very different from Bardaisan's outlook was that of **Tatian the Assyrian**. As a young man, Tatian traveled from his birthplace in Assyria or Syria to Rome, where around 150 he was converted to Christianity, and studied with Justin Martyr. Later on, however—perhaps around 170—Tatian left Rome and returned to the East, where he founded his own sect called the Encratites. We know little about this group, but Tatian is known for his extreme asceticism and for his condemnation of Greek philosophical thinking in his *Address to the Greeks*. Perhaps Tatian's greatest contribution to theology is his *Diatesseron*, which was a kind of harmony of the four Gospels, written originally in Syriac. This was practically the only version of the Gospels used in the Syrian church in the third and fourth century, and it was used in the church in China in the sixth century and as a basis of the ninth-century Saxon version of the Gospels, the *Heliand*. There is evidence that Tatian brought the gospel as far east as Arbela, the capital of the Persian-dominated kingdom of Adiabene. Tatian wrote several other works, but all of them have been lost; around 180 he disappears from history.[48]

There are, of course, *many* more theologians from this formative period of Christian theology that we might discuss with profit, but what we are presenting in these chapters represents what Aidan Nichols calls in his own brief survey of Christian theology a "rough and ready"[49] overview. Suffice it here to mention works like the early-second-century *Epistle of Barnabas* (somewhat similar to the *Didache*), the second century *Epistle to Diognetus* with its famous lines of Christians being "in the world, but not of the world," the late-first-century *Shepherd of Hermas*, which had so much influence in the second and third centuries, and the works of **Papias of Hierapolis** in Asia Minor and **Cyprian of Carthage**, with his important controversy with the bishop of Rome over Rome's authority.

THEOLOGY FROM 300 TO 600

The Council of Nicaea

Perhaps the most important event for both the church's life and the development of Christian theology in the period from 300 to 600 c.e. was the

Council of Nicaea. The council took place in 325 and is important especially for its definition of Jesus' full divinity: "God from God, light from light, true God from true God . . . one in being (*homoousios*) with the Father."[50] Nicaea marked a watershed moment for theology in several ways. In the first place, it represented a move *beyond* the scriptural formulations for an understanding of the identity of Jesus in terms of Hellenistic culture, while at the same time recognizing Scripture—and not Greek philosophy—as the norm for Christian faith. Second, it set a process in motion that would not come to an end for the next several hundred years, as Christian doctrine and Christian theology sought to balance faith in Jesus' true divinity with the truth of his full humanity. So much of the theology of the next centuries would revolve around trinitarian theology and Christology. Third, Nicaea was the first of the twenty-one general or ecumenical councils of the church up to our day, signaling a powerful way by which the church would make its major decisions for the next thousand years. After the Council of Constance (1414-1418), the authority of councils was tempered somewhat with the growing centralization of the papacy and the growth of papal authority, but up until our day an ecumenical council working together with the pope is the primary authority in the church.

The occasion for this first council was the controversy stirred by Arius (ca. 250-336), a brilliant preacher and pastor of one of Alexandria's several churches in the years just after Constantine had declared Christianity a legitimate—and favored—religion in the Roman empire. At a time of division in the empire, and when its borders were being challenged by migrating tribes from the north and the east, one of Constantine's immediate predecessors, Diocletian (and after him his successor Galerius), had tried to unify the empire by outlawing any religion but that of the Roman state. For Christians this meant, from 303 until 311, one of the worst systematic persecutions they had suffered, with the confiscation of scriptural writings, the prohibition of meetings, and the execution of members.

It was only when Constantine took up the Christians' cause after his victory in 312 at the Milvan Bridge outside Rome that Christians found themselves to be out of danger. Persecution of Christians did not work. The blood of the Christian martyrs proved only to be like seed, as Tertullian had said. And so Constantine seized upon this rapidly growing religion as *his* way to unify the empire. Constantine, writes David Edwards, "turned to the Church because Christianity spoke about Christ but it seems that he turned to Christ because he needed help in what really interested him: first the conquest and then the reconstruction of the empire. He was a Christian version of Diocletian."[51] He issued the Edict of Milan or the Edict of Toleration in 313.

But now, in Alexandria and increasingly across the empire, the dispute started by **Arius** was creating division, not unity. Arius's concern was, in the best tradition of Platonic philosophy, to preserve the utter transcendence of God. In the Platonic understanding, God was so transcendent that there was no way God could get involved *directly* in saving or even creating the world. To do such "dirty work,"[52] God had to create a "demiurge" or "craftsman" to fashion the world. This, said Arius, was what Jesus was: the first of all creation, *almost* fully divine—certainly greater than other creatures—but created nonetheless. Through him, God had created the universe and God had further acted to redeem humankind, but, as Arius insisted, "there was a time when the Word was not."

Arius's effort, as we might express it today, was an attempt to contextualize theology within the parameters of Platonic philosophy. But he also had recourse to Scripture: Does the Letter to the Colossians not speak of Christ as "firstborn of all creation" (Col. 1:15)? Doesn't Jesus say in John's Gospel that "the Father is greater than I" (John 14:28)? Alexander, the bishop of Alexandria, however, and even the ordinary people of that great Egyptian city, said no. If Jesus was not truly God, then God had not really involved Godself with humanity—as Alexander's deacon Athanasius (ca. 293-373) would put it later: "What has not been assumed has not been redeemed." Furthermore, people said, we pray to Christ as to God—have all our prayers been to a creature? And Scripture also attests to Jesus' divinity: "The Word was God" (John 1:1), wrote John, and "whoever has seen me has seen the Father" (14:9).

The controversy was tearing the empire apart. Gregory of Nyssa's (ca. 335-after 394) description of the controversy in his time—a century afterwards—is still probably a good description of what was happening in the 320s: "One could not go into the marketplace to exchange money, buy bread, or discuss the merits of bathing without getting involved in a discussion with merchants and others about whether 'God the Son' is subordinate to 'God the Father,' begotten or unbegotten, created *ex nihilo* or an ordinary man."[53]

And so Constantine called the bishops of the empire together at his summer palace in Nicaea, a town just outside the city he had built as the new capital of the empire—Constantinople. There were about 220 to 250 bishops in attendance, mostly from Asia Minor and North Africa, although there seems to have been one bishop, John, who represented the bishops of India and Persia, and there was present an East Syrian bishop James (or Jacob) of Nisibis.[54] The bishop of Rome was absent, but he sent two legates. There were about a dozen bishops who sided with Arius, but the group was overwhelmingly on the side of Alexander and Athanasius.

Constantine presided at the sessions and seems to have been the one to propose a term that *had* at one point been considered heretical—*homoousios*, or "of one substance"—to express Jesus' true divinity. This was a radical move, since the term belonged to Greek philosophical thought and was not scriptural, but it was the word that the assembly approved and incorporated into its famous creed.

In many ways, however, Nicaea hardly solved the controversy that Arius had begun. Even Constantine wavered in his commitment to the orthodox formula, and there were times when the majority of the empire's bishops favored the Arian position. Arianism's advantages were clear. While it denied Jesus' divinity, it did uphold Jesus' humanity, which after Nicaea was also in danger of being denied. The next centuries would witness a struggle for a balance between the two aspects of orthodox christological doctrine. This struggle would not end until the Second Council of Nicaea in 787, where Jesus' true incarnation as a human being was used as an argument for the legitimacy of "icons" or images of Jesus and the saints. Nicaea represents the great moment of clarification for the doctrine of the Trinity, and it is the beginning of the refinement of the church's doctrine about Jesus, or Christology. Much of the theological activity in the eastern part of the empire is concerned with these issues in the next several centuries.

Athanasius of Alexandria and the Four Cappadocians

The great champion of Nicaea's doctrine of "one substance" was **Athanasius**, who, as was mentioned above, attended the council as a deacon from Alexandria, but who became bishop in 328. Athanasius paid a high price for his orthodoxy. In his long, forty-five-year tenure as bishop, as emperors accepted or did not accept the Nicene formula, he was exiled no fewer than five times, for a total of sixteen years away from his see. Among many works, Athanasius's major writings might be three especially: *On the Incarnation of the Word of God*, *Orations against the Arians*, and his *Life of Antony*, the famous hermit of the Egyptian desert who was his staunch supporter. The U.S. Anglo church historian Bernard McGinn cites the noted British theologian C. S. Lewis who said of Athanasius's work on the incarnation that "only a master mind could . . . have written so deeply on such a subject with classical simplicity."[55] Athanasius insisted on the necessity of the incarnation of the very Word made flesh to reveal God's fullness to humankind and to effect human salvation. The ultimate reason for the incarnation is to bring about *theōsis*, or "deification," a theme that is a central one in Eastern theology: God "assumed humanity that we might become God."[56] Athanasius's *Life of Antony* was wildly popular and was translated into several languages very quickly. It fired the imagination of Christians and was strongly influential in the rapid development of monasticism in Egypt, and then in Ireland, Asia Minor, and Europe in the next centuries. The book was also one of the major influences on Augustine's (354-430) conversion in the latter part of the fourth century.

Athanasius is the earliest of great saints and theologians who have been recognized as "doctors of the church." The title doctor, now bestowed upon women and men in the Western church by the bishop of Rome but earlier given much

more by the consensus of the church, has been given—up to the present day—
to only thirty-three theologians according to three criteria: holiness of life (all
of them are canonized saints), greatness of theological teaching, and significant
impact on Christian thought and life. Many, like Athanasius, are bishops, but a
good number are priests, and three (Catherine of Siena [1347-1380], Teresa of
Avila [1515-1582], and Thérèse of Lisieux [1873-1897]) are women. We will
meet many of these doctors in the pages that follow.[57]

In Cappadocia, what is now eastern Turkey, there lived a group of four
theologians who were also champions of Nicaea, and moved the Nicene
doctrine forward to include the acknowledgment of the full divinity of the
Holy Spirit. The first of these, **Basil of Caesarea** (ca. 329-379), is considered
"the most influential of all the Greek bishops of the fourth century"[58] (he is
also an official "doctor" of the church). Basil, successor of the great church
historian Eusebius as bishop of Caesarea, was most concerned with refuting
"Neo-Arians" like Eunomius (d. ca. 393). For Basil, God exists in three "persons" (*hypostases* or *prosopa*) and one "substance" (*ousia*). There is "one ultimate
Beginning of all existing things, creating through the Son and perfecting in
the Spirit."[59] Through him the phrase "one substance and three persons (or
hypostases)" became the touchstone of trinitarian orthodoxy in both East and
West. Besides major works on trinitarian theology—*Against Eunomius* and
On the Holy Spirit—Basil wrote a monastic rule that had a major influence on
both Eastern and Western monasticism.

Both Basil's best friend and his younger brother bore the name of Gregory.
His best friend, **Gregory Nanzianzen** (329-389) also opposed Eunomius,
who, like Arius, basically understood God as totally nonrelational. For Gregory Nanzianzen (also a doctor of the church), however, as for all the Cappadocians, God was in God's very *essence* relational, something he argued in his
major work, the *Theological Orations*. In a memorable sentence, he wrote: "The
three most ancient opinions concerning God are Anarchia [there is *no* God],
Polyarchia [there are many gods], and Monarchia [there is only *one* God]."
Gregory chooses Monarchia, but not in the ordinary sense that it appears in
Platonic philosophy. For him, Monarchy is "not . . . limited to a single person,
but a monarchy constituted by equal dignity of nature, accord of will, identity
of movement, and the return to unity of those who come from it."[60] Basil's
brother, **Gregory of Nyssa** (ca. 335-after 394) has not made it into the official
canon of doctors of the church, but theologians today credit him with some of
the most seminal ideas about God's trinitarian nature, especially on the divinity of the Holy Spirit.[61] All three of these bishops were major figures at the
Council of Constantinople in 381, in which Nicaea was confirmed and the full
divinity of the Holy Spirit was declared.

Traditionally, historians of theology have spoken of the *three* Cappadocians.
The eminent historian of doctrine Jaroslav Pelikan, however, includes Basil's

and Gregory of Nyssa's older sister **Macrina** in the group as well. Her brother Gregory wrote an important biography of her entitled *Life of Macrina*, and in his *On the Soul and the Resurrection* he called her "sister and teacher at the same time."[62] This points to Macrina's great learning in both philosophy and theology, expressed again by Gregory when he wrote that, on her deathbed, she was the only person he knew that could answer unbelievers' objections to the resurrection.[63] What is intriguing is whether Macrina was responsible also for at least the great insights into trinitarian thinking that her brothers and their friend had developed.

Ephrem the Syrian and Syriac Christianity

We have already met James (or Jacob) of Nisibis, the city on the border between the Roman and Persian empires. In 325, James returned from the Council of Nicaea and set up what was to be an important theological school, where many Greek works were translated into Syriac. James eventually placed a native of Nisibis, the deacon **Ephrem** (309-373) in charge of the school. Ephrem remained the school's head, even when it had to be transferred to Edessa in 363 when the city was taken over from the Romans by the Persians, who were extremely hostile to Christianity.[64]

Syriac Christian theology was very different from the way theology had developed in the West in Greek-speaking areas, or even farther West in Latin-speaking North Africa and Europe. It was less doctrinally focused and more interested in symbols or mysteries. Ephrem was a major figure in developing this kind of theology. He wrote some theology in prose, but much if not most of his theological output was written in the form of poetry and hymns, and over four hundred of these still survive. In the fifth century, another Syriac theologian, Theodoret of Cyrrhus (d. 466) called Ephrem "the lyre of the Spirit, who daily waters the Syrian nation with streams of grace."[65] Some of Ephrem's most important poetic works are his *Hymns of Paradise*, the *Hymns of Nisibis*, *On the Nativity*, and *On the Church*. His *Hymns on the Pascal Feast* is, sadly, very anti-Jewish. This might be explained (not excused!), however, by the fact that Syriac Christianity was culturally very close to Judaism; that it was where Jewish Christianity flourished much longer than it did farther West within Hellenistic culture; and that Judaism itself was very strong in this area of Mesopotamia (present-day Iraq and Iran). Ephrem's anti-Judaism, in other words, was the result of an inter-family squabble, which is often the most bitter kind.

Ephrem is the only officially proclaimed doctor of the church from the non-Byzantine East,[66] or perhaps we could say he is the only fully (West) Asian doctor. He accepted Nicene orthodoxy, but nowhere in his works does the word *homoousios* ("of one substance") appear. He does reflect, however, on one of the main reasons that the proponents of Nicene give for Jesus full divinity: the importance of human divinization or *theōsis*. He wrote, "The Deity imprinted itself on to humanity, so that humanity might also be cut into the seal of the Divinity."[67]

Ephrem also spoke of the Eucharist as life-giving medicine and had a well-developed Mariology as well. Feminist scholars today note that he also imaged the Holy Spirit in female terms. For example, we read in *On the Nativity* that "it is the Holy Spirit, Who for their sake by quiet contemplation in them stirs them up to see by Her the Savior for whom they yearned."[68]

As Indian theologians Kuncheria Pathil and Dominic Veliath express it, Ephrem's is a theology that is "unhellenized" and "uneuropeanized." "As such, Ephraem constitutes a link between European, Asian and African Christianity, and provides a refreshing counterbalance to an overly cerebral tradition of theological inquiry."[69] Theology that is expressed in the form of art (from Roman catacomb paintings to a Filipino *pasyon* to the South African Keiskamma Altarpiece) all have the Syriac tradition pioneered by Bardaisan and developed by Ephrem to stand on.

As a theologian in the Syriac tradition, of course, Ephrem was not alone. He is part of a "long list"[70] that includes his contemporary **Aphrahat** (270-345), known for his *Demonstrations*, some of which, like Ephrem, but in a more positive way, are written as dialogues with Jews.[71] Aphrahat was a monk and possibly a bishop in a monastery near Mosul in modern-day Iraq. We might also mention Antioch-born **Diodore of Tarsus** (d. 390), who like the Cappadocians was a major figure at the Council of Constantinople in 381, and who was a strong opponent of the cosmic dualism of the Manicheans. Also opposed to the Manicheans was **Titus**, bishop of Bostra in modern-day Syria, who died in 378. Naming these three is merely scratching the surface, but it is important to recognize the vitality of a theology that was not at all Western in its expression.

Perhaps the most influential theologian on later generations—both in the East and in the West—wrote from the year 482 into the beginning of the sixth century.[72] This was the anonymous Syrian monk who for centuries was known as **Dionysius the Areopagite**, a convert of St. Paul as a result of his speech at the Areopagus recorded in Acts 17. He was identified with Denis, the first bishop of Paris. Already in the twelfth century, Peter Abelard (1079-1142) challenged this latter identification, but it was only in 1895 that scholars proved that the writer depended heavily on the thought of Proclus, a fifth-century Neoplatonic writer in Athens, Greece.[73] Contemporary theologians know him as **"Pseudo-Dionysius."**

Four major works make up the Dionysian corpus: *The Celestial Hierarchy, The Ecclesiastical Hierarchy, On the Divine Names,* and *Mystical Theology.* In typical Neoplatonic fashion, Pseudo-Dionysius sees reality as hierarchically structured, with the different degrees of hierarchy emanating from and leading to God ("hierarchy" literally means "holy order," or "holy rule"). Above all names and knowledge, we read in *On the Divine Names*, there is God, who doesn't so much "exist" as grant existence to everything else. Emanating from the triune God (Pseudo-Dionysius writes in *The Celestial Hierarchy*) are three degrees of celestial choirs, each of these divided into three themselves: (1) seraphim, cherubim, and thrones, (2) dominions, virtues, and powers, and (3) principalities, archangels, and angels. In *The Ecclesiastical Hierarchy*, the church is divided into two hierarchical levels, each also consisting of three levels. The first level consists of the clergy: bishops, priests, and deacons; the second level is made up of monks, laypeople, and those who are members of the church but not able to receive communion. These last are made up of three levels: the catechumens (those not yet baptized), the energumens (those not yet exorcised), and the penitents (those baptized but excluded from the altar while doing penance for sins). This threefold pattern repeats itself in the *Mystical Theology*, in which Pseudo-Dionysius speaks of the journey to Christian perfection as involving a purgative stage in which the soul is purified from imperfections, an illuminative stage by which the soul is filled with divine light, and a unitive stage by which the soul is united to God in vision.[74]

Readers will see immediately the influence of Pseudo-Dionysius on subsequent theology. The theology of angels or "angelology" was shaped by his work on the celestial hierarchy, as a reading of the prefaces to our Eucharistic Prayers will show. The medieval church in the West found a ready scheme in Pseudo-Dionysius's treatise on the church to blend with Europe's highly structured feudal society, and spiritual writers through the ages have used his scheme of spiritual growth to explain the stages of Christian perfection. Because of his supposed apostolic status he was one of the most frequently quoted authors in theological writings of both the East and the West into the seventeenth century, especially in the works of Maximus the Confessor (580-662), Gregory Palamas (ca. 1296-1359), Albert the Great (ca. 1200-1280), and Thomas Aquinas (1224-1274).[75]

Theology in the West

Even though Constantine had moved the center of the empire to Constantinople (modern Istanbul) in the East, Christianity continued to flourish in the West—in North Africa, Italy, and even in the more remote territories of the empire in Gaul. **Hilary of Poitiers** (312-367) in Gaul was born just as Constantine was coming to power. His learning in the Latin classics, Bernard McGinn observes, points to the fact that his family was aristocratic[76]—most probably wealthy Roman citizens. Although he eventually became a presbyter and a bishop, Hilary was married and a father—the only one of the church's doctors to be such (Augustine was a father, but never married). He was the first Western bishop to recognize the danger of Arianism, and he tried to refute the heresy in his major work, *The Trinity*. McGinn notes Hilary's courage to work through theological issues of the day that were still being developed, and although his theology leads to several errors—regarding Jesus' true humanity, for example—his basic approach to theology was a humble one. One passage illustrates this humility and echoes nicely what we said in chapter 1 about any language about God: "The perfection of learning is to know God in such a way that, although you realize he is not unknown, you know that he may not be described. We must believe in him, understand him, adore him, and by such actions we shall make him known."[77]

A younger contemporary of Hilary was **Ambrose** (339-397), born on the frontiers of the empire at Trier (in modern-day Germany). While serving as governor of Milan in 374 and still a catechumen, Ambrose was chosen bishop of that important city. Like almost every theologian of his time, Ambrose was opposed to Arianism and wrote treatises against it, notably *On Faith to the Emperor Gratian* and *On the Holy Spirit*. He was a pioneer in using hymnody in liturgical celebrations, and his work *On Duties* is perhaps the first comprehensive survey of Christian ethics. He is remembered as well as the counselor of Monica (322-387), the persistent mother of Augustine, and the person perhaps most responsible for Augustine's conversion. As such, Ambrose is responsible for the spiritual nurture of the theologian who is arguably, with Thomas Aquinas (1224-1274) almost a millennium later, the greatest theologian in the Western church: **Augustine of Hippo**.

Augustine in North Africa

Augustine was born in 354 in the North African town of Thagaste (in modern-day Algeria) some forty years after Christianity had been made a legal and favored religion in the empire. According to the custom of the time, and perhaps because his father was not Christian, Augustine was not baptized as an infant or a young man. When he went to study at Carthage, "a cauldron of illicit loves leapt and boiled"[78] around him, and he lived what he described as a rather dissolute life. Eventually he joined the Manichean religion (founded in third-century Persia by the prophet Mani [216-276]), but had more questions than answers. Despite the pleas and prayers of his mother, Monica, Augustine resisted Christianity, and at one point—without telling his mother—sailed off to Italy and settled in Milan as a teacher of rhetoric. Monica followed, and eventually, through the influence of Ambrose and much personal searching, Augustine became a catechumen and was baptized at Milan. Soon after, he and his mother decided to return to Africa, but after an amazing conversation/theological reflection as they were preparing to sail home, Monica rather suddenly took sick and died.[79] Augustine returned to North Africa intending to live a quiet, contemplative life as a monk, but was soon called to ordination as a presbyter in the North African town of Hippo, and upon the death of the bishop there, he was chosen as his successor.

Augustine's work is "staggering in quantity—his own incomplete review of his books numbered ninety-three."[80] His influence on Western theological thought is enormous. After citations of Scripture, Augustine is the theologian most cited by Aquinas in his own large body of works, and he is at the root of the Protestant Reformation in the sixteenth century. The Council of Trent's Decree on Justification, says Henry Chadwick, "was a mosaic of Augustinian phrases, so anti-Pelagian that the Protestants could not bring themselves to believe in its sincerity."[81] Augustine is at the root as well of the Jansenist controversy in the seventeenth and eighteenth century (in which both sides appealed to his authority), and he is the spirit behind the movement of "radical orthodoxy" or "neo-Augustinian" movement in the Catholic Church today. He is in every way a "doctor"—teacher—of the church. Bernard McGinn remarks that if, in the words of the British/American philosopher Alfred North Whitehead (1861-1947), all Western philosophy is a series of footnotes to Plato, it is true as well to say that the "history of Western theology is a series of footnotes to Augustine."[82]

Augustine was not a systematic theologian like Origen. His writings were mostly "occasional," that is, written for one reason or another—a homily, catechetical instruction, to refute a particular opinion. It was in the context of a controversy with the schismatic group led by another African bishop, Donatus—the Donatists—that he developed the principles upon which later sacramental theology was based. The Donatists had their origin in a controversy that went back to the Diocletian persecution in the early fourth century. Their position was that any person who had denied his or her faith in order to save their lives during the persecution had to be baptized again in order to be reinstated into the church. In the case of an unfaithful ordained person, he lost his office and could not be reordained. If a bishop, presbyter, or deacon resumed his office after being readmitted into the church, none of the sacraments that he administered were valid, because the validity of the sacrament depended on the worthiness of the minister.

Augustine strongly disagreed. For him, once a person was baptized or ordained she or he was sealed with an invisible, indelible mark—what Tertullian had spoken of as a "character." And as for a sacrament's efficacy because of the worthiness of the minister, Augustine judged that such a position would make the church depend too much on the clergy. "The sacrament is Christ's," writes British church historian Henry Chadwick (1920-2008), "not the minister's personal property, and salvation is always and throughout the work of God," not a human accomplishment.[83] For Augustine, a sacrament is celebrated by three participants: a recipient, God, and an authorized minister; only the first two, however, are necessary for its efficacy. The minister is "only an instrument of God's action. This means that a sacrament is quite valid apart from the moral virtues or defects of the one administering it."[84] This position is very much the basis for the later Western articulation of sacramental efficacy as *ex opere operato* (literally: from the work done, meaning that a sacrament is valid despite the holiness or worthiness of the minister).

Augustine's controversy with the doctrines of the popular ascetic and spiritual counselor Pelagius (354-420/440) helped bring to expression the doctrine we know as "original sin." Pelagius, a native of Britain, had settled in Rome after traveling in the East, where Christian attitudes to human nature were much more positive than what Augustine had personally experienced and had written about. Shocked by the moral corruption of members of the Roman church, Pelagius had begun to preach that moral reform was a matter of willpower and human effort. Once one had decided to reform one's life, God's grace could then come to assist the person, but the original effort was up to the person alone. Ultimately, as Chadwick explains it, "Grace is assisting, not all-controlling."[85] Just as men rowing a boat *can* bring their craft to shore by their own power, but find it easier to use a sail, so it is that God's grace, together with the example of Christ, helps women and men get to their heavenly destination.[86]

Not so, Augustine was convinced. Both he and Pelagius had many positions in common, and early on Augustine expressed his admiration for Pelagius's writings.[87] Ultimately, however, Augustine would insist that without God's prior help, God's action in grace, humanity was helpless to move at all. This was because humanity, in Adam, had fallen from a state of true freedom to slavery to sin. Adam's sin was humanity's *original* sin, and human guilt from this sin was handed on to Adam's descendants in the very act of human generation. This is why, Augustine argued, Christians universally brought their newborn children to be baptized. Baptism was God's great gift to the church for the salvation of humankind. It was the way that God's grace first comes to sinful humanity and gives them the possibility of salvation. Without it, even innocent children could not reach eternal life (although this is somewhat unclear in Augustine's thought as a whole).[88] Pelagius's position was a denial of the necessity of God's grace, and it even put the necessity of the sacraments in jeopardy.

Augustine worked out his ideas against Pelagius and his supporters in a number of letters and treatises over several years.[89] While, as Peter Brown argues, Augustine's position is ultimately the more pastoral and even the more human—Pelagius's ideal was that every Christian should live the strict life of a monk[90]—Chadwick notes two emphases in Augustine's arguments that would have a strong and negative influence on later theology. The first was his pejorative view of sexuality and sexual activity, one that suggested that "even within marriage the sexual act cannot be done without some taint of cupidity"[91]: sexual activity, in other words, was always in some degree sinful. Second, the absolute necessity of grace for which Augustine argued forced him to admit that there was *some kind* of predestination at work in God's providence. For Augustine, that predestination was only for the elect, while others would be given sufficient grace to choose salvation. But inevitably his disciples (like Gottschalk in the ninth century, Calvin in the sixteenth, and Jansenius in the seventeenth) drew the logical conclusion of *double* predestination—both to salvation and to perdition.[92]

The "Pelagian controversy," as it came to be called, took place in the years after the unthinkable had happened: in 410 the city of Rome had been sacked by the Goths led by Alaric. The discussion this event provoked about divine providence led Augustine to begin writing one of the greatest theological works of all time, the "large and arduous work"[93] that he entitled *De Civitate Dei* or *The City of God*. The book was to take him thirteen years to complete; he began writing at fifty-nine and finished it when he was seventy-two.[94] This great theology of history insists that *real* history is not what goes on in the passage of time, but within the interior drama of "two loves [that] built two cities, earthly love of self even unto contempt of God and heavenly love of God unto contempt of self."[95] Augustine in his old age became more and more pessimistic about the possibility of human progress and the goodness of human culture—a position that has ramifications in our own day as neo-Augustinians (among whom is no less than our present pope, Benedict XVI) express their suspicion of contemporary efforts of inculturation.[96]

Augustine is the author of several more theological masterpieces, for example, his *Confessions*, his *Homilies on the Gospel of John*, his *On Christian Doctrine*, and—perhaps his "most profound work"[97]—*On the Trinity*.[98] This last work has also had immense influence in the Western development of this central doctrine of Christianity. Among the many analogies Augustine proposes for an approach to understanding the Trinity, the most important is his "psychological analogy," based on the working of the human mind in memory, understanding, and will (or love).

As great as Augustine's contribution to trinitarian theology was, however, contemporary scholars point out how tragic it was that Augustine was not very familiar with the more dynamic and historically oriented understandings of theologians like the four Cappadocians. While these Asian thinkers took diversity and salvation history as a point of departure for their understanding of the one Christian God, Augustine's concern was more with how to explain God's diversity in the light of Christian monotheism. The result, according to scholars like U.S. feminist theologian Catherine M. LaCugna, is that trinitarian theology became more and more abstract and separated from the concrete way that God revealed Godself through Christ in the Spirit.[99]

Jerome, Marcella, Paula, Melania, and Eustochium

Augustine's great contemporary was **Jerome** (347-420), who wrote him from Bethlehem in the last year of his (Jerome's) life that he (Augustine) had practically "refounded the old faith"[100]—high praise indeed from that holy but irascible man. Jerome himself might also be called someone who had himself "refounded the faith," in that he was the *spirit* behind, if not the sole translator of, the rendering of the Christian Bible from its original languages of Hebrew and Greek into elegant, readable Latin. It was so accessible to ordinary Latin speakers that it was called the "Vulgate" (the "popular" version, from that Latin *vulgus*, the root of our English word "vulgar" or "of the people"). I say that Jerome was not the *sole* translator because with him worked a number of learned women: **Marcella** (325-410), **Paula** (347-404), **Melania the Younger** (383-439), and Paula's daughter **Eustochium** (368-419/20). All these women were learned in both Greek and Latin and no doubt helped Jerome in his daunting task; and they certainly supported him with their wealth as well. History, however, has given him most of the credit for the work.[101]

Jerome was born in Dalmatia (in the area of today's Balkan States), was educated in Rome, and spent some time as a monk in the desert near Aleppo in northern Syria. It was there that he perfected his Greek and began to learn Hebrew, but he soon set off for Jerusalem. He returned to Rome and was secretary for Pope Damasus I, and this is where he first met the holy women Marcella and Paula. They and a number of women lived together in a monastery in Rome and Jerome taught them how to sing the psalms in Hebrew and practice the interpretation of Scripture.[102] In 384, Pope Damasus died, and for a number of reasons Jerome left Rome for the Holy Land, settling with Paula and her daughter Eustochium in a monastery that they founded in Bethlehem. Paula died in 404, but Jerome was joined in 417 by Melania the Younger.

It was in Bethlehem where the bulk of the Bible was translated, although it was begun at Damasus's invitation in 382, and did not include parts of the New Testament and the books not in the Hebrew Bible. It was from Jerusalem that Jerome wrote a number of homilies, Scripture commentaries and many letters. He was a lover of Scripture—one of his most famous phrases is "ignorance of Scripture is ignorance of Christ"[103]—but he is also noted for his strong temper and, despite his clear affection for women, he is remembered in his writings for several strong misogynist statements.[104] As we have said, Christian tradition consists of *both* grace and malpractice, and Jerome seems to exemplify this to a very high degree.

Western Monasticism in Ireland and Europe

Another contemporary of Augustine and of Jerome and his female companions was **Patrick**, the evangelizer of Ireland (389-461). Though not a monk himself, Christian Ireland soon was covered with monasteries of both men and women. Some of these, like the great monastery presided over by Abbess **Bridget of Kildare** (450-525), were "double monasteries" where both men and women lived and worshiped together. Irish or Celtic monasteries were places of culture, art, and education. As Thomas Cahill has popularly explained it, at a time when continental Europe was being invaded and pillaged by the migrating peoples from the east and the north (often called the "barbarian invasions"), Irish monks copied both Christian manuscripts and manuscripts of pre-Christian authors, and in this way preserved the classical literature of the crumbling Western empire and the literature of the patristic church as well. The Irish church's great contribution to theology, therefore, was most likely that of the preservation of the past. The monasteries became universities, open to commoners and noblefolk as well, often from the ravaged shores of England and the Continent beyond. Eventually monks like **Columba** (521-597) and **Columbanus** (540-615) left Ireland to establish monasteries in the newly inhabited territories of the migrant peoples, and brought the learning of the classical period back to Europe. This is why, as Cahill suggests, the Irish "saved civilization."[105]

One other major contribution to the history of theology coming from Ireland was the development of the sacrament of penance as we know it today. In Ireland of the fifth and sixth centuries, women and men would travel to monasteries to consult with holy men and women and confess their faults, failings, and sins to them. U.S. Anglo liturgist Regis Duffy (1935-2006) suggests that the practice was most likely rooted in pre-Christian Irish legal customs.[106] The monk and nun counselors would then propose "tariff penances"—particular prayers or sets of prayers to be said to "atone" for the matters that were confessed. Gradually books appeared to help the "confessors" assign proper penances—e.g., three Our Fathers for lying to one's wife; five "Aves" for an impure thought. Gradually, too, this practice—perhaps through the Irish monasteries in Britain and Europe—began to take hold throughout the West, and gradually it began to replace the more formal, harsher practice of penance that was the earlier practice of the church. When this began to happen, however, the role of confessor began to be taken over by priests, and by the eleventh and twelfth centuries this form of penance was understood as one of the official "sacraments" of the church. This is a fine example of both inculturation (in Ireland and in the wider church) and the development of tradition that we discussed in chapter 5.

Almost a century after Patrick's evangelization of Ireland, **Benedict of Nursia** (480-550) and his twin sister, **Scholastica** (480-543), were born. Benedict is the author of one of the great documents of the Christian tradition, the *Rule of Benedict*, and he and Scholastica may well be considered to be the co-founders of Western monasticism. Monasteries soon sprang up all over Europe, and Benedictine monks, like those in and from Ireland, took up the task of preserving the culture of antiquity when that culture was in virtual collapse in the West and (as we shall see) under siege from Islam in the East. This they did by copying classical manuscripts and by collecting scriptural and "patristic" passages around particular theological themes in works called *catenae* (from the Latin for "chains") and *florilegia* ("bouquets" of quotations). Their contribution to theology at this time was found not in breaking new ground but in preserving the past—exactly what the context demanded.

In 590, a Benedictine monk was elected to the papacy; he is known in history as **Gregory the Great** (540-604). Gregory is important for bringing both a pastoral sense and great prestige to the papacy. Gregory was the first to use the phrase *servus servorum Dei* ("servant of the servants of God") to describe papal ministry, and he had a strong concern for evangelization. In one of his most famous decisions, he sent a party of forty monks under the leadership of Augustine of Canterbury (as he was later called) to evangelize England, and he is famous for a letter to Augustine that laid down important principles of what we would call today inculturation. His work entitled *Dialogues* had a strong influence on subsequent devotions to the saints, and his chapter on Benedict and Scholastica was one of the reasons that Benedict's rule became so popular in Europe in the next several centuries. Gregory's masterpiece, according to Bernard McGinn, was his *Moralia on Job*, and, in addition to many homilies and several Scripture commentaries, he wrote a famous work of pastoral theology entitled *The Pastoral Rule*. After Augustine of Hippo, he is perhaps the most quoted author in medieval theology. McGinn quotes Patrick Carry: "Benedict gave Western monks a rule; Gregory gave them a mysticism."[107]

We cannot leave this section without a short mention of Benedict's great contemporary, **Anicius Manlius Boethius** (480-524), a layman. Boethius was a member of an old Roman senatorial family and had been educated in Athens. He was, as German philosopher Josef Pieper (1904-1997) describes him, rooted in the ancient, classical world but eager to embrace the new world that was being born with the great migrations—yet he was not fully at home in either.[108] A powerful official at the court of the Arian king of the Goths, Theodoric, he was also a formidable translator, philosopher, and theologian. Like Tertullian, Boethius is responsible for several Latin terms that have become foundational in the Western theological vocabulary (for example, *principium* [principle], *definire* [define], *subjectum* [subject]), and is single-handedly responsible for translating much of Aristotle and Plato as well. His work on the Trinity has earned him the title "the first scholastic,"[109] and his greatest work—written while waiting execution for treason—was entitled *The Consolation of Philosophy*. This last work is one of the great works of world literature, and although there is nothing specifically *Christian* in it, it was used by English Catholics in the seventeenth century when they themselves were imprisoned for their faith.[110] Pieper makes the point that much of Boethius's influence during the Middle Ages is anonymous, but his thought is nevertheless a genuine cornerstone of that great era of Western thought.[111]

THEOLOGY FROM 600 TO 1000

Christian Theology in Dialogue with Islam

One of the most crucial moments in the history of Christianity was the emergence of Islam in the seventh century. In a few decades, much of Christian Africa and western Asia became Muslim, the Roman empire in the East was confined to the Byzantine empire, and Islam had conquered much of the Iberian peninsula. Islam's origins are traced to the Arabian prophet Muhammad (ca. 570 - 632 in Christian reckoning), who at the age of forty began to receive revelations from God (Allah) that he wrote down in magnificent Arabic. Islam's quick expansion, however, did not stamp out Christianity completely, and in fact there continued to exist a number of vital Christian communities, especially in Ethiopia, Egypt, and Syria. Christian theology continued to thrive as well, and a good bit of it was developed in dialogue or contention with Islam.

One of the greatest theologians of this era was the monk **Maximus the Confessor** (580-662). He was born and educated in Constantinople, lived as a monk in North Africa, traveled to Rome to fight the "monotheletist" heresy, which claimed that Christ had only one will. Maximus died in exile in what is now Georgia in western Asia. He was a great spiritual writer, especially in the area of "apophatic," or negative, theology, and, as we pointed out above, was strongly influenced by the theology of Pseudo-Dionysius. But he also wrote in the area of doctrine, composing works on both Christology and the Trinity.[112] Maximus lived at the beginning of the Muslim expansion, saw Muslims as "wild and untamed beasts,"[113] and called on Christians of the time to rely more fully on God alone.

One of the most significant theologians of the time was **John of Damascus** (ca. 675-749), an Arab Christian who served as a government official under Muslim rule and who ended his life as a monk near Jerusalem. Perhaps John's most important contribution to theology was his opposition to the movement in his day (called "iconoclasm") that tried to prohibit the veneration of images—a movement no doubt influenced by Islamic prohibitions of the same. His basic argument revolved around the reality of the incarnation: if Christ could not be pictured, then he was not truly human. As the fullness of God was revealed in Jesus' flesh, so God's presence and the presence of the saints are revealed through their images or "icons." "I do not venerate matter, but I venerate the Creator of matter who for my sake became matter," he wrote.[114] John is included in the official list of doctors of the church.

About 755 an anonymous treatise entitled *On the Triune Nature of God* appeared as the first known Christian work of theology to be written in Arabic. This work, which used the ideas, cadences, and vocabulary of both the Bible and the Qur'an, was intended as a pastoral guide for Arab Christians who lived under Muslim rule. In the following example from the introduction to the work, one can see the strong influence of both Scriptures: "You are the merciful one, the merciful Lord of mercy / You sat upon the throne, / were exalted above all creatures, / and filled all things."[115]

Another document that evidences how Christian theology was done in the context of Islamic culture is the one written by **Timothy I**, patriarch of Baghdad in 781. This is a report of a two-day dialogue that Timothy (d. 832) had with the Muslim caliph Al Mahdi. While he is clear that "Muhammad was neither the Holy Spirit nor a prophet like Moses,"[116] there was much, he said, that Muhammad did indeed get right, and so he is worthy of Christian respect. While Timothy and Al Mahdi agree strongly on the oneness of God, they have a lively debate about the Christian doctrine of the Trinity in decidedly non-Western terminology. Norris points out, however, that the agreement between caliph and patriarch has "at least one dreadful aspect," and that is the agreement "that they both properly hated Jews."[117] Other Arabic Christian apologies in the Muslim context were written in the ninth century by **Abraham of Tiberius** and **Theodore Abu Qurrah** (d. ca. 830); a homily by the deacon **Gregory Dekapolites** (d. ca. 842) of Constantinople presents a rather mixed view of Islam. All of these works, however, are interesting insofar as Christian theologians were definitely taking Islam with utmost seriousness and were doing theology out of their very particular context.

Christian Theology in China

Almost from the beginning of Christianity, as we have seen, Christians in the churches of Syria and Persia had spread the gospel eastward, often along the fabled trade route called the Silk Road. In the early seventeenth century, workers near the modern Chinese city of Xian, site of the ancient capital of Ch'ang-an, found a carved column that was dated to 781. On the column was recorded the history of an East Syrian monk named **Alopen**, who had arrived with a number of companions in the capital in 635 and had established a monastery. At the top of the column are a cloud and a lotus flower (a Buddhist symbol), atop of which sits a cross, and the text, in rather poor Chinese, gives a brief summary of Christian beliefs written with a Chinese flavor and then tells the story of Alopen. Alopen is described as arriving in Ch'ang-an with "sutras and images," about which, Dale Irvin and Scott Sunquist say: "We are left to speculate what these might have included: copies of Christian scriptures, no doubt, perhaps liturgical texts, catechetical literature, and a cross."[118] The emperor, hearing of Alopen's arrival, invited him to translate the texts that he had brought for inclusion in the imperial library. When the translations were completed, the inscription says, the emperor gave his approval to Alopen's teachings.

From the same period—dating as early as 638—are four treatises that may have been translated by Alopen and his companions from the original Syriac, but could also have been the first Christian documents written in Chinese.[119] One of these documents, entitled the *Jesus-Messiah Sutra*, uses the term "Buddha" for God, while the others use the Chinese term *I-shen* (the one God). The Holy Spirit is spoken of as the "Cool Wind" or the "Pure Wind." All four documents are very sensitive to Chinese culture and present Christianity in a thoroughly Asian way while preserving its distinctiveness as well.[120]

The author of the inscription in 781 was a bishop by the name of **Ching-Ching** (**Adam** in Syriac). He is said to have translated some thirty Christian books into Chinese and was also sought out by Buddhist missionary monks to help them translate their Scriptures into Chinese as well. These scholars lived in monasteries that were very near each other, and the Buddhist monastery still exists today.[121] This is an amazing early example of interreligious cooperation and, no doubt, dialogue and inculturation.

Christian Theology in Europe

Since the fourth century, as we have noted, Christianity in Europe was marked by the collapse of Roman antiquity and the movement of peoples from the north and the east. These peoples had been evangelized by monks from Ireland, Britain, and Italy, and the monks also brought education and preserved the classical past through the copying and preservation of texts. Much of this history was recorded by a monk of the northern English monastery of Jarrow, **Bede**, called The Venerable (673-735). Bede told the story, among others, of Abbess Hilda (614-680), who presided over the famous double monastery (men and women) at Whitby on England's northern coast and who presided as well over the Synod of Whitby in 664, where the monasteries of England decided to follow Roman and not Celtic liturgical customs. Bede also told the story of the monk **Caedmon** (d. 380), who wrote religious poetry of great theological depth in English and so is the first known poet in the English language. From English monasteries, too, came Boniface (672-754) and his relative Leoba (710-782), who were evangelizers of the tribes of what is now Germany. Under the deacon **Alcuin of York** (735-804), Charlemagne's (747-814) Europe experienced an intellectual renaissance. Alcuin is responsible for developing a Latin script that was easier to read than what had been used up until his day. He also developed the pronunciation of Latin that is used even today, and invented the indication of *Anno Domini* (A.D.—in the year of the Lord) for dates.

Charlemagne had a "shadow side" in that he engaged in a thirty-three year war with the Saxons and forced them to become Christian (against Alcuin's futile objections) and imposed as well Roman culture and customs. Thus, the Saxons were given no room to develop their own expression of the Christian religion. Around the year 830, however, an anonymous monk of Fulda (the monastery founded by Boniface in 744) wrote an amazing work. It is entitled *The Heliand* (The Savior) and is a beautiful and powerful retelling of the gospel story in the vocabulary and worldview of Saxon or northern German culture. As a prominent scholar of *The Heliand* expresses it, this unknown monk "envisioned dynamic poetic equivalents so that the impact of the original text, in its Mediterranean cultural context, might be transferred by poetry analogously to a new North-Sea context. Such a task of inculturation had not been undertaken since the evangelists themselves."[122] To give just a few examples of this remarkable work of inculturation, the scribes of the Gospels become the "lawspeakers," reflecting the Saxon notion of law that was part of the oral tradition. The prophets become "soothsayers," and the three wise men become "strong, clear-minded thanes." The disciples are described as the "warrior-companions of Jesus," and Jesus himself is spoken of as "best of healers," "best of rescuers," "chieftain of the clans."[123] What the *Heliand* shows is that, while northern Europe had become Christian, its Christianity had become in turn very much Germanized.[124]

A significant development in theology took place at the beginning of the ninth century: the "eucharistic controversy" between **Paschasius Radbertus** (ca. 790-865) on one side and **Rhabanus Maurus** (784-856) and **Ratramnus of Corbie** (d. ca. 868) on the other. Paschasius was abbot of the Benedictine monastery at Corbie in today's France and, in 833, wrote the first extensive treatise on the Eucharist. Paschasius's thesis was basically that in the Eucharist is present the "true body" of Christ, born of Mary—that eucharistic presence is indeed the *physical* presence of Christ. Rhabanus, abbot of Fulda and then archbishop of Mainz in Germany, thought that this position was too crude, and he was joined in his criticism by Paschasius's fellow monk at Corbie, Ratramnus. Their position was that Christ's presence in the Eucharist is more *spiritual*: it is a mystical, even symbolic—yet nevertheless real—presence. Although the controversy was not resolved and in fact *both* positions were orthodox, this discussion among some of the greatest theologians of their time laid the foundation for a further controversy in the eleventh century involving **Berengarius of Tours** (999-1088), and for the later doctrine (defined in 1215 at the Fourth Lateran Council) of eucharistic transubstantiation.[125]

On December 31, 1980, Pope John Paul II declared Saints **Cyril** (ca. 827-

869) and **Methodius** (ca. 815-885) co-patrons of Europe with Saint Benedict, on whom we have reflected above.[126] Cyril and Methodius were brothers from what is today the city of Salonika in the Balkan States. In 863 they were sent by the Byzantine emperor to evangelize the Slavic peoples in what is now the Czech Republic, Slovakia, and Poland. What is significant about their work of evangelization for the history of theology is that they employed what we would call today a method of inculturation. They learned the local language, invented what we know as the "Cyrillic alphabet," and translated the Scriptures into Old Slavonic. Although they encountered much opposition from Latin missionaries in the area, they appealed to Rome and were vindicated in their approach. The translation that they made of the Scriptures must surely have been a culturally sensitive presentation of the faith that they brought.

CONCLUSION

As Christianity approached the celebration of its first millennium it was flourishing in Europe and in the Byzantine empire in western Asia. But these two Christian centers were virtually surrounded and greatly beleaguered by a powerful and sophisticated Muslim world, stretching from Asia, across northern Africa and into what is today Spain and Portugal. Islam had practically cut off regular communication between East and West, and Europe had begun to assert its independence from the East. In the eighth and ninth centuries the patriarch of the West at Rome gained more and more prestige and power, and the rulers of Europe after Constantine began to call themselves Holy Roman Emperors. The West had developed its own distinct style of doing theology in the light of the near destruction of the heritage of the classical world and the incorporation of the vibrant cultures of northern Europe. The middle of the eleventh century would see the formal break between Eastern and Western Christianity that has lasted up until our own day, and it would see the beginnings of a flowering of theology that would be one of the treasures of Western civilization. And, despite being surrounded by Islam, Eastern theology would flourish as well. This, and more, is the subject for our next chapter.

QUESTIONS FOR REFLECTION

1. Why do we speak about the New Testament as a collection of theologies?
2. Why do you think Origen and Tertullian had such different approaches to doing theology?
3. The Council of Nicaea may well be the most important council in the church's history. Why do you think that is the case?
4. Why do you think we can talk about Augustine as a "contextual" theologian?

5. Why can we speak of Christian theology as "global" even in these first ten centuries?
6. What were some of the challenges of Islam for Christian theologizing?

SUGGESTIONS FOR FURTHER READING AND STUDY

F. C. Burkitt, *Early Christianity outside the Roman Empire* (Piscataway, N.J.: Gorgias Press, 2002 [originally published in 1899]).

Justo L. González, *A History of Christian Thought*, vol. 1, *From the Beginnings to the Council of Chalcedon*, Revised Edition (Nashville, Tenn.: Abingdon Press, 1989).

Michael Green, *Evangelism in the Early Church* (Grand Rapids: William B. Eerdmans, 1970).

Philip Jenkins, *The Lost History of Christianity: The Thousand-Year Golden Age of the Church in the Middle East, Africa, and Asia—and How It Died* (New York: Harper Collins, 2008).

Mary T. Malone, *Women and Christianity*, vol. 1, *The First Thousand Years* (Maryknoll, N.Y.: Orbis Books, 2001).

Bernard McGinn, *The Doctors of the Church: Thirty-Three Men and Women Who Shaped Christianity* (New York: Crossroad, 1999).

G. Ronald Murphy, *The Saxon Savior: The Transformation of the Gospel in the Ninth Century Heliand* (Oxford: Oxford University Press, 1989).

Martin Palmer, ed., *The Jesus Sutras: Rediscovering the Lost Scrolls of Taoist Christianity* (New York: Ballantine Wellspring, 2001).

James C. Russell, *The Germanization of Early Medieval Christianity: A Sociohistorical Approach to Religious Transformation* (New York: Oxford University Press, 1994).

Jaroslav Pelikan, *Christianity and Classical Culture: The Metamorphosis of Natural Theology in the Christian Encounter with Hellenism* (New Haven: Yale University Press, 1993).

Jaroslav Pelikan, *The Christian Tradition 1: The Emergence of the Catholic Tradition (100-600)* (Chicago: University of Chicago Press, 1971).

Kenneth Sawyer and Youhannh Youssef, "Early Christianity in North Africa," in Ogbu U. Kalu, ed., *African Christianity: An African Story* (Trenton, N.J./Asmara, Eritrea: Africa World Press, 2007), 41-65.

11

Christian Theology from 1000 to 1700

THE FIRST HALF of the second millennium of Christianity saw three major divisions within the Christian church. Two of these divisions endure until today: the schism between East and West in 1054 and the break in the West between Catholics and Protestants in 1517. Both have colored much of the theologizing done in these centuries. A third schism, the Great Western Schism from 1378 to 1417, came at the end of a period in the West when culture and theology were flourishing as perhaps never before. It was finally resolved at the Council of Constance (1414-1418) after all three men who had claimed the papacy finally resigned, and a new pope, Martin V, was elected. In many ways, however, this schism greatly weakened the prestige of the papacy and the church and prepared the way for the more permanent break in 1517.

Christianity and Islam continued, tragically, to be enemies. The first centuries of this period witnessed the time of the Christian Crusades against the Muslims—perhaps well intentioned but, as Frederick Norris says, Christians' "worst débâcle, with the single exception of the European Holocaust"[1] (in the twentieth century). In 1453, when Constantinople and the Byzantine empire fell to Muslim armies, Christianity became for the first time a *Western* religion, and "the dominant culture of western Europe was virtually synonymous with Latin Christianity."[2] Islam threatened the West as well, although victories in Spain in 1492, at Lepanto in 1571, and at Vienna in 1683 stemmed the tide of Islamic expansion.[3] In the midst of both Muslim occupation and Christian–Muslim hostilities, however, theology was able to be done in the Orthodox churches and in Christian–Muslim dialogue in the West.

The victories in Spain and at Lepanto came at a time when Europe was achieving unprecedented power and wealth, resulting in a period of national expansion and colonialism that ended only in the middle of the twentieth century. The last two hundred years of the period we are reflecting on in this chapter began the process of what we now call globalization. Christianity at this time became a global religion, and Christian theology was being done on every continent in the world.

If the theologians of the eleventh to eighteenth centuries are not as foundational for Christian theology as those in the first millennium, many of them certainly number among the most eminent. Women and men like Anselm, Thomas Aquinas, Gregory Palamas, Hildegard of Bingen, Teresa of Avila, Martin Luther,

Bartolomé de Las Casas, Sor Juana de la Cruz, Matteo Ricci, and Charles de Condren have built on the foundations of the past and have thought through the Christian gospel in their own times and with their own faith.

Formal, academic theology, of course, represents only the tip of the iceberg. Theology was being done as well in the architecture of the great European gothic cathedrals, in the art of Latin American *santeros*, in the music of Palestrina in Italy and anonymous composers in Bolivia and Paraguay, in the lessons of Vietnamese catechists, and in the popular religiosity of the Christian people everywhere. This chapter will be even sketchier than the previous one (it is embarrassing to know how much more is left out than included!), but my hope is that readers will continue to get a glimpse of the amazing reality that is the Christian tradition, forged as faith interacts in dialogue with history and culture.

THEOLOGY FROM 1000 TO 1500

The East-West Schism of 1054

On July 16, 1054, the Roman delegation from Pope Leo IX (1002-1054), led by French cardinal Humbert of Silva Candida (ca. 1000-1061) placed a bull of excommunication of Michael Cerularius (1000-1059), patriarch of Constantinople, on the altar of Hagia Sophia. Thus symbolically began the one-thousand-year division between the East and the West, even though its roots go back several hundred years prior to that incident, and the theological disputes that brought it on were tangled with politics and the forces of history. The years since the Council of Nicaea in 325 had seen the churches of the East and the West grow slowly apart as they became more and more different culturally, had developed distinct theologies, and—because of Islam—had become more and more isolated geographically from one another. Even at this stage in 1054 the union of the church could have been saved. As Dale Irvin and Scott Sunquist point out, what was much more decisive for the division was the tragic sack of Constantinople by crusaders in 1204.[4]

Already in 858, Byzantine emperor Michael III deposed the Patriarch Ignatius (797-897), appointing in his place the brilliant theologian **Photius** (ca. 820-893). Ignatius appealed to Rome, and Pope Nicholas I (820-867) declared Photius to be in schism. Photius replied by declaring Rome to be heretical on several grounds. Among the alleged heresies were eating milk products during Lent, using unleavened bread for the Eucharist and, most significantly, introducing the phrase in the creed that the Holy Spirit proceeds from the Father *and the Son (filioque)*.

Photius later wrote a treatise entitled *On the Mystagogy of the Holy Spirit*, in which he laid out his position on the Spirit more clearly. Even though several important Western theologians (e.g., Augustine) had accepted the Latin formula, Photius argued that the *filioque* formula introduced two causes into the Trinity, compromising the notion that the Father was the sole "origin" of the trinitarian persons—a strong conviction in Greek trinitarian thought.

While communion between Rome and Constantinople was eventually restored, the theological divisions still lay under the surface. When mixed with the growing claims of the Roman papacy, however, they continued to be a threat to schism. Things began to come to a head when Pope Benedict VIII (d. 1024) officially permitted the *filioque* to be included in the creed, ratifying what had in fact been a long-standing practice in the West. In 1054, during a conflict with the Normans, on the one hand, and the Byzantine empire, on the other, Pope Leo IX sent his delegation to Constantinople, and although Cardinal Humbert and his companions were received by the emperor, they were not received by the patriarch, Cerularius. Humbert eventually lost his patience waiting for Cerularius to grant him an audience, and so served the bull of excommunication, which was promptly reciprocated by the patriarch.

Attempts were made afterward to heal the division, especially at the Council of Florence in 1439. In the "Decree of Union with the Greek Church," both formulas of procession ("from the Father and the Son" and "from the Father through the Son") were accepted as orthodox: "All were aiming at the same meaning in different words,"[5] and both leavened and unleavened bread were accepted as valid for the eucharistic celebration.[6] But Florence could not bring the two churches together again. In our own day, even though the bull of excommunication was rescinded by both pope and patriarch after Vatican II, the divisions, rooted so tragically in a mixture of theology and politics, still remain. But efforts at reunion continue. It is said, for example, that when John Paul II would recite the Nicene Creed in ceremonies with Orthodox bishops he would always use the formula "from the Father, *through the Son*" rather than the Western formula "from the Father *and* the Son."

Anselm and the Beginnings of Scholasticism

Unfortunately, by 1054 the Western church could quite easily get along without the Eastern. This was because, around the year 1000, as U.S. Anglo historian Richard Tarnas says, "cultural activity in the West began to quicken on many fronts."[7] This was particularly true for theology. Until now, as we have said, theology in the West had been mainly confined to preserving the tradition of the past. Gradually, however, although this kind of theology did not altogether cease, a new kind of theology was coming into being. This was a theology that not only prized preserving the faith but also applied human reason to understand the faith more deeply. An early example of this new kind of theology appeared with the eucharistic controversies of the ninth century;

in the eleventh century a real pioneer of such theology emerged in the person of **Anselm of Canterbury** (1033-1109).

Anselm was a native of what is today Italy and became the abbot of the French abbey of Bec. It was here that he did most of his writing, but in 1093 he was made archbishop of Canterbury in England. Anselm is important in the history of theology for three things in particular. First, very much in the spirit of Augustine of Hippo, he understands theology as involving both faith and reason, as we have noted in chapter 2 of this book. As he writes in the preface to his *Proslogion:* "I have written the following short work . . . from the point of view of someone trying to raise his mind to the contemplation of God, and seeking to understand what he believes." And, a little later, echoing Augustine even more: "I do not seek to understand so I may believe, but I believe so that I may understand; and what is more, I believe that unless I do believe I shall not understand."[8]

Anselm's second contribution to theology is the formulation of the "ontological proof," for the existence of God. God is, writes Anselm, "that thing than which nothing greater can be thought." And since "something than which nothing greater can be thought so truly exists that it is not possible to think that it as not existing," God necessarily exists.[9] This argument has been criticized by theologians ever since, but both U.S. Anglo philosopher Charles Hartshorne (1897-2000) and Swiss theologian Karl Barth (1886-1968) have found it useful. In the preface to his own short work on the proof, Barth wrote that it is "a model piece of good, penetrating and neat theology."[10]

Third, and perhaps most influential in the history of theology, is Anselm's work on the incarnation, *Cur Deus Homo* (Why God Became Human). Rooting himself in medieval feudal culture and Frankish law, Anselm speaks of God becoming human in order to make satisfaction for Adam and Eve's sin, which was an infinite offense against God's infinite honor. Since only an infinite person could make such satisfaction, God himself had to become incarnate and die. Norris remarks how "this argument became a source of significant penetration of the gospel among the Frankish people,"[11] and so a model of contextual theology. U.S. feminist theologian Elizabeth Johnson once commented that she sometimes thinks, for this explanation, "Anselm should be considered the most successful theologian of all time. . . . It was never declared a dogma but might just as well have been, so dominant has been [his formulation's] influence in theology, preaching, devotion, and the penitential system of the Church, up to our own day."[12]

The theologian who strongly objected to Anselm's "satisfaction theory" was **Peter Abelard** (1079-1142), although he may have had in mind more the thought of his contemporary Hugh of St. Victor (1078-1141).[13] Thinking, as many theologians do today as well, that the satisfaction theory is repugnant, Abelard proposed what has come to be called the "exemplar theory" of redemption. The older theory was based on the idea that at Christ's death something changed in *God*—God became reconciled to humanity when Jesus satisfied God's honor. Abelard's theory, in contrast, posits that through the cross something *can* change in men and women; God is always willing to forgive and enter into relationship, and the cross demonstrates or is an example of how deep that love is. Women and men recognize that love and their hearts are moved to accept that love.[14]

In an age that was still suspicious of "dialectics," or the use of reason in theologizing, Abelard was its champion. In *Sic et Non* (Yes and No) he demonstrated not just the validity of reasoning in theological work but its *necessity*. The work consisted of 158 questions whose answers in classical theological sources contradict one another. Abelard's point was that it is not enough to quote sources, as had much of the traditional theology up to his time. Rather, one needs to question the sources, reflect on them, and come to one's own answer through the use of reason.[15] Although Abelard did not provide this rational reflection in *Sic et Non*, the method he implied was mirrored in his teaching, which consisted, first, in reading before his students various opinions, pointing out the differences among them, and finally proposing his own opinion—his *sententia* or "sentence."[16] In this way Abelard is partly responsible for a new way of doing theology that began in his own time and was perfected in the thirteenth century: the *quaestio*, or question. We will speak of this form in more detail when we discuss the work of Thomas Aquinas below.

Abelard is also famous (or infamous) for his love affair with his young student **Heloise** (1101-1162). David L. Edwards, quoting from Abelard's autobiography, says that this affair was the result of Abelard's "exceptional good looks as well as [his] great reputation," and a young woman who "did not rank last in beauty, while in learning she stood supreme."[17] Abelard persuaded Heloise's uncle, a canon of Notre Dame in Paris, to let him lodge in his house so he could tutor the young woman, and they soon fell in love and married secretly. When the uncle heard of the scandal he whisked Heloise off to a convent and had a gang of thugs castrate Abelard. Abelard became a monk and continued his controversial career.

Years later the two corresponded, a correspondence that contains some of the most important writing by a woman at this time. Much of it may even have been an inspiration for some of Abelard's most profound theological thought. Indeed, it can be shown that Heloise expressed many of Abelard's ideas before he did.[18]

Abelard had joined Anselm of Canterbury in developing a new kind of theology: one taught in the universities (schools) that were springing up all over Europe in his time (and therefore described as "scholastic" theology). But this new theology was not without its strong critics. The most forceful of these, perhaps, was **Bernard** (1090-1153), abbot of the monastery at Clairvaux in France. For Bernard there was no place in theology for dialectics, or "scrutiny," as he called it. Theology could be done only out of wonder.[19] Bernard was the prime exemplar of what can be called "monastic theology," among whom could also be numbered Rupert of Deutz (1075-1129), Peter the Venerable (1092-1156), and William of St. Thierry (1085-1148). Although they perhaps evidence a move toward the "scholastic" perspective, the canons of the Augustinian abbey of St. Victor in Paris, Hugh (1096-1141) and Richard (d. 1173), can also be seen as basically monastic theologians.[20]

Hugh of St. Victor is described as the most significant of many monks of St. Victor (called the "Victorines"), and he "is the era's outstanding example of the attempt to render theology scientific while maintaining its monastic character."[21] Among many things, he has the distinction of writing the first medieval "*summa*," or summary of Christian doctrine, *The Christian Mysteries of the Faith*.[22] Hugh's most important disciple, **Richard**, was of Scottish origin. He left no comprehensive summary of the faith, but his work on the Trinity is one that pioneers what we call today the "social doctrine of the Trinity." If God is love, Richard reasons, and love is self-diffusive and self-giving, God must be a loving community in God's own self.[23]

The twelfth century was rich with many notable theologians, especially in northern France and at the University of Paris, recognized officially only in 1200 but already taking shape as a number of schools run by independent scholars began to coalesce into one larger entity. As we leave this section, which outlines the rise of the scholastic method, however, it will be important to spend a few moments on the theologian who, if not the most original, had a major impact on theology of the future. This was the Italian **Peter Lombard** (ca. 1100-1161), who is often called the "Master of the Sentences."[24] Lombard was both a biblical scholar and a systematic theologian, but he is best known for his theological work, especially his *Four Books of Sentences*. Written toward the end of his life in 1155-1157, Lombard's work "did more than any other text to shape the discipline of medieval scholastic theology."[25] Although many theologians of the day had written books of Sentences (literally, "opinions"), Peter Lombard's work was probably the most comprehensive and clearest treatment of the entire content of theology, and he was also able to link the four parts—God and Trinity (I), creation and sin (II), the incarnation and the virtues (III), and the sacraments and the "last things" (IV)—together in a way that showed the coherence of the church's doctrinal system. In the centuries to come—in some cases even into the early seventeenth century—a commentary on the *Sentences* was a standard exercise for theologians aspiring to teach theology in the universities.[26]

Among the most important contributions of the *Sentences* to theology at this time was Lombard's theology of the sacraments, found in Book IV. Although the number of the sacraments was not officially set at the time (the number would be set at the Council of Trent in the sixteenth century), Lombard accepted the opinion that there were seven. Of these, he said, only baptism, confirmation, and orders were nonrepeatable, and sacraments convey grace objectively (*ex opere operato*) when properly administered and received with the proper intention. Without the right intention, however, the one receiving a sacrament only goes through the motions (what was called the *sacramentum tantum* or the "sign alone") and does not receive the grace that the sacrament symbolizes (what was called the *res sacramenti*). In all of this the *Sentences* did not break particularly new ground, but Lombard's wealth of citations from biblical and patristic sources and his general balance of opinion made much of what he said about sacraments the standard sacramental understanding of the Catholic Church.

High Scholasticism

At the beginning of the thirteenth century the stage was set in Europe for what is still considered one of the greatest periods in the history of theology, East or West. Europe had fully emerged from the times when its peoples and cultures were being destroyed by invading tribes from the north and east, and these peoples had virtually all become Christian by the end of the tenth century. The Continent enjoyed relative economic prosperity, and major cities—Paris, London, Bologna, Naples, Cologne—began to spring up. The cathedral and monastic schools that had been centers of theology began to develop into universities: Paris was the center of theological studies; Bologna was renowned for its courses on law; Naples was a center of the study of Aristotle and Muslim and Jewish texts. Breakthroughs in architecture enabled the building of the great gothic cathedrals like those in Paris and Chartres. Spain was occupied for the most part by Muslims, but theirs was a benign rule and, for the most part, Christians and Jews were tolerated and often collaborated with Islamic scholars. Elsewhere, however, Islam was the object of a series of Crusades, beginning at the end of the eleventh century and called throughout the thirteenth with disastrous results. The church, too, was experiencing a great vitality with the emergence of a number of reform movements (e.g., the Beguines) and a new kind of religious life: Dominic of Caleruega founded the Order of Preachers (Dominicans) and Francis of Assisi founded the Order of Friars Minor (Franciscans) in the first decades of the thirteenth century. It is from these two orders especially that came the major figures of what history calls "high scholasticism"—the Dominicans Albert of Lauingen (ca. 1200-1280) and Thomas Aquinas (1225/27-1274), and the Franciscan Bonaventure of Bagnoregio (ca. 1217-1274).

Albert was born in Lauingen on the Danube and was first known as "Albert the German" when he began to teach in Paris. Later, because of his immense learning and influence on the theological scene, he was known as "Albert the Great." He entered the Dominicans in 1223 and eventually taught in Paris and Cologne.[27] He was a rather controversial figure in that, in addition to theological studies, he read and wrote commentaries on the works of Aristotle, whose works had recently become available from Latin translations made from Arabic. Aristotle was still considered a dangerous figure, but Albert saw the many possibilities in Aristotle's emphasis on the universal in the particular and highly recommended his study. His writings are filled with firsthand knowledge: "I saw," "I observed," "I witnessed," "I consulted."[28] Albert's theology, however, was more Neoplatonic and Augustinian, and so traditional, but his huge literary output would, says Justo González, leave "a vast encyclopedia of all the knowledge of his time."[29] It would be Albert's student, Thomas Aquinas, who would develop the implications of Albert's Aristotelianism. Thomas would habitually refer to Aristotle as "the Philosopher."

Legend has it that **Aquinas** was so silent in Albert's classes in Cologne, where he had gone to study theology as a young Dominican, that his fellow students nicknamed him "the Dumb Ox"—until Thomas answered a question so profoundly that the class was left amazed. But legend is exactly what the story is along with the legend that Aquinas was grossly fat.[30] Thomas O'Meara, in contrast, describes Aquinas as "a man of unusual energy, generosity (he composed twenty-six works at the request of others), and courage. . . . People who knew him described him as approachable, patient, and kind. His writings present the same image of their author."[31]

These writings are voluminous. They consist of philosophical works, commentaries on Aristotle, small works called "disputed questions," twenty Scripture commentaries, sermons, poetry (he is the author of the "Pange Lingua," the last two verses of which are those of the hymn "Tantum Ergo"), and his great systematic works, the *Summa Contra Gentiles* and the *Summa Theologiae*. He wrote all these works while teaching in Paris (two separate times), Naples, Rome, and Viterbo; there are estimates that he walked some nine thousand miles in his travels. All in all, Aquinas was an extraordinary man and rightly called the era's most significant theologian, if not the most significant theologian in the church's history.

He was born outside of the town of Aquino, about halfway between Rome and Naples. At the age of about fifteen he began studies at the University of Naples, in an atmosphere where Christian, Jewish, and Muslim scholars were free to exchange ideas, and where Arab astronomy and Greek medicine were studied, along with the texts of Aristotle. Although later study with Albert would deepen his appreciation of Aristotle, Thomas was introduced to Aristotle by Peter of Ireland (ca. 1200-1260).[32] During his time in Naples, Thomas became acquainted with the relatively new Dominican Order (Aquinas was born only a few years after Dominic's death in 1221), and, not without opposition from his family, he decided to enter. This took him to Paris for novitiate, and studies in Cologne, and then he began his short but amazing career of teaching and writing.

Aquinas's work, using Aristotle in a way that harmonized his thought with

Christian faith, was revolutionary and, says O'Meara, ushered in a new age of Christian theologizing.

> For the third time, after Origen in the third century and Augustine in the fifth, the Christian faith perceived that it could employ (but not be absorbed by) the ideas of a new age, culture, and science. The struggle of the thirteenth century swirled around Aristotle, because he brought a spirit of criticism over against piety, a realism in the structure of the human personality over against the reduction of faith or grace to signs or stories. The instincts and faculties of human life enhanced (but did not replace) the world of grace and faith. Faith was not just religious information about curious mysteries, but a knowing supported by the will, a cognition which gave access to a real world.[33]

While this balance between "the instincts and faculties of human life" and "the world of grace and faith"—faith and reason—is evident in every one of Aquinas's many works, it is perhaps most evident in his greatest (although unfinished) work, the *Summa Theologiae*. This work is structured, many have suggested, like a medieval cathedral, with many details contributing to the development of the entire building. The structure of the content is developed in a pattern of a movement out of God and then a movement back—what is called an *Exitus-Reditus* scheme—that might be pictured as a large U, or even a circle.[34] Part I begins with the nature of God and God's creation of the world. Part II is divided again into two parts, each dealing with humanity and human acts. Part III reflects on the incarnation and the sacraments, or the way humanity can return back to God. The sacraments treated, however, are only baptism, confirmation, eucharist, and (partially) penance. He died (in 1274) before he completed his masterpiece, and the work was completed in what is called the "Supplement," compiled from his commentary on Lombard's *Sentences* by his friend Reginald of Piperno (1230-1290). This section completes the treatment of the sacraments and closes the work with a section on eschatology, or the return of humanity to God after death and at the end of time.

Aquinas works out this survey of Christian doctrine by dividing the three parts into a number of "Questions." Each Question is then divided into "Articles." If the Parts are the great vaults of the cathedral, the Questions are its pillars, and the Articles are building stones, the luminous windows, and the proliferation of sculptures. The form of the Articles is what came to be called the *quaestio*, a form of theologizing already implicit in Abelard and Lombard, but developed even further in this period.[35] Each Article proceeds in the same way. Aquinas first states a thesis—for example, in the famous Article 3 of Part I Question II (cited I.II.3): "Whether God exists." Then Aquinas gives a number of objections to the thesis stated, using the words *videtur quod non* ("it seems that . . . not"). After this he states his own position on the thesis, beginning with the word *respondeo*

("I answer")—in I.II.3 this consists of Aquinas's "five proofs." This is followed by a short answer to the objections that had been made previously, and then he moves on to the next Article or begins the next Question.

Aquinas's early education in Naples and study of Aristotle with Albert almost certainly influenced an aspect of his theology that has resonance today as we speak of doing theology in "global perspective." There is evidence in Aquinas's writings that he was familiar with the writings of the Spanish-born Jewish philosopher Moses Maimonides (1138-1204) and the Iranian-born Muslim thinker Avicenna or Ibn Sina (980-1037). In the *Summa*, Question XIII, for example, where he discusses how we can speak of God, he engages in a subtle dialogue with them, explaining that even though we can never speak of God in *literal* ways, we can nevertheless speak of God by using metaphor and analogy.[36]

We could say much more, of course, about Thomas Aquinas's immense contribution to the theological enterprise as a whole, but we need to move on to consider his great contemporary, **Bonaventure of Bagnoregio** (or Bagnorea). Bonaventure was the name he was given when he entered the Franciscan Order in 1243 (his original name was John). He had come to Paris to study theology there, and after entering the order he continued his studies under the eminent British Franciscan Alexander of Hales (ca. 1183-1245). He eventually became a professor at the university, at the same time that Aquinas was teaching there. Unlike Aquinas, however, he did not spend his life as a university professor. In 1257 Bonaventure was elected Franciscan minister general and in 1273, a year before his death, he was named cardinal and bishop of the Diocese of Albano near Rome.[37]

Bonaventure's theological output was impressive, as the ten volumes of his collected works attest.[38] Bonaventure wrote commentaries on Scripture, and considered the Scriptures the "primary authority" for theology: "The whole of Scripture is the heart of God, the mouth of God, the tongue of God, the pen of God. . . ."[39] He wrote the classic spiritual text, *Journey of the Mind to God*, a longer and shorter life of St. Francis, and a wonderful survey of theology entitled *Breviloquium*.[40] His theology, says U.S. Anglo Franciscan scholar Zachary Hayes, is "unabashedly Christocentric," even though this Christocentrism is located within a rich understanding of the Trinity.[41]

Although he read and admired the works of Aristotle, Bonaventure was not as positive about using "the Philosopher" as was Aquinas. Bonaventure's theology was ultimately more contemplative, more Augustinian, and more in the "monastic" style that we discussed earlier. Zachary Hayes, however, warns that we should not make too much of Bonaventure's more cautious attitude. "To be convinced that Aristotle is wrong on a specific point or to think that an Aristotelian position might be good but not fully adequate is not to be against Aristotle in principle. It simply indicates an ability to read even an outstanding author with a critical sense."[42] There is, nevertheless, a subtle difference between the Dominican and Franciscan schools that becomes more evident at the end of the century and the first half of the next (which we will discuss below). The difference also attests to the fact that there is and there always has been a healthy pluralism in Christian theology.

Although it does not fit in the category of a *scholastic* theology, the great work of **Dante Alighieri** (1265-1321), *The Divine Comedy*, was profoundly influenced by, among others, the *Journey of the Mind to God* by Bonaventure and the works of Aquinas.[43] It ranks, say some scholars, with Anselm's *Why God Became Human* and Aquinas's *Summa Theologiae*, as one of the three greatest works of theology in the Middle Ages in the West, and summarizes masterfully the moral, religious, and cosmological views of the entire era.[44] As is well known, this epic poem is a journey through the tortures of hell, up through the seven-storied mountain of purgatory, ending with a tour of the beatitude in heaven. There is not space here to develop all of Dante's powerful images of punishment, purification, and bliss, but we might simply point out that among other contributions of the work, it gave the doctrine of purgatory "an enduring place in human memory," making a "vast symphony" out of the various strands of tradition that had come together in the theology of Dante's time.[45] And, interesting in this history of theology, it points to the fact that some of the most significant theological literature is not always the most academic and cerebral. *The Divine Comedy* is not only great theology. It is also a great read.

Another figure who does not fit the mold of academic theology—although she is a doctor of the church—is the Third Order Dominican mystic and activist **Catherine of Siena** (1347-1380). Catherine, says Bernard McGinn, is representative of the new role that some women began to take in the twelfth and thirteenth centuries. She spent several years enclosed in a room attached to her parents' house in Siena, but at a certain point she left her enclosure and devoted herself to works of charity around the city. She even began to travel around Italy to negotiate peace treaties between warring cities, and even traveled to Avignon to persuade the pope to return to Rome. Her major work, the *Dialogue*, written in Italian, is far from the nuanced theology of the Scholastics, but this does not make it "naive, superficial, or unoriginal."[46] In a much more experiential fashion, Catherine's theology expresses the same reflections on the redemption that Anselm and Aquinas had articulated.

Theology in Dialogue with Islam

Throughout this period, as we have said, Islam was perceived as an enemy of Christianity, and the various Crusades from the eleventh century to the thirteenth (and even beyond) were the ways in which many Christians encountered it. There were other encounters, however, that were more gentle and dialogical. Though there is no written record of the conversation, **Francis of Assisi** is noted for his meeting with Sultan Al-Malik al-Kamil in 1219, a meeting that impressed Francis very much and influenced his instructions to missionaries in the Rule of 1221.[47] Frederick W. Norris also reports on a gentler approach to Muslims that "tiptoed through some of the written works"[48] of this period.

In the early eleventh century, **Elias of Nisibis** (d. 1049), an East Syrian theologian, strongly upheld that orthodox Christians have the same doctrine of monotheism that the Qur'an has, in contrast to Christian heretics like Marcionites, Manicheans, or Tritheists. In the twelfth century there is a record of a monk named **George**, in a debate or dialogue in a Muslim leader's court, who defended the worship of the cross in the face of Muslims' accusations of idolatry. Also in the twelfth century, **Paul of Antioch** wrote a letter to his Muslim friends, and while he defended the Christian doctrines of the Trinity and the incarnation, he quoted the Qur'an to support his views that these doctrines did not necessarily contradict Muslim understandings of God's oneness.[49]

The most prolific writer in dialogue with Islam in this period was a native of the Spanish island of Majorca, in the culture where Jewish, Muslim, and Christian dialogue flourished. His name is **Ramón Llull** (1235-1315), and he is named not only as one of the greatest missionaries in Christian history but as perhaps the first theologian who reflected systematically on the church's mission.[50] A layman all his life, after a profound conversion he provided for his wife and children and gave the rest of his fortune to the poor, becoming a Franciscan tertiary. In an effort to convert Muslims to what he was convinced was the true faith, Llull studied philosophy and Arabic, lectured at the University of Paris and the University of Montpellier and wrote prolifically in the areas of philosophy, apologetics and mysticism, poetry, and even novels. Llull's driving idea was that Muslims would be converted only by providing good reasons for doing so. He wanted to establish a school for missionaries who would learn Arabic, study Islamic philosophy, and try to develop a relevant approach to Muslims. He was basically unsuccessful. He made several missionary trips to Algeria, but was soon arrested and imprisoned before being deported back to Spain. On a missionary trip in 1315, however, he was executed by his Muslim captors.

These theologies are not examples of the same kind of interreligious dialogue in which Christians engage today, after the breakthroughs of the Second Vatican Council. Still, the evidence points to the fact that Christians at this time in both East and West were engaged in conversations with peoples of other faiths. And while these examples are not of major movements in Christian theology, they do represent a constant tradition in Christian theology that has finally come into its own in our own time.

Mystical Theology

It is important not to give the impression that what was going on in theology in the twelfth and thirteenth centuries was simply an intellectual exercise. Indeed, many of the major theologians of this period also wrote what we would call today "mystical theology"—and indeed, for the medieval mind, any authentic theology had a mystical component. Bernard of Clairvaux, William of St. Thierry (ca. 1075-1148), Hugh and Richard of St. Victor, and Thomas Aquinas were all mystical writers. Bonaventure's *Journey of the Mind into God* was the "strongest expression" of a "new synthesis of the intellectual and affective cognition of God."[51] There are, however, a number of theologians who wrote in a particularly mystical vein, and we will focus on them in this section. While most of the theologians we have sketched so far in this section have been men (and clerics, for the most part), several of the mystical theologians we will mention here will be women.

The first theologian we will consider here, **Hildegard of Bingen** (1098-1179), is described by Robert Ellsberg as "by any standard one of the remarkable figures of her age: abbess and foundress of a Benedictine religious community; author and theologian; prophet and preacher; musician and composer; poet and artist; doctor and pharmacist."[52] Irish feminist historian Mary T. Malone is equally lavish in her praise, writing that Hildegard is "one of the most accomplished persons, male or female, in the whole western Christian tradition."[53]

At the age of eight, Hildegard was given over to the care of Jutta of Spanheim (1091-1136), who was attached to the Benedictine Monastery of St. Disibode. At fifteen she officially entered Jutta's community and, at Jutta's death, was elected abbess of the women in this double monastery. She went on to found her own monastery at Bingen, and from there she undertook a number of "preaching tours" of Europe, advocating both monastic and ecclesiastical reform.

She had had visions from the age of five, but it was only much later, at the age of forty-nine, that she wrote to Bernard of Clairvaux, the archbishop of Mainz, and the pope himself for approval of what she would like to write down. With their approval Hildegard began to write, and "from this time on, writings poured forth . . . in a never-ending stream."[54] She completed her most famous work *Scivias* (a shortened form of the Latin for "Know the Ways of the Lord"), and then wrote a second book of visions, *The Book of Life's Merits*. This was followed by works in science, a nine-volume work entitled *Physics*, and a book entitled *Causes and Cures*, which is one of the basic books in the history of Western pharmacy.

Hildegard's mystical theology was thoroughly trinitarian. *Scivias*, "a kind of visionary guide to Christian doctrine,"[55] is written using extraordinary images rather than plain prose. The book is composed of six visions of God the Father, seven of the Son, and thirteen visions of the Spirit. The Spirit is described by one of Hildegard's favorite images—*viriditas*, or "greenness"—signifying freshness, fertility, life, divine presence. God is described as a Living Light, and creation is depicted as a "cosmic dance in this light."[56] Men and women, though different in makeup, are nevertheless equal and so created in the image of God. Because of such equality, God could be imaged as both male and female. All of these are extraordinary ideas for their day, as well as our own.

Scholars today are recognizing more and more the importance of the lay movement of women and men during this time called the Beguines/Beghards. These were women and men—but especially women—who lived together in community, and prayed together, but who did not take religious vows and supported themselves by manual labor.[57] Committed to simple, evangelical living and witnessing to church reform, a number of Beguine women have emerged as important figures in Christian history: Mary of Oignies (1175-1213); Juliana of Cornillon (1192-1258), who was important for her advocacy of the feast of Corpus Christi; Marguerite Porete (d. 1310) who authored *The Mirror of Simple Souls*; and **Mechtilde of Magdeburg** (1210-1282), whose life and work we will outline here.

Mechtilde joined the Beguine community in Magdeburg, Germany, at about the age of eighteen, and after forty years there moved to the great Benedictine monastery at Helfta, where Gertrude of Hackenborn (1232-1292) was abbess. It was there that she wrote her extraordinary work, *The Flowing Light of the Godhead*. Mechtilde's key image in the book is "flowing." Not only, she says, did the book flow to her from God; God's love itself is an "overflow . . . which never stands still and always flows effortlessly and without ceasing."[58] Creation itself and God's grace within it also flow from God, but even *God as such* in God's trinitarian existence is flow. In the Trinity, the Father is the "restless Godhead" who is an "overflowing spring"; the Son is "the mercy which always has flowed and ever shall flow from God and ever returns in his Son."[59] This is again extraordinary language with a definite contemporary ring.

We turn now to the great German Dominican mystic John Eckhart of Hocheim, known more widely as **Meister Eckhart** (1260-1327). Eckhart entered the Dominicans at fifteen, studied in Cologne under Albert the Great, and finished his education in Paris. He taught in Paris at two separate times and was involved all his life in the administration of the Dominican Order and in its chief purpose, preaching. He wrote in Latin but was also one of the first theologians to write in German.[60] Toward the end of his life several of his more controversial propositions—some of which might have been taken for pantheism—were condemned in Cologne, and soon after his death they were condemned by the pope himself.[61]

Although Eckhart was clearly innocent of the charges, perhaps the church's hesitations were not without justification. This is because Eckhart is notoriously difficult to understand and interpret, because at the heart of his theology is a conviction that any knowledge of God is knowledge of what God is not, and that the greatest knowledge we can have of God is always built on the deeper awareness that we know nothing at all. Knowing the real God is to break through to the "God beyond God."[62] Theology's task "was not so much to reveal a set of truths about God as it was to frame the appropriate paradoxes that would serve to highlight the inherent limitations of our minds and to mark off in some way the boundaries of the unknown territory where God dwells."[63]

Eckhart had a wide influence, especially on his students and fellow Dominicans Johannes Tauler (1300-1361) and Henry Suso (ca. 1295-1366), who also were significant mystical theologians. His work also influenced another mystical writer, John Ruysbroeck (1293-1381), who in turn had a strong influence on Gerard Groote (1340-1384), the founder of the Brothers of the Common Life. The Brothers became advocates of a new kind of spirituality that was called the *devotio moderna*, or "new devotion," which emphasized the holiness of everyday lay life over a monastic life that withdrew from the world.[64] This perspective would fit very well with Eckhart's mysticism, which ultimately, for all its emphasis on *not* knowing, calls on Christians not to seek the extraordinary "but to attain true insight into the meaning of the ordinary."[65] It would have been farthest from Eckhart's mind, but it was this point of view that contributed to the ideas that would coalesce around the great Reformers who would emerge in the sixteenth century.

One final mystical writer whom we should at least treat briefly here is the Englishwoman **Julian of Norwich** (ca. 1342-1416). In May of 1373 the young Julian lay dying. A priest anointed her and left her with a crucifix, and subsequently she received fifteen visions which are the basis for her works.[66] These works—a shorter and a longer version of a text entitled *Showings* or *Revelations of Divine Love*—were written down only twenty years later. They are extraordinary. Many of the revelations focus on the passion of Christ, but others reflect on the nature of God as love, in language that is very stirring and has been an inspiration for feminist theologians in our time as they construct powerful new ways of speaking of the trinitarian God. Of many examples, let me just give one short quotation, from the longer text, Chapter 59: "As truly as God is our Father, so truly is God our Mother. Our Father wills, our Mother works, our good Lord the Holy Spirit confirms." Early on in the text, in chapter 5 in the long text, Julian has what has become a famous vision of "something small, no bigger than a hazelnut, lying in the palm of my hand." She wonders if it will fall into nothingness since it is so small, but then realizes that this and everything created by God has meaning and goodness. And yet, she says, "We need to have knowledge of this, so that we may delight in despising as nothing everything created, so as to love and have uncreated God."[67] This is obviously a paradox, but it illustrates Julian's sense of the immanence of God in creation along with an understanding of how everything needs to yearn for God's transcendence. Ultimately, Julian writes quoting Christ in another famous passage, "Sin is necessary, but all will be well, and all will be well, and every kind of thing will be well."[68]

The mystical theology of the High Middle Ages in the West was for many centuries sidelined in the history of theology. It is only recently that its wealth has been discovered, and it is making a difference in the way that theology is done today.

Later Scholasticism and Its Critics

Aquinas and Bonaventure had disagreed somewhat on the relation of faith to reason. Aquinas was more positive toward reason, and at the heart of his theology was the "analogy of being," or the conviction that there was real continuity, despite difference, between what human reason could conceive and experience and what God was in Godself. Bonaventure, on the other hand, was more skeptical of the powers of reason and relied more on God's action in revelation to lead humanity to God. In the generation after these theological giants, the disagreements between the "Dominican school" and the "Franciscan school" became even more pronounced, to the extent that for a time Franciscans were forbidden even to study Aquinas.[69] Two theologians of the Franciscan school were particularly opposed to Aquinas's synthesis of faith and reason: John Duns Scotus (ca. 1265-1308) and William of Ockham (1285-1347). Their thought is difficult and subtle (Scotus is called *doctor subtilis* or "the subtle doctor"), but they had a profound influence on the direction of the theology of their time, and in many ways paved the way for the major theological disruption that would take place in the fifteenth and sixteenth centuries.

Scotus was born in the Scottish border country and taught at Cambridge, Oxford, Paris, and Cologne. One of his central tenets was that the human mind could not know God at all on its own, and so any kind of "natural theology" on account of the analogy of being was utterly impossible. Because of this, the only real theologian is God, since only God knows Godself. If human beings did theology, then, they could only do it by reflecting on what God had given in revelation. For Scotus, however, God has selected what should be revealed to humanity. Because of this, while we can *approach* an understanding of God through practicing our faith and the use of our reason, we can never be sure that what we know of God is really what God is like.[70] God's selectivity is based on God's sovereign will, and so, similarly, God can and is free to do exactly what God wants.

This means that there is no *law* that even God must obey, but whatever God wills or ordains is lawful and good. God's commandments are good, for example, not in themselves but because they are what God wants. The incarnation was not so much a necessity, as Anselm would say, to make satisfaction for offended divine honor; God willed to become human from the very beginning of creation and would have done so even if humanity had not sinned.[71] Scotus was also—over against the hesitancy of Aquinas—a champion of the doctrine of Mary's Immaculate Conception (not declared a dogma until 1854). His terse argument for it is also based on God's absolute power and will: *Potuit, decuit. Ergo fecit*—God *could* do it. It was fitting. So God did it.[72]

An even more radical emphasis on God's will was developed by **William of Ockham**. Ockham was born in an English village by that name and educated at Oxford. He was a controversial figure, particularly because of his association with the radical, anti-ecclesiastical thought of the "Spiritual Franciscans," who were influenced by the writings of the then long-dead southern Italian theologian Joachim of Fiore (ca. 1132-1202).[73] Even more strongly than Scotus, Ockham rejected the use of reason in theology. Like Scotus, his theology is quite tedious, and he was an advocate of a philosophical position called nominalism. This was a position that denied any kind of universal or general thinking. As a result of this, Ockham insisted, only faith can lead us to the truth, and so we must simply adhere to what God has revealed and willed. God could have decided differently, but the fact is God decided to save humanity through Jesus Christ, the sacraments, and the church. God could have become incarnate in a totally different way than God did. We can never understand why God acted in the way God did.[74]

One begins to see aspects of Luther in this position—his strong distrust of reason, his emphasis on faith alone, and his emphasis on the Scriptures. What Luther did not accept, however, was Ockham's insistence on the necessary mediating role of the church, but that was because of other influences that were in the air in the century or so afterwards.

Not all Christians appreciated the theology of these late scholastics, with all its distinctions and subtleties. Less than a hundred years after Ockham's death, John Gerson (1363-1429) begged his colleagues "not to waste time on such philosophical disputes which had little connection with the challenges of the Christian life or the urgent needs of the Church."[75] Those who continued to advocate Scotus's and Ockham's nominalism were hailed as "dunces."[76] We have already mentioned the emergence of the Brothers of the Common Life in northern Europe. Out of this movement came one of the most-read spiritual classics of all time, *The Imitation of Christ*, written by Thomas Hemerken, popularly known as **Thomas à Kempis** (ca. 1380-1471). A famous passage reflects a strong critique of the scholastic theology of the day: "What good does it do to speak learnedly about the Trinity if, lacking humility, you displease the Trinity? Indeed it is not learning that makes a man holy and just, but a virtuous life makes him pleasing to God. I would rather feel contrition than know how to define it."[77]

Also associated with the Brothers of the Common Life at the turn of the fifteenth century was **Erasmus of Rotterdam** (ca. 1466-1536). In his great spoof of monks, ignorant priests, celibacy, and relics (topics that would soon loom large on the theological scene) entitled *The Praise of Folly*, Erasmus also mocks the "divines" or professors of theology. He says what excites them are questions like whether there was any instant of time in the generation of the Second Person; whether there be more than one filiation in Christ; whether it be a possible proposition that God the Father hates the Son; or whether it was possible that Christ could have taken upon Him the likeness of a woman, or of the devil, or of an ass, or of a stone, or of a gourd; and then how that gourd should have preached, wrought miracles, or been hung on the cross.... There are infinite of these subtle trifles, and others more subtle than these, of notions, relations, instants, formalities, quiddities, haecceities, which no one can perceive without a Lynceus whose eyes could look through a stone wall and discover those things through the thickest darkness that never were.[78]

The first scholastics were bold innovators in response to the new context of an emerging Europe. That context had changed now, and Western theology was on the brink of something new. Catholic scholastic theology would not die, but it would be challenged by new ways of thinking and, for Europeans, the discovery of new peoples and new worlds.

Theology at the End of the Byzantine Empire

As Europe was becoming wealthier and stronger militarily, the Christian Byzantine empire was getting weaker and more vulnerable in the face of a vibrant and flourishing Muslim culture (although it began to decline after 1200).[79] Much of the theological debate after 1054 until the empire's fall in 1453 had to do with reunion with Rome and the issues that had precipitated the schism. A strong supporter of reunion was Patriarch John XI of Constantinople (ca. 1225-1297), but most of the people of the empire and Byzantine theologians were opposed, like Patriarch German II, who was patriarch from 1223 to 1240. As we mentioned at the beginning of this chapter, the Council of Florence in 1439 came to an agreement on the major issues of the schism, but in 1443 the patriarchs of Alexandria, Antioch, and Jerusalem condemned the council's decisions, and these decisions were still being debated when Constantinople fell ten years later. Justo González wryly refers to an author who remarked that ten thousand Turks ready for battle would not make as much noise as one hundred Christians discussing theology![80]

Another area of controversy that eventually involved Byzantium's greatest theologian, **Gregory Palamas** (1296-1359), was over the question of "Hesychasm," that is, the practice of meditation while reciting the "Jesus Prayer" ("Lord Jesus Christ, have mercy upon me"). The practice goes back to the tenth century with Symeon, called the "New Theologian" (949-1022), one of the greatest and most beloved theologians of the East, and was revived by Gregory of Sinai (ca. 1260-1346).

Another monk, **Barlaam of Calabria** (ca. 1290-1348), who was trained in

Western scholasticism, ridiculed the practice. The Hesychasts claimed, through their practice, to see the very divine light the disciples saw surrounding Jesus at the transfiguration, but, said Barlaam, no one can see God. Barlaam's attack brought Gregory into the controversy, but Gregory put it terms of the theology of the Trinity. In a very famous distinction, Gregory argued that, while we cannot know God in Godself or essence, we can know God from God's effects or "energies." Thus, the Eastern practice was indeed orthodox.[81] In 1351, a council condemned the anti-Hesychast position.

While little serious theology seems to have been done in Russia during this time, the turn of the fourteenth century witnessed the last great East Syrian theologian, the Patriarch of Nisibis **Ebedjesu bar Berika** (d. 1318). Many of Ebedjesu's works are lost,[82] but what survives is his *Book of the Pearl on the Truth of Christian Doctrine*, a work of systematic theology. Besides what one might expect—an exposition of "Nestorian" christological doctrine—there is something perhaps quite unexpected. Ebedjesu argued that the patriarch of Rome (the pope) had the place of honor among all the patriarchs of the Christian world.

The Coptic (Egyptian) church, though like the East Syrian church not in communion with Rome, produced works of Scripture scholarship, polemics, and summaries of Christian doctrine, although these, González says, were not very original. Nevertheless, it is important to note that theology was still being done in North Africa in the midst of Muslim rule, and we could mention in particular **Fadail Ibn al'Assal** and **Abul-Barakat Ibn Kabar** (d. 1320).[83]

In the Syrian Orthodox church we should mention **Gregory Bar-Hebraeus** (1226-1286) as one of that church's most eminent theologians. **Gregory of Datev** (b. 1346) was familiar with Latin Christianity but strenuously defended the theology of the Armenian Orthodox church. Once more, it is important to recognize the fact that both of these men were practicing Christian theology as a minority voice in their cultures.

Christian Theology in 1500

By 1500 Christianity was for the first time a Western religion. The Byzantine empire had fallen, Europe had emerged as the center of the world's power (although Islam remained a force to be reckoned with, as did China as well), and the European exploration/invasion/encounter with Latin America, parts of Africa, and Asia had begun. In Europe, a theology of the church had developed that focused more and more on institution and hierarchy, as both were challenged by secular rulers and reform movements, whether heretical, like the Waldensians, or loyal and orthodox, like the Franciscan movement. Scholastic theologians had refined the church's doctrines and had developed a strong theology of the sacraments that stressed eucharistic presence and priestly powers of consecration and absolution, but rather downplayed Christian baptismal dignity and responsibilities. In a fascinating development, the doctrine of purgatory became central in Christianity, and the church's power through indulgences and the celebration of Mass was stressed to perhaps exaggerated lengths. Canadian philosopher Charles Taylor points out the fascinating cooperation here between popular religious sensibilities and official theology.[84] The papacy was powerful, but wounded and corrupt after the "Babylonian Captivity" at Avignon and the scandal of the Great Western Schism.

People were hungering for more. The Renaissance of the fifteenth century had opened up once more the riches of the Bible and the earliest theologians. Movements like the Brothers of the Common Life were experiencing that Christians could live holy lives despite the church and its rituals. This paved the way for the number of "Reformations"[85] that climaxed in the sixteenth century. In the newly evangelized lands that Europe was colonizing, new issues and situations demanded new theological answers. Christianity and theology had experienced a marvelous era in five hundred years since the first millennium, but something new was afoot. In the next five hundred years Christianity was to change dramatically—more than anyone could imagine as the fifteenth century came to a close.

THEOLOGY FROM 1500 TO 1700

Historian Justo González has suggested that as a result of the shift in the center of gravity in the population of today's church, the emphasis placed on the Protestant and Catholic Reformations in traditional histories of the church "will take second place to the Spanish and Portuguese invasion of the Western Hemisphere, and to the ensuing colonial expansion of Western Europe."[86] González's point is certainly not to denigrate the Reformation(s) period, but only to emphasize the fact that any history, history of theology, or theology as such needs to recognize the truly *catholic* and global nature of Christianity in today's world. This is why we will begin our survey of this complex and rich period of Christian theologizing with an outline of the theology that was being done in what today we call the "global south." We will focus on theologizing in Latin America and Asia, since European interest in Africa developed a bit later than the sixteenth and seventeenth centuries, and theology in North America is connected for the most part more closely with the theology of the Protestant Reformation.

Theology in Latin America and Asia

Indigenous local theologizing began as soon as women and men tried to make sense of the new faith that they had received from the colonizers and conquerers. The example of the complex theology surrounding the Virgin of Guadalupe in Mexico is a case in point, as is the Virgin of La Cobra (La Caridad) in Cuba.[87] However, for the most part and with few exceptions, theologizing in this first part of the colonial era was done by foreigners and evangelizers, even if they were strongly identified with the people whom they served. While our focus here will be on theology that has been preserved in writing, we must never forget that most of the theological reflection of this time was expressed in architecture (e.g., the marvelous churches in the colonial Philippines), art (the magnificent altar pieces in Latin American cathedrals), music (witness the recently discovered music of anonymous Bolivian composers), popular devotions to Mary and the saints, or catechetical lessons in indigenous languages such as Japanese, Vietnamese, or Qechua. In many ways—and this is true of all places and all times—it is this theologizing that has captured the minds and hearts of ordinary people, as contemporary contextual theologians have realized in our own day.[88]

Latin America

In 1492, the same year that Columbus reached the island of Hispaniola (today the Dominican Republic and Haiti) and Europeans first caught a glimpse of what was for them a whole new world, Spain had finally succeeded in its *reconquista* (reconquest) of the Iberian peninsula. After some seven centuries of Muslim rule, Muslims (and also Jews) had been driven out of Spain or forced to convert to Christianity. In the "new world," the spirit of reconquest would continue, as Spain sought to expand its empire and enrich its treasuries with new sources of revenue. As Spain, and eventually Portugal, accomplished this, the cost to the indigenous population was immense: "Neither the Crusades nor the Holocaust [in the twentieth century] caused as much death as did Christendom's conquest of America."[89] The conquerers were clear that they wanted to bring Christianity, for that was the only way that the indigenous peoples could be saved. Evangelization was nevertheless linked to a system called the *encomienda* (a right to indigenous peoples' labor) that virtually enslaved the population and deprived it of its human dignity.[90]

It was in this context that some of the first theologizing in Latin America was done. In the first decades of the sixteenth century, in a letter that cannot be dated exactly, the Dominican superior in Hispaniola, **Pedro de Córdoba** (ca. 1460-1525) laments how the indigenous peoples of the island have been "destroyed in body and soul."[91] It would be better if the local population had not been made to convert to Christianity at all rather "than to have the name of Christ blasphemed as is now the case."[92] Since the conversion of the local peoples had been part of the rationale for Spain's conquest of the "Indies," as the Spanish called them, de Córdoba's argument called into question Spain's entire enterprise there.[93]

De Córdoba and his fellow Dominicans chose their best preacher, **Antonio de Montesinos** (ca. 1480-1540) to deliver a powerful, controversial sermon in the Santo Domingo cathedral on the Sunday before Christmas in 1511. The sermon infuriated the rich landowners who were exploiting the people, but the text was nevertheless widely circulated both on the island and in Spain. As a result, Montesinos was summoned back to Spain to defend his position before the King—which was exactly what the Dominican community had hoped would happen.[94] A famous passage of the sermon reveals that Montesinos had minced no words:

> . . . you are in mortal sin, and live and die therein by reason of the cruelty and tyranny that you practice on these innocent people. Tell me, by what right or justice do you hold these Indians in such cruel and horrible slavery? By why right do you wage such detestable wars on these people . . . ? . . . Are they not men? Do they not have rational souls? Are you not bound to love them as you love yourselves? . . . Be sure that in your present state you can no more be saved than the Moors or Turks who do not have and do not want the faith of Jesus Christ.[95]

It is not certain whether a young **Bartolomé de Las Casas** (1474-1566) was in the congregation on that day, but he might well have been. He had come to Hispaniola in 1502 and had returned as a priest and *encomendero* a few years later. In 1514 he underwent a profound conversion, eventually joined the Dominican Order, and became known as the "Defender of the Indians."[96] The rest of his life was spent, in his own words, "going and coming from the Indies to Castile, and from Castile to the Indies, many times."[97] In an amazingly large number of writings (his complete works in Spanish run to fourteen volumes), in theological and legal debates and in constant political negotiations, Las Casas called for a recognition of the religious and personal freedom of the indigenous populations of the Spanish-occupied territories. "God has a very fresh and living memory," he writes, "of the smallest and most forgotten."[98]

Though going against the majority of theologians of his time regarding the salvation of those who did not profess explicit faith in Christ, Las Casas found the red thread in the Christian tradition from Justin Martyr through Aquinas that argued for the universal salvific will of God and the possibility of implicit Christian faith.[99] In his seminal work on Las Casas, Gustavo Gutiérrez acknowledges that he was certainly not the lone voice that argued in this way. Nevertheless, he says, he was "perhaps the one who drilled the deepest into what was occurring in the Indies and best articulated a theological reflection on the basis of those events. . . ."[100]

Around the turn of the seventeenth century, the indigenous Peruvian **Felipe Guamán Poma de Ayala** (ca. 1550-1615) wrote a remarkable book, addressed to King Philip III of Spain, in which he writes firsthand of the injustices done to his people at the hands of the colonizers. He writes that he has "walked through the world *in search of Christ's poor*," and calls for the conversion not only of his own people, but of Christians as well.[101] Here we have a rare but powerful theological statement from the grassroots.

There are a number of manuscripts from early-sixteenth-century Mexico, often written by indigenous Christians, that collectively go by the name of **"Testarian manuscripts."** These, writes Orlando Espín, are full catechisms and prayer books that use indigenous pictographs to represent the doctrinal and ethical teachings of the missionaries. Some of the pictographs are traditional; some of them have been developed specifically to convey the new and strange truths of Christianity. Espín points out that the commentaries in the local language explaining the pictographs do not follow them exactly, suggesting that "the missionaries could not impose orthodox European concepts without the free, cultural filtering done by the native authors." In this way, the message of evangelization "could be more than the strictly orthodox teaching of the friars."[102]

Perhaps the most important event in the evangelization of the Americas in the sixteenth century was the series of apparitions of the Virgin of Guadalupe in 1531 to a simple Mexican peasant named Juan Diego. While there is evidence of a chapel dedicated to *la Virgén* on the hill of Tepeyac where she originally appeared, devotion to Guadalupe achieved popularity only in the mid-seventeenth century when two accounts of the apparition and the miracles associated with it were published, both written by Mexican-born Spanish priests. The first, written in 1648, was in Spanish by diocesan priest **Miguel Sánchez**, entitled *Image of the Virgin Mary, Mother of God of Guadalupe*. This is "the first presently known account of the Mexican appearances of the Virgin of Guadalupe."[103] Beginning in the eighteenth century, however, another account, published the following year in 1649, took on more importance, even though it is similar in almost every way to Sánchez's account. This text was written in Nahuatl, an indigenous language of Mexico and was aimed more at the common people than at the Spanish elite. The name of the volume was *Hue tlamahuiçoltica*, but known more popularly as *The Nican mapohua* and it was written by the parish priest of the shrine of Guadalupe, **Luis Laso de la Vega**.

In both versions we have a narration of the familiar story: the appearance of a "beautiful lady" to the peasant Juan Diego, her request for a shrine, the hesitancy of the bishop and his conversion when he saw the image of the Virgin miraculously painted on the *tilma* or cloak of Juan Diego. In oral tradition, and then in written form over a century later, we have the first indigenous reflections on Mariology—or perhaps even on the doctrine of God[104]—in the Americas.

No reflections on Latin American theologizing at this time, however brief, can omit the person and the work of one of the most amazing women in Latin

American church history. This is **Juana Inés de la Cruz** (1651-1694), popularly known as Sor Juana. Poet, dramatist, scholar, theologian, and feminist, her work constitutes "one of the great literary outputs of the baroque era."[105] In 1690, with a critique of a sermon that she had read, she wrote the first work of theology written by a woman in the Americas. Not surprisingly, however, her foray into the world of clerics and men got her into trouble. After writing a brilliant response to her critics ("You foolish men, accusing women for lacking reason when you yourselves are the reason for the lack"[106]), she stopped writing altogether and died soon after.

Asia

Spain and Portugal were expanding into Asia as well, although, with the exception of the Philippines, not as conquerers of territory but as traders out of small colonies in places like Goa in India and Malacca in what is today Malaysia. Missionaries had gone to India, only to find Christians already there for centuries, and from India, men like Francis Xavier (1506-1552) traveled to Japan and even tried to reach China.

Later Jesuits were more successful in gaining entrance into the Middle Kingdom, as China called itself. Chief among these is **Matteo Ricci** (1552-1610). Ricci was a protegé of his Jesuit superior Alessandro Valignano (1539-1606), and Valignano was convinced that true evangelization of Asia was going to take place only when Asians could express the faith in their own terms. To evangelize was not to make people Spanish or Portuguese, but Christian. The church was not tied to one culture, but could adapt to any.[107] Ricci learned Mandarin Chinese and devoted himself to the study of Confucian classical literature. He was so successful at this that he was accepted as a member of the scholarly class and given a Chinese name, Li Madou. In his conversations with Confucian scholars, sharing with them as well the best of Western technology and science (like clocks, maps, sundials, and mathematics), Ricci had the "opportunity to lay the foundation for the same sort of marriage between a philosophy, Confucianism, and the Christian faith as Thomas Aquinas had performed with Aristotelianism."[108] In 1982, Pope John Paul II praised Ricci's work as being equal to that of Justin Martyr and Origen "in their effort to translate the message of faith in terms understandable to the culture of their times."[109]

Two other Jesuits who need to be mentioned in any survey of theology in Asia at this time are **Robert de Nobili** (1577-1656) in India and **Alexandre de Rhodes** (1591-1660) in Vietnam. On arriving in India in 1606, de Nobili realized that, for Indians, becoming Christian meant becoming European—something that he was convinced was not at all the case. His response was to learn Indian languages, to dress in the saffron robes of a Hindu *sannyasi*, and to devote himself to a life of prayer and meditation. De Nobili was the first European to learn Sanskrit, the language of the Hindu Scriptures, and this enabled him to dialogue with Hindu scholars and to begin thinking about

Christian doctrine in Indian ways. His goal was to establish a seminary where Christian doctrine could be taught based on Hindu philosophy, but this idea never came to fruition. He wrote voluminously in three Indian languages and European languages as well. He is always cited as a pioneer of a theology that takes risks in taking culture and local religious practice seriously.[110]

Although he was expelled from Vietnam several times and died not in Vietnam but as a missionary in Persia, Alexandre de Rhodes is the founder of Vietnamese Christianity. Like de Nobili, he was convinced that learning the language and culture of a country was the only true way of preparing to evangelize it. His great contribution to Vietnamese theology was the publication in 1651 of his *Catechismus*, a course on the entire Christian doctrinal tradition. It was written in the romanized Vietnam script that de Rhodes himself invented (the alphabet still used today), used new words for God (e.g., the Noble Lord of Heaven and Earth, the Noble Supreme Lord), and integrated many Vietnamese proverbs and sayings.[111] Peter Phan judges that what de Rhodes accomplished in inculturating the gospel is hardly what we would be satisfied with today. Nevertheless, what he *did* accomplish "far surpassed what the official church of his times could have dreamed of, even in its most catholic moments."[112]

One final example of Asian theologizing comes from the Philippines. This is a Tagalog version of the "Our Father" found in the 1593 *Doctrina Christiana*, a catechism originally written in 1582. Printed in both Spanish and Tagalog and based on Nahuatl catechisms used in Mexico, it was the first book printed in the Philippines, and originally the work of Franciscan **Juan de Plasencia** (d. 1590), a Spanish missionary.[113] In a short article reflecting on the 1593 version of the prayer, Filipino theologian José de Mesa points out that it is a much more inculturated translation than the current one in use in the Philippines today (for example: one of the petitions reads "give us today our daily rice"). De Mesa observes that the first missionaries in the Philippines were quite sensitive to the local culture, and used it as a guide as they helped local people understand the riches of the gospel.[114]

Reformations in the West

While the European colonization and Christian evangelization of Latin America and Asia were taking place, northern Europe was being rocked by a reform movement that was splitting the church apart in ways that Rome had never imagined. There had been reform movements before that had challenged the legitimacy of the church. There had been anti-Roman movements in the Middle Ages such as that led by Peter Waldo (d. 1218), and the movements sparked by John Wyclif (1324-1384) in England and Jan Hus (1369-1415) in Bohemia (today's Czech Republic). But these had been rather easily suppressed.[115]

At the turn of the sixteenth century, however, a number of factors made things ripe for more radical reform. The Catholic hierarchy was corrupt, with many bishops never even setting foot in their dioceses even though they collected revenues from them. The popes, in order to collect money for a restoration of Rome in grand Renaissance style, promoted the sale of indulgences in a way that bordered on the heretical. There was a general atmosphere, with wider education and literacy, of opposition to any authority that stood in the way of a warmer, more personal relationship with God, and there was a real longing to throw off many of the accretions developed in the medieval church and to get back to the sources of Christianity, especially Scripture. In this context there emerged several great theologians who were able to articulate the Christian faith in fresh ways for these new times. Some did this in opposition to Rome; others defended the Roman church while advocating reform in it as well.

Luther

Perhaps the most creative of these theologians was the German **Martin Luther** (1483-1546), whose personal struggles and religious breakthrough grounded the entire Protestant (as it came to be called) reform movement. Like Augustine whom he admired, Luther was not a systematic thinker. Rather, with the exception of his two catechisms, his theology was forged in the midst of controversy and was more pastoral than academic.[116] Nevertheless, what always anchors his theologizing is the insight that grace has been freely given through the work of Jesus Christ, and only by faith in him (*sola fide*, "by faith alone") can we grasp that grace and be saved.

Luther, perhaps even more than other people of his time, had been terrified of hell. He himself had said that he entered the Augustinian monastery to escape hell, and even after entering monastic life and being ordained to the priesthood he struggled mightily with anxieties and scrupulosity.[117] One day, however, while meditating on Paul's Letter to the Romans he had a deep realization that nothing he could *do* would save him. Salvation was a gift, already accomplished by God in Christ, and all he had to do was accept that in faith: "The righteousness of God," Paul wrote, "has been manifested apart from the law . . . through faith in Jesus Christ for all who believe" (Rom. 3:21-22).

The way to encounter Christ in faith was through the Scriptures, "the cradle in which the Saviour lies."[118] What was important was not all the practices that had developed in the church, especially in the previous thousand years: Masses for the dead, the veneration of relics, devotions to the saints, procuring indulgences. Only through Scripture (*sola Scriptura*, "by Scripture alone") can we meet the living Christ. Certainly, many things in the tradition were still valid, but they must not obscure the center of Christian faith.

Luther's intention at the beginning was to call the Roman church to reform, but as he encountered more and more opposition—and ultimately excommunication—he became more radical. He began in 1517 with the publication of ninety-five provocative but basically orthodox theses especially aimed against the way money was being raised through the granting of indulgences. By 1520, now considered a heretic in Rome, he published his *Appeal to the Christian Nobility of the German Nation*, which called for the reform of the clergy, the marriage of clergy, the extension of the chalice to the laity at Mass, and the basing of theology on the Bible.[119] He eventually accepted only two sacraments—baptism and Eucharist—since only they, he said, had a clear basis in the New Testament. He denied the authority of the papacy, wrote against the sacrificial nature of the Mass, and proposed the equality of all Christians—thus denying any difference between lay and ordained Christians.[120]

Luther's life was lived in controversy, both with Rome and with other reformers such as Ulrich Zwingli (1484-1531) in Switzerland and fellow Augustinian Andreas Karlstadt (1486-1541). As he grew older he relied on the milder-tempered Philip Melanchthon (1497-1560) to draft confessions of faith that tried to achieve concord among his colleagues and with Rome as well.[121] The most important of these was the Augsburg Confession of 1530, but while it settled some Protestant controversies it could not restore unity with Rome. Despite the efforts of Cardinal Gaspar Contarini in 1541 (1483-1542) on the Catholic side, the breach had grown too wide.

By the end of the 1530s Henry VIII had been declared head of the church in England and had broken with Rome, and Protestantism had spread to France, Switzerland, and other parts of northern Europe as well.

Calvin

Another major theological voice against Rome was **John Calvin** (1509-1564). Calvin was a great organizer of people as well as thoughts, and he used them totally "in the service of God as he understood God."[122] Born in France, he studied classics at the University of Paris and then studied classics and law at the University of Orléans and Bourges. When he was about twenty he had a "sudden conversion to teachableness,"[123] and began to read Luther with much appreciation, as well as other reform theologians. He began to write and in 1536 published the first version of the *Institutes of the Christian Religion*, his major work and one of the great classics of theology. The *Institutes* underwent a number of revisions from that time until 1559. Soon after finishing the first edition of the *Institutes*, Calvin was called by the head of the reformed church in Geneva, Guillaume Farel (1489-1565), to help lead the church there. He was not appreciated in Geneva, however, and both he and Farel were expelled from the city in 1538. In 1541 Calvin was recalled to Geneva and stayed there, as leader of the church, for the rest of his life.

As with Luther and the other Reformers, Scripture stood at the center of Calvin's thought, and his goal was always to give every Christian direct access to the Scriptures. In Geneva he preached four times a week, wrote commentaries on almost every book of the Bible, and established a school to train pastors and preachers of the Word.[124] Calvin's vision of the church was "a school in which all are students as well as teachers, being instructed by God through Christ by the doctrine of the Holy Spirit set forth in Scripture."[125] His great objection to Rome was that it taught that images (statues, stained glass) were the way simple people were nourished in their faith, and not through the Scriptures.

Although Calvin's doctrine of "double predestination" is not the center of his theology,[126] it certainly looms large in it. As he puts it very plainly in the *Institutes*: "As Scripture, then, clearly shows, we say that God once established by his eternal and unchangeable plan those whom he long before determined once for all to receive into salvation, and those whom, in the other hand, he would devote to destruction."[127] Like Augustine before him, Calvin saw this doctrine more as a consolation for Christian life than as a threat. Rather than worry about whether one can save oneself through one's own works, the Christian need only put his or her faith in Christ, whose death has made satisfaction for human sin. One can never really know whether one has been elected or not, but the fact that one *has* faith in Christ and strives to live a good life is a good indication that she or he has indeed been chosen.

Although Calvin softened the teaching on predestination in his own pastoral practice,[128] Catholics and Protestants alike were nevertheless offended at the doctrine, which had been condemned previously in the fifth, sixth, and ninth centuries.[129] Catholics condemned the doctrine of predestination at Trent (DS 1567/ND 1967). On the Protestant side, the Dutch Reformed theologian Jacobus Hermanzoon, who is known by the name Arminius (1559-1609), proposed a more moderate doctrine of election, but the Synod of Dort of 1618-1619 upheld Calvin's stricter view as orthodox Reformed theology.[130]

Like Luther, Calvin also denied all the sacraments except baptism and Eucharist, but unlike Luther he did not accept the real presence in the Eucharist. Reception of the sacrament unites us spiritually to Christ, but Christ's body remains in heaven and is not actually present on the altar. For Calvin, Rome's error was to think that "we feed on the Body and Blood of Christ with our mouths, and not with our souls."[131]

Scotland, England, and the Radical Reformation

Reformed theology was taken to Scotland by **John Knox** (ca. 1513-1572). Knox was influenced by Calvin, but perhaps even more influenced by Ulrich Zwingli and Heinrich Bullinger (1504-1575), with whom he stayed in Zurich. One way that Bullinger's influence is seen is in Knox's treatise on predestination, where, in subtle but crucial contrast to Calvin, Knox situates the doctrine of predestination in a discussion of the nature of God, instead of—as Calvin did in the *Institutes*—in the context of the doctrine of grace and the experience of salvation. While this was his "only major theological treatise," Knox's collected works run to six volumes.[132]

Even though he broke with Rome, Henry VIII's intention was not to change much of the theology or liturgy of the English church. However, the Reformation in England was under the influence of both Lutheran and Reformed theology. One of the architects of the theology of the Church of England was **Thomas Cramner** (1489-1556), who gave the church a first version of its liturgical treasure, *The Book of Common Prayer*. Other important English theologians were **John Jewel** (1522-1571), who wrote an *Apology of the Church of England*, and **Richard Hooker** (1554-1600), whose *Of the Lawes of Ecclesiasticall Politie* is one of the most important theological works of the Elizabethan period, and who is being read today more and more as a *Reformed* theologian.[133]

We need to mention, too, theologians of what is called the "Radical Reformation." Because these theologians insisted on limiting baptism to adults, and so called for the re-baptism of those already baptized as infants, they became known as "Anabaptists." Anabaptists tried to live simply, to reproduce the first Christian communities. They had no liturgy beyond listening to the Word of God and they would have no link to any government. One of these, the Dutchman **Menno Simons** (1496-1561) was the founder of the Mennonites. Another, the German **Thomas Müntzer**, who advocated violence against oppressive government, was killed in the peasant revolt in Münster in 1534.

The Catholic Reformation and the Council of Trent

At first, the Catholic Church didn't take Luther or the rest of the Reformers very seriously, even though there were strong voices among its theologians and hierarchy for reform even before 1517. One of the most eminent theologians of the time and one of theology's most important interpreters of Thomas Aquinas, **Thomas de Vio Cajetan** (1469-1534), had studied Luther's works and met with him personally in 1518, but the two came to no resolution. **Johann Eck** (1486-1543) also debated with Luther, but the result was the same.[134] At a council in Regensburg, Cardinal Gaspar Contarini, much of whose theology was close to Luther's, had come close to reconciliation with the Protestant theological positions,[135] but ultimately met resistance from both sides. This was in 1541, and by then it was clear that Protestant and Catholic theologies were—at least at that time—irreconcilable.

In the years following 1517 there were strong movements for the pope to call a council to reform the church and answer the challenges of the Reformers, but Rome was hesitant. One reason was that the Catholic Church did not want to give the impression that it was taking its critics too seriously. Second, the Protestant side had called for a council, but wanted both clergy and laity to take part, with little if any papal interference. This was simply unacceptable. Third, the experience of the aftermath of the Great Western Schism with the emergence of the theory of "Conciliarism" (that a council was a greater authority than the pope) was something to which Rome was keenly allergic. Finally, there was politics: Rome was afraid of the interference of Francis I of France; Francis was suspicious of Rome's ties with Emperor Charles V. After a long delay, Paul III called for an ecumenical council to take place in the more neutral territory of Trent in northern Italy, and it finally had its opening session in December of 1545. It had taken almost twenty years for Rome to begin the serious reform and theological clarification that was demanded by the tragic division of Western Christianity.[136]

The council had no real intention of reconciliation with Luther, Calvin, and the other Reformers. Its goal was much more to make Catholicism secure in areas where it was in danger of being overwhelmed by the new movements: for example, northern Italy and France. As Bishop Pietro Bertano said in 1547, if the council "will not help those already lost to the Church, it will at least help those still in danger of becoming lost." This it would do by stating—often for the first time—the clear teaching of the church and by subjecting the church to a thorough and much needed internal reform.[137]

In some ways this defensive concentration on what were certainly pressing problems in Europe was unfortunate. Had the council been able to focus on problems encountered in Latin America and Asia it would have been more inclusive of the entire church. But there were only European bishops and abbots present. The bishop of Mexico City, Juan de Zumárraga (the bishop in the story of the Guadalupe apparitions), had intended to attend the council. He wanted to "communicate the problems of the new Christians and request help from the pope and the coming Council," but he died before he was able to leave Mexico.[138]

The council had a troubled history. It met in three stages, from 1545 to 1548, from 1551 to 1552, and then from 1562 to 1563. At first it was not very well attended. Some popes refused to reconvene it. But in the end what the Council of Trent accomplished would shape the theology and discipline of the church well into the twentieth century. In terms of doctrine, it did not set out to clarify the whole of Christian faith. Rather, it focused only on those things about which Rome and the Reformers had disagreed. One of its major documents was its Decree on Justification, which in many ways agrees with Luther's perspective but insists on the importance of human cooperation with God's grace. The council affirmed the centrality of Scripture, but Christian faith, it said, was not based on Scripture alone, but also on "unwritten traditions which have come down to us" (DS 1501/ND 210). It set the number of books in the Bible at seventy-two, in contradistinction to the Protestants' refusal to accept books like Sirach or the Book of Wisdom, and it declared that Jerome's Vulgate translation of the Bible is the official Catholic version of the Bible for use in public readings, debates, and preaching (DS 1502-1503, 1506/ND 211-212, 214).

The number of sacraments was declared to be "not more nor fewer than seven" (DS 1601/ND 1311). Eucharistic transubstantiation was affirmed as was the sacrificial character of the Mass, and it was stated clearly that the eucharistic presence was of "the total and whole Christ . . . under whichever species [the sacrament] is received" (DS 1729/ND [1539]). The four "minor orders" were declared as legitimate, the doctrine of purgatory was upheld, and the veneration of relics was upheld, as was the practice of indulgences—even though their abuse was acknowledged and moderation encouraged (DS 1835/ ND 1686). Trent emphasized the power and dignity of the priesthood and of the episcopacy (although the episcopacy's sacramental nature would have to wait until Vatican II to be recognized); and, of course, it insisted on the legitimacy and centrality of the papacy.

Besides issuing doctrinal decrees, Trent enacted many practical reforms. Chief among these were reforms concerning bishops, who would be the main agents of implementation after the council concluded. A bishop had be legitimately born, ordained a priest at least six months before his consecration, of a mature age, and normally hold a degree in law or theology. He had to reside in his diocese, and in his diocese his principal duty was to preach, to administer the sacraments, and to supervise his clergy—not far from the theology of the episcopate today, rooted in Christ's threefold office of prophet, priest, and ruler/servant. Very significantly as well, Trent mandated—for the first time in history—a training program for clergy. This was to develop in the next several hundred years into the modern seminary.

Catholicism's best theologians attended the council. Several theologians from the celebrated University of Salamanca in Spain were present. **Domingo de Soto** (1494-1560) was present at the first two periods of the council as the emperor's representative. De Soto was the pupil of the learned Francisco de Vitoria (1485-1546), and a good friend of Bartolomé de Las Casas. Like Las Casas, his theology was quite open to the possibility of salvation of non-Christians by "implicit faith"—that they lived a life that was faithful to the gospel, even if they did not know it or profess it explicitly. The other Salamancan present at the earlier periods of Trent was the Franciscan **Andrés de Vega** (d. 1560), an associate of de Soto and one who in his theological writing made "many very precise references"[139] to the issue of salvation for non-Christians in Latin America. He is the author of a commentary on the council's Decree on Justification.

A third Salamancan theologian was **Melchior Cano** (1509-1560). Cano's most famous and very influential work was entitled *De Locis Theologicis* (On the Sources of Theology). Cano spoke of ten major sources of theology—for example, Scripture, oral tradition, the Roman church, reason, history—and he proposed a new way of doing theology. One gathered data from the sources and then showed how they agreed with reason and logic. This method would be developed in the theological "manuals" or "handbooks" in the post-Tridentine years.[140]

Present at all three periods of the council was **Girolamo Seripando** (1492-1563), first as prior general of the Augustinians (Luther's former order), and then as cardinal president of the assembly and papal legate. Although his Augustinian theology of original sin and justification was not accepted by the council, he nevertheless had a strong influence on the final formulation of the decrees on these doctrines.[141] Finally, we can mention the Jesuit **Diego Lainez** (1512-1565). Lainez was present during the first two periods, where he strongly upheld the doctrine of the papacy, opposed Calvin's understanding of predestination, and was one of the authors of the document on justification. In the final session he attended as the successor of Ignatius Loyola (1492-1556) as Jesuit superior general.[142]

Teresa of Avila and John of the Cross

Before leaving this incredibly complex theological scene in the sixteenth century, we need to refer briefly to two of the most influential spiritual writers and mystics in the history of spirituality and theology: the Spanish Carmelites **Teresa of Ávila** (1515-1582) and **John of the Cross** (1542-1591). Both are doctors of the church (Teresa was the first woman to be declared so in 1970). They both were also involved in the reform of their Order, and their writings represent "one of the high points in the history of Christian mysticism."[143] Teresa's *The Interior Castle* is the most mature of her writings, which include her autobiography and *The Way of Perfection*. John's work is comprised of prose, but especially of poetry, including his famous "On a Dark Night," which speaks of the "dark night of the soul." Once again in the case of John we have an example of penetrating theology written in nondiscursive form.[144]

Of course, brilliant theology was also produced by some of the most important artists and musicians in history, for example **Michelangelo Buonarroti** (1475-1564), **Leonardo da Vinci** (1452-1519), and **Giovanni Pierluigi da Palestrina** (1514-1594).

Theology in Europe after the Council of Trent

We might speak of three types of theology being written in the aftermath of the Council of Trent and into the seventeenth century. First, on the Catholic side, there are theologies of controversy, typified by the works of the German Jesuit **Peter Canisius** (1521-1597), whose catechism based on Trent went through two hundred editions in his lifetime, and the Italian Jesuit **Robert Bellarmine** (1542-1621), who is famous for stressing the importance of the church's institutional nature in the manner of the Kingdom of France or the Republic of Venice.[145] On the Protestant side, first of all, was **Martin Chemnitz** (1522-1586). He is considered the Protestant counterpart of Bellarmine, and much of Catholic polemic theology was a refutation of the charges that he made in his works. Later we can speak of Prussian **Abraham Calov** (1612-1686) and—perhaps more irenic in spirit and systematic—the German **Johann Andreas Quenstedt** (1617-1688). This type of polemic theology persisted—especially on the Catholic side—up until the twentieth century.

A second type of theology was a kind that became more and more specialized and focused, the beginnings of what we speak of today as the various theological disciplines such as "dogmatic" theology or moral theology. As Aidan Nichols describes it, theologians who began to practice these specialties "thought of themselves as experts in one or another of these fields, and got on with digging their own gardens without worrying too much about what others were doing with theirs."[146] In the case of both "dogmatic" and moral disciplines, theology was developing into a rather arid exposition of church doctrines, expressed in one of the texts of the time as the treatment of those things "defined or handed out as dogmas in the Council of Trent, or explained in the Catechism of this same council."[147]

Third, and most important, there appeared a large number of writings of spiritual, ascetical, or mystical theology. We have mentioned the works of Teresa and John of the Cross above. We need also to mention the various members of the "French school" of spirituality which began with **Cardinal Pierre de Bérulle** (1575-1629) and continued with **Madeleine de St. Joseph** (1578-1637), **Charles de Condren** (1588-1641), **Jean-Jacques Olier** (1608-1657), and **John Eudes** (1601-1680). Space does not allow us to go into any real detail, but the French school is largely responsible for the later development of devotion to the Sacred Heart and the profound theology surrounding it, as well as the development of the seminary system envisioned by the Council of Trent and a rich, if rather baroque, theology of the priesthood. This theology held sway in the church up until Vatican II, and in many ways still persists in theologies of the priesthood today. Finally, **Francis de Sales** (1567-1622), a doctor of the church, is important for his *Introduction to the Devout Life*, a marvelous introduction to spirituality aimed at lay women and men at work in the world.[148]

The seventeenth century also witnessed the **Jansenist Controversy**. The controversy has deep roots, going back to the controversies over grace and free will that involved the Dutch theologian **Michael Baius** (1513-1589) and the Spanish Dominican and Jesuit theologians **Domingo Bañez** (1528-1604) and **Luís de Molina** (1535-1600). In the wake of these controversies **Cornelius Jansen** (1585-1638), bishop of Ypres in Holland, wrote a book entitled *Augustinus* (Augustine) that was published posthumously in 1640. The book caused a stir, arguing that God does not give grace to everyone, and that the minority of human beings will be saved. The theory was taken up by some, particularly those in religious life, and resulted in a very negative view of the human person and discouragement of frequent communion. Even though it was condemned in 1643, it had a major influence on much of the spirituality and theology throughout the next several centuries.[149]

THEOLOGY IN 1700

This has been a such long chapter because there is simply so much theology to survey in the period from the turn of the second millennium until the century after the reformations in Western Christianity. Although there were still pockets of vibrant Christianity in western Asia (Turkey, Iraq, the Balkans), and in Egypt and Ethiopia in Africa, the major "theological action" of Christianity was in Europe and—as we are discovering more and more today—in areas of European expansion in Latin America and Asia. In the seventeenth century, France and England began to colonize North America, and Catholic theology began to be done as Native Americans were catechized in what is today Canada and northern New York. It began in a Calvinist key in the sermons and conversations of settlers in today's New England, who saw themselves in a new promised land that held out new hope for Christianity. Harvard College was founded in 1636 and so was the first theology school in North America (the University of Santo Tomás, of course, was founded in the Philippines in 1511, also as a school of theology). In the mid-seventeenth century much of the work that theologians like Ricci and de Nobili accomplished was destroyed when Rome condemned their work in what came to be called the Rites Controversy.

As always, theology flourished in the arts. **Gian Lorezo Bernini's** (1598-1680) works inside and outside St. Peter's in Rome reflect the theology of the papacy at the time; **Claudio Monteverdi's** (1567-1653) revolutionary music reflected contemporary Catholic devotion to the Blessed Virgin Mary.

The theology of the next three centuries, the subject of the final chapters of this book, will be done in dialogue with—and, for Catholics until the mid-twentieth century, in opposition to—the great philosophical and scientific revolutions of their times. It will also be carried out in the context of the demise of a European hegemony in Christianity which, in the year 1700, was surely unimaginable.

QUESTIONS FOR REFLECTION

1. Why was the schism between East and West so tragic? What are its effects today?

2. Which understanding of Jesus' death on the cross do you think is better: Anselm's or Abelard's?
3. What might be the advantages and disadvantages of "dialectics" for theology?
4. What do you think are the greatest accomplishments of Aquinas and Bonaventure?
5. Do you think that mystics like Hildegard and Eckhart are theologians as important as Anselm, Aquinas, and Ramón Llull? Why or why not?
6. What is the importance of the theology done in Latin America and Asia in the sixteenth and seventeenth centuries?
7. Do you think the Protestant Reformation of the sixteenth century had to happen? Why or why not?
8. Why is the Council of Trent important in the history of theology?

SUGGESTIONS FOR FURTHER READING AND STUDY

N. S. Davidson, *The Counter Reformation* (Oxford: Basil Blackwell, 1987).

G. R. Evans, ed., *The Medieval Theologians: An Introduction to Theology in the Medieval Period* (Oxford: Blackwell, 2001).

Justo L. González, *A History of Christian Thought*, vol. 2, *From Augustine to the Eve of the Reformation*, rev. ed. (Nashville, Tenn.: Abingdon Press, 1971).

———, *A History of Christian Thought*, vol. 3, *From the Protestant Reformation to the Twentieth Century*, rev. ed. (Nashville, Tenn.: Abingdon Press, 1975).

Gustavo Gutiérrez, *Las Casas: In Search of the Poor of Jesus Christ* (Maryknoll, N.Y.: Orbis Books, 1993).

Carter Lindberg, ed., *The Reformation Theologians: An Introduction to Theology in the Early Modern Period* (Oxford: Blackwell, 2002).

Mary T. Malone, *Women and Christianity*, vol. 2, *From 1000 to the Reformation* (Maryknoll, N.Y.: Orbis Books, 2002).

———, *Women and Christianity*, vol. 3, *From the Reformation to the 21st Century* (Maryknoll, N.Y.: Orbis Books, 2003).

Bernard McGinn, *The Doctors of the Church: Thirty-Three Men and Women Who Shaped Christianity* (New York: Crossroad, 1999).

Thomas F. O'Meara, *Thomas Aquinas: Theologian* (Notre Dame, Ind.: University of Notre Dame Press, 1997).

Kenan B. Osborne, ed., *The History of Franciscan Theology* (St. Bonaventure, N.Y.: Franciscan Institute, 1994).

Andrew C. Ross, *A Vision Betrayed: The Jesuits in Japan and China, 1542-1742* (Maryknoll, N.Y.: Orbis Books, 1994).

12

Christian Theology in the Eighteenth and Nineteenth Centuries

T HE END OF THE WARS OF RELIGION (the Thirty Years' War) in the middle of the seventeenth century left Europe exhausted and disillusioned.
Already at the end of the seventeenth century there was a growing sense that
science and human reason were surer guides to life than religion, and this
sense developed in the eighteenth century into what history calls the Enlightenment. The Enlightenment gave birth to philosophies that were based on
human reason and experience, and gave birth as well to the American (1776)
and French (1789) Revolutions and their experiments in democracy. Although
those experiments had tragic effects in France, the world never would be the
same. The coming two centuries would see the spread of the conviction that
human beings were born with "created equal with certain inalienable rights,"
entitled to "liberty, equality and fraternity."

Catholics and Protestants responded to the Enlightenment differently. While
some Catholics showed an openness to the new philosophy of individual experience and democratic ideas, official Catholicism in Rome was firm in its opposition, especially after the anticlerical developments of the French Revolution.
This climaxed in 1864 with Pius IX's publication of *The Syllabus of Errors* and
the First Vatican Council's declaration of papal infallibility in 1870. Although
not all Protestants sought to accommodate Enlightenment thought and democratic ideals, there did develop through the nineteenth century a theology that
attempted to engage the thought of such great philosophers as Immanuel Kant
(1724-1804) and Georg Wilhelm Friedrich Hegel (1770-1831).

The nineteenth century was also a time of worldwide colonial expansion on
the part of Europe and (later) the United States, mostly for the exploitation
of the world's natural resources for the burgeoning factories of the indus-
trial revolution. Hand in hand with this colonialism—although often critical
of its excesses—was the great missionary movement in both Protestantism
and Catholicism. Although there had been some missionary activity among
Protestants earlier, there was a virtual of explosion of activity after the 1792
publication of an essay by the Englishman **William Carey** (1761-1834) on
the obligation of Christians to convert those who had not yet heard the gospel.[1] Women's participation in the movement outnumbered men's two to one,

and so a lot of theologizing "on the ground" was by women—and often for women.[2]

At the end of the eighteenth century, as a result of the suppression of the Jesuits in 1793 and the disasters of the French Revolution, there had been left only a few hundred Catholic missionaries throughout the world.[3] After 1815, however, the church experienced an amazing multiplication of men's and women's missionary congregations. Many of these were dedicated to the Sacred Heart and to Mary under various titles, reflecting the popular religious devotions of the day. Several founders of these new congregations had visions of missionary activity and theology that anticipated developments in the next century. **Francis Libermann** (1802-1852), for example, founder of the Spiritans, wrote to his missionaries in Africa that they should "put off Europe, its customs, its spirit. . . . Become Negroes to the Negroes, in order to form them as they should be, not in the fashion of Europe, but allow them to keep what is peculiar to them."[4] Cardinal **Charles Lavigerie** (1825-1892), founder of the Missionaries of Africa, gave his congregation a habit that was similar to the robes Muslims wore in North Africa and insisted on language learning and respect for local cultures.[5]

The missionary movement among both Catholics and Protestants sent thousands of missionaries (in Protestantism the majority were women) to Asia, Oceania, Australia, New Zealand, Africa, and Latin America. Whenever women and men in these places embraced Christianity, theologizing had begun in these new and challenging contexts.

As in every time in the history of the World Christian Movement, the eighteenth and nineteenth centuries produced women and men who are giants in the history of theology. Theologians like Jonathan Edwards (1703-1758), Friedrich Schleiermacher (1768-1834), Johann Adam Möhler (1796-1838), Sojourner Truth (1797-1833), Søren Kierkegaard (1813-1855), John Henry Newman (1801-1890), and Thérèse of Lisieux (1873-1897) have all engaged in theologizing in a way that captured some of the breakthroughs and agonies of their time. Each of these theologians, along with the many others on whom this chapter will (always all too briefly) focus, have dealt in their own way with the turn to the individual and individual experience that Descartes articulated as this era was beginning. In this way, they have maintained and contributed to the continuing conversation that is the Christian theological tradition.

THEOLOGY IN THE EIGHTEENTH CENTURY

Anglican and Protestant Theology

British theology in the eighteenth century was largely influenced by the European Enlightenment's confidence in the powers of human reason. Although appearing in the last half decade of the seventeenth century, **John Locke's** *Reasonableness of Christianity* in 1695 breathed the spirit of the period we are focusing on here. **John Toland's** (1670-1722) *Christianity Not Mysterious* (1696) and **Matthew Tindal's** (1657-1733) *Christianity as Old as the Creation* (1730) took things one step further: Christian revelation could be discovered through the use of reason itself.[6] **Joseph Butler** (1692-1752) was a bit less confident in reason in his 1736 *Analogy of Religion*. For him reason was certainly important, but it could not provide ultimate certainty.

Among Protestants in Germany **Hermann Samuel Reimarus** (1694-1768) was the first to begin what would be later called "the quest for the historical Jesus." His conviction was that it was possible to go behind the New Testament texts, which depicted Jesus in terms that the Enlightenment mind could not accept (divine, a miracle worker, savior) and uncover the real Jesus of history. For Reimarus, Jesus was a great moral teacher, whose teachings rational women and men could understand. **Gotthold Ephraim Lessing** (1729-1781), however, who actually published Reimarus's work in 1774, denied that any historical fact could be the basis on which one built one's faith. For him, there existed a "great ugly ditch" between the accidental facts of history and the truths of reason. In this way he very much undermined the truth of the Bible, which became "irrelevant to a reasonable religion."[7]

In reaction both to a rigid and arid Protestant orthodoxy that had developed after the Reformation and to a theology that was moving away from the Bible, there arose a movement within Lutheranism called Pietism. Its founder was **Philip Jakob Spener** (1635-1705) and his collaborator and successor was **August Hermann Francke** (1663-1727). Pietism gained influence in the German church and beyond. Its theology was less preoccupied with controversy, more focused on the Bible and on participating in works of charity. The movement was later led by **Nicolaus Ludwig von Zinzendorf** (1700-1760), who has been called the greatest German evangelical after Luther. His writings call for a warm, almost erotic, relationship with Christ as the center of Christian religion. Also significant about the Pietists is that they engaged in mission work, especially in India, several decades before the "official" beginning of the Protestant missionary movement sparked by William Carey.[8]

In Britain, Pietism's move to a warmer, more personal religion was taken up by **John Wesley** (1703-1791). Wesley studied at Oxford and was ordained an Anglican priest in 1728. He went to Georgia as a missionary of the Church of England but was a dismal failure. Returning to England, he began to associate with the Moravian Brethren, a Pietist group, and on May 24, 1738, he had a deep experience of conversion as he attended a prayer meeting at the Aldersgate-Street church: "About a quarter before nine, while [a reading from Luther] was describing the change which God works in the heart through faith in Christ, I felt my heart strangely warmed. I felt I did trust in Christ, Christ alone for salvation: And an assurance was given me, that he had taken away *my* sins, even *mine*, and saved *me* from the law of sin and death."[9] Wesley did not accept Calvin's understanding of "unconditional predestination," for while he thought that even though God predestined some people to eternal happiness, it was always on the condition of free acceptance of and cooperation with God's grace. When Wesley was accused of subscribing to the theology of **Jakob Arminius** (ca. 1559-1609), he freely admitted that this was the case.[10] John's brother **Charles Wesley** (1707-1788), was the author of a great number (over 5,500!) of richly theological hymns, including "O, For a Thousand Tongues to Sing," "Jesus Lover of My Soul," and "Hark! The Herald Angels Sing."[11]

Perhaps the greatest Protestant theologian of the age lived and worked in the British colony of Massachusetts. **Jonathan Edwards** (1703-1758) was born in the colony of Connecticut. He studied at Yale, married, and succeeded his father-in-law as the pastor of the Congregational (Reformed) Church in Northampton, Massachusetts. He was a successful pastor there, and he was one of the most effective preachers during the "Great Awakening," that period of religious fervor that swept through the colonies in the decades of the 1730s and '40s. In 1750, however, in a dispute over who was to be admitted to the Lord's Supper at his church, he was dismissed by his congregation and worked until 1757 among Native Americans at Stockbridge, Massachusetts. All through his time as pastor and then at Stockbridge, Edwards studied deeply and wrote prolifically. In 1757 he was invited to become president of the College of New Jersey (later Princeton University), but after he was voluntarily inoculated for smallpox he fell ill and died within a few months, in 1758.

We might note four things for which Edwards is remembered. First of all, even as a college student he was impressed by the empirical methodology of John Locke, and this led him to emphasize experience in his theology, and one of his most important works is entitled *Treatise on Religious Affections*, written in 1746. Second, at the heart of Edwards's theology is Calvin's notion of the sovereignty of God. Edwards, like Calvin, believed strongly in the doctrine of double or unconditional predestination, and this is reflected in his work *The Freedom of the Will*, written at Stockbridge in 1574. Again, like Calvin, he understood the doctrine as a consoling one, putting Christians' anxieties about salvation at rest, and he was enthralled by God's "excellence," as he called it. Third, his *The Life of David Brainard* of 1749 proved to be a spiritual classic and was read widely both in the colonies and abroad. Brainard was a missionary among the Native Americans in Massachusetts, and the zeal and holiness of his life that Edwards narrated inspired an entire generation of missionaries in America and Britain. Finally, although it is in many ways untypical of his theology, Edwards's sermon entitled "Sinners in the Hands of an Angry God," in which he memorably compares sinners in God's hands to an insect being held over a flame, is— perhaps unfortunately—his most widely read work.[12]

One more North American colonial writer worth mentioning is the remarkable Quaker **John Woolman** (1720-1772). Woolman spoke of his conversion as being convinced that the "inward spiritual life and the outward exercise of justice are inseparable."[13] This commitment to justice is evidenced in his strong opposition to slavery and in his respect for the culture and religion of the Native Americans. Woolman's *Journal* is a marvelous spiritual classic, offering arguments against slavery as incompatible with the gospel, and narrating his journeys among Native Americans. Contemporary theologians look to Woolman as a resource for an ecological theology, for a liberation theology for the more affluent nations of North America, Europe, Australia, and New Zealand, and even for a theology of religious pluralism that both acknowledges other religions with respect but still upholds Christian particularity.[14]

Catholic and Orthodox Theology

Aidan Nichols remarks that "the eighteenth century is perhaps the least creative of the modern centuries for Catholic theology"—and perhaps also one of the least explored.[15] It was in this century that the so-called theological manual began to replace Aquinas's *Summa Theologiae* as the basic text in seminaries. The aim of these new texts was not so much to help students understand the faith or think theologically for themselves, but to pass on the correct teaching of the church as articulated at Trent and against Protestantism.

Theology continued to be divided into various specializations and subdisciplines: homiletics, catechetics, pastoral theology, and church history. One of these newer disciplines was moral theology, and a major figure to emerge in this field was **Alphonsus de Liguori** (1696-1787), doctor of the church and founder of the Redemptorist Order (1749). In his work *Moral Theology*, published in two volumes, he began to articulate his perspective of "equiprobabilism," which was a kind of a middle course between positions that were too rigid or too lax. Other famous works of Alphonsus were his works of devotional piety: *Visits to the Blessed Sacrament, Novena to the Sacred Heart of Jesus*, and especially his *Glories of Mary*, based on the Marian hymn, "Salve Regina" ("Hail Holy Queen").[16]

We need to glance briefly at the state of theology in the churches of the East, although there is not much to report. Many of the churches in the East and North Africa were under Muslim rule, and while worship and monastic life were allowed, no evangelizing activity was permitted and the churches and monasteries tended to look inward. After John of Damascus, theology was regarded as complete, with nothing more to add, and so it was more about preserving the past than actively engaging issues in the present. But theologizing was being done as people professed their faith as a Christian minority, and as Byzantine chant was sung in monasteries like those on Mount Athos in Greece and at St. Catherine's on Mount Sinai.

In Russia many priests were illiterate, and scholarship and theological speculation were discouraged, even though there were some scholarly monks/bishops like **Tikhon of Zadonsk** (1724-1783).[17] Kiev was a center of learning, but what was studied there were the works of Reformed, Lutheran, and Roman Catholic theologians from the West.[18] Just prior to the eighteenth century, in 1672, a synod in Jerusalem approved as "the faith of the Eastern Church"[19] the Confession of Faith of **Diostheus** (1641-1707), patriarch of Jerusalem. Twentieth-century Orthodox theologian John Meyendorf has called the Confession "the most important Orthodox dogmatic text of this period."[20]

Theology and the Arts

The eighteenth century was the century of some of the West's most brilliant composers, and many of them composed explicitly religious music. **Johann Sebastian Bach** (1685-1750) wrote more than two hundred cantatas, the majority of which were originally performed on various Sundays of the year at Lutheran church services. In addition, his works on the passions of St. Matthew and St. John are masterful interpretations of the gospel narratives, interspersed with powerful chorales and hymns. **George Friedrich Handel's** (1685-1759) *Messiah* of 1742 weaves together scriptural passages from the Old and New Testament in a powerful interpretation of the meaning of Jesus of Nazareth. Finally, although we could name many more, **Wolfgang Amadeus Mozart** (1756-1791), even beyond his religious works like the *Requiem* and the motet *Ave Verum*, helps listeners hear the voice of God. The great twentieth-century theologian Karl Barth once wrote that "when the angels go about their task of praising God, they play only Bach," but "that when they are together *en famille* they play Mozart and that then too the good God listens with special pleasure."[21] This was also the age of baroque and rococo art and architecture, and "with all its figures, it is an affirmation that there is a world of grace whence come these angels and saints. . . . Grace, in the fresco and the sculptured group, becomes concrete. . . ."[22] In the sterner architecture of Calvinist churches in Europe and North America, the centrality of the pulpit reflects Protestant emphasis on the Word and the sermon.

CATHOLIC THEOLOGY IN THE NINETEENTH CENTURY

Romantic Idealism in Germany

At the beginning of the nineteenth century, in the wake of the Enlightenment and the French Revolution, Rome was definitely opposed to the movements that were influencing the modern world in the West. Says Thomas O'Meara,

"Rome rejected not only the institutions of the modern world—democracy, science, development—but rejected new forms of cultural life such as subjectivity, evolution, freedom. Rome dreamt and cultivated happier, theonomous, sacramental times of the past."[23] This attitude of opposition to and fear of the contemporary would persist all through the century—and well into the next century. However, from about 1790 until 1848, especially in Germany, there emerged a theological movement centered at the University of Tübingen and inspired by the philosopher Friedrich Wilhelm Joseph Schelling that made an authentic attempt to dialogue with the spirit of the times. This movement breaks the stereotype that, in the nineteenth century, Catholicism was "a well-planted garden with a neoscholastic statue at its entrance and closure." Rather, for about fifty years in Germany, "Catholicism creatively engaged with the culture of the time," assuming that "it could find a new synthesis through post-Kantian idealism as it had previously with Plotinus and Aristotle."[24]

The context of this German theological movement was Romanticism. The end of the eighteenth century saw something new emerge, a way of thinking and being in the world that was very different from the measured spirit of the Enlightenment and its reliance on reason. Romanticism stressed intuition over reason, the solitary hero rather than the social contract, nature with all its variation rather than a mechanical, ordered universe. The measured couplets of Alexander Pope (1688-1744) gave way to the lush poetry of William Wordsworth (1770-1850) and William Blake (1757-1827), and Johann Wolfgang von Goethe (1749-1832). The restrained music of Joseph Haydn (1732-1809) gave way to the massive symphonies of Ludwig von Beethoven (1770-1827).

It was in this context that **Friedrich Wilhelm Joseph Schelling** (1775-1854), "the mentor of German Catholic intellectuals,"[25] worked out his philosophy. His focus was thoroughly modern, rooted in philosophers from Descartes to Kant, and yet going beyond them in his Romantic age. His philosophy reflected on "self, freedom, system, the absolute, insight in mind and process in universe and history,"[26] and at many points his thought connected with Catholic sensibilities.

In 1822 the Protestant duke of Württemberg established a Catholic faculty of theology, which would exist alongside the Protestant faculty, at the University of Tübingen in the Black Forest of Germany. As it developed, the theology of Tübingen displayed two characteristic features: a commitment to the study of the broad Christian tradition—liturgy, the early and medieval theologians—and an openness to the Romantic culture sweeping Germany at the time.[27] The founder of the school, **Johann Sebastian Drey** (1777-1853), had an exciting vision of a theology that embraced history and mystery, and his understanding of revelation was as an explicitation of a deep, primal experience of "an eternal and absolute ground"[28] made clearest in Christ. He was the teacher at Tübingen of the three great figures of the school, all Catholic priests, **Johann Adam Möhler** (1796-1838), **Franz Anton Staudenmaier**

(1800-1856), and **Johann Evangelist Kuhn** (1806-1887), and it was through these students that Drey made his most enduring contribution to theology.

Of the three, Möhler was to have the greatest impact on future theology, even though he was practically forgotten when he died at the young age of forty-two. In 1825 he published the first of his two seminal works, *The Unity of the Church*. Möhler had chosen to study history, and he discovered in the church's earliest theologians a theology quite similar to the theology that Drey had developed through the works of Schelling. The church is much more than the visible institution that it had understood itself to be after Trent. Rather, the church was, in its deepest identity, a community enlivened by the presence of the Holy Spirit. The church is dynamic—always changing with culture and history, and yet always keeping its identity as God's people. Its principle "is not canon law but an unpredictable development."[29] In the same way, Christian tradition is always the same because it always changes: "It is not a collection of writings but the community's consciousness bearing and reflecting upon revelation under the silent direction of the Spirit."[30] This ecclesiology and theology of tradition are not very far from that laid out in Vatican II.

Möhler's second masterpiece, *Symbolik*, or *Symbolism*, was inspired by Hegel. *Symbolism* is a systematic theology, treating theological anthropology, the doctrine of justification, the doctrine of the church, and eschatology. But it is more than that. It attempts to show, in regard to each element of the "Symbols" or creedal statements of faith, how the various Protestant groups and the Catholic Church differ from one another. The polemical aspect is a bit hard to read today—and it subjected Möhler to heavy criticism when he published it—but what is important is "its attempt to understand the Catholic tradition as a coherent, systematic world-view responding to human beings' deepest needs and capacities."[31]

The Roman School

To much of what the Tübingen school was attempting to do, of course, as well as to similar attempts elsewhere, Rome was fundamentally opposed. In France, **Félicité Robert de Lamennais** (1813-1854), together with his friends **Henri Lacordaire** (1802-1861—the famous Dominican preacher) and **Charles de Montalembert** (1810-1870) published the first modern Catholic daily newspaper, *L'Avenir*, in which democratic ideas and separation of church and state were advocated. This brought strong sanctions from Gregory XVI in 1832 and 1834 in the encyclicals *Mirari Vos* and *Singulari Quaedam*.[32]

In Italy, the work of the brilliant philosopher and theologian **Antonio Rosmini Serbati** (1797-1855) was under suspicion from Rome during his life and was condemned over thirty years after his death, in 1887. Rosmini was an early advocate of a renewed study of Aquinas, but more inspired by

Augustine and Bonaventure than by the neoscholastic thought of his day. He was a prodigious writer, with his collected works numbering sixty volumes. His theology bears an uncanny resemblance to the twentieth-century German theologian Karl Rahner (whom we will discuss in the next chapter).[33]

The main reason for the suspicion of all these—and many more[34]—theologians was that all of them accepted in one way or another the Enlightenment's emphasis on individual human experience as a key element of theological reflection. The danger, Rome saw, was a kind of subjectivism that would lose sight of the objective truths of the faith, upheld and taught by the Roman magisterium. This can explain, therefore, the "meteoric rise" of the Roman school of theology, one that came to be called "neoscholasticism."[35]

Already in 1810 the Collegio Alberoni in Piacenza, Italy, had become a school in which manuals inspired by Aquinas were used. In 1824 Gregory XVI restored the Roman College—eventually named the Pontifical Gregorian University in 1873—to the Jesuits, who had been suppressed in 1793 and restored in 1814. The College soon became a major center of neo-Thomist/neoscholastic theology, especially with the presence of **Giovanni Perrone** (1794-1876), who was a major influence on Pius IX's declaration of the dogma of the Immaculate Conception in 1854. In 1843, **Joseph Kleutgen** (1811-1883) was appointed to the Roman College, and he was an especially outspoken opponent of the more innovative German theologians. His two volumes on the philosophy and theology of "former times" (*Vorzeit*) were major arguments against the "German school" of theology, some theologians of which were condemned as heretics through his and Perrone's influence.

Not all the theologians at the Roman College were strict neoscholastics, and some were even opposed to the movement, even though they wrote in Latin and used scholastic expressions in their writings. They were, however, strong supporters of papal authority and more interested in offering arguments from scriptural, theological, and magisterial authority rather than engaging in speculation.[36] Among the Italian seminarians converted to the neo-Thomist approach, however, was Giovanni Pecci, the future **Leo XIII** (1810-1903), whose encyclical *Aeterni Patris* in 1879 mandated that all seminaries teach the philosophy and theology of Thomas Aquinas. Both Perrone and Kleutgen were highly involved in writing drafts of the encyclical.[37]

After 1848, when the Tübingen school had begun to fade, several French and German theologians had been censured by Rome. Pius IX (1792-1878), elected as a liberal in 1846, began to turn more and more against anything contemporary or innovative, and Roman theology had the upper hand in directing Catholic theology. In 1864 Pius IX issued his *Syllabus of Errors*: eighty propositions that condemn, among others, pantheism, rationalism, separation of church and state, and infringement by governments of the rites of the papacy. The last proposition is the most famous. It condemns the idea that "the Roman Pontiff can, and ought to, reconcile himself, and come to terms with progress, liberalism and modern civilization" (see DS 2901-2980). In 1870, Pius IX convoked the First Vatican Council, which issued an important decree on the relation between faith and reason (*Dei Filius* [DS 3000-345/ ND 113-139]) and assured the authority of the pope by declaring his universal jurisdiction and infallibility (*Pastor Aeternus* [DS 350-375/ND 818-839]).

Newman, Brownson, and Thérèse

Neoscholasticism, with strict fidelity to the Roman magisterium as it had expressed itself in the *Syllabus*, at Vatican I, and in other documents, dominated Catholic theology in the second half of the nineteenth century. There were certainly those who moved in another direction, but these were relatively few. One great example of these theologians who "marched to a different drum" was **John Henry Newman** (1801-1890), whose life spanned the entire nineteenth century. Newman was born an Anglican, was ordained an Anglican priest, and was vicar of St. Mary's Church at Oxford. As a young man he was quite taken with Enlightenment ideas, but as he grew older he became much more cautious about the role of reason in the life of faith. He also became more and more "catholic" in his ecclesiology, and joined a number of Anglican theologians seeking to make the church both more holy and more catholic. As he continued to study the earliest theologians of the church he became more and more convinced that it was Rome, despite its development of doctrines not found strictly in the Scriptures or the fathers, that held the fullness of the truth. This was the conclusion he came to after writing *An Essay on the Development of Christian Doctrine*, and although he was often suspect by Anglicans and Catholics alike he took the bold step of joining the Catholic Church in 1845. As he wrote in his autobiography, *Apologia pro Vita Sua* twenty years later, he had now no experience of a deeper faith or deeper fervor, "but it was like coming into port after a rough sea; and my happiness on that score remains to this day without interruption."[38]

Newman was never attracted to neoscholasticism. He was much more of a patristic scholar. Nevertheless his powers of reflection were immense, as evidenced by his most theoretical and technical work, *An Essay in Aid of a Grammar of Assent*.[39] "Assent" here means the assent of faith, and the entire work is an attempt to persuade the reader that while faith is not *rational* it is nevertheless *reasonable*. In many ways Newman's whole argument is found in the epigram from St. Ambrose on the title page of the work: "Not through dialectics [i.e., rational argument] did it please God to fashion God's people." Newman begins by distinguishing *real* assent from *notional* assent: faith is not just the acceptance of ideas as true; it is an acceptance of truth that is self-involving. The real assent of faith assents to truths that "have an influence both on the individual and on society, which mere notions cannot exert."[40] We come to real assent not through rational argument, but through an argument of "converging probabilities" that Newman calls the "informal inference" or the "illative sense."[41] Just as one assents to the fact that Great Britain is an island not by actually walking its perimeter but by accepting the testimony of trusted maps and teachers; or just as "regular polygon, inscribed in a circle, its sides being continually diminished, tends to become that circle,"[42] we can see how a number of arguments for faith do not *prove decisively* but make it necessary to assent to truth. At a certain point, in fact, it is more logical to *believe* than to remain skeptical. In a powerful, engaging way, Newman argues for faith in a very different way than the dry neoscholastic manuals.

Newman was always controversial and not always accepted by his fellow Catholics. In an essay published in 1859 entitled "On Consulting the Laity in Matters of Faith," Newman marshaled his expertise in patristic thought to argue that there needs to be a wider dialogue between hierarchy and laity in the church. In the fourth century, he points out, the church could well have gone Arian had it only been up to the bishops, but the sense of the faith with which the laity is also endowed called the hierarchy back to true orthodoxy. Newman was against a declaration at Vatican I on the pope's infallibility, arguing that it was "inopportune." Of course, when the council declared the dogma, he accepted it. But when he was made a cardinal by Leo XIII in his first consistory, people said that it only proved that no one in Rome had read his writings. Robert Ellsberg ends his reflection on Newman's life with the following words: "If he was anything he was a realist. Thus, he preserved his optimism by counting on the long run. One of his favorite mottoes was 'Everything in its time.' Pope Paul VI must have recognized the truth of this saying when he called Vatican II 'Newman's Council.'"[43]

Before we leave this sketch of Catholic theology in the nineteenth century, I want to acknowledge two other important theologians: the U.S. American **Orestes Brownson** (1803-1876) and **Thérèse of Lisieux** (1893-1897). Brownson was a colorful character, whose spiritual journey took him through Congregationalism, Universalism, freethinking, Unitarianism, and Transcendentalism before he converted to Catholicism in 1844.[44] Brownson lived at a time when anti-Catholic sentiment was high in the United States, and he wrote very much in Catholics' defense. He was also an opponent of slavery in the United States and wrote works critical of the U.S. bishops in this regard. He was in addition a strong supporter of the "Americanization" of the church, an idea that, years after his death, would be condemned by Rome as "Americanism." In his later years, though, he became quite supportive of the move to declare papal infallibility.[45]

Thérèse is in many ways an unlikely theologian, and yet Pope John Paul II declared her a doctor of the church in 1997. Bernard McGinn calls her "the doctor of pure love."[46] Her writing, especially her autobiography entitled *Story of a Soul*, reflects much of the saccharine piety of late nineteenth-century

Catholicism—perhaps too often dismissed as an inferior kind of Christian expression of faith. And yet, as Swiss theologian Hans Urs von Balthasar expresses it, "She penetrates straight through all triviality and counterfeit to the simple, naked truth of the gospel."[47] Thérèse offers little in the way of close theological analysis; she probably could not understand the neoscholastic theology so prominent in the France of her day, let alone the lofty works of a Möhler or a Newman. But she accomplished what every true theologian aims at: a clear, passionate understanding of her faith.

PROTESTANT AND ANGLICAN THEOLOGY IN THE NINETEENTH CENTURY

Theology on the European Continent

Perhaps the most influential theologian of the nineteenth century was the great German thinker who is rightly called "the father of modern theology,"[48] **Friedrich Daniel Ernst Schleiermacher** (1768-1834). Schleiermacher was brought up as a Pietist (Moravian Brethren) and was educated at the Pietist University of Halle. Despite his very sophisticated theological thinking, his influence by Kant, and his later reputation as a "liberal" theologian, he never forsook his Pietist roots. He himself called himself a "Herrnhuter [i.e. a Pietist] of a higher order"; British theologian Brian Gerrish calls him a "liberal evangelical."[49]

Schleiermacher's project in theology was one deeply rooted in the context of his times. He accepted Kant's devastating critique of the possibility of a rational, philosophical knowledge of God, but he was critical nonetheless of Kant's alternative that religion was found in ethics. For him, religion was not found in right knowledge or in right action but in direct, immediate experience—what he called "feeling." Religion "has to do . . . with the infinite universal wholeness of all things, of that all-embracing totality which may or may not be labeled 'God,' but which includes and enfolds everything within itself."[50]

This conviction was the basic idea in one of his most important and influential works, *Addresses on Religion, to Its Cultured Despisers*. In this more apologetic work, Schleiermacher plays down the importance of theology, but in *The Christian Faith*, in two editions of 1821-1822 and 1830-1831, Schleiermacher laid out a brilliant systematic theology that was based on his fundamental insight.[51] As he expressed it in a letter to his friend Friedrich Lücke in 1829, religion is not so much the "daughter of theology," but theology is the "daughter of religion":[52] theology, in other words, could be based only on experience.

It was from this perspective that *The Christian Faith*, "perhaps the most influential theological work of the nineteenth century,"[53] was developed. The foundation of religion is that feeling (more of a consciousness than an emotion) of being part of an encompassing whole, a sense of wonder, contingency, graciousness—a God-consciousness. This leads to an understanding, on the one hand, of the doctrine of creation and, on the other hand—because we cannot live in constant awareness of such grace—of the doctrine of sin. Only Jesus of Nazareth had the fullness of God-consciousness, and so in communion with him we can achieve redemption. We do not do this alone, however; we do it as the church as "regenerate individuals" come together "to form a system of mutual interaction and co-operation."[54] The church moves toward the consummation of history when all the elect will share Christ's perfect sense of the presence of God.

For Schleiermacher, doctrines and their formulations—creation, original sin, virgin birth, Trinity, resurrection, and so on—are expressions of the more basic experience of God on which religion is based. They are "accounts of the Christian religious affections set forth in speech."[55] It would be a mistake, then, he says, to take them literally or to understand the Scriptures as a collection of divine truths.[56] This might have persuaded people with an Enlightenment mind-set, but it brought criticism both from Catholic quarters in his own day, and in the twentieth century from neo-orthodox theologians led by Karl Barth.[57] Nevertheless, "He so anticipated what was to come that he remains still the great point of departure for modern Protestant theology."[58]

Although there appeared many important theologians in the generation between Schleiermacher and **Albrecht Ritschl** (1822-1889), Ritschl represents in many ways a continuation of Schleiermacher's theological project and, even more than Schleiermacher, is the founder of what came to be called "liberal theology." Where Ritschl differs from his predecessor, however, is in his aversion to experience as the basis for Christian life—he called it mysticism—and in his insistence on the importance of historical revelation.[59] In his three-volume systematic work *The Christian Doctrine of Justification and Reconciliation*, he argued that it is only when Christians get back to the Jesus of the Gospels that they discover the love of God revealed by him, a love that draws us into community to work for the reconciliation of humanity called the Reign of God.[60] Justo González observes that Ritschl's real significance for theology is how he exemplifies the way Protestant theology will develop through the rest of the nineteenth century up until the First World War. The "liberal theology" he set in motion has four major characteristics: (1) it emphasizes the love of God over the God of judgment who calls into question all human activity; (2) it downplays the reality of sin and the human need for grace; (3) it emphasizes the historical study of the Scriptures and doctrines to "get behind" the accretions of Greek philosophy; and (4) it de-emphasizes the truth of doctrine and emphasizes value and morality.[61]

A clear expression of what Ritschl's theology implied was given at the very beginning of the twentieth century in the little book entitled *What Is Christianity?* by **Adolf von Harnack** (1851-1930). What was at the heart of

Christianity was Jesus' teaching, which could be summarized in three points: the coming of the Reign of God, the Fatherhood of God and the worth of the human soul, and the command of love. The gospel of Jesus was about the Father, not himself, and so the reflections on Jesus' divinity that were evident in the New Testament itself and in the early church needed to be de-Hellenized. In Harnack's massive *History of Dogma* he speaks of the later doctrines of the incarnation and the Trinity as the influence of the Greek spirit upon the church. While such acceptance of Hellenistic philosophy was necessary at the time for the survival of the church, the spirit of the times of his day called the church to shed this Greek "husk" to reveal the "kernel" of authentic Christianity—not in doctrines but in practice of love in the world.[62]

We can only mention other prominent members of the Ritschlian school. Perhaps the most famous are **Wilhelm Herrmann** (1846-1922), **Julius Kaftan** (1848-1926), and **Theodor Haering** (1848-1928). We need to turn now to several figures influenced in one way or another by the philosophy of Georg Wilhelm Friedrich Hegel.

To risk oversimplifying Hegel's complex, comprehensive, and dense thought—for him reality was the unfolding of the principle of rationality in the universe, which he called Spirit. How this unfolding took place was in a threefold but never-ending movement of a thesis being proposed, clashing with an opposite idea—an antithesis—and being resolved into a synthesis, which then becomes a thesis as the process continues and reality proceeds in its evolution. History, therefore, was not a process that revealed a reality behind it, but reality itself, the key to connecting with Absolute Reality as realized itself through the dialectical process.[63] Hegel's system eventually collapsed under the weight of its own inclusiveness, but he influenced a number of theologians in several ways.

The first of these is **Ferdinand Christian Baur** (1792-1860). Baur was a contemporary of Möhler in the Protestant faculty at Tübingen and was a pioneer in biblical criticism. In distinguishing the different New Testament theologies of the Gospels and of Paul, he made use of the Hegelian dialectic to show that Christianity emerged as a dialectical movement between an earlier theology inspired by Peter and a later one inspired by Paul, which the New Testament was attempting to reconcile in a synthesis. Baur saw this working as well in the history of doctrine, and while there is clearly some truth in his theories—witness the development of Christology from the fourth to the eighth centuries—one can understand how such ideas would challenge the "objectivity" of revelation on which Catholic theology was based.

The year 1835 saw the publication of **David Friedrich Strauss's** (1808-1874) *Life of Jesus*, translated into English by George Eliot (**Mary Ann Evans** [1819-1880]). Strauss developed the idea that the portrait of Jesus in the New Testament was a *myth*—not so much in the sense that it was untrue, but that it was a symbolic interpretation of how people of faith tried to understand

Jesus' significance. For Strauss, however, the meaning of Jesus was that he was the first person in history to discover that God and humanity were one reality. Basing his thought on one of Hegel's key ideas—that the finite was ultimately identical with Infinite Mind or Spirit—Jesus the miracle worker points to how humanity ultimately is the shaper of nature, his sinlessness points to humanity's own sinlessness and inevitable progress toward perfection, symbolized by Jesus' death, resurrection and ascension into glory.[64] In this he was akin to the thought of **Ludwig Feuerbach** (1804-1872), who argued in works like *The Essence of Christianity* (1841 [also translated by George Eliot]) and *The Essence of Religion* (1853) that God was simply the projection of what humanity would like to be, and theology is ultimately anthropology.

Along the same lines was the philosophy of **Karl Marx** (1818-1883), whose thought would be so influential in the twentieth century. Marx taught that religion was an "ideology" whose function was to serve the established order, which was directed by those who were economically privileged. Marx employed Hegel's dialectic to show that this order would inevitably be overturned, and that this time of "utopia" could be hastened if the economically underprivileged would band together in revolution.[65]

Strauss's work continued what Reimarus and Lessing had begun in the previous century, what **Albert Schweitzer** (1875-1965) described as "the quest of the historical Jesus" in a book by that title in 1906. The subtitle of the book was "from Reimarus to Wrede," and the work surveyed biblical scholarship through the nineteenth century. Such scholarship, said Schweitzer, simply projected its own liberal ideas onto Jesus. The real Jesus of history, however, argued Schweitzer, was a very different character from more traditional portraits of him (e.g., miracle worker, son of God), and he differed as well from the portraits of Jesus as moral teacher or an embodiment of nineteenth-century white male European ideals. He was, rather, a man driven by his vision of the imminent coming of the Reign of God, willing to throw himself on the wheel of fate to bring about the end of history. Jesus was mistaken, but we can imitate his teachings and his own courage in the face of opposition to his vision. Schweitzer's little book shaped much of New Testament scholarship and Christology of the twentieth century and reinstated an eschatological vision of Christianity, which had strong implications for theologies of mission and of the church.[66]

Very much opposed to the Hegelian system of dialectics and rationalism is the theologian who is "at once the most attracting and the most repelling theologian of the nineteenth century,"[67] **Søren Kierkegaard** (1813-1855). For him, Christianity was something that was to be accepted not because of reasonable arguments but by a leap of faith. Christianity was a difficult religion to live, but people had tamed it and made it something middle class and easily acceptable. Kierkegaard insisted, however, that there is "an enormous gap between the highest level of human decency and the Christian life,"[68] because, more fundamentally, there exists an "infinite qualitative difference" between humanity and God.[69] Kierkegaard was despised in his own country of Denmark during his life—much of which was his own fault. In later years he was rediscovered and has been hailed as one of the first existentialist philosophers. His strong apophatic approach to the knowledge of God made him a strong influence on Karl Barth in the twentieth century.

Theology in Britain and North America

Although British theology does not often receive much mention in histories of theology, there was considerable theological activity going on in both England and Scotland during the nineteenth century. In England, the great romantic poet **Samuel Taylor Coleridge** (1772-1834) was one of the few British thinkers familiar with German theology. Like Schleiermacher, he had a strong sense of experiential nature of religion. In Scotland both **Thomas Erskine** (1788-1870) and **John McCleod Campbell** (1800-1872) opposed the rigid Calvinism that had developed within the Scottish church and were pioneers in doing theology out of a faith in the radically personal nature of God. In his *The Nature of Atonement*, McCleod Campbell rejected the common "penal theories" of the doctrine, calling for a doctrine based more on God's mercy and love—very similar to Abelard's exemplar theory in the twelfth century.[70] Coleridge, Erskine, and McLeod Campbell had a profound influence on **Frederick Dennison Maurice** (1805-1872), who ranks with Newman as one of the most important English theologians of the entire century. He too was against the rigidity of Calvinist theology, and insisted that Christianity was at its core about reconciliation and the Reign of God. His two-volume work *The Kingdom of Christ* was published in 1842.[71]

In the aftermath of the publication of Darwin's *Origin of Species* in 1859, and in the context of the scientific revolution in general, British theologians, as well as Christian zoologists, geologists, and psychologists took up the challenges that these revolutionary ideas proposed with an openness that was not so common a few decades later among Christian believers. Taking natural selection seriously meant thinking differently about traditional understandings of divine providence, omnipotence, the reality of evil, the nature and purpose of miracles, human origins, original sin, the nature of free will, and even the uniqueness of Christianity. These writers were mostly Anglicans, but among them were Evangelicals and even Roman Catholics. We can only mention a few names here, but they are thinkers who certainly deserve more research: Christian evolutionist **Aubry Moore** (1843-1890); **James Martineau** (1805-1900) and **F. R. Tennant** (1866-1957) and their contributions to a post-Darwin theodicy; **Baden Powell** (1796-1860) and his reflections on the possibility of miracles; **Frederick Temple** (1821-1902) together with his colleagues who published *Essays and Reviews* in 1860 (a collection of essays that attempted to take science and historical criticism seriously). Finally, we may mention **J. N. Farquar** (1861-1929), missionary to India, whose ground-breaking book *The Crown of Hinduism* reflected on Christianity as the *fulfillment of* and not simply the *replacement of* Indian religion.[72]

In North America, one of the most influential religious thinkers of the period was **Ralph Waldo Emerson** (1803-1882). Already as a student at Harvard he had been influenced by the emerging historical-critical scholarship in Germany, soon to bear fruit in scholars like Baur and Strauss, and his ideas bear the stamp of German thought. For Emerson, Christianity was burdened by two basic mistakes: it was too preoccupied with the person of Jesus of Nazareth, and that led to a neglect of the "God within," the "Oversoul" or the "Self." He was also influenced by recent "discoveries" on the part of European scholars of Indian, Persian, and Chinese Scriptures, and he became a pioneer in the United States in the study of these Asian religions. During his life Emerson became a "cultural icon," and his ideas are often said to be the basis of "American religion": the conviction that God speaks in the deepest self of the individual, and a conviction as well that holds the dogmas of religion in high suspicion. Perhaps his ideas can best be summarized in "Self Reliance," published in 1841 and "arguably America's most famous and controversial essay."[73]

The life of Swiss-born **Philip Schaff** (1819-1893) "provides a window into nearly a whole century of religious developments in both the United States and western Europe."[74] A student of, among others, F. C. Baur at Tübingen, Schaff was one of the first to introduce to the United States the breakthroughs in theology that were taking place in Germany at the beginning of the century. He came to the United States in 1844 and taught at the Reformed seminary in Mercersberg, Pennsylvania (founding what came to be called "Mercersberg Theology"). From 1870 until the end of his life he taught at Union Theological Seminary in New York City. Schaff proposed a move away from the individualist and rationalist understandings of Protestantism as they had developed and called for a move toward a more ecclesial and sacramental understanding of the church. This he called "'ecclesial catholicism,' the grand synthesis of Protestantism and Roman Catholicism, both leaving behind their imperfections."[75] Schaff's literary output was immense, but we might highlight his three-volume collection of Christian creeds entitled *The Creeds of Christendom*, published in 1877 and, until the appearance of the four-volume set edited by Jarosalv Pelikan and Valerie Hotchkiss at the beginning of our present century, was the unsurpassed collection of creedal statements in English.[76]

There are several more significant U.S. American theologians whom we could sketch here,[77] but let me conclude this section with brief portraits of two U.S. American women, **Sojourner Truth** (1797-1883) and **Elizabeth Cady Stanton** (1815-1902). Sojourner Truth was born a slave in New York state and was known originally as Isabella. She became a free woman in 1827 and in

1843 she changed her name in order better to reflect her mission as someone who traveled constantly speaking the truth about slavery and women's rights. In 1850 Olive Gilbert wrote her biography, in which is contained a marvelous narration of her conversion ("Oh, God, I did not know you were so big").[78] Sojourner Truth's most famous speech may have been at a women's convention in Akron, Ohio, in 1851 when she reflected on objections to women's equality: "And ain't I a woman? I have borne thirteen children, and seen most all sold off to slavery, and when I cried out with my mother's grief, none but Jesus heard me! And ain't I a woman? ... Then that little man in black there, he says women can't have as much rights as men, 'cause Christ wasn't a woman! Where did your Christ come from? Where did your Christ come from? From God and a woman! Man had nothing to do with Him."[79]

Elizabeth Cady Stanton was a leader in the "first wave" of the feminist movement in the United States and believed that the Bible was actually an obstacle to the achievement of women's equality. To rectify this she gathered a group of learned women to write a commentary on the Bible that focused on those passages that dealt with women. This was published as *The Woman's Bible* in 1895 and 1898, and was an early attempt to unmask the patriarchy that was present in the Bible, or at least in male interpretations of it. To this pioneering and courageous work feminists in the twentieth and twenty-first centuries owe an immeasurable debt.[80]

THEOLOGY FROM 1900 TO THE GREAT WAR

Protestant Theology

In many ways theology in the period from 1900 until 1914 and the start of World War I (often called the Great War) continues much of the agenda of the nineteenth century. In Europe, especially in Germany, the liberal Protestant theology of Ritschl is carried on in the work and teaching of Adolf Harnack and Wilhelm Herrmann. An important voice at this time was also the German church historian **Ernst Troeltsch** (1865-1923). In *The Absoluteness of Christianity* (1901) he argued that no religion, even Christianity, can be absolutely valid. When one accepts a particular religion, that religion can become normative for that person, but it can never be a validity that is objectively universal. Troeltsch's studies paved the way for the comparative study of religion that developed in the twentieth century, often with the unfortunate results that religion could be studied without any personal involvement or faith commitment.[81] This is the way, however, in which "religious studies" in our own day have developed.

Another major theological figure at this time in the Protestant world was one of the principal leaders of the "social gospel" movement, **Walter**

Rauschenbusch (1861-1918). Rauschenbusch was born of German parents in Rochester, New York, and at an early age was sent to Germany for elementary and secondary education. He attended Rochester Theological Seminary, where he came under the influence of the nineteenth-century German liberal theologians, from Schleiermacher to Harnack. Accepting a call to a pastorate in Hell's Kitchen, one of the most poverty-stricken areas of New York City, he was strongly affected by the challenge to combine his strong commitment to personal religion with a commitment as well to an understanding of the gospel which stood for social justice. What became increasingly clear to him was the centrality of the Reign of God in Jesus' preaching. Jesus' vision was certainly one of individual repentance and acceptance of God's love, but that acceptance involved Christians in contributing to and embodying in their lives a new social order that was taking shape even in the present age.

As Rauschenbusch began to speak and write widely on the topic, an invitation came from the Rochester seminary to join the faculty, and in 1907 his first book in English, *Christianity and the Social Order*, appeared. It immediately made an impact on the American scene and beyond because it spoke to problems that were being exposed as well in the secular press. More works followed, including in 1910 *For God and the People: Prayers of the Social Awakening*, and in 1912 his most expansive work, *Christianizing the Social Order*. This latter expressed the hope that the United States could be converted into a true Christian society, embodying the values of God's Reign.

Rauschenbusch was perhaps too optimistic in his hopes for social reform, even though—contrary to some critics—he did have a strong sense of human sinfulness and saw original sin as a corrective embedded in the tradition that emphasized human solidarity rather than individualism. His great merit was to recognize how his own context—his congregation's poverty and the situation of injustice in the midst of incredible wealth—needed to shape the way Christianity was lived out and thought about theologically. His ideas suffered neglect after World War I, but his vision has surfaced again in our own day. Perhaps in the light of the theology of liberation, theologians today recognize him as "a much more profound theologian than was thought at an earlier time."[82]

Although its roots go back into the Wesleyan holiness movements of the nineteenth century, many trace the origins of Pentecostalism to the Azusa Street revival in Los Angeles, California, in 1906. The leader was the African American preacher **William J. Seymour** (1870-1922), who edited a free, four-page paper, *The Apostolic Faith*, that did not theologize in a theoretical way but gave accounts of the miracles of healing and the speaking in tongues that were having an impact on the entire nation. As blacks, whites, Chinese, and even Jews came to hear Seymour preach, it seemed as if racial discrimination was being wiped away: "The color line was washed away by the blood."[83] Pentecostal theology, until recently, has been more in the genre of the sermon, testimony, and hymn.[84] The church on Azusa Street sent out missionaries to all parts of the world almost immediately, and today Pentecostalism—with a growing body of formal theology—is the fastest growing Christian body in the world.

Catholic Theology

In Catholicism there was still official opposition to any theology that did not conform to the neoscholastic mode.[85] This is most evident in Rome's reaction to a number of theologians who were branded "Modernists" in the Decree *Lamentabili* (DS 3401-3466) and **Pius X's** (1835-1914) encyclical *Pascendi* in 1907. Among these theologians were the French biblical scholar **Alfred Loisy** (1857-1940), the English theologian **George Tyrrell** (1861-1909), the great British writer on mysticism **Baron Friedrich von Hügel** (1852-1925), and the English writer **Maude Dominica Petre** (1863-1942). All of these thinkers had worked at the end of the nineteenth century to reconcile Christian thinking with the radical challenges posed by their contemporaries, but Rome was only threatened by such efforts. After the condemnation of Modernism, all Catholic clergy were obliged to take an oath against what were understood as Modernist positions (DS 3537-3550/ND 143/1-13), and it was common knowledge that clergy and laity alike were encouraged to report theologians suspected of Modernist ideas to ecclesiastical authorities. This atmosphere persisted up until the eve of Vatican II, and, as we will see, several of the major architects of that council were indeed suspected of Modernist ideas during their careers.

Something was brewing, however, even before the war. **Maurice Blondel** (1861-1949), although under some suspicion, began to develop a powerful theology of "immanentism" which is rooted in human experience.[86] At the same time, and in support of Blondel's vision from a more Thomistic perspective, **Pierre Rousselot** (1878-1915) demonstrated that Aquinas's philosophy was not ultimately based on an arid rationalism, but on a dynamic intellectualism that tended toward objectivity in individual judgment. It was a *transcendental* Thomism that would be developed more fully by some of the greatest Catholic theologians of the twentieth century, Karl Rahner and Bernard Lonergan.[87]

CONCLUSION

The eighteenth century was not the greatest of centuries for Christian theology. Christianity was caught in the grip of Enlightenment thinking, and when it was not co-opted by it, was struggling against it. Perhaps the brilliance of the music and other arts in the eighteenth century hold the best theological reflection of the age. The breakthroughs of individual dignity and autonomy, however, had a marked influence on the development of science and democracy, and all three of these revolutions would shape the way Christians theologized in the next century. Experience in theology, the accuracy of the Bible, and the importance of human rights and participation in government would be questions with which people of faith would have to wrestle up to our own "postmodern" time.

Quite in contrast to the eighteenth, the nineteenth century was one of brilliant and creative theological thinking. It also produced major challenges to theology as scholars proposed ways of thinking that went beyond the bounds of traditional Christian methods of interpreting the Bible and orthodoxy of doctrine. It was a time, however, that was very Eurocentric, with European Christianity at the height of its development. What is clear is that there was very little formal theologizing by people who were not Europeans or North Americans during this period, or if there was it was basically under the influence of Western theology and theologians. And while there is evidence of some theologizing by women (and I have given only a few examples), theology was mostly done by men.

All of this will change, however, by the last third of the twentieth century, when the contextual nature of Christian theologizing will become much more obvious, and when theology will for the first time—at least at a conscious and intentional level—become an activity in which Christians of both genders will be engaged in all parts of the world.

QUESTIONS FOR REFLECTION

1. Why might we say that the eighteenth century saw better theology in the music and the arts than in formal theology?
2. What was so important about the theology of the Tübingen school? Why do you think that Roman theology was so opposed to it?
3. Why do you think Newman is such an important figure in nineteenth-century theology?
4. What do you think was important about liberal Protestant theology, from Schleiermacher onward? Why do you think it is dangerous?
5. Why is the work of Sojourner Truth and Elizabeth Cady Stanton important for contemporary feminist theology?
6. Why do you think Rome was so concerned about "modernism"?

SUGGESTIONS FOR FURTHER READING AND STUDY

Justo L. González, *A History of Christian Thought*, vol. 3, *From the Protestant Reformation to the Twentieth Century*, rev. ed. (Nashville, Tenn.: Abingdon Press, 1975).

Alasdair I. C. Heron, *A Century of Protestant Theology* (Philadelphia: Westminster Press, 1980).

Mary T. Malone, *Women and Christianity*, vol. 3, *From the Reformation to the 21ˢᵗ Century* (Maryknoll, N.Y.: Orbis Books, 2003).

Gerald A. McCool, *Catholic Theology in the Nineteenth Century: The Quest for a Unitary Method* (New York: Seabury Press, 1977).

Bernard McGinn, *The Doctors of the Church: Thirty-Three Men and Women Who Shaped Christianity* (New York: Crossroad, 1999).

John Meyendorf, *Rome, Constantinople, Moscow: Historical and Theological Studies* (Crestwood, N.Y.: St. Vladimir's Seminary Press, 1996).

Thomas F. O'Meara, *Romantic Idealism and Roman Catholicism: Schelling and the Theologians* (Notre Dame, Ind.: University of Notre Dame Press, 1982).

Mark G. Toulouse and James O. Duke, eds., *Makers of Christian Theology in America* (Nashville, Tenn.: Abingdon Press, 1997).

13

Christian Theology from the Twentieth Century to the Present

THE TWENTIETH CENTURY, the "short century" in the phrase of Eric Hobsbawm,[1] began in 1914 with the beginning of the Great War and ended in 1989 with the demise of Communism in the Soviet Union. Within that time the world that had been dominated politically and culturally by the West changed dramatically. Already in the 1920s under the leadership of Mohandas K. Gandhi, India was demanding independence from Great Britain, a goal that was achieved in 1947. Four hundred years of colonialism by Spain and then the United States ended in 1946 in the Philippines, and The Netherlands recognized Indonesian independence in 1949. Beginning with Ghana (Britain's Gold Coast) in 1957, state after state in Africa shed their colonial status, as was the case of many other nations in the Caribbean and the Pacific. The result of this was, on the one hand, a rise in national and cultural identity that demanded that any understanding of faith be sought in particular cultural and historical contexts. On the other hand—at least for many of these nations—there was a revival of local religious identity which called into question traditional Christian understandings of its own exclusivism. Both of these results generated new ways of doing theology as the twentieth century came to a close and a new millennium began.

The twentieth century saw unprecedented developments in both the secular and religious worlds. It was marked by two global wars and a "cold war" that threatened nuclear destruction of the entire planet. It was marked as well by a growing cooperation among the Christian churches, by a growing secularization in the West (including Australia and New Zealand), and by the phenomenon of globalization and the rise of ecological consciousness. The West grew and prospered economically while poverty increased in Latin America, Asia, and Africa.

By the end of the twentieth century, the demographic center of Christianity had shifted from Europe and North America, and Christianity had become a global reality. Karl Rahner suggested that this era of the global or world church was only the second truly major epoch in Christianity, equal in significance to the time when, in Jerusalem, it was decided that new members of Greek culture need not conform to all the cultural and religious practices of

Judaism. The event that signaled this new era for all churches was the Second Vatican Council (1962-1965), when, for the first time in history, bishops who were born on every continent were present at an ecumenical council.

At this writing we are well into the twenty-first century, a century that began, in some ways, on September 11, 2001, with the terrorist destruction of the World Trade Center in New York City in the United States. It is a time when theology needs to be done in dialogue with other religions, in the context of the ambiguities of globalization, and in the context as well of global warming and the threat of ecological destruction. Theology needs to be done both in the context of local situations and concrete social locations, but also in global perspective, as this series and this present book are attempting to do.

THEOLOGY FROM 1914 TO THE SECOND VATICAN COUNCIL

The period from the outbreak of the Great War until the time of the Second Vatican Council (1962-1965) was one of truly amazing theological reflection in the Christian churches, whether Protestant, Evangelical, Catholic, or Orthodox. Even though it took place within the Catholic Church, and even though the significance of the council is being debated within Catholicism, I am using the council as a marker because it is almost certainly the most significant religious "event"[2] of the twentieth century. At Vatican II the Catholic Church opened its doors not only to the contemporary world but also to other Christian churches and to other religions as well. It created an atmosphere of dialogue and openness that went a long way toward quelling the polemical attitudes of Christian churches to one another. After Vatican II, although Protestants, Catholics, and Orthodox maintained their distinct traditions, Christian theologians dialogued with one another, read one another, and profited from one another's distinctiveness. In many ways, after Vatican II what mattered more in theology was not so much one's church affiliation as one's "social location": one's gender, one's culture, one's generational identity—in short, one's *context*. The post–Vatican II era has seen the development of a truly global theology, articulated within Catholicism, Protestantism, Evangelicalism, and Pentecostalism. Such a development, however, was in large part prepared for by the theological ferment of the period—scarred by two World Wars, the Holocaust, and the rise of Communism—that preceded it.

Protestant and Orthodox Theology

Undoubtedly the most significant theologian of the twentieth century was **Karl Barth** (1886-1968). Born in Basel, Switzerland, and educated in the relatively conservative University of Berne, Barth completed his theological education (although he never received the doctorate) in the heady atmosphere of Berlin and Marburg in Germany. There he studied under Harnack and Herrmann, imbibed their ideas eagerly, and was convinced of the truth of the liberal theology that they taught.

In 1911 Barth became pastor of the small Swiss village of Safenwil, and as he began to preach week after week to these poor, working-class women and men, he began to doubt the optimism of the liberal theologians. Then, at the outbreak of World War I he was appalled to see that among the ninety-three intellectuals who had signed a declaration supporting Germany's role in the fighting, his theological mentors were among them. His disenchantment was complete. As he studied the Letter to the Romans and produced a commentary on it, he began to understand theology in a way that stood the theology of Schleiermacher and his liberal successors on its head.

Even though Schleiermacher was right that religion was rooted in human experience, Barth noted, what Schleiermacher had missed was that Christianity was not a religion. *Religion*, always a human construction, inevitably leads to idolatry, the worship of a false God. On the contrary, the God of the Bible is *not* accessible to human experience. Rather, as Kierkegaard had insisted, there exists an "infinite qualitative difference" between God and humanity, time and eternity.[3] There is no "analogy of being," says Barth. That idea, presented so clearly by the Catholic theologian **Erich Przywara** (1889-1972), is "the intention of Antichrist, and I think that because of it one cannot become Catholic."[4] If humanity is to know the true God, the God of the Bible, God has to reach out to women and men, and this God has done most fully and perfectly in Jesus of Nazareth. God in Christ both *condemns* all human efforts of religion, and yet *accepts* humanity in that very rejection: "The No that meets us is *God's* No. What we lack is just what helps us. . . . What cancels all the truth of the world is just what founds it. Exactly because God's No is complete, it is also his Yes."[5]

When his *Epistle to the Romans* began to get a very positive reception in the German-speaking theological world, Barth was called to teach at several universities in Germany. In 1935, however, as a consequence of his involvement in the publication of the famous Barmen Declaration against Hitler's attempt to co-opt the German church, he was dismissed from his post (then in Bonn) and took up a position at the University of Basel in Switzerland. He remained there the rest of his life, lecturing to a whole generation of future pastors and theologians, and completing his *magnum opus*, the *Church Dogmatics*. This immense, thirteen-volume work was never finished, but Barth did succeed in finishing the first four of five projected parts. Part I (or volume I as he called the major parts) focused on revelation and, in a bold innovation, presented it as a trinitarian process. Volume II treated the doctrine of God; volume III reflected on creation; volume IV spoke of reconciliation and treated Christology. The projected volume V was to treat the theme of eschatology. Together with Origen's *First Principles*, the *Summa Theologiae* of Aquinas and Calvin's *Institutes*, Barth's *Dogmatics* ranks as the one of the greatest works of systematic theology in Christian theological history.

Barth virtually shaped the direction of theology in the twentieth century, but he certainly had his critics. After the publication of *The Epistle to the Romans*, a group of theologians, including **Emil Brunner** (1899-1966) and **Rudolf Bultmann** (1884-1976), allied themselves with Barth and began to speak in terms of "dialectical theology," because of "the interplay of the 'No' and the 'Yes' of the Word" to humanity.[6] Bultmann became one of the leading New Testament scholars of the century, emphasizing the "mythological" character of the Gospel narratives and, under the influence of **Martin Heidegger's** (1889-1976) philosophy, interpreting the New Testament in terms of existentialist thought. This was far indeed from Barth's position. Eventually, Brunner began to see at least *some* truth to the idea of a natural theology built on the analogy of being—to which Barth responded with a resounding No. Relations between Barth and Brunner were strained for the rest of their lives—Barth compared themselves to an elephant and a whale, both God's creatures who could never meet.[7] At the end of Brunner's life, however, Barth sent him a reconciling message, implicitly acknowledging a softening of his message as it has appeared in the essay "The Humanity of God": "'Commended to *our* God,' even by me. And tell him, *Yes*, that the time when I thought that I had to say 'no' to him is now long past, since we all live only by virtue of the fact that a great and merciful God says his gracious Yes to all of us."[8]

Barth's theology is radically Christocentric. It is Christ who makes the unknowable God knowable, who shows us in his person and cross what the true God "looks like." Over the desk in his study hung a reproduction of Holbein's painting of the crucifixion (on which the Keiskamma Altarpiece to which we referred in chapter 3 is based). In the picture John the Baptist (anachronistically) is present, pointing with an enlarged index finger to the crucified Christ. Such, said Barth, is the task of the theologian: to point to Christ.[9] Toward the end of his life he was on the Swiss radio program "Music for a Guest." He requested only Mozart (his favorite composer) and spoke of his career, ending with these words: "The last word which I have to say as a theologian and also as a politician is not a term like 'grace,' but a name, 'Jesus Christ.'"

An early adherent of "dialectical theology" was the young **Dietrich Bonhoeffer** (1906-1945). Bonhoeffer had been educated in liberal theology at Berlin, but when he read Barth it was "like a liberation." In Barth he "discovered a theological freedom and courage that well suited his own independence and intellectual temperament."[10] He would need that "courage and freedom," for he found himself in the 1930s involved in the Confessing Church, which was founded as a result of the Barmen Declaration. He was also one of the leaders of the clandestine seminary that trained clergy for the church and was eventually shut down by the Gestapo.

It was in these years at the seminary that Bonhoeffer wrote one of his most famous works, *The Cost of Discipleship*, and his work on seminary community, *Life Together*, influenced by Benedict's *Rule*.[11] During World War II he worked for the German army in counterintelligence, but he was arrested in 1943 for taking part in a plot to assassinate Hitler. It was in prison that he wrote the work that has had the greatest influence on twentieth-century theology, a collection of letters and fragments published as *Letters and Papers from Prison*. The work's power lies in the theological experiments in which Bonhoeffer engages in the papers and letters he wrote— "'lightning flashes' of theological thought," as one commentator has put it.[12] Such "lightning flashes" were lines like ". . . we cannot be honest unless we recognize that we have to live in the world *etsi deus non daretur* [as if God does not exist]"; "God lets himself be pushed out of the world on to the cross"; "only the suffering God can help."[13] Bonhoeffer never developed these ideas, since he was executed on April 9, 1945 (just a week before the prison camp in which he was held was liberated by the Allied Forces). It would have been interesting to see how he would have done it. His thought—particularly some of his fragmentary sayings—were hugely influential in the theology of secularization and the Death of God movement in the 1960s. These movements have passed in the twenty-first century, but his works still ring with mighty challenge today as Christians still look for holiness in their everyday lives.

Another theological giant of the first part of the twentieth century is **Paul Tillich** (1886-1965). Born and educated in Germany, Tillich left Germany as Hitler came into power and spent the rest of his life teaching in the United States. He was relatively unknown until 1948, when a book of his sermons, entitled *The Shaking of the Foundations*, became, surprisingly, a national best-seller in the United States. Afterwards Tillich went on to become perhaps the most eminent theologian in his adopted nation and was also acclaimed around the world.

Tillich's "principal goal was to make Christianity understandable and persuasive to religiously skeptical people, modern in culture and secular in sensibility."[14] He did this by using what he called a "method of correlation," which attempted to explain Christian faith "through existential questions and theological answers in mutual interdependence."[15] His major work, the three-volume *Systematic Theology*, used this method in all of its five parts. In each part a fundamental human question was given an answer with a symbol or doctrine from the Christian tradition. Part I asks the question about whether we can know the truth, and the answer given is the Christian doctrine of revelation. Part II correlates the question of finitude and contingency with the doctrine of God—the "ground of Being," human beings' "ultimate concern."[16] In the third part Tillich poses the question of human alienation through sin, and then speaks of Jesus Christ as the "New Being" who restores humanity to right relation with itself, the world, and Being Itself.[17] Part IV develops the idea of the "Spiritual Presence" in answer to the question of life's ambiguities, and Part V proposes that the doctrine of the Kingdom of God is the answer to the question of the meaning of history.

The three volumes of *Systematic Theology* are written in sometimes stirring prose, and run to some eight hundred pages with no footnotes or references. Here and in many other works Tillich offers many fresh ideas and images to explain traditional theological concepts: for example, faith is the state of being "ultimately concerned," and *always* involves doubt;[18] the need to move away from both "autonomy" (self-direction) and "heteronomy" (being directed by others), to "theonomy" (living by the direction of God);[19] grace as "acceptance."[20] Tillich's concern to communicate the faith in ways that twentieth-century women and men could understand ranks him among those theologians who have practiced inculturation in the past, and makes him a forerunner of those who would practice it in the future. From the beginning of his career to the end, he was a theologian of culture.[21]

Although Tillich taught at both Harvard and the University of Chicago, the bulk of his teaching career was spent at Union Theological Seminary in New York City (1933-1955). Tillich's colleague on the faculty of Union was the influential social ethicist **Reinhold Niebuhr** (1892-1971), who at the peak of his career was the most well known religious figure in the United States. At the heart of his vision was a phrase that appeared in his 1932 book *Moral Man and Immoral Society*: "Christian Realism."[22] Niebuhr was wary of simple answers to what were really very complex questions in politics and human social life, and he was especially critical of those who saw the American way of life as the epitome of Christianity's meaning. Humanity itself, and human society, is shot through with ambiguity, and while there is much good in both, human beings must never be so naive as to think that any situation is beyond critique. This attitude is summed up well in one of Niebuhr's most famous aphorisms: "Man's capacity for justice makes democracy possible; but man's inclination to injustice makes democracy necessary."[23]

Niebuhr's masterwork, *The Nature and Destiny of Man*, also had Christian Realism at its heart. Humanity is not evil in its bodily existence or in its limited knowledge. Rather, it is when we try to deny our finitude by dominating others or obeying others rather than God that we experience sin. We transcend our finitude not by trying to be like God but by trusting God and imitating Christ, whose combination of perfect freedom and human finitude shows the way of true humanity.[24]

Toward the end of *Moral Man and Immoral Society* Niebuhr explains that a society can be changed only when those who want change use power, but he insists that such power need not be violent. This idea, together with the idea of nonviolent resistance in the life of Mohandas K. Gandhi in India, the idea of civil disobedience in the nineteenth-century U.S. literary figure Henry David Thoreau, and the social gospel thought of Walter Rauschenbusch became the starting point for the vision and theology of **Martin Luther King, Jr.** (1929-1968). A Baptist minister, educated at Morehouse College and Crozer Seminary in Pennsylvania, King completed the doctorate at Boston University, where he studied the personalist theology of Borden Parker Bowne (1847-1910) and Edgar Sheffield Brightman (1884-1953).[25] Although he considered an academic career, King accepted an offer to be pastor at Dexter Avenue Baptist Church in Montgomery, Alabama, and this set the stage for his role in history. In December 1955, Rosa Parks was arrested because she refused to move from the "white section" of a Montgomery bus, and King emerged as the leader of what became the Montgomery Bus Boycott. Soon he was the national leader of a vigorous and tumultuous civil rights movement that was to change U.S. history, a leadership that he held until he was tragically assassinated on April 4, 1968.

In his thirteen years of leadership in the civil rights movement, King was to deliver sermons and write books that are considered some of the most powerful contextual theology ever written. Deeply biblical and rooted in the best values of his country and culture, King's theologizing is moving and memorable. His "I Have a Dream" speech at the Lincoln Memorial in 1963 is one of the most quoted and influential texts in U.S. culture; his "Letter from the Birmingham Jail" is an eloquent defense of his ministry and of his vision. Among many powerful quotations, let me choose just one:

> We're going to win our freedom because both the sacred heritage of our nation and the eternal will of the almighty God are embodied in our echoing demands. And so, however dark it is, however deep the angry feelings are, and however violent explosions are, I can still sing "We Shall Overcome." We shall overcome because the arc of the moral universe is long, but it bends toward justice. We shall overcome because Carlyle is right: "No lie can live forever." We shall overcome because William Cullen Bryant is right: "Truth, crushed to earth, will rise again."[26]

King's commitment to justice and eloquent articulation of it became an inspiration for many other movements of civil rights and liberation—among Latino/as in the United States, among victims of apartheid in South Africa, among the poor of Asia, and among Latin Americans who gave birth to liberation theology in the late 1960s and 1970s.

Three Russian Orthodox theologians stand out in this period.[27] **Sergei Nikolaevich Bulgakov** (1871-1944) was expelled from Soviet Russia in 1923 and lived the rest of his life in Paris. Highly unsystematic and often obscure, his ecclesiology was highly influential in the growing ecumenical movement after the Great War. He was one of the first to use the term "panentheism"— that the world dwells within the reality of God, and he was fascinated by female imagery for the Godhead. He was also the only theologian of the twentieth century to use *kenosis*—self-emptying—as a normative concept for all language about God, and in this way anticipates contemporary understandings of God as suffering with humanity.

Vladimir Nikolaevich Lossky (1903-1958), also an exile in Paris, was a theological opponent of Bulgakov but was nevertheless a brilliant patristic scholar and writer on Meister Eckhart. **Georgii Vasilievich Florovsky** (1893-1979) taught in Paris, and then in the 1950s moved to the United States and taught at Harvard and Princeton. His 1937 masterpiece, *The Ways of Russian Theology*, tried to expose the many false turns in the history of theology in Russia as a result of the continued influence of Western thought. The remedy, not surprising for an Orthodox theologian, was to return to the earliest theologians of the church. His work also encompassed important thinking in ecclesiology and Mariology.[28] Orthodox theology is not always as well known in the West as it should be, but these theologians had a profound influence especially on the renewal of Catholic theology, which we will discuss in the following section.

Catholic Theology

After the First World War there developed several new directions in the scholastic revival mandated by Leo XIII in *Aeterni Patris*. This came about as "the excesses of antimodernist vigilantes" weakened, and the church became a bit more open to democracy.[29] Three "schools" began to take shape, each associated with the name of a significant Thomist philosopher, and all more open to both democracy and secular culture. **Jacques Maritain** (1882-1973) was the spokesperson for the "traditional Thomism" still taught in the world's seminaries, although his thought had "a breadth, urbanity, and flexibility" which other Thomists—like **Reginald Garrigou-Lagrange** (1877-1964) of the Angelicum in Rome—did not.[30] **Étienne Gilson** (1884-1978) took a more historical turn, while **Joseph Maréchal** (1878-1944) built on the work of Blondel and Rousselot to develop a "Transcendental Thomism" that put Aquinas's thought in a critical dialogue with the thought of Kant.

It was particularly from the second two schools that renewal began to develop within Catholic theology. From the historical approach to Thomism comes the groundbreaking work of **Marie-Dominique Chenu** (1895-1990) and **Yves Congar** (1904-1995). From the school of Transcendental Thomism emerges the theology of perhaps the two most important Catholic theologians of the century, **Karl Rahner** (1904-1984) and **Bernard J. F. Lonergan** (1904-1984).

The context of Catholic renewal is shaped also by several movements that actually go back to the nineteenth century. Under the influence of German pioneers like Baur and Strauss, and later Julius Wellhausen (1844-1918) and Hermann Gunkel (1862-1932), a biblical renewal slowly began to develop in Catholicism. It was embodied in the great founder of Jerusalem's École Biblique, **Marie-Joseph Lagrange** (1855-1938) and began really to flourish after the publication of **Pope Pius XII's** (1876-1958) 1943 encyclical *Divino Afflante Spiritu*. A patristic revival also had begun, with roots in the immense work of **Jacques Paul Migne's** (1800-1875) collections of texts of the theologians of the early church in both Latin and Greek. In addition to these two movements were the liturgical renewal, promoted especially by the Benedictines **Prosper Guéranger** (1805-1875) and **Odo Casel** (1886-1948) and the ecumenical movement, already on the horizons even at the all-Protestant Edinburgh Missionary Conference of 1910. At the conference, a letter of greeting was read from Bishop Geremia Bonomelli of Cremona, Italy, expressing hope in future cooperation among all Christian groups.[31]

It was in this atmosphere of Thomistic renewal and a return to the sources that **Marie-Dominique Chenu** was professor and then rector at the Dominican theologate at Le Saulchoir in Belgium. Like his friend Etienne Gilson, Chenu saw the importance of a historical recovery of the thought of Aquinas, and so devoted his life to that work. Although not an original thinker, his contributions to the history of theology were truly significant, as witnessed by his works (to name a few) *Aquinas and His Role in Theology; Nature, Man and Society in the Twelfth Century*, and *Toward Understanding St. Thomas*. He was a leader in the movement that came to be known as *ressourcement*, and trained a whole generation of students, the most famous of whom was **Yves Congar**.

Congar, as he would have admitted, was not a speculative theologian, but "his work magnificently demonstrates the value of historical research and documentation for renewing theology and reforming church structures and ways of worship and devotion."[32] In 1939 he wrote one of the first Catholic contributions to the ecumenical movement, entitled *Christianity Divided*. In 1953 his *Lay People in the Church* represented perhaps the first systematic reflection on the theology of the laity.

Because of such pioneering work—and of publishing a controversial book, never published in English, on church reform—Congar came under suspicion by Rome and was even for a time exiled from his teaching at Le Saulchoir. However, by the time of the Second Vatican Council he was numbered among the *periti*, or official theological advisors, who helped in the drafting of the council documents. Congar's influence can be seen in the documents on the church, the laity, the church in the modern world, revelation, ecumenism and the church's missionary activity.[33] Toward the end of his life he published a three-volume work on the Holy Spirit that, while quite unsystematic, is a treasure-trove of historical information on the Spirit in both Eastern and Western theology.

Although perhaps more influenced by the "Transcendental Thomist" school,[34] **Henri de Lubac** (1896-1991) represents another major figure of the movement of *ressourcement*. Teaching at the Jesuit theologate in Lyons, France, de Lubac wrote voluminously on the social nature of Catholicism, on medieval exegesis, on atheism, and on the theology of his friend Pierre Teilhard de Chardin, whose work we will reflect on shortly. Perhaps his greatest contribution to theology, however, are his books on the Eucharist and on the relation between nature and grace.

Corpus Mysticum: Eucharist and the Church in the Middle Ages is a stunning example of how historical research can contribute to the renewal of theology. De Lubac's research into patristic and early medieval texts discovered that, while originally the *church* was considered the *true* body of Christ and the Eucharist was understood as the *mystical* body of Christ whose purpose was the edification (i.e., building up) of the church, in the tenth and eleventh centuries, with a shift "from symbolism to dialectics," the focus began to be on the *Eucharist* as the true body, with the church becoming peripheral as the *mystical* body. Renewal in the church needs not so much to reverse the understanding again as to recognize that "the Church and the eucharist make each other, every day, each by the other." Celebrating the Eucharist is the way that Christians are nourished to be the body of Christ in the world.[35]

De Lubac's book *Surnaturel: Études Historiques* (Supernatural: Historical Studies) has as its thesis that the common distinction between natural and supernatural, nature and grace, is actually a false one, and not really part of the theology of Thomas Aquinas. The very fact that men and women are created in the image of God points to the fact that they are already graced. While the discussion is a very technical one, its implications are very practical. They point to the graced nature of human culture and to the possibility of salvation even without explicit knowledge of or faith in Christ. The theologian we will discuss next, the German Jesuit **Karl Rahner**, will complement de Lubac's historical scholarship and develop the idea of a "graced world" as one of the key insights of his magnificent theological system.

In a sense, Rahner *does not* have a system. Although he did write a kind of systematic theology entitled *Foundations of Christian Faith*, it is not anywhere near as complete as the systems of Barth or Tillich.[36] In another sense, however, Rahner is one of the most systematic thinkers in Christian history. Even though most of his writings are more in the form of occasional essays (for example, his twenty-three-volume *Theological Investigations*) and shorter books, everything he wrote is based on one fundamental insight, which he called the "supernatural existential"—the simple fact that *everything* in creation and in human life is already graced, and that humanity is inescapably caught up and surrounded by "Holy or Gracious Mystery."[37]

Man is a spirit, that is, he lives his life in a perpetual reaching out towards the absolute, in openness to God. This openness to God is not a contingency which can emerge here or there at will in man, but is the condition for the possibility of that which man is and has to be, even in the most forlorn and mundane life. The only thing which makes him a man is that he is forever on the road to God whether he is clearly aware of the fact or not, whether he wants to be or not, for he is always the infinite openness to the infinite for God.[38]

This openness to God, says Rahner, is already grace, and it already says something about the one who does indeed fill it—like a keyhole says something about the key that fits into it.[39] The openness does not *have* to be fulfilled, but if it is, it will be by a freedom-respecting gift that fills that openness. In fact, Christians believe, God *has* offered this gift in revelation, and so revelation is not essentially an extrinsic list of propositions but a personal offer. This offer is accepted as human beings struggle to live life authentically, for the offer is in the warp and woof of everyday life. But this offer is also given in history, through the history of Israel, the event of Jesus of Nazareth, and his continuing presence in the Christian church. In offering God's gift of self, God shows us the inner reality of the divine nature, for the Holy Mystery of the Father is revealed by the incarnate Son through the power of the Holy Spirit. The doctrine of the Trinity, like all Christian doctrines, is not simply a piece of information but a "real symbol" that tells us as much about ourselves as it does about God. Since God's offer is to all humanity—one cannot be human without being on the road to God—grace is universal, and so salvation is possible outside the boundaries of the Christian church and Christian faith, even though grace is always offered through the grace of Christ and faith is always *implicit* faith in Christ (Rahner's famous theory of the "anonymous Christian").

Except for the years during and immediately after World War II, Rahner spent many years teaching theology at the Universities of Innsbruck (1937-1938, 1948-1964), Munich (1964-1967), and Münster (1967-1971), and as late as 1962 he had conflicts with Rome. But as Vatican II started he was appointed a *peritus*, or official advisor, and had a profound effect on many of the council's documents. Already in his lifetime he became "the most influential and widely-read Catholic theologian of the twentieth century,"[40] and despite important critiques by theologians like **Johann Baptist Metz** (1928-) urging a more socially conscious and political theology,[41] his theology remains one of the most exciting in the church today. Many of his ideas—the holiness of the everyday, the universal reality of grace, for example—are basic for constructing contextual theologies in local cultures and situations today.

Some theologians would contend, however, that the work of Rahner's fellow Jesuit **Bernard J. F. Lonergan** holds more promise for the future. Lonergan was born in Canada and educated in England and Rome. He taught theology in Canada, for twelve years at the Gregorian University in Rome, and then at Toronto, Harvard, and Boston College. He wrote major works on the doctrine of grace, the procession of the Word in the writings of Aquinas, and on the doctrine of the Trinity and Christology, but his most well known and probably most important works are a massive study of human understanding (*Insight: A Study of Human Understanding* [1957]) and *Method in Theology* (1972).

Lonergan's ideas converge around the notions of self-transcendence, horizon, and conversion. First, if human beings are honest, they will recognize an ineluctable, spontaneous dynamic in themselves that he names the "pure desire to know."[42] This is a dynamic of *self-transcendence*. The authentic person is one who tries to obey the "transcendental precepts": "Be attentive, Be intelligent, Be reasonable, Be responsible."[43]

The more one knows, the more questions emerge, and openness to these questions moves one to levels of consciousness and breadth of knowledge that continue to expand one's *horizon*. One not only knows what one knows (the "known known"), but moves to know what one does not know (the "known unknown"), which pushes one to begin to move into a horizon that is totally unknown (the "unknown unknown").[44] As we move beyond our own horizons into ever new ones, we are faced with the possibility and the reality of *conversion*, and this can be on the intellectual level (reality is not something just "out there" but something I participate in creating), the moral level (I act not just for pleasure or to maintain order but because something is simply good), or the religious (I recognize that this dynamic is something given to me in freedom and in love).[45]

For Lonergan, one can only properly do theology if one has experienced religious conversion, for while theology certainly involves meticulous research and rational reflection, its purpose is ultimately to penetrate the mystery of God's love that is poured into our hearts by the Holy Spirit (Rom. 5:5) and to communicate such understanding to the Christian people. It is only from this perspective that we can understand Christian doctrines and how they are related to one another, for they are not simply a list of truths but the various ways that Christians express this very basic experience of grace.

Lonergan has a loyal following of disciples today who see his thought as truly seminal for a theology that can answer some of the vexing questions that the contemporary world has posed for religious faith. Theology, in Lonergan's words, "mediates between a cultural matrix and the significance and role of religion in that matrix."[46]

Although his influence has been stronger after Vatican II than before, we must make brief mention of the Swiss theologian **Hans Urs von Balthasar** (1905-1988) and his close associate and friend **Adrienne von Speyer** (1902-1967). Von Balthasar's theology is worked out with the conviction that while humanity can indeed come to an understanding of God and God's dramatic work in history, Christians need always to be aware that the *dissimilarities* in our knowledge of God are always greater than the *similarities*, and that the dissimilarities should function to break and to judge the language we use in theology.[47] In this regard he is close to the theology of Karl Barth, whose work he greatly admired and which influenced him considerably in his work. Also influential were the mystical visions of von Speyer, especially in terms of his Christology.[48]

Balthasar tended to be critical of developments in the church that, in his opinion, were too open to the world or too welcoming to secular movements or to the truth in non-Christian religions.[49] Nevertheless, his theology is many-faceted and, especially for "neo-Augustinian" theologians today, holds out much promise for future development.

Four other important theologians, among many significant ones in this marvelous period of theological history, deserve mention as we end this section. **Edward Schillebeeckx** (1914-) has perhaps, like von Balthasar, had more influence in the years since Vatican II with his important books on Christology and ministry, books that have shaped much of the current debate in these areas. However, in his work on the sacraments in the late 1950s, *Christ the Sacrament of the Encounter with God*, he treated the sacraments from a more personalist and existentialist perspective than previous scholastic works.[50] His approach has had a profound influence on sacramental theology ever since and has found many echoes in the documents of the council.

The scientist and mystic **Teilhard de Chardin's** (1881-1955) vision of cosmic and human evolution culminating in Christ can be seen in several of Vatican II's documents, especially the Pastoral Constitution on the Church in the Modern World. **Joseph Ratzinger** (1927-), who eventually became **Pope Benedict XVI** in 2005, was a young theologian in the 1950s and '60s, but he had already made an impression as a professor of theology at Bonn and Münster. In his younger years he was an admirer of Rahner and the theology of de Lubac and was an official theological advisor at the council. Like Balthasar, however, he was disillusioned by some of the post–Vatican II chaos in the church, and he became wary of contemporary culture and experience.

Finally, **John Courtney Murray's** (1904-1967) careful work on relations between church and state were hugely influential in the council's document on religious freedom. As Murray himself wrote, the council's teaching on freedom of conscience and the human right to freedom of religion was "a significant event in the history of the Church." Murray's work also helped in persuading the council to accept the notion of the development of doctrine.[51]

THEOLOGY FROM VATICAN II TO THE PRESENT

Practically every theologian that we have considered in the previous section contributed in some way to the event that was the Second Vatican Council.

When the newly elected Pope John XXIII announced the council in January 1959, he surprised almost everyone. At one level the Catholic Church was in the best "shape" that it had been for centuries, and the prestige of the pope during the papacy of Pius XII was at an all-time high. At another level, however, Pope John recognized the importance of the theological ferment that had been going on from the end of the nineteenth century and realized that the church at last needed to come to terms with the contemporary world.

The council proved to be a "new Pentecost," a genuine moment of renewal for the church throughout the world. During the first session in 1962, the bishops rejected the draft documents that had been prepared in basically neo-scholastic form by members of the Roman curia and demanded documents that were more scripturally and patristically based. The council began with a discussion of the liturgy and at the second session (1963) approved a document that called for a renewal of the sacramental rites, the Liturgy of the Hours, and an adaptation of the liturgy to local cultures and languages.

The document on the church moves from understanding the church as an institution to understanding it as a community, the people of God. While acknowledging that the church is a hierarchical community, the council articulated a more fundamental equality of all Christians based on their baptism. The document recognizes the importance of the bishop's role in the church and reestablished the diaconate as a permanent order in the church, available to married men. The possibility of salvation outside of explicit faith in Christ is clearly taught, and the presence of God's grace both in other Christian bodies and in non-Christian religions is acknowledged (this is developed even more in the decrees on ecumenism and other religions).

The document on revelation explains revelation as God's personal offer of friendship, encourages all Christians to read and study the Bible, and speaks of tradition not so much as a body of doctrines but as a dynamic within the church of handing on the faith. The document on the church in the modern world acknowledges some Christian blame for atheism, recognizes the goodness and even helpfulness of the secular world, and, for the first time in a church document, speaks of the importance of human culture (as does the document on the missionary nature of the church). These are only a few of the breakthroughs of the council, some of which were stunning reversals of position from previous Roman teachings. The work of theologians which had been disparaged in the past or rejected outright—for example, Möhler, Newman, Congar, Rahner—was vindicated.[52]

Vatican II's repeated teaching on the goodness of local cultures and the necessity to perform liturgy, preach, and do theology in dialogue with them opened up the possibility for a new pluralism in theology, and the years after Vatican II have seen that pluralism flourish. What we can present here is only the briefest of treatments and will not touch every movement in theology today, but I hope that it can capture the dazzling array of ways of doing theology that the council made possible. Some of richness of that pluralism, I further hope, has been reflected in the content and method of this book. We begin with Latin American theologies since their influence has been so pervasive in the last half-century and then branch out to theologies in other local cultures and particular social locations.

Theologies in Latin America

"When we speak of theology in Latin America, we must speak of the theology of liberation. Here, for the first time in the history of our subcontinent, a theology is appearing that belongs to us—a theological reflection incarnate in the situation and the persons and peoples of America."[53] Certainly there had been a Latin American theology before, as we saw in the last chapter, but it was a theology done more by lone, often prophetic, voices. Now, in the wake of Vatican II, a whole new way of doing theology had emerged. It is a theology that starts with the concrete experience of the masses of Latin American poor and moves not just to a deeper *understanding* of the faith (although it has offered startling insights into traditional doctrines and practices). Rather it leads to a new way of acting (and continuous reflection on acting) that helps the poor in the struggle for their liberation from the sinful structures that oppress them and involve them in those structures' sinfulness.

Liberation theology has its origins in the legacy of Catholic social teaching begun already in 1893 by **Pope Leo XIII** (1810-1903). More proximately, however, its origins can be traced to the second Conference of Latin American Bishops held in Medellín, Colombia, in 1968. The theme of the conference was "The Church in the Present-Day Transformation of Latin America in the Light of the Council." At that conference a new way of doing theology was introduced, based on the "see, judge, and act" model used in the Young Christian Worker movement in Europe in the 1930s. Each of the sixteen documents that were issued at Medellín began with a sociohistorical analysis of a particular reality (e.g., justice, family, the church), followed by a reflection based on Christian doctrine, with conclusions for action to which the Latin American church committed itself.

A few years later one of the theologians at the conference, **Gustavo Gutiérrez** (1928-) from Peru published the book that was to give "form and direction" to Latin American theology throughout the 1970s and beyond: *A Theology of Liberation*.[54] The book laid down the principles of liberation theology method and presented a short overview of what the basic doctrines of Christianity—for example, God, Christ, church, eschatology—might look like from a liberation perspective. Gutiérrez soon emerged as the "father" of the movement, publishing a number of important works, one of the most important of which is his *Las Casas: In Search of the Poor of Jesus Christ*.[55] There followed a massive outpouring of works ranging from theological method to works on ecclesiology, Christology, Mariology, ecology, and feminist issues by such noted theologians as the Brazilians **Clodovis Boff** (1944-) and **Leonardo Boff** (1938-), **Ivone Gebara** (1944-), and **Maria Clara Lucchetti Bingemer** (1949-), Uruguayan **Juan Luis Segundo** (1925-1996), Spanish **Ignacio Ellacuría** (1930-1989), and the Argentinian United Methodist **José Míguez Bonino** (1924-)—to name only a few of the most famous.

Much Latin American theology, however, is not done by professional theologians at all, but is done in the context of small Christian communities reflecting on the relevance of faith for daily, basic issues. It is done also in marvelous songs that are sung by these communities and in chapels and churches, and it is done in art, such as the colorful art of El Salvador and the powerful sculptures of Peruvian **Edilberto Mérida** (1927-).

Liberation theology was early on influenced by the political theology developed in Germany in the 1960s by German theologians **Jürgen Moltmann** (1926-) and **Johann Baptist Metz** (1928-), and also by the concerns and methods of Karl Marx.[56] Because of this latter influence, liberation theology has often been criticized, especially by several cautionary statements from Rome. In the last decades, however, it has been influenced by Latin American popular religion, indigenous cultures, the Catholic Charismatic movement, the challenge of Pentecostalism, Latin American feminism, and minority groups such as indigenous peoples and those of the African diaspora.[57] Now that Latin America has found its voice, it holds immense promise for the future.

Caribbean theologies also reflect a liberation perspective. Chief among these is Antiguan Kortright Davis' *Emancipation Still Comin': Explorations in Caribbean Emancipatory Theology*. Surveys of Carribean theology can be found in works edited by Patrick Anthony from St. Lucia and Howard Gregory from Jamaica.[58]

Asian Theologies

Although Christians are a tiny minority in Asia, they have a strong identity, and Asian Christians are engaged in some of the most exciting and creative theologizing in the world today. Just browsing through the three-volume work edited by Aotearoa New Zealand theologian John C. England is enough to boggle the mind![59] The Federation of Asian Bishops' Conference, a Catholic body that goes back to the 1970s in the wake of Vatican II, has perhaps best expressed the agenda for Asian theology today: it must engage in a "threefold dialogue" with Asia's poor, with Asia's cultures, and with Asia's religions.[60] The geographical extent of Asia is immense, and its cultures are complex and incredibly varied. For our purposes we might divide Asia into South Asia (e.g., India, Pakistan, Bangladesh, and Sri Lanka), Southeast Asia (e.g., Vietnam,

Philippines, Indonesia, Malaysia), Northeast Asia (Japan, Korea, China, and Taiwan), and West Asia (Kazakstan, Uzbekistan, the "Middle East," Turkey).

Theology in South Asia focuses particularly on issues emerging from efforts of interreligious dialogue with three of the great religions in the world: Hinduism, Islam, and Buddhism. In India, of particular interest is the dialogue with Hinduism, and this has seriously engaged Indian theologians. Towering, perhaps, above all Indian theologians in **Raimon Panikkar** (1918-). His theological output has been immense, and he writes about a new way of thinking about Christianity that integrates the riches of other religious ways into its heart. In books like *Christophany: The Fullness of Man* (2004) and *The Trinity and the Religious Experience of Man* (1973), he has written profoundly about Christology and the Trinity, and has opened up astonishing ways of thinking about traditional Christian doctrines. Other important Indian theologians— again, to name only a few—are the Protestants **M. M. Thomas** (1916-1997) and **Stanley J. Samartha** (1920-2001), and Catholics **George Soares-Prabhu** (1929-1995), **Samuel Rayan** (1920-), **D. S. Amalorpavadass** (1932-1990), and **Michael Amaladoss** (1936-).[61] A strong movement in India as well is the development of "Dalit theology," a theology that springs up from the experience of "outcastes" in Indian society. It is a theology of hope and resistance by the poorest of the poor in India, and similar in this way to Latin American liberation theology.[62] In Sri Lanka, we need to mention the work of **Aloysius Pieris** (1934-), who has attempted in his work to combine a fine sensitivity to Buddhism with a deep commitment to justice and liberation. South Asia, too, has a growing body of feminist theological reflection.[63]

In Southeast Asia lies the only majority Christian country in Asia: the Philippines. Immediately after Vatican II perhaps the most eminent Filipino theologian was **Catalino G. Arévalo** (1925-), often called the "Dean of Filipino theologians."[64] He has been a major contributor to the work of the FABC, a member of the Vatican's International Theological Commission, and a pioneer in developing a Filipino liberation theology by doing a "theology of the signs of the times."[65] Maryknoll sister **Virginia Fabella** is one of the founders of the Ecumenical Association of Third World Theologians (EATWOT) and has edited a number of important Asian and majority world collections of theology, including several feminist anthologies. **Emerito Nacpil**[66] is a United Methodist bishop, but in the years right after Vatican II he was one of the leaders of contextualization efforts in the Philippines and Asia, and author of the "critical Asian principle," a declaration promoting the independence of Asian theological thinking. Other theologians of note are **José M. de Mesa** (1946-), who has spoken eloquently for the use of Filipino culture as the "guide" for theology,[67] Pioneer Filipino philosopher and theologian **Leonardo N. Mercado** (1935-), and younger theologians **Gemma T. Cruz** (1970-), and **Timoteo D. Gener**. Musicians like **Raul Caga** (1965-) are writing popular yet substantial religious music. Theology is also flourishing in Indonesia, often in dialogue with Islam, but the majority of theologizing is done in Indonesian. One important exception (though there are others) is **Robert Hardawiryana** (1926-), who, like Arévalo, has had a major influence on FABC documents as well as official Catholic documents in Indonesia.[68] In Malaysia we can mention **Edmund Kee Fook Chia** (1962), even though he teaches in the U.S., and Methodist bishop and theologian **Hwa Yung** (1948-).[69]

The church in China in northeast Asia has had a complex, sometimes tragic history since the Communist takeover in 1949. In the last several decades China has been somewhat open to religion, and theological schools and seminaries have begun to flourish. Much theological reflection is being done in Chinese, which will almost certainly be one of the main theological languages in the future. In Protestant theology the key figure in both church and theology has been Bishop **K. H. Ting** (**Ding Guangxun** [1915-]). Ting has written in many areas—for example, on the Incarnation, Christology, ecclesiology, God—and begins from the Chinese context in a way that "creatively merges western theology and Chinese culture."[70] The art of **He Qi** gives a powerful Chinese interpretation to biblical scenes. In Japan, perhaps the most famous Protestant theologian, highly influenced by Barth, is **Kitamori Kazoh** (1916-1996), whose 1946 *Theology of the Pain of God* has become a classic in twentieth-century theology. The work of **Kosuke Koyama** (1929-2009), who retired in the United States, having served as a missionary in Thailand, is an outstanding example of Asian contextual theology. Also important in Japanese theology—and well known throughout the world—is the novelist **Endo Shusaku** (1923-1996), whose novel *Silence* on the seventeenth-century persecution of Christians and *A Life of Jesus* are important as theology as well as literature.[71]

Theologies in Australia, New Zealand, and Oceania

Evidence of the vitality of Australian theology is seen by glancing at one of the world's most important and interesting theological journals, *The Australian E-Journal of Theology*, published by the Australian Catholic University and edited by **Gerard Hall**.[72] Names like **Neil Ormerod, David Coffey, Denis Edwards, Anne Hunt, Patricia Fox,** and **Anthony Kelly** are well-known names around the English-speaking theological world, and the scholars have offered major contributions in theological method, ecclesiology, and work on the doctrine of the Trinity and other classical theological themes.[73] In 2000, **Gideon Goosen**, himself an eminent Australian lay theologian, published *Australian Theologies: Themes and Methodologies into the Third Millennium*.[74] The book provides a marvelous and exhaustive survey of the plurality of theologies being done in Australia: works in aboriginal theology, ecological theology, feminist theologies, and theology and economics. Goosen concludes at the end of his survey that a "modest start" in constructing Australian theologies has been made, and he remarks that he knows no Australian theologian today who writes as if "theology were above context."[75]

Such a conclusion could also be made for theology in Aotearoa New Zealand. Perhaps the leading Catholic theologian in the country today is **Neil Darragh**, a parish priest and professor who combines pastoral experience and considerable scholarly skill. Among his works is a very useful introduction to theology and, in the context of environment-conscious New Zealand, a book on ecology.[76] A number of Catholic theologians, among them **Helen Bergin**, **Susan Smith**, **Henare Tate**, and **John Dunn**, have published a book on New Zealand spirituality. Susan Smith and Anglican **Cathy Ross** have both published landmark books on women in mission.[77] Presbyterian **Peter Matheson** has surveyed the past and present state of theology in the country.[78]

A New Zealand theologian, **Philip Gibbs** (1947-) is also one of the leading theologians in Oceania. Based in Papua-New Guinea, Gibbs has produced fine studies in contextual theology in that country, but he has also—perhaps more significantly—helped many ordained, religious, and lay leaders to begin to articulate their faith in the PNG context.[79] Several decades ago the journal *Point* published a fascinating study of Melanesian theologies, of which many contributions were by indigenous Melanesian people.[80] Noteworthy as well is the work of Irish Columban missionary **Frank Hoare** and his reflections on contextual theological issues in Fiji.[81]

African Theologies

Even before Vatican II, African theologians were discussing the importance of developing a truly African theology. A famous example of this discussion is a debate that took place between Belgian **Alfred Vanneste**, the dean of a theology faculty in Kinshasa, Congo, and **Tharcisse Tshibangu** (1933-), then a student, later bishop of Mbujimayi, Congo. Tshibangu delivered a paper entitled "Towards a Theology with an African Slant," and noted several aspects of African culture that could be used to develop an African theology: the African sense of life, symbolism, and intuition, as well as resources in traditional religions. In answer, Vanneste delivered his paper entitled "First, a True Theology," emphasizing the universality of Christianity and the universality of theology.[82] Ultimately, of course, Tshibangu's view prevailed, as expressed so powerfully by Pope Paul VI in 1969: "You may, and you must, have an African Christianity."[83]

African theology, like Asian and Latin American theology, is concerned with two perspectives from which to do theological reflection. On the one hand, closer to the Latin American emphasis, African theology focuses on the poverty and marginalization of African peoples, and calls for liberation. This was particularly true in South Africa during the apartheid years, and is reflected in the theology of South Africans **Allan Boesak** (1945-), **Takatso Mofokeng**, and **Itumuleng Mosala**.[84] It is evident also, however, in the work of the Congolese Catholic **Bénézet Bujo**.[85] The other perspective, closer to the Asian emphasis, focuses on African cultural values and the resources to be found in African Traditional Religions. Kenyan Protestant theologian **John S. Mbiti** (1931-) was one of the first to take up this theological task, insisting that God "was not a stranger in Africa prior to the coming of missionaries," for they did not bring God, but God brought them to complete Africans' knowledge of God through the gospel.[86] Tanzanian Catholic theologian **Charles Nyamiti** has pioneered a Christology that images Jesus as Ancestor, a resonant African theme that is not without its problems but can be argued as valued nonetheless. Others, such as Bishop **Anselme T. Sannon** of Burkina Faso, image Jesus as Master of Initiation, or, like **François Kabasélé**, speak of Christ as Chief.[87] Tanzanian **Laurenti Magesa** and Nigerian **E. E. Uzukwu** take up the idea of the Roman Catholic African Synod of 1994 and reflect on the church as God's extended family, another African image that finds deep resonance in African hearts.[88]

Women are also active in the creation of an African theology today. Two of the best known are Ghanaian **Mercy Amba Oduyoye** and Kenyan **Musimbi Kanyoro**, and they have both been involved in editing collections of African women's theology.[89] In 1989 Oduyoye founded the Circle of Concerned African Women Theologians, a group that engages in interreligious dialogue, builds solidarity among women, and attempts to identify the most crucial issues for continued theological reflection. One of the areas of special concern that has emerged is the effort to find more inclusive images for God.[90]

These short paragraphs, of course, just scratch the surface of a lively theological world that includes Pentecostals, Evangelicals, Catholics, and members of the huge number of African Independent/Initiated Churches. Much African theology takes place in local languages, and so passes "under the radar" of other people in the world. An example of such is the powerful Christology of the Ghanaian laywoman **Afua Kuma**, in a small book of prayers in Twi.[91] Africans are deeply religious by nature and, as John Mbiti points out eloquently, "Much of the theological activity in Christian Africa today is being done as oral theology, from the living experiences of Christians . . . theology in the open, from the pulpit, in the marketplace, in the home as people pray or read and discuss the Scriptures."[92]

Theologies in Europe and North America

We come finally to theologies being done in Europe and North America, until the end of the twentieth century the center of Christianity but now somewhat at the periphery in terms the world's Christian population. Nevertheless, the "global north" remains a major center of theological activity, with venerable theological schools with rich traditions and ample library and theological resources. The future of theology will almost certainly be with the countries of Asia, Latin America, Africa, and Oceania, and among the various subaltern groups in the North, but for the moment European and North American theologizing is thriving. This section will survey very briefly some of the various theologies being done by "majority" persons[93] in these regions. Then it will point to some of the important theology being done by the subaltern groups mentioned above.

Theologies of the European and North American "Majority"
A major issue with which European and North American theologians are concerned is that of the relation of Christianity to other religious ways. One of the most widely read—and controversial—works in this area is U.S. Catholic lay theologian **Paul F. Knitter's** (1939-) *No Other Name*, published in 1985. Knitter lays out several possible approaches to the question, and argues himself for a model of religious pluralism that acknowledges the crucial importance of Christ, and yet denies that in him alone can human beings find salvation. Knitter's work was the stimulus for a lively debate in the last several decades, involving theologians such as Britain's **John Hick** (1922-), Indian **Gavin D'Costa** (1958-), and U.S. Evangelicals **Harold Netland** (1955-), and **S. Mark Heim**.[94] The question of the relation between Christianity and other religious ways has also shaped the emerging discipline of "comparative theology." One engages in comparative theology by studying carefully the texts and practices of another religion, and then reflecting on how what one has studied can illumine and challenge the Christian tradition. Both of the chief practitioners of comparative theology are scholars from the United States: the Jesuit **Francis X. Clooney** and the layman **James Fredericks**.[95]

    Carl F. Henry (1913-2003) was until his death the leading Evangelical theologian in the United States. Today, prominent Evangelicals include U.S. Americans **Donald A. Carson** (1946-), **Miroslav Volf** (born in today's Croatia in 1956), **Kevin Vanhoozer** (1957-), and British **Alister McGrath** (1953-).[96] Greek Orthodox bishop and theologian **John Zizioulas's** work has had immense influence on Western theology, especially his book *Being as Communion: Studies in Personhood*.

    Some of the more prominent systematic theologians today are the German Catholic layman **Peter Hünermann**, the U.S. Americans **David Tracy** (1939-), **Thomas F. O'Meara, Elizabeth A. Johnson** (1941-), **Richard R. Gaillardetz, Bradford Hinze,** and **Terrence Tilley**, Canadian **Douglas John Hall** (1928-), and the British theologian, now archbishop of Canterbury, **Rowan Williams** (1950-).[97]

British theologian **Paul Heelas** has gathered an important group of scholars from both Europe and the United States to reflect on religion and modernity in his collection *Religion, Modernity and Post-Modernity*; **John Milbank** (1952-) and **Stanley Hauerwas** (1940-) are both major spokespersons for a theology that is extremely critical of modernity and its intellectual tools.[98] Milbank, along with **Catherine Pickstock**, is highly influential in the movement of Radical Orthodoxy, a movement that looks to Karl Barth for its origin and spirit.[99]

Feminist theology is also an important, highly influential theological movement in Europe and North America. Perhaps the best introduction to contemporary feminism (with reference to subaltern feminisms as well) is U.S. American **Anne Clifford's** *Introducing Feminist Theology*. Among important feminist theologians we could mention the German **Elizabeth Moltmann Wendel**, **Rosemary Radford Ruether** (1936-), **Elizabeth A. Johnson**, and **Letty M. Russell** (1929-2007).

We have often cited the work of **Robert J. Schreiter** (1947-) in this book. Schreiter is on the cutting edge of several movements of contemporary theology. His 1985 work on contextual theology has become a classic in the field, as has his work on reconciliation and peacemaking. In 2008, together with **Vincent Miller**, Schreiter edited a special issue of *Theological Studies* in which a number of scholars reflected on the issue of globalization.[100]

Theologies of Ecology have been written by Americans **Larry Rasmussen**, **Rosemary Radford Ruether**, and **Sallie McFague** (1934-); and **John Haught** is the leading voice in the dialogue between religion and science, particularly in the context of the challenge of evolution.[101]

This very sketchy overview of European and North American theology done by participants in the "majority" culture gives at least a sense of the variety and intensity of theology in the "global North" today. Although there may be some tendencies to ignore or go counter to concrete circumstances of culture and situations in doing theology (and there are some "neo-Augustinian" theologies that do want to do that),[102] the vast majority recognize the importance of context in any theological effort.

Theologies of Subaltern Groups in Europe and North America

Although there are certainly European theologies done by immigrant groups in Europe, we will focus here on subaltern theologies in North America, since these are much more developed. Once again, we can only give a "bird's-eye view" of complex and vital movements, but what we sketch here will provide a relatively adequate introduction to very significant theological activity.

Black Theology. African American womanist **Shawn Copeland** (1947-) writes that while the term "black theology" may have been used earlier, the term was not claimed until **James Cone** (1947-) published his *Black Theology and Black*

Power in 1969.[103] Cone writes that he was completely unaware of developments in Latin American liberation theology when he wrote the book, but there is a remarkable similarity between his thought and that of theologians like Gustavo Gutiérrez. As he says in the preface to his second book, *A Black Theology of Liberation* (1970), "Christianity is essentially a religion of liberation. . . . Any theology that is indifferent to the theme of liberation is not Christian theology."[104] Cone's 1970 work was a short *summa* of Christian theology, treating all the major doctrines and interpreting them from the perspective of African Americans' struggle for dignity and freedom. For Cone, sin is basically being "white," that is, caught up in a blindness of the fact that God is on the side of the oppressed. Not only does this mean that God is on the side of blacks, however. It means that God and Jesus *are* black, so close is their identification with those who suffer.

Copeland traces three distinct phases in the development of black theology in the United States. A first phase was a *formative* one that grew out of the great civil rights movement of the 1950s and 1960s, as African American leaders grew disenchanted with the moderate position of Martin Luther King Jr. and gravitated toward the movements of "Black Power" inspired by Malcolm X and adopted by members of the Student Non-Violent Coordinating Committee (SNCC). Cone came on the scene in a second phase of *academic development*, when, led by Cone, theologians like Cone's brother **Cecil, Major Jones, J. Deotis Roberts** (1927-) and **Gayraud Wilmore** emerged. A third phase began about 1976 and involved black theology in a critique of "capitalist civilization," which was at the heart of racial oppression. In addition, as a result of a critique by Cone's student **Jacqueline Grant**, black theology began to recognize the existence of sexism within the black community, and so there soon emerged a "womanist" black theology pioneered by Grant, **Katie G. Cannon, Delores Williams**, and several others.[105]

All the theologians mentioned so far in this section have been Protestant, but there are a number of major Catholic contributors to black and womanist theology, among whom number **Shawn Copeland, Jamie T. Phelps**, and **Bryan Massingale**. On several occasions, black Catholic theologians have had joint consultations with Latino/a theologians, to whom we turn next.[106]

Latino/a Theology. We have seen in chapter 11, Hispanic or (preferred today) Latino/a theology goes back to the beginning of the great encounter of Latin American peoples with European explorers or invaders, but contemporary Latino/a theology is perhaps traced to the groundbreaking work of Mexican-American **Virgilio P. Elizondo** (1935-) with the publication of his doctoral dissertation *Mestizaje: The Dialectic of Cultural Birth and the Gospel* in 1978. Gradually, through the 1980s and '90s, theologians such as **María Pilar Aquino** (1956-), **Orlando O. Espín** (1947-), **Arturo Bañuelas, Roberto Goizueta** (1954-), **Alan Figueroa Deck**, and **Gary Riebe-Estrella** (1946-) began to pursue doctoral studies and to publish, mostly in anthologies, some explor-atory essays[107] (one prominent Latino theologian, **Jean-Pierre Ruiz** described Latino/a theology as possessing an "anthological imagination"). Latino/a theol-ogy has certainly been influenced by Latin American liberation theology, but it draws much more on the values of Latino/a culture in all its variety in the United States, as well as the rich theology implicit in Latino/a popular religion.

A third source, which is actually the context of the first two, is *lo cotidiano*, or the events and rhythms of everyday life. It is in the everyday, Latino/a theo-logians insist, that revelation happens and theology begins to be done. In fact, writes Espín, "Revelation could *only* happen (as revelation) in *lo cotidiano*."[108] For Latino/as, theology is constructed from one's daily life and culture, from the viewpoint of a people often marginalized because of their race or legal status in the country.

In 1988 Bañuelas and Espín collaborated to found the Academy of His-panic Theologians in the United States, and the Academy began to publish its own journal, *Journal of Hispanic/Latino Theology*, which has been a rich source of Latino/a theological reflection in the last two decades. Orlando Espín has organized several colloquia of colleagues with the result that two important books have been published, one on the themes of systematic theology, and the other on the theology of tradition (which we have cited several times in chapter 5).[109]

As in black theology, Latina women have claimed a distinctive voice in theologizing. Cuban-American **Ada María Isasi-Díaz** (1943-) has coined the term "*mujerista* theology," after the Spanish word *mujer* (woman), to empha-size the particular perspective of Latinas who, like black women, are victims of a double oppression—from white, racist society, on the one hand, and from Latino men with their *machismo*, on the other. The term also points to the fact that Latina women do theology out of their own experience of popular religiosity and *lo cotidiano* (the "everyday"—a term that has taken on great importance in Latino theologizing). Not all Latinas accept the term *mujerista*, but it is widely referred to. More and more women, in any case, are writ-ing theology, among whom are **Carmen Nanko-Fernández** (1958-), **Nancy Pineda-Madrid**, and **Michelle González**—women who are doing theology *Latinamente* from fresh perspectives.[110]

Because Latino/as in the United States are overwhelmingly Catholic (although this is changing), most Latino/a theologians are Catholic. There are, however, several important Protestant contributors, chief among whom is the eminent historian of doctrine and systematic theologian **Justo L. González** (1937-). González's work is wide-ranging, and his publications are numerous. We have quoted often from his three-volume history of doctrine, *A History of Christian Thought*. In the area of doctrinal history he has published a short his-tory of Christian thought, and he has also—among many other works—writ-ten a short by splendid systematic theology "from a Hispanic perspective."[111]

Asian American and Native American Theologies. It is noteworthy that in her survey of U.S. American subaltern theologies, Shawn Copeland focused only on black theology, Latino/a theology, and Native American theology—and not Asian theology. The omission reflects the fact that, until recently, the presence and importance of Asian Americans has been relatively neglected by U.S. theologians. This is perhaps a result of the few numbers of Asians in the country until after the Hart-Celler Immigration Act of 1965 reversed laws like the Chinese Exclusion Acts of the late nineteenth century.

Jonathan Y. Tan's introduction to Asian American theologies, however, reveals that Asians have of course been in the United States a long time, and, like black and Latino/a theology, Asian American theology goes back to the 1960s and '70s.[112] Tan writes of a first generation of Asian American theologians, the Japanese American Methodist **Roy Isao Sano**, influenced by black liberation theology; Korean American Methodist **Jung Young Lee** (d. 1996) and his contributions in theological method and trinitarian theology; and Chinese American Presbyterian **David Ng** (d. 1997) and his vision of the church as an inclusive, multicultural community.[113] Tan writes of a current second generation of theologians who have broad theological interests, and come from the whole spectrum of Asian ethnic groups in the United States. They not only oppose external challenges of racism and discrimination, as did the first generation, but they focus on internal challenges to their identity and culture.[114] Like other contextual theologians, their starting point is not so much biblical texts or church doctrines, but everyday challenges, everyday life, and cultural values and practices.

In the second generation there are feminist theologians, like Korean American **Chung Hyun Kyung**, best remembered for her provocative address on the Holy Spirit at the 1991 Canberra Assembly of the World Council of Churches and author of *Struggle to Be the Sun Again: Introducing Asian Women's Theology*. Tan himself is a Catholic, as is Vietnamese American **Peter C. Phan** (1943-), one of the most prolific of Asian American theologians. Phan is a patristic scholar and the author of studies on Karl Rahner, but in the last decades he has dedicated himself to Asian American theology. In many ways his *magnum opus* is his translation of Alexandre de Rhodes's Vietnamese catechism, which he published with an extensive introduction.[115] Among his many works we can mention his three volumes of collected essays in mission and inculturation, Asian American theology, and interreligious dialogue.[116] Phan's learning is broad and his energy is immense. Among many projects he is also the general editor of this series on theology in global perspective. Another theologian of wide interests and learning is **Amos Yong**, a Malaysian American Pentecostal. Yong's work deals particularly with the possibilities, from his church tradition, of interreligious dialogue.[117]

One of the challenges of Native American theologies to much of traditional Christian theology—including, in some ways, black, Latino/a, and Asian American theologies—is the Native American centrality of *space* over *time*. Christianity is an *eschatological* religion, but Native American religions revolve around sacred spaces. This is the task of **Vine Deloria** in *God is Red*: to develop "the importance of regaining a sense of space and environment in the midst of time."[118] **George Tinker's** *Missionary Conquest: The Gospel and Native American Cultural Genocide* attempts to expose Euro-American efforts to destroy Native American cultural values and structures, based on a theology of America as the "City on the Hill," the New Israel with a clear, manifest destiny to occupy the land. His is an uncomfortable theology, to say the least, but it is one that is ultimately salutary to the dominant U.S. American culture.

CONCLUSION

When the twentieth century began, most Christians had no idea of the epochal shifts that would take place within the new century. The nineteenth century had been an "Age of Progress," and so people were horrified at the destruction of the Great War. The war was fought, in the famous words of U.S. president Woodrow Wilson, "to make the world safe for democracy." But an unfair treaty at war's end only spawned a more horrible war, along with a Holocaust of six million Jews and the aftermath of almost half a century of cold war between the West and the Soviet Union. The cold war came to an end between 1989 and 1991 with the tearing down of the Berlin Wall and the demise of the Soviet Union, but instead of a time of prosperity and peace, the majority of the world has continued in the beginning of the twenty-first century to experience poverty and violence, and many innocent people have fallen victim to senseless acts of terrorism.

At the same time, the last one hundred years have seen unprecedented developments. No one could have anticipated the speed of the "independence" movements in the middle of the twentieth century. No one could have predicted the renaissance of local religions in all parts of the world. No one could have foreseen the phenomenal growth of Christianity in Asia, Africa, Latin America, and Oceania. In addition, technology has revolutionized both travel and communication and has brought on the phenomenon of globalization with its considerable advantages and disadvantages.

This is the context of Christian theologizing from the beginning of the "short" twentieth century until our present day. Karl Barth and Paul Tillich were both deeply engaged in trying to interpret faith in the contexts of their day. Vatican II was an attempt of the Catholic Church to finally "open the windows" to the contemporary world. Africans, Asians, Latino/as in North America, African Americans, and Christians committed to ecology and dialogue with science are all attempting to understand their faith in their particular contexts—just as did the authors of the New Testament, Anselm in feudal Europe, Luther in a corrupt church. Theology is faith seeking understanding. It has sought that understanding through the ages, and it will continue to do so in the midst of constantly changing cultures and historical events.

QUESTIONS FOR REFLECTION

1. Karl Barth and Karl Rahner are often spoken of as the greatest theologians of the twentieth century? Do you agree? If so, why do you think this is so? If not, why do you disagree?
2. Should we speak of Martin Luther King Jr. as a great theologian of the twentieth century? Why or Why not?
3. What do you think is so important about liberation theology?
4. Why do you think we can speak only of "contextual" or "local" theologies today?
5. Many names are mentioned in this chapter. Can you think of any other theologians from your own culture or ethnic group that should be given mention here?
6. Why is the Second Vatican Council considered such an important event in the history of theology?

SUGGESTIONS FOR FURTHER READING AND STUDY

Giuseppe Alberigo and Joseph Komonchak, eds., *History of Vatican II*, 5 vols. (Maryknoll, N.Y.: Orbis Books; Leuven: Peeters, 1995, 1997, 2000, 2003, 2006).

Gregory Baum, *The Twentieth Century: A Theological Overview* (Maryknoll, N.Y.: Orbis Books, 1999).

Eberhard Busch, *Karl Barth: His Life from Letters and Autobiographical Texts* (Philadelphia: Fortress Press, 1975).

James H. Cone and Gayraud S. Wilmore, *Black Theology: A Documentary History*, 2 vols. (Maryknoll, N.Y.: Orbis Books, 1993).

Ignacio Ellacuría and Jon Sobrino, eds., *Mysterium Liberationis: Fundamental Concepts of Liberation Theology* (Maryknoll, N.Y.: Orbis Books, 1993).

John C. England, Jose Kuttianimattathil, John M. Prior, Lily A. Quintos, David Suh Kwang-sun, Janice Wickeri, eds., *Asian Christian Theologies: A Research Guide to Authors, Movements, Sources*, 3 vols. (Delhi: ISPCK; Maryknoll, N.Y.: Orbis Books, 2002, 2003, 2004).

David Ford, ed., *The Modern Theologians*, 2nd ed. (Oxford: Blackwell, 1997).

Franz-Josef Eilers, ed., *For All the Peoples of Asia*, vol. 2, *Federation of Asian Bishops' Conferences Documents from 1992 to 1996*; vol. 3, *Federation of Asian Bishops' Conferences Documents from 1997 to 2001* (Quezon City, Philippines: Claretian Publications, 1997, 2002).

Gaudencio Rosales and Catalino G. Arévalo, eds., *For All the Peoples of Asia*, vol. 1,

Federation of Asian Bishops' Conferences Documents from 1970 to 1991 (Quezon City, Philippines: Claretian Publications; Maryknoll, N.Y.: Orbis Books, 1992).

David G. Schultenover, ed., *Vatican II: Did Anything Happen?* (New York: Continuum, 2007).

Timothy C. Tennent, *Theology in the Context of World Christianity: How the Global Church Is Influencing the Way We Think About and Discuss Theology* (Grand Rapids: Zondervan, 2007).

David Tracy, *The Achievement of Bernard Lonergan* (New York: Herder & Herder, 1970).

Conclusion

Theology is faith seeking—faith seeking *understanding*, faith seeking *together* in community, faith seeking through various *methods*, faith seeking in active conversation with the riches of tradition *through history*. This book has been an attempt to introduce readers to the great adventure of seeking that theology is. Our perspective has been that of Catholicism, but I hope I have succeeded in showing that a truly *Catholic* theology is one that is in dialogue with other Christian women and men, and with women and men of entirely different faiths. Our perspective has attempted to be *global*, even though, because of the limits of my own training and facility in many non-European languages I may not have always succeeded.

What I hope I have accomplished, however, is the realization on the part of my readers that theology is something that every Christian can do, or better, is something that every Christian actually *does*—in every situation, in every social location, in every culture in our globalized world and global church. Yes, to do theology accurately, to do theology as a ministry in the church, we do need to know the Christian tradition and we do have to respect (and, if need be, to be critical of) the wisdom of our church leaders. Yes, we need the skills of methods and the knowledge of history, and the help of our great ancestors in the faith. But in the end this is all secondary. What matters is that we keep seeking, as best we can, to understand the Mystery that surrounds us, in whatever context we live.

Notes

INTRODUCTION

1. Dorothee Sölle, *Thinking about God: An Introduction to Theology* (London: SCM; Philadelphia: Trinity Press International, 1990); Peter C. Hodgson and Robert H. King, eds., *Readings in Christian Theology* (Philadelphia: Fortress Press, 1985); and *Christian Theology: An Introduction to Its Traditions and Tasks* (1982; newly updated ed., Minneapolis: Fortress Press, 1994); Alister E. McGrath, *Christian Theology: An Introduction* (Oxford/Malden, Mass.: Blackwell, 2001).

2. Kuncheria Pathil and Dominic Veliath, *An Introduction to Theology*, Indian Theological Series (Bangalore: Theological Publications in India, 2003); Aidan Nichols, *The Shape of Catholic Theology: An Introduction to Its Sources, Principles, and History* (Collegeville, Minn.: Liturgical Press, 1991); José M. de Mesa and Lode Wostyn, *Doing Theology: Basic Realities and Processes* (Manila: Wellspring Books, 1982).

3. See Richard P. McBrien, *Catholicism*, 2 vols. (Minneapolis: Winston Press, 1980), 2:1169-86; see also Thomas H. Groome, *What Makes Us Catholic: Eight Gifts for Life* (San Francisco: HarperSanFrancisco, 2002).

4. See Andrew M. Greeley, *The Catholic Imagination* (Berkeley: University of California Press, 2001).

5. See Vatican Council II's Constitution on Divine Revelation, *Dei Verbum* (DV) 2: "Through this revelation, therefore, the invisible God . . . out of the abundance of love speaks to women and men as friends . . . and lives among them, so that God may invite and take them into fellowship with Godself."

6. See DS 3016. The Latin text speaks of the connection of the *mysteries* with each other, but I think the context is clear that "mysteries" here would mean the same as "doctrines." The other two ways that Vatican I speaks of coming to an understanding of doctrines is (1) by analogy and (2) by reflecting on the eschatological aspect of every doctrine—their connection with the "final end of humanity," as the text says. In her book in this series, Australian theologian Anne Hunt uses this comparative method to probe the doctrine of the Trinity. See *The Trinity* (Maryknoll, N.Y.: Orbis Books, 2005), esp. 3-4.

7. Rebecca Button Prichard, *Sensing the Spirit: The Holy Spirit in Feminist Perspective* (St. Louis, Mo.: Chalice Press, 1999), 7.

8. Ibid.

9. For further reflections on this important fact, see my book *Models of Contextual Theology*, Faith and Culture Series (Maryknoll, N.Y.: Orbis Books, 2002).

10. See Amy-Jill Levine, "Hermeneutics of Suspicion," in Letty M. Russell and J. Shannon Clarkson, eds., *Dictionary of Feminist Theologies* (Louisville, Ky.: Westminster John Knox Press, 1996), 140-41.

11. Karl Rahner, "Toward a Fundamental Interpretation of Vatican II," *Theological Studies* 40, no. 4 (1979): 716-27.

1. MYSTERY AND REVELATION

1. John Macquarrie, *God-talk: An Examination of the Language and Logic of Theology* (London: SCM Press, 1967); Rosemary Radford Ruether, *Sexism and God-Talk: Toward a Feminist Theology* (Boston: Beacon Press, 1993).

2. René Latourelle, *Theology: Science of Salvation* (Staten Island, N.Y.: Alba House, 1969), 3. More precisely, Latourelle says that theology is knowledge of God in a double sense—it is the knowledge that God has of Godself (and so *God's* knowledge) and the knowledge that human beings have of, or *about*, God. As a human endeavor, however, theology has this more objective sense.

3. Thomas Aquinas, *Summa Theologiae*, part I, question 1, article 7. See *St. Thomas Aquinas, Summa Theologiae*, volume I (1a 1), *Christian Theology*, trans. Thomas Gilby (New York: McGraw-Hill; London: Eyre & Spotswoodie, 1963), 25-28.

4. Ludwig Ott, *Fundamentals of Catholic Dogma* (St. Louis, Mo.: B. Herder, 1957), 1.

5. Stanley J. Samartha, "The Asian Context: Sources and Trends," in R. S. Sugirtharajah, ed., *Voices from the Margins: Interpreting the Bible in the Third World* (Maryknoll, N.Y.: Orbis Books, 1991), 48.

6. Ronaldo Muñoz, *The God of Christians* (Maryknoll, N.Y.: Orbis Books, 1990), 4.

7. Gregory of Nyssa, *De beatitudinibus*, PG 44, column 1263, *Oratio* VI, 41. Also found in *The Liturgy of the Hours*, Office of Readings for Thursday of the Twelfth Week in Ordinary Time.

8. Augustine, *Sermo LII*, chapter VI, 16, PL 38, col. 360.

9. Isidore of Seville, *Sentences* 1.2.4, *Santos Padres Españoles*, volume 2 (Madrid, 1971–), 229. Quoted in Jaroslav Pelikan, *The Christian Tradition: A History of the Development of Doctrine*, volume 3, *The Growth of Medieval Theology (600-1300)* (Chicago: University of Chicago Press, 1971–89), 20.

10. Thomas Aquinas, *Summa Theologiae*, part I, question 3, article 3, in *St. Thomas Aquinas, Summa Theologica*, volume 1, trans. Fathers of the English Dominican Province (New York: Benziger Brothers, 1947), 14.

11. Ibid., part I, question 3, article 10, Dominican Province translation, 69.

12. I owe this expression from the sport of archery to Professor David Burrell in his seminar on Aquinas at the University of Notre Dame. For Burrell's more formal treatment, see his essay "Aquinas: Articulating Transcendence," in *Exercises in Religious Understanding* (Notre Dame, Ind.: University of Notre Dame Press, 1974), 80-140, esp. 132-33.

13. Cited in Thomas F. O'Meara, *Thomas Aquinas: Theologian* (Notre Dame, Ind.: University of Notre Dame Press, 1997), 31. O'Meara, referring to the work of James A. Weisheipl, suggests that the cause of his lethargy might have been either overwork or, more likely, a stroke or a brain tumor. But O'Meara, like Weisheipl, does not discount the mystical in this experience. See James A. Weisheipl, *Friar Thomas d'Aquino* (New York: Doubleday, 1974), 321-22.

14. See Joseph Campbell (with Bill Moyers), *The Power of Myth* (New York: Doubleday, 1988), 49.

15. David L. Edwards, *Christianity: The First Two Thousand Years* (Maryknoll, N.Y.: Orbis Books, 1997), 261.

16. Pascal's *Memorial*, quoted in Hans Küng, *Does God Exist? An Answer for Today* (New York: Vintage Books, 1981), 57.

17. Quoted in Shaun McCarty, *Partners in the Divine Dance of Our 3-Personed God* (New York/Mahwah, N.J.: Paulist Press, Illumination Books, 1996), 20.

18. See Eberhard Busch, *Karl Barth: His Life from Letters and Autobiographical Texts* (Philadelphia: Fortress Press, 1976), 116.

19. Paul Tillich, *Dynamics of Faith* (New York: Harper Torchbooks, 1958), 61.

20. Michael McCauley, "The Deep Mystery of God," *America* 191, no. 11 (October 18, 2004): 17.

21. Elizabeth A. Johnson, *She Who Is: The Mystery of God in Feminist Theological Discourse* (New York: Crossroad, 1992), 105.

22. See Sheldon B. Kopp, *If You Meet the Buddha on the Road, Kill Him! The Pilgrimage of Psychotherapy Patients* (Toronto/New York: Bantam Books, 1976).

23. Kena Upanishad, Part 2, in Juan Mascaró, trans., *The Upanishads* (Hammondsworth, Middlesex, England: Penguin Books, 1965), 52.

24. Lao Tsu, *Tao Te Ching*, 1, trans. Gia-Fu Feng and Jane English (New York: Vintage Books, 1972).

25. Quoted in Fazlur Rahman, *Major Themes of the Qur'an*, 2nd ed. (Minneapolis, Minn.: Biblioteca Islamica, 1994), 4.

26. Martin Buber, *I and Thou* (New York: Charles Scribner's Sons, 1958), 160.

27. Gregory of Nyssa, *Homily VII in Cant.*, PG 44, col. 941c, quoted in Yves Congar, *I Believe in the Holy Spirit* 1 (3 vols. in 1; New York: Crossroad, 1997), 77.

28. John Sanders, *The God Who Risks: A Theology of Providence* (Downers Grove, Ill.: InterVarsity Press, 1998), 281.

29. Hilary of Poitiers, *De Trinitate* 12.56, SC 462, 466, quoted in Congar, *I Believe*, 3:213.

30. Gabriel Marcel, *Being and Having* (New York: Harper Torchbooks, 1965), 117.

31. Ibid. The distinction between problem and mystery is something that Marcel says is basic to his entire thought (see Gabriel Marcel, "Creative Fidelity," in *Creative Fidelity* [New York: Farrar, Straus, 1964], 152). For a full treatment of the distinction as it is developed throughout Marcel's thought, see Albert B. Randall, *The Mystery of Hope in the Philosophy of Gabriel Marcel 1888-1973: Hope and Homo Viator* (Lewiston, N.Y./Queenston, Ont./ Lampeter, U.K.: Edwin Mellen Press, 1992), 121-93.

32. "Immortal, Invisible, God Only Wise," words by Walter Chalmers Smith (1824-1908), 1867.

33. John Haught, *Mystery and Promise: A Theology of Revelation* (Collegeville, Minn.: Liturgical Press, 1993), 46-47.

34. Buber, *I and Thou*, 3-34.

35. John Macmurray, *Persons in Relation* (New York: Harper, 1961), 28-29.

36. Catherine Mowry LaCugna, *God for Us: The Trinity and Christian Life* (San Francisco: HarperSanFrancisco, 1991), 323. See also LaCugna's chapter "The Trinitarian Mystery of God" in Francis Schüssler Fiorenza and John Galvin, eds. *Systematic Theology: Roman Catholic Perspectives* (Minneapolis, Minn.: Fortress Press, 1991), 1:156-57.

37. Irenaeus of Lyons, *Adversus Haereses* 4.14.3; SC 100, 542, 546. The passage is also found in Office of Readings, Wednesday of Second Week of Lent.

38. Georges Bernanos, *Diary of a Country Priest* (New York: Macmillan, 1937); Gerard Manley Hopkins, "God's Grandeur," in *A Hopkins Reader*, ed. John Pick (New York: Oxford University Press, 1953), 13.

39. John Wood Oman, *Honest Religion* (Cambridge: Cambridge University Press, 1941), 194. I am following closely my description of Oman's experience in my book *John Oman and His Doctrine of God* (Cambridge: Cambridge University Press, 1992), 58-59.

40. John V. Taylor, *The Go-Between God: The Holy Spirit and the Christian Mission* (New York: Oxford University Press, 1979), 19.

41. Flannery O'Connor, "The Teaching of Literature," quoted in Robert Coles, *Flannery O'Connor's South* (Baton Rouge: Louisiana State University Press, 1980), 104.

42. Edmund Chia, *Towards a Theology of Dialogue: Schillebeeckx's Method as Bridge between Vatican's Dominus Iesus and Asia's FABC Theology* (Bangkok, Thailand: Privately printed, 2003), 220. The quotation is from "Edward Schillebeeckx: An Orientation to His Thought," in Robert J. Schreiter, ed., *The Schillebeeckx Reader* (New York: Crossroad, 1984), 17.

43. See David Tracy, *Blessed Rage for Order* (New York: Seabury Press, 1975), 93.

44. Ma. Christina A. Astorga, "Culture, Religion, and Moral Vision: A Theological

Discourse on the Filipino People Power Revolution of 1986," *Theological Studies* 67, no. 3 (September 2006): 567-601.

45. Tracy, *Blessed Rage*, 93.

46. Roberto S. Goizueta, *Caminemos con Jesús: Toward a Hispanic/Latino Theology of Accompaniment* (Maryknoll, N.Y.: Orbis Books, 1995), 49-50.

47. Hildegard of Bingen, *Scivias*, "Declaration," trans. Mother Columba Hart and Jane Bishop, Classics of Western Spirituality (New York/Mahwah, N.J.: Paulist Press, 1990), 59.

48. Augustine of Hippo, *Confessions*, 8, 12.

49. Robert Ellsberg, *All Saints: Daily Reflections on Saints, Prophets, and Witnesses for Our Time* (New York: Crossroad, 1997), 34.

50. Douglas John Hall, *Thinking the Faith: Christian Theology in a North American Context* (Minneapolis, Minn.: Augsburg Fortress, 1989), 443.

51. See Edward Schillebeeckx, *Jesus: An Experiment in Christology* (New York: Vintage Books, 1981), 548-50. We will reflect on the nature of doctrine in part 2 (chapter 5); however, for a fine short introduction to the notion of doctrine, see Justo L. González, *A Concise History of Christian Doctrine* (Nashville, Tenn.: Abingdon Press, 2005), 2-14.

52. Juan Luis Segundo, *Christ in the Spiritual Exercises of St. Ignatius* (Maryknoll, N.Y.: Orbis Books, 1987), 22-26.

53. See Justo L. González, *A History of Christian Thought*, vol. 1, *From the Beginnings to the Council of Chalcedon*, rev. ed. (Nashville, Tenn.: Abingdon Press, 1987), 298. See also Walter Kasper, *The God of Jesus Christ* (New York: Crossroad, 1984), 183.

54. See Dale T. Irvin and Scott W. Sunquist, *History of the World Christian Movement*, vol. 1, *Earliest Christianity to 1453* (Maryknoll, N.Y.: Orbis Books, 2001), 174.

55. G. van Noort, *Dogmatic Theology*, vol. 1, *The True Religion*, from the 5th ed., ed. J. P. Verhaar (Westminster, Md.: Newman Press, 1955), 34-35.

56. Aidan Nichols, *The Shape of Catholic Theology: An Introduction to Its Sources, Principles, and History* (Collegeville, Minn.: Liturgical Press, 1991), 273.

57. Hall, *Thinking the Faith*, 406.

58. José M. de Mesa, *Why Theology Is Never Far from Home* (Manila: De La Salle University Press, 2003), xiv.

59. Ibid., xiv-xv.

2. FAITH AND THEOLOGY

1. Henri J. M. Nouwen, *Creative Ministry* (Garden City, N.Y.: Doubleday Image Books, 1978), 17.

2. José M. de Mesa and Lode Wostyn, *Doing Theology: Basic Realities and Processes* (Quezon City, Philippines: Claretian Publications, 1990), 48.

3. My student Becky Otte warns of the gender stereotype at work here and suggests other images of gift exchange, such as between friends or parents giving a gift to their child or children. While I certainly agree with Becky's caution here, I decided to use the image of a man giving flowers to a woman because it better illustrates, I believe, how the gift of *self*—the heart—is offered and received and reciprocated. But again, Becky's point is well taken.

4. Here and in the next several paragraphs I am following my former teacher Juan Alfaro. See his *Fides, Spes, Caritas* (Rome: Pontifical Gregorian University, 1968), 186-97. See also Juan Alfaro, "II. Faith," in Karl Rahner et al., eds., *Sacramentum Mundi: An Encyclopedia of Theology*, vol. 2 (London: Burns & Oates, 1968), 313-22, esp. 321; and Avery Dulles, *The Assurance of Things Hoped For: A Theology of Christian Faith* (Oxford/New York: Oxford University Press, 1994), 186.

5. John F. Haught, *God after Darwin: A Theology of Evolution* (Boulder, Colo.: Westview Press, 2000). See, for example, Haught's development on p. 47.

6. See Ernest Weekly, "believe," *A Concise Etymological Dictionary of Modern English* (New York: E. P. Dutton, 1952), 39.

7. Dulles, *Assurance of Things Hoped For*, 186.

8. See, for example, Pablo Richard, "Theology in the Theology of Liberation," in Ignacio Ellacuría and Jon Sobrino, eds., *Mysterium Liberationis: Fundamental Concepts of Liberation Theology* (Maryknoll, N.Y.: Orbis Books, 1993), 154-60; Joyce Ann Mercer, "Faith," in Letty M. Russell and J. Shannon Clarkson, eds., *Dictionary of Feminist Theologies* (Louisville, Ky.: Westminster John Knox Press, 1996), 96-97; James D. Whitehead and Evelyn Eaton Whitehead, *Method in Ministry: Theological Reflection and Christian Ministry*, rev. ed. (Kansas City, Mo.: Sheed & Ward, 1995).

9. Mercer, "Faith," 96.

10. Dulles, *Assurance of Things Hoped For*, 186.

11. Walter M. Abbott, ed., *The Documents of Vatican II* (New York: Herder & Herder/ Association Press, 1966), 113 n. 7.

12. William James, *The Varieties of Religious Experience* (New York: Collier, 1961), 140.

13. Dag Hammerskjöld, *Markings*, trans. W. H. Auden and Leif Sjöberg (London: Faber & Faber, 1964), 169 (Whitsunday, 1961).

14. See Dulles, *Assurance of Things Hope For*, 224-26. Dulles cites texts from the Second Council of Orange, the Council of Trent, and Vatican II, as well as texts from Scripture and from Aquinas.

15. Ibid., 227.

16. John D. Davies, *Beginning Now* (London: Collins, 1971), 219-20, quoted in John V. Taylor, *The Go-Between God: The Holy Spirit and the Christian Mission* (New York: Oxford University Press, 1979), 173.

17. Hans Küng, *On Being a Christian* (Garden City, N.Y.: Doubleday, 1976), 74-75.

18. Paul Tillich, *Dynamics of Faith* (New York: Harper Torchbooks, 1958), 20.

19. Ibid., 16.

20. Karl Rahner, *Hearers of the Word* (New York: Herder & Herder, 1969), esp. 53-68.

21. For the term "eros of the mind," see Bernard J. F. Lonergan, *Insight: A Study of Human Understanding* (New York: Philosophical Library, 1957), 221; the quotation is on p. 638.

22. Ibid., 10.

23. The ad was in the magazine *Outside* (November 1999), the page (unnumbered) after page 41.

24. René Latourelle, *Theology: Science of Salvation* (Staten Island, N.Y.: Alba House, 1969), 30.

25. Anselm of Canterbury, *Proslogion*, *The Prayers and Meditations of Saint Anselm*, trans. in Sister Benedicta Ward, S.L.G. (Middlesex, U.K./New York: Penguin Books, 1973), 239.

26. Sacred Congregation for Education, "The Theological Formation of Future Priests" (Vatican City: Vatican Polyglot Press, 1976), 10, #19.

27. Richard P. McBrien, *Catholicism*, 2 vols. (Minneapolis: Winston Press, 1980), 1:60-61.

28. John Paul II, encyclical letter *Fides et Ratio* 105 (henceforth FR), http://www.vatican .va/holy_father/...C_15101998_fides-et-ratio_en.shtml. Note 128 of the encyclical makes reference to Bonaventure's work: *Prologus*, 4: *Opera Omnia* (Florence, 1891), vol. 5:296.

29. Douglas John Hall, *Thinking the Faith: Christian Theology in a North American Context* (Minneapolis: Augsburg Fortress, 1989), 255.

30. See Roger Haight, *An Alternative Vision: An Interpretation of Liberation Theology* (New York/Mahwah, N.J.: Paulist Press, 1985), 64-82.

31. Aloysius Pieris, *An Asian Theology of Liberation* (Maryknoll, N.Y.: Orbis Books, 1988), 45-50.

32. Dorothee Sölle, *Thinking about God: An Introduction to Theology* (London: SCM; Philadelphia: Trinity Press International, 1990), 4.

33. Kosuke Koyama, *Water Buffalo Theology* (Maryknoll, N.Y.: Orbis Books, 1999), 142.

34. Robert J. Schreiter, *Constructing Local Theologies* (Maryknoll, N.Y.: Orbis Books, 1985), 119-20. Schreiter's five criteria are as follows: (1) the cohesiveness of Christian performance, (2) the worshiping context and Christian performance, (3) the praxis of the community and Christian performance, (4) the judgment of other churches and Christian performance [this is the one I am referring to here], and (5) the challenge to other churches and Christian performance. See Schreiter, 117-21, and my discussion of Schreiter's criteria in *Models of Contextual Theology* (Maryknoll, N.Y.: Orbis Books, 2004), 22-25.

35. David Tracy, *Blessed Rage for Order: The New Pluralism in Theology* (New York: Seabury Press, 1975), 22.

36. See Blaise Pascal, *Pensées*, 474, in Jacques Chevalier, ed., Pascal, *Oeuvres Completes* (Paris: Gallimard, Bibliothéque de la Pleiade, 1954), 1221. The noted twentieth-century spiritual writer John Dunne quotes Pascal's phrase "The heart has its reasons that reasons do not know" as the basis for his book *The Reasons of the Heart* (Notre Dame, Ind.: University of Notre Dame Press, 1979). See John Henry Newman, *An Essay in Aid of a Grammar of Assent* (Notre Dame, Ind.: University of Notre Dame Press, 1979). Cardinal Newman speaks of reasoning by means of "informal inference" or the employment of the "illative sense." Newman speaks of "converging probabilities" in several places in this work, e.g., pp. 281-82: ". . . the mind itself is more versatile and vigorous than any of its works. . . . It determines what science cannot determine, the limit of converging probablilities and the reasons sufficient for a proof." See also Michael Polanyi, *Personal Knowledge: Towards a Post-Critical Philosophy* (Chicago: University of Chicago Press, 1962).

37. Hall, *Thinking the Faith*, 383.

38. See Néstor Oscar Míguez, "Hermeneutical Circle," in Virginia Fabella and R. S. Sugirtharajah, eds., *Dictionary of Third World Theologies* (Maryknoll, N.Y.: Orbis Books, 2000), 97; Amy-Jill Levine, "Hermeneutics of Suspicion," in Letty M. Russell and J. Shannon Clarkson, eds., *Dictionary of Feminist Theologies* (Louisville, Ky.: Westminster John Knox Press, 1996), 140-41; José M. de Mesa, *Why Theology Is Never Far from Home* (Manila: De La Salle University Press, 2003), 111-95.

39. Fritz Buri, *Thinking Faith* (Philadelphia: Fortress Press, 1968), 86-87. Quoted in Hall, *Thinking the Faith*, 57.

40. Hall, *Thinking the Faith*, 251.

41. Tertullian, *On the Flesh of Christ* 5, quoted in Ed L. Miller, ed., *Classical Statements on Faith and Reason* (New York: Random House, 1970), xi. Miller's book is a fine collection of texts that deal with the question of the relationship between faith and reason, and he provides a short but excellent introduction to the topic on pp. ix-xv.

42. Tertullian, *Proscriptions against the Heretics* 7, in Miller, *Classical Statements*, 5.

43. Karl Barth, *The Epistle to the Romans* (London: Oxford University Press, H. Milford, 1933), 143-44, quoted in Gerald O'Collins, *The Case against Dogma* (New York: Paulist Press, 1975), 14.

44. Miller, *Classical Statements*, xi.

45. Clement of Alexandria, *Stromata* 1.2, in Miller, *Classical Statements*, 12.

46. Harold O. J. Brown, "On Method and Means in Theology," in John D. Woodbridge and Thomas Edward McComiskey, eds., *Doing Theology in Today's World* (Grand Rapids: Zondervan, 1991), 147.

47. See McBrien, *Catholicism*, 2:1174.

48. Aidan Nichols, *The Shape of Catholic Theology: An Introduction to Its Sources, Principles, and History* (Collegeville, Minn.: Liturgical Press, 1991), 13-14.

49. Augustine, *In Johannis Evangelium* 39.6, in John Chapin, ed., *The Book of Catholic Quotations* (New York: Farrar, Straus & Cudahy, 1956), 57.

50. See Eugene TeSelle, "Faith," in Allan D. Fitzgerald, ed., *Augustine through the Ages* (Grand Rapids: William B. Eerdmans, 1999), 347-50. The quotation is from *De Praedestinatione Sanctorum* 2.5, PL 44:963, quoted in FR 79.

51. Blaise Pascal in Chapin, *Catholic Quotations*, 332.

52. These words appear as the epigraph on the first page of Louis J. Luzbetak's *The Church and Cultures* (Maryknoll, N.Y.: Orbis Books, 1988). The Web page http://www.quotationspage.com/quote/24949.html gives the reference as *Science, Philosophy and Religion: A Symposium*, 1941.

3. FAITH SEEKING UNDERSTANDING

1. See http://worldmusiccentral.org/article.php/the_rough_guide_to_turkish_cafe.

2. See http://worldmusiccentral.org/article.php/k_naan_earthdance_2008.

3. See http://www.npr.org/templates/story/story.php?storyId=15400402 for a program from U.S. National Public Radio on how chicha music had its origins in U.S. rock 'n' roll and has expanded from Peru throughout Latin America.

4. Michael Amaladoss, foreword to Jojo M. Fung, *Shoes-Off Barefoot We Walk: A Theology of Shoes-Off* (Kuala Lumpur: Longman Malaysia, 1992), xi.

5. Quoted in Fredrica Harris Thompsett, *We Are Theologians: Strengthening the People of the Episcopal Church* (Cambridge, Mass.: Cowley, 1989), 68.

6. John Shea, "Theology at the Grassroots," *Church* 3 (Spring 1986): 3-7.

7. Quoted in Philip and Sally Sharper, eds., *The Gospel in Art by the Peasants of Solentiname* (Maryknoll, N.Y.: Orbis Books; Dublin: Gill and Macmillan, 1984), 69. See Ernesto Cardenal, *The Gospel of Solentiname*, 4 vols. (Maryknoll, N.Y.: Orbis Books, 1976, 1978, 1979, 1982).

8. Ian M. Fraser, "Theology at the Base," in Samuel Amirtham and John S. Pobee, eds., *Theology by the People: Reflections on Doing Theology in Community* (Geneva: World Council of Churches, 1986), 62.

9. Sadayanday Batumalai, *An Introduction to Asian Theology* (Delhi: Indian Society for Promoting Christian Knowledge, 1991), 7.

10. Aidan Nichols, *The Shape of Catholic Theology: An Introduction to Its Sources, Principles, and History* (Collegeville, Minn.: Liturgical Press, 1991), 32.

11. Howard W. Stone and James O. Duke, *How to Think Theologically* (Minneapolis: Fortress Press, 1996), 16-19.

12. René Latourelle, *Theology: Science of Salvation* (Staten Island, N.Y.: Alba House, 1969), 8.

13. Clodovis Boff, "Epistemology and Method of the Theology of Liberation," in Ignacio Ellacuría and Jon Sobrino, eds., *Mysterium Liberationis: Fundamental Concepts of Liberation Theology* (Maryknoll, N.Y.: Orbis Books, 1993), 66-72.

14. Peter Schineller, "Inculturation and Modernity," *Sedos Bulletin* 2 (February 15, 1988): 47.

15. Leonardo N. Mercado, *Elements of Filipino Theology* (Tacloban, Philippines: Divine Word University, 1975), 13. Amirtham and Pobee, *Theology by the People*, 7.

16. Patricia O'Connell Killen, "Assisting Adults to Think Theologically," in James D. Whitehead and Evelyn Eaton Whitehead, *Method in Ministry: Theological Reflection and Christian Ministry*, rev. ed. (Kansas City, Mo.: Sheed & Ward, 1995), 103-11.

17. See, for example, Timoteo D. Gener, "Every Filipino Christian a Theologian: A Way of Advancing Local Theology for the 21ˢᵗ Century," in E. Acoba et al., *Doing Theology in the Philippines* (Quezon City / Manila: Asian Theological Seminary / OMF Literature Inc., 2005), 3-23.

18. Stone and Duke, *How to Think Theologically*, 6.

19. Michael H. Taylor, "People at Work," in Amirtham and Pobee, *Theology by the People*, 124.

20. See Joseph G. Healey, ed., *Once upon a Time in Africa: Stories of Wisdom and Joy* (Maryknoll, N.Y.: Orbis Books, 2004), 49; see also Satish Kumar, "You Are, Therefore I Am," http://www.resurgence.org/resurgence/issues/kumar199.htm; "I Am Because We Are," http://livingtheology.net/?p=38.

21. See Yves M. Congar, *Tradition and Traditions: An Historical and Theological Essay* (London: Burns & Oates, 1966). Three significant books on tradition are John E. Theil, *Senses of Tradition: Continuity and Development in Catholic Faith* (New York: Oxford University Press, 2000); Jan H. Pranger, *Redeeming Tradition: Inculturation, Contextualization, and Tradition in a Postcolonial Perspective* (Privately published as a doctoral dissertation at the University of Groningen, Holland); and Orlando O. Espín and Gary Macy, eds., *Futuring Our Past: Explorations in the Theology of Tradition* (Maryknoll, N.Y.: Orbis Books, 2006).

22. Letty M. Russell, *Church in the Round: Feminist Interpretation of the Church* (Louisville, Ky.: Westminster John Knox Press, 1993), 35-45.

23. Dorothy Day, "Letter to an Agnostic," *America* (August 4, 1934), republished in *America* (April 17, 1999): 7.

24. Jaroslav Pelikan, *The Vindication of Tradition* (New Haven: Yale University Press, 1984), 65.

25. See Gary Riebe-Estrella, "Tradition as Conversation," in Espín and Macy, *Futuring Our Past*, 141-56.

26. International Theological Commission, *Theses on the Relationship between the Ecclesiastical Magisterium and Theology* (Washington, D.C.: United States Catholic Conference, 1977).

27. See Richard R. Gaillardetz, *By What Authority? A Primer on Scripture, the Magisterium, and the Sense of the Faithful* (Collegeville, Minn.: Liturgical Press, 2003), 121-45; Robert McClory, *Faithful Dissenters: Stories of Men and Women Who Loved and Changed the Church* (Maryknoll, N.Y.: Orbis Books, 2000).

28. *Catechism of the Catholic Church* (New York: Doubleday Image Books, 1994); Heinrich Denzinger and Adolf Schönmetzer, *Enchiridion Symbolorum, Definitionum et Declarationum de Rebus Fidei et Morum*, 34th ed. (Barcelona/Freiburg/Rome/New York: Herder, 1967); Jaroslav Pelikan and Valerie Hotchkiss, eds., *Creeds and Confessions of Faith in the Christian Tradition* (New Haven: Yale University Press, 2003).

29. On *habitus*, see especially Edward Farley, *Theologia: The Fragmentation and Unity of Theological Education* (Philadelphia: Fortress Press, 1983); on "theologizing person," see Eugene Kennedy, *Comfort My People: The Pastoral Presence of the Church* (New York: Sheed & Ward, 1968), 137-51.

30. The Mudflower Collective, *God's Fierce Whimsy: Feminism and Theological Education* (New York: Pilgrim Press, 1985), 140.

31. Martin Luther, *Weimar Aufgabe* 5.162.28. One sees several variants of Luther's dictum. See, for example, Douglas John Hall, *Thinking the Faith: Christian Theology in a North American Context* (Minneapolis: Augsburg Fortress, 1989), 237-38.

32. Stephen B. Bevans, *Models of Contextual Theology* (Maryknoll, N.Y.: Orbis Books, 2002), 3-15.

33. Robert J. Schreiter, *Constructing Local Theologies* (Maryknoll, N.Y.: Orbis Books, 1985), 4.

34. John Paul II, Address to the Italian National Congress of the Ecclesial Movement for Cultural Commitment, January 16, 1982, *L'Osservatore Romano* (English edition), June 28, 1982, 7.

35. Andrew F. Walls, "The Great Commission 1910-2010," lecture delivered at the University of Edinburgh, 2002. See http://www.towards2010.org.uk/downloads/t2010 paper01walls.pdf, 9.

36. See Juan Alfaro, *Fides, Spes, Caritas* (Rome: Pontifical Gregorian University, 1968); see also Avery Dulles, *The Assurance of Things Hoped For: A Theology of Christian Faith* (New York: Oxford University Press, 1994), 186.

37. Karl Barth, *Church Dogmatics* I/2 (Edinburgh: T&T Clark, 1956), 792.

38. "Ecumenical Dialogue of Third World Theologians, Dar es Salaam, Tanzania, August 5-12, 1976. Final Statement," in Sergio Torres and Virginia Fabella, eds., *The Emergent Gospel* (Maryknoll, N.Y.: Orbis Books, 1978), 269.

39. Karl Rahner, "A Theology That We Can Live With," in *Theological Investigations* XXI (New York: Crossroad, 1988), 100.

40. Gustavo Gutiérrez, *A Theology of Liberation* (Maryknoll, NY: Orbis Books, 1973), 13.

41. Fraser, "Theology at the Base," 55.

42. Nichols, *Shape of Catholic Theology*, 26.

43. Geoffrey Wainwright, "Theology as Churchly Reflection," in Theodore W. Jennings, ed., *The Vocation of the Theologian* (Philadelphia: Fortress Press, 1985), 18-20.

44. Karl Barth, *Evangelical Theology: An Introduction*, Fontana Library (London: Collins, 1963), 149.

45. Hall, *Thinking the Faith*, 289.

46. Charles Journet, *The Wisdom of Faith: An Introduction to Theology* (Westminster, Md.: Newman Press, 1952), 49-50.

47. Quoted in Thompsett, *We Are Theologians*, 57.

48. Henri Nouwen, *In the Name of Jesus: Reflections on Christian Leadership* (New York: Crossroad, 1996), 68.

49. David Tracy, *Blessed Rage for Order: The New Pluralism in Theology* (New York: Seabury Press, 1975), 45-46.

50. Whitehead and Whitehead, *Method in Ministry*, 103-11.

51. Martin Kähler, *Schriften zur Christologie und Mission* (1908; repr., Munich: Chr. Kaiser Verlag, 1971), 189-90; Martin Hengel, "The Origins of the Christian Mission," in idem, *Between Jesus and Paul: Studies in the Earliest History of Christianity* (London: SCM, 1983), 53. Both are quoted in David J. Bosch, *Transforming Mission: Paradigm Shifts in Theology of Mission* (Maryknoll, N.Y.: Orbis Books, 1991), 16 and 15 respectively.

52. Farley, *Theologia*, 31, 77.

53. See Jürgen Schuster, "Karl Hartenstein: Mission as a Focus on the End," *Mission Studies* 19, 1, 37 (2002): 53-81; Wilhelm Andersen, *Towards a Theology of Mission: A Study of the Encounter between the Missionary Enterprise and the Church and Its Theology*, IMC Research Pamphlet no. 2 (London: SCM Press, 1955).

54. J. Andrew Kirk, *The Mission of Theology and Theology as Mission* (Valley Forge, Pa.: Trinity Press International, 1997), 51. See also the work of U.S. Latino (Puerto Rican) missiologist Carlos F. Cardoza-Orlandi, *Mission: An Essential Guide* (Nashville, Tenn.: Abingdon Press, 2002); and Peter C. Phan, "Proclamation of the Reign of God as Mission of the Church: What for, to Whom, by Whom, with Whom and How?" in idem, *In Our Own Tongues: Perspectives from Asia on Mission and Inculturation* (Maryknoll, N.Y.: Orbis Books, 2003), 32-44.

55. Stephen Bevans, "Wisdom from the Margins: Systematic Theology and the Missiological Imagination," in Richard C. Sparks, ed., *Proceedings of the Fifty-sixth Annual Convention, The Catholic Theological Society of America* (Berkeley, Calif.: Catholic Theological Society of America, 2001), 21-42.

56. Federation of Asian Bishops' Conferences, Office of Theological Concerns, "The Spirit at Work in Asia Today," in Franz-Josef Eilers, ed., *For All the Peoples of Asia*, vol. 3 (Quezon City, Philippines: Claretian Publications, 2002), 320.

57. See Stephen Bevans, "The Church as Creation of the Holy Spirit: Unpacking a Missionary Image," *Missiology: An International Review* 35, no. 1 (January 2007): 5-21.

58. Wilhelm Andersen, "Further Toward a Theology of Mission," in Gerald H. Anderson, ed., *The Theology of the Christian Mission* (Nashville, Tenn.: Abingdon Press, 1961), 313.

59. Robert Ellsberg, *All Saints: Daily Reflections on Saints, Prophets, and Witnesses for Our Time* (New York: Crossroad, 1997), 128.

60. See "The Keiskamma Altarpiece," *UCLA AIDS Institute Insider* 5, 1 (Summer 2007): 5-10; and Carol Brown, "Hope Restored, History Reclaimed," ibid., 11-17. See also the Web site http://www.keiskamma.org/art/keiskamma-altarpiece.

61. David Tracy, *The Analogical Imagination: Christian Theology and the Culture of Pluralism* (New York: Crossroad, 1981), 116.

PART II. FAITH SEEKING TOGETHER

1. Gustavo Gutiérrez, "The Task of Theology and Ecclesial Experience," in Leonardo Boff and Virgilio Elizondo, eds., *La Iglesia Popular: Between Fear and Hope. Concilium* 176 (Edinburgh: T&T Clark, 1984), 63.

2. Helmut Thielicke, *A Little Exercise for Young Theologians* (Grand Rapids: William B. Eerdmans, 1962), 4-5.

3. Geoffrey Wainwright, "Churchly Reflection," in Theodore W. Jennings Jr., ed., *The Vocation of the Theologian* (Philadelphia: Fortress Press, 1985), 19.

4. Michael H. Taylor, "People at Work," in Samuel Amirtham and John S. Pobee, eds., *Theology by the People: Reflections on Doing Theology in Community* (Geneva: World Council of Churches, 1986), 124.

5. Bishop James Malone, "How Bishops and Theologians Relate," *Origins* 16, no. 9 (July 31, 1986), 172.

4. THE COMMUNITY AS SOURCE OF THEOLOGY

1. Reinhold Niebuhr, *The Nature and Destiny of Man: A Christian Interpretation* (London: Nisbet, 1941), 20.

2. René Descartes, *Discourse on Method and Meditations*, trans. Lawrence J. Lafleur (Indianapolis: Bobbs-Merrill Educational, 1960), 24.

3. This term is used by Robert Bellah and his colleagues to describe the basic reality of human persons prior to being linked together, by necessity, in society. See Robert Bellah, Richard Madsen, William M. Sullivan, Ann Swidler, and Steven M. Tipton, *Habits of the Heart: Individualism and Commitment in American Life* (New York: Harper & Row, 1985), 142-63, 244.

4. These words are definitely *attributed* to Luther. See "Memorable Quotes from Martin Luther," http://imdb.com/title/tt0309820/quotes. In August Franzen and John P. Dolan's *A History of the Church* (Montreal: Palm, 1968), 275, Luther is quoted in this way: "Unless

I am convinced by the testimony of the Scriptures or by clear reason (for I do not trust either in the pope or in councils alone, since it is well known that they have often erred and contradicted themselves), I am bound by the Scriptures I have quoted, and my conscience is captive to the Word of God. I cannot and will not retract anything, since it is neither safe nor right to go against conscience. May God help me, Amen."

5. Immanuel Kant, "What Is Enlightenment?" (1784), http://www.fordham.edu/HALSALL/MOD/kant-whatis.html.

6. See Frank G. Kirkpatrick's excellent development of what he calls the "atomistic/contractarian model of community" in his *Community: A Trinity of Models* (Washington, D.C.: Georgetown University Press, 1986), 13-61.

7. The text of the Declaration of Independence is from http://www.archives.gov/national-archives-experience/charters/declaration_transcript.html, the Web site of the United States' National Archives.

8. John Wood Oman, *Grace and Personality*, 3rd rev. ed. (Cambridge: Cambridge University Press, 1925), 58.

9. For a deeper development of Oman's thought, see Stephen Bevans, *John Oman and His Doctrine of God* (Cambridge: Cambridge University Press, 1992), 63-81.

10. Martin Buber, *I and Thou*, 2nd ed. (New York: Charles Scribner's Sons, 1958), 11.

11. See Josiah Royce, *The Problem of Christianity* (Chicago: University of Chicago Press, 1968), 248.

12. Frank Oppenheim, "A Roycean Response to the Challenge of Individualism," in Donald L. Gelpi, ed., *Beyond Individualism: Toward a Retrieval of Moral Discourse in America* (Notre Dame, Ind.: University of Notre Dame Press, 1989), 97.

13. John Macmurray, *Persons in Relation*, Gifford Lectures 1954 (London: Faber & Faber, 1961; repr., Atlantic Highlands, N.J./London: Humanities Press International, 1991), 11, 15. See also John Macmurray, *The Self as Agent* (Atlantic Highlands, N.J./London: Humanities Press International, 1991).

14. Macmurray, *Persons in Relation*, 24.

15. For a marvelous exposition of Macmurray's thought, see Kirkpatrick, *Community*, 146-220.

16. What follows relies strongly on Fr. Mercado's text: Leonardo N. Mercado, *Elements of Filipino Theology* (Tacloban, Philippines: Divine Word University Publications, 1975), 54-58.

17. These are terms in anthropology. See, for example, Donn V. Hart, *Compadrinazgo: Ritual Kinship in the Philippines* (DeKalb, Ill.: Northern Illinois University Press, 1977).

18. See, for example, Pham Van Bich, *The Vietnamese Family in Change: The Case of the Red River Delta* (Richmond, Surrey, England: Curzon Press, 1999), 18-19.

19. E.g., Gary Riebe-Estrella, "Understanding Cultural Difference: Attitudes and Frameworks," in Stephen Bevans and Roger Schroeder, eds., *Word Remembered, Word Proclaimed: Selected Papers from Symposia Celebrating the SVD Centennial in North America* (Nettetal, Germany: Steyler Verlag, 1997), 227-36; Gary Riebe-Estrella, "*Pueblo* and Church," in Orlando O. Espín and Miguel H. Díaz, eds., *From the Heart of Our People: Latino/a Explorations in Catholic Systematic Theology* (Maryknoll, N.Y.: Orbis Books, 1999), 172-88; Richard A. Shweder and Edmund J. Bourne, "Does the Concept of Person Vary Cross-Culturally?" in Richard A. Shweder and Edmund J. Bourne, eds., *Culture Theory: Essays on Mind, Self and Emotion* (Cambridge: Cambridge University Press, 1984), 158-99.

20. Riebe Estrella, "Understanding Cultural Difference," 231.

21. Ibid.

22. Riebe-Estrella, "*Pueblo* and Church," 173-74.

23. Bernice Letlhare, "Corporate Personality in Botswana and Israel: A Religio-

Cultural Comparison," in Gerald O. West and Musa W. Dube, eds., *The Bible in Africa: Transactions, Trajectories and Trends* (Leiden: Brill, 2000), 477.

24. Ibid., 478. Letlhare refers here to Gabriel M. Setiloane, *The Image of God among the Sotho- Tswana* (Rotterdam: Balkema, 1976), 36-39.

25. John Paul II, *Ecclesia in Africa* (EiAf), 43. See http://www.vatican.va/holy_father/john_paul_ii/apost_exhortations/documents/hf_jp-ii_exh_14091995_ecclesia-in-africa_en.html. For a fine study of this communal African worldview, see Casimir Ebuziem, "'Umuna bu ihe' As Ministry: Contribution of Indigenous Igbo Values to Emerging Lay Leadership in Nigeria" (D.Min. thesis, Catholic Theological Union, Chicago, 2007).

26. Parker J. Palmer, *The Courage to Teach* (San Francisco: Jossey-Bass, 1998), 95.

27. Ibid.

28. Ibid., 95-96.

29. Ibid., 97, quoting Ian Barbour, *Religion in an Age of Science* (San Francisco: Harper-SanFrancisco, 1990), 220-21.

30. Denis Edwards, *Breath of Life: A Theology of the Creator Spirit* (Maryknoll, N.Y.: Orbis Books, 2004), 13.

31. Eduard Schweizer, *The Church as the Body of Christ* (Richmond, Va.: John Knox, 1964), 21.

32. See H. Wheeler Robinson, "The Hebrew Conception of Corporate Personality," in *Corporate Personality in Ancient Israel*, rev. ed. (Philadelphia: Fortress Press, 1980), 37-42.

33. See, for example, Elizabeth Johnson, *She Who Is: The Mystery of God in Feminist Discourse* (New York: Crossroad, 1992), 156-58; Gerhard Lohfink, *Jesus and Community* (Philadelphia: Fortress Press, 1984), 31-73.

34. S. Mark Heim, *The Depth of the Riches: A Trinitarian Theology of Religious Ends* (Grand Rapids: William B. Eerdmans, 2001), 53.

35. Thomas Aquinas, "Colloquium super *Credo in Deum*," *Opuscula theologica* 2 (Taurini, 1954), 216-17. See the Office of Readings, Saturday of the Thirty-third Week of the Year.

36. Heim, *Depth of the Riches*, 108.

37. Ibid., 104. The quotation from the *Inferno* is Canto XXXIV, 28, in Allen Mandelbaum, trans., *The Divine Comedy* (New York/Toronto: Everyman's Library, Alfred A. Knopf, 1995), 210.

38. Leonardo Boff, "Trinity," in Ignacio Ellacuría and Jon Sobrino, eds. *Mysterium Liberationis: Fundamental Concepts of Liberation Theology* (Maryknoll, N.Y.: Orbis Books, 1993), 389.

39. See, for example, Johnson, *She Who Is*, 191-223; Catherine Mowry LaCugna, "God in Communion with Us," in Catherine Mowry LaCugna, ed., *Freeing Theology: The Essentials of Theology in Feminist Perspective* (San Francisco: HarperSanFrancisco, 1993), 83-114; Patricia Fox, "The Trinity as Transforming Symbol: Exploring the Trinitarian Theology of Two Roman Catholic Feminist Theologians," *Pacifica* 7 (1994): 273-94.

40. Susan Niditch, "Genesis," in *The Women's Bible Commentary*, ed. Carol A. Newsom and Sharon H. Ringe (Louisville, Ky.: Westminster John Knox Press, 1992), 13.

41. Robert Bellarmine, *De Controversiis*, volume 2, book 3, chapter 2 (Naples: Giuliano, 1857), 75, quoted in Avery Dulles, *Models of the Church* (New York: Doubleday Image Books, 1974), 39 n. 1.

42. See Michael A. Fahey, "Church," in Francis Schüssler Fiorenza and John P. Galvin, eds., *Systematic Theology: Roman Catholic Perspectives* (Minneapolis: Fortress Press, 1991), 32. The term "perfect society" is often understood in the moral sense, but this is not the way in which it should be understood. Fahey uses the term in the same sense as "visible society," and explains that "the 'perfect' character of the society called church was an apologetic

attempt to assert the church's independence from the state." The term "enjoyed widespread support" after Trent in the sixteenth century until the time of Vatican II in the 1960s.

43. James D. Whitehead, "Christian Images of Community: Power and Leadership," in Michael A. Cowan, ed., *Alternative Futures for Worship*, vol. 6, *Leadership Ministry in Community* (Collegeville, Minn.: Liturgical Press, 1987), 23-37.

44. On the importance of the place of the chapter on the people of God in Vatican II's document on the church and its theological significance, see Gérard Philips, "Dogmatic Constitution on the Church: History of the Constitution," in Herbert Vorgrimler, ed., *Commentary on the Documents of Vatican II*, vol. 1 (New York: Herder & Herder, 1967), 110. See also Alois Grillmeier, "Chapter II: The People of God," in ibid., 153.

45. See Leonardo Boff, *Ecclesiogenesis: The Base Communities Reinvent the Church* (Maryknoll, N.Y.: Orbis Books, 1986), 25. The reference to Congar is "My Pathfindings in the Theology of Laity and Ministries," *The Jurist* 2 (1972): 169-88.

46. The document, admittedly, is a bit oblique about Christians' share in Jesus' office of king. The last two sections of paragraph 12, however, do deal with the charismatic structure of the church, whereby all Christians are called to some kind of ministry. Footnote 42 of the Abbott edition of the Vatican II documents says that in paragraph 13 "the People of God is considered in its relationship to Christ as King." See Walter M. Abbott, ed., *The Documents of Vatican II* (New York: Herder & Herder / Association Press, 1966), 30.

47. Abbott, *Documents of Vatican II*, 29 n. 40.

48. Paul Crowley, "Catholicity, Inculturation and Newman's *Sensus Fidelium*," *Heythrop Journal* 32, no. 7 (April 1992): 161.

49. Johann Adam Möhler, *Symbolism, or Exposition of the Doctrinal Differences between Catholics and Protestants* (London: Gibbings, 1906), 277, quoted in Avery Dulles, *The Craft of Theology: From Symbol to System* (New York: Crossroad, 1992), 9.

50. John Henry Newman, *On Consulting the Faithful in Matters of Doctrine* (Kansas City, Mo.: Sheed & Ward, 1985), 73, quoted in Dulles, *Craft of Theology*, 9.

51. Orlando O. Espín, "Tradition and Popular Religion," in Arturo J. Bañuelas, ed., *Mestizo Christianity: Theology from the Latino Perspective* (Maryknoll, N.Y.: Orbis Books, 1995), 148-74.

52. Crowley, "Catholicity," 165-66.

53. Newman, *Consulting the Faithful*, 109. See also Newman's *The Arians of the Fourth Century* (London/New York: Longmans, Green, 1997).

54. See U.S. Catholic Bishops, "The Challenge of Peace: God's Promise and Our Response" and "Economic Justice for All," in David J. O'Brien and Thomas A. Shannon, eds., *Catholic Social Thought: The Documentary Heritage* (Maryknoll, N.Y.: Orbis Books, 1992), 492-571 and 572-680. Although they differ in their critique, strong voices of opposition to the perspectives of the bishops have been Michael Novak and Michael J. Baxter. See Novak's *The Spirit of Democratic Capitalism* (Washington, D.C.: American Enterprise Institute, 1982); and Michael J. Baxter, "Writing History in a World without Ends: An Evangelical Catholic Critique of United States Catholic History," *Pro Ecclesia* 5 (Fall 1996): 440-69.

55. This refers to the famous dictum of Thomas Aquinas and other Thomistic theologians that "grace perfects nature." On this, for example, see Thomas Aquinas, *Summa Theologiae*, I, LXII, 5, Respondeo.

56. Palmer, *Courage to Teach*, 90.

57. Mary Benet McKinney, *Sharing Wisdom: A Process for Group Decision Making* (Valencia, Calif.: Tabor, 1987), 12.

58. Ibid., 13.

59. See *The Rule of St. Benedict*, ed. Timothy Fry (Collegeville, Minn.: Liturgical Press, 1981), 3.3.

60. See Riebe-Estrella, "Understanding Cultural Difference"; on *pastoral de conjunto*, see Ana María Pineda, "*Pastoral de Conjunto*," in Bañuelas, *Mestizo Christianity*, 128-31; on *teología de/en conjunto* see Arturo J. Bañuelas, "U.S. Hispanic Theology: An Initial Assessment," in Bañuelas, 73, 76; see also Eduardo C. Fernández, *La Cosecha: Harvesting Contemporary United States Hispanic Theology (1972-1998)* (Collegeville, Minn.: Liturgical Press, A Michael Glazier Book, 2000), 57; J. D. Rodríguez and L. I. Martel-Otero, eds., *Teología en conjunto: A Collaborative Hispanic Protestant Theology* (Louisville, Ky.: Westminster John Knox Press, 1997).

61. Espín and Díaz, eds., *From the Heart* (see n. 19 above); Orlando O. Espín and Gary Macy, eds., *Futuring Our Past: Explorations in the Theology of Tradition* (Maryknoll, N.Y.: Orbis Books, 2006).

62. Justo L. González, *Mañana: Christian Theology from a Hispanic Perspective* (Nashville, Tenn.: Abingdon, 1990), 29-30.

63. Rebecca Chopp, *Saving Work: Feminist Practices of Theological Education* (Louisville, Ky.: Westminster John Knox Press, 1995), 72-75.

64. Vincent J. Donovan, *The Church in the Midst of Creation* (Maryknoll, N.Y.: Orbis Books, 1989), 146-56.

65. Ibid., 149.

66. David Tracy, *Plurality and Ambiguity: Hermeneutics, Religion, Hope* (San Francisco: Harper & Row, 1987), 19.

5. COMMUNITY AS SOURCE AND PARAMETER OF THEOLOGY

1. We will refer to this idea of "classics" once again in this chapter, and in more detail. For a definition and development of the notion, see David Tracy, *The Analogical Imagination: Christian Theology and the Culture of Pluralism* (New York: Crossroad, 1981), 99-229.

2. Gerald O'Collins, *Fundamental Theology* (New York/Ramsey, N.J.: Paulist Press, 1981), 193.

3. Ibid.

4. Stephen Still, quoted in Robert L. Kinast, "Experiencing the Tradition through Theological Reflection," *New Theology Review* 8, no. 1 (February 1995): 15.

5. See Gabriel M. Setiloane, *The Image of God among the Sotho-Tswana* (Rotterdam: Balkema, 1976), 36-39.

6. John Macmurray, *Persons in Relation* (Atlantic Highlands, N.J./London: Humanities Press International, 1991), 128. The quotation is from Macmurray, not a direct quotation from Plato.

7. See, for example, the studies and cases reported at http://www.feralchildren.com/en/showchild.php?ch=hesse.

8. See http://africanhistory.about.com/library/weekly/aa080601a.htm. See also the short article, "Slave Trade, Abolition of," *Oxford Encyclopedia of World History* (Oxford/New York: Oxford University Press, 1998), 615. The *Oxford Encyclopedia* reports that there were some four million slaves in the United States at the time of Abraham Lincoln's "Emancipation Proclamation" in 1863, and that slavery was not abolished in Cuba until 1886 and in Brazil in 1888.

9. Jon Butler, "African Spiritual Holocaust," in *Awash in a Sea of Faith: Christianizing the American People* (Cambridge, MA: Harvard University Press, 1990), 129-63.

10. Alex Haley, *Roots: The Saga of an American Family* (New York: Dell Paperback, 1976).

11. Orlando Espín and Gary Macy, eds., *Futuring Our Past: Explorations in the Theology of Tradition* (Maryknoll, N.Y.: Orbis Books, 2006).

12. Quoted by Delwin Brown, *Boundaries of Our Habitations: Tradition and Theological Construction* (Albany: State University of New York Press, 1994), 84-85.

13. Sigfried Widenhoffer, "A Theory of Tradition," xeroxed working paper, 6.

14. Karl-Heinz Weger, "Tradition," in Karl Rahner, ed., *Sacramentum Mundi: An Encyclopedia of Theology*, vol. 6 (New York: Herder & Herder; London: Burns & Oates, 1970), 269.

15. Miguel Díaz, "A Trinitarian Approach to the Community-Building Process of Tradition: Oneness as Diversity in Christian Traditioning," in Espín and Macy, *Futuring Our Past*, 158.

16. Orlando O. Espín, "Traditioning: Culture, Daily Life and Popular Religion, and Their Impact on Christian Tradition," in Espín and Macy, *Futuring Our Past*, 5-6.

17. Weger, "Tradition," 270.

18. Avery Dulles, *The Craft of Theology: From Symbol to System* (New York: Crossroad, 1992), 103.

19. Espín, "Traditioning," 11.

20. Yves Congar, *Tradition and Traditions: An Historical and a Theological Essay* (New York: Macmillan, 1967).

21. Tracy, *Analogical Imagination*, 99-229.

22. Aidan Nichols, *The Shape of Catholic Theology: An Introduction to Its Sources, Principles, and History* (Collegeville, Minn.: Liturgical Press, 1991), 171. Nichols cites Rupert of Deutz, *De Omnipotentia Dei*, XXVII. For a more in-depth introduction to Scripture as source of theology, see Nichols, 97-180.

23. Nichols, *Shape of Catholic Theology*, 172. The reference is to Hugh of St. Victor, *Eruditio didascalia*, IV, 4.

24. For excerpts of the texts of Perpetua, Jerome on Paula, and Egeria and citations of the full texts, see Barbara J. MacHaffie, ed., *Readings in Her Story: Women in Christian Tradition* (Minneapolis: Augsburg/Fortress, 1992), 24-27, 33-40, 40-43. The quotation about Macrina is from Dale T. Irvin and Scott W. Sunquist, *History of the World Christian Movement*, vol. 1, *Earliest Christianity to 1453* (Maryknoll, N.Y.: Orbis Books, 2001), 185. For feminist scholarship on "mothers" of the church, see Mary T. Malone, *Women and Christianity*, vol. 1, *The First Thousand Years* (Maryknoll, N.Y.: Orbis Books, 2000).

25. For more information on doctors of the church, see Bernard McGinn, *The Doctors of the Church: Thirty-three Men and Women Who Shaped Christianity* (New York: Crossroad, 1999).

26. Jaroslav Pelikan, *Credo: Historical and Theological Guide to Creeds and Confessions of Faith in the Christian Tradition* (New Haven/London: Yale University Press, 2003), 166-67.

27. Nichols, *Shape of Catholic Theology*, 187. For a fuller development of the liturgy as source of theology, see 181-99.

28. Jaroslav Pelikan, *The Illustrated Jesus through the Centuries* (New Haven: Yale University Press, 1997); *Jesus through the Centuries: His Place in the History of Culture* (New Haven: Yale University Press, 1985); *Mary: Images of the Mother of Jesus in Jewish and Christian Perspective* (Philadelphia: Fortress Press, 1986); *Mary through the Centuries: Her Place in the History of Culture* (New Haven: Yale University Press, 1996).

29. Dorothy Day, "Letter to an Agnostic," *America* (August 4, 1934), republished in *America* 108, no. 13 (April 17, 1999): 7.

30. Gary Riebe-Estrella, "Tradition as Conversation," in Espín and Macy, *Futuring Our Past*, 141.

31. Ivone Gebara, "Women Doing Theology in Latin America," in Ursula King, ed., *Feminist Theology from the Third World* (Maryknoll, N.Y.: Orbis Books, 1994), 56-57.

32. González has published a book based on his Zenos Lectures and several other series of lectures that he has given. See Justo L. González, *The Changing Shape of Church History* (St. Louis, Mo.: Chalice Press, 2002).

33. James D. Whitehead and Evelyn Eaton Whitehead, *Method in Ministry: Theological Reflection and Christian Ministry*, rev. ed. (Kansas City, Mo.: Sheed & Ward, 1995), 7-9.

34. Justo González, "A Response to Virgilio Elizondo," in Paul Crowley, ed., *Proceedings of the Forty-Eighth Annual Convention*, Catholic Theological Society of America, 1993, 14.

35. On the pluriformity of the New Testament, see, for example, James D. G. Dunn, *Unity and Diversity in the New Testament: An Inquiry into the Character of Earliest Christianity* (Philadelphia: Westminster Press, 1977).

36. Dale T. Irvin, *Christian Histories, Christian Traditioning: Rendering Accounts* (Maryknoll, N.Y.: Orbis Books, 1998).

37. On this last tension, see Robert J. Schreiter, "Two Forms of Catholicity in a Time of Globalization," *Himig Ugnayan* 8 (2007): 1-17; and Timothy Radcliffe, *What Is the Point of Being Christian* (London/New York: Burns & Oates, 2005).

38. Espín, "Traditioning," 8.

39. Whitehead and Whitehead, *Method in Ministry*, 8.

40. Anne Carr, *Transforming Grace: Christian Tradition and Women's Experience* (San Francisco: HarperSanFrancisco, 1990), 160-61.

41. Letty Russell, *Church in the Round: Feminist Interpretation of the Church* (Louisville, Ky.: Westminster John Knox Press, 1993), 201.

42. Irvin, *Christian Histories*, 15.

43. See Alasdair MacIntyre, *After Virtue*, 2nd ed. (Notre Dame, Ind.: University of Notre Dame Press, 1984), 222; Kathryn Tanner, "Postmodern Challenges to 'Tradition,'" *Louvain Studies* 28 (2003): 175-93.

44. Douglas John Hall, *Thinking the Faith: Christian Theology in a North American Context* (Minneapolis: Augsburg Fortress, 1989), 264.

45. See http://www.brainyquote.com/quotes/quotes/w/williamfau141196.html.

46. Gabriel Marcel, "Creative Fidelity," in *Creative Fidelity* (New York: Farrar, Straus, 1964), 147-74.

47. Irvin, *Christian Histories*, 149, note 52, quoting Eugen Rosenstock-Huessy, *The Christian Future, or, the Modern Mind Outrun* (New York: Harper & Row, 1966), 130 (emphasis in the original).

48. David Coward, review of Joan E. DeJean, *Ancients against Moderns: Culture Wars and the Making of a Fin de Siècle* (Chicago: University of Chicago Press, 1997), in the *New York Review of Books* (April 27, 1997): 28.

49. John Oman, *Vision and Authority, or The Throne of St. Peter*, new rev. ed. (London: Hodder & Stoughton, 1928; 1st ed., 1902), 7-8.

50. T. S. Eliot, quoted in Cornel West, *Keeping Faith: Philosophy and Race in America* (New York: Routledge, 1993), 9.

51. West made these remarks at a session on North American Contextual Theology at the 1995 meeting of the Catholic Theological Society in New York City. The quotation is from the report written by John J. Markey in Paul Crowley, ed., *Proceedings of the Fiftieth Annual Convention*, 253. What follows the quotation are my own recollections of the session.

52. Jaroslav Pelikan, *The Vindication of Tradition* (New Haven: Yale University Press, 1984), 65.

53. Hall, *Thinking the Faith*, 272; see 271-72 for his full argument.

6. COMMUNITY AS THE PARAMETER OF THEOLOGY

1. For the quotation from William Faulkner, see http://www.brainyquote.com/quotes/quotes/w/williamfau141196.html. See also T. S. Eliot, *Selected Essays* (San Diego: Harcourt Brace Jovanovich, 1978), 4, quoted in Dale T. Irvin, *Christian Histories, Christian Traditioning: Rendering Accounts* (Maryknoll, N.Y.: Orbis Books, 1998), 28, 149 n. 51.

2. See Francis A. Sullivan, *Magisterium: Teaching Authority in the Catholic Church* (New York/Ramsey, N.J.: Paulist Press, 1983), 24.

3. Gerald O'Collins, *Fundamental Theology* (New York/Ramsey, N.J.: Paulist Press, 1981), 186.

4. Thomas Aquinas, *Quodlibet*, 3, q. 4, a. 1, quoted in Francis A. Sullivan, *Creative Fidelity: Weighing and Interpreting Documents of the Magisterium* (New York/Mahwah, N.J.: Paulist Press, 1996), 1, 185 n. 1. See also Richard R. Gaillardetz, *By What Authority? A Primer on Scripture, the Magisterium, and the Sense of the Faithful* (Collegeville, Minn.: Liturgical Press, 2003), 60.

5. For a more developed theology of ordained ministry along this line, see Stephen Bevans, "The Service of Ordering: Reflections on the Identity of the Priest," *Emmanuel* 101, no. 7 (September 1995): 397-406; and Susan K. Wood, ed., *Ordering the Baptismal Priesthood: Theologies of Lay and Ordained Ministry* (Collegeville, Minn.: Liturgical Press, 2003).

6. Avery Dulles, "Authority and Pluralism in the Church," in idem, *The Survival of Dogma: Faith, Authority and Dogma in a Changing World* (Garden City, N.Y.: Doubleday Image Books, 1973), 108-9.

7. Ibid., 108.

8. Monika Hellwig, *What Are the Theologians Saying Now? A Retrospective on Several Decades* (Westminster, Md.: Christian Classics, 1992), 20.

9. George Lindbeck, *The Nature of Doctrine: Religion and Theology in a Post-Liberal Age* (Philadelphia: Fortress Press, 1984).

10. Sullivan, *Creative Fidelity*, 33.

11. Justo L. González, *A Concise History of Christian Doctrine* (Nashville, Tenn.: Abingdon Press, 2005), 6-7.

12. Sullivan, *Creative Fidelity*, 34.

13. Alister E. McGrath, "Doctrine and Dogma," in Alister E. McGrath, ed., *The Blackwell Encyclopedia of Modern Christian Thought* (Oxford/Cambridge, Mass.: Blackwell, 1993), 112. McGrath's article (112-19) offers as well a fine synthesis of Lindbeck's thought on the nature of doctrine.

14. Francis Sullivan points to five instances in the church's history "when a pope, acting independently of an ecumenical council, exercised his teaching authority to define dogmas of faith." Even if one would accept all five instances, or, as some theologians suggest, *seven* or even *twelve*, we are still talking about a rare exercise of the magisterium's authority. See Sullivan, *Creative Fidelity*, 84-86.

15. Kenneth Untener, "If a Pope Resigns . . . ," *America* 182, no. 10 (March 25, 2000): 22.

16. Ibid.

17. Charles Curran, "Public Dissent in the Church," *Origins* 16 (1986): 178.

18. Juan Alfaro, "Theology and the Magisterium," in René Latourelle and Gerald O'Collins, eds., *Problems and Perspectives of Fundamental Theology* (New York/Ramsey, N.J.: Paulist Press, 1982), 347.

19. Karl Rahner, "The Development of Dogma," in *Theological Investigations*, vol. 1 (Baltimore: Helicon Press; London: Darton, Longman & Todd, 1961), 49.

20. John of the Cross, *The Ascent of Mount Carmel* 2.22, 3, in *The Collected Words of St. John of the Cross*, rev. ed. (Washington, D.C.: Institute of Carmelite Studies, 1991), 230, quoted in Sullivan, *Creative Fidelity*, 30. The text is also found in the Office of Readings of the Roman Breviary for Monday, second week in Advent.

21. Sullivan, *Creative Fidelity*, 23, quoting the Congregation for the Doctrine of the Faith, *Instruction on the Ecclesial Vocation of the Theologian*, 24. See http://www.vatican.va/roman_ curia/congregations/cfaith/documents/rc_con_cfaith_doc_19900524_theologian-vocation_en.html.

22. See Sullivan, *Creative Fidelity*, 12-27, for an in-depth reflection on these various levels of teaching and responses required to the magisterium's teaching.

23. Ibid., 84-85.

24. See Gaillardetz, *By What Authority?*, 84-86.

25. Richard R. Gaillardetz, *Teaching with Authority: A Theology of the Magisterium of the Church* (Collegeville, Minn.: Liturgical Press, 1997), 271.

26. *Instruction on the Ecclesial Vocation of the Theologian*, 34.

27. Raymond E. Brown, *Priest and Bishops: Biblical Reflections* (London: Geoffrey Chapman, 1971), 76-77 (quotation from 77).

28. I have embellished the cardinal's remarks a bit here, but have been true to what he said some thirty years ago.

29. O'Collins, *Fundamental Theology*, 189. See also the text of the International Theological Commission, *Theses on the Relationship between the Ecclesiastical Magisterium and Theology* (Washington, D.C.: United States Catholic Conference, 1977), thesis 6 (p. 5).

30. Avery Dulles, "Doctrinal Authority in the Church," in idem, *Survival of Dogma*, 102-3.

31. Bernard Lonergan, "Cognitional Structure," in Frederick E. Crowe, ed., *Collection: Papers by Bernard Lonergan, S.J.* (New York: Herder & Herder, 1967), 221-39; see also David Tracy, *The Achievement of Bernard Lonergan* (New York: Herder & Herder, 1970), 123-32.

32. Bishop James Malone, "How Bishops and Theologians Relate," *Origins* 16, no. 9 (July 31, 1986): 174.

33. René Latourelle, *Theology: Science of Salvation* (Staten Island, N.Y.: Alba House, 1969), 49.

34. International Theological Commission, thesis 5.2; the quotation is taken from Paul VI, "Address to the International Congress on the Theology of Vatican II," AAS 58 (1966): 890.

35. Quoted in Sullivan, *Creative Fidelity*, 175.

36. Malone, "Bishops and Theologians," 172.

37. See Robert McClory, *Faithful Dissenters: Stories of Men and Women Who Loved and Changed the Church* (Maryknoll, N.Y.: Orbis Books, 2000).

38. Malone, "Bishops and Theologians," 172.

39. Quoted in Dulles, *Survival of Dogma*, 104. The quotation is from the same discourse quoted above.

40. Joseph Ratzinger, "The Church and the Theologian," *Origins* 15, no. 47 (May 8, 1986): 769.

41. Latourelle, *Theology*, 50.

42. See Gaillardetz, *By What Authority?* 134-43. The quotation is from Cardinal Joseph Ratzinger, "Theology Is Not Private Idea of Theologian," *L'Osservatore Romano* (English edition, July 2, 1990): 5.

43. John Paul II, apostolic letter *Ordinatio Sacerdotalis*, 4. http://www.vatican.va/holy_father/john_paul_ii/apost_letters/documents/hf_jp-ii_apl_22051994_ordinatio-sacerdotalis_en.html.

44. For a more detailed discussion of reception, with an ample bibliography, see Gaillardetz, *Teaching with Authority*, 227-54 and idem, *By What Authority?* 107-20.

45. Pius X, *Vehementer Nos*, quoted in Michael Fahey, "Church," in Francis Schüssler Fiorenza and John Galvin, eds., *Systematic Theology: Roman Catholic Perspectives*, vol. 2 (Minneapolis: Fortress Press, 1991), 32.

46. Gaillardetz, *Teaching with Authority*, 250.

47. Ladislaus Örsy, *The Church: Learning and Teaching* (Wilmington, Del.: Michael Glazier, 1987), 90-91.

48. See Avery Dulles, "Authority and Conscience: Two Needed Voices in the Church," *Church* 2, no. 3 (Fall 1986): 12.

49. Avery Dulles, "The Magisterium and Theological Dissent," in idem, *The Craft of Theology* (New York: Crossroad, 1992), 111-12.

50. Gaillardetz, *Teaching with Authority*, 268. Gaillardetz refers to Richard A. McCormick, *Corrective Vision: Explorations in Moral Theology* (Kansas City, Mo.: Sheed & Ward, 1994), 85.

51. Örsy, *Church*, 93.

52. Gaillardetz, *Teaching with Authority*, 270.

53. O'Collins, *Fundamental Theology*, 15.

PART III. THE WAY FAITH SEEKS

1. Gustavo Gutiérrez, *A Theology of Liberation* (Maryknoll, N.Y.: Orbis Books, 1973), 15.

2. Bernard Lonergan, *Method in Theology* (New York: Herder & Herder, 1972), 4.

3. J. J. Mueller, *What Are They Saying about Theological Method?* (New York/Ramsey, N.J.: Paulist Press, 1984), 2.

4. Francis Schüssler Fiorenza, "Systematic Theology: Task and Methods," in Francis Schüssler Fiorenza and John P. Galvin, eds., *Systematic Theology: Roman Catholic Perspectives* (Minneapolis: Fortress Press, 1991), 1-87.

7. HISTORICAL INVESTIGATION AND
THEOLOGICAL REFLECTION

1. Thomas Aquinas, *In Aristotelis Libros de Caelo et Mundo*, 1, 22, quoted in Thomas F. O'Meara, *Thomas Aquinas, Theologian* (Notre Dame, Ind.: University of Notre Dame Press, 1997), 37 n. 85.

2. John Paul II, *Fides et Ratio*, 65. See http://www.vatican.va/edocs/ENG0216/__PE.HTM. See also *The Theological Formation of Future Priests* (Vatican City: Vatican Polyglot Press, 1976), 29.

3. Vatican II uses the term "dogmatic theology" to refer to what I am calling in this book "systematic theology." The latter term is preferred, I believe, because theology deals not just with "dogmas," which, as we have seen in the previous chapter, have a rather narrow sense as doctrines that are solemnly defined by the church's magisterium as pertaining to revelation. Theology, rather, deals with the spectrum of the church's doctrines and does

it in a way that is systematic—showing those doctrines' connections with each other and constructing a way of interpreting the whole of revelation by the way that the doctrines are ordered one to the other. I would understand dogmatic theology, doctrinal theology, and systematic theology to be roughly synonymous with one another, however.

4. Augustine, *De Trinitate*, 1.2.4. See PL vol. 42, col. 822.

5. Thomas Aquinas, *Quodlibet* IV, articulus 3. See http://www.corpusthomisticum.org/q04.html#67602.

6. Francis A. Sullivan, *Creative Fidelity: Weighing and Interpreting Documents of the Magisterium* (New York/Mahwah, N.J.: Paulist Press, 1996), 2.

7. Edward Weekly, *A Concise Etymological Dictionary of Modern English* (New York: E. P. Dutton, 1952), under "speculate."

8. Walter Kasper, *The Methods of Dogmatic Theology* (Shannon, Ireland: Ecclesia Press, 1969), 26.

9. Bernard Lonergan, *Method in Theology* (New York: Herder & Herder, 1972), 355.

10. Ibid., 350.

11. James D. Whitehead and Evelyn Eaton Whitehead, *Method in Ministry: Theological Reflection and Christian Ministry*, rev. ed. (Kansas City, Mo.: Sheed & Ward, 1995), 9.

12. Anne Hunt, *Trinity: Nexus of the Mysteries of Christian Faith*, Theology in Global Perspective (Maryknoll, N.Y.: Orbis Books, 2005), 3.

13. See Sallie McFague, *Models of God* (Philadelphia: Fortress Press, 1987). For the images of God as dance and stranger, see Stephen Bevans, "Reimagining God and Mission," in Ross Langmead, ed., *Reimagining God and Mission: Perspectives from Australia* (Adelaide: ATF Press, 2007), 3-23. For the images of compassionate adversary and fertile emptiness, see Jane Kopas, *Seeking the Hidden God* (Maryknoll, N.Y.: Orbis Books, 2005).

14. See, for example, the essays by African theologians Anselme T. Sanon, François Kabaseélé, and Cécé Kolié in Robert J. Schreiter, ed., *Faces of Jesus in Africa* (Maryknoll, N.Y.: Orbis Books, 1991).

15. José M. de Mesa, "The Resurrection in the Filipino Context," in *In Solidarity with the Culture: Studies in Theological Re-rooting*, Maryhill Studies 4 (Quezon City, Philippines: Maryhill School of Theology, 1987), 102-46.

16. See the chapter, "Liberation Theology between Resistance and Reconstruction," in Robert J. Schreiter, *The New Catholicity: Theology between the Local and the Global* (Maryknoll, N.Y.: Orbis Books, 1997), 98-115.

17. Hunt, *Trinity*, 3-4.

18. Thomas Aquinas, quoted in O'Meara, *Thomas Aquinas*, 150. See also 3Sent. D. 13.q,1, a.1, ad 5.

19. See, for example, José M. de Mesa, "Understanding God's 'Kagandahang-Loob,'" "'Loob' and Prayer," and "'Utang na Loob' and Marriage," in *In Solidarity with the Culture*, 43-55, 56-67, 68-74; John R. Pesebre, "Balik-Loob: Towards a Filipino Evangelical Theology of Repentance," in ATS Forum Contributors, *Doing Theology in the Philippines* (Quezon City: Asian Theological Seminary; Manila: OMF Literature, 2005), 117-30.

20. Theological Advisory Commission, "Asian Christian Perspectives on Harmony," in Franz-Josef Eilers, ed., *For All the People of Asia*, vol. 2, *Federation of Asian Bishops' Conferences Documents from 1992 to 1996* (Quezon City: Claretian Publications, 1997), 232.

21. Rosemary Radford Ruether, *Sexism and God-Talk: Toward a Feminist Theology*, Tenth Anniversary Edition (Boston: Beacon Press, 1993), 19.

22. It is feminist New Testament scholar Barbara Reid who proposes that the persistent widow in Luke 18:1-7 is in fact an image of God. For her very creative and convincing interpretation, see her *Choosing the Better Part? Women in the Gospel of Luke* (Collegeville, Minn.: Liturgical Press, 1996), 190-94.

23. See Sally B. Purvis, "Cross," in Letty M. Russell and J. Shannon Clarkson, *Dictionary of Feminist Theologies* (Louisville, Ky.: Westminster John Knox Press, 1996), 61-63.

24. Gustavo Gutiérrez, *A Theology of Liberation* (Maryknoll, N.Y.: Orbis Books, 1973), 15.

25. Roger Haight, *An Alternative Vision: An Interpretation of Liberation Theology* (New York/Ramsey, N.J.: Paulist Press, 1985); Robert McAfee Brown, *Theology in a New Key: Responding to Liberation Themes* (Philadelphia: Westminster Press, 1978); Juan Luis Segundo, *Liberation of Theology* (Maryknoll, N.Y.: Orbis Books, 1976).

26. Jon Sobrino, "El conocimiento teológico en la teología europea y latinoamericana," in *Liberación y cautiverio: Debates en torno al método de la teología en América Latina* (Mexico City: Comité Organizador, 1975), 177-207. An English summary of the talk is given in Alfred T. Hennelly, "Theological Method: The Southern Exposure," *Theological Studies* 38, no. 4 (December 1977): 718-25.

27. Mircea Eliade, *No Souvenirs: Journals 1957-1969* (London: Routledge & Kegan Paul, 1978), 213-14.

28. John W. Oman, *Grace and Personality* (Cambridge: Cambridge University Press, 1917), 4.

29. Karl Marx, *Theses on Feuerbach*, 11, in L. D. Easton and K. H. Guddat, eds. and trans., *Writings of the Young Marx on Philosophy and Society* (Garden City, N.Y.: Doubleday Anchor Books, 1967), 402.

30. Hennelly, "Theological Method," 721. The quote by Sobrino is quoted by Hennelly.

31. José Miguez Bonino, *Doing Theology in a Revolutionary Situation* (Philadelphia: Fortress Press, 1975), 72.

32. Gutiérrez, *Theology of Liberation*, 6-15.

33. Brown, *Theology in a New Key*, 71.

34. Gutiérrez, *Theology of Liberation*, 11.

35. Clodovis Boff, "Epistemology and Method of the Theology of Liberation," in Ignacio Ellacuría and Jon Sobrino, eds., *Mysterium Liberationis: Fundamental Concepts of Liberation Theology* (Maryknoll, N.Y.: Orbis Books, 1993), 73.

36. Ibid., 74-79.

37. Ibid., 79-83.

38. Ibid., 83-84.

39. Ibid., 83.

40. Ada María Isasi-Díaz, "The Task of Hispanic Women's Liberation Theology— *Mujeristas*: Who We Are and What We Are About," in Ursula King, ed., *Feminist Theology from the Third World* (Maryknoll, N.Y.: Orbis Books, 1994), 90-91.

8. CONTEXTUAL METHODS

1. Francis Schüssler Fiorenza, "Systematic Theology: Task and Methods," in Francis Schüssler Fiorenza and John P. Galvin, eds., *Systematic Theology: Roman Catholic Perspectives* (Minneapolis: Fortress Press, 1991), 1-87; J. J. Mueller, *What Are They Saying about Theological Method?* (New York/Ramsey, N.J.: Paulist Press, 1984).

2. See Stephen B. Bevans, *Models of Contextual Theology*, rev. and expanded ed. (Maryknoll, N.Y.: Orbis Books, 2002). This chapter is a summary of what has been expressed more fully in this book.

3. Charles H. Kraft, *Christianity in Culture: A Study of Dynamic Biblical Theologizing in Cross-Cultural Perspective* (Maryknoll, N.Y.: Orbis Books, 1979), 296.

4. See, for example, Pope John Paul II's remarks on inculturation in RM 52-54. See also the International Theological Commission, "Faith and Inculturation" (1987), in James A.

Scherer and Stephen B. Bevans, eds., *New Directions in Mission and Evangelization 1: Basic Statements 1974-1991* (Maryknoll, N.Y.: Orbis Books, 1992), 154-61; and the Theological Advisory Commission of the Federation of Asian Bishops' Conferences, "Theses on Inculturation," in James A. Scherer and Stephen B. Bevans, eds., *New Directions in Mission and Evangelization 3: Faith and Culture* (Maryknoll, N.Y.: Orbis Books, 1999), 91-103. It must be admitted that the present pope, Benedict XVI, is somewhat hesitant about inculturation or contextual theology. Such hesitation can be seen in his now-famous speech at the University of Regensburg in September of 2006. See http://www.vatican.va/holy_father/benedict_xvi/speeches/2006/september/documents/hf_ben-xvi_spe_20060912_university-regensburg_en.html.

5. Avery Dulles, *Models of Revelation* (New York: Doubleday, 1983), 30.

6. The phrase is referred to by Ian Barbour, *Myths, Models and Paradigms: A Comparative Study in Science and Religion* (New York: Harper & Row, 1974), 7. See Reinhold Niebuhr, *The Nature and Destiny of Man,* vol. 2 (New York: Charles Scribner's Sons, 1943), 50.

7. Dulles, *Models of Revelation*, 29-48.

8. H. Richard Niebuhr, *Christ and Culture* (New York: Harper Torchbooks, 1975).

9. Avery Dulles, *Models of the Church* (Garden City, N.Y.: Doubleday Image Books, 1974).

10. Kraft, *Christianity in Culture*, 264, 269ff.

11. See the note on Acts 17:28 in *The Catholic Study Bible*, ed. Donald Senior (New York/Oxford: Oxford University Press, 1990), "The New Testament," 212.

12. John Paul II, encyclical letter *Slavorum Apostoli*, 11. See http://www.vatican.va/edocs/ ENG0220/__P3.HTM.

13. John XXIII, "Pope John's Opening Speech to the Council," in Walter M. Abbott, ed., *The Documents of Vatican II* (New York: Herder & Herder/Association Press, 1966), 714-15.

14. Bruce Fleming, *Contextualization of Theology: An Evangelical Assessment* (Pasadena, Calif.: William Carey Library, 1980), 66.

15. See, for example, Barbara Reid, *The Gospel according to Matthew*, New Collegeville Bible Commentary (Collegeville, Minn.: Liturgical Press, 2005), 84.

16. Justin Martyr, *Second Apology*, 8.1; for the use of the phrase in Justin's writings, see also Justin Martyr, *First Apology* 46, in *The First and Second Apologies*, trans. Leslie William Barnard, Ancient Christian Writers 56 (Mahwah, N.J.: Paulist Press, 1997).

17. Andrew F. Walls, "Culture and Coherence in Christian History," in *The Missionary Movement in Christian History: Studies in the Transmission of Faith* (Maryknoll, N.Y.: Orbis Books, 1997), 22, 25.

18. This passage appears in Warren's preface to the seven books in the Christian Presence Series (London: SCM Press, 1959-1966), which included books by Kenneth Cragg, George Appleton, Raymond Hummer, John V. Taylor, William Steward, Martin Jarrett-Kerr, and Peter Schneider. Each book in the series "began with a general introduction . . . at the end of which was a comment on that particular volume" (Graham Kings, *Christianity Connected: Hindus, Muslims and the World in the Letters of Max Warren and Roger Hooker* [Utrecht, The Netherlands: Boekencentrum, 2002], 123). See, for example, the preface to John V. Taylor, *The Primal Vision* (London: SCM Press, 1963), 10.

19. See, for example, Leonardo N. Mercado, *Elements of Filipino Theology* (Tacloban City, Philippines: Divine Word University Publications, 1975); *Inculturation and Filipino Theology* (Manila: Divine Word Publications, 1992); Leonardo N. Mercado, ed., *Doing Filipino Theology* (Manila: Divine Word Publications, 1997). See in this last volume Mercado's "A Synthesis of Doing Filipino Theology," 157-77.

20. See, for example, Laurenti Magesa, *Anatomy of Inculturation: Transforming the*

Church in Africa (Maryknoll, N.Y.: Orbis Books, 2004); and Diego Irarrázaval, *Incultura-tion: New Dawn of the Church in Latin America* (Maryknoll, N.Y.: Orbis Books, 2000).

21. James D. Whitehead and Evelyn Eaton Whitehead, *Method in Ministry: Theological Reflection and Christian Ministry*, rev. ed. (Kansas City, Mo.: Sheed & Ward, 1995), 3-99.

22. Justo L. González, *Christian Thought Revisited: Three Types of Theology*, rev. ed. (Maryknoll, N.Y.: Orbis Books, 1999), 137-38.

23. Karl Barth, *Church Dogmatics* I, 2 (Edinburgh: T. & T. Clark, 1956), 792.

24. Jon Sobrino, "El conocimiento teológico en la teología europea y latinoamericana," in *Liberación y cautiverio: Debates en torno al método de la toología en América Latina* (Mexico City: Comité Organizador, 1975), 207, quoted in Alfred T. Hennelly, "Theological Method: The Southern Exposure," *Theological Studies* 38, no. 4 (December 1977): 724.

25. See Robert J. Schreiter, *Constructing Local Theologies* (Maryknoll, N.Y.: Orbis Books, 1985), 117-21.

26. See Congregation for the Doctrine of the Faith, *Instruction on Certain Aspects of the Theology of Liberation*, http://www.vatican.va/roman_curia/congregations/cfaith/documents/ rc_con_cfaith_doc_19840806_theology-liberation_en.html.

27. Gustavo Gutiérrez, *A Theology of Liberation* (Maryknoll, N.Y.: Orbis Books, 1973); Jean-Marc Éla, *My Faith as an African* (Maryknoll, N.Y.: Orbis Books; London: Geoffrey Chapman, 1988); Aloysius Pieris, *An Asian Theology of Liberation* (Maryknoll, N.Y.: Orbis Books, 1988); Elisabeth Schüssler Fiorenza, *Wisdom Ways: Introducing Feminist Biblical Interpretation* (Maryknoll, N.Y.: Orbis Books, 2001); Ada María Isasi-Díaz, *En la Lucha/ In the Struggle: Elaborating a Mujerista Theology* (Minneapolis: Fortress Press, 1993).

28. "Conclusions of the Theological Consultation," in Gaudencio Rosales and Catalino G. Arévalo, eds., *For All the Peoples of Asia: Federation of Asian Bishops' Conferences Documents from 1970 to 1991* (Quezon City, Philippines: Claretian Publications; Maryknoll, N.Y.: Orbis Books, 1992), 347 (#53); see also Stephen Bevans, "Inculturation of Theology in Asia (The Federation of Asian Bishops' Conferences, 1970-1995), *Studia Missionalia* 45 (1996): 11-14.

29. David Tracy, *Plurality and Ambiguity: Hermeneutics, Religion, Hope* (San Francisco: Harper & Row, 1987), 19.

30. Horacio de la Costa, "A Commencement of Teaching," in *The Background of Nation-alism and Other Essays* (Manila: Solidaridad, 1965), 70.

31. See José M. de Mesa, *In Solidarity with the Culture: Studies in Theological Re-Root-ing* (Quezon City, Philippines: Maryhill School of Theology, 1991); *Why Theology Is Never Far from Home* (Manila: De La Salle University Press, 2003); *Mga Aral sa Daan: Dulog at Paraang kultural sa kristolohiya* (Manila: De La Salle Unversity Press, 2004).

32. The best introduction to Koyama's work is his *Water Buffalo Theology* in the twenty-fifth anniversary edition (Maryknoll, N.Y.: Orbis Books, 1999). See also Dale T. Irvin and Akintunde E. Akinade, eds., *The Agitated Mind of God: The Theology of Kosuke Koyama* (Maryknoll, N.Y.: Orbis Books, 1996). This volume contains a bibliography of Koyama up to 1995.

33. Bernard J. F. Lonergan, *Method in Theology* (New York: Herder & Herder, 1972), 292.

34. Ibid., 231; Tracy, *Plurality and Ambiguity*, 19.

35. Carl Rogers, *On Becoming a Person: A Therapist's View of Psychotherapy* (Boston: Houghton Mifflin Company, 1961), 25.

36. Justo L. González, *Mañana: Christian Theology from a Hispanic Perspective* (Nash-ville, Tenn.: Abingdon Press, 1990). Two other more recent works by González also reflect a use of the transcendental model: *The Acts of the Apostles: The Gospel of the Holy Spirit* (Mary-knoll, N.Y.: Orbis Books, 2001) and *The Changing Shape of Church History* (St. Louis: Chal-ice Press, 2002).

37. Sallie McFague, *Metaphorical Theology: Models of God in Religious Language* (Philadelphia: Fortress Press, 1982; second printing, with an additional preface, 1985); *Models of God: Theology for an Ecological, Nuclear Age* (Philadelphia: Fortress Press, 1987); *Life Abundant: Rethinking Theology and Economy for a Planet in Peril* (Minneapolis: Fortress Press, 2000); *A New Climate for Theology: God, the World, and Global Warming* (Minneapolis: Fortress Press, 2008).

38. "Contrast community" is proposed by Gerhard Lohfink in *Jesus and Community: The Social Dimension of Christian Faith* (Philadelphia: Fortress Press, 1984).

39. Tertullian, *Praescription of Heretics*, 7; *Letter to Diognetus*, 5, in the translation of Dale T. Irvin and Scott W. Sunquist, *History of the World Christian Movement*, vol. 1 (Maryknoll, N.Y.: Orbis Books, 2001), 96.

40. See Geoffrey Wainwright, *Lesslie Newbigin: A Theological Life* (New York/Oxford: Oxford University Press, 2000), 390.

41. Stanley Hauerwas and William H. Willimon, *Resident Aliens* (Nashville, Tenn.: Abingdon Press, 1989), 47.

42. See Alfred G. Hogg, *The Christian Message to the Hindu: Being the Duff Missionary Lectures for Nineteen Forty-Five on the Challenge of the Gospel in India* (London: SCM Press, 1945), 9-46; Hendrik Kraemer, "Continuity and Discontinuity," in *The Authority of Faith: The Madras Series*, vol. 1 (New York/London: International Missionary Council, 1939), 4.

43. Paul VI, "Closing Discourse to All-Africa Symposium," quoted in Aylward Shorter, *African Christian Theology* (Maryknoll, N.Y.: Orbis Books), 20.

9. CATHOLIC METHOD

1. Andrew M. Greeley, "The Catholic Imagination of Bruce Springsteen," *America* 158, no. 5 (February 6, 1988): 110-14. I intentionally say "try" to leave the church. The explanatory note at the beginning of Greeley's article reads: "Because Bruce Springsteen's imagination was shaped as Catholic in the early years of his life, he is both a liturgist and a superb example of why Catholics cannot leave the church" (p. 110).

2. Richard P. McBrien, *Catholicism*, 2 vols. (Minneapolis: Winston Press, 1980), 2:1183.

3. The first two sections of this chapter are a revision of my article "Reaching for Fidelity: Roman Catholic Theology Today," in John D. Woodbridge and Thomas Edward McComiskey, eds., *Doing Theology in Today's World: Essays in Honor of Kenneth S. Kantzer* (Grand Rapids: Zondervan, 1991), 321-38.

4. Karl Barth, "Foreword" to *Church Dogmatics*, I.1, *The Doctrine of the Word of God* (Edinburgh: T. & T. Clark, 1936; repr., 1960), x.

5. Karl Barth, "The Humanity of God," in *The Humanity of God* (Richmond: John Knox, 1960), 37-65; for his message to Emil Brunner, see Eberhard Busch, *Karl Barth: His Life from Letters and Autobiographical Texts* (Philadelphia: Fortress Press, 1976), 195-96 and 476-77. Brunner was at one time an ally of Barth but because Barth compromised in his idea of "natural theology," their relationship became quite strained.

6. See Thomas F. O'Meara, *Fundamentalism: A Catholic Perspective* (New York: Paulist Press, 1990), 82-83.

7. David Tracy, *The Analogical Imagination: Christian Theology and the Culture of Pluralism* (New York: Crossroad, 1981), 410.

8. Andrew M. Greeley, *The Catholic Imagination* (Berkeley/Los Angeles/London: University of California Press, 2000), 1-21.

9. McBrien, *Catholicism*, 2:1180.

10. See Julian of Norwich, *Showings*, part 1, chapter 5: http://www.umilta.net/love1.html; Joseph Mary Plunkett, "I See His Blood upon the Rose": http://www.umilta.net/love1.html; Gerard Manley Hopkins, "God's Grandeur": http://www.bartleby.com/122/7.html.

11. Paul VI, the opening speech at the Second Session of the Second Vatican Council, September 29, 1963, in *Il Concilio Vaticano* (Bologna: Edizioni Dehoniane, 1968), 96. The pope was referring to the mystery that is the church, but Richard McBrien takes this phrase in a wider sense as a way of describing a sacrament. See Richard P. McBrien, "Roman Catholicism," in Lindsay Jones, ed., *The Encyclopedia of Religion* (Detroit: Thomson Gale, 2005), 12:7881.

12. Lawrence Cunningham, *The Catholic Experience* (New York: Crossroad, 1985), 115.

13. See Thomas H. Groome, *What Makes Us Catholic: Eight Gifts for Life* (San Francisco: HarperSanFrancisco, 2002), 92.

14. See Ada María Isasi-Díaz, "Lo Cotidiano: A Key Element of Mujerista Theology," *Journal of Hispanic/Latino Theology*, 10, 1 (2002): 5-17. See also Roberto S. Goizueta, *Caminemos con Jesús: Toward a Hispanic/Latino Theology of Accompaniment* (Maryknoll, N.Y.: Orbis Books, 1995), 47-76.

15. Friedrich Schleiermacher, *The Christian Faith*, Thesis 24 (Philadelphia: Fortress Press, 1976; 1st ed., 1928), 103.

16. McBrien, *Catholicism*, 2:1173.

17. Rosemary Haughton, *The Catholic Thing* (Springfield, Ill.: Templegate, 1979), 59.

18. See, for example, Theological Advisory Commission, "Asian Christian Perspectives on Harmony," in Franz-Josef Eilers, ed., *For All the Peoples of Asia: Federation of Asian Bishops' Conferences Documents from 1992 to 1996* (Quezon City, Philippines: Claretian Publications), 229-98; Joseph Komonchak, *Foundations in Ecclesiology*, Lonergan Workshop Monographs 11 (Boston: Lonergan Institute, Boston College, 1995); Donald L. Gelpi, ed., *Beyond Individualism: Toward a Retrieval of Moral Discourse in America* (Notre Dame, Ind.: University of Notre Dame Press, 1989); Donald L. Gelpi, *Inculturating American Theology: An Experiment in Foundational Method* (Atlanta: Scholars Press, 1988); John Haught, *God after Darwin: A Theology of Evolution* (Boulder, Colo.: Westview Press, 2000).

19. See Francis X. Clooney, "The Emerging Field of Comparative Theology: A Bibliographical Review (1989-1995)," *Theological Studies* 56, no. 3 (March 1995): 521-50; James L. Fredericks, *Buddhists and Christians: Through Comparative Theology to Solidarity* (Maryknoll, N.Y.: Orbis Books, 2004).

20. Timothy Radcliffe, *What Is the Point of Being Christian?* (London: Burns & Oates; New York: Continuum, 2006), 164-78; Robert J. Schreiter, "Two Forms of Catholicity in a Time of Globalization," *Himig Ugnayan* 8 (2007): 1-17.

21. Haughton, *Catholic Thing*, 15-16.

22. Stephen Happel and David Tracy, *A Catholic Vision* (Philadelphia: Fortress Press, 1984), 14.

23. McBrien, *Catholicism*, 2:1174-75; Avery Dulles, *The Reshaping of Catholicism: Current Changes in the Theology of the Church* (New York: Harper & Row, 1988), 72.

24. J. J. Connelley, "The Task of Theology," *Proceedings of the Catholic Theological Society of America* (1974), 1-58. The three principles referred to in the text are laid out on pp. 42-53.

25. McBrien, *Catholicism*, 1176-1180.

26. Even though he himself was not Catholic, the late U.S. Anglo anthropologist and long-time missionary to India Paul Hiebert (1933-2007) was very catholic in his thought and contributed a fine article to the literature on critical realism. See his "Epistemological Foundations for Science and Theology" and "The Missiological Implications of an Epis-

temological Shift," in his *Anthropological Reflections on Missiological Issues* (Grand Rapids: Baker, 1994), 19-34 and 35-51.

27. See Juan Luis Segundo, *Christ in the Spiritual Exercises of St. Ignatius* (Maryknoll, N.Y.: Orbis Books, 1987), 22-26; see Roger Haight, *Jesus: Symbol of God* (Maryknoll, N.Y.: Orbis Books, 1999), 88.

28. Augustine, Letter 187, 34 in *The Works of St. Augustine: A Translation for the 21ˢᵗ Century, Letters 156-210*, ed. Boniface Ramsey, trans. Roland Teske (Hyde Park, N.Y.: New City Press, 2004), 246-47 (I originally found the quotation in Robert Kress, *The Church: Communion, Sacrament, Communication* [Mahwah, N.J.: Paulist Press, 1985], 138); Edward Schillebeeckx, *Christ the Sacrament of the Encounter with God* (New York: Sheed & Ward, 1963).

29. Thomas F. O'Meara, "The Future of Catholicism," inaugural lecture as William K. Warren Professor of Theology at the University of Notre Dame (October 15, 1986), 3.

30. Haughton, *Catholic Thing*, 9-11. All quotations in the following paragraphs are from these pages.

31. Happel and Tracy, *Catholic Vision*, 31.

32. See David Tracy, *Blessed Rage for Order: The New Pluralism in Theology* (New York: Seabury Press, 1975), 29 and passim. Tracy is indebted to Schubert Ogden's essay "What Is Theology?" in Ogden, *On Theology* (New York: Harper & Row, 1986), 1-21.

33. O'Meara, *Fundamentalism*, 1. I owe much in this section to this excellent book, as the reader will readily see.

34. Richard P. McBrien, "Threat of Catholic Fundamentalism," *The Catholic Transcript* (July 25, 1985): 5, quoted in O'Meara, *Fundamentalism*, 66.

35. O'Meara, *Fundamentalism*, 7-8.

36. Benedict XVI in the press conference on the plane en route to Brazil, see http://www.vatican.va/holy_father/benedict_xvi/speeches/2007/may/documents/hf_ben-xvi_spe_20070509_interview-brazil_en.html; see also http://www.catholic.org/international/international_story.php?id=24732 for an article on the bishops' implementation of the Aparecida document.

37. Federation of Asian Bishops' Conferences, "A Renewed Church in Asia: A Mission of Love and Service" (2000), in Franz-Josef Eilers, ed., *For All the Peoples of Asia: Federation of Asian Bishops' Conferences Documents from 1997 to 2001*, vol. 3 (Quezon City, Philippines: Claretian Publications, 2002), 6-7.

38. Martin E. Marty and R. Scott Appleby, eds., *Fundamentalisms Observed* (Chicago/London: University of Chicago Press, 1991). The project itself is entitled "The Fundamentalism Project," and when completed it consisted of four additional volumes: *Fundamentalisms and Society* (1992), *Fundamentalisms and the State* (1992), *Accounting for Fundamentalisms* (1994), and *Fundamentalisms Comprehended* (1995). This is certainly the most complete study of fundamentalism that exists.

39. Marty and Appleby, *Fundamentalisms Observed*, ix.

40. Bruce B. Lawrence, *Defenders of God: The Fundamentalist Revolt against the Modern Age* (San Francisco: Harper & Row, 1989), 2-3.

41. Marty and Appleby, *Fundamentalisms Observed*, ix.

42. O'Meara, *Fundamentalism*, 87.

43. Ibid.

44. See the Pontifical Biblical Commission, "The Interpretation of the Bible in the Church" (1993), http://catholic-resources.org/ChurchDocs/PBC_Interp.htm.

45. See the famous hymn, "There's a Wideness in God's Mercy": http://catholic-resources.org/ ChurchDocs/PBC_Interp.htm. The phrase is also the title of a book by the Evangelical theologian Clark Pinnock, who after publishing it received the scorn of many

of his Evangelical colleagues. See Clark Pinnock, *A Wideness in God's Mercy: The Uniqueness of Jesus Christ in a World of Religions* (Grand Rapids: William B. Eerdmans, 1992).

46. O'Meara, *Fundamentalism*, 84.

47. Ibid., 92.

PART IV. FAITH SEEKING THROUGH THE AGES

1. Alister E. McGrath, *Christian Theology: An Introduction* (Oxford/Cambridge, Mass.: Blackwell, 1994), 3.

2. Ibid.

3. James D. Whitehead and Evelyn Eaton Whitehead, *Method in Ministry: Theological Reflection and Christian Ministry*, rev. ed. (Kansas City, Mo.: Sheed & Ward, 1995), 9.

10. CHRISTIAN THEOLOGY
FROM THE BEGINNINGS TO 1000

1. Rodney Stark, *The Rise of Christianity: How the Obscure, Marginal Jesus Movement Became the Dominant Religious Force in the Western World in a Few Centuries* (San Francisco: HarperSanFrancisco, 1997), 6-7. Stark, a sociologist of religion, calculates that at a 40 percent increase per decade, if the Christian population was 1,000 in 40 C.E., it would have reached 6,299,832 by the year 300. If the population of the Roman empire was about sixty million, this would be 10.5 percent of the people. These figures are somewhat contested by scholars, but what seems to be the case is that Constantine legalized and favored Christianity in 313 as a way of unifying the empire. He saw, as it were, the handwriting on the wall: with a 40-percent increase per decade, the Christian population, Stark projects, would have increased to 33,882,008 in the year 350, or 56.5 percent of the population.

2. Michael Green, *Evangelism in the Early Church* (Grand Rapids: William B. Eerdmans, 1970), 173.

3. Stephen B. Bevans and Roger P. Schroeder, *Constants in Context: A Theology of Mission for Today* (Maryknoll, N.Y.: Orbis Books, 2004), 78.

4. Dale T. Irvin and Scott W. Sunquist, *History of the World Christian Movement*, vol. 1, *Earliest Christianity to 1453* (Maryknoll, N.Y.: Orbis Books, 2001), 111-14.

5. Frederick W. Norris, *Christianity: A Short Global History* (Oxford: OneWorld, 2002), 88.

6. Ibid., 93.

7. Green, *Evangelism in the Early Church*, 173.

8. We start our history of theology with the New Testament, but it is important to recognize the contextual nature of the Old Testament Scriptures as well. In the Book of Genesis alone, scholars have now long recognized, a final editor has woven strands of the older "Yahwist" theology together with the later "Priestly," "Elohist," and even "Deuteronomic" theologies. The prophets and their editors came out of very particular historical circumstances and borrowed culturally conditioned historical forms like the "trial narrative." Wisdom literature was written at a time when Israel was being influenced or even threatened by Hellenistic culture. See, for example, the work of the longtime missionary to India and French biblical scholar Lucien Legrand, *The Bible on Culture* (Maryknoll, N.Y.: Orbis Books, 2000) and the work of Nigerian Old Testament scholar James Chukwuma Okoye, *Israel and the Nations* (Maryknoll, N.Y.: Orbis Books, 2006).

9. Aidan Nichols, *The Shape of Catholic Theology: An Introduction to Its Sources, Principles and History* (Collegeville, Minn.: Liturgical Press, 1991), 269.

10. Raymond E. Brown, *An Introduction to the New Testament* (New York: Doubleday, 1997), 110.

11. British Orthodox theologian Andrew Louth remarks that the "mothers" are "perhaps no less important for being largely unknown by name." He points out also that, for the Orthodox tradition, the "patristic" period "refers to the period between the apostolic period and now," to those men and women who have "handed on to us the faith." See Andrew Louth, *Wisdom of the Byzantine Church: Evagrios of Pontos and Maximos the Confessor*, The 1997 Paine Lectures in Religion at the University of Missouri-Columbia (Columbia: University of Missouri, 1998), 3.

12. Alister McGrath, *Christian Theology: An Introduction* (Oxford/Cambridge, Mass.: Blackwell, 1994), 8.

13. Nichols, *Shape of Catholic Theology*, 286. De Lubac spoke of renewal in the *Western* church. I would think this is true in every part of the church, even though the Eastern church has always stayed close to the "patristic" witness.

14. The text of the *Didache* may be found in John W. Coakley and Andrea Sterk, eds., *Readings in World Christian History*, vol. 1, *Earliest Christianity to 1453* (Maryknoll, N.Y.: Orbis Books, 2004), 12-16. References will be given in the text, according to chapter and section, e.g., 1.3.

15. Maxwell Staniforth, introduction to the Letters of Ignatius of Antioch, in *Early Christian Writings* (Middlesex, England: Penguin Books, 1968), 65.

16. See Paul Bernier, *Ministry in the Church: A Historical and Pastoral Approach* (Mystic, Conn.: Twenty-Third Publications, 1992), 23-26.

17. Richard R. Gaillardetz, *Ecclesiology for a Global Church: A People Called and Sent*, Theology in Global Perspective (Maryknoll, N.Y.: Orbis Books, 2008), 252.

18. The translation is by Maxwell Staniforth, in *Early Christian Writings*, 77-78.

19. Stark, *Rise of Christianity*, 179, quoting W. H. C. Frend, *Martyrdom and Persecution in the Early Church* (Oxford: Basil Blackwell, 1965), 413.

20. Tertullian, *Apology* 50, in Alexander Roberts and James Donaldson, eds., *Ante-Nicene Christian Library*, Volume XI, The Writings of Tertullian, Volume I (Edinburgh: T. & T. Clark, 1866), 139.

21. The text can be found at http://www.earlychristianwritings.com/text/martyrdom polycarp-hoole.html.

22. The text can be found in Coakley and Sterk, *Readings*, 1:30-37.

23. The text can be found in ibid., 24-30.

24. Justo L. González, *A History of Christian Thought*, vol. 1, *From the Beginnings to the Council of Chalcedon*, rev. ed. (Nashville, Tenn.: Abingdon Press, 1989), 101.

25. Justin Martyr, *First Apology* 46.3-4, quoted in González, *History*, 103.

26. Justin Martyr, *Second Apology* 10.2-3, quoted in González, *History*, 103-4.

27. Bevans and Schroeder, *Constants in Context*, 85.

28. Irvin and Sunquist, *History*, 123.

29. Clement of Alexandria, *Miscellanies* 1.5, quoted in Irvin and Sunquist, *History*, 123.

30. David L. Edwards, *Christianity: The First Two Thousand Years* (Maryknoll, N.Y.: Orbis Books, 1997), 68.

31. Hans Küng, *Christianity: Essence, History, and Future* (New York: Continuum, 1995), 163.

32. Ibid.; González, *History*, 208.

33. González, *History*, 209.

34. Ibid., 210.

35. Justo L. González, *Christian Thought Revisited: Three Types of Theology*, rev. ed. (Maryknoll, N.Y.: Orbis Books, 1999), 25.

36. Irvin and Sunquist, *History*, 124.

37. González, *Christian Thought*, 4.

38. Tertullian was one of the first Christian theologians to reflect on the reality of God as Trinity. Nigerian theologian A. Okechukwu Ogbonnaya suggests that Tertullian's approach to trinitarian theology was influenced by African understandings of a communitarian God—something rather ironic given Tertullian's opposition to any human reasoning or experience in the doing of theology. See A. Okechukwu Ogbonnaya, "African Communal Analysis of Tertullian's Divinity," in his *On Communitarian Divinity: An African Interpretation of the Trinity* (St. Paul: Paragon House, 1998), 51-74.

39. Some of these words and sayings are cited in Edwards, *Christianity*, 61-62.

40. *First Letter of Clement* 20.11, quoted in González, *Christian Thought*, 20.

41. González, *Christian Thought*, 20-22.

42. Ibid., 33-36.

43. Ibid., 15

44. Irenaeus, *Adversus Haereses* 4 prologue, quoted in González, *Christian Thought*, 141.

45. For what follows, see Robin E. Waterfield, *Christians in Persia* (New York: Barnes & Noble, 1973), 16-17; Irvin and Sunquist, *History*, 125-26; Bevans and Schroeder, *Constants in Context*, 75-78; J. P. Arendzen, "Bardesanes and Bardesenites (*Bar-Daisan*)," *The Catholic Encyclopedia*, vol. 3 (1907), http://www.newadvent.org/cathen/02293a.htm; Alberto Camplani, "Bardaisan," *Encyclopedia of Religion*, 2nd ed., ed. Lindsay Jones (Detroit: Macmillan Reference USA, 2005), 2:786-87.

46. Arendzen, "Bardesanes."

47. Irvin and Sunquist, *History*, 126.

48. See Bevans and Schroeder, *Constants in Context*, 78; González, *History*, 109-12; Patrick J. Healey, "Tatian," *The Catholic Encyclopedia*, vol. 14 (1912), http://www.newadvent.org/cathen/14464b.htm; M. Whittaker, "Tatian," *New Catholic Encyclopedia*, 2nd ed. (Detroit: Thomson Gale, 2003), 13:764-65.

49. Nichols, *Shape of Catholic Theology*, 263.

50. The Nicene Creed. See the text in Coakley and Sterk, *Readings*, 1:101. See also Jaroslav Pelikan and Valerie Hotchkiss, eds., *Creeds and Confessions of Faith in the Christian Tradition*, vol. 1, *Early, Eastern, and Medieval* (New Haven: Yale University Press, 2003), 158-59.

51. David Edwards, *Christianity*, 70.

52. Ibid., 97. On this Platonic understanding of God and its theological implications, see also Justo L. González, *A Concise History of Christian Doctrine* (Nashville, Tenn.: Abingdon Press, 2005), 72-77.

53. Catherine Mowry LaCugna, "The Trinitarian Mystery of God," in John Galvin and Francis Schüssler Fiorenza, eds., *Systematic Theology: Roman Catholic Perspectives*, vol. 1 (Minneapolis: Fortress Press, 1991), 152. LaCugna refers to Gregory of Nyssa, *De Deitate Filii et Spiritus Sancti*, PG 46:557.

54. Irvin and Sunquist, *History*, 114; Waterfield, *Christians in Persia*, 20.

55. Bernard McGinn, "Athanasius of Alexandria," in his *The Doctors of the Church: Thirty-Three Men and Women Who Shaped Christianity* (New York: Crossroad, 1999), 27.

56. Athanasius of Alexandria, in R. W. Thomson, trans., *De Incarnatione*, chapter 54 (London: Oxford University Press, 1971), quoted in McGinn, *Doctors*, 29.

57. See Orlando Espín, "Doctors of the Church," in idem and James B. Nickoloff, eds.,

An Introductory Dictionary of Theology and Religious Studies (Collegeville, Minn.: Liturgical Press, 2007), 360; McGinn, *Doctors*, 1-21.

58. McGinn, *Doctors*, 43. On Basil's doctrine of the Holy Spirit, see the work of the Australian theologian Denis Edwards, "Basil on the Holy Spirit," in his *Breath of Life: A Theology of the Creator Spirit* (Maryknoll, N.Y.: Orbis Books, 2004), 16-30.

59. Basil of Caesarea, *On the Holy Spirit* 16.38, quoted in McGinn, *Doctors*, 45.

60. Gregory Nanzianzen, *Theological Orations* 29.2, PG 36:76, quoted in Catherine Mowry LaCugna, "God in Communion with Us: The Trinity," in Catherine Mowry LaCugna, ed., *Freeing Theology: The Essentials of Theology in Feminist Perspective* (San Francisco: HarperSanFrancisco, 1993), 87 n. 4.

61. See Gregory of Nyssa's *On the Deity of the Son and the Holy Spirit*, PG 46:554-76, and *On the Holy Spirit against the Macedonians*, PG 45:1301-34.

62. Gregory of Nyssa, *Life of Macrina*; *On the Soul and the Resurrection* 1, trans. Catharine R. Roth (Crestwood, N.Y.: St. Vladimir's Seminary Press, 1993), 27, quoted in Jaroslav Pelikan, *Christianity and Classical Culture: The Metamorphosis of Natural Theology in the Christian Encounter with Hellenism* (Chicago: University of Chicago Press, 1971), 8.

63. See Gregory of Nyssa, *On the Soul and the Resurrection*, trans. Catharine R. Roth, 103.

64. See Waterfield, *Christians in Persia*, 20 and McGinn, *Doctors*, 31-35.

65. Theodoret of Cyrrhus, Letter 146, quoted in McGinn, *Doctors*, 32.

66. McGinn, *Doctors*, 31.

67. Ephrem the Syrian, *On the Nativity* 1.99, in Coakley and Sterk, *Readings*, 1:117, quoted in McGinn, *Doctors*, 34.

68. Ephrem the Syrian, *On the Nativity* 1.51, in Coakley and Sterk, *Readings*, 1:115.

69. Kuncheria Pathil and Dominic Veliath, *An Introduction to Theology*, Indian Theological Series (Bangalore: Theological Publications in India, 2003), 120. See their treatment of Ephrem on pp. 119-25.

70. Francis X. E. Albert, "Aphraates," *The Catholic Encyclopedia*, vol. 1 (1907), http://www.newadvent.org/cathen/01593c.htm.

71. Norris, *Christianity*, 41. See F. C. Burkitt, *Early Christianity outside the Roman Empire* ((Piscataway, N.J.: Gorgias Press, 2002 [originally published in 1899]).

72. Gary Macy, "Dionysius the Areopagite (Pseudo)," in Orlando O. Espín and James B. Nickoloff, eds., *An Introductory Dictionary of Theology and Religious Studies* (Collegeville, Minn.: Liturgical Press, 2007), 351.

73. See ibid. and Donald Duclow, "Dionysius the Areopagite," in *Encyclopedia of Religion*, 2nd ed., ed. Lindsay Jones (Detroit: Macmillan Reference USA, 2005), 4:2355.

74. See Justo L. González, *A History of Christian Thought*, vol. 2, *From Augustine to the Eve of the Reformation* (Nashville, Tenn.: Abingdon Press, 1971), 93-96.

75. Francis X. Murphy, "Pseudo-Dionysius," *New Catholic Encyclopedia*, 2nd ed. (Detroit: Thomson Gale, 2003), 11:801.

76. McGinn, *Doctors*, 36.

77. Hilary of Poitiers, *The Trinity* 2.7, quoted in McGinn, *Doctors*, 38.

78. Augustine, *Confessions* 3.1, in *The Confessions of St. Augustine*, trans. Frank J. Sheed (New York: Sheed & Ward, 1942), 35.

79. Augustine, *Confessions* 9.10-11, trans. Sheed, 163-66.

80. Garry Wills, *Saint Augustine* (New York: Viking/Penguin Books, 1999), xii.

81. Henry Chadwick, *Augustine* (Oxford: Oxford University Press, 1986), 118-19.

82. McGinn, *Doctors*, 66.

83. Chadwick, *Augustine*, 79.

84. González, *Concise History*, 153.
85. Chadwick, *Augustine*, 108.
86. See ibid.
87. Peter Brown, *Augustine of Hippo: A Biography*, rev. ed. (Berkeley/Los Angeles: University of California Press, 2000), 342.
88. See Chadwick, *Augustine*, 111. In Augustine's earlier writing he had suggested that unbaptized infants might "find their destiny in neither heaven nor hell" (ibid.)—but in a liminal state, a *limbus*, or what posterity would call "Limbo." On April 19, 2007, the International Theological Commission of the Congregation for the Doctrine of the Faith issued a statement affirming that, though Limbo remains a viable theological doctrine, it was never one officially taught by the Catholic Church. See International Theological Commission, "The Hope of Salvation for Infants Who Die without Being Baptized," http://www.vatican.va/roman_curia/congregations/cfaith/cti_documents/rc_con_cfaith_doc_20070419_un-baptised-infants_en.html, 40-41.
89. See Peter Holmes, trans., *The Anti-Pelagian Works of Saint Augustine, Bishop of Hippo,* in *Works of Aurelius Augustine, Bishop of Hippo*, vols. 4, 12, and 15 (Edinburgh: T&T Clark, 1872). See Brown, *Augustine*, 340-410.
90. Brown, *Augustine*, 348.
91. Chadwick, *Augustine*, 114.
92. Ibid., 116.
93. See ibid., 97.
94. Ibid.
95. *City of God* 14.28, quoted in McGinn, *Doctors*, 69.
96. See Robert J. Schreiter, "Two Forms of Catholicity in a Time of Globalization," *Himig Ugnayan* 8 (2007): 1-17.
97. McGinn, *Doctors*, 69.
98. See Augustine, *The Works of St. Augustine: A Translation for the 21ˢᵗ Century*, ed. John E. Rotelle (Brooklyn, N.Y.: New City Press): *Confessions*, trans. Maria Boulding (1997); *Teaching Christianity* (De Doctrina Christiana), trans. Edmund Hill (1996); *The Trinity* (De Trinitate), trans. Edmund Hill (1991). Augustine, *Homilies on the Gospel according to St. John*, trans. H. Browne (Oxford: J. H. Parker, 1848-49).
99. Catherine M. LaCugna, *God for Us: The Trinity and Christian Life* (San Francisco: HarperSanFrancisco, 1991), esp. 81-109.
100. Jerome, Epistle 195, quoted in Chadwick, *Augustine*, 117.
101. See Mary T. Malone, *Women and Christianity*, vol. 1, *The First Thousand Years* (Maryknoll, N.Y.: Orbis Books, 2000), 135-40; see also Robert Ellsberg, *All Saints: Daily Reflections on Saints, Prophets and Witnesses for Our Time* (New York: Crossroad, 1997), 47, 55-56, 570-71.
102. Malone, *Women*, 136.
103. Jerome, *In Isaiam*, 1-2, PL 24:17.
104. See McGinn, *Doctors*, 63 and Malone, *Women*, 158-61.
105. See Thomas Cahill, *How the Irish Saved Civilization: The Untold Story of Ireland's Heroic Role from the Fall of Rome to the Rise of Medieval Europe* (New York: Nan F. Talese/Doubleday, 1995), especially 145-96.
106. Regis A. Duffy, "Sacraments," in Francis Schüssler Fiorenza and John Galvin, eds., *Systematic Theology: Roman Catholic Perspectives*, vol. 2 (Minneapolis: Fortress Press, 1991), 238-39.
107. McGinn, *Doctors*, 85. McGinn speaks of Gregory's "masterpiece" on p. 87. See also González, *History of Christian Thought*, 2:71-74.

108. Josef Pieper, *Scholasticism: Personalities and Problems in Medieval Philosophy* (New York/Toronto: McGraw-Hill, 1960), 26-27.

109. Ibid., 36. Pieper cites Martin Grabmann, *Die Geschichte der scholastichen Methode*, I (Freiburg, 1909), 148.

110. Ellsberg, *All Saints*, 462.

111. Pieper, *Scholasticism*, 30-31.

112. See Louth, *Wisdom*, 12-45.

113. Norris, *Christianity*, 79.

114. Quoted in David Edwards, *Christianity*, 119. See John of Damascus, *On the Divine Images*, in Coakley and Sterk, *Readings*, 1:289-97.

115. See Norris, *Christianity*, 81. The citation is from a handout given at a lecture at Catholic Theological Union, November 7, 2006, by Mark N. Swanson of the Lutheran School of Theology at Chicago. The lecture was entitled "A Neglected Chapter in Global Christian History: The Arabic Christian Tradition." For the full text of this important work, see Margaret Dunlop Gibson, ed., *An Arabic Version of the Acts of the Apostles and the Seven Catholic Epistles from an Eighth or Ninth Century MS, in the Convent of St. Catherine on Mount Sinai, with a Treatise on the Triune Nature of God*, Studia Sinaitica 7 (London: Cambridge University Press, 1899; repr., Piscataway, N.J.: Gorgias Press, 2003).

116. Norris, *Christianity*, 82.

117. Ibid. For part of the text of the dialogue, see Coakley and Sterk, *Readings*, 231-32.

118. Irvin and Sunquist, *History*, 1:317.

119. Ibid. Irvin and Sunquist make reference to P. Y. Saeki, *The Nestorian Documents and Relics in China* (Tokyo: Academy of Oriental Culture Tokyo Institute, 1937), 121. The text of the inscription can be found in Coakley and Sterk, *Readings*, 1:243-47.

120. See Irvin and Sunquist, *History*, 318. See also Martin Palmer, ed. *The Jesus Sutras: Rediscovering the Lost Scrolls of Taoist Christianity* (New York: Ballantine Wellspring, 2001); and Ray Riegert and Thomas Moore, eds., *The Lost Sutras of Jesus: Unlocking the Ancient Wisdom of the Xian Monks* (Berkeley, Calif.: Ulysses Press, 2006). Part of the text of these documents can be found in Coakley and Sterk, *Readings*, 247-51.

121. Norris, *Christianity*, 88. My colleague Roger Schroeder visited this Buddhist monastery near Xian in the summer of 2007 and tells of a wonderful encounter with one of the monks there.

122. G. Ronald Murphy, *The Saxon Savior: The Transformation of the Gospel in the Ninth Century Heliand* (Oxford: Oxford University Press, 1989). See also G. Ronald Murphy, trans., *The Heliand: The Saxon Gospel* (Oxford: Oxford University Press, 1992); and Douglas Hayward, "Contextualizing the Gospel among the Saxons: An Example from the Ninth Century of the Cultural Adaptation of the Gospel as Found in *The Heliand*," *Missiology: An International Review* 22, no. 4 (October 1994): 439-53.

123. See Hayward, "Contextualizing the Gospel," 445.

124. See the important work by James C. Russell, *The Germanization of Early Medieval Christianity: A Sociohistorical Approach to Religious Transformation* (New York: Oxford University Press, 1994).

125. See Ralph McInerny, *A History of Western Philosophy*, vol. 2, http://maritain.nd.edu/jmc/etext/hwp206.htm. See also González, *History of Christian Thought*, 2:118-22.

126. John Paul II, *Slavorum Apostoli*, 1. See http://www.vatican.va/edocs/ENG0220/__P1.HTM.

11. CHRISTIAN THEOLOGY FROM 1000 TO 1700

1. Frederick W. Norris, *Christianity: A Short Global History* (Oxford: OneWorld, 2002), 108.

2. Dale Irvin and Scott Sunquist, *History of the World Christian Movement*, vol. 1, *Earliest Christianity to 1453* (Maryknoll, N.Y.: Orbis Books, 2001), 504.

3. See Stephen B. Bevans and Roger P. Schroeder, *Constants in Context: A Theology of Mission for Today* (Maryknoll, N.Y.: Orbis Books, 2004), 174; J. B. Heffernan, "Lepanto, Battle of," *New Catholic Encyclopedia* (New York: McGraw Hill, 1967), 3:665-66; G. Winner and E. P. Colbert, "Vienna," *New Catholic Encyclopedia*, 14:654.

4. Irvin and Sunquist, *History*, 392. In summarizing the complex events that follow I am relying closely on Irvin and Sunquist, 369-71 and 390-93.

5. "Decree of Union with the Greek Church," Florence, January 1439, 6, in Jaroslav Pelikan and Valerie Hotchkiss, eds., *Creeds and Confessions of Faith in the Christian Tradition*, vol. 1, *Early, Eastern and Medieval* (New Haven: Yale University Press, 2003), 754.

6. Ibid., 10, in Pelikan and Hotchkiss, 754-55.

7. Richard Tarnas, *The Passion of the Western Mind: Understanding the Ideas That Have Shaped Our World View* (New York: Ballantine Books, 1991), 173.

8. Anselm of Canterbury, *Proslogion*, preface and chapter 1, lines 154-57, in *The Prayers and Meditations of St. Anselm*, translated and with an introduction by Sister Benedicta Ward, S.L.G. (Harmondsworth, England: Penguin Books, 1973), 238 and 244.

9. Ibid., chapter 2, lines 158-60; chapter 3, lines 195-96.

10. See Norris, *Christianity*, 103-4; and Karl Barth, *Anselm: Fides Quaerens Intellectum* (Cleveland/New York: Meridian Books, 1960), 9.

11. Norris, *Christianity*, 103.

12. Elizabeth A. Johnson, "Jesus and Salvation," in The Catholic Theological Society, *Proceedings of the Forty-Ninth Annual Convention*, ed. Paul Crowley (Santa Clara University, 1994), 5. A good portion of the text of *Cur Deus Homo* can be found in John W. Coakley and Andrea Sterk, eds., *Readings in World Christian History*, vol. 1, *Earliest Christianity to 1453* (Maryknoll, N.Y.: Orbis Books, 2004), 339-46.

13. See M. T. Clanchy, *Abelard: A Medieval Life* (Oxford: Blackwell, 1997), 283.

14. Abelard's ideas are expressed in a number of his works. See Clanchy, *Abelard*, 283-87.

15. Justo González, *A History of Christian Thought*, vol. 2, *From Augustine to the Eve of the Reformation*, rev. ed. (Nashville, Tenn.: Abingdon Press, 1971), 171-72.

16. David L. Edwards, *Christianity: The First Two Thousand Years* (Maryknoll, N.Y.: Orbis Books, 1997), 238.

17. Edwards, *Christianity*, 239, quoting Abelard's *History of My Calamities*. The text can be found in J. T. Muckle, *The Story of Abelard's Adventures: A Translation with Notes of the Historia Calamitatum* (Toronto: Pontifical Institute of Medieval Studies, 1954), 25.

18. See Clanchy, *Abelard*, 278.

19. Aidan Nichols, *The Shape of Catholic Theology* (Collegeville, Minn.: Liturgical Press, 1991), 293, quoting Bernard, Sermon 36, PL 183:967.

20. For more detailed treatment of Bernard, William, and the "Victorines," see Emero Stiegman, "Bernard of Clairvaux, William of St. Thierry, the Victorines," in G. R. Evans, ed., *The Medieval Theologians: An Introduction to Theology in the Medieval Period* (Oxford: Blackwell, 2001), 129-55.

21. Stiegman, "Bernard," 142.

22. Ibid., 142-43.

23. Ibid., 46.

24. Nichols, *Shape of Catholic Theology*, 295. In her essay "Peter Lombard" in Evans, *Medieval Theologians*, 168, Marcia L. Colish writes that Lombard was born between 1095 and 1100 and died in 1161. Nichols gives the date of his death as 1160.

25. Colish, "Peter Lombard," 182.

26. Ibid.; see also Nichols, *Shape of Catholic Theology*, 295.

27. See Thomas F. O'Meara, *Thomas Aquinas: Theologian* (Notre Dame, Ind.: University of Notre Dame Press, 1997),13.

28. See Bernard McGinn, *The Doctors of the Church: Thirty-Three Men and Women Who Shaped Christianity* (Mahwah, N.J.: Paulist Press, 1999), 115.

29. González, *History of Christian Thought*, 2:258. Here I am relying heavily on González, 258-60.

30. O'Meara, *Thomas Aquinas*, 33. However, McGinn does quote a similar legend about Aquinas as "dumb ox" (*Doctors*, 124).

31. O'Meara, *Thomas Aquinas*, 34.

32. Ibid., 4.

33. Ibid., 26-27.

34. See the various diagrams in ibid., 56-68. See also the very convenient edition of the *Summa* on the "New Advent" Web site, http://www.newadvent.org/summa/.

35. See Nichols, *Shape of Catholic Theology*, 297.

36. See David B. Burrell, *Knowing the Unknowable God: Aquinas, Maimonides, Ibn Sina* (Notre Dame, Ind.: University of Notre Dame Press, 1986). I was privileged to participate in a seminar conducted by David Burrell on this subject at the University of Notre Dame in the fall semester of 1982.

37. See the sketch of Bonaventure's life in Michael Robson, "Saint Bonaventure," in Evans, *Medieval Theologians*, 187.

38. *Bonaventurae Opera Omnia*, 10 vols. (Quaracchi: Collegio San Bonaventura, 1882-1902).

39. Robson, "Saint Bonaventure," quoting Bonaventure's *Collationes in Hexaemeron* 12, no. 17 in *Bonaventurae Opera Omnia*, 5:387.

40. Bonaventure, *The Journey of the Mind to God*, ed. Stephen F. Brown (Indianapolis: Hacket, 1993); *The Major Legend of St. Francis (1260-1263)* and *The Min or Legend*, in Regis Armstrong, J. A. Wayne Hellmann, and William J. Short, eds., *Francis of Assisi: Early Documents*, vol. 2, *The Founder* (New York/London/Manila: New City Press, 2000), 525-683 and 684-717; *Breviloquium*, trans. Erwin Esser Nemmers (St. Louis, Mo.: Herder, 1946).

41. Zachary Hayes, "Bonaventure: Mystery of the Triune God," in Kenan B. Osborne, ed., *The History of Franciscan Theology* (St. Bonaventure, N.Y.: Franciscan Institute, 1994), 51. See also Zachary Hayes, *The Hidden Center: Spirituality and Speculative Christology in St. Bonaventure* (New York: Paulist Press, 1981).

42. Hayes, "Bonaventure: Mystery of the Triune God," 44.

43. See S. Mark Heim, *The Depth of the Riches: A Trinitarian Theology of Religious Ends* (Grand Rapids: William B. Eerdmans, 2001), 98-99.

44. See Tarnas, *Passion of the Western Mind*, 192.

45. See Jacques Le Goff, *The Birth of Purgatory* (Chicago: University of Chicago Press, 1984), 334. For theological reflections on Dante's masterpiece, see Heim, 96-117 and Le Goff, 334-355. Le Goff's notes also indicate important commentaries on the poem.

46. McGinn, *Doctors*, 134.

47. See Bevans and Schroeder, *Constants in Context*, 143.

48. Norris, *Christianity*, 111.

49. Ibid., 111-12.

50. See Bevans and Schroeder, *Constants in Context*, 151, who refer to Stephen Neill, *History of Christian Missions*, rev. ed. (New York: Penguin Books, 1986), 114-15.

51. Oliver Davies, "Late Medieval Theologians," in Evans, *Medieval Theologians*, 223.

52. Robert Ellsberg, *All Saints: Daily Reflections on Saints, Prophets, and Witnesses for Our Time* (New York: Crossroad, 1997), 405.

53. Mary T. Malone, *Women and Christianity*, vol. 2, *From 1000 to the Reformation* (Maryknoll, N.Y.: Orbis Books, 2002), 108.

54. Ibid., 111.

55. Ibid., 112.

56. Ibid., 114.

57. See Bevans and Schroeder, *Constants in Context*, 146-47. See also E. W. McDonnell, *The Beguines and Beghards in Medieval Culture: With Special Emphasis on the Belgian Scene* (New Brunswick, N.J.: Rutgers University Press, 1954).

58. Mechtilde of Magdeburg, *The Flowing Light of the Godhead*, book VII, chapter 55, as quoted in Davies, "Late Medieval Theologians," 228. Text trans. Frank Tobin, Classics of Western Spirituality 92 (New York: Paulist Press, 1998).

59. Ibid., book V, chapter 26, as quoted in Davies, "Late Medieval Theologians," 228.

60. Davies, "Late Medieval Theologians," 226.

61. See the fuller version of Eckhart's biography in Edmund Colledge's introduction ("Historical Data") in Edmund Colledge and Bernard McGinn, eds., *Meister Eckhart: The Essential Sermons, Commentaries, Treatises, and Defense* (New York: Paulist Press, 1981), 5-23.

62. Bernard McGinn, "Introduction," "Theological Summary," in Colledge and McGinn, *Meister Eckhart*, 31.

63. Ibid.

64. González, *History of Christian Thought*, 1:324-25.

65. McGinn, "Theological Summary," 61.

66. See Julian of Norwich, *Showings*, chapter 3, ed. Edmund Colledge and James Walsh, Classics of Western Spirituality (New York: Paulist Press, 1978), 179-180. See also Barbara J. MacHaffie, "Jesus as Mother," in *Readings in Her Story: Women in Christian Tradition* (Minneapolis: Fortress Press, 1992), 63; Davies, "Late Medieval Theologians," 229.

67. *Showings*, chapter 5, in Colledge and Walsh, 183.

68. *Showings*, chapter 27, in Colledge and Walsh, 225.

69. Edwards, *Christianity*, 243.

70. See Nichols, *Shape of Catholic Theology*, 304-5.

71. See Edwards, *Christianity*, 243-44.

72. See R. Rosini, OFM, *Mariologia del beato Giovanni Duns Scoto* (Castelpetroso, 1994), 80 n. 16.

73. Joachim is an immensely important figure in the late Middle Ages, but a survey like this cannot fully do him justice. See Irvin and Sunquist, *History*, 1:419-21.

74. See ibid., 434; see also Edwards, *Christianity*, 244.

75. Edwards, *Christianity*, 245.

76. Ibid.

77. Thomas à Kempis, *The Imitation of Christ*, book I, chapter I. See http://www.leaderu.com/ cyber/books/imitation/imb1c01-10.html#RTFToC13.

78. Erasmus of Rotterdam, *The Praise of Folly*, "Oration: Great Illuminated Divines." See http://www.fordham.edu/halsall/mod/1509erasmus-folly.html.

79. See J. J. Saunders, *A History of Medieval Islam* (London: Routledge and Kegan Paul, 1965), 187-99. In this entire section I am relying heavily on González, *History of Christian Thought*, 2:292-303.

80. González, *History of Christian Thought*, 297.

81. See Catherine M. LaCugna's fine treatment of Gregory Palamas in her *God for Us: The Trinity and Christian Life* (San Francisco: HarperSanFrancisco, 1991), 181-205.

82. I discovered this fact (and Ebedjesu's death date) on "WikiSyr." See http://www.wikisyr.com/pmwiki.php?n=Menu.EbedjesuDeNisibe. González refers to an article in the *Dictionnaire de Théologie Catholique* (Paris: Letouzey et Ané, 1903-1950), 4:1485-86. See González, *History of Christian Thought*, 2:299 n. 23.

83. González (*History of Christian Thought*, 2:300 n. 28) cites the article in the *DThC* by Eugene Tisserant, "Kabar, Abul-Barakat Ibn," *DThC* 8:2293-95.

84. See Charles Taylor, *A Secular Age* (Cambridge, Mass.: Harvard University Press, 2007), 69-70.

85. See Edwards, *Christianity*, 281, where he insists on the importance of using the plural here.

86. Justo L. González, *The Changing Shape of Church History* (St. Louis, Mo.: Chalice Press, 2002), 44.

87. See, for example, Virgilio Elizondo, *Guadalupe: Mother of the New Creation* (Maryknoll, N.Y.: Orbis Books, 1997); and Miguel H. Díaz, "A Trinitarian Approach to the Community-Building Process of Tradition: Oneness as Diversity in Christian Traditioning," in Orlando O. Espín and Gary Macy, eds., *Futuring Our Past: Explorations in the Theology of Tradition* (Maryknoll, N.Y.: Orbis Books, 2006), 165-70.

88. To give just one example, see Orlando Espín, *The Faith of the People* (Maryknoll, N.Y.: Orbis Books, 1997).

89. Norris, *Christianity*, 144.

90. See Justo L. González, "Voices of Compassion," *Missiology: An International Review* 20, no. 2 (April 1992): 165-66.

91. Ibid., 166. González refers to Gustavo Gutiérrez's article "En busca de los probres de Jesucristo," *Mensaje* [Lima, Peru]: 507.

92. González, "Voices of Compassion," 166, referring to Gutiérrez, 508.

93. González, "Voices of Compassion," 166.

94. Ibid., 167.

95. The text is found in H. McKennie Goodpasture, ed., *Cross and Sword: An Eyewitness History of Christianity in Latin America* (Maryknoll, N.Y.: Orbis Books, 1989), 11-12. The section quoted is from p. 12. Goodpasture has excerpted the text from Bartolomé de Las Casas's posthumously published work *History of the Indies* in Benjamin Keen, ed., *Latin American Civilization*, 3rd ed. (Atlanta, Ga.: Houghton Mifflin, 1974), 1:170-71.

96. Bevans and Schroeder, *Constants in Context*, 176.

97. Bartolomé de Las Casas, *Obras escogidas*, vol. 5, ed. J. L. Pérez de Tudela (Madrid: BAE, 1957/58), 539b, quoted in Gustavo Gutiérrez, *Las Casas: In Search of the Poor of Jesus Christ* (Maryknoll, N.Y.: Orbis Books, 1993), 4-5.

98. Las Casas, *Obras Escogidas*, vol. 5, 44b, quoted in Gutiérrez, *Las Casas*, 194.

99. Gutiérrez, *Las Casas*, 241-71.

100. Ibid., 5.

101. Felipe Guamán Poma de Ayala, *El primer nueva corónica y buen gobierno*, ed. J. Murra and Rolena Adorno, 3 vols. (Mexico City: Siglo XXI, 1980), 1109, quoted in Gutiérrez, *Las Casas*, 11. See also Gutiérrez's fuller treatment of the work in *Las Casas*, 444-52. There is a discussion among scholars today about the identity of Guamán. Some claim that he is a Spaniard writing under a pseudonym.

102. Orlando O. Espín, "Trinitarian Monotheism and the Birth of Popular Catholicism: The Case of Sixteenth-Century Mexico," *Missiology: An International Review* 20, no. 2 (April 1992): 184. Espín cites several sources for a deeper development of these remarkable manuscripts.

103. *The Story of Guadalupe: Luis Laso de la Vega's* Hue tlamahuiçoltica *of 1649*, Lisa Sousa, Stafford Poole, and James Lockhart, eds. and trans. (Palo Alto, CA: Stanford University Press, 1998), 1-2.

104. See Gary Riebe-Estrella, "La Virgén: A Mexican Perspective," *New Theology Review* 12, no. 2 (May 1999): 39-47; see also Ana Castillo, ed., *Goddess of the Americas, La Diosa de las Americas* (New York: Riverhead Books, 1996).

105. Ellsberg, *All Saints*, 492.

106. Quoted in ibid., 493.

107. See Andrew C. Ross, *A Vision Betrayed: The Jesuits in Japan and China, 1542-1742* (Maryknoll, N.Y.: Orbis Books, 1994), xiii-xv.

108. Ibid., 128.

109. John Paul II, "Father Matteo Ricci: Bridge to China," address delivered to participants of the concluding session of the International Ricci Studies Congress, October, 25, 1982, *The Pope Speaks* 28, no. 2 (1983): 101.

110. See Bevans and Schroeder, *Constants in Context*, 189-90. See also Michael Amaladoss, "Nobili, Robert de," *Biographical Dictionary of Christian Missions*, ed. Gerald H. Anderson (New York: Macmillan Reference USA, 1997), 498-99.

111. See the remarkable work on de Rhodes by Peter C. Phan, *Mission and Catechesis: Alexandre de Rhodes and Inculturation in Seventeenth-Century Vietnam* (Maryknoll, N.Y.: Orbis Books, 1998). Referred to here are pp. 135-37 and 139-40, but see also 107-202. The complete text of de Rhodes's catechism is found on pp. 211-315.

112. Ibid., 202.

113. See José Femilou D. Gutay, "Life and Works of Fray Juan de Plasencia," unpublished manuscript shared with me by José M. de Mesa.

114. See José M. de Mesa, "The 'Ama Namin' in the Doctrina Christiana of 1593: A Filipino Cultural-Theological Reading," in ATS Forum, *Doing Theology in the Philippines* (Quezon City: Asian Theological Seminary; Manila: OFM Literature, 2005), 150-58.

115. See Edwards, *Christianity*, 265-68.

116. See Alister McGrath, *Christian Theology: An Introduction* (Oxford: Blackwell, 1994), 64.

117. See Edwards, *Christianity*, 296.

118. Ibid., 297.

119. Ibid., 302.

120. For a good overview of Luther's theology, see Oswald Bayer, "Martin Luther (1483-1546)," in Carter Lindberg, ed., *The Reformation Theologians: An Introduction to Theology in the Early Modern Period* (Oxford: Blackwell, 2002), 51-66. Obviously there is much more to Luther's theology than I have sketched here, but I hope that, for our purposes in this survey, what I have summarized gets to the heart of Luther's thought.

121. See Edwards, *Christianity*, 305-6.

122. Ibid., 310.

123. *Calvin: Commentaries*, trans. Joseph Haroutunian (Philadelphia: Westminster Press, 1958), 52, quoted in Randall C. Zachman, "John Calvin (1509-1564)," in Lindberg, *Reformation Theologians*, 185.

124. Edwards, *Christianity*, 311; Zachman, "John Calvin," 187.

125. Zachman, "John Calvin," 190.

126. See McGrath, *Christian Theology*, 64.

127. John Calvin, *Institutes*, XXI, Summary, in *Calvin: Institutes of the Christian Religion*, 2, ed. John T. McNeil (Philadelphia: Westminster Press, 1960), 931.

128. See *Institutes*, XXI.1, in McNeil, *Calvin*, 922; and Edwards, *Christianity*, 315, 318.

129. The condemnations took place at the Council of Arles in 475 (DS 330-342), the Second Council of Orange in 529 (DS 396-397/ND 1922), the Council of Quercy in 853 (DS 621-624), and the Council of Valencia in 855 (DS 625-633).

130. Edwards, *Christianity*, 315.

131. See Zachman, "John Calvin," 193-94.

132. See Justo L. González, *A History of Christian Thought*, vol. 3, *From the Protestant Reformation to the Twentieth Century*, rev. ed. (Nashville, Tenn.: Abingdon Press, 1975), 291.

133. See Peter Newman Brooks, "Thomas Cranmer (1489-1556)," in Lindberg, *Reformation Theologians*, 239-52; González, *History of Christian Thought*, 3:185-87; and Daniel F. Eppley, "Richard Hooker (1554-1600), in Lindberg, 266.

134. See Jared Wicks, "Thomas de Vio Cajetan (1469-1534)," in Lindberg, *Reformation Theologians*, 269-83.

135. N. S. Davidson, *The Counter Reformation* (Oxford: Basil Blackwell, 1987), 7-8.

136. See Christopher Belitto, *The General Councils: A History of the Twenty-One Church Councils from Nicaea to Vatican II* (Mahwah, N.J.: Paulist Press, 2002), 101; and August Franzen and John P. Dolan, *A History of the Church* (Montreal: Palm Publishers, 1968), 315.

137. See Davidson, *Counter Reformation*, 9. The quotation from Bishop Bertano is quoted by Davidson from G. Bushbell, ed., *Concilium Tridentinum: Diariorum, actorum, epistolarum, tractatuum nova collectio* (Freiburg, 1916), 10:762.

138. See Casiano Floristán, "Evangelization of the 'New World': An Old World Perspective," *Missiology: An International Review* 20, no. 2 (April 1992): 142.

139. Gutiérrez, *Las Casas*, 246.

140. See González, *History of Christian Thought*, 214.

141. See "Seripando, Girolamo," in T. C. O'Brien, ed., *The Encyclopedic Dictionary of the Western Churches* (Washington, D.C.: Corpus Publications, 1970), 711-12.

142. "Lainez, Diego (1512-65)," in Orlando O. Espín and James B. Nickoloff, eds., *An Introductory Dictionary of Theology and Religious Studies* (Collegeville, Minn.: Liturgical Press/A Michael Glazier Book, 2007), 727.

143. McGinn, *Doctors*, 139.

144. See ibid., 140-41 and 148-50. See *The Collected Works of St. Teresa of Avila*, trans. Kieran Kavanaugh and Otilio Rodríguez, 2 vols. (Washington, D.C.: Institute of Carmelite Studies, 1980); and *The Collected Works of John of the Cross*, trans. Kieran Kavanaugh and Otilio Rodríguez (Washington, D.C.: Institute of Carmelite Studies, 1991).

145. See Avery Dulles, *Models of the Church* (Garden City, N.Y.: Image Books, 1974), 21-22. For a further elaboration of the Catholic controversialists, see González, *History of Christian Thought*, 199-207.

146. Nichols, *Shape of Catholic Theology*, 318.

147. See William M. Thompson, "Introduction, I, Historical Aspects of the French School," in *Bérulle and the French School: Selected Writings*, ed. William H. Thompson (New York/Mahwah, N.J.: Paulist Press, 1989), 7. The quotation is from Noel Alexandre, *Theologia dogmatica et moralis* (1693), 1, pref., cited by Yves Congar, *A History of Theology* (Garden City, N.Y.: Doubleday, 1968), 178.

148. See Thompson, *Bérulle and the French School*, for a good introduction to the French school and a selection of their writings. On Francis de Sales, see McGinn, *Doctors*, 160-64.

149. See Davidson, *Counter Reformation*, 12-14; Edwards, *Christianity*, 373-74.

12. CHRISTIAN THEOLOGY
IN THE EIGHTEENTH AND NINETENTH CENTURIES

1. See Stephen B. Bevans and Roger P. Schroeder, *Constants in Context: A Theology of Mission for Today* (Maryknoll, N.Y.: Orbis Books, 2004), 211. Carey's title is *An Inquiry into the Obligations of Christians to Use Means for the Conversion of the Heathens.*

2. See Dana L. Robert, ed., *Gospel Bearers, Gender Barriers: Missionary Women in the Twentieth Century* (Maryknoll, N.Y.: Orbis Books, 2002), xi.

3. Kenneth Scott Latourette, *A History of Christianity*, vol. 2, *Reformation to the Present* (New York: Harper & Row, 1953), 1012.

4. Marc R. Spindler, "Libermann, François Marie Paul," in Gerald H. Anderson, ed., *Biographical Dictionary of Christian Missions* (New York: Simon & Schuster, 1998), 399.

5. Adrian Hastings, "Lavigerie, Charles Martial Allemande," in Anderson, *Biographical Dictionary*, 387.

6. Ibid.; Gerald R. Cragg, *The Church and the Age of Reason* (New York: Penguin Books, 1960), 159, and 163-64.

7. David L. Edwards, *Christianity: The First Two Thousand Years* (Maryknoll, N.Y.: Orbis Books, 1997), 356. See also Alister McGrath, *Christian Theology: An Introduction* (Cambridge, Mass./Oxford: Blackwell, 1994), 85-86 (for Reimarus) and 84 (for Lessing).

8. On Pietism, see Cragg, *Church and the Age of Reason*, 100-106.

9. *The Works of John Wesley* (Grand Rapids: Zondervan, 1958/59), 1:103, quoted in Justo L. González, *A History of Christian Thought*, vol. 3, *From the Protestant Reformation to the Twentieth Century*, rev. ed. (Nashville, Tenn.: Abingdon Press, 1975), 308-9.

10. See González, *History of Christian Thought*, 3:312-313.

11. See http://www.wholesomewords.org/biography/biorpcwesley.html.

12. On Edwards, see González, *History of Christian Thought*, 316-17, and Stephen J. Stein, "Jonathan Edwards (1703-1758)," in Mark G. Toulouse and James O. Duke, eds., *Makers of Christian Theology in America* (Nashville, Tenn.: Abingdon Press, 1997), 55-63. See also *The Works of Jonathan Edwards* (New Haven: Yale University Press, 1957–).

13. Michael L. Birkel, "John Woolman (1720-1772)," in Toulouse and Duke, *Makers of Christian Theology*, 79.

14. Ibid., 81. See *The Journal of John Woolman and A Plea for the Poor* (Secaucus, N.J.: Citadel Press, 1961).

15. Aidan Nichols, *The Shape of Catholic Theology* (Collegeville, Minn.: Liturgical Press, 1991), 321 and n. 149.

16. See Bernard McGinn, *The Doctors of the Church: Thirty-Three Men and Women Who Shaped Christianity* (New York: Crossroad, 1999), 165-68.

17. See Robert Ellsberg, "St. Tikhon of Zadonsk," in his *All Saints: Daily Reflections on Saints, Prophets, and Witnesses for Our Time* (New York: Crossroad, 1997), 349-50.

18. See Cragg, *Church and the Age of Reason*, 115-16.

19. "Diostheus and the Synod of Jerusalem, *Confession*, 1672," Decree 18, in Jaroslav Pelikan and Valerie Hotchkiss, eds., *Creeds and Confessions of Faith in the Christian Tradition*, vol. 1, *Early, Eastern and Medieval* (New Haven: Yale University Press, 2003), 635. The entire text is found on pages 615-35.

20. John Meyendorf, *Rome, Constantinople, Moscow: Historical and Theological Studies* (Crestwood, N.Y.: St. Vladimir's Seminary Press, 1996), 86, quoted in Pelikan and Hotchkiss, *Creeds*, 614.

21. Quoted in Ellsberg, "Wolfgang Amadeus Mozart," in *All Saints*, 530. On Bach, Vivaldi, Handel, and Mozart, see Geoffrey Hindley, ed., *The Larousse Encyclopedia of Music* (New York: Crescent Books, 1990), 197-201, 206, 214-17, 241-44.

22. Thomas F. O'Meara, *Theology of Ministry*, completely rev. ed. (Mahwah, N.J.: Paulist Press, 1999), 116.

23. Thomas F. O'Meara, *Romantic Idealism and Roman Catholicism: Schelling and the Theologians* (Notre Dame, Ind.: University of Notre Dame Press, 1982), 3.

24. Ibid., 4.

25. Ibid.

26. Ibid., 7.

27. Ibid., 326-27.

28. Johann Sebastian Drey, *Kurze Einleitung*, A Short Introduction to the Study of Theology (Tübingen, 1819), 1, quoted in O'Meara, *Romantic Idealism*, 98; see also p. 95.

29. O'Meara, *Romantic Idealism*, 151. I am relying heavily here on O'Meara's development of Möhler's thought on pp. 146-53.

30. Ibid., 151. The text is found in Johann Adam Möhler, *Unity of the Church or The Principle of Catholicism, Presented in the Spirit of the Church Fathers of the First Three Centuries*, ed. and trans. Peter C. Erb (Washington, D.C.: Catholic University of America Press, 1996).

31. Michael J. Himes, "Introduction" to the English translation of Johann Adam Möhler, *Symbolism: Exposition of the Doctrinal Differences between Catholics and Protestants as Evidenced by Their Symbolical Writings* (New York: Crossroad, 1997), xvii.

32. See August Franzen and John P. Dolan, *History of the Church* (Montreal: Palm Publishers, 1965), 362-65. For the text of the encyclicals, see http://www.papalencyclicals.net/ Greg16/g16mirar.htm and http://www.papalencyclicals. net/Greg16/g16singu.htm.

33. See ND, pp. 50-51. See also Gerald A. McCool, *Catholic Theology in the Nineteenth Century: The Quest for a Unitary Method* (New York: Seabury Press, 1977), 111-12, 119-25.

34. McCool's work, cited above, lays out in great detail the struggles of more "open" theology in the nineteenth century, Rome's action, and the eventual ascendancy of neo-scholasticism.

35. Nichols, *Shape of Catholic Theology*, 328.

36. See McCool, *Catholic Theology*, 83.

37. See ibid., 81-87, 129-44, 226-40.

38. John Henry Cardinal Newman, *Apologia Pro Vita Sua* (New York: Longmans, Green, 1897), 238.

39. Nicholas Lash, "Introduction," to John Henry Newman, *An Essay in Aid of a Grammar of Assent* (Notre Dame, Ind.: University of Notre Dame Press, 1979), 3.

40. Newman, *Essay in Aid of a Grammar of Assent*, 76.

41. Ibid., 230-60, 270-99.

42. Ibid., 253.

43. Ellsberg, *All Saints*, 87.

44. See the introductory remarks on Orestes Brownson in Toulouse and Duke, *Makers of Christian Theology*, 211.

45. "Brownson, Orestes," in Orlando O. Espín and James B. Nickoloff, *An Introductory Dictionary of Theology and Religious Studies* (Collegeville, Minn.: Liturgical Press, 2007), 165.

46. McGinn, *Doctors*, 169.

47. Quoted in ibid., 171.

48. The title is commonly used. I am quoting here from Alasdair I. C. Heron, *A Century of Protestant Theology* (Philadelphia: Westminster Press, 1980), 23. I am relying heavily on this fine work in this entire section.

49. See Brian A. Gerrish, *A Prince of the Church: Schleiermacher and the Beginnings of Modern Theology* (Philadelphia: Fortress Press, 1981), 31-33.

50. Heron, *Century*, 24.

51. González, *History of Christian Thought*, 3:349.

52. Friedrich Schleiermacher, First Letter to Dr. Lücke, in James Duke and Francis Fiorenza, trans., *On the* Glaubenslehre: *Two Letters to Dr. Lücke* (Chico, Calif.: Scholars Press, 1981), 40-41.

53. González, *History of Christian Thought*, 3:349.

54. Friedrich Schleiermacher, *The Christian Faith*, 2nd ed., §115, ed. H. R. Mackintosh and J. S. Stewart (Philadelphia: Fortress Press, 1928), 532.

55. Ibid. §15, 76.

56. See Heron, *Century*, 27.

57. See, for example, the critique of Staudenmaier, who claims that Schleiermacher builds his system not on the objectivity of Christ but the subjectivity of the human person: O'Meara, *Romantic Idealism*, 140, 219 n. 5. One of Barth's famous lines is "one can *not* speak of God simply by speaking of man in a loud voice," quoted in Gerrish, *Prince*, 13.

58. Heron, *Century*, 31.

59. Ibid., 33.

60. Ibid., 36.

61. González, *History of Christian Thought*, 3:376-77.

62. Heron, *Century*, 36.

63. Ibid., 38-42; González, *History of Christian Thought*, 3:362-64.

64. Heron, *Century*, 44.

65. Ibid., 44-45.

66. For a concise summary of this very complex history, see Walter Kasper, *Jesus the Christ* (London: Burns & Oates; New York: Paulist Press, 1976), 29-32. See also González, *History of Christian Thought*, 3:377-82; and Heron, *Century*, 51-55.

67. González, *History of Christian Thought*, 364.

68. Ibid., 365.

69. Quoted in Heron, *Century*, 47.

70. See ibid., 62-63; see also Brian A. Gerrish, "The Protest of Grace: John McCleod Campbell on the Atonement," in idem, *Tradition and the Modern World: Reformed Theology in the Nineteenth Century* (Chicago: University of Chicago Press, 1978), 71-98.

71. Heron, *Century*, 63-64; the bibliographical reference is found in James C. Livingston, *Religious Thought in the Victorian Age: Challenges and Reconceptions* (New York: Continuum; London: T. & T. Clark, 2007), 290.

72. Livingston's book (n. 71 above) treats these and many more religious thinkers of the nineteenth century in some detail.

73. Alan D. Hodder, "Ralph Waldo Emerson (1803-1882)," in Toulouse and Duke, *Makers of Christian Theology*, 196. See Hodder's entire essay, pp. 192-99.

74. Klaus Penzel, "Philip Schaff (1819-1893)," in Toulouse and Duke, *Makers of Christian Theology*, 236.

75. Ibid., 237.

76. I have cited the Pelikan / Hotchkiss work (vol. 1) several times in this chapter.

77. For further reading, see Toulouse and Duke, and their companion volume, *Sources of Christian Theology in America* (Nashville, Tenn.: Abingdon Press, 1999). The companion volume contains selected texts and helpful, short introductions to each theologian and religious thinker.

78. Part of the text is found in Rosemary Radford Ruether and Rosemary Skinner Keller, eds., *In Their Own Voices: Four Centuries of American Women's Religious Writing* (San Francisco: HarperSanFrancisco, 1995), 173-74.

79. See Sojourner Truth, "Ain't I a Woman?": http://afroamhistory.about.com/library/blsojourner_truth_womanspeech.htm.

80. See part of the text of *The Woman's Bible* in Barbara J. MacHaffie, ed. *Readings in Her Story: Women in Christian Tradition* (Minneapolis: Fortress Press, 1992), 157-62.

81. See Heron, *Century*, 57-60.

82. González, *History of Christian Thought*, 384. On Rauschenbusch, see Robert T. Handy, "Walter Rauschenbusch (1861-1918)," in Toulouse and Duke, *Makers of Christian Theology*, 341-47 and González, 382-84.

83. Frank Bartleman, *How Pentecost Came to Los Angeles* (1925), quoted in Vinay Samuel, *The Holiness-Pentecostal Tradition: Charismatic Movements in the Twentieth Century* (Grand Rapids: William B. Eerdmans, 1971), 99.

84. See Harvey Cox, *Fire from Heaven: The Rise of Pentecostal Spirituality and the Reshaping of Religion in the Twenty-First Century* (Cambridge, Mass.: Da Capo Press, 1995), 201.

85. See McCool, *Catholic Theology*, 241-49.

86. For a simple explanation of Blondel and a systematic development of what his philosophy implied for theology, see Gregory Baum, *Man Becoming: God in Secular Experience* (New York: Herder & Herder, 1970).

87. See McCool, *Catholic Theology*, 249-51.

13. CHRISTIAN THEOLOGY
FROM THE TWENTIETH CENTURY TO THE PRESENT

1. Eric Hobsbawm, *The Age of Extremes: The Short Twentieth Century (1914-1991)* (New York: Pantheon Books, 1995).

2. Joseph A. Komanchak, "Vatican II as an 'Event,'" in David G. Schultenover, ed., *Vatican II: Did Anything Happen?* (New York: Continuum, 2007), 24-51.

3. See Robert W. Jensen, "Karl Barth," in David Ford, ed., *The Modern Theologians*, 2nd ed. (Oxford: Blackwell, 1997), 26. Jensen refers to the German edition of *The Epistle to the Romans*, *Der Romerbrief*, 7, where Barth quotes Kierkegaard.

4. Karl Barth, Foreword to *Church Dogmatics* I.1, *The Doctrine of the Word of God* (Edinburgh: T. & T. Clark, 1936), x. See also Barth's citation of Przywara on p. 44. For a discussion of Barth's relationship with Przywara, see Thomas F. O'Meara, *Erich Przywara, S.J.: His Theology and His World* (Notre Dame, Ind.: University of Notre Dame Press, 2002), 99-107.

5. Barth, *Der Romerbrief*, 16, quoted in Jensen, "Karl Barth," 26.

6. Alasdair I. C. Heron, *A Century of Protestant Theology* (Philadelphia: Westminster Press, 1980), 78.

7. Ibid., 90.

8. Quoted in Eberhard Busch, *Karl Barth: His Life from Letters and Autobiographical Texts* (Philadelphia: Fortress Press, 1975), 476-77.

9. See the picture of Barth's study in ibid., 418, and the frontispiece of the book.

10. Charles Marsh, "Dietrich Bonhoeffer," in Ford, *Modern Theologians*, 39. Marsh refers to Bonhoeffer's biography by his friend Eberhard Bethge, *Dietrich Bonhoeffer: A Biography* (Minneapolis: Fortress Press, 2000).

11. Marsh, "Dietrich Bonhoeffer," 46.

12. Wayne Whitson Floyd, Jr., "Style and the Critique of Metaphysics: The Letter as Form in Bonhoeffer and Adorno," in Wayne Whitson Floyd, Jr., and Charles Marsh, Jr.,

eds., *Theology and the Practice of Responsibility: Essays in Dietrich Bonhoeffer* (Valley Forge, Pa.: Trinity Press International, 1994), quoted in Marsh, "Dietrich Bonhoeffer," 47.

13. Dietrich Bonhoeffer, *Letters and Papers from Prison*, new greatly enlarged edition, ed. Eberhard Bethge (New York: Collier Books, 1972), 360, 361.

14. David H. Kelsey, "Paul Tillich," in Ford, *Modern Theologians*, 87.

15. Paul Tillich, *Systematic Theology*, 3 vols. in 1 (Chicago: University of Chicago Press; New York: Harper & Row, 1967), 1:60.

16. See ibid., 1:211, 235.

17. See ibid., 2:118-38.

18. Paul Tillich, *Dynamics of Faith* (New York: Harper Torchbooks, 1957), 1, 16-22.

19. For example, Tillich, *Systematic Theology*, 1:83-86.

20. Paul Tillich, "You Are Accepted," in his *The Shaking of the Foundations*. See http://www.religion-online.org/showchapter.asp?title=378&C=84.

21. See James J. Bacik, *Contemporary Theologians* (Chicago: Thomas More Press, 1989), 115.

22. See Robin W. Lovin, "Reinhold Niebuhr (1892-1971)," in Ford, *Modern Theologians*, 413.

23. Reinhold Niebuhr, *The Children of Light and the Children of Darkness* (New York: Charles Scribner's Sons, 1972), xiii, quoted in Lovin, "Reinhold Niebuhr," 418.

24. Lovin, "Reinhold Niebuhr," 416.

25. See Stephen B. Oates, *Let the Trumpet Sound: The Life of Martin Luther King, Jr.* (New York: New American Library, 1982), 34, 39.

26. Martin Luther King, Jr., "Remaining Awake through a Great Revolution," speech delivered at the National Cathedral, Washington, D.C., on March 31, 1968. Congressional Record, April 9, 1968. See http://www.africanamericans.com/MLKRemainingAwake ThroughGreat Revolution.htm.

27. I am relying on Rowan Williams, "Eastern Orthodox Theology," in Ford, *Modern Theologians*, 502-10, for the development of this paragraph.

28. See John H. Erickson, "Georges Florovsky (1893-1979)," in Mark G. Toulouse and James O. Duke, eds., *Makers of Christian Theology in America* (Nashville, Tenn.: Abingdom Press, 1997), 495-97.

29. See Gerald A. McCool, *Catholic Theology in the Nineteenth Century: The Quest for a Unitary Method* (New York: Seabury Press, 1977), 251.

30. Ibid., 252.

31. See Joan Delaney, "From Cremona to Edinburgh: Bishop Bonomelli and the Missionary Conference of 1910," *Ecumenical Review* (July 2000). Http://findarticles.com/p/articles/mi_m2065/is_3_52/ai_66279082. It is important to note that one of the protégés of Bonomelli was a young priest from his diocese named Angelo Roncalli, the future John XXIII.

32. Fergus Kerr, "French Theology: Yves Congar and Henri de Lubac," in Ford, *Modern Theologians*, 107.

33. An inside look at his work at the council can be found in his two-volume journal that he kept during the four sessions. See Yves Congar, *Mon Journal du Concile* (Paris: Les Éditions du Cerf, 2002).

34. See McCool, *Catholic Theology*, 258.

35. See Kerr, "French Theology," 109-10. The quotations are from *Corpus Mysticum* but are not referenced in the article.

36. This is the point of Joseph A. Di Noia in his essay "Karl Rahner," in Ford, *Modern Theologians*, 120.

37. "Karl Rahner: Finding God in Daily Life," in Bacik, *Contemporary Theologians*, 20.

38. Karl Rahner, *Hearers of the Word* (New York: Herder & Herder, 1969), 66.

39. See Karl Rahner, *Foundations of Christian Faith* (New York: Seabury Press, 1978), 98, quoted in Neil Ormerod, *Introducing Contemporary Theologies: The What and the Who of Theology Today* (Newton, NSW, Australia: E. J. Dwyer, 1990), 97.

40. Di Noia, "Karl Rahner," 118.

41. See Bacik, "Johann Metz," in idem, *Contemporary Theologians*, 151-64.

42. Bernard J. F. Lonergan, *Insight: A Study of Human Understanding* (New York: Philosophical Library, 1957), 348-49.

43. Bernard J. F. Lonergan, *Method in Theology* (New York: Herder & Herder, 1972), 231.

44. See David Tracy, *The Achievement of Bernard Lonergan* (New York: Herder & Herder, 1970), 1-21.

45. Longeran, *Method in Theology*, 237-44.

46. Ibid., xi.

47. See John Riches and Ben Quash, "Hans Urs von Balthasar," in Ford, *Modern Theologians*, 136.

48. Ibid., 135, 143.

49. Ibid., 136.

50. See Robert J. Schreiter, "Edward Schillebeeckx," in Ford, *Modern Theologians*, 153.

51. John Courtney Murray, introduction to Vatican II's Declaration on Religious Freedom (*Dignitatis Humanae*), in Walter M. Abbott, ed., *The Documents of Vatican II* (New York: Herder & Herder/Association Press, 1966), 673.

52. For a fine overview of the results of the council, see Robert J. Schreiter, "The Impact of Vatican II," in Gregory Baum, ed., *The Twentieth Century: A Theological Overview* (Maryknoll, N.Y.: Orbis Books, 1999), 158-72; see also Giuseppe Alberigo, *A Brief History of Vatican II* (Maryknoll, N.Y.: Orbis Books, 2006).

53. Roberto Oliveros, "History of the Theology of Liberation," in Ignacio Ellacuría and Jon Sobrino, eds., *Mysterium Liberationis: Fundamental Concepts of Liberation Theology* (Maryknoll, N.Y.: Orbis Books, 1993), 3.

54. Ibid., 16.

55. For a more detailed treatment of Gutiérrez, see Luis Rivera Rodríguez, "Gutiérrez, Gustavo (1928-)," in Justo L. González, ed. *The Westminster Dictionary of Theologians* (Louisville, Ky.: Westminster John Knox Press, 2006), 163-64. See also James B. Nickoloff, "Gutiérrez, Gustavo (1928-)" in Espín and Nickoloff, eds., 526-27; Bacik, 165-77; and Ormerod, 129-38.

56. See Rebecca Chopp, "Latin American Liberation Theology," in Ford, *Modern Theologians*, 410-11.

57. See, for example, Diego Irarrázaval, *Inculturation: New Dawn of the Church in Latin America* (Maryknoll, N.Y.: Orbis Books, 2000); Manuel M. Marzal, Eugenio Maurer, Xavier Albó, Bartomeu Melià, *The Indian Face of God in Latin America* (Maryknoll, N.Y.: Orbis Books, 1996); Paulo Suess, "Evangelization and Inculturation: Concepts, Options, Perspectives," in James A. Scherer and Stephen B. Bevans, eds., *New Directions in Mission and Evangelization 3* (Maryknoll, N.Y.: Orbis Books, 1999), 159-74; María Pilar Aquino, "Feminist Theology, Latin America," in Letty M. Russell and J. Shannon Clarkson, eds. *Dictionary of Feminist Theologies* (Louisville, Ky.: Westminster John Knox Press, 1996), 114-17.

58. Patrick Anthony, ed., *Theology in the Carribean Today 1: Perspectives* (St. Lucia: Archdiocesan Pastoral Centre, 1994); Howard Gregory, ed., *Carribean Theology: Preparing for the Challenges Ahead* (Jamaica: Canoe Press, University of the West Indies, 1995).

59. John C. England, Jose Kuttianimattahil, John M. Prior, Lily A. Quintos, David Suh

Kwang-sun, Janice Wickeri, eds., *Asian Christian Theologies: A Research Guide to Authors, Movements, Sources*, 3 vols. (Delhi: ISPCK and Claretian Pubishers; Maryknoll, N.Y.: Orbis Books, 2002, 2003, 2004).

60. The first statement of this was at the first conference of the Federation of Asian Bishops' Conferences (FABC) in 1974. See "Evangelization in Modern Day Asia," in Gaudencio Rosales and Catalino Arévalo, eds., *For All the Peoples of Asia: Federation of Asian Bishops' Conferences Documents from 1970 to 1991*, vol. 1 (Quezon City, Philippines: Claretian Publications, 1997), 11-25. The "threefold dialogue" is repeated regularly in subsequent documents. See Stephen Bevans, "Inculturation of Theology in Asia (The Federation of Asian Bishops' Conferences, 1970-1995), *Studia Missionalia* 45 (1996): 9-10.

61. Although I am writing much of this section out of my own general knowledge, I have relied somewhat in this section on George Gispert-Sauch, "Asian Theology," in Ford, *Modern Theologians*, 458-68.

62. Dalit theology has inspired a considerable literature. See, for example, Sathianathan Clarke, *Dalits and Christianity: Subaltern Religion and Liberation Theology in India* (New Delhi: Oxford University Press, 1998).

63. See Aruna Gnanadason, "Feminist Theologies, South Asian," in Russell and Clarkson, *Dictionary*, 110-12.

64. England et al., *Asian Christian Theologies*, 2:385.

65. Catalino G. Arévalo, "On the Theology of the Signs of the Times," *Philippine Priests' Forum* 4, no. 4 (1972), cited in England et al., *Asian Christian Theologies*, 386.

66. For some of the theologians in the pages that follow, I have not been able to ascertain birth (and death) dates.

67. José M. de Mesa, *Why Theology Is Never Far from Home* (Manila: De La Salle University Press, 2003). See the entries on Filipino theology in England et al., *Asian Christian Theologies*, 331-497.

68. See England et al., *Asian Christian Theologies*, 178. See the large section on Indonesian theologians, 2:122-243.

69. See the extensive section on Malyasia and Singapore in ibid., 245-330.

70. Ibid., 3:181.

71. See the important dissertation by Malaysian theologian How Chuang Chua, "Japanese Perspectives on the Death of Christ: A Study in Contextualized Christology" (Trinity International University, Deerfiled, Ill., March 2007).

72. See http://dlibrary.acu.edu.au/research/theology/ejournal/.

73. For example, Neil J. Ormerod, "The Structure of a Systematic Ecclesiology," *Theological Studies* 63, no. 1 (March 2002): 3-30; idem, "Two Points or Four? Rahner and Lonergan on Trinity, Incaration, Grace, and Beatific Vision," *Theological Studies* 68, no. 3 (September 2007): 661-73; David Coffey, *Deus Trinitas: The Doctrine of the Triune God* (New York: Oxford University Press, 1999); Anne Hunt, *Trinity: Nexus of the Mysteries of Faith*, Theology in Global Perspective (Maryknoll, N.Y.: Orbis Books, 2005); Patricia Fox, *God as Communon: John Zizioulas, Elizabeth Johnson, and the Retrieval of the Symbol of the Triune God* (Collegeville, Minn.: Liturgical Press, 2001); Anthony Kelly, *Eschatology and Hope*, Theology in Global Perspective (Maryknoll, N.Y.: Orbis Books, 2006).

74. Gideon Goosen, *Australian Theologies: Themes and Methodologies in the Third Millennium* (Strathfield, NSW: St. Pauls Publications, 2000).

75. Ibid., 293.

76. Neil Darragh, *Doing Theology Ourselves: A Guide to Research and Action* (Auckland: Accent Publications, 1995), and *At Home in the Earth: Seeking an Earth-centered Spirituality* (Auckland: Accent Publications, 2000.

77. Susan Smith and Helen Bergin, eds., *He Kupu Whakawairua: Spirituality in Aotearoa*

New Zealand: Catholic Voices (Auckland: Accent Publications, 2002); Susan Smith, *Women in Mission: From the New Testament to Today* (Maryknoll, N.Y.: Orbis Books, 2007); Cathy Ross, *Women with a Mission, Rediscovering Missionary Wives in Early New Zealand* (Auckland: Penguin, 2006).

78. Peter Matheson, "The Contours of Christian Theology in Aotearoa New Zealand," in Susan Emilsen and William W. Emilsen, *Mapping the Landscape: Essays in Australian and New Zealand Christianity* (New York: Peter Lang, 2000), 255-72.

79. See Philip Gibbs, ed., *Alive in Christ: The Synod for Oceania and the Catholic Church in Papua New Guinea*, Point No. 30 (Goroka, Papua-New Guinea: Melanesian Institute, 2006).

80. John D'Arcy May, ed., *Living Theology in Melanesia: A Reader*, Point No. 8 (Goroka: Melanesian Association of Theological Schools and the Melanesian Institute, 1985).

81. For example, Frank Hoare, "Community Polarization around Cultural Adaptation in the Liturgy in a Fiji Indian Catholic Community," *Mission Studies* 18, no. 1 (2001): 130-53.

82. See Bénézet Bujo, *African Theology in Its Social Context* (Maryknoll, N.Y.: Orbis Books, 1992), 59-60.

83. Paul VI, "Closing Discourse to All-Africa Symposium," quoted in Aylward Shorter, *African Christian Theology* (Maryknoll, N.Y.: Orbis Books, 1975), 20.

84. See John de Gruchy, "African Theology: South Africa," in Ford., *Modern Theologians*, 448.

85. See Bujo, *African Christian Theology*, 15-16.

86. Kwame Bediako, "African Theology," in Ford, *Modern Theologians*, 433.

87. See the essays in Robert J. Schreiter, ed., *Faces of Jesus in Africa* (Maryknoll, N.Y.: Orbis Books, 1991).

88. Laurenti Magesa, "Christ's Spirit as Empowerment of the Church-As-Family," *Sedos Bulletin* (www.sedos.com), 2000.

89. See Musimbi Kanyoro and Nyambura Njoroge, eds., *Growing in Faith: African Women in the Household of God* (Nairobi: Acton Publishers, 1996); and Mercy Amba Oduyoye and Musimbi Kanyoro, eds., *The Will to Arrive: Women, Tradition, and the Church in Africa* (Maryknoll, N.Y.: Orbis Books, 1992).

90. Mercy Amba Oduyoye, "Third World Women's Theologies: African," in Virginia Fabella and R. S. Sugirtharajah, eds., *Dictionary of Third World Theologies* (Maryknoll, N.Y.: Orbis Books, 2000), 219-20.

91. Afua Kuma, *Jesus of the Deep Forest: The Praises and Prayers of Afua Kuma* (Accra, Ghana, 1981).

92. John S. Mbiti, *Bible and Theology in African Christianity* (Nairobi, 1986), 229, quoted in Bediako, "African Theology," 435.

93. I say "majority" persons with some sense of nuance. At the moment there are more white Europeans and North Americans doing theology than blacks, Asians, Pacific Islanders and Latino/as. Very probably, however, this majority position may shift, as more and more subaltern persons begin to do theology out of their own contexts. Whites might then still be in the majority numerically, but they will be in the minority when all the subaltern theologians are taken together. This is already the case within the general population in certain areas of North America (e.g., Los Angeles, California).

94. See, for example, John Hick and Paul F. Knitter, eds., *The Myth of Christian Uniqueness: Towards a Pluralistic Theology of Religions* (Maryknoll, N.Y.: Orbis Books, 1987); Gavin D'Costa, ed., *Christian Uniqueness Reconsidered: The Myth of a Pluralistic Theology of Religions* (Maryknoll, N.Y.: Orbis Books, 1990); Gavin D'Costa, *The Meeting of Religions and the Trinity* (Maryknoll, N.Y.: Orbis Books, 2000); Harold Netland, *Dissonant Voices: Religious*

Pluralism and the Question of Truth (Grand Rapids: William B. Eerdmans, 1991); idem, *Encountering Religious Pluralism: The Challenge to Christian Faith and Mission* (Downers Grove, Ill.: InterVarsity Press, 2001); S. Mark Heim, *The Depth of the Riches: A Trinitarian Theology of Religious Ends* (Grand Rapids: William B. Eerdmans, 2001).

95. See Paul F. Knitter, *Introducing Theologies of Religions* (Maryknoll, N.Y.: Orbis Books, 2002); S. Mark Heim, *The Depth of the Riches: A Trinitarian Theology of Religious Ends* (Grand Rapids: William B. Eerdmans, 2001); Francis X. Clooney, "The Emerging Field of Comparative Theology: A Bibliographical Review (1989-1995)," *Theological Studies* 56, no. 3 (March 1995): 521-50; James L. Fredericks, *Buddhists and Christians: Through Comparative Theology to Solidarity* (Maryknoll, N.Y.: Orbis Books, 2004).

96. See, for example, Ray S. Anderson, "Evangelical Theology," in Ford, *Modern Theologians*, 481-98; D. A. Carson, *Christ and Culture Revisited* (Grand Rapids: William B. Eerdmans, 2008); Miroslav Volf, *After Our Likeness: The Church as the Image of the Trinity* (Grand Rapids: William B. Eerdmans, 1998); Kevin J. Vanhoozer, *The Drama of Doctrine: A Canonical-Linguistic Approach to Christian Theology* (Louisville, Ky.: Westminster John Knox Press, 2005); We have cited Alister McGrath's *Christian Theology: An Introduction* several times in this book.

97. See the immense commentary on Vatican II edited by Hünermann, together with Bernd Jochen Hiberath, *Herders Theologischer Kommentar zum Zweiten Vatikanischen Konzil* (Freiburg: Herder, 2005); David Tracy's bibliography is very large, and he is considered perhaps the most important Catholic theologian in the United States. See, for example, his small but important work, *Plurality and Ambiguity: Hermeneutics, Religion, Hope* (San Francisco: Harper & Row, 1987). See, among others, Gaillardetz's volume of ecclesiology in this series, *Ecclesiology for a Global Church: A People Called and Sent* (Maryknoll, N.Y.: Orbis Books, 2008). Elizabeth Johnson's best known work is *She Who Is: The Mystery of God in Feminist Theology* (New York: Crossroad, 1992). Hinze has written an important book on dialogue in the church, *Practices of Dialogue in the Roman Catholic Church: Aims and Obstacles, Lessons and Laments* (New York: Continuum, 2006). Among Tilley's works see *Inventing Catholic Tradition* (Maryknoll, N.Y.: Orbis Books, 2000), *History, Theology and Faith: Dissolving the Modern Problematic* (Maryknoll, N.Y.: Orbis Books, 2004), and *The Disciples' Jesus: Christology and Reconciling Practice* (Maryknoll, N.Y.: Orbis Books, 2008). See Douglas John Hall's marvelous three-volume systematic theology, *Thinking the Faith*, *Professing the Faith*, and *Confessing the Faith* (Minneapolis: Fortress Press, 1989, 1993, 1996). From Williams's many writings, see his *Arius: Heresy and Tradition*, rev. ed. (Grand Rapids: William B. Eerdmans, 2001).

98. John Milbank, *Theology and Social Theory: Beyond Secular Reason* (Oxford: Blackwell, 1990); Perhaps Hauerwas's most accessible work is the book he wrote with William Willimon, *Resident Aliens: Life in the Christian Colony* (Nashville, Tenn.: Abingdon Press, 1989).

99. John Milbank, Catherine Pickstock, and Graham Ward, eds., *Radical Orthodoxy: A New Theology* (London: Routledge, 1999).

100. Robert J. Schreiter, *Constructing Local Theologies* (Maryknoll, N.Y.: Orbis Books, 1985); *Reconciliation: Mission and Ministry in a Changing Social Order* (Maryknoll, N.Y.: Orbis Books, 1992); *The New Catholicity: Theology between the Global and the Local* (Maryknoll, N.Y.: Orbis Books, 1997); "Theology and Globalization," *Theological Studies* 69, no. 2 (June 2008).

101. Larry L. Rasmussen, *Earth Community, Earth Ethics* (Maryknoll, N.Y.: Orbis Books, 1996), Rosemary Radford Ruether, *Gaia and God: An Ecofeminist Theology of Earth Healing* (San Francisco: HarperSanFrancisco, 1992); Sallie McFague, *Life Abundant: Rethinking Theology and Economy for a Planet in Peril* (Minneapolis: Fortress Press, 2001); John F. Haught, *God after Darwin: A Theology of Evolution* (Boulder, Colo.: Westview Press,

2000) and *Christianity and Science: Toward a Theology of Nature* (Maryknoll, N.Y.: Orbis Books, 2007).

102. See Robert J. Schreiter, "Two Forms of Catholicity in a Time of Globalization," *Himig Ugnayan* 8 (2007): 1-17.

103. Shawn Copeland, "Black, Hispanic/Latino, and Native American Theologies," in Ford, *Modern Theologians*, 359.

104. James H. Cone, "Preface to the 1970 Edition," *A Black Theology of Liberation*, 2nd ed. (Maryknoll, N.Y.: Orbis Books, 1986), vii.

105. See Copeland, "Black," 360-62; Cecil Wayne Cone, *The Identity Crisis in Black Theology* (Nashville, Tenn.: AMEC, 1975); Major J. Jones, *The Color of God: The Concept of God in Afro-American Thought* (Macon, Ga.: Mercer University Press, 1987); David Emmanuel Goatley, ed., *Black Religion, Black Theology: The Collected Essays of J. Deotis Roberts* (Harrisburg, Pa.: Trinity Press International, 2003); Gayraud S. Wilmore, *Black Religion and Black Radicalism: An Interpretation of the Religious History of African Americans* (Maryknoll, N.Y.: Orbis Books, 1998); Jacquelyn Grant, *White Women's Christ and Black Women's Jesus: Feminist Christology and Womanist Response* (Atlanta, Ga.: Scholars Press, 1989); Katie G. Cannon, *Katie's Canon: Womanism and the Soul of the Black Community* (New York: Continuum, 1995); Delores S. Williams, *Sisters in the Wilderness: The Challenge of Womanist God-talk* (Maryknoll, N.Y.: Orbis Books, 1993).

106. All three of these Catholic theologians have contributed, for example, to Jamie T. Phelps, ed., *Black and Catholic: The Challenge and Gift of Black Folk: Contributions of African American Experience and Thought to Catholic Theology* (Milwaukee, Wis.: Marquette University Press, 1997). All three again contributed to a special issue of *Theological Studies*, "The Catholic Reception of Black Theology," 61, no. 4 (December 2000).

107. See Arturo J. Bañuelas, ed., *Mestizo Christianity: Theology from the Latino Perspective* (Maryknoll, N.Y.: Orbis Books, 1995); see also the special issue of *Theological Studies*, "Encountering Latino and Latina Catholic Theology," 65, no. 2 (June 2004).

108. Orlando O. Espín, "Traditioning: Culture, Daily Life and Popular Religion, and Their Impact on Christian Tradition," in Orlando O. Espín and Gary Macy, eds., *Futuring Our Past: Explorations in the Theology of Tradition* (Maryknoll, N.Y.: Orbis Books, 2006), 5.

109. Orlando O. Espín and Miguel H. Díaz, eds., *From the Heart of Our People: Latino/a Explorations in Catholic Systematic Theology* (Maryknoll, N.Y.: Orbis Books, 1999); the book on tradition is cited above, edited by Espín and Macy.

110. See Ada María Isasi-Díaz, *En la Lucha—In the Struggle: A Hispanic Women's Liberation Theology* (Minneapolis: Fortress Press, 1993); Carmen M. Nanko-Fernández, "From Pájaro to Paraclete: Retrieving the Spirit of God in the Company of Mary," *Journal of Hispanic/Latino Theology*, http://www.latinotheology.org/2007/company_of_mary; Nancy Pineda-Madrid, "Traditioning: The Formation of Community, the Transmission of Faith," in Espín and Macy, eds., *Futuring Our Past*, 204-26; Michelle A. González, "What about Mulatez? An Afro-Cuban Contribution," in Espín and Macy, 180-203.

111. Justo L. González, *A Concise History of Christian Doctrine* (Nashville, Tenn.: Abingdon Press, 2005); *Mañana: Christian Theology from a Hispanic Perspective* (Nashville, Tenn.: Abingdon Press, 1990).

112. See Jonathan Y. Tan, *Introducing Asian American Theologies* (Maryknoll, N.Y.: Orbis Books, 2008).

113. Roy Isao Sano, *Amerasian Theology of Liberation: A Reader*. Monograph available at the Pacific and Asian Center for Theology and Strategies Collection, Graduate Theological Union Archives, Berkeley, CA, 1973; Jung Young Lee, *Marginality: The Key to Multicultural Theology* (Minneapolis: Fortress Press, 1995); idem, *The Trinity in Asian Perspective* (Nash-

ville, Tenn.: Abingdon Press, 1999); David Ng, ed., *People on the Way: Asian North Americans Discovering Christ, Culture and Community* (Valley Forge, Pa.: Judson Press, 1996).

114. Tan, *Introducing*, 99-101.

115. Peter C. Phan, *Mission and Cathechesis: Alexandre de Rhodes and Inculturation in Seventeenth-Century Vietnam* (Maryknoll, N.Y.: Orbis Books, 1998).

116. Peter C. Phan, *In Our Own Tongues: Perspectives from Asia on Mission and Inculturation* (Maryknoll, N.Y.: Orbis Books, 2003); *Christianity with an Asian Face: Asian Theology in the Making* (Maryknoll, N.Y.: Orbis Books, 2003), and *Being Religious Interreligiously: Asian Perspectives on Interfaith Dialogue* (Maryknoll, N.Y.: Orbis Books, 2004).

117. See Amos Yong, *Beyond the Impasse: Toward a Pneumatological Theology of Religions* (Grand Rapids: Baker Book Company, 2003); and *Hospitality and the Other: Pentecost, Christian Practices, and the Neighbor* (Maryknoll, N.Y.: Orbis Books, 2008).

118. Quoted from Robert Allen Warrior, *Tribal Secrets: Recovering American Indian Intellectual Traditions* (Minneapolis: University of Minnesota Press, 1994) in Copeland, "Black," 380.

Index